W9-CGQ-477

PLACE IN RETURN BOX to remove this checkout from your record.
TO AVOID FINES return on or before date due.
MAY BE RECALLED with earlier due date if requested.

DATE DUE	DATE DUE	DATE DUE
DEC 28 402003		
JAN 1 2 2009		
121708		
FEB 0 4 2012		
042914		

The Revolution of American Conservatism

The

Revolution of

American Conservatism

The Federalist Party in the
Era of Jeffersonian Democracy

DAVID HACKETT FISCHER

The University of Chicago Press
Chicago and London

The University of Chicago Press, Chicago 60637
The University of Chicago Press, Ltd., London .

Copyright © 1965 by David Hackett Fischer. All rights reserved
Originally published 1965. Midway Reprint 1975
Printed in the United States of America

International Standard Book Number: 0-226-25135-7
Library of Congress Catalog Card Number: 75-29561

for Judith

Contents

Tables

Acknowledgments

Seven years ago, a good friend, Francis Haber, first turned my thoughts toward the Federalists. An early effort, which grew from his suggestion, was an undergraduate thesis which Shaw Livermore wisely and patiently directed. In the history department of The John Hopkins University, where a preliminary draft was submitted as a dissertation, I received much helpful counsel from C. Vann Woodward, Frederic C. Lane, Charles A. Barker, and most of all, Wilson Smith. It is also a pleasure to acknowledge the encouragement and friendly criticism of Richard McCormick, Noble Cunningham, and my colleagues at Brandeis, John Roche, Marvin Meyers and Leonard Levy. The costs of research were defrayed by generous grants from the Colonial Dames of America, The Johns Hopkins University, and Brandeis University.

To Miss Jeannette Hopkins and the suffering staff of Harper & Row, my most sincere gratitude is due for the practiced speed and skill with which they have edited an intricate manuscript, for the unfailing courtesy and patience which they have extended to an aggravating author, and for the generosity with which they have undertaken to publish a book with many costly appendages.

Without the support and inspiration of my parents I could not have begun. Nor would I be finished without the help of Judith, my wife, who served as collaborator and critic. To her this work is dedicated.

Wayland, Massachusetts   D.H.F.
January 1965

Introduction

I fear Federalism will not only die, but all remembrance of it be lost.

—FISHER AMES, 1807

In the year 1810, two elderly American gentlemen reflected sadly upon what they took to be the ruins of a republic. "The times are really altered, [compared] to what they were thirty years ago," David Sewall wrote to Robert Treat Paine. "The Patriotism and genuine American spirit which then glowed is greatly depreciated, and seems degenerated into selfishness and democracy." Paine replied sympathetically, "The times are *really* altered, and that spirit which once was so successfully exerted to procure and protect the substantial liberty and happiness of the country . . . has unhappily taken the course you have described."[1]

I

No major problem in American history is more difficult to discuss reasonably—and is more in need of reasonable discussion—than the expansion of political democracy. A profusion of interpretations and a paucity of facts have together bred bewilderment and despair among serious students of the problem. Confusion is compounded, of course, by conceptual conflict. An outspoken colonial historian has argued that America was a "middle-class democracy" long before the Revolution. An eccentric politician insists that America has never been a democracy, and hopes that we shall never become one. Clearly, they are not discussing the same thing.[2]

Democracy as an ideal, as a philosophical conception, does not admit of easy explication. But the process of political democratization may be specified more simply as the expansion of voter participation within an increasingly open and free electoral process. To say this is to specify

[1] David Sewall to Robert Treat Paine, 27 July 1810; Paine to Sewall, 17 Aug. 1810, Robert Treat Paine Papers, Mass. Hist. Soc.; punctuation is modified throughout.
[2] Robert E. Brown, *Middle-Class Democracy and the Revolution in Massachusetts, 1691–1780.* (Ithaca, 1955), pp. v–viii, 401–408; Barry Goldwater, *The Conscience of a Conservative* (N.Y., 1960), pp. 15–24.

xi

but two variables of many, but it will serve as a working definition for the purposes of this investigation.

The process of democratization has been continuous in American political history; scholars have observed and described it in every period. But it is surely true that more significant changes have occurred in some periods than in others, and that the process, though continuous, has not been constant. To examine a part of the problem is difficult because there are few fixed reference points. But perhaps it is possible to begin by agreeing upon two generalized assumptions which, though not supported by a consensus of expert opinion, would appear to be sustained by a majority (the majoritarian idea, it seems, has even invaded the academy).

The first rests upon a cluster of revisionist studies of the Jacksonian era, which conclude that the process of democratization was far advanced before Jackson reached the White House, before Tocqueville crossed the coast. "Political democracy," Marvin Meyers has written, "was the medium more than the achievement of the Jacksonian party," a precondition more than a consequence of the election of 1828. The expansive ideals of equality and liberty would, of course, continue to ramify in new and surprising ways after 1828, but by that date they had already wrought radical changes in the structure of American politics. Richard P. McCormick and J. R. Pole have recently buttressed this assumption with voting statistics.[3]

A second generalized assumption concerns the structure of American politics before 1800. Bernard Bailyn has given it intelligent expression: "Nowhere in the eighteenth-century America was there 'democracy'— middle-class or otherwise, as we use the term." The political role of the people was effectively limited, not by property qualifications for voting and officeholding, but by the much greater weight of habit and custom. "In stable governments," Fisher Ames observed, "usages become laws. Things wear a certain channel for themselves."[4] It would appear to have

---

[3] Marvin Meyers, *The Jacksonian Persuasion, Politics and Belief* (Stanford, 1957), p. 4; Richard P. McCormick, "New Perspectives on Jacksonian Politics," *American Historical Review*, LXV (1960), 288–301; J. R. Pole, "Suffrage and Representation in Massachusetts; A Statistical Note," *William and Mary Quarterly*, 3d. ser., XIV (1957), 560; XV (1958), 412–426; "Suffrage and Representation in New Jersey, 1774 to 1844," *New Jersey Historical Society Proceedings*, LXXI (1953), 38; "Election Statistics in Pennsylvania, 1790–1840, *Pennsylvania Magazine of History and Biography*, LXXXII (1958), 217; "Constitutional Reform and Election Statistics in Maryland, 1790–1812," *Maryland Historical Magazine*, LV (1955), 275–292; "Representation and Authority in Virginia from the Revolution to Reform," *Journal of Southern History*, XXIV (1958), 16–50; "Election Statistics in North Carolina to 1861," *ibid.*, 225–228.

[4] Bernard Bailyn, "Political Experience and Enlightenment Ideas in Eighteenth Century America," *Amer. Hist. Rev.*, LXVII (1962), 339–351, esp. 346; J. R. Pole, "Historians and the Problem of Early American Democracy," *ibid.*, LXVII (1962), 626–646; Fisher Ames to Josiah Quincy, Jan. 20, 1806, in Ames, *Works*, I, 349.

been thus in colonial America. A few prominent families, possessed of wealth and distinctions, monopolized offices and power in every colony.

The politics of New Hampshire were dominated during the eighteenth century by a single family, the Wentworths. In Boston, great power lay in the hands of Hutchinsons, Sewalls, Wheelwrights, and Olivers; other Massachusetts towns were controlled in similar fashion by a few families whose names regularly recur upon the lists of officeholders. In Connecticut there was an ascendancy of Allyns, Huntingtons, Pitkins, Stanleys, and Walcotts; a recent study of the structure of power in a single town, Kent, has shown the "top offices were filled by a small group or clique of the town's wealthiest men." Even in Rhode Island where, as John Adams wrote, "there has been no Clergy, no Church, and I had almost said no State, and some People say no religion, there has been a constant respect for certain old Families."[5]

The elitist pattern of politics and society in eighteenth-century New England was even more apparent in the middle and southern colonies. New York, before the War for Independence, was largely governed by Bayards and De Lanceys, Heathcotes, Johnsons, Livingstons, Coldens, Morrises, Nicollses, Pells, Philipses, Rapaljes, Remsens, Schuylers, Smiths, Stuyvesants, Van Cortlandts and Van Rensselaers. The predominant families of proprietary Pennsylvania were Penns, Allens, Assetons, Fishbournes, Hamiltons, Hills, Lloyds, Logans, Norrises and Pembertons; of Maryland, Bordleys, Calverts, Carrolls, Darnalls, Dulanys, Lloyds, Ogles and Taskers. Similar lists could be recited for Virginia, the Carolinas, and Georgia.[6]

The industrious researches of Robert Brown have conclusively established the important point that the political power of the colonial elite did not derive from economic restrictions upon the exercise of voting. Brown has shown that the suffrage was open, in Massachusetts, to most adult white males; and it may be granted, in Bailyn's words, that "what has been proved about the franchise in early Massachusetts—that it was open for practically the entire adult male population—can be proved to

---

[5] Leonard W. Labaree, *Conservatism in Early American History*, 2d. edn. (Ithaca, 1959), pp. 1–31; see also Benjamin W. Labaree, *Patriots and Partisans, The Merchants of Newburyport, 1764–1815* (Cambridge 1962), p. 15; Robert J. Taylor, *Western Massachusetts in the Revolution* (Providence, 1954), pp. 11–26; and John Cary, "Statistical Method and the Brown Thesis on Colonial Democracy," *William and Mary Quarterly*, XX (1963), 250–264; Charles S. Grant, *Democracy in the Connecticut Frontier-Town of Kent* (New York, 1961), p. 152; Oscar Zeichner, *Connecticut's Years of Controversy, 1750–1776* (Chapel Hill, 1949), pp. 3–19; John Adams to Thomas Jefferson, Nov. 15, 1813, *Adams-Jefferson Letters*, ed. Cappon, II, 400; David S. Lovejoy, *Rhode Island Politics and the American Revolution, 1760–1776* (Providence, 1958), pp. 5–31.

[6] Charles S. Sydnor, *Gentlemen Freeholders*, pp. 60–77; Jack P. Greene, *The Quest for Power* (Chapel Hill, 1963), pp. 11, passim; Roy Smith, *South Carolina as a Royal Province, 1719–1776* (New York, 1903), p. 87; Frederick B. Tolles, *Meeting House and Counting House* (Chapel Hill, 1948), pp. 109–143; Labaree, *Conservatism in Early American History*, pp. 1–32. The work of an older generation of historians

a lesser or greater extent for all the colonies." It is also true, of course, that many members of the ruling elites were parvenu, that their wealth was often new wealth. Both popular participation and social mobility were far more extensive in colonial America than in the mother country, or in any other eighteenth-century state.[7]

Nevertheless, Bagehot's phrase for nineteenth-century England, a "deferential society," would appear to describe eighteenth-century America. Men were trained from childhood to show deference to their betters, and to expect it from their inferiors. The "habit of subordination," as a Federalist later labeled it, served to cement a functional society more effectively than legislative restraints or constitutional restrictions. The dropping of a curtsy, the doffing of a cap, the raising of a deferential finger to the brow—these were the superficial symbols of a spirit which ran deep and strong in the minds and hearts of men. A fundamental distinction between the "multitude" and the "people of the better sort" expressed itself in manners, speech, and modes of dress. A nineteenth-century historian of Portsmouth, New Hampshire, recalled "earlier times, when scarlet colored broadcloth cloaks, worn by our *Warners, Jaffreys, Cutts* and other gentlemen of the old school of politeness, good order and decorum, warned the boys of *severe reprehension*, if not *rods* which awaited them for any neglect of respectful recognition of the approach of these august personages, by the *low bow*, or *doffed hat*, or both."[8]

The "habit of subordination" also expressed itself in the low level of voter participation in colonial elections. Despite competition between individual candidates or between rival "connexions," which often took place in an unsystematic fashion, the deferential spirit resulted in desultory attendance at the polls, and the "best people" with only occasional difficulty managed the affairs of their communities.[9]

If these assumptions about the Jacksonian era and the colonial period are correct, then it follows that between 1760 and 1820 two major changes occurred in the structure of American politics. Many more people exercised their electoral privileges. They did so within an in-

---

is still useful and relevant here; see esp. Carl Lotus Becker, *History of Political Parties in the Province of New York, 1760–1776* (Madison, 1909; 2d. edn. 1960), ch. I. Becker's conclusions on local conventions have been challenged by Luetscher; and his assumption of a restricted suffrage is open to question. But his work has permanent value for its description of social patterns and political structure.

[7] Bailyn, "Political Experience and Enlightenment Ideas," p. 346; Brown, *Middle-Class Democracy and the Revolution in Mass.*, passim. Robert and Katherine Brown, *Virginia 1705–1786; Aristocracy or Democracy?* (East Lansing; 1964), passim.

[8] Charles Brewster, *Rambles About Portsmouth*, 2 vols. (Portsmouth, 1869), II, 117.

[9] Brown concedes that voter participation was generally low in the colonial era. See *Middle-Class Democracy and the Revolution in Massachusetts*, pp. 51–52, 397 (the turnout in Boston in 1763, a peak figure, was low in percentage of adult males); and see Brown and Brown, *Virginia 1705–1786; Democracy or Aristocracy?*, pp. 146, 163.

creasingly open and free electoral process. With these hypotheses in mind, I examined the voting statistics compiled by McCormick and Pole. The work of both scholars shows that a sudden expansion of popular participation did in fact take place within a very narrow time span— the sixteen-year period from 1800 to 1816. Before 1795, participation appears to have ranged between 15 and 40 per cent of adult males in nearly all states, with no clear upward tendencies. From 1796 to 1799, a slow but significant rise was perceptible, especially in the middle states. In 1800 there appears to have been a sudden jump, followed in the next few years by a falling off. But from 1804 to 1816, in a majority of states, an extraordinary surge carried voter participation in state elections to unprecedented heights—68 to 98 per cent of adult males. This level has been maintained ever since, with many fluctuations, of which the most important was a falling off in the period 1824–1840, the Age of Jackson![10]

In a few states voting qualifications were eased within the period 1800–1816, but in most states they were not. The revision of suffrage requirements followed, rather than preceded, the expansion of voter participation. An explanation must be found elsewhere.

The principal issues of the period, the embargoes and the War of 1812, were of course bitterly controversial, but intrinsically no more interesting than the imperial questions of the 1760s and early 1770s, or the constitutional issues of the late 1770s and 1780s, or the pressing problems of the 1790s. Why did the explosive expansion of participation come when it did? Two alternative hypotheses come to mind. First, the Jeffersonian movement might have been solely responsible for quickening popular interest in political questions, and for the expansion of the democratic principle. Seymour Lipset has summarized this possible interpretation in a sentence: "The almost unchallenged rule of the Virginia Dynasty and the Democratic-Republican Party served to legitimate national authority and democratic rights."[11] A second hypothesis would be that organized party rivalry gained a new intensity in the period 1800–1816—a two-party rivalry more competitive than ever before; and that the central and transcendent fact of competition served to stimulate an expansion of popular participation.

[10] See statistics of McCormick and Pole, summarized in ch. IX below (Tables XXII, XXIV, XXV, pp. 370, 373–374). It will be noted that the expansion of popular participation is apparent in state elections. The Jacksonian era may have been a period of expanded voter participation in presidential contests, but not in the electoral process. A minor premise of this investigation is that more significant things were happening to the structure of American politics on the local than on the national level—more significant because the people were more interested in local affairs. Evidence appears not only in voting statistics but also in impressionist statements of contemporary observers. See, e.g., Israel Pickens to William Lenoir, Jan. 29, 1816, in the Lenoir Papers, Southern Hist. Coll., Univ. of N. C.

[11] Seymour Martin Lipset, *The First New Nation* (New York, 1963), p. 45.

Standard works on the Jeffersonian era (there are remarkably few of them) tend to support the first hypothesis. They do not generally indicate that party competition was unusually keen in the period 1804–1816; indeed, most suggest the opposite, arguing that the Federalist Party was moribund after 1804, unresponsive to the Jeffersonian movement, unyielding in its stubborn conservatism, unwilling and unable to compete for popular support.[12]

2

Historians have not been attentive to the men who called themselves Federalists in the age of Jefferson. The prevailing interpretation calls to mind the Scottish poet's satirical strictures upon another great party in adversity:

> Awa, Whigs, awa!
> Awa, Whigs, awa!
> Ye're but a pack o' traitor louns,
> Ye'll do nae good at a'.

> Our thrissles flourish'd fresh and fair,
> And Bonnie bloom'd our roses;
> But Whigs cam' like a frost in June,
> And wither'd a' our posies.

Even John Bach McMaster, who openly admitted that one of the purposes of his history was to "show up" Thomas Jefferson, dismissed the Federalists after 1800 as "mere obstructionists, a sect of the political world which, of all other sects, is most to be despised." And Albert J.

---

[12] The origins of this interpretation are to be found partly in the earliest histories of the Federal Party by descendants of Federalist leaders, who emphasized what appeared to them to be the most admirable features of that political group—its honest and independent leaders who remained stubbornly loyal to their own ideals in defiance of popular opinion. There were such Federalists as these, but as a generalized view of the Federal Party it is not merely inaccurate but in the case of Dwight and Sullivan positively deceitful. It has contributed to present misunderstandings. See Theodore Dwight, *History of the Hartford Convention* (New York, 1833); William Sullivan, *Familiar Letters on Public Characters and Public Events* (Boston, 1834); Henry Cabot Lodge, *Life and Letters of George Cabot* (Boston, 1877); Charles R. King, *The Life and Correspondence of Rufus King*, 6 vols. (New York, 1894–1900); Edmund Quincy, *Life of Josiah Quincy* (Boston, 1867); Theophilus Parsons, Jr., *Memoir of Theophilus Parsons* (Boston, 1859); Octavius Pickering and C. W. Upham, *The Life of Timothy Pickering* 4 vols. (Boston, 1867–1873); William Plumer, Jr., *Life of William Plumer* (Boston, 1856); Simeon E. Baldwin, *Life and Letters of Simeon Baldwin* (New Haven, n.d.); Thomas Wentworth Higginson, *Life of Stephen Higginson* (Boston, 1907); Richard Hildreth, *The History of the United States*, 6 vols. (New York, 1849–1856). The standard view has also developed from another tradition of filiopietism, the accumulated antipathies of the Adams family, which culminated in Henry Adams' magnificent *History of the United States*, 9 vols. (New York, 1889–1891). I have discussed this work at greater length in "The Myth of the Essex Junto," *William and Mary Quarterly*, 3d. ser., XXI (1964), 191–235.

Beveridge, whose admiration for one Federalist, John Marshall, is well known, had little sympathy for Marshall's political friends. The Federal Party after 1800 was, in his judgment, "reduced to a grumbling company of out of date gentlemen. . . . They had repudiated democracy, and assumed an attitude of insolent superiority, mournful of a glorious past, despairing of a worthy future."[13]

Students of parties and political machinery have generally concluded that the Federalists disdained formal political organization and competition in the Jeffersonian era. George D. Luetscher, in an able and important monograph on early American politics, suggested that the Federalists were destroyed because they refused to develop an organization and to compete actively with the Jeffersonians. He contended that his rule was proved by one exception, Delaware, where Federalists did develop effective party machinery, competed energetically, and managed to retain power throughout the Jeffersonian era.[14]

There are a few exceptional works—a splendid study of Delaware politics by John A. Munroe, an excellent biography of William Plumer, and an important and provocative monograph on New York politics by Dixon Ryan Fox. But the great majority of studies of the Jeffersonian era are, understandably, centered upon the Jeffersonians. The standard

[13] John Bach McMaster, *A History of the People of the United States*, 9 vols. (New York, 1883–1927), II, 629; his view of Jefferson is quoted in Eric Goldman, *John Bach McMaster, American Historian* (Philadelphia, 1943), p. 123; A. J. Beveridge, *Life of John Marshall*, 4 vols. (Boston, 1916–1919), III, 256–257; IV, 6; see also James Schouler, *History of the United States under the Constitution*, 6 vols. (New York, 1881–1899), II, 430; Vernon Louis Parrington, *Main Currents in American Thought*, Harvest Books ed., 2 vols. (New York, 1927), II, 271; Claude G. Bowers, *Jefferson in Power: the Death Struggle of the Federalists* (Boston, 1936), p. 487; Henry Adams, *History of the United States*, 9 vols. (New York, 1889–1891), I, 88; Edward Channing, *A History of the United States*, 6 vols. (New York, 1905–1925), IV, 164. A Jeffersonian historian, Claude G. Bowers, began his study of Jefferson's administration with the astonishing statement that "anti-Jeffersonian historians have been much too tender with the Federalists in their days of degeneracy and treason." Mr. Bowers announced that he would set the record straight. He offered an account of the "death struggle of this once great party" as "a warning to all succeeding political parties and politicians that public opinion cannot be defied with impunity" (Bowers, pp. v–vii). For a Madisonian variant of the Jeffersonian theme see Irving Brant, *James Madison*, 6 vols. (Indianapolis, 1941–1961). Although Brant bitterly assails Henry Adams's cavalier treatment of Madison, he merely accepts Adams's interpretation of the Federalists after 1800. The economic interpretation of Charles Beard and the frontier thesis of Frederick Jackson Turner harmonized readily with this interpretation. John D. Barnhart, *Valley of Democracy; The Frontier versus the Plantation in the Ohio Valley, 1775–1818* (Bloomington, 1953), pp. 159, 174; Homer C. Hockett, "Federalism and the West," *Essays in American History dedicated to Frederick Jackson Turner* (New York, 1910), p. 114; and "Western Influences on Political Parties to 1825," *Ohio State University Studies*, IV (1916).

[14] George D. Luetscher, *Early Political Machinery in the United States* (Philadelphia, 1903), pp. 102–103, 150–151. Luetscher's thesis reappears, slightly modified, in J. R. Pole, "Jeffersonian Democracy and the Federalist Dilemma in New Jersey, 1798–1812," *Proceedings of the New Jersey Hist. Soc.*, LXXIV (1956), 292.

interpretation of the Federalists remains unchanged from Henry Adams to the most recent surveys of the period.[15]

3

The following account is frankly revisionist. Its purpose is to suggest that a younger generation of Federalists—the most obscure leaders of a major party in American political history—responded to the Jeffersonian movement with energy, flexibility and effect. It will be argued that they deliberately tried to create popularly oriented vote-seeking political

[15] John A. Munroe, *Federalist Delaware, 1775–1815* (New Brunswick, 1954); Lynn W. Turner, *William Plumer* (Chapel Hill, 1962); Dixon Ryan Fox, *The Decline of Aristocracy in the Politics of New York* (New York, 1919); Paul Goodman, *The Democratic-Republicans of Massachusetts* (Cambridge, 1964). In at least two instances, fine Jeffersonian-centered studies have accurately and suggestively appraised the activity of their opponents. See Noble Cunningham, *The Jeffersonian Republicans in Power* (Chapel Hill, 1963) and Sanford Higginbotham, *The Keystone in the Democratic Arch: Pennsylvania Politics, 1800–1816* (Harrisburg, 1952). Other Jefferson-centered studies include James Truslow Adams, *New England in the Republic* (Boston, 1926); Chilton Williamson, *Vermont in Quandary: 1763–1825* (Montpelier, 1949); William A. Robinson, *Jeffersonian Democracy in New England* (New Haven, 1916); Walter R. Fee, *The Transition from Aristocracy to Democracy in New Jersey* (Somerville, 1933); Charles Henry Ambler, *Sectionalism in Virginia from 1776 to 1861* (Chicago, 1910); Joseph I. Shulim, *The Old Dominion and Napoleon Bonaparte* (New York, 1952); Delbert H. Gilpatrick, *Jeffersonian Democracy in North Carolina, 1789–1816* (New York, 1931); John Harold Wolfe, *Jeffersonian Democracy in South Carolina* (Chapel Hill, 1940); Ulrich B. Phillips, "Georgia and State Rights," in *American Historical Association Report*, 1901, II; William T. Utter, *The Frontier State, 1803–1825*, vol. II in *The History of the State of Ohio*, ed. C. F. Wittke, (Columbus, 1942). There are two useful biographies of latter-day Federalists, Samuel Eliot Morison, *Life and letters of Harrison Gray Otis*, 2 vols. (Boston, 1913), which is discussed in my "Myth of the Essex Junto," and Morton Borden's *The Federalism of James Bayard* (New York, 1955). Both defend one Federalist while dismissing the rest in traditional fashion. Morison's work, however contains one chapter, "The Federalist Machine," which is very helpful for present purposes. For the most recent statements of the standard view see Shaw Livermore, *The Twilight of Federalism* (Princeton, 1962), pp. 6–9, 28–30; William Chambers, *Political Parties in a New Nation* (New York, 1963), pp. 183 *passim*; and Lipset, *The First New Nation*, p. 45. These are all works of high importance; the behavior of Federalists in the period 1800–1814 is central to none of them. Mr. Lipset's sociological insights have been very helpful in many ways; Mr. Chambers' reformulation of the role of parties in the republic—as artifacts essential to the operation of the government—was very useful; and Mr. Livermore's discussion of the Federalists after their party fell apart was often suggestive. All three works relied primarily upon secondary sources in the period 1800–1814; their restatements of the standard view are evidence of the consensual support which it has attracted. Less helpful in this context is Mr. Louis Hartz' brilliantly intuitive single-factor synthesis of American history. The Federalists, he suggests, were not aristocrats but whiggish liberals who misunderstood their own society. The Federalists, he writes, "deserve all of the criticism they have received, but not for the reason they have received it. Their crime was not villainy but stupidity, and perhaps in politics a man ought to know that if he is guilty of the second, he is going to be charged with the first. What is remarkable is how long the American Whigs [and Federalists] managed to endure the strange abuse of a liberal community without waking up to the logic behind it. Here they were in a setting where the democracy

organizations which might defeat Jefferson with his own weapons. The younger Federalists successfully established these party organizations in at least ten states. They sponsored partisan newspapers and secret political societies on an unprecedented scale, and borrowed Jeffersonian electioneering techniques, rhetoric, and issues for their own elitist purposes.

The young Federalists were, of course, conspicuously unsuccessful in their effort to recover power from their opponents. They never overcame the heavy handicap of a late start, after their adversaries were well organized, after their adversaries' principles and prejudices had been widely disseminated, after Federalism itself had become a byword for repression and antirepublican ideas, a synonym for privilege and political depravity. Young Federalists were hindered by older colleagues who refused to cooperate, and even opposed any effort to borrow Jeffersonian techniques. Jeffersonians themselves proved to be extraordinarily resourceful as the rivalry became more intense. And finally, after fourteen years of slow political starvation, the chance coincidence of events at Hartford, Ghent, and New Orleans came as a crushing blow to the frail structure of the Federalist cause.

But if the young Federalists were unsuccessful in their own particular purposes, their partisan activity remains doubly significant. Firstly, by offering close competition to the Jeffersonians in a contest for popular favor, they helped to stimulate an increase in popular interest in politics. The fact of intensive party rivalry would explain, better than any other, the extraordinary surge of voter participation in the Jeffersonian era and other important changes which will be discussed in chapter IX.

Secondly, the political ethics and behavior of younger Federalists contrast in striking ways with the conduct of older colleagues who had grown to maturity in a different political environment. The juxtaposition of two generations of Federalist leaders is itself an important measure of change in the structure of society and politics during the New Republic. For this reason, we shall begin not with the younger Federalists but with their elders, the "gentlemen of the old school."

4

But before beginning, it is necessary to note that there are at least five things which this study is not. It is not a traditional narrative history of the Federal Party from the election of 1800 to the election of 1816. The political history of the New Republic stands in need of intensive

---

was closer to them than anywhere else in the West, and yet instead of embracing it they feared it and fought it" (*The Liberal Tradition in America* [New York, 1955]), p. 101. As I hope to demonstrate, Mr. Hartz has misread the political ideals of the older Federalists and mistaken the political behavior of their younger colleagues.

analysis, which is impossible within the narrow limits of a narrative framework. Second, this investigation is not primarily an effort to explain the ultimate disintegration of the Federal Party. The outline of an interpretation appears above; illustrative material will appear throughout the following chapters. The problem is admittedly important, but not as interesting or as significant as the extended effort of some Federalists to preserve and to improve their party in the Jeffersonian era.

Third, this is not a study of the social sources of partisan allegiance. The problem is briefly discussed in Appendix I. But though relevant, it is peripheral to the present study. Fourth, no simple homogenization of American politics is intended. Younger Federalists did not become Jeffersonians. Emulation encapsulated fundamental disagreement.

Finally, the following chapters are not a reductive argument that young Federalists themselves were the cause of an expansion of popular participation in politics. Competition between two parties was the crucial fact; party interaction was the agency of change. And in this interaction, Democratic-Republicans rather than Federal Republicans remained predominant. The period 1800–1816 must remain, of course, the Jeffersonian era; if Federal antagonists are the focus of concern in the following pages, it is because a generation of Jeffersonian scholars has inaccurately estimated their role and mistaken their relevance.

This work is an essay, in the most literal sense. It does not pretend to be definitive in hypothesis or conclusion. A proper piece of historical research ought to raise more questions than it answers—to close a few avenues, but to open many more. To that purpose this project is addressed.

The Revolution of American Conservatism

I

Federalists of the Old School

> *We have frequently seen that the pliant Twig will by bending,*
> *retain its situation, when, by force of the torrent, the sturdy*
> *Oak will be torn up by the roots. No man, however, will be so*
> *foolish as to say that the former is so reputable as the latter,*
> *or that we may rest in safety our weight against one, as well*
> *as against the other.*
>
> —STEPHEN HIGGINSON, 1789

The men who called themselves Federalists in 1800 were as multifarious
as any major party in American politics. Even in an investigation which
is limited to leaders of the first rank, we must deal with a broad variety
of principle and purpose. Other scholars have discussed these variations
in economic, social, and geographic terms, but there was also a temporal
dimension of Federalist thought which has been generally overlooked.
Benjamin Chew (1722–1810) and James Buchanan (1791–1868) both
called themselves Federalists, but their attitudes and behavior were very
different. The difference constituted nothing less than a revolution in the
form and function of leadership in American politics.

In this chapter I propose to examine the ideals—even idealism—of
the gentlemen of the "old school,"[1] the most mature leaders of the federal
cause in 1800. Born between 1720 and 1760,[2] they were part of the
generation that had waged the War for Independence. As younger men
they had been capable of extraordinarily effective political leadership.
But at the end of the eighteenth century, after the French Revolution had
burst upon the world, their attitudes and assumptions were increasingly
anachronistic. Political conditions in Europe and America were changing
rapidly, but the ancient ideals of the old school were not easily abandoned. With uniform tenacity these aging statesmen resisted "Brutus"

---

[1] For the use of "old school" in this context see Joseph Dennie to Winthrop
Sargent, Mar. 4, 1803, Sargent Papers, Mass. Hist. Soc.; (Newburyport, Mass.)
Repertory, Oct. 22, 1803, Jan. 21, 1804; (Portland, Me.) *Eastern Argus*, Apr. 13, 1804;
Elisha Boudinot to Timothy Pickering, Feb. 24, 1807, Pickering Papers, Mass. Hist.
Soc.; Anna Cabot Lowell to Anne Grant, Nov. 8, 1809, Mass. Hist. Soc. *Proceedings*,
2d Series XVIII (1904), 309.

[2] See App. II, for sketches of Federalist leaders in the Jeffersonian era.

haircuts, pantaloons, and ideology; stubbornly clinging to tiewigs, small-clothes, and traditional Whiggish principles.[3]

Any attempt to set up a single individual as typical of the ideals of the old school must necessarily fail. The two conventional models—Hamilton and Adams—are especially poor choices, for each of these great men was doubly exceptional. But without seeking to homogenize Federalism into a single personality, we might begin with two leaders whom Federalists themselves regarded as paragons rather than proto-types, as representative men in Emerson's elevated sense.

I

In the collective esteem of New England Federalism, no man stood quite as high as George Cabot (1752–1823). To Fisher Ames he was the "keeper of my conscience and judgment." To another Friend of Order he was the "Nestor of the federal cause." The son of a moderately prosperous North Shore merchant, Cabot's beginnings were unpromising. Never a bookish sort, he was required to withdraw from Harvard College in his freshman year on account of rebelliousness and "the great neglect of his exercises." He was promptly sent to sea under a stern captain, and at the age of seventeen was master of a schooner in transatlantic trade.[4]

Whether or not the Revolution was a social movement, it substantially changed Cabot's social circumstances. He associated himself with the American cause and reaped a fortune from the risk-ridden business of privateering. By 1780, his family was thought to be "by far the most wealthy in New England." Though Cabot thus belonged to the newly rich of the Revolution, there was nothing of an *arriviste* in his demeanor. He matured into a splendid figure of a gentleman, tall and straight as a grenadier, with alert penetrating blue eyes, ruddy complexion, and

---

[3] It is presently unfashionable to interpret the founding fathers as idealists who based their behavior upon a rigid conception of the body politic as it ought to be. The scholarship of the past half century, from Charles Beard to mid-century historians as diverse as Daniel Boorstin, John P. Roche, and Merrill Peterson, has tended to stress the pragmatic genius of early American statesmen. Ironically, the only Federalist recently reinterpreted as an idealist is Alexander Hamilton, perhaps the most hardheaded of the lot. See Daniel Boorstin, *The Genius of American Politics* (Chicago, 1953); John P. Roche, "The Founding Fathers: A Reform Caucus in Action," *The American Political Science Review*, LV (1961), 799–806; Merrill Peterson, "Henry Adams on Jefferson the President," *Virginia Quarterly Review*, LXIII (1963), 187–201; for Hamilton, see Cecilia M. Kenyon, "Alexander Hamilton: Rousseau of the Right," *Political Science Quarterly*, LXXV (1958), 161–178; and Broadus Mitchell, *Alexander Hamilton; the National Adventure, 1788–1804* (New York, 1962), pp. 117–118.

[4] Fisher Ames to Timothy Pickering, Mar. 24, 1806, in Ames, *Works*, I, 376; Peter Parley [Samuel G. Goodrich], *Recollections of a Lifetime*, 2 vols. (New York, 1856), II, 36; Sullivan, *Familiar Letters*, 373; W. C. Lane, "The Rebellion of 1766 in Harvard College," *Colonial Society of Mass. Transactions*, X (1905), 54–55; L. V. Briggs, *History and Genealogy of the Cabot Family*, 2 vols. (Boston, 1927), I, 66–107; Lodge, *Cabot*, pp. 8–15.

fine white hair queued neatly behind him. "In aspect and appearance he was strikingly dignified," a contemporary wrote. "Such was the effect of his presence that in a crowded room, and amid other men of mark, when you once became conscious that he was there, you could hardly forget it. You seemed always to see him, as a traveller in Switzerland sees Mont Blanc towering above the other mountains."[5]

Temperament, circumstance, and conviction combined to make Cabot into an elitist, deeply conscious of differences among men. His social attitudes were epitomized in his relations with the man who tilled his country estate. "The labor of my farm," he wrote candidly, "is performed altogether by a tenant, to whom I give specific benefits, that he may have no control over the management, and the benefits are liberal, that he may be happy, and tied to me by his interest." Equality of condition was nothing better than a bad joke. "It was observed here," Cabot wrote to a New York Federalist after a riot in which Hamilton was reportedly felled by a flying cobblestone, "that your Jacobins were prudent to endeavor to knock out Hamilton's brains, to reduce him to an equality with themselves."[6]

From this consciousness of inequality, Cabot derived his conception of society as an organism, a physical and moral entity composed of many different kinds of parts, "a perfect whole," as one of his friends wrote, "in which the general harmony may be preserved, each one learning his proper place and keeping to it." Without possessing any extended notion of egalitarianism, Cabot was a collectivist. He even spoke in Rousseau's terms of the "general will," by which he meant the common good rather than the wishes of a majority.[7]

The government Cabot envisioned for the "great family" which was

[5] Samuel Curwen to William Brown, Feb. 10, 1780, in *Journal and Letters of Samuel Curwen*, ed. G. A. Ward (Boston, 1842), pp. 233–234; Octavius Howe, "Beverly Privateers in the Revolution," *Colonial Society of Mass. Publications*, XXIV (1924), 324, 421, passim; K. W. Porter, *Jacksons and Lees*, 2 vols. (Cambridge, 1937), I, 22–25; East, *Business Enterprise in the American Revolutionary Era*, p. 228; [Goodrich], *Recollections*, II, 36; see also Wilson, *Aristocracy of Boston*, p. 10.

[6] Cabot to Wolcott, Aug. 3, 1801, and Cabot to King, July 27, 1795, in Lodge, *Cabot*, pp. 323, 82–83.

[7] Cabot to Timothy Pickering, Aug. 31, 1796, Cabot to Goodhue, May 5, 1790, and Cabot to Parsons, Aug. 12, 1794, in Lodge, *Cabot*, pp. 110, 36–7, 78–9; [Jonathan Jackson], *Thoughts upon the Political Situation of the United States* . . . (Worcester, 1788), pp. 49, 53, 58, 171. For the same holistic conception of society see the [Philadelphia] *Political and Commercial Register*, July 6, 1804, in which a correspondent discussed the commonwealth in terms of its "head, viscera, members and organs." Ruminating on the election of 1800, he commented, "our body politic is turned completely upside down—the head is prostrated on the earth, while the heels are exalted in the air. But can we long exist in this way? Men do sometimes stand upon their heads but if they do not in a short time resume their natural position they infallibly die." Another metaphorical statement of the same idea was a building in which the stones were the people, and the cement was the "public will" (ibid., July 13, 1804). For a graphic example of this kind of social holism, see the title page of Thomas Hobbes, *Leviathan* (London, 1651).

society is not easily described in twentieth-century terms. Democracy he despised as "government of the worst." But he cannot be catalogued simply as an antidemocrat. In a world of arbitrary power and inherited privilege he was committed, mind and heart—and pocketbook—to republicanism. A republic, as John Adams truly said, can be anything or nothing, but to Cabot it was something both familiar and precise. It meant the traditional polity of Massachusetts Bay, which a distinguished New England divine had neatly summarized as *a speaking* Aristocracy *in the face of a silent* Democracy." All of the people participated in the choice of "rulers" but only the "better sort" of people were chosen. The noun "ruler" was often used by Puritans and Federalists. It was used precisely, for they expected statesmen to govern according to the whisperings of conscience rather than the wishes of constituents.[8]

The New England way was government by consent, but the people consented to men rather than to measures. It was representative government, but the concept of representation was *in personam*. In John Cotton's terms it was a popular state but not a democracy. "Though it be a *status popularis,* where a people choose their owne governors; yet the government is not a democracy, if it be administered, not by the people, but by the governors, whether one (for then it is a monarchy, though elective) or by many, for then (as you know) it is aristocracy."[9]

The cement of this political system was the deferential spirit of eighteenth-century Anglo-American society, in which the "multitude" were trained from birth to "submit to that subordination necessary in the free'est [sic] states," and the "natural rulers of society" were accustomed to expect it. The system could function only as long as "the most reputable class," in Cabot's words, could "keep the people steady," could keep up the spirit of restraint and subordination. The problem, as Cabot saw it, was not a matter of repression but of persuasion, not of restraint but of education. Checks and balances, property qualifications, constitutional restraints which were the focus of discussion in 1787 were never of primary significance in his political thought. His purpose was not to institutionalize social conflict, but to preserve social harmony. His goal was not merely to secure a branch of the government as a sanctuary for the "wise and good," but to place all power in their hands, with the consent of the people.[10]

For the preservation of this model commonwealth, Cabot and his friends in eastern Massachusetts relied upon education in the broadest

[8] Cotton Mather, *Magnalia Christi Americana* . . . (Hartford, 1820), I, 395; see also Perry Miller, *The New England Mind: The Seventeenth Century* (Cambridge, Mass., 1954), pp. 398–462, and *Orthodoxy in Massachusetts, 1630–1650* (Cambridge, Mass., 1933), pp. 186, passim.

[9] B. Katherine Brown, "A Note on the Puritan Concept of Aristocracy," *Mississippi Valley Historical Review*, XLI (1954–1955), p. 106.

[10] Cabot to King, Aug. 14, 1795, in Lodge, *Cabot*, pp. 85–86.

sense. "The people must be *taught* to confide in and reverence their rulers," Stephen Higginson declared. "It is necessary to pay great attention to the education of youth," Jonathan Jackson wrote, "teaching them their just rights, at the same time they are taught proper subordination." Most education happens outside the classroom; Cabot and his friends believed that institutions other than formal schools might serve educational purposes. A "well-regulated family," the churches, even the militia might be a means of inculcating "the discipline of the mind, subordination."[11]

But he recognized no legitimate role for a political party. Extraconstitutional machinery, mass meetings of the people, semipermanent committees of correspondence smacked of subversion and the spirit of faction. When the Jeffersonian movement began to develop, Cabot recoiled from the form as well as from the substance of its protest. "After all," he asked, "where is the boasted advantage of a representation system . . . if the resort to popular meetings is necessary?"[12]

In Cabot's social attitudes there was of course much self-interest, but little self-indulgence. The burden of respectability rested heavily upon him. He worried himself with the thought that he was failing in his duty. Though he held many responsible positions, he criticized himself for "an aversion to all sorts of responsibility, founded upon an anxiety lest I should not properly acquit myself."[13]

Cabot and his colleagues agreed that if the "best people" properly acquitted themselves, the republic would be safe. But in the 1780s there were disturbing signs of misbehavior among the "natural rulers of society." There was, for example, the case of Robert Morris, who turned the perquisites of public office to private advantage without scruple or restraint. Morris was a "commercial man," a moderate Whig, a friend to "high-toned government," whose principles, in so far as he had any, were basically harmonious with those of Cabot and his mercantile friends in Massachusetts. Yet they bitterly excoriated the "most scandalous conduct" of "Mr. Financier" and prayed for his retirement.[14]

[11] Higginson to Pickering, May 27, 1797, in Pickering Papers; Jackson, *Political Situation*, p. 27; Ames, "Schoolbooks," *Works*, II, 405–406; Porter, *Jacksons and Lees*, I, 119; Parsons, *Memoir*, p. 23. See also *Kendall* v. *Inhabitants of Kingston, Mass. Repts.*, V (1809), 524–535, esp. 530–535.

[12] Cabot to King, Aug. 14, 1795, in Lodge, *Cabot*, 85. See also B. Goodhue to S. Goodhue, Jan. 9, Apr. 9, 1796, Goodhue Papers, Essex Institute.

[13] Cabot to Pickering, Feb. 17, 1808, in Pickering Papers, Mass. Hist. Soc.; see also Cabot to Wolcott, Apr. 21, 1798, Cabot to Pickering, Apr. 2, 1808, Cabot to Gore, Apr. 17, 1797, in Lodge, *Cabot*, pp. 159, 390, 132.

[14] Clarence L. Ver Steeg, *Robert Morris, Revolutionary Financier* (Philadelphia, 1954), pp. 22–27; Ferguson, *Power of the Purse*, pp. 70–105. See Higginson to Arthur Lee, [Oct.] 1783, in Jameson, ed., *Letters of Higginson*, ed. Jameson, 711–713; Robert A. East, "Massachusetts Conservatives in the Critical Period," in *The Era of the American Revolution*, ed. Richard B. Morris, (New York, 1939), pp. 349–391, esp. p. 368; Samuel Osgood to Higginson, Feb. 2, 1784, in *Letters of Members*

The misbehavior of Robert Morris was less distressing than another kind of corruption personified in a second great "commercial character," John Hancock, who had formed the disagreeable habit of yielding to political opinions merely because they were popular. Cabot made no distinction in value between the malefactions of Morris and Hancock. To alter one's public conduct for the sake of a vote was as fundamentally dishonest as to change it for a dollar. Cabot believed that to give way before "merely popular opinion" was doubly disagreeable because usually it was unnecessary. What was popular was vaporous and transient, mere whipsyllabub, a puff of air. "Popular gales sometimes blow hard, but they don't blow long," he wrote. "The man who has the courage to face them will at last *out*face them."[15] In a curious way, Cabot was an idealist who rested his behavior upon a conception of society as it ought to be. The fact that his ideals cannot be comprehended in the familiar American formulas of liberty, equality, and majority rule does not mean that they were dishonest or unsustained.

Cabot's idealism was in harmony with his interests as he conceived them. But at the end of the eighteenth century it was incompatible with the changing realities of American politics. During the War for Independence the cement of Cabot's commonwealth had begun to crumble. As another Federalist wrote in 1787, "the people turned against their teachers the doctrines which were inculcated in order to effect the late revolution." In this context, when things began to go wrong, Cabot and his colleagues delivered themselves of dark comments upon the nature of their species, not as detached rational judgments but impassioned Jeremiads, in traditional New England style.[16]

George Cabot's principles, it must be quickly noted, were not peculiar to New England. Striking similarities appear in the attitudes of a New Yorker, John Jay (1745–1829). Even more than Cabot, Jay personified the virtues which gentlemen of the old school valued most dearly—all the qualities of mind and character summarized by the Romans in the word *gravitas*. In 1800, Jay was fifty-five years old, a gentleman farmer of independent means, a distinguished statesman of

---

of the Continental Congress, ed. Edmund C. Burnett, VII (Washington, 1934), 430–436; Higginson to Hamilton, Nov. 11, 1789, in *Papers of Alexander Hamilton,* ed. Harold C. Syrett, V (New York, 1962), 507–511, quotation on p. 507.

[15] Higginson, *Laco,* 8, 14, 22; Pickering to Jacob Ashton, Oct. 29, 1816 in Upham, *Pickering,* IV, 277; Pickering to James Pindell, Jan. 27, 1814, in Pickering Papers; Cabot to Wolcott, Apr. 7, 1797, in Lodge, *Cabot,* p. 120. I read "last" for "least".

[16] Ames, "Camillus No. 1," *Works,* II, 101; see also Stephen Higginson to [?], Apr. 1784, in *Letters of Higginson,* pp. 713–719, esp. p. 716; and Jackson, *Political Situation,* p. 132; Cabot to Pickering, Apr. 10, 1804, in Pickering Papers, Mass. Hist. Soc.; Cabot to Parsons, Aug. 12, 1794, in Lodge, *Cabot,* p. 79. Here again Perry Miller's work on the Puritans is suggestive; cf. *The New England Mind: From Colony to Province* (Cambridge, Mass., 1953), pp. 19–39.

broad experience and bright achievement, a devout Christian who combined the honest piety of his Huguenot forebears with the flamboyant lights-and-incense devotionalism of his adopted Anglican church.[17]

Jay's political and social assumptions were essentially identical with Cabot's. The conceptual unit of his thought was society rather than the individual. Jay is principally remembered for his role in a rebellion which had liberty as its watchword. But as early as March 1776 he was apprehensive of "licentiousness" in American society. "Liberty and reformation may run mad," he declared, "and madness of any kind is no blessing." Freedom was a word which—like many Founding fathers— he rarely used. Liberty he chose to define in terms of the common good. "Civil liberty," Jay wrote, "consists not in a right to every man to do just as he pleases, but it consists in an equal right to all the citizens to have, enjoy, and to do, in peace, security, and without molestation, whatever the equal and constitutional laws of the country admit to be consistent with the public good."[18]

Equality of right, but inequality of condition, were fundamental to his thought. "Those who write for the public," he declared, "write for the simple as well as the wise." From an assumption of inequality he derived his collectivistic conception of society and his preference for positive government. "The mass of men," he observed, "are neither wise nor good, and virtue, like the other resources of a country, can only be drawn to a point and exerted by strong circumstances ably managed, or a strong government ably administered.[19]

Jay, like Cabot, was an elitist, but not an extreme antidemocrat. He believed that popular participation was essential to the stability of a republic, and he favored a broad electorate for the choice of both legis-

[17] Frank Monaghan, *John Jay, Defender of Liberty* (New York, 1935), pp. 16–22, 25, 42–43, 68, 72, 94–95, 218–219, 428; John Jay to Jedidiah Morse, Jan. 1, 1813, John Jay to Timothy Pickering, Aug. 17, 1795, in *The Correspondence and Public Papers of John Jay*, ed. Henry P. Johnston, 4 vols. (New York, 1890–1893), IV, 365–367, 185. Not many Federalists of the old school could conceivably be called devout, but Jay was clearly an exception. See Jay to Gouverneur Morris, Oct. 28, 1816, ibid., IV, 393–394.

[18] Jay to Alexander MacDougall, Mar. 23, 1776, Jay to William Vaughan, May 26, 1796; Jay, "Charge to the Grand Jury of Ulster County," 1777; Jay, "An Address to the People of the State of New York," 1788; Jay, "Charge to the Grand Juries of the Eastern Circuit," in Johnston, *Jay*, I, 49–51; IV, 217–218; I, 164; III, 297; III, 395. See also W. F. Craven, *Legend of the Founding Fathers*, p. 55.

[19] Jay to Rufus King, Dec. 22, 1793, in King Papers, New York Hist. Soc.; partly printed in King, *Life and Corres. of King*, I, 509–510. See also Jay to Thomas Jefferson, Sep. 8, 1787, Jay to George Washington, June 27, 1786; Jay to John Hartley, Jan. 8, 1795; Jay to Lord Lansdowne, Apr. 20, 1786, in Johnston, *Jay*, III, 191–194, 204–205; IV, 153, 160–162; Gottfried Dietze, *The Federalist; A Classic on Federalism and Free Government* (Baltimore, 1960), p. 78. Jay grew steadily more pessimistic about the nature of man as he grew older and American politics became more democratic; cf. Jay, "Address to the People of the State of New York," (New York, 1788), pp. 3–4; and Jay to Richard Peters, Mar. 14, 1815, in Johnston, *Jay*, IV, 386–388.

lators and the executive. He persisted in this opinion, despite the French Revolution, despite demagogic assaults upon his character in 1795, despite the fact that he was once attacked and nearly killed by a Manhattan mob and carried home to his frantic wife with blood streaming from "two large holes in his forehead." As late as 1810 he wrote to his English friend William Wilberforce, "The French Revolution has so discredited democracy, and it has so few influential advocates in Europe, that I doubt its giving you much more trouble. On the contrary, there seems to be a danger of its depreciating too much. Without a portion of it there can be no free government.[20]

Jay believed that the people must choose their own governors, but he was unwilling to see them govern themselves. In New York he tried to reduce property qualifications for voting, but at the same time a favorite political maxim was "those who own the country ought to govern it." The reconciliation of these apparently divergent commitments lay not in the constitutional constructions of 1787 but in the deferential spirit of colonial society. "Our government should in some degree be suited to our manners and circumstances," he wrote, "and they, you know, are not strictly democratical."[21]

The "habit of subordination" was not, perhaps, as deeply rooted in the middle states as in the orderly towns of New England. But it was clearly present during Jay's formative years. "We were accustomed to look upon gentlefolk as beings of a superior order," one man recalled. "For my part, I was quite shy of them and kept off at a humble distance. A periwig in those days was a distinguishing badge of gentlefolk, and when I saw a man riding the road near our house with a wig on, it would so alarm my fears and give me such a disagreeable feeling that I daresay I would run off as for my life."[22]

Jay's conservative idealism derived from his remembrance of the past, from his cherished recollection of deference and distinctions in colonial society. He believed at the end of the century that enough remained of both to sustain a model commonwealth of the kind that he and Cabot idealized. In private correspondence and public statements

[20] Jay to Wilberforce, Oct. 25, 1810, in Johnston, *Jay*, IV, 335–336; Monaghan, *Jay*, pp. 94–97; *Journals of the Provincial Congress . . . of New York*, 2 vols. (Albany, 1842), I, 867; Hammond, *Political Parties in New York*, I, 93. Contemporaries believed that the Jeffersonian movement began with Jefferson's jealousy of Jay. See John Adams to J. Q. Adams, Dec. 24, 1804, in Adams Family Papers, Mass. Hist. Soc., reel 403; Fisher Ames to Thomas Dwight, Aug. 24, 1795, in Ames, *Works*, I, 172.

[21] Jay to George Washington, Jan. 7, 1787, June 27, 1786; Jay to Richard Price, Sep. 27, 1785; Johnston, *Jay*, III, 226–229, 203–205, 168–169. Jay's conception of representation was *in personam*. See Jay to Col. Floyd, n.d., Johnston, *Jay*, I, 217.

[22] Devereux Jarret, *Autobiography* (Baltimore, 1806), p. 14; Hilliard, *Jeremiah Mason*, p. 157; Charles Biddle, *Autobiography*, pp. 330–331n; Carl Becker, *The History of Political Parties in the Province of New York, 1760–1776*, 2nd pr. (Madison, 1960), pp. 13–17.

he declared confidently that "social harmony" could be preserved if the "virtuous and wise," "the rational and well-intentioned," "the better sort of people" were firmly united and faithful to their special obligations. "If the sound and leading friends of their country could concur in opinion as to men and measures," he wrote, "their efforts would probably be successful; but unfortunately there is too little unanimity in many points, and the want of it exposes us to the hazard of many evils."[23]

Jay's sense of public responsibility bore heavily upon him. "We must go home to be happy," he declared, "and our home is not in this world. Here we have nothing to do but our duty." But he drove himself to the mark, and sought to drive others too. In 1796, during the domestic crisis caused by his controversial treaty, he was provoked to comment, "It seems strange, but so it is in all republics, that many excellent men who are happy in their families and fortunes and in the esteem of society and of their friends, who enjoy their villas and their gardens and neglect not to guard their trees and vines from caterpillars and their favorite plants and flowers from nipping frosts, yet omit attending to the political grubs, who are constantly and insiduously labouring to wound and prey upon the roots of all their temporal enjoyments."[24]

Political parties, to Jay as to Cabot, constituted a threat to social solidarity, an impediment to good order, a breeding ground for the political grubs whose existence he lamented. His stubborn refusal, as governor of New York, to limit appointments to Federalists provoked at least one of them to become a Jeffersonian. In 1800 he refused to allow supporters to tinker with state election laws for partisan advantage, though the practice was commonly resorted to by Federalists and "Anti's" in many other states. On still another occasion he issued a quaint public declaration: "Every consideration of propriety forbids that differences in opinion respecting candidates should suspend that natural good humor which harmonizes society."[25]

Society above the individual and "high-toned" government above them

---

[23] Jay to Lindley Murray, Aug. 22, 1794; Jay to Theophilus Parsons, July 1, 1800; Johnston, *Jay*, IV, 51–52, 274–275; Jay to Pickering, Dec. 24, 1808, in Pickering Papers, Mass. Hist. Soc.

[24] Jay to Lowell, Feb. 29, 1796, Johnston, *Jay*, IV, 204–205; Monaghan, *Jay*, pp. 413–414, 422; George S. Hilliard, *Memoir, Autobiography and Correspondence of Jeremiah Mason* (Kansas City, 1917).

[25] Jay to James Duane, Sep. 16, 1795; Schuyler to Jay, May 7, 1800; Jay to Richard Hatfield et al., Nov. 8, 1800; Jay to George Washington, Sep. 13, 1794, Feb. 25, 1795; Johnston, *Jay*, IV, 191–194, 273, 278–280, 59, 160–161. The renegade Federalist was Ambrose Spencer; [New York] *Evening Post*, Jan. 25, 1802. Hammond, *History of Political Parties in the State of New York*, II, 71; Cabot to Christopher Gore, May 2, 1799, Lodge, *Cabot*, p. 231; Robert Troup to Rufus King, May 6, 1799, Mar. 9, Nov. 9, 1800; May 27, 1801; King, *Life and Correspondence of King*, III, 14, 208, 331, 458. For Jay's family, which in its organization reflected his politics and in its tone revealed his personality, see Mrs. Jay to Jay, Dec. 28, 1778, Johnston, *Jay*, I, 184–185.

both; a consciousness of class distinctions but not of class conflict; a faith that the people could choose their own governors, but not that they could govern themselves; a feeling that party organization was an engine of social disorganization—this was the substance of Jay's social thought, the marrow of his political idealism. Stiff in his self-righteousness, stubborn in his sense of rectitude, he personified the Old School in both its strength and weaknesses.

2

Federalists of the old school did not comprise a tidy socioeconomic interest group. The principles personified by Cabot and Jay were shaped and colored by a rich variety of social, geographic, economic, ethnic, psychological, and religious factors. To discuss this diversity in comprehensive fashion is beyond the scope of this essay. But a brief sampling of variations may serve to display more clearly the underlying theme, and at the same time to indicate the way in which an idealized pattern of political leadership was actually practiced in eighteenth-century America.

It is well known that Federalism flourished within sight of salt water. The explanation is not necessarily economic. By 1800 many small tidewater communities had reached a state of social equilibrium which reinforced both the prejudices and the power of the gentlemen of the old school. And in seafaring centers, the division between fo'c'sle and quarterdeck was carried into politics—"Jefferson seemed but a mutineering first mate, and his 'rights of man' but the black flag of a rebellious crew."[26]

An illustration is the career of Captain Thomas Truxtun (1755–1822) a hero of our "quasi-war" with France. Forty-five years old in 1800, Truxton had spent thirty-three of them at sea; he had joined his first ship at the age of twelve, when the death of his father, an English barrister practicing in New York, shattered the fortunes of his family. During the War of Independence, Truxtun won fame as a privateersman. When Congress organized the Navy in the 1790s, he was honored with a coveted command—the new live-oak frigate *Constellation*.[27]

Captain Truxtun's famous adventures in *Constellation* have been chronicled elsewhere. Our business is with the way he ran his ship. A "happy and well-governed" vessel in his estimation was one whose

[26] Thomas Wentworth Higginson, *Life and Times of Stephen Higginson* (Boston, 1907), p. 42; Labaree, *Patriots and Partisans*, pp. 11–14, has recently made the same point. For the relationship of social stability to partisan commitment, see Rowland Berthoff's brilliant and suggestive "The American Social Order; A Conservative Hypothesis," *Amer. Hist. Rev.*, LXV (1960), 495–514.

[27] Eugene S. Ferguson, *Truxtun of the Constellation; The Life of Commodore Thomas Truxtun, U.S. Navy, 1755–1822* (Baltimore, 1956), pp. 3, 5–13, 17–19, 23–47, 100–122.

officers were able "to keep alive a good Subordination." This he managed to accomplish without resorting to either cruelty or terror. Though his best friends admitted that he was a "Proud and tyrannical" commander, he was never a brutal one. In his entire naval career he punished but one man with the lash, when other American frigate captains were flogging six a day. In his standing orders, Truxtun required his officers to be "Civil and polite to everyone . . . for Civility does not interfere with discipline."[28]

Truxtun's discipline rested mainly on the force of his personality, reinforced by the open and habitual display of deference. "No officer must attempt to offer an opinion to me," he ordered, "without its first being previously asked." Commissioned officers were instructed to avoid "improper familiarity with the Petty Officers." When common seamen found it necessary to address a superior they were required to "Speak holding their hats in hand."[29]

His methods appear to have been most remarkably effective. USS *Constellation* was no more free of grousing than any other man-of-war, but by and large the crew seems to have internalized Truxtun's values. "There is one thing certain," an unfriendly observer noted, "that his word is a Law here, which may not be his fault, as mankind will be Blinded in the radiance of Glory." The life of the Captain, in the center of this "petty kingdom," was not, of course, an easy one. Few men could meet the cost. "No society, no smiles," a junior officer wrote, "wrapped up in his notions of his own dignity, and the means of preserving it, he shuts himself up from all around him. He stands alone, without the friendship or sympathy of one on board; a solitary being in the midst of the ocean."[30]

When Captain Truxtun came ashore, he carried his quarterdeck habits with him. Jeffersonian commercial and naval policy might have been enough to have made him a Federalist, but the habit of command provided a broader basis for rapport with the principles of Cabot and Jay. After the fashion of old-school Federalism, his first response to the Jeffersonian movement was to turn his back upon it. "I wish to know no man that is not a real and true patriot," he wrote. Nominated for

---

[28] Ibid., pp. 140, 144–151. Truxtun made disciples by the success of his discipline. When Lt. John Rodgers, first lieutenant in *Constellation*, succeeded to his own command, a visitor noted that "the order on board was *Great, & Probably* too much all *a mode L'Truxtun*" [sic]. Ibid., p. 148.

[29] Ibid., pp. 141–203.

[30] David Porter, *Constantinople and Environs* (New York, 1835), II, 10; Truxtun to James McHenry, Mar. 3, 1797, Steiner, *McHenry*, p. 251; "If the chinese system is not to be adopted in the United States, and the people of our towns continue their commercial habits of trading beyond the sea, it is evident [that we must have] . . . a Navy to defend our rights, and support the honor and dignity of our flag." Biddle, *Autobiography*, p. 414; E. S. Ferguson, . . . *Description of the Truxtun-Biddle Letters* (Philadelphia, 1947), p. 18; Ferguson, *Truxtun*, pp. 256–257.

office by "Friends of Order" after his retirement, he steadfastly refused to court a following, to electioneer in any way. Captain Truxtun was not averse to the introduction of organization to politics. On an earlier election day, when *Constellation* lay at a wharf in Philadelphia, her company marched to the polls and voted by divisions. But the idea of appealing for popular support was beneath consideration. Altogether, Truxtun's political attitudes were summed up in a single metaphor by another salt-water Federalist. "In the political ship there must be common seamen as well as pilots," wrote Theophilus Parsons, "and a mutiny of the crew may as effectually destroy her as a division among the officers."[31]

Federalists of the old school were not, of course, confined to coastal communities. William Sullivan, in his memoirs, described another group of like-minded men whose physical environment was far removed from Truxtun's. "There was a class of persons, no longer known," he wrote in 1834, "who might be called the gentry of the interior. They held very considerable landed estates, in imitation of landholders in England. These persons were the great men in their respective counties. They held civil and military offices, and were members of the General Court. This sort of personal dignity disappeared before the end of the last century."[32]

By 1800, the "gentry of the interior" were indeed a disappearing breed. But more than a few still survived, struggling to preserve their ancient privileges. Charles Cotesworth Pinckney of South Carolina is an example; so too is Charles Carroll of Carrollton in Maryland. But none serves better to illustrate the type than Theodore Sedgwick (1746–1813) of Berkshire County, Massachusetts. The first Sedgwick in America was Theodore's great-great-grandfather, Major Robert Sedgwick, wealthy brewer, patron of Harvard, Cromwellian soldier, and sometime governor of Jamaica. At the end of the eighteenth century, Theodore Sedgwick's social and economic situation was stabilized, if not by his family roots or his education at Yale, then by three successive matrimonial alliances with the ruling families of western Massachusetts.[33]

When the war came in 1775, Sedgwick made a most reluctant rebel. He prized his Tory friends, and nourished a fear of social disorganization which foreshadowed his Federalist commitment. As late as May 1776, he was unable to accept the idea of independence; as early as August of the same year he was troubled by the spirit of "licentiousness" which he

[31] Parsons to Timothy Pickering, n.d. [Dec. 1, 1797?], Parsons, *Memoir of Parsons*, pp. 122–124; [Hartford] *American Mercury*, Dec. 2, 1802; Truxtun to Biddle, July 11, 1807, Biddle, *Autobiography*, p. 413; Ferguson, *Truxtun*, p. 258.

[32] Sullivan, *Familiar Letters*, p. 2.

[33] The three families were the Masons, Dwights, and Russells. H. D. Sedgwick, "The Sedgwicks of Berkshire," *Berkshire Hist. Soc. Collections*, III (1899–1913), 91–106, esp. 91–92; Mary E. Dewey, ed., *Life and Letters of Catherine Maria Sedgwick* (New York, 1871), pp. 13–37.

sensed in the people. To Aaron Burr he wrote, "In the confusion which was at once the cause and consequence of a dissolution of Government, men's minds as well as actions became regardless of all legal restraint. . . . The people were the fountain of all honor. The first thing they did was to withdraw all confidence from everyone who had ever any connexion with government."[34]

The events of the 1780s did not ease Sedgwick's mind. In 1787 he wrote to Rufus King, "Every man of observation is convinced that the end of government, security, cannot be attained by the exercise of principles founded on democratic equality. A war is now actually levied, on virtue, property and distinctions in the community, and however there may be an appearance of a temporary cessation of hostilities, yet the flame will again and again break out."[35]

Doubts and mental hesitations notwithstanding, Sedgwick committed himself unequivocally to the Whig cause. At the end of the war, he more than any other single figure dominated the politics of his county. There was a bad moment during Shays' Rebellion, when angry men with sprigs of hemlock in their hats overran Sedgwick's estate and sacked his mansion. But in his bids for public office during the 1780s and 1790s, Sedgwick secured pluralities with astonishing regularity.[36]

The means by which Sedgwick controlled his county ought not to be confused with the methods of a modern party machine.[37] The principal prop beneath his power was the habit of deference in the people. It was slipping, as Shays' Rebellion showed, but not yet down. Every act of Sedgwick's was designed to buttress it. Firstly, he sought to strengthen "the influence of numerous connexions formed into a phalanx by family compact," as a Jeffersonian described it. Sedgwicks, Dwights, Van Schaicks, Worthingtons, Masons, and Sergeants were intertwined in one extended cousinage, one "union of political influence" which allowed of no alternative to rule by the wise and good.[38]

Secondly, Sedgwick endeavored to promote "good order" in Berkshire County by means of an alliance with the established Congregational

[34] Theodore Sedgwick to Aaron Burr, Aug. 7, 1776, in Davis, Memoirs of Burr, I, 92–93; Lee Nathaniel Newcomer, The Embattled Farmers; A Massachusetts Countryside in the American Revolution (New York, 1953), p. 99.

[35] Theodore Sedgwick to Rufus King, June 18, 1787, in King, Life and Correspondence of King, I, 223–224.

[36] In an incident long cherished by the ruling families of the county, a devoted family retainer saved the Sedgwick silver by distracting the rioters. Marion L. Starkey, A Little Rebellion (New York, 1955), p. 177.

[37] See the unpubl. diss. (Harvard, 1952) by Richard E. Welch, Jr., "Theodore Sedgwick, 1746–1813; Federalist."

[38] [Barnabas Bidwell], The Honorable Mr. Sedgwicks Political Last Will and Testament, with an Inventory and Appraisal of the Legacies therein Bequeathed (Stockbridge?, 1800), p. 5; Dewey, ed., Life and Letters of Catherine Maria Sedgwick, p. 49.

Church. Though he personally found Unitarianism attractive, his heresy remained a closely guarded secret until he made a deathbed confession to William Ellery Channing. In addition to the church, he used "the liberal puffs of a devoted newspaper." The Stockbridge *Western Star* was one of the few journals outside the great cities for which regular Federalist patronage can be substantiated. Sedgwick's support consisted mainly of "occasional advertisements, and dinners and treats for the editor," and "at one time a *douceur* of twenty dollars." The political coverage of the *Western Star* was at best sporadic during the 1780s and 1790s, but the talents of its editor were a welcome addition to the arsenal of order.[39]

But Sedgwick's mainstay was much the same as Thomas Truxtun's— an insistence upon an open and habitual display of subordination. Sedgwick was known as "the kindest of neighbors, not less among the very poor than the well-to-do." But for the former the price of Sedgwick's generosity was some small token of submission. "He was born too soon to relish the freedoms of democracy," his daughter wrote. "I have seen his brow lower when a free-and-easy mechanic came to the *front* door, and upon one occasion I remember his turning off the 'east steps' (I am *sure* not kicking, but the demonstration was unequivocal) a grown-up lad who kept his hat on after being told to take it off."[40]

Theodore Sedgwick was not one of the brightest stars in the Federal firmament. But like his russet-coated ancestor, he knew what he fought for and loved what he knew. In his instinctive commitment to the "cause of order," in the very mediocrity of his talents, Sedgwick was a more representative member of the old school than his more brilliant and famous associates.[41]

Some of the more cacophonous variations on our theme appear wherever old-school Federalism intersected with the frontier. An illustration is the public career of William Cooper (1754–1809), founder of Cooperstown, N.Y., father of James Fenimore Cooper, and one of the most picturesque political characters in the new republic.

Cooper was nearly as self-made as a man can be. Son of a poor Pennsylvania Quaker, he eloped with an heiress and extracted a small fortune

[39] Richard D. Birdsall, *Berkshire County, A Cultural History* (New Haven, 1959), pp. 51, 183–184; [Bidwell], *Sedgwick's Political Will*, p. 5; Henry Van Schaack to Theodore Sedgwick, Feb. 9, 1801, in Sedgwick Papers, Mass. Hist. Soc.; see below ch. VII. Bidwell's remarks bring to mind the fact that "liberal" in its present political usage is anachronistic when applied to the politics of the new republic. "Conservative," however, was just coming in: e.g., "to influence the country into the adoption of conservatory principles." Jacob Wagner to Pickering, May 13, 1808, in Pickering Papers, Mass. Hist. Soc.; the earliest usage I have found.

[40] Dewey, ed., *Life and Letters of Catherine Maria Sedgwick*, pp. 49–50; H. D. Sedgwick, "The Sedgwicks of Berkshire," p. 96.

[41] H. D. Sedgwick, "The Sedgwicks of Berkshire," p. 94; Sir Charles Firth, *Oliver Cromwell and the Rule of the Puritans in England* (London, 1900; World's Classics edition, 1953), p. 90.

from a series of intricate but invariably successful land speculations. During the War of Independence he purchased a large tract in the upper Susquehanna Valley, and sold it in small sections to farmers who were willing to make Cooperstown their home. By 1805 he calculated that he had settled some 40,000 souls upon 750,000 acres of virgin soil, an achievement quite possibly without parallel in the history of the westward movement.[42]

Like Cabot's social attitudes, Cooper's social relationships are not easily conceived in twentieth-century terms. Unlike Truxtun, he combined an open display of elitism with an intimacy with the people. Cooper always cherished his emblems of superiority. Before the Susquehanna Valley was laced with open roads, he contrived to import a little carriage, lashed across the gunwales of two canoes, and proudly traveled about in it with files of men on either side struggling to prevent the vehicle from capsizing on the rough and rock-strewn ground. But he never held himself aloof from his neighbors, high or low. He was a frequent visitor to Cooperstown's Red Lion Tavern, where he drank with the men of the village and responded to their humor with his hearty laughter. A tall, powerful man, he boasted that he could throw any man in the county— at least once the courts investigated a "bruising match" between Cooper and another settler.[43]

This American Squire Western described the method by which he controlled the politics of Cooperstown as "the art of hook and snivery." It was an unholy combination of persuasion, flattery, force, fraud, bribery, favoritism, imposition, intimidation, demagoguery, arm-twisting and elbow-bending, which went on the whole year round. Cooper was always on hand at a wedding, even in the humblest cabins. At a marriage in one poor settler's hovel he stood before the couple in his high old-fashioned riding boots mud-spattered to the hip, solemnly pronounced them man and wife, turned down a gratuity, gave the bride "a good hearty kiss or rather smack, remarking that he always claimed that as his fee," took a hearty swig of rum, swallowed a chunk of wedding cake, and was off to his next appointment.[44]

Cooper was most active in this fashion just at election-time. In the midst of one campaign a friend wrote, "Reports say, that you was very civil to the young and handsome of the sex, that you flattered the old

[42] Lyman H. Butterfield, "Judge William Cooper (1754–1809): A Sketch of his Character and Accomplishment," *New York History*, XXX (1949), 386; Butterfield, "Cooper's Inheritance," ibid., XXXV (1954), 6–43; Moss Kent to James Kent, Apr. 21, May 5, July 8, 1796, in Kent Papers, Library of Congress; Hudson *Northern Whig*, Jan. 18, 1810. James Fenimore Cooper sketched his father in *The Pioneers* as Judge Marmaduke Temple.

[43] Butterfield, "Cooper's Inheritance," p. 21; and "Judge William Cooper," pp. 397–401. See also James Fenimore Cooper's sketch of Judge Temple in *The Pioneers*.

[44] Butterfield, "Cooper's Inheritance," p. 396.

and ugly, and even embraced the toothless and decrepit, in order to obtain votes—when will you write a treatise on electioneering? Whenever you do, afford a few copies only to your friends." Cooper's electioneering continued after the election had ended. If the returns showed a plurality for his hand-picked candidates (they often did, for he hand-picked the election judges too), the people would be rewarded with a celebration. In 1792, he made elaborate plans to celebrate an anticipated Federalist victory by arranging to "Illuminate as well the town as the lake on which we shall raise bonfires on Platforms, cannonading, musick, Horns and Conche Shells, turn out all the wine in my cellar, etc."[45]

Cooper much preferred the carrot to the stick. "So, in rural phrase," he wrote candidly, "may we compare the poor settler to the creature of draft. Unsustained, over-loaded, and oppressed, he yields no profit; well-treated, in good heart, and gently driven, his labor is lighter and profit more." But he was known to use the hook, as well as "snivery." Cooper bullied recalcitrant citizens who insisted upon voting as they pleased, threatening to foreclose a mortgage or withhold a coveted favor. When a Jeffersonian tried to organize a following in Cooperstown, Cooper placed him in irons and packed him off to New York City for trial under the Sedition Law.[46]

William Cooper's techniques bear a certain superficial resemblance to those of a twentieth-century political leader; but the differences are fundamental. Implicit even in his most intimate gestures was an elitistic spirit, an expectation of deference. He never appealed for support on a basis of equality, nor tried to construct a broadly based and efficiently organized political party. Indeed, his treatment of Federalists who refused to recognize his paternal authority could be almost as harsh as his punishment of Jeffersonians. Cooper never "offered" himself in the Jeffersonian sense; instead he invited the people to acknowledge his supremacy and their subordination. In return he promised benevolence, affection, and security. As Erich Fromm has suggested, it could be a deeply satisfying arrangement for many more people than Cooper, even on the frontier.

Cabot, Jay, Truxtun, Sedgwick, Cooper—these are representative Federalists of the old school. The list embraces a variety of interests and circumstances. Old family and new, urban and rural, from the quarter-

---

[45] Philip Schuyler to Cooper, 1 May 1792; Cooper to Stephen Van Rensselaer, 2 May 1792; James Fenimore Cooper, *Legends and Traditions of a Northern County* (Cooperstown, 1936), pp. 117, 123; for Cooper's use of popular rhetoric, see *Annals of Congress*, 4th Cong., 1st Sess., p. 541.

[46] William Cooper, *Guide to the Wilderness* (Cooperstown, N.Y., 1936), p. 8; Henry W. Boynton, *James Fenimore Cooper* (New York, 1931), p. 13; James Morton Smith, *Freedom's Fetters* (Ithaca, N.Y., 1956), p. 394; Moss Kent to James Kent, April 21, May 5, July 8, 1796, in Kent Papers, Library of Congress; for Cooper's activity in 1796–1797 see [Cooperstown, N.Y.] *Otsego Herald*, 15 Dec. 1796, 2 Feb. 1797.

deck of *Constellation* to the green hills of Berkshire County, Federalists lived in many different situations. There were other dimensions beyond these—we have neglected southern Federalists such as Pinckney or Carroll, or for that matter George Washington, all of whom show a basic identity with the principles examined here.[47] We have ignored the variety of Federalism which flourished in the fashionable salons of Philadelphia and New York, and was personified by Gouverneur Morris (1752–1816), a "pleasurable man" whose character revealed none of the *gravitas* that appeared in Cabot and Jay, but whose principles in an effete and even Frenchified way were remarkably similar.[48]

All of these men were deeply conscious of inequalities; all tended to think in terms of society rather than the individual, of maximal rather than minimal government. All hoped to sustain a governing elite with the consent of the people, by reinforcing the deferential spirit of colonial society. All sought not to institutionalize social conflict but to strengthen social harmony. All bitterly opposed the "spirit of party" at the same time that they sought to exclude "disorganizers" from the government. If their political ideals must be summarized in a slogan, then let it be Samuel Stone's—"*a speaking* aristocracy *in the face of a silent* democracy."

3

There were, of course, exceptions. Not every Federalist was able to endorse these central ideas of the old school. One dissenter was that "queer gentleman" John Adams (1735–1826). His political ideas need no exposition here. Every informed student of early American politics is familiar with his hope that deep human drives could be harnessed to the wheels and gears of a balanced constitution.[49]

Less familiar, perhaps, is Adams' curious relationship with other Federalists. The gentlemen of the old school read his treatises and generally praised them. One believed that Adams' chef d'œuvre was "rather an encomium on the British constitution than a defence of

[47] For George Washington see Harold W. Bradley's "The Political Thinking of George Washington," *Journal of Southern History*, XI (1945), 469–486; and Saul K. Padover, "George Washington—Portrait of a True Conservative," *Social Research*, XXII (1955) 199–222.

[48] For Gouverneur Morris see esp. Morris to Aaron Ogden, Dec. 28, 1804, Morris to John Dickinson, May 23, 1803, Morris to Uriah Tracy, Jan. 5, 1804, in Morris Papers, Library of Congress; Anne Cary Morris, ed., *The Diary and Letters of Gouverneur Morris*, 2 vols. (New York, 1888), II, 471–476; Morris, "Equality," [1796?], in Morris Papers, Columbia University Library.

[49] For Adams as that "queer gentlemen," see John Rutledge, Jr. to Harrison Gray Otis, June 6, 1809, in Otis Papers, Mass. Hist. Soc. Adams' notion of a balanced constitution is most conveniently contained in his famous correspondence with Jefferson, especially his letters of June 25, July 9, July 13, 1813, and Nov. 13, 1815; Cappon, ed. *Adams-Jefferson Letters*, II, 334, 352, 355, 456.

the American systems." But altogether, their relations with Adams the philosopher were superficially harmonious.[50]

Not so their relations with Adams the politician. By 1800, after three years of his administration, many federal leaders so thoroughly misunderstood him that they believed he had taken leave of his senses. "With regard to Mr. A.," wrote Ebenezer Mattoon, "it is impossible to calculate upon him. It would puzzle the angels to develop the motives of his conduct." Another Federalist, John Steele of North Carolina, wrote home that "Mr. Adams has lately acted so strange a part that many do not hesitate to assert he is deranged in his intellect. The democrats laugh, but Federalists lament that there should be any cause for such an opinion."[51]

The violent quarrels between Adams and other Federalists in 1799–1800 were not merely a matter of appointments, the army, and foreign affairs, but a clash of conflicting political conceptions. Adams never shared the dream of social harmony. His balanced constitution was directly designed to institutionalize social conflicts of the kind which other Federalists hoped to prevent. Equally important was the fact that Adams conceived of the balance as a machine which would restrain both democracy and aristocracy from gaining a predominance. In the light of the structure of colonial society it could be argued that the latter was a prior objective.[52]

Federalists of the old school visualized the balanced constitution as an essentially antipopular device. When they praised Adams, it was his

[50] W. R. Davie to James Iredell, Aug. 6, 1787, in Iredell Papers, Duke University Library. For Jeffersonian criticism see Barnabas Bidwell to Ephraim Kirby, Sep. 20, 1802, in Kirby Papers, Duke. Wrote Kirby: "If the people could be convinced that our late president's favorite . . . model is the English government . . . could it not have a very great political effect?" See also Mahlon Dickerson's mistaken opinion that the *Defence* was "a weak attempt to support aristocracy." Diary, Oct. 15, 1798, in Dickerson Papers, N.J. Hist. Soc.

[51] Ebenezer Mattoon to Thomas Dwight, Mar. 2, 1801, in Dwight-Howard Papers, Mass. Hist. Soc.; John Steele to Miss Anne Steele, n.d., in Steele Papers, II, Southern Hist. Coll., Univ. of N. C.; see also "the unsteady temper of our late president," Gouverneur Morris to John Parish, Nov. 13, 1801, in Morris Papers, Library of Congress; "credulity easily imposed upon by flattery, an overweening fondness for self. . . . Happy it would have been . . . had he died 12 years ago," Charles Cotesworth Pinckney to Pickering, Dec. 31, 1808, in Pickering Papers, Mass. Hist. Soc.; "those sportive humors for which our chief is distinguished," Wolcott to Pickering, Dec. 28, 1800, in Pickering Papers, Mass. Hist. Soc.; "What is the charm that attaches the east so much to Mr. A? It can be nothing personal," Bayard to Hamilton, in Bayard Papers, N.Y. Public Library; also Bayard to ?, Jan. 30, 1801, in Ely Papers, N.J. Hist. Soc.; John Rutledge, Jr., to Fisher Ames, Aug. 22, 1800, Houghton Library, Harvard University; McHenry to Pickering, Mar. 20, 1809, in Pickering Papers, Mass. Hist. Soc.; Wm. Plumer, Diary, 1800, in Plumer Papers, Library of Congress.

[52] Scarcely any leading Federalists continued to stand by Adams in 1800. It is interesting that those who did were almost invariably merchants or commercial lawyers—Otis, Champlin, Chase, Craik, the Trumbulls, Dexter, and Stoddert; cf. Dauer, *Adams Federalists*, pp. 260–265.

strictures upon absolute democracy which they singled out for special commendation. They liked the way in which he exposed the "terrors of democracy." He was a sort of political astronomer, who had discovered the comet of democracy, measured the heat of its fiery tail, and accurately forecast its course.[53]

The relations between Adams and the Federalists of the old school were further complicated by semantical confusion. Both repudiated "aristocracy" as a form of government, but Adams defined the word more broadly (or more literally). Aristocrats, for Adams, were "all those men who can command, influence or procure more than an average number of votes . . . every man who can and will influence one man to vote besides himself." He saw a danger of oligarchical usurpation not merely in hereditary privilege but also in the talents and distinctions of a natural elite. The ability to control this natural aristocracy was for him the supreme test of a constitution. To Thomas Jefferson he wrote, "your *aristoi* are the most difficult animals to manage, of anything in the whole Theory and practice of Government. They will not suffer themselves to be governed. They not only exert their own Subtilty Industry and courage, but they employ the Commonalty to knock to pieces every Plan and Model that the most honest Architects in Legislation can invent to keep them in bounds."[54]

The gentlemen of the old school agreed that an aristocratic predominance was undesirable, but they merely meant that the natural elite should not be permitted to make itself into a hereditary caste and that the people should not be excluded from the political process. To Adams it meant much more. When Federalists of the old school read the written arguments of Adams the philosopher, they could ignore this crucial difference in word meaning. But when they confronted Adams the statesman, they were forced to face the man in his totality. The day of reckoning arrived in 1799, when Adams suddenly concluded that the balance was heavy on the side of the *aristoi* and threw his weight against them. Taken aback, the Federalists accounted for his action by questioning his sanity. Adams reciprocated, in his quaint way, by cursing their "stiff-rumped stupidity."[55]

[53] Edmund Quincy, *Josiah Quincy*, p. 70; Schouler, *History of U. S.*, I, 392; for the interpretation of the balance as an essentially antipopular device by other old-school Federalists, see "Plebicola" in [Baltimore] *Federal Gazette*, Aug. 25, 28, 1801; see also Elias Boudinot, speaking for "we old fashioned folks" in a letter to Pickering, June 3, 1808, in Pickering Papers, Mass. Hist. Soc.

[54] Adams to Thomas Jefferson, July 9, 1813, Cappon, ed., *Adams-Jefferson Letters*, II, 352.

[55] Pickering to W. W. Van Ness, Jan. 25, 1814, in Pickering Papers, Mass. Hist. Soc.; John Adams to J. Q. Adams, Dec. 14, 1804, in Adams Family Papers, reel 403. This brief sketch has been deliberately limited to contrasts between Adams and other old-school Federalists. There are, of course, significant comparisons to be made.

In the eccentric thought of John Adams, the disintegration of the holistic ideals of the old school was already apparent. In the attitudes of a much younger man, the same process was even more fully developed. Alexander Hamilton (1755?–1804) laughed at the illusions of his friends. "Among Federalists," he wrote in 1800, "old errors are not cured. They also continue to dream, though not so preposterously as their opponents. All will be well, (say they) when the power once more gets back into Federal hands. The people, convinced by experience of their error, will repose a *permanent* confidence in good men. *Risum teneatis?*"[56]

In the considered opinion of a close friend, Gouverneur Morris, Hamilton's lack of rapport with other Federalists was owing to his origins. "From his situation in early life," Morris observed, "it was not to be expected that he should have a fellow-feeling with those who idly supposed themselves to be the natural aristocracy of this country." Hamilton, indeed, had no connection with the colonial past. He did not reach the mainland until 1772, when the imperial dispute had passed the point of no return and society was distracted by riots and rescues, alarums and excursions. The turbulence of the '70s prevented Hamilton from conceptualizing in terms of social harmony, as did Jay and Cabot and Washington. It was difficult if not impossible for anyone who arrived as late as Hamilton to place much credence in the idea of a silent multitude and a speaking elite.[57]

The difference between Hamilton and Jay, it will be noted, was as much a matter of age as of social and geographic origins. The importance of the time factor is apparent in the fact that Hamilton was joined in his dissent by another prodigy, Fisher Ames (1758–1808), who also came late upon the scene and advanced with great rapidity. Ames had once shared the happy dream of a speaking aristocracy and a silent democracy, but it was not deeply imbedded in his mind and at the end of the eighteenth century he abandoned it. In disillusionment and despair he wrote, "We have thought that virtue, with so many bright rewards, had some silent power; and that, with ten thousand charms, she could always command a hundred thousand votes. Alas! These illusions are as thin as the gloss on other bubbles."[58]

[56] Hamilton to Rufus King, June 3, 1800, King, *Life and Correspondence of King*, IV, 134.

[57] Morris to Robert Walsh, Feb. 5, 1811, in Anne Cary Morris, *Dairy and Letters of Gouverneur Morris*, II, 522–525; for Morris's intimacy and deep affection for Hamilton see David B. Ogden to Wm. Meredith, July 12, 1804, in Meredith Papers, Hist. Soc. of Penna., which reported that Morris was "almost overcome with grief at witnessing the last moments of the man whom of all men he loved most on earth."

[58] Fisher Ames, "No Revolutionist," Nov. 1801., *Works*, II, 205. "Our good men *feel* better towards the government than they talk or reason," he wrote. "They really believe seven-eighths of the democratic lying theories invented and propagated to subvert all government." Ames to Gore, Nov. 10, 1799, *Works*, I, 266; see also Ames to Pickering, Nov. 5, 1799, *Works*, I, 262.

By 1800, Ames was speaking of other Federalists in Hamilton's terms. "Their confidence is so blind and they are acted upon so little by their fears, their trust in the sinless perfection of a democracy is so entire, that perhaps suffering severely is the only mode of teaching," he wrote. The men who called themselves Federal Republicans insisted upon a fundamental distinction between republicanism and democracy, the difference being the strength of "good order" and "subordination" in the former. Ames and Hamilton could not agree that the difference could be maintained in America; neither of these younger men could trust to the deferential spirit. "We are democrats," Ames insisted, "we pretend to be republicans. Experience will punish and teach."[59]

Fisher Ames was not a notably stable individual. His surviving works suggest a manic-depressive psychosis—and his principles were as unstable as his personality. "I am habitually a zealot in politics," he wrote. "It is, I fancy, constitutional, and so the cure desperate. I burn and freeze, am lethargic, raving, sanguine and despondent, as often as the wind shifts."[60]

There were other Federalists who manifested similar symptoms. Most of them were very near to Ames's age—Robert Troup (1757–1832), William Vans Murray (1760–1803), Jeremiah Smith (1759–1842), Christopher Gore (1758–1827)—too young to find old-school doctrines acceptable, too old to acquiesce in new realities. As political events progressed from bad to worse in the 1790s, these transitional figures were driven to desperate expedients. In fear and confusion, some of them looked with favor upon extreme antipopular restraints which were rarely countenanced by gentlemen of the old school.[61]

[59] Fisher Ames to Theodore Dwight, Mar. 19, 1801, Ames, *Works*, I, 293; Ames to Thomas Dwight, Oct. 20, 1700, *Works*, I, 260. See also Ames to Gore, July 28, 1798, *Works*, I, 237. It is in this context that we should read another startling statement of Ames's: "Indeed it is notorious, that there was scarcely an advocate for the federal Constitution who was not anxious, from the first, to hazard the experiment of an unprecedented and almost unqualified proportion of democracy, both in constructing and administering the government, and who did not rely with confidence, if not blind presumption, on its success. This is certain, the body of the federalists were always, and yet are, essentially democratic in their political notions." "The Dangers of American Liberty," 1805, *Works*, II, 348; see also the definitions in Ames to Pickering, Jan. 12, 1807, Ames, *Works*, I, 386: "A republic tends, experience says, irresistibly towards licentiousness, and that a licentious republic, or democracy, is of all governments that very one in which the wise and good are most completely reduced to impotence."

[60] He remained, in his own words, "a stubborn hoper," at the same time that he feared for the worst. But his hopes were lacking in a rational foundation; in moments of optimism he turned back to the doctrines of the old school, because he had nowhere else to go. "I am no royalist, Anglo-American, nor tory," he declared. "I only ask how our government is to be supported;—and I answer by miracle. The miracle of virtue, that loves others first, then one's self." Ames to Thomas Dwight, Dec. 21, 1792, *Works*, I, 126; Ames to Pickering, Mar. 16, 1806, in Pickering Papers, Mass. Hist. Soc.; Ames to Richard Peters, Dec. 14, 1806, *Works*, I, 377; see also Ames to Gore, Feb. 24, 1803, *Works*, I, 319.

[61] These men are listed as "transitional figures" in Appendix II.

The first was the use of the bayonet. In the summer of 1798, when the Western world was in flames and Jeffersonians were speaking publicly of armed resistance to the government, a few Federalists lost their heads. Among them was William Barry Grove (1764–1818) of North Carolina. In a letter to the Secretary of War he requested a supply of arms and ammunition from the federal arsenal in Wilmington, North Carolina.

"In this part of the state," he wrote from Fayetteville, "we have few grumbletonians and still fewer jacobins. I am persuaded you may with safety confide in us so far as to lend us some of those arms which are and must be useless in their present situation, and may eventually be wanting in the hands of active citizens to keep a certain class of people in order. . . . The arms would be as safe as if they are in one of the arsenals, and might be of infinite service in keeping up a proper respect and confidence in the government."[62]

Grove was not alone in his belief that a little violence might promote the cause of order. But as we have seen, gentlemen of the old school generally agreed that in a republic stability derived only from consent. Even Hamilton, in more reflective moments stood with them on this point. "In politics as in religion," he wrote "it is equally absurd to aim at making proselytes by fire and sword. Heresies in either can rarely be cured by persecution."[63]

Other Federalists in Ames's age-group had second thoughts about republicanism itself. How many is difficult to say. Because the prevailing climate of opinion prevented them from speaking candidly, it is impossible to estimate their numbers with precision. Thomas Jefferson affected to believe that they were the very soul of Federalism, which is of course absurd. They were never more than a handful, but were to be found even in that ancient refuge of regicides, Connecticut.[64]

A pair of Connecticut Yankees may serve to illustrate the type. One was John Allen (1763–1812), a shambling, sharp-tempered Litchfield lawyer who was most remarkable for the width of his body and the narrowness of his mind. His speeches in Congress Hall on the subject of democracy were famous for violence and vituperation. At the climax of one such oration, Allen fainted dead away, and lay senseless upon the floor until a team of Federalists dragged his mountainous body into the lobby.[65]

[62] William Barry Grove to James McHenry, Aug. 20, 1798, in McHenry Papers, Duke University Library.

[63] Stephen G. Kurtz, *The Presidency of John Adams* (Philadelphia, 1957), pp. 316–317, 323, 354–356; Hamilton, Federalist #1, in Van Doren, ed., *The Federalist*, pp. 1–5.

[64] Thomas Jefferson to W. C. C. Claiborne, 1803, in A. A. Lipscomb & A. L. Bergh, eds., *The Writings of Thomas Jefferson*, 20 vols. (Washington, 1903), XIV, 488.

[65] Charles Swain Hall, *Benjamin Tallmadge* (New York, 1943), p. 94.

The other royalist was Uriah Tracy (1755–1807), also a lawyer of Litchfield, whose rudeness and bigotry were noxious even to his Federal colleagues. Many Federalists despised the people, but Tracy genuinely hated them. "They are vicious," he wrote brutally, "and love vicious men for their leaders." For Jeffersonians he had nothing but loathing. "Democrats are alike the world over," he declared, "when men worship the Devil is it strange that they should become Devilish?" The revolutionary changes then progressing in the structure of American politics provoked him to comment that "the herd have begun to walk on their hind legs."[66]

Once, in Connecticut, Tracy and Allen cornered a visitor from New York whom they mistook for a Federalist. Allen opened the conversation with customary *savoir-faire:* "Damn you, Tracy!" he exploded. "Speak out! Be Plain!" At that signal, Uriah Tracy began to argue that "it was a damned farce to suppose that a republican government could exist," that America must inevitably have her own king and aristocracy.[67]

On another occasion Tracy engaged in a political discussion with a Connecticut clergyman whom he naturally assumed to be a fellow "friend of order." Afterwards the minister, Stanley Griswold, "a correct honest man"—and a secret admirer of Thomas Jefferson—made a record of the conversation, in which Tracy reportedly declared that "the people of this country have too much liberty and equality. They know too much and are too great politicians—they are too free from taxes and not obliged to labor hard enough—so long as this is the case they cannot be governed; government must be weak and constantly in danger of opposition and an overthrow. This state of liberty and equality must be broken up, and we must have a king here, but he must not be called king, as it would startle the old whigs—but he must have the essential requisites of a king. And we must have a body of nobility, but they must not be called noblemen for the same reason, yet must have all the essentials of a body of noblemen. We must have an established religion and an established clergy. The people must be reduced to a condition of hard labor and ignorance, and then they will be safely governed."[68]

[66] William Plumer, *Diary*, Jan. 12, 1806, in Plumer Papers, Library of Congress; Uriah Tracy to John Rutledge, Jr., Aug. 18, 1803, Jan. 12, 1805, in Rutledge Papers, Southern Hist. Coll., Univ. of N. C.; Pickering to George Cabot, Mar. 16, 1808, in Lodge, *Cabot*, p. 388; for similar comments by John Allen, see *Annals of Congress*, 5th Cong. 1st sess., cols. 709–710, 715, 774, 854, 1578, 1580, 1970, 2089, 2090, 2091, 2093; Tracy to King, Mar. 12, 1806, in King, *Life and Correspondence of King*, IV, 500.

[67] Thomas Hortell to Ephraim Kirby, Feb. 23, 1801, in Kirby Papers, Duke University Library.

[68] Stanley Griswold to Ephraim Kirby, Feb. 23, 1801, in Kirby Papers, Duke University Library. For the description of Griswold see *Dictionary of American Biography*, VIII, 13. When these private and confidential letters were later made public by Connecticut Republicans, Tracy and Allen protested that they were misquoted, issued statements testifying to each other's republicanism, and collected affadavits from other Federalists. The Jeffersonians replied with more

To Jeffersonians, Uriah Tracy was the cloven foot of Federalism. They rejoiced whenever he appeared against them. In the midst of a Connecticut campaign one of them wrote happily, "Tracy, you know, is in the field. . . . So fortunate an event was hardly to be hoped. He is in morals and politics a perfect federalist and it is considered as very momentous at this crisis to rend the veil and to display the monster federalism naked."[69] But even among "high-toned" Federalists, Tracy was an eccentric. That he favored the introduction of hereditary forms is less significant than the fact that he recognized the necessity of disguising them. Altogether, these two Connecticut cryptoroyalists, Uriah Tracy and John Allen, are themselves the fullest measure of America's republican commitment.

Other Federalists in Ames's unhappy age-group preferred to seek a radical but nonviolent solution within the broad framework of republicanism. Noah Webster (1758–1843), for example, reasoned from an assumption that the youth of the republic were principally responsible for the political troubles of the 1790s to the conclusion that a startling alteration in age requirements might restore social and political harmony. "It would be better for the people," he wrote; "they would be more free and more happy—if all were deprived of the right of suffrage until they are 45 years of age, and if no man was eligible to an important office until he is fifty, that is, if all powers of government were vested in our old men who have lost their ambition chiefly and have learned wisdom by experience; but to tell this to the people would be treason. We have grown so wise of late years as to reject the maxims of Moses, Lycurgus and the patriarchs; we have, by the constitutions of government and the preposterous use made of doctrines of *equality*, stripped *old* men of their dignity and *wise* men of their influence, and long, long are we to feel the mischievous effects of our modern policy."[70]

There were other schemes, so fantastic as to be burlesques of the innovations of the 1770s and 1780s—proposals for the organization of the American governments on the lines of a joint-stock venture, in which men would receive votes in proportion to their economic resources; suggestions by Federalists who trusted more to chance than to the people's choice that public officers be selected by lot. The number and variety of radical remedies which these bewildered physicians prescribed

---

evidence. See [Walpole, N.H.] *Political Observatory*, Jan. 28, Feb. 20, Apr. 24, 1804. On another occasion Tracy said that "the people ought to put on their leather aprons and attend to their own business and let politics and the concerns of government alone." Ibid., Jan. 28, 1804.

[69] Alexander Wolcott to Ephraim Kirby, Sep. 23, 1803, in Ephraim Kirby Papers, Duke University Library.

[70] Noah Webster to Benjamin Rush, Dec. 15, 1800, in Harry R. Warfel, *Letters of Noah Webster* (New York, 1953), pp. 229–230.

for the body politic is itself an indication that the disease which they diagnosed was systemic, advanced, and incurable.[71]

4

The Jeffersonian victories in 1800 were, of course, a heavy blow to gentlemen of the old school. In the midst of bitter disagreements, "Jacobins" and "Monocrats" managed to agree that the elections constituted a peaceable revolution in the structure of American politics. There were few formal institutional reforms, scarcely any constitutional revisions. But the triumph of Thomas Jefferson (whatever his own values and purposes may have been) symbolized changes of sweeping significance which were gradually taking place in the minds and hearts of men. The expansive ideals of liberty, equality, and majoritarianism were affirmed with unprecedented force and clarity; the old-fashioned elitism, the orders and distinctions, the postures of deference and subordination which had prevailed in eighteenth-century America were dealt a killing blow.[72]

Election returns did not immediately destroy the illusions of the older Federalists—ancient principles died a lingering death. Many gentlemen found comfort in the thought that the people's "unaccountable infatuation for bad men" could only be temporary. Charles Cotesworth Pinckney confidently predicted that Jefferson's followers would "proceed on their mad and wicked career, and the people's eyes will be opened." Others expected that democrats, like thieves, would fall out among themselves. "When these gentry find that there are more PIGS than TEATS," a Connecticut Federalist wrote happily, "what a squealing there will be in the hog pen."[73]

But in the meantime, there seemed little for good men to do. "When the people have been long enough drunk they will get sober," wrote

[71] Chilton Williamson, *American Suffrage from Property to Democracy, 1760–1860* (Princeton, 1960), pp. 170–171; *American Register* (1809) II, 15–18.

[72] Thomas Jefferson to Spencer Roane, Sep. 6, 1819, in P. L. Ford, ed., *The Works of Thomas Jefferson*, 12 vols. (New York, 1904–5), XII, 136; Fisher Ames, "The Dangers of American Liberty," 1805, Ames, *Works*, II, 344–399.

[73] Daniel Dewey to Theodore Sedgwick, Dec. 8, 1800, in Sedgwick Papers, Mass. Hist. Soc.; C. C. Pinckney to Alexander Hamilton, May 3, 1802, in Hamilton Papers, Library of Congress. "I think there is still virtue enough left in the community to understand, after the present clamour has subsided, the real interests of the country, and to restore to honest men the confidence which they have lost." Roger Griswold to John Rutledge, Dec. 14, 1801, in Rutledge Papers, Southern Hist. Coll., Univ. of N. C. "The people are as completely blinded as were the Sodomites who would have defiled the men of God—a thick film is upon their eyes, which it would seem nothing short of a miraculous power can remove. When their city is in flames, they will see the error of their ways." Josiah Dwight to Thomas Dwight, Aug. 15, 1803, in Dwight-Howard Papers, Mass. Hist. Soc.

Gouverneur Morris, "but while the frolic lasts, to reason with them is useless."[74] The political revolution of 1800 manifested itself not merely in the defeat of the Federalists of the old school, but also in their disengagement. A remarkable number withdrew not merely from politics but from society as well. Thomas Truxtun, finding the navy uncongenial after Thomas Jefferson became his commander-in-chief, placed the proverbial oar upon his shoulder and moved inland to a New Jersey farm. A visitor found him ensconced in his study, "arrayed in his uniform coat, cocked hat and cockade, a flannel petticoat in place of breeches, and his feet rolled up in pieces of the same texture."[75]

Cabot, Jay, Adams, and later Morris retired to their country estates. Charles Cotesworth Pinckney isolated himself on an island off the Carolina coast; Theodore Sedgwick immured himself within his Berkshire mansion. "The aristocracy of virtue is destroyed; personal influence is at an end," he growled. "I would never have abandoned the government personally, but from the most complete conviction that the people would make an experiment of democracy." Only William Cooper lingered behind, until 1809, when he met an appropriate end in a tavern brawl, struck down by a democrat.[76]

Men of Ames's age-group were less resigned, more pessimistic than older colleagues. Fisher Ames himself could manage nothing better than a cynical jest. "Though I indulge no hope," he wrote, I derive much entertainment from the squabbles in Madam Liberty's family. After so many liberties have been taken with her, she is no longer a *miss* and a virgin, though she may still be a goddess." But humor such as this rang

[74] Gouverneur Morris to Roger Griswold, Nov. 3, 1803, in Morris Papers, Library of Congress. "The least [the Federalists] attempt, the better," wrote Francis Dana. "Let them stand still on terra firma and see the salvation of the Lord, if it is ordained to visit our unhappy country." Gouverneur Morris wrote pointedly to his Jeffersonian friend, R. R. Livingston, "Tis better to suffer with the virtuous and wise than to reign in bad company." Francis Dana to Stephen Higginson, n.d., "Sunday, P.M." [1804?], Pickering Papers, Mass. Hist. Soc.; Morris to R. R. Livingston, Sep. 6, 1805, in Morris Papers, Library of Congress. At least one Federalist actually rejoiced in his removal from office. "I am so far from being mortified or depressed in spirit on account of being removed," he wrote, "that I rather glory in the circumstances. By this act of injustice I am placed upon the list of a goodly number of political martyrs who have gone before me, at the head of whom I consider General Washington, for although he escaped a violent death, yet how they have traduced him! To be counted one of his disciples and suffer death for adhering to his principles, *what an honour!* Was it *possible* for Mr. Jefferson to have done me a *greater?* Certainly *not!*" Rufus Putnam to Pickering, Jan. 5, 1804, Pickering Papers, Mass. Hist. Soc. See also John Trumbull to Rufus King, Nov. 21, 1810, in King, *Life and Correspondence of King*, V, 226; James Hillhouse to Noah Webster, Mar. 22, 1808, in Noah Webster Papers, New York Public Library.

[75] Katherine Beekman, "A Colonial Capital," *N.J. Hist. Soc. Proceedings*, 4 ser., III (1918), 15.

[76] Cabot to Oliver Wolcott, Mar. 26, 1798, in Lodge, *Cabot*, p. 150; Monaghan, *Jay*, pp. 427–435; King to Christopher Gore, Nov. 20, 1803, Robert Troup to King, May 6, 1802, in King, *Life and Corrsp. King*, IV, 326, 120; Butterfield, "Judge William Cooper," 402; Sedgwick to King, Dec. 14, 1801, King Papers, N. Y. Hist. Soc.

hollow. Ames and his contemporaries were reduced to despondency as they recognized that their nation had indeed degenerated into a democracy. "It is time to leave the pumps and take to the long-boat," wrote Jeremiah Smith, "a majority must and will do what they please. A paper constitution affords no security." Despondency gave way to alarm. "Our days are made heavy with the pressure of anxiety, and our nights restless with visions of horror," Ames wrote. "We listen to the clank of chains, and overhear the whispers of assassins. We mark the barbarous dissonance of mingled rage and triumph in the yell of an infatuated mob; we see the dismal glare of their burnings, and scent the loathsome steam of human victims offered in sacrifice."[77]

[77] Fisher Ames, "The Dangers of American Liberty," 1805, Ames, *Works*, II, 354; Fisher Ames to Timothy Pickering, Mar. 10, 1806, Ames, *Works*, I, 369. "I fear your severe account of our present legislature [N.C.] is but too correct. I sometimes feel strongly disposed to dissent from the established republican apothegm, 'The will of the majority is the interest of the majority.'" Edwin J. Osborne to William Gaston, Dec. 14, 1800, in Gaston Papers, Southern Hist. Coll., Univ. of N. C. See also John Marshall to H. G. Otis, Aug. 5, 1800, in Otis Papers, Mass. Hist. Soc.; Rufus King to Christopher Gore, May 8, 1816, in King, *Life and Corresp. King*, V, 534; Ames to Pickering, Nov. 6, 1807, Ames, *Works*, I, 293. Thomas Dwight believed that the experiment which the people were making with their government would cost "the lives of thousands and tens of thousands of human beings." Dwight to John Williams, Feb. 11, 1802, May 19, 1803, in Dwight-Howard Papers, Mass. Hist. Soc. Richard Peters was troubled at night by "political visions," "*Blue Devils*" which "dance in the most diabolical gambols" inside his brain. Peters to Pickering, Nov. 3, 1807, in Pickering Papers, Mass. Hist. Soc. H. W. Dwight, declared, "If the United States are not and that without the least possible delay, Politically, Physically, & Morally damned, it will not be because they do not deserve it. Individually, and in Church and State, I am more than ever convinced of the Doctrine of *Total Depravity*, and that there is great wrath laid in store for us as a nation. May the Almighty have compassion and save us. Ourselves we cannot save." Dwight to Sedgwick, Mar. 31, 1800, in Sedgwick Papers, Mass. Hist. Soc. The most tangible evidence of Federal fears was the fall of stocks. See [Boston] *Independent Chronicle*, Aug. 17, 1801; Jonathan Ogden to William Meredith, Feb. 23, 1801, in Meredith Papers, Hist. Soc. of Penna. T. B. Adams to J. Q. Adams, Jan. 15, 1801, in Adams Family Papers, Mass. Hist. Soc., reel 400. For other expressions of hysteria see [Hartford] *Connecticut Courant*, May 19, 1800; Henry Van Schaak to Oliver Wendell, Jan. 15, 1800, in Van Schaack Papers, Library of Congress; Manasseh Cutler, Diary, May 2, 1800, in W. P. and J. P. Cutler, *Life, Journals and Correspondence of Rev. Manasseh Cutler*, 2 vols. (Cincinnati, 1888), II, 107. "The wisest provisions in the government of a democratic state are of little use and they can be but of short continuance, unless there could be one provision established as the basis of all others, and that is, that the populace should become rational, and never entrust the administration to any but the most wise and virtuous men. The prospect is dreadful to our posterity, but it is involved as surely as destiny in the nature of things. We have no superior order of citizens, no hereditary object of superstitious veneration but a useless superstition, and the chaos of the populace always creates a devouring monster." Samuel Stanhope Smith to Pickering, Dec. 28, 1803, in Pickering Papers, Mass. Hist. Soc. Many similar letters could be quoted: "I cannot endure that state of society wherein the men of talents, of mental endowments, 'whose hearts are pure and whose hands are clean,' are least in honor and estimation among us. When such men are awed into forbearance or stand mute through terror, it is time to despair for the commonwealth." T. B. Adams to J. Q. Adams, Nov. 10, 1802, in Adams Family Papers, Mass. Hist. Soc., reel 401; Smith to Plumer, Jan. 28, 1804, Plumer Papers, Library of Congress.

The events of Jefferson's first administration were even more disheartening than his election. Neither the hopes of the older men nor the fears of Fisher Ames proved to be realistic. Each year, in every state, Federalists of the old school watched their opponents gather strength and popularity. Worse than defeat, in terms of its psychological impact, was the dismal fact that their nation prospered mightily without their leadership. The government did not disintegrate; no mobs of shoeless democrats stalked across the countryside. After a slight recession, business actually began to boom. No wonder that some of the Federalists became desperate men!

II

The Young Federalists

"We must have a new set of leaders. . . . Let us have men who can relax their principles of morality as occasion may require and adapt themselves to circumstances."
—WILLIAM PLUMER, 1803[1]

The defeat of such Federalists as John Jay and George Cabot did not mark the death of Federalism. As the gentlemen of the old school were making a rather ungentlemanly departure from public life, another group of Federalist leaders began to replace them—a fresh generation of dynamic young men who brought new life to a lost cause, new strength to the shattered enterprises of the old school.

Together, of course, these two generations of American conservatives shared more than merely a party name. Both were elitists in their social attitudes; both agreed that "men of talents should give, not receive direction from the multitude." Both tended to identify talents and virtue with birth and breeding, with blood and wealth, with beauty and refinement in dress, demeanor, and physical appearance.[2]

But if elitist purposes remained constant, electoral practices did not. In the midst of many changes, the younger Federalists moved uncertainly toward new patterns of political behavior which contrasted sharply with the precepts of the old school. The contrast between the two generations of American conservatives was itself a measure of change in the political structure of the new republic.

I

Born between 1760 and 1789, the second generation of Federalists matured in an "age of convulsions and overturning," a period in which, as John Quincy Adams observed, change itself appeared to be the only constant. Not least among these many changes in America was an

[1] William Plumer to Jeremiah Smith, 21 Nov., 25 Dec. 1801, in John H. Morison, ed., *The Life of Jeremiah Smith* (Boston, 1845), pp. 213–25.

[2] Plumer, "Autobiography," in Plumer Papers, Library of Congress; "Apollo views, with honest pride, His fav'rites all on Fed'ral side." [Boston] *New England Palladium*, 6 Nov. 1804; "There is a stronger affinity than many people believe between the accomplishments of the mind and the body." Harrison Gray Otis to Miss Sophia H. Otis, 30 July 1810, in Otis Papers, Mass. Hist. Soc.

alteration in the relationship between gentlemen and politics. Federal gentlemen of the old school were products of a society which had expected and even required men of wealth and reputation to take leading parts in the affairs of the commonwealth. Public office was at once an eighteenth-century gentleman's sacred right, his special property, and his saving obligation.[3]

But by the century's end a perceptible gap was opening between politics and people "of the better sort." An important study, "The American Business Elite," by a history-minded sociologist, C. Wright Mills, offers striking evidence of political disengagement by men of property in the generation of the young Federalists (see Table I). In the genera-

Table I. Political Offices Held by "The American Business Elite"

Generation born between	Per cent holding 3 or more offices	Per cent holding 1 or 2 offices	Total per cent holding office	Per cent holding no office
1570–1699	45.09	23.53	68.62	31.38
1700–1729	51.11	17.77	68.88	31.12
1730–1759[a]	50.40	20.80	71.20	28.80
1760–1789[b]	20.27	26.14	46.41	53.59
1790–1819	18.67	25.56	44.23	55.77
1820–1849	17.80	20.50	38.30	61.70
1850–1879	11.45	27.71	39.16	60.84

SOURCE: C. Wright Mills, "The American Business Elite: A Collective Portrait," *Tasks of Economic History*, (Dec. 1945), pp. 20–44.

[a] Generation of the old-school Federalists.
[b] Generation of the young Federalists.

tion of the old-school Federalists, 71 per cent of Mills's business leaders held public office, a figure near to that for earlier age-groups. But in the generation of the young Federalists, participation in public affairs dropped suddenly to 46 per cent and continued to fall very slowly thereafter.

This startling change might be explained in several ways. Perhaps men of wealth were being driven out of politics by other men who practiced the arts of popular politics with greater freedom, power, and effect. This was the view of a British traveler in the new nation. "The leading Federalists," he wrote, "are gentlemen of fortune, talents and education, the natural leaders of the country. The leaders of the democratic party, on the other hand, are for the most part, what may be called politicians of fortune; adventurers who follow politics as a profession. With them

[3] Charles S. Sydnor, *Gentlemen Freeholders: Political Practices in Washington's Virginia* (Chapel Hill, 1952), p. 131, passim; Henry Steele Commager, "Leadership in 18th Century America and Today," Daedalus, XCI (1961), 652–673.

politics are a pecuniary, with the Federalists, they are a secondary consideration. The democrats being men of inferior birth and breeding to the Federalists, can more easily mix with the rabble, and practice the tribunitian arts. They affect, with their dress and manners, to regard themselves as of the Plebian order, and condescend to a familiarity of intercourse with the vulgar from which gentlemen would revolt."[4]

Jeffersonians, of course, sought a different explanation. One Republican suggested that "the wealthy and powerful, in whom philanthropy is absorbed in self, and patriotism in the aggrandizement of their families," were not driven out of politics, but were distracted from pursuit of the public interest by proposals of private gain.[5] Young Federalists who remained active in politics registered similar complaints against the political apathy of their wealthy friends after 1800. "Talents among us are employed to get riches," one of them wrote, "and wealth is used only to buy distinction and pleasure. When property is threatened, its possessors are impatient to enjoy the present moment and careless of futurity." In the private correspondence of leading young Federalists no theme is more common than this lament that the "natural rulers" of the nation had abdicated their public responsibilities.[6]

Whatever the explanation, the brute fact of a bifurcation between politics and propriety (in Harrington's double meaning) is clear, in this and other evidence. Changing attitudes and assumptions appeared in the changing connotation of words such as "politics" and "politician." Before 1800 both appear to have been neutral in themselves. Hamilton in *The Federalist Papers*, for example, spoke of "the little arts of the

[4] "A View of the State of Parties in the United States of America," 2d edn., (Edinburgh, 1812), pp. 50–51.

[5] "To the Citizens of Newcastle County" (1804), broadsides in coll. of Amer. Antiq. Soc.

[6] [Boston] *New England Palladium*, 4 Jan. 1803; "Many of our Gentlemen of Large Fortune take no part in the public affairs & hope to compromise with the fury of democracy by their inactivity and even submission. It is true everywhere." H. W. DeSaussure to John Rutledge, 23 Aug. 1801, in Rutledge Papers, Univ. of N. C.; see also [Boston] *Centinel*, 29 Mar. 1800; [Boston] *New England Palladium*, 9 Nov. 1804; Cabot to John Rutledge, 15 Aug. 1808, in Rutledge Papers, Univ. N. C.; William Gaston to Rutledge, 17 Jan. 1809, ibid.; N. Saltonstall to Leverett Saltonstall, 4 Mar. 1808, in Saltonstall Papers, Mass. Hist. Soc.; Pickering to Hazen Kimball, 5 Jan. 1814, in Pickering Papers, Mass. Hist. Soc. For contrasting statements in the preceding decade see Higginson to Hamilton, 11 Nov. 1789, in Syrett, ed., *Hamilton Papers*, V, 507; Gore to King, 15 Mar. 1794, 6 Nov. 1794, in *King*, I, 575, 552; ". . . many of our gentlemen of large fortunes who are reluctant to take any part in the public affairs ought to be called into service and strongly urged not to compromise into the fury of democracy, by their inactivity." Rutledge to Harrison Gray Otis, 15 Sep. 1801, in Otis Papers, Mass. Hist. Soc.; "The solicitude which *moderate* Federalists evince for acquiring property, while Democrats are attacking the *right of property*, and will, if their schemes succeed, destroy the distinction of *meum* and *tuum*, puts one in mind of a very wise old woman, who, when her house was on fire, in order to secure her most valuable effects, *locked them in a closet* which was a part of the burning building." [Boston] *N. Eng. Palladium*, 15 Jan. 1805.

little politician" at one point, and of "wise politicians" at another.[7] After 1800, however, both words usually bore negative connotations. Fisher Ames wrote of his "pigsty and politics, two scurvy subjects that should be coupled together." Timothy Pickering equated "the *public cheat*" with "the *politician.*" This usage was not limited merely to disgruntled Federalists. In 1812 a Republican explained, "what I mean by *politics* are those petty topics of ribaldry and abuse which *newspaper-readers* are continually babbling about." John Randolph of Roanoke spoke bitterly of "the refuse of the retail trade of politics." And a lady of no particular persuasion disturbed Mrs. John Quincy Adams by observing that her son "is formed for a politician; he understands the art of *twisting* a subject better than any child she ever saw."[8]

With the decline of deference, politics itself had become a dirty business, in the judgment of the "better sort of people," a low trade from which neither honor nor reputation could be gained. Gentlemen of the old school, who had been educated to regard public affairs as their private responsibility, advised their sons after 1800 to keep clear.[9] The fastidious needed no urging. The North Carolina Federalist who, in 1803, repudiated a nomination because he was "unwilling to make enemies and have my character bandied about through so many counties," personifies a prejudice which has pervaded American society from his time to ours.[10]

[7] Hamilton, Federalist #11, 25, in Van Doren, ed., *The Federalist*, pp. 63–70, 157–162; see also George Cabot to Christopher Gore, Jan. 21, 1800, in Lodge, *Cabot*, p. 268; [Baltimore] *Federal Republican*, 14 Oct. 1809.

[8] John Campbell to David Campbell, 10 Aug. 1812, in Campbell Papers, Duke University Library; Fisher Ames to Gore, 7 Nov. 1802, in Ames, *Works*, I, 304; [Boston] *New England Palladium*, 20 Apr. 1813; Louisa Catherine Adams to John Quincy Adams, 10 June 1804, in Adams Family Papers, reel 403; see also Francis Scott Key to John Randolph, 13 Aug. 1813, in B. C. Howard Papers, Md. Hist. Soc.

[9] William C. Cummings to Thomas Cummings, Sep. 15, 1806, in Cummings Papers, Duke Univ. Library.

[10] Robert Williams to John Haywood, 20 June 1803, in Haywood Papers, Univ. of N. C.; see also T. B. Adams to J. Q. Adams, 10 Nov. 1802, in Adams Family Papers, reel 401. See also the exchange between Littleton W. Tazewell and John Randolph of Roanoke. "How fast is this government of ours settling into aristocracy; and into aristocracy of the worst kind, the aristocracy supported by intrigue," Tazewell wrote. "While I am railing at your conduct and deploring the sad effect likely to result from the precedent thereafter, I am aware of the difficulties of accomplishing the admirable end you have in view, and of counteracting the plans of your adversaries, without resorting to some such expedient and fighting with their weapons—I am not enough of a casuist however yet to justify means by ends, or to extol evil when practiced for the attainment of good—Republican virtue should disdain such shifts—If liberty cannot be preserved without them, it is not worth the preservation, for too surely this present antidote will prove its bane hereafter." 4 Mar. 1804, in Tazewell Papers, Va. State Library. Randolph impatiently replied, "Your remarks on the mode in which men are brought forward to public notice are forcibly striking. Yet as you cannot devise a remedy, it appears to be one of those inherent evils of our system (what system is without them?) to which we must submit. Instead of railing at the thing, I wish you would come to participate in it." 21 Apr. 1804, in Tazewell Papers, Va. State Library.

2

The younger Federalists who became active in public affairs after 1800 faced a double-ended dilemma. They meant to preserve as much of the elitism of early American society as possible, but in a new Republican context in which the "multitude" were being invited to participate more actively, more meaningfully in politics, and in which their "natural leaders" were turning to private affairs. Younger Federalists nourished a traditional respect for "orders and distinctions" in society, but ancient axioms of the old school, time-honored techniques of political management, were reduced to mere irrelevancies.

In the midst of conflict and discontinuities of so many kinds, many members of the new generation of Federalism undertook a new experiment in elitist politics—endeavoring to turn the forms of democracy against its substance, to combine the rhetoric of popular government with the hard reality of the iron law of oligarchy. In place of the happy vision of a silent multitude and a speaking elite, they substituted an uglier but more workable arrangement—a silent elite in the midst of a speaking multitude. "You must get close to the people in order to manage them," a young Federalist candidly declared; "there is no better way."[11]

The shield and weapon of Federalism in the political arena, the engine of its new-modeled elitism, the essential political artifact, was party. Young Federalists who actively supported the cause positively defended the partisan spirit which united them, even if it divided the nation. They condoned otherwise indefensible tactics as necessary for "the good of the party." They preached submission to party discipline as a cardinal virtue of politics. "It is manifest," one of them wrote, "that the politician is bound to support the principles of his party, and not to represent his own opinion."[12]

Young Federalists could find comfort and assurance in a biblical injunction. "Unto the pure all things are pure," Paul had written. They were bound together in a cause which in its righteousness served to sanctify the most ignoble means. The good of the cause itself became the measure of morality. "As a party we stand on the most elevated ground," wrote Alexander Contee Hanson in the midst of one of the most squalid political campaigns in the history of the state. "Besides justice, honor and everything else that can recommend a cause Providence seems to be on our side." Psychic identity was extraordinarily complete. In 1817, when Hanson learned of an internecine quarrel which promised to disrupt the Federal organization in Maryland, he wrote, "I tremble for

[11] John Carlyle Herbert to Vergil Maxcy, 11 Apr. 1816, in Galloway-Maxcy-Markoe Papers, Library of Congress.
[12] D. B. Ogden to Stephen Van Rensselaer, 24 Jan. 1813, in Ogden Papers, N. Y. Hist. Soc.; [New York, N. Y.] *Evening Post*, 4 May 1810.

the party. When the news first came, I felt exactly as if I saw one of my children on the eave of a high house hanging on by the nails."[13]

Federalists spoke of the federal party as the "spartan band" which stood militantly between civilization and barbarism. It is psychologically significant to note that a military metaphor was characteristic. No sense of social harmony, such as had appeared in the mellower notions of the old school, manifested itself in the social and political thought of younger Federalists. To the class consciousness of the old school, younger men added a new sense of class conflict. The world was returned to a Hobbesian state of nature—a state of selfishness and strife, of turmoil and trouble. The political world became a battlefield. The other party was the enemy, and a no man's land lay in between. "There could be no half-way change," William Sullivan wrote. "The convert could do nothing short of what was done by a deserter from the army."[14]

Young Federalists understood that their Federal party could serve their purposes only if it were purged of anti-Republican connotations which Jeffersonians had so skillfully fastened to it in the 1790s. With varying degrees of resolution they undertook to adjust its reputation to popular prejudices and to purify its name of oligarchic imputations, at the same time that they sought to promote oligarchical purposes. The emblem of Federalism was changed after 1800 from the black cockade— which despite its honorable revolutionary origins had become a malodorous symbol of malevolent repression during the 1790s—to the white rose, which despite its Bourbon associations, retained the scent of purity and innocence.[15]

If the very name Federalist could not be cleansed, then in the interest of the new *sub rosa* elitism, it too must be abandoned. A variety of party names was suggested—Federal-Republican, Republican-Federal, American-Republican, American-Whig, True-Republican, True-American, even Democratic-Federalist. "Names are influential things," a Connecticut Federalist declared, "and much has been effected by the term Democratic Republican. In my opinion it is time to leave this distinction."[16]

[13] Hanson to William Gaston, 12 June 1814, in Gaston Papers, Univ. of N. C.; Hanson to G. C. Washington, 16 Dec. 1817, in Hanson-Washington Papers, Md. Hist. Soc.

[14] Simeon Baldwin to Elizabeth Baldwin, 10 Jan. 1803, in Baldwin Papers, Yale University; Sullivan, *Familiar Letters*, p. 189.

[15] [Boston, Mass.] *New England Palladium*, 15 July 1814.

[16] E. Goodrich to S. Baldwin, 20 Feb. 1804, in Baldwin Papers, Yale Univ.; Troup to King, 11 Apr. 1807, *King*, V, 31; [Boston] *New England Palladium*, 11 Feb. 1812; Fox, *Decline of Aristocracy in New York*, p. 87; Higginbotham, *Keystone in the Democratic Arch*, pp. 14, 217, 233. "All those who have jealousies in proportion to their understanding—all who are governed by names instead of substance are in favor of Stanford [a conservative Republican candidate for governor in N. C.]. Among them you here of nothing but tories, Monarchists, Warhawks,

All of this contrasted sharply with the convictions and the conduct of old-school gentlemen. The two generations regarded each other with a mixture of friendly disapproval, impatient frustration, and outright distrust. Older men dismissed the younger generation as a pack of popularity-hunters. The younger generation in turn anathematized its elders —"Sere and yellow leaves falling around us," Verplanck called them— for their failure to adapt themselves to political reality. A young New York Federalist wrote thus of John Jay: "While I shall ever do justice to his integrity of character, I cannot but think there has been wanting a *knowledge of men,* and a disregard of the causes of popular impression (which are often trifling and capricious) with too unbending and inflexible dispositions on various occasions."[17]

There were, of course, members of the younger generation who disagreed: the Federalist literati who managed American magazines which so closely resembled the *Anti-Jacobin*—magazines such as *The Analectic,* the *Monthly Anthology,* and the *Port-Folio*—would continue to think and to speak like the men of the old school. Mercantile men in their counting houses would mutter about the decline of public virtue as they laid up great stores of private treasure. There were ministers who found strength in biblical counsel to "hearken not unto the people, for the cause was from the Lord," and scholars who found comfort in the career of Aristides the Just. But these men and others who disapproved of any attempt to abandon the ethics of the old school generally disapproved of politics as well. They appear to have had small influence upon the conduct of a Federalist opposition.

3

Contrasts between the two generations of Federalists might be clarified and specified by close inspection of a few individuals among the younger men. Limitations of time and space, of the author's energy and the reader's fortitude, require that we restrict our attention to no more

---

Oppressors, British partizans, taxmakers applied to the name of Federalists— Indeed the word Federalist alone without the aid of expletives represents to their affrighted imaginations every thing that is base and infamous. . . . We began wrong—Prejudices ought to have been dissipated by the Mirror of Truth long before the champion of correct principles had been introduced upon the stage. . . . The magic of these words are as potent as the voice of fate." Unsigned letter to Duncan Cameron, 21 July [1808], in Cameron Papers, Univ. of N. C. See also Richard Peters to Pickering 9 Jan. 1804, in Pickering Papers, Mass. Hist. Soc. The same sentiment strengthened older Federalists in their determination to withdraw. "The Federalists will never regain the ascendance *eo nomine*," Peters wrote, "They put off the day when they would recover influence." Ibid., 15 Mar. 1808; and see also Adair to Henry Clay, 15 Aug. 1805, *Clay Papers,* I, 196.

[17] Gulian Verplanck, *Oration* (New York, 1809), p. 11, Thomas R. Gold to Theodore Sedgwick, Nov. 5, 1800, in Sedgwick Papers, Mass. Hist. Soc.

than a half dozen. They will be the six young Federalists who were most prominent in 1800.[18]

Among the six were four "hot-headed youths," as a Jeffersonian editor described them, who sat together in the Fifth and Sixth Congresses. Sometimes they were also called "Harpies," after the oldest, most experienced, and most garrulous of them, Robert Goodloe Harper (c. 1765–1825), representative from South Carolina's Ninety Six district. Harper was not an attractive person, even to his political associates. Acquaintances were quick to notice his obsessive egoism and compulsive ambition for wealth, fame, and power. We might take the measure of the man in his characteristic Congressional pose—in his pompous, pretentious, pidgeon-breasted posture, thumbs hooked in figured waistcoat, chin tucked in spotless cravat, mouth turned up at the corners in an infuriating smile of insolent self-satisfaction.[19]

Harper's early career was marked by a high degree of social and geographic mobility. The son of a self-made southern planter, Harper was born in Virginia, raised in North Carolina, and educated in New Jersey. After graduating from Princeton in 1785, he set out to seek his fortune among the sandy hills, scrubby pines, and dour Scots of the South Carolina upcountry. In that unlikely setting, his considerable talents for full-blown oratory and fine-spun pamphleteering quickly brought him public recognition. In 1795, at the age of thirty, he was sent to Congress Hall in Philadelphia, where after a flirtation with the developing Republican "interest," he attached himself firmly to the "Friends of Order."[20]

Harper's Federalist commitment appears to have been less a matter of conviction than of temperament and circumstance. A close acquaintance and quondam friend observed that he was "seduced from the arms of the Jacobins by the good tables of the merchants of Philadelphia." Appeals to principle were occasions for slogans rather than serious thought. Indeed, he criticized Jefferson less for his theories than for his theorizing. The master of Monticello, in Harper's confirmed judgment, was a "weak wavering indecisive character, deliberating when he ought to act."[21]

During his six years in Congress, Harper distinguished himself primarily for the virulence of his attacks upon Jefferson's "Jacobinical" adherents. Many times he hinted of dark plots and secret combinations

[18] Sketches of other younger Federalists appear in Appendix II.

[19] [Philadelphia] *Aurora*, 21 Dec. 1798; J. S. Watson to David Watson, n.d., "Letters from William and Mary College," *Va. Mag. Hist. & Biog.*, xxix (1921), 160–170; see also Ames to Gore, 28 July 1798, Ames, *Works*, I, 236; Gallatin to wife, 19 Dec. 1797, in Henry Adams, *Writings of Albert Gallatin* (Philadelphia, 1879), I, 188.

[20] See my unpubl. thesis (Princeton, 1958) "Robert Goodloe Harper," pp. 2–111.

[21] William Cobbett, *Porcupine's Works* (London, 1801), IX, 331; Harper to Constituents, 5 Jan. 1797, in Elizabeth Donnan, ed., "The Papers of James A. Bayard," *Amer. Hist. Assn. Annual Report for 1913* (Washington, 1915), II, 23.

against the Constitution and the common good. But despite frequent prodding by enemies and friends, he never produced much in the way of evidence. In manners and tactics this short, stocky little man was the McCarthy of his generation, a reckless and irresponsible demagogue.[22]

But for all his bumptious, blustering manner, Harper was a subtle and skillful politician whose conception of political leadership contrasted sharply with the attitudes of his senior colleagues. While Congressional gentlemen of the old school piously declaimed against the dishonesty of representatives who pandered to the prejudices of the people and to the interests of their constituents, Harper sat at his desk writing friendly, folksy letters to the good citizens of Ninety Six district. He was the only Federalist who commanded a steady following among the yeoman farmers of the South Carolina upcountry.[23]

Harper, unlike older Federalists, acknowledged the power of the people, without condescension, as a fact of political life, and without nostalgia for the ancient habit of subordination. "Sir!" he declared. "The people are not truly estimated by those gentlemen. They are not the blind, ignorant herd which those gentlemen take them to be. They will do in the future what they have always done heretofore—they will judge of the measures of government by the measures themselves." The ancient ideal of a speaking aristocracy in the face of a silent democracy did not appear in the public attitudes of this latter-day Federalist.[24]

Harper also diverged from old-school axioms in his attitudes toward party, which he defended as useful and even desirable in the new republic. "While opposite parties in the Government struggle for preeminence," he declared, "they are like persons engaged in an exhibition before the public, who are obliged to display superior merit and superior excellence in order to gain the prize. The public is the judge, the two parties are the combatants, and that party which possess power must employ it properly, must conduct the government wisely, in order to ensure public approbation, and retain their power. In this contention, while the two parties draw different ways, a middle course is produced generally conformable to public good. Party spirit, therefore, and the contentions to which it gives rise, neither alarms nor displeases me. It might, indeed, sometimes run into excess and produce mischief, as the wind may sometimes be converted into a storm, or fire give rise to a

[22] See particularly *Annals of Congress*, 5th Cong., 2d Sess., col. 192f, 1972–1992 (29 May 1797, 18–19 June 1798).

[23] Harper wrote at least eighteen printed letters to his constituents in six years, a number greater than that which can be assigned to any other contemporary Congressman. They appear in Donnan, "Papers of James Bayard," and in Harper's *Select Works* (Baltimore, 1814); on representation, cf. *Select Works*, p. 42.

[24] *Annals of Congress*, 5th Cong., 1st Sess., col. 172 (29 May 1797); tense and person are changed throughout in quotations from the *Annals*.

conflagration, but its general effects, like those of the great elements of nature, I have no doubt, are beneficial."[25] Throughout his public career, Harper would always be a party man. "Our strength is in union," he wrote to a young Federalist. "We had better slacken our course a little, to wait for our friends than to leave them so far behind as to produce danger of disunion."[26]

The old Federalists publicly encouraged Harper to contribute his talents to the arsenal of respectability, but privately they had grave misgivings about the man himself and his methods. Their attitudes were epitomized in the reaction of Charles Carroll of Carrollton when he discovered to his horror that Harper was seriously courting his daughter. The crusty old Maryland gentleman first quietly discouraged the match, then sternly forbade Harper to call. Only when the young couple announced their own engagement as a *fait accompli* and threatened to elope did Mr. Carroll give his grudging consent.[27]

Early in 1801 the Federalists sponsored a series of testimonial dinners for Oliver Wolcott, Junior. At one, a gentleman of the old school proposed a toast to the good old way: "Talents and virtue in individuals, and good sense in the community, properly to appreciate them." At another dinner for Wolcott in the same year, Harper rose out of his seat to salute an altogether different sentiment: "The Federal Party. Public spirit its guide, honourable feeling its cement, and public good its object."[27a]

If Robert Goodloe Harper were captain of the Federal crew in the Fifth and Sixth Congresses, as Admiral Morison has called him, the first lieutenant was Morison's ancestor, Harrison Gray Otis (1765–1848), of Boston.[28] Like Harper, he was handsome, eloquent, and self-assured. To all of these qualities Otis added a certain elegance. Mr. Morison tells a characteristic story of his ancestor. "It is related," he writes, "that he once met on the street a married couple of his acquaintance, as the lady was arranging the shirt ruffles of her untidy spouse. 'There—look at Mr. Otis's bosom!' said she, pointing to his immaculate ruffles. 'Madam,' said Otis, with one of his best bows, 'If your husband could look within my bosom, he would die of jealousy.' "[29]

Otis was the scion of a distinguished Boston family, a graduate of

---

[25] Ibid., 5 Cong., 2d Sess., col. 874 (19 Jan. 1798).

[26] Robert Goodloe Harper to Alexander Contee Hanson, 4 Mar. 1810, in Harper Papers, Library of Congress.

[27] Charles Carroll to Richard Caton, 8 Sep. 1800, in Harper-Pennington Coll., Md. Hist. Soc.

[27a] [Hartford, Conn.] *Connecticut Courant*, Feb. 16, 23, 1801.

[28] S. E. Morison, *Otis*, I, 85; this work is, of course, the principal source for Otis's Life. It should be supplemented, however, by Otis letters in the John Rutledge Papers, Southern Hist. Coll., Univ. of N. C.

[29] Ibid., I, 219.

Harvard, and an able lawyer-politician in his own right. His splendid command of the language was the delight and despair of his colleagues. When one of them heard that Noah Webster was about to bring out a dictionary with three thousand new words in it, he quipped, "For Heaven's sake, don't let Otis get hold of it."[30]

It was Otis' eloquence which made his reputation. He first attracted notice and admiration by his oratory in the Boston Town Meeting, particularly by the famous "second shirt speech" in which he denounced Albert Gallatin as "a vagrant foreigner" who "came to this country without a second shirt to his back, a man who in comparison to Washington is like a satyre to Hyperian [sic]."[31]

Otis, like Harper, was no theoretician. His federalism was not carefully thought out, but was intuitive, temperamental, environmental. An appeal to principle was for him an exercise in rhetoric rather than reason. He had little use for political philosophy; the report of the Hartford Convention, which probably came from his pen, attacked broadly the "profligacy and folly of political theorists."[32]

Otis was an elitist by birth and breeding. He contemptuously considered democracy "government by acclamation," and he called the people "the duped and deluded mob whose hosannas and execrations are as much mechanical and responsive as the pipes of an organ."[33] Once he wished that "Jacobinism was an indictable offence."[34] When he thought of the "mob" about him, he sometimes feared the worst. "The wonder with me," he wrote once, "is and always has been that the sovereign people have not long since been excited to revolutionary movements."[35]

Yet Otis had genuine respect for the power of the voting public, as an amusing incident shows. During the crisis of 1798, he declared in Congress, "I do not wish to invite hordes of wild Irishmen, nor the turbulent and disorderly of all parts of the world to come here with a view to disturb our tranquillity, after having succeeded in the overthrow of their own governments." His words were picked up by the newspapers and soon a ditty was circulating in the streets of Boston, addressed to Otis:

---

[30] Ibid., I, 41.

[31] Ibid., I, 56. "From his cradle as from Plato's, swarmed the Hyblean [sic] bees, and left the honies of eloquence on his tongue." S. L. Knapp, *Oration before the Associated Disciples of Washington* (1812) 11-12 Knapp describes Otis as "bland and conciliatory."

[32] [Boston, Mass.] *New England Palladium*, Jan. 10, 1815.

[33] Harrison Gray Otis to John Rutledge, Jr., Oct. 18, 1801, Aug. 8, 1802, in Rutledge Papers, Southern Hist. Coll., Univ. of N. C.

[34] Harrison Gray Otis to Theodore Sedgwick, Apr. 13, 1800, in Sedgwick Papers, Mass. Hist. Soc.

[35] Harrison Gray Otis to John Rutledge, Aug. 25, 1800, in Rutledge Papers, Southern Hist. Coll., Univ. of N. C.

> Young man. We would have you remember
> While we in this country do tarry,
> The "Wild Irish" will choose a new member
> And will ne'er vote again for *young Harry*.

Otis promptly explained away his remarks.[36]

Harrison Gray Otis was a party politician who placed a high premium on loyalty, discipline, and close cooperation. He had little admiration for the heterogeneity, diversity, and disorganization that characterized old-school federalism. Borrowing an adjective from Joseph Lancaster, the man who was then bringing order and system to mass education, Otis declared, "It is easier to manage the town of B[oston] by a *Lancastrian* system of political discipline than to institute numerous schools."[37]

The gentlemen of the old school distrusted Otis as much as they disliked Harper. Stephen Higginson said of him, "For the sake of an additional vote, or the rise of one grade in the scale of promotion, [Otis] would sell any and all parties or persons in succession till he reaches the top. Whoever trusts him will be betrayed."[38]

Otis, in turn, reprobated the independence and unbending integrity of the old school gentlemen, whom he described as "silly casuists" who "would sacrifice their party to save their theory."[39] Of the Essex clique he wrote, "There is not one of these sworn brothers who is, or ever was, a politician, or ever had what old John Adams calls the tact of the feelings and passions of mankind; but they are men of probity, of talent, of influence, and the Federal party may say of them, *Non possum vivere sine te nec cum te.*"[40]

A third member of the young Federalist clique in Congress during the last years of the eighteenth century was John Rutledge, Junior (1766–1819), the representative from Orangeburg district, South Carolina.[41] Born into a family of public distinction and private wealth, he derived his education from a tutor and a tour of Europe. When he returned to America, he alternated his time between South Carolina and summer homes in New England.

Rutledge's travels had taken him to France in time to witness the

36 Morison, *Otis*, I, 108.

37 Harrison Gray Otis to William Sullivan, Jan. 19, 1822, in Misc. Mss., New York Public Library.

38 Stephen Higginson to Timothy Pickering, Jan. 12, 1800, May 11, 1797, in Pickering Papers, Mass. Hist. Soc.; J. F. Jameson, ed., "Letters of Stephen Higginson, 1783–1804," *American Historical Association Annual Report for 1896* (Washington, 1897), I, 833, 798.

39 Harrison Gray Otis to Theodore Sedgwick, Apr. 13, 1800, in Sedgwick Papers, Mass. Hist. Soc.

40 "It isn't possible to live without you or with you," Harrison Gray Otis to Josiah Quincy, n.d., in Edmund Quincy, *Josiah Quincy*, pp. 241–242.

41 John Rutledge needs study; he does not have a biography in the DAB. There is nothing other than a brief article by Elizabeth Cometti, "John Rutledge, Jr., Federalist," *Journal of Southern History*, XIII (May 1947), 186–219.

beginning of the Revolution. Like Americans and Englishmen of all political persuasions, he approved of it at first. He became a friend of Thomas Paine and a correspondent of Jefferson.[42] But as the Revolution drifted to the left, John Rutledge shifted to the right. He returned to America, where, as early as 1794, he was described as "a decided Federalist and a promoter of federal measures." As such, he was elected to the Fifth, Sixth, and Seventh Congresses.[43]

In his politics John Rutledge resembled Harper and Harrison Gray Otis. His hatred of "the gallic mania," his fear of the "fire of democracy"[44] was conditioned by temperament and social circumstances. He, too, was afraid to venture forth upon "the dark and dangerous ocean of theoretical experiment."[45] But although Rutledge was not a theoretician, he was an effective forensic orator who spoke "with ease, fluency and grace."[46]

Rutledge was a party man. He regarded the old-school gentlemen, the "great men,"[47] as he sarcastically called them, with a mixture of admiration and disapproval. Like Harper and Otis, and unlike the old-school gentlemen, he tended to view the Federal Party as a symbol of hope and an instrument of political salvation. "Let us keep up the spirits of our party and depend upon it, 'le bon temps reviendrai,'" he wrote.[48]

These three young Federalist Congressmen, Harper, Otis and Rutledge, were remarkably similar in many ways. Each of them showed the same distaste for theoretical thought, the same assumption that the world was a realm of conflict. Each of them despised the people but respected their power. Each accepted the idea of party and looked to the Federal Party as the only weapon which could defeat the Jeffersonians. Each of them manifested the same mixture of admiration and disapproval in their attitudes toward the gentlemen of the old school.

The fourth young Federalist in Congress, however, was made in another mold. Compared with Harper, James A. Bayard (1767–1815), the representative from Delaware, was a man of moderation.[49] His Federalist colleagues considered him less moderate than lax. They were

---

[42] Ibid., pp. 187, 203n.

[43] Charles Cotesworth Pinckney to Timothy Pickering, Oct. 5, 1794; cited by Cometti, "Rutledge," p. 188. It should be noted that in 1796 "Federalist" was still rather an ambiguous label. Rutledge was friendly with Jefferson until the XYZ Affair, and voted for him and Thomas Pinckney in 1796.

[44] Annals of Congress, 6th Cong. 1st Sess., cols. 230–232.

[45] Cometti, "Rutledge," p. 190; John Rutledge to Fisher Ames, Aug. 22, 1800, in Misc. File, Houghton Library, Harvard Univ. This letter is wrongly attributed to John Rutledge, Senior.

[46] Cometti, "Rutledge," p. 189.

[47] John Rutledge to Bishop Robert Smith (his father-in-law), Dec. 7, 1799, in Rutledge Papers, Southern Hist. Coll., Univ. of N. C.; Cometti, "Rutledge," p. 191.

[48] John Rutledge to Harrison Gray Otis, Feb. 15, 1803, in Otis Papers, Mass. Hist. Soc.

[49] A standard work is Morton Borden, The Federalism of James A. Bayard (New York, 1955).

appalled by his personal habits. He drank heavily by even their liberal standards, gambled incessantly, and worst of all, he fraternized with Democrats.[50]

Bayard was a well-bred gentleman, abundantly endowed with charm and presence. He had an open, easy-going personality and an affable, engaging manner. Unlike his three young colleagues he seldom expressed a disapproval of the old-school gentlemen or a contempt for the people. But in many other ways he was quite similar to Harper, Otis, and Rutledge. Bayard was not a theoretical sort of man. For an eloquent lawyer-statesman, a man who was considered the best extempore speaker in the Congress, he was curiously inarticulate about political fundamentals. To a Jeffersonian friend and fishing partner, he declared, "I do not know in what the difference exists as to our opinions upon the material principles of politicks, [but] I believe you are a little more *peopleick* than myself."[51]

Bayard was not as strongly partisan as Harper, Otis, and Rutledge, but he was emphatically partisan nonetheless. More than any other single individual, he was the leader of the Federal Party in Delaware. On election eves, his letters to Federalist friends and colleagues were couched in the imperative: "You will take care upon the whole to satisfy and please the People," he wrote to one of them. "Many things however apparently popular are not always so, and you will consult deliberately and attentively that good understanding which God has given you in order to discover the means of healing the differences and cementing the interests of the Party which it concerns us all so much to support."[52]

As this letter shows quite clearly, James A. Bayard had considerable respect for the voting power of the people. In his make-up there was very little of the unbending, self-righteous independence that characterized the gentlemen of the old school. He willingly recognized the fact that in America the people and their opinions were sovereign.

After these four young Congressmen, the most notable young Federalist in 1801 was the President's son, John Quincy Adams (1767–1848). He was quite unlike the others. In the long history of the republic, few men who have won high office have been as disagreeable as he. Even Bayard, who could manage to get along with nearly anybody, found him "singularly cold and repulsive."[53] His own wife, Louisa Catherine

[50] Jeremiah Mason to Jesse Appleton, Jan. 29, 1814, in Hilliard, *Mason*, pp. 79–81; see also the opinions of Plumer and John Quincy Adams cited in Borden, Bayard, pp. 157–162.

[51] James A. Bayard to Caesar A. Rodney, Feb. 24, 1804, in Bayard Letterbook, New York Public Library; Borden, *Bayard*, p. 13.

[52] James A. Bayard to William Hill Wells, Jan. 12, 1812, in Donnan, *Bayard*, p. 188; Borden, who stresses Bayard's moderation and independence, ignores this significant document.

[53] Diary, Aug. 3, 1813, in Donnan, Bayard, p. 427.

Adams, thought his character was marred by "unnecessary harshness and severity of character."[54] The Federalists tended to humor him as an "eccentric."[55] By the time he came to prominence, they had given up trying to understand the Adamses. Even when John Quincy Adams committed the ultimate, unforgivable act of political apostasy, many Federalists merely shrugged their shoulders. "Considering how apt he is to be violent," George Cabot wrote, "I did not find him more so than I had expected."[56]

The contrast between John Quincy Adams and the young Federalists in Congress is in many ways sharp and extreme. They were extroverts; he was shy and withdrawn. They were shallow men, bored by appeals to political fundamentals; he meditated and wrote profoundly upon all manner of subjects. On winter mornings he wakened before dawn to work at his desk while Bayard, Harper, and Rutledge were still abed sleeping off their midnight revelry. In the realm of political thought he read the masters—Hobbes, Filmer, Sydney, and Locke. Yet for all these contrasts there are significant comparisons to be made. Like the others—more than the others—young Adams was devoured by the "glorious fault," political ambition. Even in 1808, at the nadir of his career, when he stood alone, without a friend or a following, the presidential fever burned fiercely inside him. To John Quincy Adams nothing ever seemed quite as important as his own political future.

Adams and his history-minded family have painstakingly pictured him as an independent statesman, untrammeled by the web of party dependency. But it was not always so. In the earliest years of the nineteenth century young Adams identified his future with the Federal Party. In the intrigues for the Massachusetts senatorships in 1802 he was the very model of a party politician, subtle and stubborn in his own interest, yet always mindful of the harmony of the whole.[57]

In the first years of the nineteenth century Adams viewed the gentlemen of the old school in much the same way that Otis and the other young men did. "Many of them," he wrote, "are too much devoted to personal and selfish views to make any sacrifice to party purposes. Such men never can be of much use, and yet they are always heavy burdens upon the party with which they are associated. In the days of Cato and Caesar, the men who had no affections but for their gardens and their

[54] Martin Duberman, *Charles Francis Adams, 1807–1886* (Boston, 1961), p. 3.
[55] Theodore Lyman to Timothy Pickering, Sep. 16, 1796, in Pickering Papers, Mass. Hist. Soc.
[56] George Cabot to Timothy Pickering, Apr. 11, 1808, in Lodge, *Cabot*, p. 392.
[57] Samuel F. Bemis, *John Quincy Adams and the Foundations of American Foreign Policy* (New York, 1949), merely restates the traditional Adams interpretation of the episode; for a more perceptive analysis of Adams's behavior on this occasion by a skilled party warrior, see Bennett Champ Clark, *John Quincy Adams, "Old Man Eloquent"* (Boston, 1932), pp. 64–74.

statues and their palaces were destined to be vanquished, and were so."[58]

The old-school gentlemen reciprocated young Adams's disapproval. Stephen Higginson wrote of him in the same way that he had written of Otis: "Like a Kite without a Tail, he will be violent and constant in his attempts to rise; but like that, he will be impelled by every eddy Wind, and will pitch on one side and on the other, as the popular currents may happen to strike."[59]

Adams's attitudes, it is true, were far from consistent. His opinions had a way of reflecting those of whomever he happened to be with at the moment. When he corresponded with Josiah Quincy, he sounded like a faithful party politician; with other men he played a different role. After a Federalist caucus in Fanueil Hall, he strolled home with "Ambi" Dexter, the moderate independent old-school Federalist, and remarked upon "the questionable nature of this party organization and its tendency under our constitution."[60] But notwithstanding this conversation with Dexter, Adams began his career as a party man and continued to act in that role until he decided that the Federal Party was doomed to everlasting defeat. Early in Jefferson's administration, he was indeed "as outrageous a Federalist as any in Massachusetts."[61]

One of John Quincy Adams's few friends was another young Federalist, William Plumer (1759–1860), of New Hampshire. To Plumer, Adams wrote, "You see more clearly and judge more coolly of men and things relating to our political world, than almost any other man with whom it has ever been my fortune to act in public life." Although a few years older than other young Federalists, Plumer had started late. After false starts in religion, medicine, and commerce, he finally found his metier as a lawyer and was admitted to the bar in 1787. While Harper, Otis, Bayard, and Rutledge were winning their reputations in Congress, Plumer was taking a leading part in the New Hampshire legislature, becoming speaker of the state House of Representatives in the 1790s.[62]

In temperament and intellect, William Plumer was closer to John Quincy Adams than the other young Federalists. But in common with them all, he feared democracy and rested his hopes upon the Federalist party. "This party spirit, like the poor, we always have with us," he

[58] John Quincy Adams to Josiah Quincy, Jr., Dec. 4, 1804, in Edmund Quincy, *Josiah Quincy*, 63–64.

[59] Stephen Higginson to Timothy Pickering, Jan. 12, 1800, Feb. 15, 1804, in Jameson, "Letters of Higginson," pp. 833, 839 f; see also Fisher Ames to Christopher Gore, Feb. 24, 1803, Ames, *Works*, I, 321.

[60] C. F. Adams, ed., *Memoirs of John Quincy Adams*, 12 vols. (Philadelphia, 1874–77), I, 467.

[61] Joseph D. Learned to John Bailey, 24 June 1823, in Bailey Papers, New York Hist. Soc.

[62] Adams to Plumer, 16 Aug. 1809, in Chamberlain Coll., Boston Public Library; Lynn W. Turner's excellent *William Plumer of New Hampshire* (Chapel Hill, 1962) has been very helpful; also useful is William Plumer, Jr., *Life of William Plumer* (Boston, 1856).

declared.[63] He had a low opinion of the "unthinking populace," the "passions of the multitude," but a healthy respect for their political power.[64]

Plumer was even more outspoken than other young Federalists in his criticism of the "old school." "We must have a new set of leaders," he declared emphatically. "Pickering, Dexter, Ames, Tracy, Ellsworth, Griswold, Wolcott, Jay, Hamilton, King, Ross, Bayard, Marshall, Harper, W. Smith &c must be abandoned. They have had their day. They cannot be sufficiently accomodating. . . . Let us have men who can relax their principles of morality as occasion may require and adapt themselves to circumstances."[65] With unabashed candor Plumer advised Jeremiah Smith to "abjure . . . that uprightness which cannot accommodate itself to events—which cannot flatter the people—that stiff, ungracious patriotism, which professes to save the people from their worst enemies, themselves."[66]

Just as Plumer went further than others in his disapproval of the old-school gentlemen, so they went further in their dislike of him. Plumer complained that the old-school gentlemen who comprised the so-called "Exeter Junto" were "cold, formal and unsocial" to him. In his diary he painfully catalogued their repeated snubs.[67]

Despite the individuality of these six young Federalists—Harper, Otis, Rutledge, Bayard, Adams, and Plumer—an essential unity is evident in their political attitudes and prejudices. They accepted the idea of party and accommodated themselves to the fact that political power was the gift of the people. Although disillusioned by the progress of democracy and disheartened by the crushing defeat of the old-school gentlemen in 1800, they were not yet disarmed of all their weapons nor prepared to abandon the political struggle.

Without the cooperation of most old-school Federalists—indeed, against the wishes of many—these young politicians labored to create a disciplined, popularly oriented, but essentially elitistic political organ-

[63] William Plumer to Jeremiah Smith, Nov. 21–Dec. 25, 1803, in J. H. Morison, *Jeremiah Smith*, pp. 213–215; William Plumer to Jeremiah Smith, Jan. 9, 1803, in Plumer Papers, Library of Congress.

[64] William Plumer to Jeremiah Smith, Jan. 9, 1802, in Plumer Papers, Library of Congress; see also, the disagreement between William Plumer and the Exeter men over fiscal policy in Turner, *Plumer*, pp. 68–69.

[65] William Plumer to Jeremiah Smith, Nov. 21–Dec. 23, 1803, in Morison, *Smith*, pp. 213–215; the inclusion of Bayard and Harper by Plumer was perhaps due to the fact that Plumer knew them mainly by reputation when he penned the letter. Plumer's positions shifted, perhaps with those of his correspondents. In the previous year he had insisted that "the use of poisoned weapons are forbid to us." Turner, *Plumer*, p. 86; he would continually bombard his son with pious exhortations to virtue in public and private life, at the same time that he confided his inner thoughts to Jeremiah Smith.

[66] Ibid.; see also Plumer's earlier and considerably more moderate statement in Turner, *Plumer*, p. 86.

[67] William Plumer, Diary, Nov. 17, 1805, in Plumer Papers, Library of Congress.

ization which might effectively challenge the power of the Jeffersonians. Their task was difficult, for they were faced with opposition on two sides —the Jeffersonians in front and the gentlemen of the old school behind. There were moments when even the most optimistic of them were reduced to despair. Even John Rutledge thought at times that "the good and true men must hang their unstrung harps on the willow."[68] Otis, in dark moments, resolved to give up politics altogether. In 1805 he made a visit to Philadelphia which is reminiscent of Gibbon's visit to Rome. Amid the vacant public buildings he mused upon the "past glories and the prosperous days of the Republic," sadly contemplated the ruins of the Federal Party, and the "reign of profligate anarchy."[69]

A few of the young Federalists, the most intelligent, slowly reached the conclusion that Federalism could never be successfully revived. John Quincy Adams was one of the first. He began to lean in this direction as early as 1802, when he was defeated as the Federalist candidate for Congress in Boston. "The cause assigned by the federalists for their failure," he noted bitterly, "is that the election day was rainy, and that a large number of strong federal votes from the remotest part of the town was lost by non-attendance. This is one of a thousand proofs how large a portion of federalism is a mere fair-weather principle, too weak to overcome a shower of rain. It shows the degree of dependence that can be placed upon such friends. As a party, their adversaries are more sure, and more earnest."[70]

Not much later, William Plumer began to think the same thoughts. "Federalism can suit only a virtuous state of society," he wrote to a friend in 1803. "Don't flatter yourselves that it is ever to have a resurrection." He concluded that the only hope was to "form a union with some of the better sort of democrats, and with some of the worst. We want the former to increase our numbers, and the latter to do our lying."[71] Adams and Plumer watched and waited for a chance to change sides, for a moment when their Jeffersonian adversaries might receive them cordially. The Great Embargo gave them their opportunity, and they made the most of it.

Other young Federalists, however, faced repeated disaster with renewed dedication. Not merely Harper, Otis, Rutledge, and Bayard but many others dedicated themselves to the future of the Federal Party.

[68] John Rutledge to Harrison Gray Otis, Aug. 17, 1804, in Otis Papers, Mass. Hist. Soc.

[69] Harrison Gray Otis to John Rutledge, June 9, 1805, in Rutledge Papers, Southern Hist. Coll., Univ. of N. C.

[70] C. F. Adams, ed., *Memoirs*, II, 256; see also John Quincy Adams to Thomas B. Adams, Nov. 26, 1804, in Adams Family Papers, reel 403; John Quincy Adams to Rufus King, Oct. 8, 1802, in W. C. Ford, ed., *Writings of John Quincy Adams*, 7 vols. (New York, 1913–1917), III, 7.

[71] William Plumer to Jeremiah Smith, Dec. 23, 1803, in Morison, *Smith*, p. 212.

Most are forgotten figures, strangers even to specialists in early American political history. A few, however, had bright political futures ahead of them. They included Josiah Quincy (1772–1864), Roger Brooke Taney (1777–1864), John Macpherson Berrien (1781–1856), Daniel Webster (1782–1852), William Gaston (1778–1844), and among the very youngest a future president, James Buchanan (1791–1868). Antaeus-like, they would gather strength from every fall.

Falls would be frequent. A Federal Party *eo nomine* would never regain the confidence of the people. But in time the tactics if not the ethics of the young Federalists would be vindicated by successive waves of Jacksonians, Whigs, and Republicans. In England, similar devices would be successfully exploited by men who called themselves "tory Democrats." Before the nineteenth century was out, the fears of that political eccentric, John Adams, would be realized—the American *aristoi* would indeed "employ the Commonalty to knock to pieces every Plan and Model that the most honest Architects in Legislation can invent to keep them in bounds."[72]

Some of the young Federalists could foresee their own defeat but not the tarnished victories of their successors. In fear more than in hope they hedged their political bets in three ways. First, some of them moved uncertainly toward a conception of minimal government which represented another departure from the ideals of the old school. "You must either make the government supreme or the people supreme," Barent Gardenier said. "I am for the latter." In 1803 a Federalist declared, "The prime duty of a free government is to treat all men alike, leaving their prosperity and success to depend upon their integrity, industry and skill."[73]

Whether or not power could be recovered by the "best people," it was clear that it would never be fully at their command. As the rich and well-born awakened to this fact, public power became an object of suspicion and hostility. The first stirrings of this consciousness came in the era of Jeffersonian democracy. Petty favors, particular alliances, would still be sought in state and national politics. Tariffs and turnpikes, grants of land and monopolistic privilege, would be demanded and received

---

[72] see above, p. 19.

[73] *Annals of Congress*, 11 Cong., 1 Sess., col. 133, 27 May 1809; [New York] *Evening Post*, 25 Apr. 8, 1803; see also [Trenton] *Federalist*, 24 June 1811; [Boston] *New England Palladium*, 20 Apr. 1810, 27 Sep. 1803; Roger Griswold to J. Rutledge, 15 Apr. 1802, in Rutledge Papers, Univ. of N.C.; "Commerce and freedom always flourish and decay together. No permanent systematic restrictions on the commerce of a country can ever be enforced, while the people are free." Josiah Dunham, *Oration . . . at Windsor*, p. 12; and see Daniel Webster and the bank, a subject on which a great change of opinion had taken place *on both sides of the house*." *Annals of Congress*, 14 Cong., 1. Sess., col. 1339, 5 Apr. 1816; and see below, ch. IX and App. II.

by every generation of American conservatives in the nineteenth century, by even the most doctrinaire of Adam Smith's disciples. But the old-school ideal of active and energetic government, deeply and broadly involved in many kinds of regulatory functions, could necessarily have little weight in the calculus of American conservatism from the generation of Harper and Otis to that of Nixon and Goldwater. As a buttress of elitism, it perished with the men of the old school. Thereafter, it could be said, in Reinhold Niebuhr's words, that "American conservatism is not conservative at all in the traditional sense; it is a part of the traditional liberal movement and it exhibits the defects of its creed; but it has not retained many of its virtues."[74]

Another striking fact about the younger generation of Federalist leaders was the way in which they returned to Christianity, with an evangelical enthusiasm rarely in evidence among gentlemen of the old school. Before the turn of the century, "a Bible was rarely to be seen in a fashionable house," even in Boston. As late as 1804, Simeon Baldwin observed that "fashion does not require people to go to church."[75]

But ten years later observers seemed generally to agree upon the fact of a "great change respecting the truth of Christianity which has taken place of late years in the minds of the educated classes, and especially among public men." Thus observed a renegade Republican, De Witt Clinton, in a conversation with Federalists of both generations who agreed entirely. "As to the fact," James Kent added, "there is no doubt, there could be no doubt."[76]

The possessing classes had particular reasons for favoring a revival of Christianity. "Take away Religion," wrote Lewis Tappan, who began his public career as a young Federalist, "and what prevents the mass of people from violating laws of God and man? There may be some, philosophical enough to be moral without the sanctions of Religion. But

[74] Reinhold Niebuhr, *Christian Realism and Political Problems* (New York, 1953), p. 55. A cluster of monographs, including Oscar and Mary Handlin, *Commonwealth: Massachusetts, 1774–1861* (New York, 1947); and Louis Hartz, *Economic Policy and Democratic Thought: Pennsylvania, 1776–1860* (Cambridge, 1948) have endeavored to demonstrate the breadth of regulatory activity and economic policy on the part of state governments; but they erect and demolish a straw man in the form of extreme laissez faire, which never has and never can exist. The questions which these investigators undertook to resolve deserve to be reopened, and re-examined by scholars with greater depth in early American economic history. It may appear that economic policy in ante-bellum American states (1815–1860) was much closer to practices in the latter part of the century than to 17th and 18th century patterns.

[75] Edward Warren, *The Life of John Collins Warren compiled chiefly from his Autobiography and Journals*, 2 vols. (Boston, 1860), I, 19; Simeon Baldwin to wife, 12 Feb. 1804, in Baldwin Papers, Yale Univ.

[76] J. M. Mathews, *Recollections of Persons and Events* (New York, 1865), pp. 71, 75; see also Clifford S. Griffin, *Their Brothers' Keepers* (New Brunswick, 1960), pp. 3–60; W. G. McLoughlin, ed., *Charles Grandison Finney, Lectures on Revivals of Religion* (Cambridge, 1960), pp. vii–lii.

the generality want its commands to restrain and regulate their conduct."[77] De Witt Clinton believed that this motive was the major one. "The twenty or thirty years which spread over the latter part of the last century and the beginning of the present, have given demonstration of the awful results to which infidelity leads. Facts speak for themselves, and too loudly to be disregarded, have shown that infidelity makes war on the social and civil welfare of man, as well as his eternal safety."[78]

But the emotional quality of the revival, the zeal which the "educated classes" manifested in the anxious seats of their churches and in the private circle of domesticity, may be evidence that they returned to religion not primarily because of what it promised to do for the people but because of what it promised to do for themselves. In a world where class conflict was added to class consciousness, where the acceleration of change was a constant, evangelical Christianity was a haven of assurance, a sanctuary from social strife.

A third way of hedging a political gamble was education—formal schooling to control the common man, not to liberate him. While Jefferson produced platitudes and ineffectual plans, Federalists even in his own state, such as Charles Fenton Mercer, labored to construct systems of public education which carried far beyond the ideas of the old school. Their purposes appeared in their infatuation with Lancastrian pedagogy, with its order, discipline, and mindless memory training, a device not merely for making mass education practicable but for making conservative education effective. The political impotence of Federalism in so many states, the intensity of party rivalry, meant that not much would be accomplished. But another generation of conservatives, Whigs such as Horace Mann and Henry Barnard and Calvin Wiley, would build with better success on foundations laid by Federal predecessors.

All of these developments, political, economic, religious, and educational, encapsulated a revolution of American conservatism which reflected a continuing revolution in the structure of American society, from organic interdependence to individual autonomy, from deference to political democracy, but most of all from open to covert elitism. The revolution had begun before the War for Independence; it would continue after the War of 1812. But in the intervening years, and especially in the period 1800–1816, it would proceed with unparalleled momentum. Ironically, the young Federalists who hoped to control its effects would contribute to both its mass and velocity by their partisan political activity. That story is the theme of the chapters which follow.

[77] Tappan to Benjamin Tappan, 21 May 1814, in Tappan Papers, Library of Congress. "It is marvellous to me that a man of sound mind, extensive observation, and fairness, can look abroad and not perceive that Christianity is the conservator of all that is dear in civil liberty and human happiness; and infidelity sets loose all the base passions of our nature." Tappan to Benjamin Tappan, 12 Dec. 1829, in Tappan Papers, Library of Congress.
[78] Mathews, *Recollections*, pp. 71, 75.

III

The Creation of the Federal Party

> *"One of two things will, I confess, take place. Either the advances of the [Jeffersonian] faction will create a federal party, or their unobstructed progress will embolden them to use their power, as all such gentry will if they dare, in acts of violence on property."*
>
> —FISHER AMES, 1803

> *"If this country is to be saved, if we are to be spared that general wreck of freedom, the country, under Providence, must owe its salvation to the Federal Party."*
>
> —DAVID B. OGDEN, 1812

> *"I prefer the household prudence of my Great-Grandmother, who cautioned those who darn stockings not to make two holes in trying to stop one."*
>
> —GOUVERNEUR MORRIS, n.d.[1]

Our understanding of political development in the new nation has been clouded by the imprecise usage of a crucial word—party. Historians have applied it without distinction to all groups which have manifested partisanship, thereby obscuring the institutional process of party growth. A party, as Webster defines it, is an "organized political group which tries to elect its candidates to office," an autonomous body with its own formal structure, stable following, and sometimes an ideological frame of reference which transcends particular issues and events.[2]

Parties, in this sense, are not as old as the American republic. They were preceded by more primitive political groups, which friends called "interests" or "connexions" and enemies condemned as "factions" or "sects," groups which existed primarily within the structure of a government. Interests or factions were little more than tenuous evanescent alliances, without organization or formal structure. An interest could perhaps be called a *partie sans parti*, a party to an argument but not an organized political group.[3]

---

[1] Fisher Ames to Thomas Dwight, 29 Nov. 1803, in Ames, *Works*, I, 335; David B. Ogden to William Meredith, 29 June 1812, in Meredith Papers, Hist. Soc. Penna.; Gouverneur Morris to [?], n.d. [c. Jan. 1813?], in Morris Papers, Library of Congress.

[2] Chambers, *Political Parties*, pp. 44–48.

[3] Joseph Charles, *Origins of the American Party System* (Williamsburg, 1956), p. 42n; Chambers, *Political Parties*, pp. 17, 26, 34–52; Seymour Martin Lipset, *The*

During the first four Congresses under the present Constitution, two interests developed in opposition to one another—a group which called itself the "Republican interest" (we call them Jeffersonians) and another which often spoke of itself as "Friends of Order," "Friends of Government," or sometimes the "federal interest." They differed from pre-Revolutionary factions primarily in that they existed on the national level. In structure and function they were very similar to the court and country connections of colonial America. In the early 1790s, these nebulous political formations had little meaning beyond the walls of Congress Hall; even within it they were loose, unstructured associations of attitude and conviction which are more clearly apparent to twentieth-century historians than they were to eighteenth-century politicians. As late as 1794, an intelligent, experienced, and unequivocably Jeffersonian representative, Nathaniel Macon, wrote home, "It is said there are two parties in Congress, but the fact I do not positively know. If there are, I know that I do not belong to either."[4]

After the epochal conflict over Jay's treaty in 1795–1796, the defeated Republican interest entered a new stage of development—gradually growing into a full-fledged party in our sense of the word. It generated its own structure of committees, sponsored open nominating meetings, founded and subsidized newspapers, collected campaign funds, and expended them on an unprecedented scale. As the "Republican interest" evolved into a "Republican Party," Federalist opponents were left far behind. "Friends of Order" were doubly reluctant to take the extraordinary step of establishing an extraconstitutional organization. Reasons of principle were reinforced by expediency. The friends of the administration had, after all, won the struggle over Jay's treaty and retained their grasp upon the government in the election of 1796. A "resort to popular meetings" appeared both improper and unnecessary.[5]

First New Nation (New York, 1963), pp. 32–35; Paul Goodman, *The Democratic-Republicans of Massachusetts* (Cambridge, 1964), 59–69.

[4] In 1787–1789, of course, a Federalist "party" briefly appeared to promote the Constitution. Though elaborately organized in at least a few urban areas (see Committee rosters dated 2 Apr. 1789 in Alexander Hamilton Papers, N.Y. Hist. Soc.) it did not perpetuate itself *qua* party. Its purpose was not to gain power within the government but to revolutionize it, and when the coup succeeded, the party dissolved in many states, leaving only its name and a few organizational remnants in Penna., N.Y., and perhaps N.J. See Cunningham, *Jeffersonian Republicans*, p. 23; Tinkcom, *Republicans and Federalists in Penna*, pp. 31, 269–73; Harry Ammon, "Formation of the Republican Party in Virginia," *Jnl. Southern Hist.*, XIX (1953), 309; Alfred Fabian Young, "The Democratic-Republican Movement in New York State, 1788–1797," unpub. diss. (Northwestern Univ. 1958); Goodman, *Democratic-Republicans of Massachusetts*, 27–29, and my own "Metamorphosis of Maryland Federalism."—Nathaniel Macon to John Steele, 11 Dec. 1794, in Kemp Battle, ed., "The Letters of Nathaniel Macon, John Steele, and William Barry Grove," *James Sprunt Historical Monographs*, III (1902), 21.

[5] All recent accounts agree; see Chambers, *Political Parties*, pp. 53–149; Charles, *American Party System*, pp. 91–140; Cunningham, *Jeffersonian Republicans.*, pp. 67–115; Stephen G. Kurtz, *The Presidency of John Adams* (Phila., 1957), pp. 59–77.

Among Jeffersonian Republicans, political necessity was indeed the mother of party invention. The tide was running against them in the period 1795–1798; a quasi-war between the American and the French republics was a near-fatal blow to the "French party" in the United States. As the people rallied to the administration, the Jeffersonians redoubled their partisan efforts, extended and refined their partisan machinery. In adversity they were forced to develop "a new political engine, the first of its kind in modern history," a tightly disciplined, efficiently organized, popularly oriented, vote-seeking party. The Federalists, however, remained an interest, a league of gentlemen, a loose confederation of men united by a certain vague attachment to Washington and the Constitution and by an antipathy to democracy, Jefferson, and the "spirit of faction." Occasional agitation among the Federalists for party organization usually came to nothing. "We are broken to pieces," Fisher Ames declared in 1797.[6]

The Federalists, of course, were never entirely unorganized during the 1790s. In all parts of the union there were the inevitable secret pacts and private understandings. Legislative caucuses met sporadically in most state capitals. There were many personal cliques and connections of the sort Sir Lewis Namier has described in the context of eighteenth-century England. In the middle states, politically the most sophisticated, the Federalists were beginning to develop formal machinery. New York Federalists seem to have moved farthest and fastest in this direction. As early as 1792 they organized committees throughout the state, and put on an impressive gubernatorial campaign. Peter Van Schaack, the "Kinderhook tory," in 1800 professed to be as busy as "a member of a *revolutionary* committee." But even in New York in 1800 there was no effective Federalist statewide organization beyond a rudimentary legislative caucus. "All our friends here are in sad anarchy," Gouverneur Morris wrote.[7]

[6] Chambers, *Political Parties in America*, p. 103. For examples of Republican organization in 1800 see [Amherst] *Village Messenger*, 14 June 1800; [Boston] *Independent Chronicle*, 30 Oct. 1800; [Hartford] *American Mercury*, 11 Sep. 1800; [Newark] *New Jersey Centinel of Freedom*, 3 June, 1–8 July, 5 Aug. 1800; Philadelphia *Aurora*, 30 Sep. 1800; [Richmond] *Virginia Argus*, 28 Mar. 1800; [Lexington] *Kentucky Gazette*, Feb. 27, 13 Mar. 1800; Cunningham, *Jeffersonian Republicans*, pp. 144–174. For Federal agitation for organization see, for example, William Vans Murray to James McHenry, Sep. 9, 1796, in B. C. Steiner, *The Life and Correspondence of James McHenry* (Cleveland, 1907), p. 197; Kurtz, *Presidency of John Adams*, 161; for continuous improvements in organization and technique see Cunningham, *Jeffersonian Republicans*, pp. 50–66 passim. Fisher Ames to Alexander Hamilton, 26 Jan. 1797, in Hamilton Papers, Library of Congress.

[7] Young, "Democratic-Republican Movement," p. 367; Peter Van Schaack to Theodore Sedgwick, Apr. 7, 1800, in Sedgwick Papers, Mass. Hist. Soc. For Federalist meetings and committees in New York in 1800 see *Albany Centinel*, 25 Mar., 22 Apr. 1800 [New York] *Commercial Advertiser*, 27 Mar. 24, Apr. 1800; Barent Gardenier et al. to Peter Van Schaack, 14 Mar. 1798, in Van Schaack Papers, Library of Congress. Gouverneur Morris to Rufus King, 4 June, 1800, in King, *Life and Correspondence of King*, III, 251.

Federalists in Pennsylvania, Delaware, New Jersey, and Virginia were not far behind their New York brethren In the first two states Federalist organizations had developed as early as 1795. In New Jersey and Virginia, Federalist organizations appeared in the campaign of 1800. Although short-lived, the network of Federalist committees in the Old Dominion constituted the most sophisticated state organization—on paper—to oppose Jefferson in 1800. But these organizations were incomplete, intermittent, and, in competition with the Jeffersonians, generally inadequate.[8]

The Federalists also possessed rudimentary organizations in the larger cities, from Charleston, where a leading Jeffersonian complained bitterly of Federalist energy and efficiency, to Salem, the sixth largest city in the nation, where party organization had recently appeared. In October 1800 a local clergyman noted in his diary, "For the first time the zeal of Caucusing has been introduced into Salem. In former times, particular men of influence have met to agree upon a Candidate for office but then the meeting was few and all upon one side. Now parties are armed at all points, and large associations are forming."[9]

But these exceptions notwithstanding, the Federalists were in a state of extreme disorganization at the end of the 1790s. Evidence of many kinds suggests that they were not merely split, as a modern party might be, but atomized. First, there is the testimony of the Federalists themselves. Fisher Ames emphatically declared, "The Federalists hardly deserve the name of a party. Their association is a loose one, formed by accident, and shaken by every prospect of labor or hazard." Robert Troup sadly wrote to a Federalist in Europe, "I cannot describe to you how broken and scattered your federal friends are! At present we have no

[8] *Address to the Federal Republicans of the State of New Jersey* (Trenton, 1800); *An Address to the Citizens of the County of Morris*, Dec. 16, 1800, broadsides, N.J. Hist. Soc.; *Newark Gazette*, Sep. 16, 1800; *Address to the Federal Republicans of Burlington County . . . by a Committee* (Trenton, 1800); *An Address to the Freemen of Pennsylvania, from the Committee of Correspondence for the city of Philadelphia* (Germantown, 1799); [Lancaster] *Journal*, 10 Sep., 22 Sep. 1800; [Philadelphia] *Aurora*, 5 Feb. 1800; [Philadelphia], *Gazette of the U.S.*, 6 Nov. 1800; [Philadelphia] *True American*, 11 Oct. 1800; *Poulson's American Daily Advertiser*, 11, 13 Oct. 1800; Sanford W. Higginbotham, *The Keystone in the Democratic Arch*, p. 19; Fee, pp. *New Jersey*, 1, 9, 134; Pole, "The Federalist Dilemma in N.J.," p. 264; Kurtz, *Presidency* of Adams, p. 426, exaggerates the extent of Federal organization in the middle states; Munroe, *Federalist Delaware*, p. 236; [Richmond] *Virginia Argus*, 28 Mar. 1800; Cunningham, *Jeff. Republicans*, pp. 152–153; see also *To the Freemen of the State of Rhode Island*, 19 Aug. 1800, broadside in Library of Congress file of the *Newport Mercury*, which shows an embryonic Federalist organization in that state. Charles A. Beard, *Economic Origins of Jeffersonian Democracy*, 2d edn. (New York, 1943), p. 377.

[9] William Bentley, *Diary*, 4 vols. (Salem, 1905–1914), II, 354. See also *Russell's Gazette*, 7 Apr. 1800; *Mass. Mercury*, 21, 28 Mar., 2 May, 1800; Georgetown *Washington Federalist*, 30 Sep. 1800. There were also Federalist legislative caucuses in New Hampshire and Massachusetts; [Portsmouth], *U.S. Oracle of the Day*, 21 June 1800; Ames to Gore, 5 Mar. 1800, in Ames, *Works* I, 277.

rallying point; and no mortal can divine where or when we shall again collect our strength!"[10]

Second, there were the taunts of Jeffersonians, even in the middle states. William Duane wrote from Philadelphia to a Connecticut Republican, "The only uniform corps here now are the *Republicans*." The *Aurora* declared that the "disorganized state" of the Federalists was "scarcely describable." In New York, Aaron Burr openly boasted of the "superior management" of the Republican cause. New Jersey Jeffersonians wrote contemptuously of the "weak strategems" of their opponents.[11]

Third, the voting behavior of Congressmen between 1798 and 1800 suggests that even the federal interests within Congress Hall were disintegrating as the Republicans were improving their party discipline. Professor Manning J. Dauer's compilation of Congressional voting statistics shows that in the last two sessions of the Fifth Congress and in the Sixth Congress the percentage of Republicans who voted independently on important issues steadily declined. But at the same time, the percentage of moderate and maverick Federalists increased considerably (see Table II).

Fourth, there were a few exceptions which serve to demonstrate the rule. Occasional efforts by Federalists to organize and unify their colleagues brought violent public reactions from their colleagues. In Maryland, for example, the Federalists of one Eastern Shore county imitated their opponents by organizing a nominating committee, but they were much embarrassed when one of their candidates self-righteously repudiated his nomination as "an unwarrantable liberty." In Montgomery County across the bay, a Federalist caucus became the principal issue of the campaign, not so much between Federalists and Republicans as among Federalists themselves.[12]

Fifth, Federalist disorganization at the turn of the century is reflected

[10] Fisher Ames to Oliver Wolcott, 3 Aug. 1800, in Hildreth, *The History of the United States*, 6 vols. (New York, 1849–1856), V, 376; see also John Adams to T.B. Adams, 11 July 1801, in Adams Family Papers, reel 401; and Henry W. De Saussure to Pickering, 12 Aug. 1800, in Pickering Papers, Mass. Hist. Soc. Robert Troup to Rufus King, 1 Oct. 1800, in King, *Life and Correspondence of King*, III, 315; see also Jonas Platt to James Kent, 25 Dec. 1800, in Kent Papers, Library of Congress; Cabot to Gore, 2 May 1799, in Lodge, *Cabot*, p. 231; Cabot to Wolcott, 3 Aug. 1801, ibid., p. 32; Hamilton to James A. Bayard, 6 Aug. 1800, in H.C. Lodge, ed., *Works of Alexander Hamilton*, 12 vols. (New York, 1904), X, 386.

[11] William Duane to Ephraim Kirby, 3 July 1800, in Kirby Papers, Duke University Library; the *Aurora's* observation is quoted in the [New York] *Commercial Advertiser*, 22 Mar. 1800; *Albany Centinel*, 13 May 1800; [Newark] *Centinel*, 16 Sep. 1800; see also 28 July 1800; see also [Philadelphia] *Aurora*, 10 Nov. 1800; Salem *Impartial Register*, 10 Nov. 1800.

[12] [Easton] *Republican Star*, 2 Oct. 1804, 15 Oct. 1805; [Georgetown, Md.] *Centinel*, 9, 12 Sep. 1800; for other Federalist protests against attempts at Federalist organization see [Portsmouth] *N.H. Gazette*, 26 Aug. 1800; [Concord] *Courier of N.H.*, 26 July, 2, 9, 16 Aug. 1800; and [Salem] *Gazette*, 25 Feb. 1800.

Table II. Voting Behavior of Federalists and Republicans in the U.S. House of Representatives, 1798–1800[a]

Session	Orthodox Republicans	Moderate Republicans	Federalists (ex-Republicans)	Per Cent Deviant
5 Congress 2	45	5	0	10
5 Congress 3	44	3	0	7
6 Congress 1	41	1	0	2
6 Congress 2	41	2	0	4

Session	Orthodox Federalists	Moderate Federalists	Republicans (ex-Federalists)	Per Cent Deviant
5 Congress 2	48	7	0	12.7
5 Congress 3	46	9	1	17.8
6 Congress 1	52	10	1	17.4
6 Congress 2	49	11	3	22.2

[a] Identities and Definitions follow Manning J. Dauer, *The Adams Federalists* (Baltimore, 1953), pp. 288–342. "Deviant" members are those whom Dauer classes as "moderate," "Federalist ex-Republican," or "Republican ex-Federalist." Percentage of Deviant members is taken of the total number (i.e., orthodox Federalists plus moderate Federalists plus Republicans–ex-Federalists). The conclusions drawn here are not those of Professor Dauer.

in a chaos of conflicting nominations, from the presidential race in which a Congressional caucus ineffectually gave equal endorsements to both leading contenders, to confused contests for the most humble local offices. In some districts no Federalists competed in elections that it was thought any Federalist might have won. In others there was a plethora of candidates. "Nearly a dozen" men competed for Vermont's eastern Congressional seat in 1800. In Baltimore County, Maryland, thirteen Federalists vied for four seats in the House of Delegates. In Essex County, Massachusetts, there were seven Federalist candidates for one place in Congress. In 1798, no less a Republican than Albert Gallatin owed his election to the fact that his opposition was split between two candidates.[13]

Some old-school gentlemen declared that a multiplicity of candidates was a positive good. "It will be the means of bringing more people to

[13] George Cabot to Oliver Wolcott, 16 Oct. 1798, in Lodge, *Cabot*, p. 173; P. Browne to Duncan Cameron, 20 Jan. 1801, in Cameron Papers, Southern Hist. Coll., Univ. of N.C.; William Barry Grove to James McHenry, 2 Aug. 1798, in McHenry Papers, Duke University Library. [Hanover, N.H.] *Dartmouth Gazette*, 25 Oct. 1800; Easton, Md. *Herald*, 6 Oct. 1802; Manasseh Cutler, *Diary*, 21 Mar. 1801, in W. P. & J. P. Cutler, *Life, Journals and Correspondence of Rev. Manasseh Cutler*, 2 vols. (Cincinnati, 1888), II, 43. For other conflicting Federalist nominations see [Brookfield Mass.] *Farmer's Journal*, 1 Apr., 3 Sep. 1800; [Leominster] *Telescope*, 20, 27 Mar. 1800; [Northampton] *Hampshire Gazette*, 2 Apr. 1800; [Portsmouth] *U.S. Oracle*, 28 June 1800. Edward Day to Samuel Hodgdon, Aug. 20, 1798, Samuel Hodgdon to Timothy Pickering, in Pickering Papers, Mass. Hist. Soc.; see also William Rawle to James Iredell, Sep. 26, 1798, in Iredell Papers, Duke University Library; [Georgetown] *Centinel*, 7 Oct. 1800.

the poles," Thomas Sims declared. "Honest well-thinking men, however limited on general subjects may be their understanding, commonly possess discernment enough to distinguish between truth and falsehood."[14]

Sixth, the disorganization of the Federalists appeared in the informality of nominating methods. In all parts of the union a favorite means of nomination was by an anonymous letter to the local newspaper. Once put "in nomination" in this fashion, it was "not customary for those so designated, publicly to decline."[15] The inevitable consequence was confusion compounded. One nominating letter to the *Centinel* in Boston began, "Mr. Russell, If you have no better list, please to insert the following. . . ."[16] Another wrote: "As I have seen no nomination list published, I take the liberty to offer the following. . . ."[17] A third: "Mr. Russell, . . . As I understand that several of our present Representatives for some time had it in contemplation to resign, I beg leave to propose to my fellow citizens the following gentlemen to represent this town. . . ." The bewildered editor commented, "*It is the first time we have heard of any intentions to resign in our present representatives.*"[18] In southern states, and occasionally in northern states, too, candidates nominated themselves on their own platform by newspaper advertisement or broadside. In 1790, for example, William Thompson "respectfully offered himself" for Boston town clerk, and declared that he would work for half the usual salary.[19]

Seventh, after the death of Washington, there was no man who was able to command the support of the Federal Party, even if it had existed. A Federalist recently returned from Europe noted, "I have not heard of any one man since my return [mentioned] as chief. It will always happen as it did after the death of Alexander among his captains. In fact we are in a strange situation."[20] When Federal leaders heard of Washington's death their hearts had overflowed with genuine grief. "The death of the General!" Henry Van Schaack exclaimed. "God help us!"[21] John Adams, writing retrospectively of 1800, declared, "The federal party has been so imprudently managed, as well as so discordantly composed that

[14] Thomas Sims to Leven Powell, 20 Feb. 1801, in William E. Dodd, ed., "Correspondence of Col. Leven Powell, M.C., relating to the election of 1800," *The John P. Branch Historical Papers of Randolph Macon College* (1901), p. 61. And where Federalist tickets did appear, there were complaints against chronic ticket-splitting among generally sympathetic voters; Portsmouth *U.S. Oracle*, 27 Nov. 1800.

[15] Thomas B. Adams to John Quincy Adams, 20 Oct. 1802, in Adams Family Papers, reel 401; Luetscher, *Early Political Machinery*, pp. 63–72.

[16] [Boston, Mass.] *Centinel*, May 6, 1797.

[17] Ibid., Mar. 8, 1800; see also Feb. 12, Mar. 15, 1800.

[18] Ibid., Apr. 11, 1801; see also Mar. 4, Oct. 28, 1801.

[19] "To the respectable CITIZENS of BOSTON," Mar. 6, 1790, broadsides, Mass. Hist. Soc.

[20] William Vans Murray to Rufus King, Apr. 5, 1802, in King, *Life and Correspondence of King*, IV, 95–96.

[21] Henry Van Schaack to Theodore Sedgwick, Dec. 26, 1799, in Sedgwick Papers, Mass. Hist. Soc.

the overthrow of the party is no wonder. The federal cause had no head."[22]

Alexander Hamilton's indiscreet pamphlet assault on John Adams ruined the reputations of both author and subject. We have already glanced at Adams's reputation among Federalist leaders.[23] In 1800 Hamilton's stock stood not much higher. He himself lamented that "his influence with the Federal Party was wholly gone."[24] More sophisticated politicians might have succeeded in rallying behind the unknown soldier, Charles Cotesworth Pinckney, but of such political tactics the gentlemen of the old school neither knew nor cared. Whether one prefers to say that the Federalists had no leader or that they had too many, the fact remains that none could lead effectively.

The Federalist predicament was the same in many of the states as it was in the nation—little organization and no effective leaders. In Massachusetts, for instance, the death of Governor Increase Sumner was, from the Federalists' viewpoint, "a deplorable event." He alone seemed able to unite the individuals of the old school behind him. Theodore Sedgwick believed that "it will be difficult if not impossible to obtain a successor in all respects his equal. Great talents aren't indispensable, but those which are so, he possessed, in an eminent degree."[25]

The old-school Federalists preferred to attack the methods of their opponents rather than to imitate them. While the Republicans organized themselves, Federalists published satirical commentaries such as "The Grand Caucus," a comedy in two acts, in which four Jeffersonians, "Will Sneakup, Esq., Obedumb Bragwell, Esq., Squire Quorom, Esq., and Lord Cockdedoodledoo," organized a "self-created convention" and after much tomfoolery emerged as its candidates for office.[26]

Privately, the Federalists spoke more seriously. Jeremiah Smith of New Hampshire described the Republican party organization in his own state with mixed horror and fascination. "Are not we fallen on evil times?" he asked. "Did you believe 15 years ago that a thing of this kind could happen in New England?"[27]

---

22 John Adams to T. B. Adams, Jan. 16, 1801, in Adams Family Papers, reel 400.
23 See above, p. 17–19.
24 Allan Nevins, *The New York Evening Post* (New York, 1922), p. 11; see also Fisher Ames to Christopher Gore, Dec. 29, 1800, in Ames, *Works*, I, 289; [Providence, R. I.] *Gazette*, Nov. 15, 1800.
25 Theodore Sedgwick to Rufus King, July 26, 1799, in King, *Life and Correspondence of King*, III, 71; see also Thomas Dwight to Theodore Sedgwick, Apr. 11, 1800, and Peter Van Schaack to Theodore Sedgwick, Jan. 29, 1800, in Sedgwick Papers, Mass. Hist. Soc; for a retrospective view of Federalist disorganization in Maryland during the election of 1800 see Robert Goodloe Harper to A. C. Hanson, Sep. 28, 1815, in Galloway-Maxcy-Markoe Papers, Library of Congress.
26 [Easton, Md.] *Herald*, Aug. 31, 1802; see also J. Laurence to Rufus King, Apr. 16, 1794, in King, *Life and Correspondence of King*, I, 561.
27 Jeremiah Smith to William Plumer, Feb. 22, 1804, in Plumer Papers, Library of Congress; see also [Hartford, Conn.] *Connecticut Courant*, June 2, Sep. 1, 8; Oct. 27, Nov. 22, Dec. 17, 1800; Fisher Ames to Thomas Dwight, Sep. 3, 1794, in Ames,

The Federalists continually expressed surprise that their "theoretical" opponents should show such a flair for organization. One of them said, "Their leaders, although in some respects visionary, are practical men in their indefatigable industry to obtain proselytes."[28] Theophilus Parsons wrote angrily, "The Jacobins appear to be completely organized throughout the United States. The principals have their agents dispersed in every direction; and the whole body act with a union to be expected only from men, in whom no moral principles exist."[29]

Some of the Federalists took pains "to keep the people steady," and to "give efficacy to the will of the wise and good."[30] They spoke to the voters in the same way that a horseman might talk to his refractory mount, alternating soft words and sharp ones, a lump of sugar and a touch of the spur. But the people were not to be treated like "a great beast"—and the Federalists were thrown from power.

We have seen how most of the gentlemen of the old school and some of the younger Federalists withdrew from politics as the first years of the new century passed slowly in succession.[31] Even among those who remained in politics there was a spirit of "incorrigible lethargy."[32] One of the few who remained active observed, "Federalism sits like a Turk benumbed with opium, a careless looker-on, or perhaps is amused to observe the ingenuity of the work of its own destruction." He concluded, "The Federalists want zeal, want plan, want union—they will soon want a hiding place."[33]

But as defeat followed political defeat, some of the Federalists were roused to action. They persuaded themselves that the creation of a federal party was necessary, if not to regain power, at least to keep the Jeffersonians from "excesses." Fisher Ames was one of the few old-school gentlemen of this persuasion. "One of two things will, I confess, take place," he wrote. "Either the advances of the [Jeffersonian] faction will create a federal party, or their unobstructed progress will embolden them to use their power, as all such gentry will if they dare, in acts of violence on property."[34]

Works, I, 148; T. Evans to Leven Powell, Oct. 30, 1800; Moss Kent to James Kent, June 24, 1795, in Kent Papers, Library of Congress; Thomas Dwight to Theodore Sedgwick, Apr. 11, 1800, in Sedgwick Papers, Mass. Hist. Soc.

[28] Robinson, *Jeff. Dem. in N. Eng.*, p. 63.

[29] Theophilus Parsons to John Jay, May 5, 1800, in Johnston, *Correspondence of Jay*, IV, 267–270.

[30] George Cabot to Oliver Wolcott, May 2, 1799, in Lodge, *Cabot*, p. 229; George Cabot to John Rutledge, Oct. 22, 1800, in Rutledge Papers, Southern Hist. Coll., Univ. of N. C.

[31] See above, p. 88.

[32] Thomas Dwight to Theodore Sedgwick, Dec. 5, 1800, in Sedgwick Papers, Mass. Hist. Soc.; see also George Cabot to Rufus King, Mar. 17, 1804, in King, *Life and Correspondence of King*, IV, 370.

[33] [Boston, Mass.] *New England Palladium*, Jan. 4, 1803.

[34] Fisher Ames to Thomas Dwight, Nov. 29, 1803, in Ames, *Works*, I, 335; see also George Cabot to Rufus King, Mar. 7, 1804, in Lodge, *Cabot*, p. 347.

Ames listened to denunciations of "party spirit," then proceeded to argue the point with his friends. "Party is an association of honest men for honest purposes, and, when the State falls into bad hands, is the only efficient defence; a champion who never flinches, a watchman who never sleeps," he wrote. "We must keep united, and keep the public with us."[35]

But Ames received little encouragement from the gentlemen of the old school. "I am almost separated from all my federal friends," he complained. "They are lazy or in despair, and they urge, with wonderful eagerness, the futility of all exertions to retrieve the public mind from its errors, or to prevent their consequences. . . . I have, over and over again, made the offer to almost every considerable man in Connecticut and New Hampshire, as well as Massachusetts, to form a phalanx to write, &c. My offers have produced some ridicule, more disgust, no cooperation."[36] In New York, Alexander Hamilton was in much the same situation, making the same suggestions to his colleagues with the same ill success.[37]

Simultaneously, however, movement was afoot among the young Federalists who were much impressed by the efficiency of Jeffersonian technique and young enough to accommodate themselves to it. Josiah Quincy was of the opinion that "a degree of organization has been effected in the opposite party unexampled, I suspect, in this country, since the revolutionary committees of 1775." Their triumph, he believed was due to this organization rather than to specific "measures."[38] The young Federalists believed that emulation was the price of political survival. "If we mean to preserve the commonwealth and New England," Harrison Gray Otis declared, "our organization must be more complete and systematic. It must extend through every county and town, and an ample fund must be provided for the distribution of political truth."[39] Henry De Saussure was of the same opinion. "It is necessary to collect our strength and subdue our grief," he wrote in 1801.[40]

[35] Fisher Ames to Theodore Dwight, Mar. 19, 1801, in Ames, *Works*, I, 293; Fisher Ames to Dwight Foster, Feb. 9, 1801, ibid., I, 291; see also Fisher Ames to Christopher Gore, Dec. 13 1802, ibid., I, 310; and Ames' careful distinction between the Federal "party" and the Jacobin "sect," *An Oration on the Sublime Virtues of General George Washington* (Boston, 1800), p. 23.

[36] Fisher Ames to Christopher Gore, Feb. 24, 1803, Dec. 14, 1802, in Ames, *Works*, I, 312, 319.

[37] Alexander Hamilton to Charles Cotesworth Pinckney, Mar. 15, 1802, in Lodge, *Works of Hamilton*, X, 428.

[38] Josiah Quincy to John Quincy Adams, Nov. 23, 1804, in Adams Family Papers, reel 403; see also Josiah Quincy to Noah Webster, June 30, 1806, in Webster Papers, New York Public Library; Robinson, *Jeff. Dem. in N. Eng.*, p. 63; Luetscher, *Political Machinery*, p. 152.

[39] Harrison Gray Otis to Woodbury Storer, Aug. 29, 1804, in Misc. Bound Manuscripts, Mass. Hist. Soc.

[40] Henry W. De Saussure to John Rutledge, Dec. 19, 1801, in Rutledge Papers, Southern Hist. Coll., Univ. of N. C.; write John Rutledge: "We must everywhere be

Similar agitation was apparent among young Federalists in almost every state. But it bore first fruit in New York, where, as we have seen, the political techniques of Federalists during the 1790s were unusually sophisticated.[41]

In January 1801, a group of Federalists who were in Albany for a session of the legislature met together at the Tontine Coffee House and created a statewide Federalist organization more complete than any that had appeared during the 1790s. The "numerous and respectable meeting" in which they convened constituted an "open" caucus, i.e., a meeting of legislators with other Federalist leaders, who attended by special invitation. A few transitional figures—Robert Troup, for example—sat in, but it was primarily an affair of younger men such as Moss Kent (1766–1838), Josiah Ogden Hoffman (1766–1837), Elisha Williams (1773–1835), W. W. Van Ness (1776–1823), Abraham Van Vechten (1762–1823), and Thomas Morris (1771–1840).[42]

The open caucus appointed a caucus subcommittee of sixteen, which in turn selected a state general committee composed of small committees from each of the four senatorial districts (see Table III). The state general committee was ostensibly sovereign; it nominated the Federalist candidate for governor and decided upon campaign strategy. But probably most of its decisions were made upon the recommendation of the caucus subcommittee. The state general committee encouraged the formation of lesser committees throughout the state. Within a month these began to appear everywhere, from New York City's first ward at the Battery, to the little town of Canandaigua in the western reaches of the state.[43] The state organization was essentially a network of committees of correspondence—the traditional American device which had been used widely for every imaginable purpose from managing a revolution to fighting yellow fever epidemics and publicizing agricultural reform.[44]

Federalists in other states followed close behind. Statewide organizations appeared in Massachusetts and New Hampshire as early as 1804, in Connecticut by 1805, in Rhode Island, Pennsylvania, Maryland, and

---

active and provident in preserving the identity and existence of our party," John Rutledge to Theodore Sedgwick, Sep. 24, 1801, in Sedgwick Papers, Mass. Hist. Soc.

[41] See above, p. 52.

[42] "Election," Jan. 28, 1801, broadsides, New York Public Library; see Table III below, p. 61.

[43] Ibid.; "Federal Republican Nominations," [1801]; "Election," Feb. 3, 1801; "At a numerous and respectable meeting," 1801; "In General Committee," 1801; Broadsides, New York Public Library; A broadside dated 1801, New York Hist. Soc.; circular dated Feb. 14, 1801 in Broadsides, Library of Congress.

[44] For committees of correspondence about epidemics, see [Baltimore, Md.] *Federal Gazette*, Sep. 22, 1800; for agricultural reform committees, see [Boston, Mass.] *New England Palladium*, Mar. 4, 1803; for an example of commercial committees of correspondence among booksellers in eastern cities, see Eben Andrews to Isaiah Thomas, Apr. 2, 1802, in Thomas Papers, American Antiquarian Society.

TABLE III. NEW YORK: FEDERALIST ORGANIZATION IN 1801

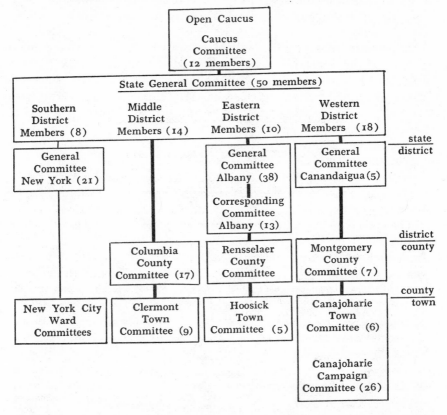

NOTE: Selected county and town committees are shown to illustrate typical patterns of local organization. Although the full extent of Federalist organization can never be known, this investigator has found evidence of committees in Albany, Chenango, Columbia, Dutchess, Greene, Herkimer, Montgomery, New York, Oneida, Ontario, Otsego, Rensselaer, Saratoga, Schoharie, Ulster, Washington, and Westchester counties. See broadsides dated Jan., Feb., and Mar. 1801 in N.Y. Hist. Soc. and N.Y. Public Library; *Albany Centinel*, Feb. 7, Mar. 6, 10, Apr. 1, 17, 1801; *Hudson Gazette*, Apr. 7, 14, 1801; [New York] *Daily Advertiser*, Apr. 25, 1801; [New York] *Spectator*, Jan. 17, 28, Feb. 3, 23, 28, Apr. 8, 11, 25, 1801; Robert Troup to Gouverneur Morris, Jan. 15, 1801, Morris Papers, Columbia University Library; Richard Varick to John Jay, Apr. 29, 1801, Columbia University Collection, Columbia University Library. The Federalists were better organized (as they were also more successful) in the western and eastern districts, rather than the southern and middle.

Virginia by 1808. Delaware, which, as we have seen, was organized as early as 1795, was possibly advanced even beyond New York (see Tables IV–X).[45]

[45] For New Hampshire, see [Walpole, N. H.] *Political Observatory*, Aug. 18, 1804; Plumer, *Life of Plumer*, pp. 313–315; for Massachusetts see Benjamin Whitwell to William Sullivan, Aug. 24, 1804, in Columbia University Collection, Columbia University; [Boston, Mass.] *New England Palladium*, May 7, 1805; William Bentley,

TABLE IV. NEW HAMPSHIRE: FEDERALIST ORGANIZATION IN 1804

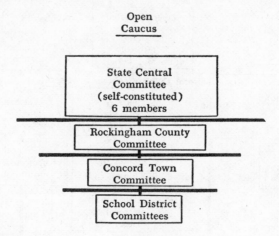

NOTE: For the existence of an open caucus see Jeremiah Smith to William Plumer, Jan. 1, 1805, Plumer Papers, Library of Congress. The central committee was organized by William Plumer, Oliver Crosby, Thomas W. Thompson, Wm. A. Kent, W. H. Woodward, and Roger Vose, without apparent approval or authorization from Federalists in the legislature. Although the full extent of low-level committees cannot be established precisely, both Federalists and Republicans declared that federal organizations existed in every county and all important towns. According to the *Political Observatory*, July 28, Aug. 18, 1804, (a Jeffersonian paper), the Federalists had formed "a system as complete as the fabled one of the *Illuminati*. "See also Plumer, *Life of Plumer*, pp. 313–315; Turner, *Plumer*, p. 144; [Portsmouth] *New Hampshire Gazette*, Sept. 11, 1804, Plumer to Thompson, Nov. 25, 1804, Plumer Papers, Library of Congress. The statement in Plumer's *Plumer*, p. 313, that this was the first party organization in New Hampshire is incorrect. The Jeffersonians were at least one year ahead. See Jeremiah Smith to Plumer Feb. 22, 1804, Plumer Papers, Library of Congress. But according to the [Walpole] *Political Observatory*, Aug. 18, 1804, the Federalist committees were "unprecedented in number."

In every instance, the organizers were young Federalists. State leaders in Massachusetts included Harrison Gray Otis, William Sullivan, and Thomas Handasyd Perkins; in Connecticut, Theodore Dwight, David

Diary, III, 221, 377; for Rhode Island, see James B. Mason to Harrison Gray Otis, July 1, 1808, in Otis Papers, Mass. Hist. Soc.; for Connecticut, see folder of miscellaneous notes and Committee Reports, 1804–1806, in Simeon Baldwin Papers, Yale University Library; [Hartford, Conn.] *Connecticut Courant*, Aug. 28, Sep. 4, 1805; for Vermont, in which the Federalists lagged behind their colleagues in other states, see [Windsor, Vt.] *Washingtonian*, May 18, 1812, July 18, 1814, July 7, 1815; for New Jersey I have found evidence only of occasional committees 1801–1808; see Pole, "The Federalist Dilemma in N. J.," pp. 266–267; Federalist organization in Pennsylvania was extensive by 1808, see [Philadelphia, Pa.] *United States Gazette*, Mar. 17–June 27, 1808; Samuel Sitgreaves to John Arndt, Sep. 1, 1807, in Personal papers misc., Library of Congress; in Maryland, county organization appeared as early as 1803; see [Baltimore, Md.] *Republican; or, anti-Democrat*, Aug. 10, 1803; [Frederick-town, Md.] *Hornet*, Aug. 16, 1803; *Frederick-town Herald*, Aug. 27, Sep. 3, 1803; by 1808 a state organization was operating, see [Baltimore, Md.] *North*

TABLE V. DELAWARE: FEDERALIST ORGANIZATION IN 1804

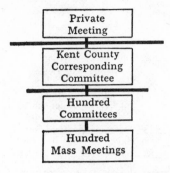

NOTE: similar organizations are known to have existed in all counties. The private meeting was held in the Wilmington residence of James Broom during August, 1804. [Dover] *Constitutionalist*, Sept. 6, 1804; [Wilmington] *Mirror of the Times*, Sept. 1, 22, 26, 1804; John Fisher to Caesar A. Rodney, Jan. 23, 1804, John Fisher Papers, N. Y. Hist. Soc. See also material cited in Luetscher, *Political Machinery*, pp. 102–103.

Daggett, and John Cotton Smith; in Vermont, Josiah Dunham; in New Hampshire, William Plumer, Thomas W. Thompson, Roger Vose, and Daniel Webster; in Rhode Island, James B. Mason; in Maryland, Robert Goodloe Harper, John Hanson Thomas, Roger Brooke Taney, and John Rousby Plater; in Delaware, James Bayard.[46] It is difficult to single out the one or two main leaders for Pennsylvania, Virginia, North Carolina, and Ohio.

These young men ruled their organizations with a firm hand. Where necessary, they dispatched orders, written in the imperative mood and couched in imperious language.[47] At the same time, young Federalists lower in the organization learned to accommodate themselves to the decisions of their superiors. In Maryland, for example, when John Carlyle Herbert was notified that he would be a candidate for an office that he couldn't win rather than for one that he could, he grumbled but submitted, "even though it promised nothing but mortification and defeat."[48]

American, Aug. 12, Sep. 5, 1808; [Baltimore, Md.] *Evening Post*, July 14, 1808; Robert Goodloe Harper to John Hanson Thomas, July 1808, in Harper-Pennington Papers, Md. Hist. Soc.; for Virginia, see Benjamin Stoddert to John Rutledge, June 4, 1807, in Rutledge Papers, Southern Hist. Coll., Univ. of N. C.; W. W. Burrows to John Rutledge, Oct. 9, 1803, Ibid.; North Carolina Federalists were slow to organize; however, see [Raleigh, N. C.] *Minerva*, July 23, 1804; Federalists in South Carolina and Georgia apparently never did create an effective organization, except in Charleston.

[46] See below, Appendix II.

[47] See, for example, Harrison Gray Otis to [Timothy Bigelow], n.d. "Tuesday," in Autograph File, Houghton Library, Harvard University.

[48] John Carlyle Herbert to Vergil Maxcy, Apr. 11, June 18, Nov. 7, 1816, in Galloway-Maxcy-Markoe Papers, Library of Congress.

TABLE VI. CONNECTICUT: FEDERALIST ORGANIZATION IN 1805

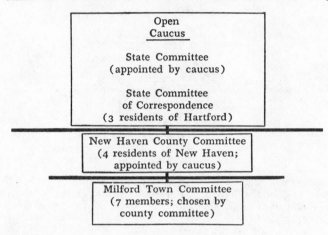

Open
Caucus

State Committee
(appointed by caucus)

State Committee
of Correspondence
(3 residents of Hartford)

New Haven County Committee
(4 residents of New Haven;
appointed by caucus)

Milford Town Committee
(7 members; chosen by
county committee)

NOTE: Within New Haven County, similar town committees functioned at Derby, Oxford, Woodbridge, Waterbury, Guilford, Branford, East Haven, North Haven, Hamden [sic], Cheshire, Wolcott, and Wallingford. The New Haven County Committee served as the committee for New Haven town. The extent of Federalist organization in other counties is not known, but county committees existed in Hartford, New London, Windham, Middlesex, and Tolland counties. From the fact that each member of every county committee was responsible for liaison with town committees in a part of his county, an extensive network of town committees might be safely assumed to have existed. See a bundle of miscellaneous circulars, mostly undated and unaddressed, in Simeon Baldwin Papers, Yale University. See also Theodore Dwight to Simeon Baldwin, Mar. 27, 1805, Baldwin Papers, Yale; for the open caucus see the [Hartford] Connecticut Courant, Aug. 28, Sep. 4, 1805. For the gradual growth of this organization see John Trumbull to John Adams, July 21, 1801, Adams Family Papers, ass. Hist. Soc., reel 401; and Uriah Tracy to John Quincy Adams, June 18, 1804, ibid., reel 403. For the comments of a Jeffersonian, see Elisha Tracy to Ephraim Kirby, Sep. 18, 1803, Kirby Papers, Duke University Library.

The writings of Federalists show a steady growth of party consciousness. They continued to attack the "spirit of faction," but made a crucial distinction between a party "grounded on principle" and a faction resting upon "self-interest," between the Federal "party" and the Jeffersonian "faction."[49]

Most of the old-school gentlemen and a few younger men dragged their feet. Service on committees and submission to committee decisions was distasteful to them. They spoke disdainfully of private meetings— "half a score of red hot feds well stuffed with brandy and conceit all talking together, each magnifying his own importance, enlarging both the circle of his influence and his influence in that circle," wrote Jeremiah Smith.[50] An aging Massachusetts Federalist, Thomas Dwight,

[49] [Boston, Mass.] New England Palladium, Aug. 13, 1805.
[50] Jeremiah Smith to William Plumer, Jan. 1, 1805, in Plumer Papers, Library of Congress.

TABLE VII. MASSACHUSETTS: FEDERALIST ORGANIZATION IN 1807

NOTE: Full extent of local organization is not known, but included the following counties: Bristol, Worcester, Middlesex, Essex, Plymouth, Hampshire, Cumberland, Barnstable, and Suffolk. Lincoln was split, with two separate organizations in full panoply. For the role of runners see below, chapter V. All committees were appointed from above and were top secret. The Boston Initial Caucus consisted of the Central Committee plus ward committees. The Grand Caucus was merely a mass meeting, a pep rally on the eve of the election which in 1807 was presided over by, of all people, John Quincy Adams. The dates were Feb. 3 for the State Caucus, Mar. 6 for the Initial Caucus, and April 1 for the Grand Caucus. See Christopher Gore to Bristol Committee, Mar. 25, 1807, Misc. Bound, Mass. Hist. Soc.; Ebenezer Bacon et al. to Silvanus Crowell et al., Broadsides, Mass. Hist. Soc.; "Federal Meeting," Mar. 7, 1807, Broadsides, Essex Institute; misc. Broadsides marked "Not in Shaw," 1807, Amer. Antiq. Soc.; [Boston] Repertory, Feb. 13, Apr. 3, 31, May 18, 1807; [Boston] Independent Chronicle, May 8, 1807, [Boston] Columbian Centinel, Mar. 21, 25, 1807; see also Morison, Otis, I, 286–320.

point-blank refused to attend a party gathering to which he had been invited. "I shall not be of the party," he said petulantly, "having inevocably [sic] determined to assert and enjoy my own personal independence."[51] Another said self-righteously, "A party must do the very thing we condemn, prefer their friends to the public good."[52]

A few transitional figures remained active, however—leaders such as Robert Troup of New York and Christopher Gore of Massachusetts.

[51] Thomas Dwight to John Williams, July 5, 1805, in Dwight-Howard Papers, Mass. Hist. Soc.

[52] Morison, Jeremiah Smith, pp. 244, 259.

TABLE VIII. RHODE ISLAND: FEDERALIST ORGANIZATION IN 1808

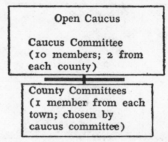

NOTE: This was the most secretive Federalist organization in the nation. It operated without public meetings, or publicity of any kind. The explanation lies in federal strategy for the Rhode Island state elections of 1808, which was to lull the Democrats into a false sense of security by pretending not to set up candidates until the last minute. In the period from 1810 to 1816, when the Federalists became more confident of their strength, their organization gradually became less clandestine.

In 1808 there may have been a "General Committee" in Providence which coordinated the efforts of the county committees when the legislature was not in session. There definitely was such a body in 1812, 1814, and 1816.

See James B. Mason to H. G. Otis, July 11, 1808, Otis Papers, Mass. Hist. Soc.; [Newport] *Mercury*, Apr. 16, July 9, 23, 30, 1808; [Bristol] *Mt. Hope Eagle*, Aug. 20, 1808; [Providence] *Columbian Phoenix*, July 9, 30, Aug. 13, 20, 1808; Providence General Committee to Henry Comstock, Nov. 9, 1812, Aug. 15, 22, 1814, Apr. 4, 1816, Broadsides, American Antiquarian Society.

These gentlemen tried to rally their friends and contemporaries, with pleas and arguments that made refusal very difficult. Christopher Gore wrote thus to Rufus King: "That you have become disgusted with the politics of our Country can excite no surprise. Some of your friends, however, complain that you do not take a more active part in the affairs of New York, and think that your exertions might materially affect the cause of order and freedom."[53] Robert Troup, in a similar letter to Rufus King, made apathy tantamount to treason. "The contest now seems to be for everything sacred in society," he wrote, "and the man who sleeps upon his post is fit for the oppression meditated against us."[54] These impassioned solicitations were not without result. George Cabot, for example, wrote to Timothy Pickering, "I am forced to work much more than I like. You draw and others drive me into the vortex of politics, which I wish to shun. You can scarcely imagine how active we are to secure the election."[55] Sometimes old-school Federalists served as front men, lending their prestige to the industry of young Federalists.[56]

But other Federalists of the old school stubbornly resisted all appeals. These gentlemen recognized no distinction between a faction and a

[53] Christopher Gore to Rufus King, May 5, 1811, in King, *Life and Correspondence of King*, V, 245.

[54] Robert Troup to Rufus King, Apr. 11, 1807, ibid., V, 29.

[55] George Cabot to Timothy Pickering, Apr. 2, 1808, in Lodge, *Cabot*, p. 390.

[56] Richard Frisby to James McHenry, May 29, 1811, in McHenry Papers, Md. Hist. Soc.

TABLE IX. NEW JERSEY: FEDERALIST ORGANIZATION IN 1808

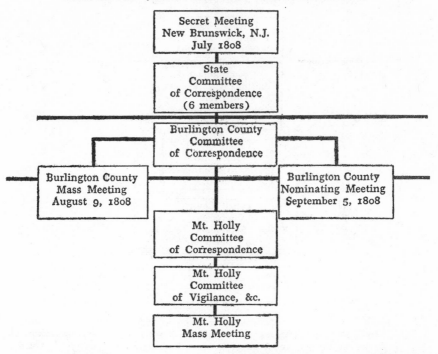

NOTE: The secret meeting in New Brunswick, which nominated congressional candidates, convened at least once again, on Sep. 2, 1808. See [Newark] *Centinel of Freedom*, July 19, Aug. 2, Sep. 13, 1808. The State Committee was appointed by this body; it included William Lawson, John Dennis, Robert Boggs, William Dunham, Daniel W. Desborough, and William B. Paterson. See Wm. Lawson *et al.* to Jacob Thompson, 1808, printed circular in Broadsides, N. J. Hist. Soc. Local committees appear to have been appointed from above. But the procedure for nominating local officers and assemblymen was at least nominally democratic. The Burlington County Mass Meeting invited Federalists in each town to elect delegates to a nominating meeting, which was done. The full extent of local organization is not known, but committees and meetings were organized in all townships in Burlington County. Similar committees are known to have existed in Bergen, Hunterdon, Middlesex, Monmouth, Salem, Somerset, and Sussex counties. See [Trenton] *Federalist*, Aug. 8–Oct. 3, 1808; Joshua M. Wallace *et al.* to George Hancock *et al.*, Oct. 26, 1808, Ely Papers, N. J. Hist. Soc. Nominations in Sussex were made by a caucus of Federalist lawyers; in Monmouth by a single mass meeting.

party. One faction was bad enough; two factions would be worse. Gouverneur Morris wrote, "I prefer the household prudence of my Great Grandmother who cautioned those who darn stockings not to make two Holes in trying to stop one."[57] Their resistance helped to drive a few

[57] Gouverneur Morris to [?], n.d. [c. Jan. 1813], in Morris Papers, Library of Congress; see also Gouverneur Morris to William Henderson, Jacob Radcliff, Samuel M. Hopkins, S. Jones, Jr., Cadwallader D. Colden, Mar. 9, 1809, in Morris Papers, Library of Congress; Peter Augustus Jay to John Jay, Sep. 11, 1812, in Jay Papers, Columbia University Library.

TABLE X. MARYLAND: FEDERALIST ORGANIZATION IN 1811

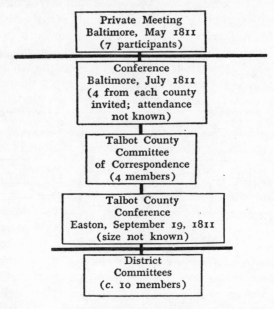

NOTE: Federalists present at the private meeting in May included Robert Goodloe Harper, James McHenry, Charles Ridgely of Hampton, John Eager Howard, James Hindman, Walter Dorsey, and Samuel Sterrett. The conference which they called together cannot be considered a convention, for they summoned specific men from the counties. See Robt. H. Goldsborough et al., to Robert Goodloe Harper et al., June 1, 1811; John Carlyle Herbert to James McHenry, June 5, 1811; Richard Frisby to McHenry, May 29, 1811; John Murray to Jacob Wagner, [Sep.] 23, 1811; all in McHenry Papers, Library of Congress; John Rousby Plater to McHenry, June 3, 1811, McHenry Papers, Md. Hist. Soc.; the last letter is published by B. C. Steiner, ed., "McHenry Letters," Southern Hist. Assn. Proceedings, IX (1905) 317–319. See also the anonymous "Three Patriots." (n. p., 1811) in Md. Hist. Soc. The Talbot County organization is detailed in P. Sherwood et al., to Benjamin Roberts et al., n.d. [c. 20 Sep. 1811] which circular fell into the hands of a Democratic editor who published it and offered to show it on request. See [Easton] Star, Oct. 1, 1811. The full extent of local organization is not known, but at least nine counties and part of a tenth were organized. They included Baltimore, Calvert, Cecil, Frederick, Kent, Prince George's, St. Mary's, Talbot, Washington, and part of Anne Arundel. See [Baltimore] Whig, Aug. 7, 1811, [Baltimore] Federal Republican, July 4, 6, 18, Sep. 18, 26, 1811; [Baltimore] American, Aug. 29, 1811; [Annapolis] Maryland Gazette, Aug. 14, 1811; [Elizabeth-town] Md. Herald, Aug. 14, 1811.

young Federalists into the Jeffersonian camp. In 1805, William Plumer began his gradual shift to the left, growling about the behavior of the old-school gentlemen and about the similarity of his labors to "those of Sisiphus."[58] But most of the young Federalists who had created state organizations were committed to them, and were prepared to manage them.

[58] William Plumer to Uriah Tracy, May 2, 1805, in Plumer Papers, Library of Congress.

A few old-school gentlemen who remained active in public life continued to behave according to the conventions of eighteenth-century politics. Timothy Pickering is a good example. This Federalist of the old school, sixty-five years old in 1810, has often been treated almost as if he were a "boss" in the modern sense of the word. But his name is conspicuously absent from Massachusetts committee rosters, even on the highest level. He seems merely to have been a figurehead, a relic of Washingtonian days gone by and a symbol of the glorious past rather than a party leader.[59]

The Federalists were understandably sensitive about their party organization. Their elaborate security measures undoubtedly are the reason that historians have been unaware of their activity.[60] But Jeffersonians were always on the alert. Even a furtive Federalist committee in Concord, New Hampshire, that convened in an empty school room at four o'clock in the morning was spotted by sharp-eyed Republicans and publicly exposed.[61] Security precautions make it difficult to know the full extent of these Federalist organizations. There seems to have been great variation from state to state and constant fluctuation from year to year. In most states north of the Potomac they grew slowly from 1804 to 1808, more swiftly from 1808 to 1814. In New York, a statewide organization appeared in 1801, then disappeared, then reappeared after the embargo and the accession of Madison.[62] In New Hampshire, the first Federalist organization, which William Plumer had founded, collapsed when he broke with his party. But young Federalists including Daniel Webster and Thomas W. Thompson created another one that proved more viable.[63] In Pennsylvania, Federalists organized active

[59] See Cabot to Pickering, Aug. 10, 1808, in Lodge, *Cabot*, p. 397, for evidence that Pickering was kept ignorant, even of national meetings, by the men who were managing the fortunes of the party.

[60] For an example of their security measures, see Robert Goodloe Harper to John Hanson Thomas, July, 1808, in Harper-Pennington Papers, Md. Hist. Soc.

[61] [Walpole, N. H.] *Political Observatory*, July 28, 1804; Robinson, *Jeff. Dem. in N. Eng.*, p. 58; for the Federalist response, see [Boston, Mass.] *New England Palladium*, May 7, 1805.

[62] For the Federalists' decline in New York, 1802–1807, see *New York Evening Post*, May 3, 1805; [Boston, Mass.] *New England Palladium*, May 7, 1807; Moss Kent to James Kent, May 17, 1806, in Kent Papers, Library of Congress; Robert Troup to Rufus King, Mar. 12, 1807, in King, *Life and Correspondence of King*, V, 12; for federal resurgence after the passage of the Embargo Act, see James Kent to Moss Kent, July 7, 1808, Moss Kent to James Kent, May 27, 1809, in Kent Papers, Library of Congress; [New York] *Evening Post*, May 4, 1808; by 1810 a statewide organization was operating more efficiently than in 1801; see [New York] *Evening Post*, Jan. 8, 11, 12, 16, 17, 22, 26, 27, 31, Feb. 2, 8, 16, 23, 1810; [Albany, N. Y.] *Balance*, Jan. 5, Mar. 27, Apr. 6, 20, 1810; [Hudson, N. Y.] *Northern Whig*, Jan. 18, 26; Mar. 22, 1810; "Federal Nomination," Apr. 5, 1810, broadsides, New York Public Library.

[63] Daniel Webster to Thomas W. Thompson, Mar. 15, 1808, in Misc. Bound Manuscripts, Mass. Hist. Soc.; Thomas W. Thompson to Daniel Webster, Feb. 17, 1810, William A. Kent to Daniel Webster, Feb. 28, 1810, in Webster Papers, Library of Congress; [Concord, N. H.] *New Hampshire Patriot*, Oct. 13, 1812, Feb. 1, 1814.

county committees in every party of the state from Bucks to Beaver, Delaware to Erie, but never succeeded in establishing an effective, unified, statewide organization.[64]

Federalist organizations were, of course, much more complete and effective in the middle states and New England than in the south and west. In Ohio, the "friends of order" were only strong enough to act as a balance between contending Republican factions. In this role, however, they had considerable influence and an impetus to organization.[65] The Federalists of western Virginia were remarkably well organized and generally successful in local elections, but were never able to compete in the politics of the state as a whole.[66] In North Carolina, the Federalists were strong and active but seem never to have created formal party organization. Instead they continued to depend upon the traditional system of connections, influence, and private arrangements between prominent men. Only in the four extreme southern and western states—South Carolina, Georgia, Kentucky, and Tennessee—were the Federalists generally without organization.[67]

The most important function of these Federalist organizations was the making of nominations. Town, county, city, ward, district, and state committees all dealt with this problem. Committees, even at the highest level, usually concerned themselves only with offices directly in the gift of the people. Candidates for appointive posts were filled by legislative caucuses.[68] As the committees began to operate in the various states, there was a sharp decrease in the number of Federalist candidates, a reaction against self-nomination, or nomination by a small clique.[69]

Fund raising was another important task. Contributions were sought from wealthy merchants and prosperous farmers, sometimes in vain. The letters of the Federalist leaders are full of bitter attacks upon the reluctance of wealthy men to offer financial support, upon the wealth

[64] Higginbotham, *The Keystone in the Democratic Arch*, pp. 19, 325.

[65] William T. Utter, *The History of the State of Ohio* (Columbus, 1941), passim. There were, however, corresponding committees in Washington County, Ohio; Cutler, *Life and Times of Ephraim Cutler*, p. 66; and in Fayette County, Kentucky; Lexington *Western Monitor*, 5 July 1816.

[66] Charles Henry Ambler, *Sectionalism in Virginia from 1776 to 1861* (Chicago, 1910), pp. 87–97.

[67] In the latter states formal political machinery was rare among Jeffersonians see Cunningham, *Jeffersonian Republicans in Power*, pp. 188, 189, 192. William Polk to Duncan Cameron, Oct. 15, 1808, Benjamin Rainey to Duncan Cameron, June 8, 1808, Cameron Papers, Southern Hist. Coll., Univ. of N. C.; William Polk to William Gaston, Feb. 23, 1813, Gaston Papers, Southern Hist. Coll., Univ. of N. C.

[68] Clement Dorsey, "An Address to the People of Charles County, in reply to 'Something Curious,'" n. p., 1817, Md. Hist. Soc.

[69] See Roger Brooke Taney, "An Address to the People of Frederick County," n. p., 1817, Md. Hist. Soc.; [Annapolis, Md.] *Maryland Gazette*, Sep. 4, 18, 25, 1806, Aug. 18, 1814; [Georgetown, Md.] *Federal Republican*, Oct. 8, 1813; [Baltimore, Md.] *Whig*, Aug. 7, 1811; [Boston, Mass.] *New England Palladium*, Mar. 25, 1808, Sep. 18, 1810.

which lay "snug in its iron chest." But there were also references to merchants whose purses were "always open to the party at election times."[70]

The systematic distribution of pamphlets, broadsides, ballots, and newspapers was another major function. Under the general direction of the state committees, county committees sought out able Federalist polemicists and commissioned them to write pamphlets. An example is a letter which Abraham Van Vechten, a young New York Federalist, sent to Alexander Hamilton: "I am enjoined by the gen'l committee to tax your goodness to prepare a short, temperant [sic] and pertinent supplementary address by way of Reply to that of our opponents. This tax will be levied and collected without communicating whence it is deriving."[71]

County committees, and in some cases, state committees, arranged for the publication of these pamphlets and distributed bundles of them to committees closest to the people.[72] In some of the better organized states, local committees were enjoined to keep abreast of public opinion in their neighborhood. If "any falsehood, misrepresentation, or embarrassment" should develop, they were responsible for correcting it as best they could. If unable to deal with it, they were instructed to seek assist-

---

[70] For evidence of systematic collection of funds, see Alexander Contee Hanson to Robert Goodloe Harper, June 6, 1814, in Harper-Pennington Papers, Md. Hist. Soc.; E. Cutts to Daniel Webster, June 23, 1815, in Webster Papers, Library of Congress; Robert Troup to Gouverneur Morris, Mar. 4, 1809, in Morris Papers, Columbia University Library; Killian K. Van Rensselaer to [?], Apr. 11, 1807, in Columbia University Coll., Columbia University Library; Warren, *Life of Warren*, I, 69; unsigned circular dtd. Jan. 1805, in Simeon Baldwin Papers, Yale University Library.

[71] Abraham Van Vechten to Alexander Hamilton, n. d. [1801?], in Hamilton Papers, Library of Congress.

[72] Circular unaddressed and unsigned, dtd. Jan. 1805, in Simeon Baldwin Papers, Yale University Library; for additional evidence of systematic distribution of circulars and pamphlets, see William Polk to Duncan Cameron, Oct. 15, 1808, in Cameron Papers, Southern Hist. Coll., Univ. of N. C.; [Boston, Mass.] *New England Palladium*, Aug. 19, 1814; "Proceedings and Address of the Convention of Delegates to the People of New Jersey," (Trenton, 1812), Library of Congress; John Carlyle Herbert to Vergil Maxcy, Apr. 11, 1816, in Galloway-Maxcy-Markoe Coll., Library of Congress; John Murray to Jacob Wagner, [July?] 23, 1811, photostat in James McHenry Papers, Library of Congress; W. V. McGroarty, "The Washington Society of Alexandria," *Tyler's Quarterly*, IX (1928), 150; [Concord, N. H.] *New Hampshire Patriot*, Sep. 1, 1812; Thomas Lenoir to William Lenoir, Aug. 5, 1806, in Lenoir Papers, Southern Hist. Coll., Univ. of N. C.; [Boston, Mass.] *New England Palladium*, Mar. 18, 1808, Sep. 27, Apr. 24, 1810, Nov. 10, 1812; Gouverneur Morris, *Diary*, Apr. 13, 1807, in Morris Papers, Library of Congress; [Easton, Md.] *Star*, Oct. 14, 1806; "For Governor Stephen Van Rensselaer," [1801], in American Broadsides, New York Hist. Soc.; Vergil Maxcy to Robert Goodloe Harper, May 3, 1820, in Harper-Pennington Papers, Md. Hist. Soc.; John Pickering to Leverett Saltonstall, July 4, 1814, in Saltonstall Papers, Mass. Hist. Soc.; John Rutledge to Harrison Gray Otis, Feb. 10, 1809, in Otis Papers, Mass. Hist. Soc.; Benjamin Whitwell to Samuel Dexter, Harrison Gray Otis, and William Sullivan, Aug. 1, 1814, in Columbia University Collection, Columbia University; William Bentley, *Diary*, III, 359 (May 14, 1808); Robert Troup to Rufus King, Apr. 11, 1807, in King, *Life and Correspondence of King*, V, 30.

ance from the county committee, which would supply information for a rebuttal.[73]

The principal responsibility of town committees, town-subcommittees, ward committees, hundred committees, and school district committees was to see that Federalist voters came to the polls. The means which they used will be discussed at some length in chapter V.

Although these Federalist organizations were popularly oriented, they were not popularly controlled. Authority passed down from the top. The purpose of the party architects, in this first stage of structural growth, was merely to consolidate the "federal" cause.

[73] Circular unaddressed and unsigned, dtd. June, 1805, in Simeon Baldwin Papers, Yale University Library.

IV

Caucus or Convention?

> "Some folks are talking of conventions. . . . Beware of extremes!"
> —ALEXANDER HAMILTON, 1792

> "Let us consult outdoors among the common voters. Some of them may know something, as well as the Court folks."
> —AN ANONYMOUS FEDERALIST, 1816[1]

I

The first stage of party development merged imperceptibly into a second. Continuing competition with Jeffersonians drove the Federalists from a caucus-committee organization toward the convention—from a cellular structure organized from the top down, to a loose confederation of local groups which sent delegates or "conferees" to central meetings. Rarely would these delegates be chosen by a free and open popular election; hardly ever would the ensuing Federalist conventions be popularly controlled in any meaningful sense. But they were forced upon the Federal parties by four needs: the need for "available" candidates, the need to have an effective way of resolving intramural disputes, the need to make nominations over which no committee had jurisdiction, and the need to keep up with the Democratic-Republicans, to maintain the appearance, at least, of respect for popular opinion. The convention was more than mere window-dressing in Federalist organizations; it became a necessary political artifact.

A single example which recapitulated the general trend was the Massachusetts gubernatorial election of 1816. In that year, the Federalists were forced to find a successor to their popular and perennial candidate Caleb Strong. The caucus committee (see Tables VII, XV) recommended that the candidate should be Harrison Gray Otis. He declined. The nomination was then given to the lieutenant governor, William Phillips, who turned it down in a fit of pique because he had not been offered it first. The trouble which ensued was vividly described by a gentleman on the scene:

---

[1] Hamilton to King, 28 June 1792, in *King*, I, 416; Edward H. Robbins to Samuel Howe, 7 Feb. 1816, in Morison, *Otis*, I, 288–89.

The President of the Senate [a young Federalist named John Phillips] and Speaker [the controversial Timothy Bigelow] were both of the Caucus Committee. The latter succeeded in a nomination from the committee to the grand body [i.e., the Legislative caucus]. All were surprised, some swore, others grew faint and complained of the air of the room, others more collected called for adjournments and succeeded, all inquiring as they came down, "What shall we do?"

Another meeting was held, a new Committee softer and smoother were recommended for another attack on the present incumbent [William Phillips, the lieutenant governor] of which your neighbor of the Senate was one. It was with difficulty they could see him, and very soon directed to inform the body that he would not be the candidate, and off they came with a flea in their ears as the saying is.

In the meantime the Speaker [Timothy Bigelow] grew sick, as you will see by the paper. A new meeting was summoned to decide on his fate, his friends flew to Medford and obtained a letter declining most fully and satisfactorily. The cry was again 'What shall we do?' Some said 'Let us consult outdoors among the common voters. Some of them may know something as well as the [General] Court folks.' Others said 'It would please them and do no hurt—advised to delay 48 hours.' In 24, they were assured Lieutenant Governor [Phillips] would stand.

A new committee appointed to wait on him with a vote that the Federal interest in this state imperiously demanded of him the sacrifice and nothing short of his compliance would satisfy the public sentiment, and to request his permission to use his name. He replied that he had consulted conscience and duty and found himself bound to assent, and from that moment was as clay in the potter's hands.[2]

These were the levers which moved the Federalists toward the convention—increasing sensitivity to public opinion and disagreements among themselves. As Federalists and Republicans "exposed" each other's organizations in the press, it became increasingly important that these organizations should at least appear to be subject to the popular will. In most states, Republicans initiated nominating conventions; Federalists followed suit.

Federal-Republican conventions first appeared in the interstices of committee organizations to decide questions which no single committee was able to resolve. In most states there were no Congressional district committees. Groups of "conferees"—delegates from county committees, assembled to nominate Congressmen.[3]

[2] Edward H. Robbins to Samuel Howe, Feb. 7, 1816, in Morison, *Otis*, I, 288–289; for other evidence of the Federalists' increasing awareness of public opinion, and of the "availability" of their candidates see Robert Troup to Rufus King, Apr. 4, 1809, in King, *Life and Correspondence of King*, V, 148; [Annapolis, Md.] *Maryland Gazette*, June 29, 1815; "To the People of Sussex County [Del.], Sep. 1, 1802, broadsides, Library of Congress; Nathan Saltonstall to Leverett Saltonstall, Mar. 2, 1804, in Saltonstall Papers, Mass. Hist. Soc.; Pole, "Federalist Dilemma in New Jersey," p. 266 and n.

[3] In Mass. and N. Y., also to nominate state senators; [Boston, Mass.] *New England Palladium*, Feb. 23, Mar. 13, 1810, Oct. 2, 1812; [Albany, N. Y.] *Balance*, Feb. 9, 1810; "Minutes and Report of a Meeting in Barnstable Congressional District," 1812, in Lemuel Shaw Papers, Mass. Hist. Soc.

These gatherings of Federalists used popular rhetoric and apparently democratic procedures with such facility that they sometimes seemed to be Jeffersonian affairs. A "Convention of Delegates" from nineteen counties in the Western Senatorial District of New York headed its report "Voice of the People." Only the text of its address and the names of its candidates showed it to be Federalist.[4] In Massachusetts an assembly of Federalists from "the several towns in the county of Worcester" billed itself as a "Republican Convention." It solemnly resolved that "in all free Constitutions the only legitimate source of power being in the people, no modification thereof can be constitutionally exercised."[5]

In nearly all of the middle states, Federalists gradually adopted delegate-meetings, conferences, or conventions on the state level. In Pennsylvania, during the campaign of 1808, their caucus arrangements broke down. Federalists proposed a nominating convention and would have held it but for the strenuous opposition of the Quids.[6] Delaware Federalists introduced statewide conventions at least as early as 1810 and continued to use them for many years.[7] Maryland Federalists had them in an embryonic form as early as 1811;[8] New York, New Jersey, and Virginia in 1812.[9] In New York, New Jersey, Delaware, and Virginia, Federal "conventions" or "nominating meetings" were publicized widely in pamphlets and newspapers. In Maryland they were secret but conventions nonetheless—meetings of delegates from the counties, chosen not by the people but by local elites for the purpose of making nominations and deciding party policy.

In New England, Federalists made no use of state nominating conventions. Legislative caucuses remained sufficiently representative. But conventions did appear in counties and Congressional districts. Samuel Eliot Morison's statement that the Federalist organization in Massachusetts "made no concessions, even in theory, to popular rights, and was frankly based upon the right of the leaders to rule the party, and

---

[4] [Albany, N. Y.] *Balance*, Feb. 9, 1810.

[5] [Boston, Mass.] *New England Palladium*, Apr. 30, 1811.

[6] See Table XI, p. 76; for Pennsylvania, see Higginbotham, *The Keystone in the Democratic Arch*, p. 155; [Philadelphia] *Gazette of the United States*, Mar. 17–June 27, 1808; *Erie Mirror*, June 2, 9, 23, 30, July 7, 14, 1808; George Latimer to James Lewis, et al., Mar. 11, 1808, in American Broadsides, New York Hist. Soc.

[7] See evidence cited in Table XVI, p. 81; Munroe, *Federalist Delaware*, pp. 235–238; Luetscher, *Early Political Machinery*, pp. 100–103, 149.

[8] For Maryland see Richard Frisby to James McHenry, May 29, 1811, in McHenry Papers, Md. Hist. Soc.; Robert H. Goldsborough et al. to Robert Goodloe Harper et al., June 1, 1811, J. C. Herbert to James McHenry, John Rousby Plater et al. to James McHenry, June 3, 1811, in B. C. Steiner, ed., "McHenry Letters," *Publications of the Southern Historical Association*, IX (1905), 317–319; for county and district committees in this pyramidal party structure, see [Easton, Md.] *Star*, Oct. 1, 1811.

[9] For New York, see Abraham Van Vechten to Theodore Dwight, Aug. 12, 1812, in New York Miscellany, New York Public Library; for New Jersey, see [Trenton, N. J.] *Federalist*, May 18–Sep. 21, 1812; for Virginia, see *Martinsburgh Gazette*, Sep. 4, 1812.

Table XI. Pennsylvania: Federalist Organization in 1808

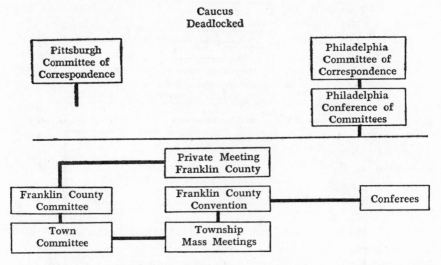

NOTE: When it was apparent that no gubernatorial candidate could be agreed upon in caucus, mass meetings, independent of each other, appointed committees of correspondence in Philadelphia and Pittsburgh, Mar. 8 and 7, respectively, and nominated James Ross. The Philadelphia Committee also called a conference of county committees in its part of the state, which undertook to organize the state by reaching the most prestigious Federalist in each Congressional District. The result was a channel of communication, but not a chain of command; Pennsylvania Federalism remained unorganized, in any effective way, above the district level. But local level organizations seem remarkably complete—they existed in Montgomery, Delaware, Beaver, Wayne, Philadelphia, Northampton, Luzerne, Chester, Westmoreland, Berks, Allegheny, Lancaster, Adams, Washington, Bucks, Lycoming, Dauphin, Venango, Butler, Mercer, Crawford, and Erie. See [Erie] *Mirror*, June 2–July 14, 1808; [Phila.] *U. S. Gazette*, Mar. 5–June 27, 1808; [Phila.] *Political and Commercial Register*, Mar. 5–Sep. 21, 1808; [Wilkesbarre] *Luzerne County Federalist*, Apr. 1–Oct. 7, 1808; Financial Records of the *Chester and Delaware Federalist*, 1808, Dreer Coll., Hist. Soc. of Penna.; George Latimer *et al.*, to James Lewis, Mar. 11, 1808, Broadsides, N. Y. Hist. Soc.; Samuel Sitgreaves to John Arndt, Sep. 1, 1808, Personal Papers Misc., Library of Congress; Higginbotham, *Keystone in the Democratic Arch*, pp. 147–176.

through it the body politic" is erroneous.[10] He overlooks these significant developments on the local level.[11]

[10] Morison, *Otis*, I, 287.

[11] Henry D. Sedgwick to William Sullivan, Apr. 26, 1811, in Columbia University Coll., Columbia University Library; [Boston, Mass.] *New England Palladium*, Feb. 16, Mar. 13, 1810; Mr. Morison's belief that the Federalist organization in Massachusetts "differed absolutely from the usual American type, in that it was thoroughly centralized" is dubious, at best. It is certainly true that the Federalists were more reluctant than their adversaries to make concessions to local readers, but they made them anyhow. And on the other side, Republican organizations were often centralized too. In Massachusetts, the nerve center of the Jeffersonian party was a Boston central committee, similar to that of the Federalists; Morison, *Otis*,

Table XII. New Jersey: Federalist Organization in 1812

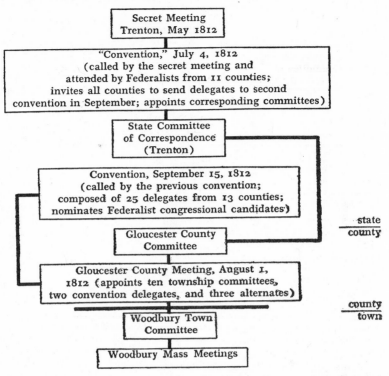

NOTE: For an "exposé" of the secret meeting in Trenton, which was held during the May term of the state Supreme Court and thus probably attended by lawyers for the most part, see [Newark] *Centinel of Freedom*, May 26, June 9, Sep.1, 22, 1812. The full extent of local organization is not known, but from the fact that a single newspaper reported committee organizations and mass meetings in nine counties, it may be assumed that New Jersey Federalists were organized throughout the greater part of the state. See [Trenton] *Federalist*, May 18, 25, June 1, 8, 15, July 20, 27, Aug. 3, 10, 17, 24; Sep. 7, 14, 21, 1812. The nine counties mentioned therein are Burlington, Cumberland, Essex, Gloucester, Hunterdon, Middlesex, Monmouth, Somerset, and Sussex.

A very thin line separated conventions from mass meetings, which were merely political rallies. In appearance they were often so similar that differentiation becomes impossible. Nevertheless, the conventions which appear in the tables[12] were genuine decision-making bodies composed of delegates who were selected, appointed, or elected at the place which they represented. There were occasions when the mass meetings

I, 287; Cunningham, *The Jeffersonian Republicans*, pp. 256–259; Robinson, *Jeff. Dem. in N. Eng.*, p. 63; Republican organization in Massachusetts appears in Jonas Godfrey to Elkaneh Tisdale, Mar. 25, 1809, and many other circulars in Broadsides, American Antiquarian Soc.

[12] See pp. 77–83.

Table XIII. New Hampshire: Federalist Organization in 1812

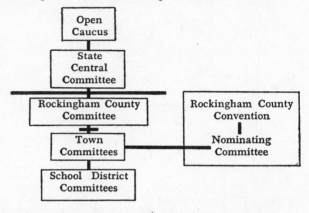

NOTE: The County Committee of Correspondence, probably appointed by the state committee, appointed one man in each town, who with two or three others of his selection composed the town committee. The latter in turn chose one man in each school district who formed a committee on that level. The County convention was a large mass meeting (1,500–3,000 depending on the county), within which a nominating committee composed of one man from each town came together. Town delegates were selected by town committees. Similar "conventions" were sponsored by Federalists in Grafton, Cheshire, Strafford, and Hillsborough. The relation of state committee to caucus is not known. See [Exeter] *Constitutionalist*, Aug. 4, 11, 18, 25, Oct. 31, 1812, Feb. 9, 1813, Feb. 1, 1814; [Windsor] *Washingtonian*, Sep. 28, 1812; [Keene] *N. H. Sentinel*, Aug. 15, Oct. 17, 31, 1812; [Concord] *N. H. Patriot*, Oct. 13, 1812; [Concord] *Gazette*, Oct. 6, 20, 1812; [Hanover] *Dartmouth Gazette*, Sep. 22, Oct. 20, 1812, Walpole *Democratic Republican*, July 27, 1812, E. Cutts to Daniel Webster, June 23, 1812, Webster Papers, Library of Congress.

went out of control, and, to the consternation of the young Federalists on the platform, became active nominating conventions.[13]

There were also occasions when a Federalist convention which had been rigged by a private meeting beforehand, was suddenly thrust upon its own devices by unforeseen contingencies. In 1816, the New York state convention was confounded when the gubernatorial candidate whom party leaders had carefully selected suddenly refused to run. This assemblage was chagrined to discover that it had indeed become a genuine nominating convention. "You can have no conception of the agitation which took place," one participant wrote.[14]

Most of the participants in Federalist conventions belonged to the younger generation. "The men who now attempt to direct their course," wrote a Republican, "are obviously *new* men, who have no great reputa-

[13] Morison, *Otis*, I, 295; the young Federalists mentioned herein comprised a third generation, born after 1790, who seldom became prominent leaders of the party; mass meetings will be discussed in ch. V below.

[14] W. A. Duer to William Henderson, Feb. 16, 1816, in King, *Life and Correspondence of King*, V, 516; David B. Ogden to Rufus King, Feb. 17, 1816 ibid., V, 513.

Table XIV. Virginia: Federalist Organization in 1812

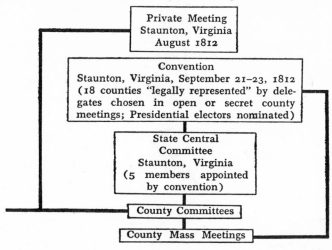

NOTE: The eighteen counties "legally represented" in convention included Augusta, Bath, Berkeley, Culpeper, Frederick, Fairfax, Fauquier, Hardy, Hampshire, Jefferson, Loudoun, Nelson, Prince William, Pendleton, Randolph, Rockbridge, Rockingham, and Westmoreland. The convention urged the formation of local committees as shown; the extent to which they were in fact formed is not known. See *Martinsburgh Gazette*, Mar. 13, 27, Apr. 3, Sep. 4, 1812; Abraham Shepherd to Timothy Pickering, Oct. 4, 1812, Pickering Papers, Mass. Hist. Soc. The State Central Committee suggested the creation of subcommittees in the counties, but their extent is not known.

tion for intelligence or prudence and are all individuals who are rather *seeking* a name than such as have acquired standing."[15]

2

It is difficult to measure precisely the impact of organization upon the outcome of elections. In most states, between 1800 and 1816 there was a clear correlation between the extent of Federalist organization and the fortunes of Federalist candidates at the polls. In Delaware and Connecticut, where Federalist party structure was elaborated, party workers energetic, and party leaders efficient, Federal victories were the constant despair of the Jeffersonians. In Massachusetts and New Hampshire, Federalist organization was slightly less efficient and Federalist candidates were slightly less successful. In Maryland, Federalists were weak and disorganized until 1808; after that date they

15 [Newark, N. J.] *Centinel of Freedom*, Sep. 1, 1812; see also "The Spirit of Seventy Six," 1810, and "Treason Detected! or the Federal Circular Exposed," 1811, Broadsides, American Antiq. Soc.; Christopher Gore to Rufus King, Oct. 5, 1812, in King, *Life and Correspondence of King*, V, 282.

Table XV. Massachusetts: Federalist Organization in 1814

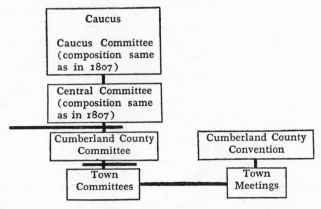

NOTE: State organization remained unchanged from 1807. Again, the extent of local organization was unknown, but Federalist conventions were held in York, Plymouth, Bristol, Essex, Middlesex, Cumberland, Lincoln, Worcester, and Washington counties. There was also a convention in Hancock which was criticized by other Federalists as being dominated by Bangor and one-fourth of the towns in the county. Suffolk County remained as organized in 1807.

See [Boston] *New England Palladium*, Mar. 22, 29, 1814; [Boston] *Repertory*, Feb. 15, Mar. 1, 14, 17, 18, 29, 1814; [New Bedford] *Mercury*, Mar. 25, 1814; [Haverhill] *Intelligencer*, Apr. 2, 1814, [Boston] *Columbian Centinel*, Mar. 12, 19, 30, 1814; Lewis Tappan, Pocket Remembrancer, Mar. 23, 1814, Tappan Papers, Library of Congress, Daniel Webster to William Sullivan, Oct. 17, 1814, Norcross Papers, Mass. Hist. Soc.; "To the Friends of Peace and Union," Mar. 8, 1814, Broadsides, Amer. Antiq. Soc.

Although there was no convention in Suffolk (Boston), the Grand Caucus in effect became one. A dissident group of very young Federalists, restive beneath the tightly controlled central committee, presented a second slate of nominees in the Grand Caucus and forced the selection of a compromise ticket. This is a clear illustration of the way in which even the most carefully planned meetings sometimes got out of control. See Morison, *Otis*, I, 295.

steadily acquired strength and structure in nearly equal measure. The New York Federalists showed discipline and unity most clearly in the period 1809–1812, when they briefly recovered their strength and the control of the legislature. The Virginia Federalists were strong and well organized in the west, weak and disorganized in the east central counties. But this correlation between strength and structure does not imply a simple causal connection. Party structure and party strength was a chicken-and-egg proposition. Strength encouraged structure, and structure increased strength. While an organized group of politicians necessarily had a great advantage over disorganized opponents, organization was not in itself necessarily decisive.

Although Federalism entered its final decline in 1816, many Federalist organizations reached a remarkable old age before they disintegrated. In Maryland, the party controlled the state until 1820; in Massachusetts,

Table XVI. Delaware: Federalist Organization in 1815

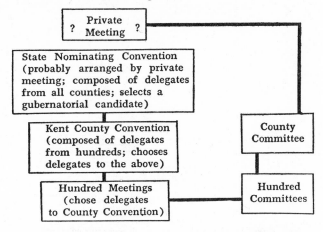

NOTE: Newcastle and Sussex counties similarly organized. There is no direct evidence of a private meeting of the most prominent Federalists in the state; its existence is assumed from the other assemblies charted above. Although there is no direct evidence of corresponding committees, these might be safely assumed to have existed. See Luetscher, *Political Machinery*, pp. 102–103, Munroe, *Federalist Delaware*, pp. 235–238.

as late as 1823; and in Delaware, even later. Late in the so-called "one party period" of American history, Federalists were still offering effective competition in many states. Even in Pennsylvania, the Federalists continued to play a significant role as late as 1823.[16]

The participation of Federalists in the Pennsylvania election of 1823 might serve to illustrate another point. In cooperation with a dissident faction of "Independent Republicans," they sponsored a "pure" state convention. Their newspapers sharply criticized the closed caucus which regular Republicans used to nominate their gubernatorial candidate, and made a campaign issue of "legislative interference in elections." The campaign was unsuccessful as far as the Federalists personally were concerned, but the attack on "legislative interference" was heard again. By 1823 King Caucus was dying. National conventions were only a decade away. "The people are sick to death of caucuses," a Federalist declared. "Strangle the monster without compunction or remorse."[17]

The practiced ease with which American politicians organized national nominating conventions during the age of Jackson was made possible by long experience with low-level conventions during the Jeffersonian

16 J. R. Pole, "Election Statistics in Pennsylvania, 1790–1840," *Pennsylvania Magazine of History and Biography*, LXXXII (1958), 217.

17 [?] to Daniel Webster, 1823, Webster Papers, Library of Congress.

Table XVII. Maryland: Federalist Organization in 1815

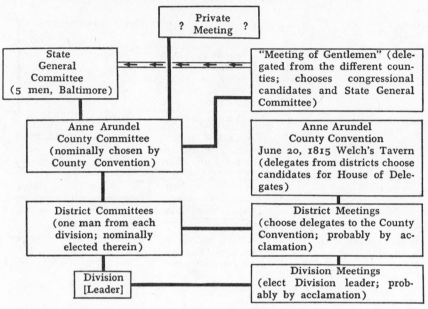

NOTE: The "meeting of gentlemen" was held at Hampton, the Ridgely estate, June 1, 1815, attendance unknown, but "large and well attended." Members of the General Committee in Baltimore included Robert Goodloe Harper, Walter Dorsey, Samuel Sterett, Richard Frisby, and G. H. Steuart. The full extent of local organization is not established except for Anne Arundel County, but according to John Murray, Anne Arundel County was the worst organized (by Federalists) in the state. The title "Leader" is borrowed from modern politics. His duties were "to attend to his division and to superintend the execution within it of all such matters connected with the Election, as may be resolved on by the county and district committee." See minutes of the Hampton Meeting, June 1, 1815, printed broadside in Galloway-Maxcy-Markoe Papers, unbound series, Library of Congress; John Murray to Jacob Wagner, July or Aug. 23, 1811, McHenry Papers, Library of Congress; [Annapolis] *Maryland Gazette*, June 29, July 20, Aug. 17, Aug. 24, Sep. 7, 1815; [Easton] *People's Monitor*, July 15, Aug. 26, 1815; [Georgetown] *Federal Republican*, Aug. 12, 1815.

era. This experience was shared by Federalists and Jeffersonians alike. The fact that this radical innovation was acceptable to the most conservative of active politicians in America is highly significant. After 1823, there would be many irreconcilable disagreements in American politics, but not over political structure. The use of conventions by Federalists is evidence of the fact that as early as 1823—and earlier— the customary forms of American politics were sustained by a genuine consensus. Thus, America avoided the tragic experience of France and Germany, escaping the bitter quarrels over not merely the role of government but its very nature.

Table XVIII. New York: Federalist Organization in 1816

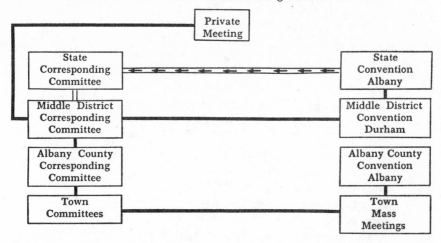

NOTE: The convention was arranged by a secret meeting of Federalists in Albany during the August 1815 term of the Supreme Court. It met February 14–15, 1816, and consisted of 106 delegates from every county in the state, who were probably appointed by county committees, and in some cases by meetings. It was not an open caucus, for only a fraction of Federalists in the legislature were invited to attend. W. A. Duer in a private letter described its participants as "the leading and most active men of the party from every part of the state." The State Committee, five men, was appointed therein. The full extent of organization is not known, but district conventions were held in the western, middle, and southern districts, at minimum, and county conventions in Rensselaer, Ontario, Columbia, Washington, Warren, Broome, Lewis, Essex, Albany, Ulster, Sullivan, Montgomery, and Otsego. Mass meetings were held in Westchester, Herkimer, and Oneida. See H. Bleecker *et al.*, to King, Feb. 16, 1816, W. A. Duer to King, Feb. 16, 1816, King, *King*, V, 506, 510; [Albany] *Advertiser*, Oct. 18, 1815, Feb. 2–Apr. 22, 1816; [Hudson] *Northern Whig*, Mar. 19, 1816; [N. Y.] *Evening Post*, Feb. 17, Mar. 7, 18, Apr. 13, 26, 29, 1816; [N. Y.] *Herald*, Apr. 26, 1816; [Salem] *Northern Post*, Mar. 14–Apr. 11, 1816; [Utica] *Patriot and Patrol*, Feb. 27, Mar. 1, 5, 19, 1816.

3

After 1800 organized Federalism was essentially a cluster of state formations. Numerous efforts were made to join these fragmented groups into a national party, but never with much success. Nevertheless, the Federalist response to the problem of national organization constituted a highly significant failure. The solution which they devised, however unsatisfactory it may have been in the light of their immediate goals, was an interesting and important step in the direction of present national party organization.[18]

[18] In part the fragmentation of Federalism after 1800 was a consequence of the decision many federal leaders made to turn their efforts toward local politics; see, e.g., Theodore Sedgwick to Alexander Hamilton, Jan. 27, 1803, in Hamilton Papers, Library of Congress.

The first attempts at national organization immediately after the election of 1800 were mainly the work of a few gentlemen of the old school. Oddly enough, Gouverneur Morris was among them. His spirits temporarily elevated by a celebration of Washington's Birthday in 1802, Morris tried to drum up enthusiasm among his friends for a chain of corresponding committees from Boston to Baltimore, with headquarters in New York City. He even suggested that these committees should be "appointed by the people," in nominating meetings. But the proposal came to nothing; Morris soon returned to his accustomed condition of despondency.[19]

Alexander Hamilton also tried to bring together the Federalists at a national meeting, in May, 1802. The occasion was a convention of the Cincinnati in the District of Columbia. He wrote to many prominent old-school gentlemen, exhorting them to attend. To Charles Cotesworth Pinckney he wrote, "I deem it was essential that there should be, without delay, a meeting and conference of a small number of leading Federalists from different states. Unless there shall be a plan of conduct proceeding from such a source, our measures will be disjointed, discordant, and of course ineffectual."[20]

Hamilton labored in vain. The few important Federalists who came to Washington were not able to agree on anything of political significance, if indeed they ever tried. There were a few similar efforts, but all in vain.[21] No interstate Federalist committees of correspondence developed during the first years of the century. No national meetings convened. As the number of Federalists in the Congress dwindled, the possibility of an effective Federalist national nominating caucus diminished proportionately.[22] The overwhelming popularity and power of Jefferson in 1804 served to stifle these feeble Federalist attempts at interstate cooperation. The presidential election came and went without an important effort by the Federalists to organize themselves above the state level.[23]

In 1808, however, the Great Embargo suddenly raised Federalist hopes as high as the presidency. During the summer of that year a Federalist

[19] Gouverneur Morris to Alexander Hamilton, Feb. 22, 1802, in Hamilton Papers, Library of Congress.

[20] Alexander Hamilton to Charles Cotesworth Pinckney, Mar. 15, 1802, in Lodge, *Works of Hamilton*, X, 428; see also Hall, *Benjamin Tallmadge*, p. 177.

[21] John Nicholas to John Rutledge, Feb. 21, 1803, in Rutledge Papers, Southern Hist. Coll., Univ. of N. C.; Theodore Sedgwick to Alexander Hamilton, Jan. 27, 1803, in Hamilton Papers, Library of Congress.

[22] Federalist Congressmen met frequently in caucus but only for consideration of legislative business; see William Plumer, *Diary*, Dec. 1, 1805, in Plumer Papers, Library of Congress.

[23] For an illustration of Federalist despair and disorganization in the 1804 campaign, see the *Lancaster Journal's* comment on an electoral ticket prepared by Federalists in Adams County, Pennsylvania: "an unavailing useless thing"; cited in Higginbotham, *The Keystone in the Demo. Arch*, p. 74.

national organization began to form for the first time. The first move was made by a Philadelphian, Charles Willing Hare. In a letter to Harrison Gray Otis, he suggested that "previous arrangements" should be made by the Federalists before the national election and invited Otis to take the initiative. "Your advice would have decisive influence with us," he declared.[24] With the advice and support of the Massachusetts caucus, Otis and other Massachusetts leaders decided "to propose a meeting of Federalists, from as many states as could be seasonably notified, at New York." A temporary target date was August 1.[25]

A committee of correspondence at Boston, composed of three young Federalists—Otis, James Lloyd, and Timothy Bigelow, together with two old-school gentlemen, Christopher Gore and George Cabot—began to write to men in other parts of the union.[26] The Massachusetts committee also sent special messengers to Vermont, New Hampshire, and Rhode Island, and corresponded with committees established in these states, thus acting as a sort of clearing committee in most of New England.

A New York committee served its adjacent states in the same fashion, keeping in close touch with Federalists in Connecticut and New Jersey. The Philadelphia committee communicated with leaders not only in eastern Pennsylvania but also in Delaware and Maryland.[27] Communica-

[24] Charles Willing Hare to Harrison Gray Otis, June 2, 1808, in Otis Papers, Mass. Hist. Soc.; Morison, *Otis*, I, 304; Theodore Sedgwick's presence in Philadelphia at this time was coincidental. According to Christopher Gore, Sedgwick had gone south "with a view of gaining some heat for his Autumnal Campaign, which is to be matrimonial, with Miss Penelope Russell, of about 40 years of age, who doesn't appear likely to be gratified with the Coldness or Imbecility of age," Christopher Gore to Rufus King, June 16, 1808, in King, *Life and Correspondence of King*, V, 10; see also Theodore Sedgwick to Harrison Gray Otis, June 6, 1808, in Otis Papers, Mass. Hist. Soc. This was not, of course, the first discussion of the presidential election. Many months earlier the Federalists had begun to debate the relative merits and pretensions of George Clinton, Monroe, etc. See Barent Gardenier to Rufus King, Jan. 16, 1808, in King, *Life and Correspondence of King*, V, 58; [Boston, Mass.] *New England Palladium*, Feb. 23, 1808; Gen. Bryan to Doctor Jones, May 14, 1808, in Calvin Jones Papers, Southern Hist. Coll., Univ. of N. C.; Elias H. Caldwell to William Gaston, June 1, 1808, in Gaston Papers, Southern Hist. Coll., Univ. of N. C.; Killian K. Van Rensselaer to Timothy Pickering, July 12, 1808, in Pickering Papers, Mass. Hist. Soc.

[25] Virginia Federalists caught between Madison and Monroe, proceeded independently to support the latter at a meeting in Richmond. See John Marshall to Charles Cotesworth Pinckney, Oct. 19, 1808, in Pinckney Papers, Library of Congress; Christopher Gore to Rufus King, June 16, 1808, in King, *Life and Correspondence of King*, V, 101.

[26] The Boston Committee of Correspondence was appointed by a special committee of twenty, which in turn had been elected by an open caucus of 300 Federalists.

[27] Charles Willing Hare to Harrison Gray Otis, June 19, 1808, Egbert Benson to Harrison Gray Otis, July 13, 1808, Abraham Van Vechten to Harrison Gray Otis, July 21, 1808, in Otis Papers, Mass. Hist. Soc.; [Harrison Gray Otis] to John Rutledge, July 3, 1808, Robert Beverley to John Rutledge, July 3, 1808, in Rutledge Papers, Southern Hist. Coll., Univ. of N. C.; Robert Goodloe Harper to J. H. Thomas, July 1808, in Harper-Pennington Papers, Md. Hist. Soc.

tion with the southern states was less complete. Individual leaders in Georgetown corresponded with Federalists in New Bern, Charleston, and Savannah. Through Harper, the Philadelphia committee contacted Archibald Lee of Virginia and Archibald Henderson of North Carolina. But with the single exception of Charleston there is no evidence of the existence of interstate Federalist committees of correspondence south of the Potomac.[28] Geographical distance itself presented a formidable obstacle to the Federalists in 1808. The date of the meeting was postponed to August 10, then to the third Monday, then to an even later date in the third week of August, in hopes of a more considerable attendance.[29]

The whole affair bore the flavor of a conspiracy. When the meeting finally took place, it was shrouded in elaborate and lamentably effective security measures. Its precise date is unknown, as are the identities of most participants. Only eight states were represented—Massachusetts, New Hampshire, Connecticut, Vermont, New York, Pennsylvania, Maryland, and South Carolina. Robert Goodloe Harper, Harrison Gray Otis, and John Rutledge were there, as were Charles Willing Hare and Thomas FitzSimons of Pennsylvania, Christopher Gore and James Lloyd of Massachusetts, and Josiah Dunham of Vermont. The names of other participants are conjectural.[30]

The meeting made two important decisions; first, that it was not in the interest of the Federalists to support a Republican, which meant thumbs down on George Clinton; second, that the most suitable Federalist candidates were Charles Cotesworth Pinckney for President and Rufus King for Vice-President.[31]

The roundabout way in which the decision of the meeting was made public is evidence of tender consciences. The Philadelphia Committee of Correspondence at first agreed to do it, but backed out when they came home and "observed something like a jealousy in our friends at having a nomination so important decided on by so small a number as we were and without any special authority." The Boston committee thereupon "leaked" the nomination to local journals, which disingenu-

[28] John M. Berrien to John Rutledge, Oct. 3, 1808, Archibald Henderson to John Rutledge, Sep. 9, 1808, in Rutledge Papers, Southern Hist. Coll., Univ. of N. C.; Samuel Eliot Morison, "First National Nominating Convention," *American Historical Review*, XVII (1911–1912), 744–765; Jacob Radcliff et al. to Harrison Gray Otis, Oct. 9, 1808, Charles Willing Hare to Harrison Gray Otis, July 12, 1808, in Otis Papers, Mass. Hist. Soc.; William Polk to Duncan Cameron, Oct. 15, 1800, in Cameron Papers, Southern Hist. Coll., Univ. of N. C.; Jacob Wagner to Timothy Pickering, Jan. 21, 1809, in Pickering Papers, Mass. Hist. Soc.

[29] Morison, "First National Nominating Convention," 753 and n.; Robert Beverley to John Rutledge, July 3, 1808, in John Rutledge Papers, Southern Hist. Coll., Univ. of N. C.

[30] Other Federalists who probably attended were Egbert Benson and Abraham Van Vechten of New York and David Daggett of Connecticut. I have found little to add to Morison's account of the meeting.

[31] Jacob Radcliff et al. to Charleston Committee of Correspondence, Sep. 1808, in Otis Papers, Mass. Hist. Soc.; Morison, *Otis*, I, 314–315.

ously published it as "information collected from every part of the union . . . without the aid of any caucus or other preliminary."[32]

Although, as has been mentioned, George Cabot and Christopher Gore lent their prestige to the enterprise, it was primarily an affair of young Federalists. Timothy Pickering, the reputed Federalist "boss," was not a participant in any way. A letter from Cabot to Pickering suggests that the latter was not even informed about the plans for the meeting until as late as August 10.[33]

Fifty years ago a historian suggested that this secret gathering constituted "the first national nominating convention." This interpretation, of course, is an overstatement. The meeting was not truly national in scope. More important, it was not a nominating convention in the modern sense, for many members of the Federal Party did not recognize its authority as legitimate or accept its decision as binding. But nevertheless, the Federalists who traveled to New York City in the summer of 1808 had taken an important step in the direction of modern party organization.[34]

Four years later, Federalist leaders took another step in the same direction. Their second national meeting, convened in New York from September 17–19, 1812, was better planned and much better attended than the first. The Philadelphia Federalists, who once again played a central role in preliminary conversations during the summer, made every effort to attract a truly representative delegation of Federalists from every state. To a North Carolina Federalist, the committee in Philadelphia wrote, "The number of delegates is left entirely to yourselves, but it is desirable that the representation from each state should be as weighty as possible in point of talent and influence—comprehending characters from different parts of the state and of different professions."[35]

The delegates were, for the most part, selected by state general com-

---

[32] Thomas FitzSimons to Harrison Gray Otis, Christopher Gore and James Lloyd, Oct. 4, 1808, in Otis Papers, Mass. Hist. Soc.; some of the younger Federalists opposed the meeting because it lent itself to misrepresentation by Democrats and because it was distasteful to gentlemen of the old school. Bayard's disapproval is described in Charles Willing Hare to Harrison Gray Otis, July 12, 1808, in Otis Papers, Mass. Hist. Soc.

[33] George Cabot to Timothy Pickering, Aug. 10, 1808, in Pickering Papers, Mass. Hist. Soc.; Lodge, *Cabot*, p. 397.

[34] Cf. Morison, "First National Nominating Convention," pp. 744, 763.

[35] James Milnor et al. to J. W. Stanly et al., Aug. 13, 1812, in Gaston Papers, Southern Hist. Coll., Univ. of N. C. The impetus came from Connecticut, but there can be little doubt of the crucial role of the Philadelphia committee. Peter A. Jay to John Jay, Sep. 17, 1812, in Jay Papers, Columbia University Library; Sullivan, *Familiar Letters* (1847 edn.), p. 350n; Milnor et al. to Otis, July 27, 1812, in Otis Papers, Mass. Hist. Soc.; Gouv. Morris to C. W. Hare, June 30, 1812, in Morris Papers, Library of Congress; Otis to Rutledge, July 31, 1812, in Rutledge Papers, Southern Hist. Coll., Univ. of N. C.; Benjamin Stoddert to Harper, Aug. 31, Sep. 1, 1812; Stoddert to J. H. Thomas, Sep. 4, 1812, Harper to Stoddert, Sep. 10, 1812, Harper to Thomas, Sep. 10, 1812, in Harper-Pennington Papers, Md. Hist. Soc.

mittees or committees of correspondence, and were thus in some degree representative of Federalist state organizations, if not of the rank and file. Altogether, more than sixty men attended from eleven states. Lengthy communications were received and read from Federalists in two others, North Carolina and Virginia. Only one state in which Federalists were active was not heard from—Ohio.[36]

Superficially, this Federalist "convention" (so it was called by Federalists themselves) contrasts sharply with the political extravaganzas which American political parties have staged every four years since the age of Jackson. It came together as quietly as possible, and its deliberations were a closely guarded secret. But once we penetrate the barred doors and bolted windows, many of the sights and sounds are familiar. Cynical party chieftains and starry-eyed visionaries, distinguished statesmen and narrow county courthouse politicians all came together in one improbable and unpredictable mass. An attempt by a few confident leaders to prearrange the nomination was conspicuously unsuccessful. Fine-spun schemes contributed less to the outcome than full-blown oratory. Conflicting groups were forced, in order to "preserve the unity of the Federalist party," to settle for a compromise that satisfied no one. In the end, more than one delegate returned home utterly bewildered by the events that had transpired.[37]

The attempt to "rig" the results of the meeting was the work of a few federal leaders in Massachusetts who believed that the only way to

[36] Among the delegates were Thomas W. Thompson of N. H., Harrison Gray Otis, Israel Thorndike, William Sullivan, Theodore Sedgwick of Mass., Josiah Ogden Hoffman, Rufus King, Peter A. Jay, George Tibbits, Gouverneur Morris, D. B. Ogden of N. Y., Elias Boudinot of N. J., Samuel Sitgreaves, Joseph Hopkinson, Horace Binney, William Meredith, and Thomas Duncan of Penna., Robert Goodloe Harper of Md., and John Rutledge of S. C. Others probably included John Noyes and Chauncey Langdon of Vt., Timothy Bigelow of Mass., Benjamin Hazard of R. I., David Daggett, Theodore Dwight, Calvin Goddard, and Samuel W. Dana of Conn. Barent Gardenier, William Coleman, and Caleb S. Riggs of N. Y., William Griffith and Richard Stockton of N. J., and A. C. Hanson of Md. Abraham Van Vechten, Harmanus Bleecker and T. P. Grosvenor were in Albany attending the New York Federalist state convention. See, in addition to material cited in n. 35 above, Horace Binney et al. to Daniel Webster, Sep. 21, 1812, in Webster Papers, Library of Congress; George Tibbits to Harrison Gray Otis, Oct. 22, 1812, in Otis Papers, Mass. Hist. Soc., Thomas W. Thompson to William Meredith, Oct. 12, 1812, in Meredith Papers, Hist. Soc. of Penna.; statements in handwriting of Rufus King, in King, Life and Correspondence of King, V, 266–271; Robert Goodloe Harper in the Georgetown Federal Republican, Nov. 16, 1812; Harrison Gray Otis in the Washington National Intelligencer, Oct. 29, 1812; [Lexington, Ky.] Reporter, Oct. 28, 1812; [Norfolk, Va.] Public Ledger, Oct. 5–7, 1812; [New York] Evening Post, Sep. 15, 1812; [New York] Public Advertiser, Sep. 19, 1812; C. C. Binney, Life of Horace Binney (Philadelphia, 1903), p. 67; Jonathan Dayton to Madison, Sep. 17, 23, 1812, cited in Brant, Madison, VI, 99.

[37] Thomas W. Thompson to William Meredith, Oct. 12, 1812, in Meredith Papers, Hist. Soc. of Penna.; Peter A. Jay to John Jay, Sep. 17, 1812, in Jay Papers, Columbia Univ. Library; George Tibbits to Harrison Gray Otis, Oct. 22, 1812, in Otis Papers, Mass. Hist. Soc.

defeat Madison and to prevent a national disaster was to support a Republican who might draw sufficient strength from his own party in the middle states to carry the election. Specifically, their hopes rested with De Witt Clinton.[38]

Against them were Federalists in New York who felt that to endorse Clinton would be to sell themselves to the lowest bidder "after the manner of a Dutch auction." In their judgment the most attractive candidate was Rufus King.[39] A third group consisted mainly of southern Federalists who argued that an avowed Federalist candidate from south of the Potomac could win enough votes in North Carolina to swing the balance. Their favorite was John Marshall.

In the convention, this third group was confounded by a letter from Charles Cotesworth Pinckney and had no influence on the outcome.[40] For three days the two others fought to a stalemate. On the last day, a brilliant speech by Harrison Gray Otis on behalf of Clinton broke the deadlock: "Mr. Otis arose, apparently much embarrassed, holding his hat in his hand, and seeming as if he were almost sorry he had arisen. Soon he warmed with the subject, his hat fell from his hand, and he poured forth a strain of eloquence that chained all present to their seats."[41]

Otis managed to carry a resolution against the nomination of a Federalist candidate, but he was unable to win an explicit endorsement of Clinton. Most of the delegates departed from New York with the understanding that the decision to make a formal nomination of Clinton would be left to the judgment of a corresponding committee in Penn-

[38] Oliver Wolcott to George Gibbs, Nov. 7, 1812, in Wolcott, Papers, Library of Congress; Christopher Gore to Rufus King, Oct. 5, 1812, in King, Life and Correspondence of King, V, 283; Gouverneur Morris, Diary, May 3, 1812, in Gouverneur Morris Papers, Library of Congress; James Milnor, Robert Wharton, Horace Binney and Andrew Bayard to Harrison Gray Otis, July 27, 1812, in Otis Papers, Mass. Hist. Soc.; Harrison Gray Otis to William Sullivan, Aug. 17, 1812, in Misc. Manuscripts, New York Public Library; Harrison Gray Otis to John Rutledge, July 31, 1812, in Rutledge Papers, Southern Hist. Coll., Univ. of N. C.

[39] Statement in King's handwriting, n. d. [1812], in King, Life and Correspondence of King, V, 265–71; Abraham Van Vechten to Theodore Dwight, Aug. 12, 1812, in Misc. Mss., New York Public Library; James Kent to Moss Kent, Nov. 10, 1812, in Kent Papers, Library of Congress; Robert Walker to Duncan Cameron, Oct. 22, 1812, in Cameron Papers, Southern Hist. Coll., Univ. of N. C.; Binney, Binney, p. 67; Morison, Otis, pp. 308–311; Murdock, "First National Nominating Convention," pp. 680–83.

[40] Pinckney wrote, "My own sentiments with regard to the most prudent conduct for the Federalists to pursue at present is on no account to think of setting up myself or any southern Federalist as a candidate . . . for by so doing the federal votes would be absolutely thrown away." Pinckney to James Milnor, Andrew Bayard, C. W. Hare, Horace Binney & John B. Wallace, Aug. 24, 1812, in Pinckney Family Papers, Library of Congress; see also Edwin Gray to L. W. Tazewell, Jan. 10, 1812, in Tazewell Papers, Virginia State Library; Benjamin Stoddert to Harper, Aug. 31, Sep. 1, 1812, in Harper-Pennington Papers, Md. Hist. Soc.

[41] Sullivan, Familiar Letters, p. 351; Peter A. Jay to John Jay, Sep. 17, 1812, in Jay Papers, Columbia Univ. Library.

sylvania, and to the flow of events in the two crucial states, Pennsylvania and North Carolina.[42]

The meeting thus ended on a note of self-abnegation. It differed, of course, in many ways from a post-Jackson nominating convention—in its secrecy, in its failure to produce a decision, in the lingering elitism of its participants. But in more important ways it was similar—it constituted a genuine decision-making body composed of delegates from vote-seeking party formations in the states. These facts would sustain John Murdock's judgment that the New York meeting in 1812 was the "first national nominating convention."[43]

Federalist strategy in the presidential campaign of 1812 was doubly unfortunate. They gained nothing by it, and lost heavily in morale. Clinton proved unable to attract Democratic votes in significant numbers. Although he piled up an impressive total of electoral votes, only twenty short of success, he failed to run as strongly as had avowed Federalist candidates in local elections. He was not able to carry as many states as the Federalists actually won in legislative and gubernatorial elections. The resolution of the New York meeting that a Federal candidate would be inexpedient in 1812 served to mask the remarkable victories of federal organizations in the states. Still greater victories in 1813 and 1814 suggest that Federalist committees and conventions functioned as efficiently as those of the Democratic-Republicans. In this context, we can comprehend Democratic denunciations of Federalists as "Jacobins" and "seditious disorganizers," which in the lexicon of early American politics meant that the Federalists were becoming very well organized indeed.[44]

[42] Peter A. Jay to John Jay, Sep. 17, 1812, in Jay Papers, Columbia Univ. Library; Thomas W. Thompson to Wm. Meredith, Oct. 12, 1812, in Meredith Papers, Hist. Soc. of Penna.; George Tibbits to Otis, Oct. 22, 1812, in Otis Papers, Mass. Hist. Soc. Irving Brant's rejection of Harper's, Otis's and Morris's accounts of the meeting as "falsehoods" is unwarranted. There is nothing contradictory in the fact that there were Federalist conversations with Clinton, and yet that no such conversations were authorized by the meeting; cf. Brant, *Madison*, VI, 101. Most younger Federalists agreed to support Clinton, but such gentlemen of the old school as King refused to go along with what was the only possibility after Otis's speech; see Rufus King to William King, Oct. 23, 1812, in King, *Life and Correspondence of King*, V, 288; see also Stoddert to Harper, Nov. 16, 1812, in Harper-Pennington Papers, Md. Hist. Soc.; [Georgetown, Md.] *Federal Republican*, Nov. 16, 1812; [Fredericktown, Md.] *Star of Federalism*, Apr. 5, 1817.

[43] Murdock, "The First National Nominating Convention," *American Historical Review*, I (1895–1896), pp. 680–683.

[44] Election results can be conveniently found in Henry Adams, *History of the U. S.*, VI, 115, 204, 209, 409–414; VII, 49, 51, 366; VIII, 9–13, 228, 238, 288–89; see also, for Republicans on Federalist organization, [Portland, Mass.] *Eastern Argus*, 9 Aug. 1804.

V

Electioneering Techniques

A man will soon, without the imputation of indelicacy, be able to hawk himself in the highways as an excellent candidate for the highest promotion, with as much freedom and vociferation as your market men now cry codfish and lobsters."

—THOMAS DWIGHT, 1789

You must get close to the people in order to manage them— there is no better way.

—JOHN CARLYLE HERBERT, 1816[1]

Generally speaking, the gentlemen of the old school did not think well of electioneering. They hoped that the people might be trusted to choose the "best men" without regard to promises or favors. This political ideal permeated American politics during the eighteenth century. Many colonies and states passed laws against electioneering. In Massachusetts, Jonathan Jackson seriously proposed that any candidate found guilty of canvassing votes should be deprived of all political privileges for life. In Virginia, as realistic a politician as James Madison expressed his "extreme distaste" for "any step which might seem to denote a solicitude" for office.[2]

It is true, of course, that many eighteenth-century gentlemen who did not approve of electioneering were forced to practice it. In the plantation states, particularly, where "treating" at the polls was familiar from colonial days, an overscrupulous office seeker was often underballoted. A candidate in eighteenth-century Virginia was virtually required to "hold a pole" before the people. One aspirant for public trust described the process in rich detail:

Perhaps you are a stranger to the term "hold a pole," of which I will inform you, viz: the candidate stands upon an eminence close to the Avenue thro, which the people pass to vie in their votes, viva voce, or by outcry. There the candidates stand ready to beg, pray and solicit the people's votes in opposition to their Competitors and the poor wretched people *are much*

[1] Thomas Dwight to Theodore Sedgwick, Feb. 7, 1789, Sedgwick Papers, Mass. Hist. Soc. John Carlyle Herbert to Vergil Maxcy, Apr. 11, 1816, in Galloway-Maxcy-Markoe Papers, Library of Congress.

[2] Madison to George Washington, Dec. 2, 1788, in Madison Papers, Library of Congress; Sydnor, p. 44. Jackson, *Political Situation.*

difficulted by the prayers and threats of those Competitors, exactly similar to the Election of the corrupt and infamous House of Commons in England. At the last election I was dragged from my lodging when at dinner, and forced upon the eminence purely against my will, but I soon disappeared and returned to my repast; and as soon as they lost sight of me they quit voting for me. Such is the pitiful and lowlived manner all the elected officers of Government come into posts of honour and profit in Virginia, by stooping into the dirt that they may ride the poor people.[3]

Political practices in Maryland were similar. A witness to one turbulent election in that state was hard put to describe it. "What confusion!" he declared. "If ever I saw a resemblence to hell, it was at Marlborough court house. Within the house, what a clatter of tongues! 'A. will thank you for your votes!'—'I am much obliged to you,' says C. 'D. is a good man,' says another. 'Won't you vote for B?' says a fourth. 'Huzza for M.' 'Damn your eyes, clear the way.'—'Who do you intend to vote for?' 'Huzza for B.' Such pulling and hauling and crowding and jostling— all speaking at once and some with a very loud voice."[4]

Vote-seeking in the southern states was not restricted to the polling places. Wherever crowds happened to gather in the weeks preceding an election, candidates were sure to be in evidence. A favorite device was to show up at a horse race or a cock fight with refreshment for the spectators. The accounts of a candidate in North Carolina contain a bill for "1 Bowl Punch at [the] race ground £1 . . 10 . ."[5] Another common strategem was to come early to a church service or a Methodist quarterly meeting, find a seat in full view of the assembled congregation, and pray louder and longer than the minister himself. A North Carolina poet satirized both of these techniques together:

> Some worked with grogg,
> Some with the jugg,
> Some sought for votes by praying;
> To church they went,
> On prayer bent,
> To see what the priest was saying.
> All must agree

[3] David Thomas to Griffith Evans, Mar. 3, 1789, *Massachusetts Historical Society Proceedings*, XLVI (1913), 371; for many other illustrations, see Sydnor, *Gentlemen Freeholders*, pp. 27–59, and Carl Bridenbaugh, *Seat of Empire: The Political Role of Eighteenth-Century Williamsburg* (Williamsburg, 1950, 1958), p. 15. Even George Washington "treated" his neighbors on election day; Freeman, *Washington*, II, 320–321.

[4] Allan B. Slauson, "Curious Customs of the Past . . . ," *Columbia Historical Society Records*, IX (1906), 111; North Carolina customs were also similar; see, e.g., the description of a candidate who "early on election morning hove into sight of the court green, in an old fashioned crazy one horse sulky, with a couple of tin cups, and a ten gallon keg between his legs"; [Raleigh, N. C.] *Star*, June 7, 1810.

[5] John Haywood to P. Casso, May 17, 1798, in Ernest Haywood Papers, Southern Hist. Coll., Univ. of N. C.

With you and me,
That interest was their object.[6]

But it should be noted that even in the southern states, where electioneering was much more widespread than in the northern states,
vote-seeking was restricted to a brief season of a few weeks. Except in
turbulent times—during the Revolution or in 1788—it was the work
of an individual or a small clique whose resources were limited. The
ideals and the realities of eighteenth-century American politics combined to inhibit the growth of systematic electioneering on a large scale.
Before the rise of the Jeffersonians, as Robinson has written, "cam-
paigning was the work of guerrillas rather than disciplined organizations."[7]

I

During the 1790s the Jeffersonians revolutionized electioneering. By
pooling their efforts they were able to sponsor campaigns far beyond
the resources of the wealthiest individuals or the busiest of cliques.
Their opponents complained bitterly of endless "dinings," "drinkings,"
and celebrations; of handbills "industriously posted along every road";
of convoys of vehicles which brought voters to the polls by the cartload;
of candidates "in perpetual motion."[8] It is true that all of these practices
can be found on a smaller scale in pre-Revolution America. But there
is a point at which a difference in degree becomes a difference in kind.
The Jeffersonians reached this point and passed it during the 1790s.

In their struggle against the Federalists, the Jeffersonians expended
astonishing amounts of money and energy. A measure of their activity
is an itemized bill for a single barbecue—one of many—which a caterer

6 William Lenoir to Gen. Rutherford, n. d. [c. 1803], typescript in Lenoir Papers,
Southern Hist. Coll., Univ. of N. C.; see also for South Carolina, Rogers, *William
Loughton Smith*, p. 165.

7 Robinson, *Jeff. Dem. in N. Eng.*, p. 56; organized electioneering was not, of
course, unknown in the middle colonies or in New England before the Revolution.
The politics of Pennsylvania generated something similar to a modern party system
as early as 1742; see [Philadelphia] *Pennsylvania Gazette*, Oct. 7, 1742; and for
graphic evidence of electioneering in Philadelphia, see cartoons dated 1765 in the
Hist. Soc. of Pa. and the American Antiquarian Society. Among New England
colonies "dirty little Rhode Island" seems to have been most sophisticated; see, e.g.,
the remarkable electioneering efforts made in 1763 by the Hopkins party, as detailed in David Lovejoy, *Rhode Island Politics and the American Revolution, 1760–
1776* (Providence, R. I., 1958), p. 24. The full extent of such practices must remain
an open question until historians are able to be more precise in their analysis of
colonial politics. But the preponderance of evidence and of informed opinion suggests that *systematic* electioneering was uncommon below the Mason-Dixon line,
and virtually unknown above it; see the judgment of Chambers, *Political Parties*,
pp. 1–33.

8 "To the People," n. d. [c. 1811], in Broadsides, Md. Hist. Soc., Charles W. Harris
to Robert W. Harris, Aug. 29, 1800, in Henry M. Wagstaff, ed., "The Harris Letters,"
The James Sprunt Studies, XIV (1916), I, 80f; [Easton, Md.] *Star*, Sep. 27, 1803,
Oct. 2, 1804; Cunningham, *Jeffersonian-Republicans*, pp. 33–45, 249–261.

submitted to the Republican committee of New York City. The total cost was $608.06!⁹

Jeffersonians carried electioneering much further than anyone might even have imagined a generation earlier. John Randolph, after he broke with his party complained that a Republican opponent had "descended to the lowest and the most disgraceful means—riding from house to house, and attending day and night meetings in the cabins and hovels of the lowest of the people. He was present at fourteen of these preachings (seven of them held at night) the week before the election."[10]

In states where written ballots were required, Republicans often furnished printed or handwritten tickets that a voter could either copy or drop into the box. For the benefit of voters who had trouble making out words, the ballots sometimes bore symbols—an American eagle by the Republican candidates, the arms of the English king next to the Federalists. The victory of the Jeffersonians was due, at least in part,

---

[9] Bill sarcastically endorsed "Thomas Winship's Modist [sic] Account for Roasting an Ox," May 1806, in McKesson Papers, New York Hist. Soc.:

Beer	£35.12.
Bread	9.16.
do.	5.00.
Wooden dishes	2.16.
Ropes	.10.
Joice [joist?], boards, planks, nails, workmanship	24.14.06.
Ox	66. .
Beer & Punch	20. .
Fire Wood	9.16.
Pepper & Salt	2. .
Stone Work & Labourers	10.00.
Sundries for basting the ox	4.00.
Timber for spit	1.00.
Labourers roasting	4.00.
Thomas Winship's superintendence	40.00.
Spars	1.04.
	243. 4. 6. or $608.06[sic]

See also list of Collections, May 1806, ibid.; Charles D. Cooper Account Book, [c. 1804], Library of Congress; see also the account of a Jeffersonian banquet for the citizens of Lancaster, Pennsylvania, on New Year's Day, 1801, which was attended by Governor McKean, members of the legislature, and other distinguished guests. "Near the head of the table, among other decorations, there was placed a pyramid covered with sugar plums. On the three sides of the base were respectively inscribed, Monarchy, Hierarchy, Aristocracy; and on the fourth side was written 200,000 in large characters. The base rested upon round and irregular pieces of sugar cake, called jumbles. It seemed to have been designed to produce a scramble and was soon demolished—pyramid, base, foundation and all. The '200,000' doubtless represents the majority by which the successful party won the [presidential] election." William Frederic Worner, "A great political meeting in Lancaster," Lancaster Co. Hist. Soc. Papers, 33 (1929), 135.

[10] John Randolph to Josiah Quincy, Apr. 19, 1813, in Edmund Quincy, Josiah Quincy, pp. 329f; see also John Randolph to Littleton Tazewell, Apr. 21, 1804, in Tazewell Papers, Virginia State Library.

to the care with which they systematized, extended, intensified, and popularized electioneering techniques.[11]

2

The Federalist gentlemen of the old school reacted in different ways to the Jeffersonian revolution in electioneering techniques. A few enlarged upon their own efforts. William Cooper is one example. Another is the transitional figure Robert Troup, who was so busy in the campaign of 1800 that he was constantly upon his feet "from 7 in the morning till 7 in the afternoon" and didn't eat dinner for three days.[12] A third is Alexander Hamilton, who had a flair for popular speaking and often "harangued" the citizenry of New York in their ward meetings.[13] A fourth is Fisher Ames. In 1798 he and several young friends sponsored a successful Federalist Fourth of July celebration in Dedham, Massachusetts, which was attended by "about sixty clergymen, gentlemen, mechanics, and farmers." After it was over Ames wrote hopefully, "The temper of the company was excellent and the progress of federalism seems to have begun."[14]

But with efforts such as these the "progress of federalism" ended more often than it began. By and large, older Federalists turned away from electioneering at the same time that Jeffersonians turned toward it. Samuel Goodrich later declared that gentlemen of the old school "did not mingle with the mass: they might be suspected of electioneering," which would have been "too degrading for them."[15] A young Fed-

[11] Bentley, *Diary*, Aug. 25, 1800, II, 346–347; see also Abraham Bloodgood to D. Fraser, Apr. 28, 1806, in McKesson Papers, New York Hist. Soc.; Middletown *Middlesex Gazette*, 5 Sep. 1800.

[12] Robert Troup to Peter Van Schaack, May 2, 1800, in Van Schaack Papers, Library of Congress.

[13] [Newark, N. J.] *Centinel of Freedom*, Apr. 28, 1801; for earlier examples see Stephen Van Rensselaer to William Cooper, Apr. 2, 1794, in William Cooper Transcripts, New York Hist. Soc.; [Boston, Mass.] *Independent Chronicle*, Oct. 15, 1795; Chilton Williamson, *American Suffrage from Property to Democracy, 1760–1860* (Princeton, 1960), p. 140.

[14] Fisher Ames to Oliver Wolcott, July 6, 1798, in George Gibbs, *Memoirs of the Administrations of Washington and John Adams, edited from the Papers of Oliver Wolcott*, 2 vols. (New York, 1846), II, 69; [Boston, Mass.] *Columbian Centinel*, July 11, 1798. For a Jeffersonian view of this "high Federalist frolic" see Warren, *Jacobin and Junto*, p. 78. At least a few gentlemen of the old school responded to Jeffersonian innovations with attempts at coercion. Federalists in parts of New England and South Carolina used colored tickets to deprive their "dependents" of the protection of secret ballot; Beard, *Economic Origins of Jeffersonian Democracy*, p. 377; see also Robinson, *Jeff. Dem. in N. Eng.*, p. 73. In Connecticut, in 1801, they passed the notorious "Stand-up Law," which required each voter to rise before his fellow townsmen as he gave his vote. In such a situation it was a courageous Jeffersonian indeed who could proclaim his true preference before the most powerful men in the community; Robinson, *Jeff. Dem. in N. Eng.*, p. 56; Williamson, *American Suffrage*, pp. 169, 183–184; Simeon E. Baldwin, "The Early History of the Ballot in Connecticut," *American Historical Association Papers*, IV (1890), p. 89; William Slade to Ephraim Kirby, Feb. 3, 1802, Philo Murray to Ephraim Kirby, Sep. 21, 1801, in Ephraim Kirby Papers, Duke University Library.

[15] Goodrich, *Recollections*, I, 237.

eralist in Massachusetts complained that in his town "not a man had been spoken to about candidates" by gentlemen of his persuasion before the election of 1800.[16] Even in New York, where Federalists were more active and better organized than anywhere else in the Union, one young man complained that they "were as usual supine till the eve of the election."[17]

The gentlemen of the old school made a virtue of their lethargy, and boasted of the "purity" of their political behavior. When Gouverneur Morris was turned out of office, he wrote proudly that he had "never sought, avoided, or resigned an office, but continued at my last post to the latest moment."[18] Sometimes they distributed handbills or inserted cards in the newspapers announcing briefly that they would not degrade themselves by solicitation. A Maryland Federalist advised the people that "as free and independent Men, you are not to be cajoled by the shew of great *personal* respect, nor caught with the miserable bait of entertainment."[19]

To Jeffersonian electioneering techniques the Federalists responded with righteous indignation. Gouverneur Morris bitterly condemned "Those brawlers, who make popularity a trade."[20] If leaders were objects of anger, "their dupes, the people" were objects of amusement. With

[16] Henry Van Schaack to Theodore Sedgwick, Apr. 7, 1800, in Sedgwick Papers, Mass. Hist. Soc.

[17] Peter Augustus Jay to John Jay, Apr. 7, 1800, in John Jay Papers, Columbia University Library.

[18] Gouverneur Morris to R. R. Livingston, [1805], in Morris, *Diary and Letters of Morris*, II, 469.

[19] "To the Voters of Talbot County," Aug. 11, 1803, in Broadsides, Mass. Hist. Soc.; some of these statements were unalloyed hypocrisy. A Federalist who declared that he would not campaign was thus pilloried in the Jeffersonian press: "How is this Gentleman who 'would not prostitute himself to party views and electioneering purposes' now employed? Not *surely* in riding all over the county, haranguing the people, and in soliciting each individual voter"; [Georgetown, Md.] *Centinel*, Sep. 23, 1800.

[20] Gouverneur Morris, "Oration on Patriotism," n. d. [1805?], in Morris Collection, Columbia Univ. Library; see also Robinson, *Jeff. Dem. in N. Eng.*, p. 54; [Boston, Mass.] *New England Palladium*, Oct. 7, 1806; "To the Electors of the Eastern District," n. d. [1798?], in American Broadsides, New York Hist. Soc. For an example of heavy-handed Federalist satire, see [Boston, Mass.] *New England Palladium*, Mar. 29, 1803:

"TIME *is Money*," said a long-faced Jacobin, as he drew his empty purse from his pocket, "for I have spent:

Two days for the Caucus at Danvers	$2.
Four days in soliciting votes	4.
Ten half days spent in certain grog shops in converting the doubtful and strengthening the weak	5.
Paid for whisky and new rum to help the cause	1.50
	12.50

But it is a good cause, and though my wife is without shoes and my children crying for bread, our party begins to triumph, and every Federalist must be ousted. Besides, when Jefferson hears how I have done and suffered, perhaps he will *create* some office for me, and then I shall no more fear the constable."

characteristic arrogance, a Federalist wrote, "I think it will be truly
laughable to see the *swinish multitude* (as Mr. Burke observes) feasting
on a Quadruped and swilling whisky to seditious toasts—God only knows
where it will end."[21]

3

Many younger Federalists took a different view. Josiah Quincy complained bitterly of the "cautious politicians" of the older generation,
"men who neither devise nor execute." He denounced the "principles"
which seemed "merely an apology of inactivity."[22] A young Federalist
in western Massachusetts, Loring Andrews, had written as early as
1798, "The fireside and the private circle will never answer to sit in
judgment upon the abettors of French intrigue. Influential characters
must be active—they must throw off all reserve—they must speak to
the people in terms, and in tone, which the apparently all-important
approaching crisis requires. They must not shelter themselves under
any assumed masks. They must go forth among the multitude and
personally discuss with them the things which appertain to their existence as an independent nation."[23]

The young Federalists at first borrowed only the most gentlemanly
techniques of the Jeffersonians. "You know, they use some weapons
which we cannot condescend to," Henry De Saussure declared. The
Jeffersonians had made extensive use of mass meetings in which voters
came together, chose a chairman, reaffirmed the right of assembly,
unanimously "nominated" candidates, passed a set of resolutions, and
adjourned.[24]

After 1800, the young Federalists borrowed this device and built their
campaigns around it. In the few parts of the union where old-school
gentlemen had used mass meetings during the 1790s, the young Federalists merely improved and enlarged. It was the custom of the "friends
of government" in Boston, for example, to assemble in the Concert Hall
on the eve of every important election.[25] After 1800, however, young
Federalists greatly expanded these meetings into "Grand Caucuses."
By 1804 they found it necessary to announce that "the Concert Hall
having been found too small, the Federalists have obtained leave to
assemble in Fanueil Hall."[26]

21 Lewis M. Ogden to William Meredith, Feb. 26, 1801, in Meredith Papers, Hist.
Soc. of Penna.
22 Josiah Quincy to John Quincy Adams, Dec. 15, 1804, in Adams Family Papers,
reel 403.
23 Loring Andrews to Peter Van Schaack, Apr. 6, 1798, in Van Schaack Papers,
Library of Congress.
24 Henry W. De Saussure to John Rutledge, Aug. 14, 1800; in Rutledge Papers,
Southern Hist. Coll., Univ. of N. C.
25 [Boston, Mass.] *Centinel*, Apr. 2, 1796, Oct. 25, 1800; not before every election,
however.
26 [Boston, Mass.] *New England Palladium*, May 8, 1804.

In little New England towns and villages, Federalists introduced mass meetings for the first time, sometimes with an embarrassed explanation that such measures were necessary to combat the spirit of Jacobinism. Thus, in Portland, Maine, a "Federal caucus" was announced in the following way: "It being discovered that the democrats had held a *secret* caucus in order to make arrangements to secure a greater number of votes for their favorites, the Federal Republicans felt themselves under a necessity of assembling in their own defence. Accordingly they met on Saturday evening to the number of about 300." After 1800, many meetings of this sort were introduced by Federalists from Maine to North Carolina.[27]

At first, these Federalist meetings were openly controlled by a few leaders, and consequently the butt of Republican satire:

FEDERAL CAUCUS
On the state of the nation.

GENERAL THUNDER took the chair.
MR. TIMID asked if it would not be best to appoint a chairman by ballot.

[27] [Boston, Mass.] *New England Palladium*, Apr. 6, 1804; for the introduction and expansion of the mass meeting by Federalists in other parts of the country, see, for New Hampshire, *Portsmouth Oracle*, Mar. 25, 1809; [Portsmouth, N.H.] *New Hampshire Gazette*, Sep. 11, 1804; [Walpole, N.H.] *Political Observatory*, Apr. 21, Aug. 18; 1804; for Vermont see [Windsor, Vt.] *Vermont Journal*, Mar. 17, 1806; [Windsor, Vt.] *Washingtonian*, May 18, 1812; for Massachusetts see [Salem, Mass.] *Register*, Feb. 28, Mar. 28, 1805; [Worcester, Mass.] *National Aegis*, Nov. 19, 1806, Dec. 25, 1816; [Boston, Mass.] *New England Palladium*, Apr. 1, May 10, Nov. 4, 1808; Mar. 5, 14, 26, 1809; Apr. 26, Sep. 17, 1811; July 14, Nov. 10, 1812; Mar. 5, 30, 1813; Apr. 1, 1814; "Extraordinary Gazette," Apr. 7, 1817, in Broadsides, New York Public Library; for Connecticut see [Hartford, Conn.] *Connecticut Courant*, June 8, 1803; for Rhode Island see *Newport Mercury*; July 30, 1808; [Providence, R.I.] *Columbian Phoenix*, July 9, 1808; for New York see broadside dated Jan. 28, 1801, in Broadsides, Library of Congress; [New York, N.Y.] *Evening Post*, Apr. 16, 23, 26, Nov. 8, 1803; Oct. 11, 1806; Mar. 24, Apr. 8, 1808; Feb. 14, Apr. 10, 14, 16, 1810; [Albany, N.Y.] *Balance*, Feb. 6, 16, Apr. 24, 1810; [Hudson, N.Y.] *Northern Whig*, Jan. 30, Feb. 15, Mar. 29, Apr. 12, May 4, 1810; for New Jersey see [Boston, Mass.] *New England Palladium*, Sep. 15, 21, 1808; Sep. 21, 1813; [Trenton, N.J.] *Federalist*, Aug. 26, 1811, Aug. 24, Sep. 14, 1807; Aug. 1, 15, 1808; May 18, June 8, July 20, 27, 1812; Fee, *Aristocracy to Democracy in N.J.*, pp. 174–75, 179–82, 188–89; for Pennsylvania, see *Pittsburgh Gazette*, Apr. 19, 1809; [Phila., Pa.] *Gazette of the United States*, July 29, Sep. 15, 17, 18, 1800, Aug. 20, 1801, Feb. 2, 10, 11, 13, 1809; Philip Shriver Klein, "Early Lancaster County Politics," *Pennsylvania History*, III (1936), 98–114; for Delaware see [Boston, Mass.] *New England Palladium*, Oct. 29, 1813; Munroe, *Federalist Delaware*, pp. 231–238; for Maryland see *Frederick-town Herald*, July 3, 1802, Aug. 27, Sep. 3, 17, 24, 1803; [Annapolis, Md.] *Maryland Gazette*, Aug. 20, Oct. 1, 1812, Sep. 29, 1814; Aug. 24, 1815; May 16, 30, 1816; Aug. 26, Sep. 16, 1819; [Baltimore, Md.] *Federal Republican*, Aug. 9, 1809; July 18, 1811; [Easton, Md.] *People's Monitor*, July 15, 1815; [Georgetown, Md.] *Federal Republican*, July 26, 1813, Aug. 12, 1815; for Virginia see *Martinsburgh Gazette*, Mar. 27, 1812, Ambler, *Sectionalism in Virginia*, pp. 90–94; for North Carolina see Alfred Moore, Jr. to John Haywood, Jan. 23, 1800, in Haywood Papers, North Carolina State Department of Archives and History, Raleigh, N.C.

GENERAL THUNDER Damn *ballots*. I'll be chairman without gentlemen, giving you that trouble. *Loud Applause*.[28]

The "nomination" of candidates in mass meetings, both Republican and Federalist, was often a sham, so transparently fraudulent that even the feeblest intelligence could penetrate it. As a consequence, more elaborate deceptions were developed. Mass meetings became "conventions," first in name and then in fact.[29] Nominating committees were "appointed" by these meetings and supposedly responsible to them.

Also, meetings of Federalists multiplied rapidly on local levels, in part because large "risings" were so obviously fraudulent. In Salem, for example, a Republican noted in 1809 that "general caucuses [meetings] seem to have lost their reputation, and have yielded to ward and other sub-divisions. In this way, conversation is personal and the disposition of citizens is known."[30] But ward and district meetings were supplements rather than substitutes for great mass meetings, which gradually grew greater. In 1808, the Boston Grand Caucus was attended by no less than four thousand Federalists![31] At a "New Hampshire rising" in 1812, two thousand spectators arrived in 500 vehicles to hear Federalist orators, including the "Godlike" Daniel Webster, "harangue" them from an open stage built specially for the purpose.[32]

The Federalists always sought to attract "the most respectable citizens of the community" to their meetings, but soon they were issuing specific invitations to less distinguished citizens. The New York Federalists arranged a meeting specially for sailors, riggers, "and others connected with commerce."[33]

The gentlemen of the old school did not at first participate in significant numbers in the systematized electioneering of their younger colleagues; but gradually they began to join in. Gouverneur Morris noted in 1809 that he had gone "for the first time in my life, to attend a popular meeting in my county." The year before, a Federalist editor

[28] [Frederick-town, Md.] *Hornet*, Aug. 9, 1803.

[29] [Boston, Mass.] *New England Palladium*, Apr. 2, 1813; the difference between a mass meeting and a nominating convention, although clear in theory, was often blurred in practice. The mass meeting gradually merged into the nominating convention.

[30] Bentley, *Diary*, III, 421.

[31] [Boston, Mass.] *New England Palladium*, July 31, 1808.

[32] *Ibid.*, Aug. 11, 1812; see also [Baltimore, Md.] *North American*, Sep. 5, 1808.

[33] [New York, N. Y.] *Evening Post*, Apr. 8, 1808; see also ibid., Apr. 14, 1810; and Eugene S. Ferguson, *Truxtun of the Constellation, The Life of Commodore Thomas Truxtun, U. S. Navy, 1755–1822* (Baltimore, 1956), p. 253; [Boston, Mass.] *New England Palladium*, May 8, 1804; earlier meetings were arranged by Federalists to consider Jay's Treaty in 1795 and 1796 in which some of the old-school gentlemen endeavored to rally "the respectable people," the "principal merchants," "the sober and discreet people"; George Cabot to Oliver Wolcott, Aug. 13, 1795, in Lodge, *Cabot*, p. 84; Kurtz, *Presidency of John Adams*, pp. 59–77, misses the essential distinction between such efforts as these to rally the opinion of "the best people" and the Jeffersonian and younger Federalists' concern with public opinion generally.

in Pennsylvania noted that at a mass meeting he noticed "the hoary heads of venerable freemen, some of whom had not attended a publick meeting in twenty years." From South Carolina, in 1800, a young Federalist reported that "all the elderly men of high character whose health will allow them . . . will come out efficiently at the election," after having been prevailed upon to do so.[34]

The old school gentlemen seem at times to have been something of a burden upon the young men who were trying to keep their party together and to keep the people with them. One elderly Pennsylvania gentleman, Charles Biddle, was a perpetual thorn in their flesh. In 1812, he was elected chairman of a meeting in Philadelphia, and candidly described his own performance: "As soon as I mentioned that we were ready for business, and requested whoever had given notice to come forward with his plan for association, immediately a little, dark-looking foreigner came forward, and, with much ceremony, handed me a paper which he begged should be read." It was a denunciation of Great Britain, and a patriotic paean to "our beloved country." Mr. Biddle continued, "It provoked me to hear a fellow lately come among us talk of 'our beloved country.' After reading them myself I put them in my pocket, telling him, with a look of contempt, that it was not the intention of the meeting to enter into such resolutions. . . . He appeared much mortified, but retired without saying anything."[35]

Jeffersonians supplemented their mass meetings with barbecues.[36] These the Federalists also sponsored, after 1800, in competition with their opponents. A proper barbecue was a costly affair. The Federalists' chronic shortage of funds sometimes crippled early efforts. In Maryland, for example, they sponsored a barbecue during the campaign of 1803 but, lacking a war chest, were forced to charge three shillings admission. Many voters who had grown accustomed to Republican largesse arrived without money in their pockets and were ignominiously turned away. A Republican editor had a field day. The dinner reportedly consisted of "eight fish, a poor grinning pig, a fattish lamb, a piece of middling of bacon, six inches square, with some boiled oysters."[37]

Similarly, in Salem, Massachusetts, the Federalists financed a public dinner by dividing their guests into three groups according to wealth,

[34] Gouverneur Morris to Jeremiah Mason, Mar. 3, 1809, in Morris Papers, Library of Congress; [Philadelphia, Pa.] *Gazette of the United States*, Apr. 27, 1808; Henry W. De Saussure to John Rutledge, Jr., Aug. 14, 1800, in Rutledge Papers, Southern Hist. Coll., Univ. of N. C.

[35] The low "fellow" happened to be James Puglia, an erudite Italian gentleman who was Mr. Biddle's superior, not merely in manners, but in intellect as well; Charles Biddle, *Autobiography* (Philadelphia, 1883), p. 336; see also ibid., pp. 329, 330, 339.

[36] Fisher Ames referred to Republicans generally as "ox-eating fools;" see Ames, *Works*, II, 206.

[37] [Easton, Md.] *Star*, Sep. 13, 1803.

and requiring some to pay sixpence, others five, and still others three and a half. A Republican noted in his diary that "it gave opportunity to laugh at such men who felt small in the last class. The populace called it Nobles, gentry and commons."[38]

The increasing volume of Federalist affairs after 1804 suggests that the young men of the party succeeded in organizing a party exchequer. In the Chesapeake country, they sponsored "turtle dinners" and "oyster roasts." On the New England coast, they invited the voters to fish fries and clambakes. Although barbecues were most common in the southern states, they were a part of Federalist campaigns in all states, even in that "land of steady habits" Connecticut. During the difficult year of the Great Embargo, barbecues were replaced by "soup houses," which a Republican described as "an electioneering shop to make federal voters."[39]

It is difficult at this late date to recover the flavor of political barbecues in the early Republic. "Electioneering Cookery" was itself a fine art.[40] Many hours before the event, "a pig or shoate" was placed "over a hole with a fire in it, split up so as not to cut through the skin of the back, through which the animal was roasted, and kept continually basted till it was done, when it became extremely delicate eating."[41]

The primary purpose of a barbecue or a fish feast or a turtle dinner was not merely to bribe the voters with a good meal and a gay afternoon, but to expose them to political propaganda. Before, during, and after the dinner, the assembled citizenry were forced to bear, with varying degrees of patience, an astonishing volume of "stump" oratory.[42]

The Federalists appear to have had difficulty mastering the strange art of "forensic degladiation," as one of them called it.[43] At first they were sometimes awkward and ineffectual in their appeals to the people. In 1803, the young Federalist Roger Brooke Taney made himself the laughing stock of western Maryland by coming to Republican barbe-

---

[38] Bentley, *Diary*, (July 28, 1808), III, 378.

[39] [Frederick-town, Md.] *Herald*, Sep. 17, 24, 1803; [Baltimore, Md.] *Federal Republican*, Oct. 6, 1809, Sep. 25, 1811; June 30, 1813; [Easton, Md.] *People's Monitor*, July 29, 1815; *Martinsburgh Gazette*, Sep. 11, 1812. A way to avoid the necessity of fund raising was to levy a contribution in goods and services upon each Federalist household—a brace of fowl from one, a round of beef from another, a ham or pig from a third, a dish of pickled beets from a fourth; Resolution, dated Oct. 5, 1810, for a dinner in Abingdon, Virginia, in Campbell Papers, Duke University Library; [Annapolis, Md.] *Maryland Gazette*, Oct. 13, 1814; [Boston, Mass.] *New England Palladium*, Mar. 3, 1815.

[40] Charles Goldsborough to Harmanus Bleecker, Apr. 27, 1813, Harriet Langdon Rice, *Harmanus Bleecker, An Albany Dutchman* (Albany, 1924), pp. 29–36.

[41] Richard Beale Davis, ed., *Augustus J. Foster, Jeffersonian America* (San Marino, Calif., 1954), pp. 203–204.

[42] For use of "stump" in this context see [Baltimore, Md.] *Federal Republican*, Oct. 7, 1809; John Fisher to Caesar Rodney, Sep. 7, 1804, in Fisher Papers, New York Hist. Soc.; Charles Fenton Mercer to John Francis Mercer, Oct. 12, 1810, in Mercer Papers, Virginia Historical Society.

[43] [Baltimore, Md.] *Federal Republican*, Oct. 7, 1809.

cues and bleating, "I am a *Republican!* A *true* Republican. My name is *Taney*—and now won't *you*—my *dear* dear fellow, won't *you* vote for me?"[44] At first, too, some of the young Federalist stump speakers addressed themselves to "the understanding and not to the passions of the audience." But it was not long before they learned the value of a choice *ad hominem* or a sly innuendo.[45]

The flavor of old-time stump speaking survives in an enthusiastic eye-witness account of an oration by a past master of the art, the young Federalist John Carlyle Herbert, of Anne Arundel County, Maryland. A "splendid and profuse" barbecue had been carefully prepared as a setting for Mr. Herbert's extraordinary talents. The spectator noted:

Immediately after dinner, Mr. John C. Herbert rose and addressed the people, in an animated speech, teeming with the most splendid declamation and poignant invective against the character of general Samuel Smith. His imagination was vivid, his style chaste and nervous, and his action and manner graceful and fascinating. He drew a glowing and highly finished picture of the private and political character of the General and deliniated each feature with the most accurate precision. He saw "his corruption and venality through the darkness beam, withdrew the veil, and gave them light in form so hideous, that even his basest friends affrighted tremble," tracing him step by step, well ripened to that maturity of depravity after which the worst examples cease to be contagious." . . . His speech was received with every mark of approbation by the people; they returned repeated huzzas.[46]

Stump oratory was, to say the least, uninhibited. In the backcountry, when one's opponent wasn't within hearing, or when the campaign was nearly at an end and there was no time for rebuttal, political speakers of both parties would hesitate at nothing. In the southern states, it was not uncommon for a speaker to accuse his absent antagonist of being at that very moment at the head of a slave rebellion.[47] In New England, a Republican said of the Federalists, "They advocated the Boston Massacre,— they approve the sanguinary KILLING OF AMERICAN SEAMEN. They

44 Carl Brent Swisher, *Roger B. Taney*. (New York, 1935), p. 46.

45 [Boston, Mass.] *New England Palladium*, Apr. 6, 1804; William Plumer to Jeremiah Smith, Mar. 10, 1801, in Plumer Papers, Library of Congress; see also the account of a Federalist electioneering canvass in Franklin County, Kentucky; Lexington *Kentucky Gazette*, 2 July, 14 Aug. 1810.

46 [Baltimore Md.] *Federal Republican*, Oct. 7, 1809; see also the following account of a Federalist "grand caucus" in Massachusetts: "Several gentlemen addressed the meeting in warm and animated speeches; in which the wretched effects of the Jeffersonian system of Embargo, Gun boats, Torpedoes, Salt Mountains and Horned Frogs—the French *liberty* of conscription, chains and dungeons, so much admired by the Democrats—were contrasted with effect, with the federal policy of Free Commerce, an efficient system of protection, a full Treasury and general prosperity—all with that true, rational and broad-bottomed liberty which our fathers fought for and transmitted to their posterity." Mar. 30, 1810, in Broadsides, American Antiquarian Society.

47 Foster, *Jeffersonian America*, p. 203.

thirst for the blood of Republicans."[48] By the time an accusation of this sort could be met, the election was over and the damage was done. In 1815, Robert Goodloe Harper was reported to be on the stump in Anne Arundel County, accusing Madison of being about to sign a treaty with the British specifically authorizing impressment—this after the war was over![49] If an opponent happened to be in the crowd, the speaker sometimes was forced to put his accusations to the test, by submitting to a fist fight or a foot race![50]

Try as they might, the young Federalists were probably never able to equal in volume the electioneering of their opponents. On the same day that John C. Herbert spoke to a Federalist gathering in Maryland, Jeffersonians sponsored no fewer than nine barbecues in the same county![51] About the same time, a busy young Federalist in another Maryland county reported, "We have had two barbecues, one last Saturday, where we had about 120 persons, and but three that were against us. Next Saturday I am to have a fish feast in a part of the county where deception has made the greatest havoc. The result I will inform you of. I have appointments in different parts of the County, two for every week . . . [torn] treating and talking."[52] The Republicans made use of many events for the purpose of attracting attention to their candidates. In the southern states, logrolling and cornshucking were particular favorites.[53] But Federalists could be resourceful, too. In Connecticut they attracted crowds by means of plowing matches, and also by a peculiar affair in which the men of New Haven County came together and built, as quickly as possible, an octagonal shepherd's house, as a test of skill with ax and adze.[54]

A measure of the expansion of electioneering activity by the Federalists after 1800 was the concern of their competitors. "Alarm! Alarm! Alarm!," cried a Republican broadside which described the "extraordinary and unparalleled exertions" of Federal agents in New York.[55] In the same state in 1809, a Republican declared that "there never was

[48] "National Honor," Apr. 4, 1808, in Broadsides, American Antiquarian Society; for an unrivalled example of pure character assassination, see also, from a York County, Pennsylvania, election of 1803, "Old Fritz Daily until the Election," in Broadsides, American Antiquarian Society.

[49] [Baltimore, Md.] Patriot. Sep. 30, Oct. 2, 1815.

[50] This was in Virginia. See [Boston, Mass.] New England Palladium, Oct. 23, 1807.

[51] [Baltimore, Md.] Federal Republican, Oct. 7, 1809.

[52] John Murray to Jacob Wagner, Aug. 23, 1811, in McHenry Papers, Library of Congress.

[53] William Barry Grove to William Gaston, July 8, 1813, in Gaston Papers, Southern Hist. Coll., Univ. of N. C.

[54] [Boston, Mass.] New England Palladium, July 10, 1810.

[55] "Alarm! Alarm! Alarm!" n.p., n.d. [1804?], in Broadsides, New York Public Library.

greater exertions made by the Federalists throughout the state, than in the time just past."[56] In 1812, a Republican completed the circle by denouncing Federal meetings as "seditious and jacobinical!"[57]

During the first fifteen years of the new century, the "season of electioneering" also grew larger. In Maryland, for example, the Federalist campaign of 1800 did not begin until the summer; by 1815 it was underway in April; in 1816, electioneering began in January![58]

Every holiday became a party celebration. It was, indeed, the rivalry between Federalists and Republicans after 1800 which helped to make the Fourth of July the event that it is today. During the 1790s Independence Day had been observed intermittently at best.[59] After 1800, however, the two parties even in the most insignificant hamlets sponsored separate celebrations which became ever more elaborate.[60] They became all-day affairs, with speeches, odes, dinners, toasts, parades, fireworks, etc. Music and songs were written specially for each occasion, and party funds were expended with a reckless and prodigal hand.[61]

Independence Day was not the only celebration which the Federalists used in a partisan manner. Their exploitation of Washington's birthday deserves a chapter in itself.[62] Local holidays also provided excuses for party celebrations—Forefather's Day in Massachusetts, Evacuation Day in New York, and in Maryland after 1814, Defender's Day. The death of

[56] Stephen Allen to B. F. Thompson, May 5, 1809, in Stephen Allen Papers, New York Hist. Soc.; see also E. Baldwin to S. Baldwin, Apr. 24, 1811, in Baldwin Papers, Yale University; Robinson, *Jeff. Dem. in N. Eng.*, p. 91; [Annapolis, Md.] *Maryland Gazette*, Apr. 11, 1816; Bentley, *Diary*, III, 221 (Apr. 1, 1806); [Wilmington, Del.] *Mirror of the Times*, Sep. 1, 1804; [Boston, Mass.] *Patriot*, Feb. 12, 1814.

[57] [Elizabethtown, N. J.] *New Jersey Journal*, Oct. 27, 1812; [Chillicothe, O.] *Supporter*, Feb. 22, 1809; [Portland, Me.] *Eastern Argus*, Mar. 30, 1804.

[58] [Annapolis, Md.] *Maryland Gazette*, Apr. 20, 1815.

[59] Bentley, *Diary*, II, 191, 276 (July 4, 1796, July 11, 1798).

[60] Ibid., III, 75 (June 27, 1804).

[61] [Boston, Mass.] *New England Palladium*, July 6, 1810; "Fourth of July," n. d. [c. 1812?] Saltonstall Papers, Mass. Hist. Soc. A measure of the Federalists' extravagance and of their improved fiscal capabilities, is a list of fireworks which they promised to set off on July 4, 1810, in Boston:

300 ¼ pound rockets.
100 ½ pound do.
12 *Paper Shells*, or *Balloons*, loaded with gold rain and variegated stars.
2 large brilliant *Suns*, four feet in diameter, charged with 54 cases brilliant fire, with a transparent face, illuminated by a verticle wheel in the centre.
2 large Pyramid Chinese *Flower Pots*, which change to fifteen *Beehives*, in miniature.
2 Diamond Pieces.
2 Columbian Pine Trees.
2 Spiral or double-coned Wheels.
3 Small verticle wheels.
2 Plural Wheels.
2 Horizontal Wheels.
3 Beehives containing 12 doz. Serpents each.
[Boston, Mass.] *New England Palladium*, June 26, 1810.

[62] See below, ch. VI.

notable old-school gentlemen was always deemed sufficient reason for a procession by young Federalists (and perhaps for rejoicing as well). The funeral of Fisher Ames, which his Jeffersonian brother refused to attend, was a particularly spectacular affair. At least a thousand people walked behind the mahogany casket through the streets of Boston.[63]

Important events in Europe were also commemorated. When Napoleon —the only man the Federalists disliked more than Jefferson—retreated from Moscow with his disintegrating army, Federalists throughout the Union sponsored appropriate "Solemnities." In Boston there was a dinner for two thousand, an address by the Russian consul, a specially written oratorio performed by two hundred musicians, and an illumination featuring transparencies of "Moscow in Flames" and of Czar Alexander.[64] Great events in America were not overlooked, either. In January 1809, Massachusetts Federalists celebrated the Enforcement Act, which was designed to make the Embargo more effective, with an elaborate "mock-Funeral" for American liberty.[65]

Electioneering did not come to an end at the elections. There was a steady growth of what might be called post-electioneering. In many parts of the country, results were never known for several days. It was customary, therefore, for both parties to celebrate a victory on election night. In western Maryland "the usual mode of merry-making and rational rejoicing" was a riotous torchlight parade through the chill autumn dusk.[66]

4

The young Federalists understood that public meetings, barbecues, processions, festivals, political funerals, and other public celebrations were not sufficient in themselves to insure the success of a campaign. It was necessary for the party to go directly after the people, to seek out each Federalist voter at his hearthside. This was the primary task of local committees whose inception was discussed in the last chapter.

The detailed instructions and documents of Federalist committees in Connecticut in the Simeon Baldwin Papers shed much light upon the means employed by these busy little cells of federalism, and the energy, efficiency and thoroughness with which they operated. Town committees were responsible for maintaining lists of all freemen in their neighborhoods. Records were kept of their attendance at elections.[67] All freemen who were not confirmed Jeffersonians were divided into groups

---

63 [Boston, Mass.] *New England Palladium*, July 8, 1808.

64 Ibid., Mar. 30, 1813.

65 Ibid., Jan. 7, 1809.

66 [Georgetown, Md.] *Federal Republican*, Oct. 11, 1813.

67 See list without title or date given by C. C. Smith to the Mass. Hist. Soc., Apr. 28, 1808, in Miscellaneous Bound Manuscripts, Mass. Hist. Soc.; see also circular dated Jan. 1805 in Simeon Baldwin Papers, Yale Univ. Library.

of eight to ten each, and were personally visited by a member of the Federalist town committee or one of the "most active, sensible, and judicious men" in the town.[68] County committees constantly exhorted their town committees to expand their efforts in extravagant language. One such message concluded, "The great object will be to get out the Freemen, and keep them out until the meeting is over. I will only add God save the Commonwealth."[69]

The Federalist town committees were instructed to "pay particular attention to young men that are coming upon the stage, that they may be early engaged on the side of truth and sound principles."[70] Each Federalist freeman was to receive a list of nominees, so that they might all "vote alike."[71] Sometimes the Federalists put symbols on their tickets, as the Republicans had done—the arms of the union by the Federalists, and a shipwreck by the Republicans.[72]

Federalists in other parts of the union seem to have been as active as those in Connecticut. Morison tells us that in Boston "vigilant ward committees made life miserable for stay-at-homes."[73] In western Massachusetts, a leading Federalist politician, Henry Van Schaak, concluded a political letter somewhat abruptly with the following apology, "I write in great haste as my carriage is waiting. You will remember that my concern is business and not elegance. I shall go to every nook in the county where I can do the best good."[74] In New York City, during the election of 1809, "every elector was served with a letter—enclosing a federal ticket, requesting him in polite terms to promote the federal candidates."[75] The door-to-door campaigns of Federalist vigilance committees in Delaware were equally thorough. A Democratic editor immortalized one committeeman, "a big man with a cocked hat," who "was seen taking a squint over the *window curtains*, perhaps after *federal recruits!*"[76] Republicans were sarcastic about these "once a year calls."[77]

[68] Circulars dated Jan. 1805, Aug. 21, 1806, in Simeon Baldwin Papers, Yale Univ. Library; see also deposition of David Page in the [Concord, N. H.] *New Hampshire Patriot*, May 7, June 21, 1814.

[69] Theodore Dwight to Simeon Baldwin, Aug. 21, 1806, in Baldwin Papers, Yale Univ. Library.

[70] Ibid.

[71] Ibid.

[72] Bentley, *Diary*, III, 349 (Mar. 14, 1808).

[73] Morison, *Otis*, I, 296.

[74] Henry Van Schaack to William Sullivan, Apr. 26, 1811, Columbia Univ. Coll., Columbia Univ. Library; for the activity of federal "agents of discord" in the "farthest counties" of Maine, see [Portland, Me.] *Eastern Argus*, Nov. 16, 1804, Mar. 26, 1812; [Boston, Mass.] *Patriot*, Feb. 12, 1814; for Essex County, see "Federal Meeting," May 12, 1809, in Broadsides, American Antiquarian Society.

[75] Stephen Allen to B. F. Thompson, May 5, 1809, in Stephen Allen Papers, New York Hist. Soc.

[76] [Wilmington, Del.] *Mirror of the Times*, Sep. 29, 1804.

[77] "New-Castle federal *sociability* commenced with the *first* instant, as is usual about *this time of year*, and more especially previous to *Important Elections*, and arose to that *alarming height* before the election of the *fifteenth*, that the Indus-

Federalists in many states made use of "runners," "riders," or vote distributors," "dapper young gentlemen,"[78] or "persons not uniformly of the first consequence,"[79] whose task it was to see that every voter had a copy of the party ticket. John Carlyle Herbert of Maryland carefully instructed a neophyte Federalist in the tricks of the trade. "Remember, my good friend," he wrote, "that everything depends upon your retaining in all the districts a *Pay* if necessary—riders and agents who ought to be constables or young men aspiring to office—to mix with the people, circulate hand bills and papers, and if necessary to apply occasional pecuniary aid to political friends in need."[80] The Federalist leaders in Salem, Massachusetts, had 120 vote distributors working, thirty in each ward in 1803.[81]

Candidates themselves went out among the people shaking the horny hands of the laborers, inquiring after families they had never seen, listening patiently to questions and grievances, discussing issues and personalities. Federalists complained bitterly of this arduous and degrading toil, but they performed it nonetheless.[82] Even Federalist candidates for the highest offices sometimes went out among the people. In 1808, James Ross, the Federalist candidate for the Pennsylvania governorship "made something of an electioneering tour in his own behalf." He spent two months on the one-week journey from Pittsburgh to Philadelphia, meeting people and making promises. Earlier in his career, Ross had sought to abolish religious tests and was charged with "atheism" by his opponents. In 1808, therefore, he made a special effort to "exhibit himself in places of worship where he has friends to introduce him."[83]

Get-out-and-vote campaigns are not a recent development in American politics. Appeals of this kind appeared regularly in Federalist papers by 1816. "Rhode Island EXPECTS EVERY MAN TO DO HIS DUTY,"

---

trious Mechanics of the town were absolutely *interrupted* in their business by frequent calls from the *Feds.* with an invitation to go to the *General Rendezvous*, opposite the *Court House* and try a *Glass of Wine*, or a little *Brandy & Water*"; [Wilmington, Del.] *Mirror of the Times*, Sep. 22, 1804.

[78] [Newport, R. I.] *Mercury*, June 27, 1800.

[79] Bentley, *Diary*, III, 17; see also [Concord, N. H.] *Courier of New Hampshire*, Mar. 3, 1803; [Windsor, Vt.] *Washingtonian*, Aug. 16, 1813.

[80] John Carlyle Herbert to Vergil Maxcy, Apr. 11, 1816, in Galloway-Maxcy-Markoe Papers, Library of Congress.

[81] Bentley, *Diary*, III, 17.

[82] Archibald D. Murphey to wife, July 24, 1814, in *Murphey Papers*, I, 73; "To the Public," n.d. [1808], in Broadsides, Md. Hist. Soc.

[83] Higginbotham, *The Keystone in the Democratic Arch*, p. 155; in 1800 John Adams himself went electioneering for the presidency after he was attacked by many old-school Federalist leaders; Kurtz, *Presidency of John Adams*, pp. 398–399; [Wilkesbarre, Pa.] *Luzerne County Federalist*, July 29, 1808; see also the description of "Jemmy Broom delivering a long speech in Brandywine hundred [Del.] in favor of federalism and of putting *himself* in the legislature" in [Wilmington, Del.] *Mirror of the Times*, Sep. 5, 1804.

wrote a "Federal Republican" in 1808.[84] In Maryland, a Federalist news-paperman wrote, "Federalists of Maryland, remember your duty! Don't you stay at home folding your arms, and yawning, with a segar in your hands, in sloth and lethargy, while the jacobins are cutting up your stage and casting it piece-meal to be devoured by the blood-hounds of their faction! No! Exert yourselves, each, as if you had your plantation and negroes at stake. . . ."[85] Federalist leaders sought to make the process of voting as convenient and easy as possible. In Salem, Massachusetts, in 1813, they spent no less than eight hundred dollars on horses and car-riages to transport electors to the polls.[86]

There was a considerable measure of corruption in Federalist elec-tioneering efforts. In 1816, when times were hard, John Carlyle Herbert advised a friend, "The plan of the campaign in Anne Arundel [County] should differ from that of last year. Private benefactions will do more good amongst the people than public feasts. This is a year of scarcity and much may be done by relieving the wants of certain persons who are pressed by the sheriff, or otherwise in need. A look at the execution docket would give you the information needed."[87]

A frequent practice was the shifting of voters from district to district as the need existed. In counties where transient farm laborers were com-mon this stratagem was difficult to detect, but in sleepy little towns like Annapolis, Maryland, it was hard to hide. Six months before the election of 1816 (the length of residence requirements in Maryland) a crowd of about forty disreputable characters suddenly appeared in the Federal-ist taverns, with no visible means of support. Forty men could swing the balance in Annapolis, where only 252 votes had been cast in 1812. The Republicans raised a great cry and forced the Federalists to withdraw their "pensioners." In nearby Prince George's County, John Carlyle Herbert was shocked by the conduct of his friends. "The affair at An-napolis," he wrote, "was certainly confided to very indiscreet managers. Never did anything which might have been prudently conducted arrive at so ridiculous a conclusion."[88]

Sometimes the old methods of coercion were resorted to. Charles Carroll of Carrollton openly pressured his employees into voting for Federalist candidates. In 1806, he wrote helpfully to a Federalist

[84] [Newport, R. I.] *Mercury*, Aug. 27, 1808; a typical exhortation was that of a Federalist meeting in Salem, Mass., May 12, 1809: "*Let it be remembered*, that if only one of the many Federalists who absented themselves from the meeting last year had voted, at least one of the Federal Candidates would have been chosen, and let this recollection induce every man to attend this year"; in Broadsides, Amer-ican Antiquarian Society.

[85] [Georgetown, Md.] *Federal Republican*, Aug. 24, 1815.

[86] Bentley, *Diary*, IV, 162.

[87] John Carlyle Herbert to Vergil Maxcy, Apr. 11, 1816, in Galloway-Maxcy-Markoe Papers, Library of Congress.

[88] Ibid.

candidate in Maryland, "I will speak to my manager and to my clerk and prevail upon them to vote for you and Col. Mercer, and to obtain as many votes for you both as electors of the Senate in this neighborhood as their influence and exertions can procure."[89]

Industry, ingenuity, and a none-too-strict sense of propriety characterized the young Federalists' adoption of electioneering techniques which had been used with such great effect against them by the Jeffersonians. Mass meetings, barbecues, stump speaking, festivals of many kinds, processions and parades, runners and riders, door-to-door canvassing, the distribution of tickets and ballots, electioneering tours by candidates, free transportation to the polls, outright bribery, and corruption of other kinds—all of these techniques and more were used by the young Federalists on a remarkably broad scale between 1800 and 1816. One particular electioneering device—also borrowed from the Jeffersonian Republicans—was used by the Federalists with great effect—secret political societies.

[89] Charles Carroll of Carrolltown to Horatio Ridout, Aug. 22, 1806, in Dreer Coll., Hist. Soc. of Pa.; "Two Letters of Charles Carroll of Carrollton," *Pennsylvania Magazine of History and Biography*, XXVIII (1904), 217; see also a somewhat similar incident in Delaware: "General Mitchell, on his way to the hundred election overtook one of the swinish multitude, trudging along, highly elated at the idea of the inestimable privilege he was about to exercise, and in a very imperious and arbitrary manner ordered him to go back, stating he had no right to a vote. . . . The honest rustic replied that he should make trial, and with uninterrupted pace pursued on"; [Wilmington, Del.] *Mirror of the Times*, Sep. 22, 1804.

VI

Federalists and the "French System of Fraternity": The Birth of the Washington Benevolent Societies

Much ill-use has been and will yet be made of secret societies.
I think with you that they should not be encouraged.
—JOHN JAY, 1799[1]

We must consider whether it be possible for us to succeed,
without, in some degree, employing the weapons which have
been employed against us.
—ALEXANDER HAMILTON, 1802[2]

Of all the political innovations which were exploited by the Jeffersonians, none was as loathsome to Federalists of the old school as semisecret fraternal organizations. Friends of order feared these "Democratic" or "Republican" societies as "the pioneers of revolution."[3] There were two distinct groups of Republican societies, two separate sequences of formation and growth.[4] The first began in 1790 and ended about 1795. It consisted of political associations founded during the first years of the French Revolution by its sympathizers, including more than a few young Federalists.[5] Most of these clubs disbanded within four or five years, their members disillusioned by the outbreak of the Terror, and discouraged by the disapproval of George Washington, who believed "self-created societies" were generally responsible for the spread of

---

[1] John Jay to Jedidiah Morse, Jan. 30, 1799, in Johnston, *Correspondence of Jay*, IV, 252–254.

[2] Alexander Hamilton to James A. Bayard, Apr. 1802, in Lodge, *Works of Hamilton*, X, 432–437.

[3] Simeon Holdfast [David Daggett], *Facts are Stubborn Things, or Nine Plain Questions to the People of Connecticut, with a Brief Reply to Each* (Hartford, 1803).

[4] It could be argued that there were actually three sequences, the first being the artisans' clubs before and during the Revolution—the Fellowship Societies, Wilkes Clubs, Mechanics Societies, the Sons of Liberty, and others; see Richard Walsh, *Charleston's Sons of Liberty* (Columbia, 1959), pp. 29–32, passim.

[5] Robert Goodloe Harper rose to the vice-presidency of Charleston's French Patriotic Society in 1792–93; see E. S. Thomas, *Reminiscences of the Last Sixty-Five Years*, 2 vols. (Hartford, 1840), I, 32; C. Fraser, *Reminiscences of Charleston* (Charleston, 1854), p. 42.

the spirit of faction during his administration and particularly to blame for the Whiskey Rebellion.[6]

During the late 1790s, however, a second group of political fraternities began to appear. Some were purely political in organization and intent, and called themselves "Republican Societies" or "Friends of the People." They appear to have been remarkably widespread—in New Jersey, Federalists complained that "Democratic Associations" had formed in six counties.[7] Their primary purpose seems to have been to encourage "friends of the people" to be friends of Thomas Jefferson in particular. A Republican association in Norfolk County, Massachusetts, for example, awarded a medal to the only Jeffersonian voter in a solidly Federalist town.[8]

Other Jeffersonian associations combined politics with benevolence and mutual financial aid, as did the Hibernian Provident Society of New York City and the St. Patrick's Benevolent Society of Philadelphia. These groups were in some instances the forerunners of insurance companies. All members contributed to a general fund from which the needy could draw.[9]

Of all Jeffersonian associations the most successful were the Tammany Societies. The origins of these famous clubs reached far back into the colonial past. They were originally social, or benevolent fraternities which did not concern themselves with politics. But during the 1790s Republicans gradually gained control over the Tammany Society of New York, drove out the Federalists, and made it an appendage of their party.[10]

[6] For a general discussion see Eugene Perry Link, *Democratic Republican Societies, 1790–1800* (New York, 1942); William Miller, "First Fruits of Republican Organization; Political Aspects of the Congressional Election of 1794," *Pennsylvania Magazine of History and Biography*, LXIII (1939), 118–143; interprets these societies as the formal machinery of the Jeffersonian movement; a contrasting and more persuasive interpretation may be found in Cunningham, *Jeffersonian Republicans*, pp. 62–66, which pictures them as auxiliaries to the main party organization.

[7] *Serious Considerations addressed to the Electors of New Jersey concerning the choice of members of the Legislature for the Ensuing Year* (1803); see also [Jno?] Williams to John Haywood, Nov. 7, 1800, in Haywood Papers, Southern Hist. Coll., Univ. of N. C.; broadside dated Apr. 14, 1804, in Broadsides, Library of Congress; [Daggett], *Facts are Stubborn Things*; [Northumberland, Pa.] *Republican Argus*, July 26, 1805; [New York, N. Y.] *Evening Post*, July 25, 1805; recent historians of the Jeffersonian movement have largely ignored this second group of Republican societies; see Link, *Democratic Republican Societies*, p. 15; Cunningham, *Jeffersonian Republicans*, p. 63; see also [Wilmington] *Mirror*, 5 Mar. 1800; [Phila.] *Aurora*, 1 Oct. 1800; [Amherst, N. H.] *Village Messenger*, 30 Aug. 1800.

[8] Bentley, *Diary*, III, 137.

[9] Broadside dtd. Apr. 14, 1804, Library of Congress; Higginbotham, *The Keystone in the Democratic Arch*, p. 215.

[10] See Tammany Society Papers, New York Public Library; Gustavus Myers, *The History of Tammany Hall*, 2d edn. (New York, 1917); William L. Utter,

Thereafter, Tammany societies spread rapidly through the northern states, from eastern New England to western Ohio, from the Canadian border to the banks of the Delaware. Wherever they appeared, the Sons of St. Tammany were enthusiastically Jeffersonian, an active and undisguised partisan undertaking. They were also an early manifestation of the taste for mummery and innocent merriment which has been a common and continuous feature of American life. On grand occasions, the "Tammannians" dressed as Indians and met in a "wigwam" for a "powwow." Their officers were sachems and sagamores, alanks, okemaws, mackawalaws and wiskinkies.[11]

Suspicious Federalists denounced the second wave of Jeffersonian societies in the same terms that Washington had used during the Whiskey Rebellion. A conservative French clergyman, the Abbé Barruel, had published a book which explained the French Revolution as an international conspiracy of Freemasons, and thus rendered all fraternal orders suspect.[12] Of the Hibernian Provident Society, a Federal meeting declared, "Such societies, when perverted from the purposes of their institution to the purposes of intrigue, are the very bane of the commonwealth."[13]

"Saint Tammany in Ohio; a Study in Frontier Politics," *Mississippi Valley Historical Review*, XV (1928), 321–340; Marcus D. Jernegan, "The Tammany Societies of Rhode Island," *Papers from the Historical Seminary of Brown University*, VIII (1897), 1–38; [Lexington, Ky.] *Gazette*, Oct. 16, 1815; and Cunningham, *Jeffersonian Republicans*, p. 181, which minimizes the role of the Tammany societies. His contention that they were not the backbone of Jeffersonian organization seems indisputable, but nevertheless they played an important role in the politics of many states.

[11] Jernegan, "The Tammany Societies of Rhode Island," pp. 12–13.

[12] Abbé Barruel, *Mémoires pour servir a l'histoire du jacobinisme*, 5 vols. (Hamburg, 1798); see Jacques Godechot, *La Grand Nation: L'Expansion Révolutionnaire de la France dans le Monde de 1789 à 1799*, 2 vols. (Paris, 1956), I, 19–22; Vernon Stauffer, *New England and the Bavarian Illuminati* (New York, 1918), pp. 103–142, 229–344; the suspicions of Jedidiah Morse notwithstanding, there is no evidence of a clear connection between American Freemasonry and either political party; see Leonard Chester to Ephraim Kirby, July 24, 1801, in Ephraim Kirby Papers, Duke University; there is also no evidence that the Order of the Cincinnati was politically active as a body.

[13] In 1803 a mass meeting in New Jersey denounced Republican clubs as dangerous and sinister. "A representative government is properly composed of electors and elected under the Constitutions," the meeting resolved. "These self-created societies are neither one nor the other, but political machines which fatal experience (nothwithstanding their fair professions) has proved to be the destroyers and the tyrants of the people"; *Serious Considerations*; see also [New Brunswick, N. J.] *Guardian*, Apr. 8, 1800; this is the earliest use of "political machine" in the modern sense which I have found; broadside dated Apr. 14, 1807, in Broadsides, Library of Congress; and John Jay to Jedidiah Morse, Jan. 30, 1799, in Johnston, *Correspondence of Jay*, IV, 252–254. A description of the Democratic Club of Hudson, N. Y., appears in Anna Bradbury, *History of the City of Hudson* (Hudson, 1908), p. 71. Its headquarters were a spare room in a store, where members gathered "round a red hot stove in an atmosphere blue with smoke, seated on old pine benches and wooden bottomed chairs with the dust and cobwebs of twenty years undisturbed on the shelves."

But as the Federalists suffered one defeat after another in the early years of the century, some of them began to have second thoughts about political societies. Alexander Hamilton was one. In a famous letter to James A. Bayard, one of the most interesting which this gifted correspondent ever wrote, he put forward an elaborate plan for the establishment of a nationwide Federalist "front" organization to be called the Christian Constitutional Society. In the name of Christ and the United States Constitution, this fraternal order was to rally the citizens of America to the cause of order.

Hamilton proposed that the Society should have a president and a national council, a subcouncil in every state, and "as many societies in each state as local circumstances may permit." The objects of the society would be three-fold:

1st. The diffusion of information. For this purpose, not only the newspapers but pamphlets must be largely employed, and to do this a fund must be created. Five dollars annually for eight years to be contributed by each member who can really afford it (taking care not to burthen less able brethren), may afford a competent fund for a competent term. It is essential to be able to disseminate *gratis* useful publications. Wherever it can be done and there is a press, clubs should be formed, to meet once a week, read the newspapers, and prepare essays, paragraphs, etc.

2nd. The use of all lawful means in *concert* [sic] to promote the election of *fit* men; a lively correspondence must be kept up between the different societies.

3rd. The promoting of institutions of a charitable and useful nature in the management of Federalists. The populous cities ought to be attended to. Perhaps it would be well to institute in such places—1st, societies for the relief of emigrants; 2d, academies, each with one professor, for instructing the different classes of mechanics. . . .[14]

Bayard praised the plan for its "great ingenuity," but thought it inadvisable and unnecessary. "An attempt at association organized into clubs on the part of the Federalists would revive a thousand jealousies now beginning to slumber," he declared. "Let us not be too impatient," Bayard cautioned, "our adversaries will soon demonstrate to the world the soundness of our doctrines and the imbecility and folly of their own."[15]

Whether or not Hamilton adumbrated his ideas to other Federalists, nothing came of them. When he died on July 12, 1804, the Christian Constitutional Society perished with him. But other men were beginning to think along the same lines. Washington's death, five years earlier, started in motion a sequence of events which ended in the growth of a network of Federalist clubs which closely resembled the Christian Con-

[14] Alexander Hamilton to James A. Bayard, Apr. 1802, Lodge, *Works of Hamilton*, X, 432.
[15] James A. Bayard to Alexander Hamilton, Apr. 25, 1802, Hamilton Papers, Library of Congress.

stitutional Society. On January 14, 1800, a month to the day after George Washington had died in his bed at Mount Vernon, a group of prominent Virginia gentlemen met at Gadsby's Tavern in Alexandria. Most of them had known Washington; many had known him well. To commemorate his name they decided to organize among themselves the "Washington Society of Alexandria." Whose idea it was is not recorded, but the energy belonged to John Carlyle Herbert, a young Federalist who has already appeared in this story. It was he who served in the crucial role of secretary at the society's inception.[16]

The constitution of the Washington Society of Alexandria began with an interesting defense of the principle of association which summed up the anti-individualist trend of Federalist thought: "As every effort of individual man, unaided by social co-operation, is comparatively weak and inefficient of the greatest moral and political ends, so particular objects of beneficence have been ever found to be advanced with most energy and effect by subordinate associations of men, pursuing sincerely, in concert, the attainment of their purpose."[17]

The constitution stipulated that the Washington Society should meet four times a year. Its anniversary, February 22, was to be observed with an oration and a solemn procession through the streets of Alexandria. Each member was to have a medal and a certificate of membership. The Society was also committed by its constitution to "aid and perpetuate certain charities which [Washington's] humane and munificent mind delighted to exercise." Among these was the "Washington Free School" to which the Society promised to donate two hundred dollars annually. Membership was by invitation only. The heavy dues, four dollars a year, suggest that only the "better sort" of people could have participated. Its first important celebration, February 22, 1800, was a rousing success.[18]

The Washington Society of Alexandria was the first and for several years the only society of its kind. Its direct political activities, at first, appear to have been minor. But it was composed of Federalists who were seeking to perpetuate the "wisdom" of Washington as "a Man and Citizen," and thereby indirectly served in the interests of federalism.[19] Other Federalists were anxious to capitalize upon the prestige and glory of the man whom they spoke of possessively as "our Washington."[20] "Should not all our YOUTH be taught to dwell on the name of WASHINGTON?" one of them asked piously.[21]

[16] William Buckner McGroarty, "The Washington Society of Alexandria," *Tyler's Quarterly Historical and Genealogical Magazine*, IX (1928), 146–159.
[17] Ibid., p. 152.
[18] Ibid., pp. 153–154.
[19] Ibid., p. 156.
[20] [New York] *Evening Post*, Mar. 29, 1808.
[21] [Philadelphia] *Gazette of the United States*, Feb. 19, 1808; "Teach your infant, in his cradle, to lisp the name of Washington"; *An Oration . . . pronounced at Windsor* (1814), p. 6.

The Federalists did indeed dwell on the name of Washington. To the "good old federal cause" he was perhaps more useful dead than alive. In 1804, four years after the birth of the Washington Society of Alexandria, Federalists in Maine made a direct effort to exploit the Washington legend for partisan purposes. One young Federalist in Augusta reported to Harrison Gray Otis that "we have not been idle in this vicinity in attempting to unite the Federalists." He reported that "a union is now effected of active and influential men belonging to the towns of Hallowell and Augusta, who have assumed the name of the Washington Association." A president and secretary were appointed, as well as a committee of six who were to communicate with "their friends in other towns" and to "receive communications from Boston."[22]

No other pro-Federalist Washington Associations are known to have appeared before 1808,[23] but in Philadelphia, New York, and Boston groups were beginning to form which called themselves "Young Federalists," and were similar to the Washington Association of Augusta, Maine, in everything but name. The "Young Federalists" of Boston helped out at election time by preparing handwritten tickets for voters,[24] and celebrated the Fourth of July in flamboyant fashion.[25]

During the hard times and political heats of the Great Embargo, the Federalist movement toward voluntary political association suddenly accelerated. Early in 1808 a group of young men in New York City decided to found a fraternal order which would combine the mummery of the Tammany Societies, the benevolent activities of the Hibernian Provident Society, the partisan enthusiasm of the Young Federalists, and the filiopietism of the Washington Society of Alexandria. The central figure was a twenty-two-year-old Federalist named Gulian Verplanck.[26]

[22] Benjamin Whitwell to Harrison Gray Otis, July 31, 1804, in Otis Papers, Mass. Hist. Soc.

[23] In Boston, a "Washington Society" founded in 1805 was Jeffersonian; see Washington Society Records, 1805–1821, Mass. Hist. Soc.

[24] [Boston] New England Palladium, May 13, 1806; for "Young Federalists" in New York, Philadelphia, Portland, and Newburyport, see John Wells to Richard Varick, July 3, 1799, in Varick Papers, New York Hist. Soc.; D. B. Ogden to William Meredith, Dec. 10, 1812, in Meredith Papers, Historical Society of Penna.; Portland Gazette, June 20, 1808; [Boston] Repertory, July 6, 1803.

[25] [Boston] New England Palladium, July 9, 1805, July 4, 10, 1806; some of these groups had begun to appear before 1800, see [Elizabethtown, N. J.] New Jersey Journal, May 7, 15, 1798; "Young Gentlemen of Boston" to Harrison Gray Otis, May 15, 1798, in Otis Papers, Mass. Hist. Soc.; other public Federalist fraternal groups included the "Anchor Club" of Philadelphia, the "Inscrutable Society" of Hanover, New Hampshire, the "Ugly Club" of Annapolis, Md., the "Society of Constitutional and Governmental Support" in Norfolk, the "Union Society" in Savannah, and the "Federalist Club" of Charleston, S. C.; Leo A. Bressler, "The Anchor Club, Defender of Federalism," Pennsylvania Magazine of History and Biography, LXXX (1956), p. 312; Wolfe, Jeff. Dem. in S. C., p. 121; [Boston] New England Palladium, July 15, 19, 1808; [Norfolk] Herald, 4, March 1795; Savannah Georgia Gazette, 9 Jan., 10 April, 19 June, 2 Oct. 1800.

[26] Robert W. July, The Essential New Yorker, Gulian Crommelin Verplanck (Durham, 1951), ch. III–IV.

A wealthy merchant named Isaac Sebring underwrote the enterprise, and old-school Federalist Richard Varick lent his political reputation. On February 22, 1809, the society held its first public meeting. It was an instant success.[27]

The Washington Benevolent Society idea spread rapidly from New York City into western New York State, and eastward to Vermont, Connecticut, and western Massachusetts. By 1810 it had reached Maryland and Rhode Island; by 1812, New Hampshire, eastern Massachusetts, Pennsylvania, New Jersey, and Ohio. A New England Republican complained that Washington Societies were "sprouting up like mushrooms in the shade."[28] A Maryland Federalist boasted that his society was "flourishing infinitely beyond our most sanguine expectations."[29]

The number of Washington Benevolent Societies which were founded by the Federalists is not easy to estimate precisely. The existence of 208 societies can be established (see Table XIX), but there were probably many more. A Vermont Republican calculated that the Federalists established "upwards of a hundred" Washington Societies in his state alone.[30]

It is even more difficult to estimate the total number of men who belonged to the Washington Benevolent Societies—so difficult, indeed, that there is no point in trying. There was an overlap of membership between county and town societies, and great variation in size. Largest and wealthiest was the Washington Society of Pennsylvania, which carried three thousand members on its rolls in 1816.[31] The Boston society, at its peak, had 1,647 paid members.[32] Some county societies were equally large—the Washington Benevolent Society of Berkshire County,

---

[27] Dixon Ryan Fox, "The Washington Benevolent Society," *Columbia University Quarterly*, XXI (1919), 27–37; E. F. Hanaburgh, "News for Bibliophiles," *The Nation*, XCVII (1913), 405.

[28] William A. Robinson, "The Washington Benevolent Society in New England; A Phase of Politics during the War of 1812," *Massachusetts Historical Society Proceedings*, XLIX (1916), 277.

[29] Alexander Contee Hanson to [?], May 11, 1811, in Leakin Papers, Md. Hist. Soc.; other societies—the "Sons of Washington" and the "American Republican Society" in Philadelphia, and the "Hamilton Society" in New York—were founded by Federalists but were eclipsed by the Washington Benevolent Societies; see [Boston] *New England Palladium*, Mar. 6, 1812; [New York] *Evening Post*, Jan. 5, 1810.

[30] [Rutland] *Herald*, May 6, 1816.

[31] *A Summary Statement of the Origin, Progress, and Present State of the Washington Benevolent Society of Pennsylvania* (Philadelphia, 1816); no less than 2,645 members had joined within two months of the society's inception. See "Declaration of the Members of the Washington Benevolent Society of Pennsylvania" [1812], Washington Benevolent Society Papers, Hist. Soc. of Penna.

[32] [Audit of Washington Benevolent Society of Massachusetts] signed N. Appleton, Feb. 8, 1814, in Washington Benevolent Society Coll., Mass. Hist. Soc.; Warren, *Life of Warren*, I, 111.

Massachusetts, numbered 2,300 in 1813. But many town societies had no more than a dozen members.[33]

Table XIX. Washington Benevolent Societies, 1800–1816[a]

Vermont

County societies:
Addison County, Chittenden County, Franklin County, Jefferson County, Orange County, Rutland County, Windham County, Windsor County

Town societies:
Bakersfield, Barnet, Barré, Bennington, Benson, Berkshire, Brandon, Brattleboro, Bridport, Bristol, Brookfield, Calais, Castleton, Chelsea, Chester, Claremont, Crofton, Fairhaven, Guildhall, Hancock, Hartford, Hartland, Jericho, Jeffry, Leicester, Londonderry, Middlebury, Monkton, Montpelier, Newbury, New Haven, Norwich, Plainfield, Putney, Randolph, Reading, Rockingham, Royalton, Saint Albans, Salisbury, Sharon, Shoreham, Springfield, Starksboro, Templeton, Vergennes, Wardsborough, Wethersfield, Westminster, Westhaven, Weybridge, Williamstown, Windsor.

New Hampshire

County societies:
Cheshire County.

Town societies:
Bedford, Boscawen, Charlestown, Claremont, Concord, Cornish, Dunbarton, Exeter, Gilmanton, Hanover, Hartford, Hopkinton, Jaffrey, Keene, Lebanon, Lancaster, Lyme, Marlborough, Norwich, Plainfield, Portsmouth, Sanbornton, Stewartstown, Tamworth, Walpole

[33] [Concord, N. H.] *New Hampshire Patriot*, May 4, 1813; Harlan H. Ballard, "A Forgotten Fraternity," *Berkshire Historical & Scientific Society Collections* (1913), pp. 279–298.
[a] This list has been compiled from A. C. Hanson to R. G. Harper, June 18, 1810, in Harper-Pennington Papers, Md. Hist. Soc.; Washington Benevolent Society MSS, Mass. Hist. Soc.; Washington Benevolent Society of Worcester Record Book, American Antiquarian Society; Washington Society MSS, New York Hist. Soc.; [Windsor, Vt.] *Washingtonian*, Feb. 3, 10, Dec. 9, 30, 1811, May 25, Apr. 4, June 15, 22, July 13, 27, Sep. 18, 28, 1812; [Rutland, Vt.] *Herald*, Mar. 18, 1812; [Boston] *New England Palladium*, Mar. 16, 1813, Mar. 4, July 18, Nov. 29, 1814; [Trenton] *Federalist*, July 6, 1812, July 24, 1815; [Westchester, Pa.] *Chester and Delaware Federalist*, Mar. 20, 1816; [Annapolis] *Maryland Gazette*, Feb. 24, 1814; Washingtoniana Pamphlets, Boston Public Library; Fourth of July Pamphlets, New York Hist. Soc.; Washington Benevolent Society Pamphlets, in the Boston Athenaeum, Mass. Hist. Soc., New York Public Library, Peabody Institute Library (Baltimore), and the Library of Congress; Charles C. Coffin, *The History of Boscawen and Webster* [N. H.] (Concord, N. H., 1878), p. 161; Addison E. Cudworth, *The History of Londonderry* [Vt.] (Montpelier, 1936), p. 51; Ebenezer Elmer, *Cumberland County* [N. J.] (Bridgeton, N. J., 1869), p. 57; Marcus W. Jernegan, *The Tammany Societies of Rhode Island* (Providence, 1897); Walter Fee, *Transition from Aristocracy to Democracy in New Jersey* (Somerville, 1937); William B. McGroarty, "The Washington Society of Alexandria," *Tyler's Quarterly*, IX, (1928), 147–167; William A. Robinson, "The Washington Benevolent Society in New England," *Massachusetts Historical Society Proceedings*, XLIX (1915–1916), 274–286; William L. Utter, "Saint Tammany in Ohio," *Mississippi Valley Historical Review*, XV (1928), 321–340; Joseph Sabin et. al, *Bibliotheca Americana*, 29 vols. (New York, 1868–1936).

Massachusetts *(includes Maine)*

County societies:
Berkshire County, Franklin County, Hampshire County, Hampden County, Plymouth County, Worcester County, Southern Part of Worcester County
Town societies:
Amherst, Athol, Augusta, Barré, Becket, Blandford, Boston, Brimfield, Brookfield, Cambridge, Charlestown, Chester, Chicopee, Deerfield, Dorchester, Easton, Fryeburg, Gloucester, Granville, Greenfield, Great Barrington, Hallowell, Hamilton, Kennebec, Knox, Lancaster and Sterling, Leominster and Fitchburg, Longmeadow, Marblehead, Nantucket, Newburyport, New Marlborough, Northampton, Northfield, Palmer, Petersham, Pittsfield, Princeton, Royalton, Salem, Springfield, Stockbridge, Templeton, Warren, Warwick, Washington, Westfield, Westminster, Wilbranham, Winchendon, Winslow, Worcester.

Rhode Island

Town societies:
Bristol, Newport, Providence

Connecticut

Town societies:
Glastonbury, Hartford, Hebron, Oxford, Tolland, Wallingford, Wethersfield

New York

County societies:
Cayuga County, Columbia County, Cortland County, Duchess County, Greene County, Herkimer County, Hudson County Montgomery County, Onondaga County, Oneida County, Ontario County, Rensselaer County, Saratoga County, Washington County.
Town societies:
Albany, Augusta, Berlin, Brookfield, Canaan, Canandaigua, Catskill, Florida, Galway, Homer, Hudson, New York City, Schenectady, Troy

New Jersey

County societies:
Burlington County, Cumberland County, Essex County, Gloucester County, Monmouth County, Sussex County
Town societies:
Bridgeton, Cranberry, Elizabethtown, Greenwich, Mount Holly, Newark, New Brunswick, Princeton, Trenton

Pennsylvania

County societies:
Chester County
Town societies:
Lancaster, Philadelphia

Maryland

County societies:
Anne Arundel County, Montgomery County, Prince George's County
Town societies:
Annapolis, Baltimore

Virginia

Town societies:
  Alexandria

Ohio

County societies:
  Washington County
Town societies:
  Marietta, Springfield, Zanesville

The Washington Benevolent Societies were aimed at all the people. The Federalists who founded them sought to attract anyone with a vote. Membership requirements were generally no more strict than those of the Boston society, which merely asked three things of its recruits—American citizenship, a "good moral character," and a "firm attachment to the constitution." The only grounds for expulsion were "abandoning the principles which entitle him to become a member," i.e., voting Democratic.[34] Dues were nominal—in Boston a two dollar initiation fee, plus one dollar a year payable quarterly.[35] The officers were empowered to exempt impoverished members from dues. In the Boston society approximately five hundred members—nearly one-third—were thus exempt from dues in 1814.[36] A life membership cost ten dollars. Additional contributions, of course, were always welcome and frequently solicited from wealthy members.[37]

At least a few societies drew in the "lower orders of society." Of the Rutland, Vermont, society, a Republican declared, "I can truly say they have some of the best characters in the town and some of the vilest. Drunkards, Liars, Whores, Counterfeiters and Thieves are not excluded. In short I can add with safety that the character of no man is enquired after. Is he a moral man is not the question. But the question is, is he a friend to the present administration or not. If he is this he is rejec[t]ed, if not then he can be admitted."[38] But the Rutland society was probably untypical. A compilation of occupations listed in the directories of the New York, Philadelphia and Boston societies shows a predominance of lawyers, merchants, shopkeepers, and mechanics. Unskilled workers such as cartmen, stevedores, and well diggers, and low prestige occupa-

---

[34] Constitution of the Washington Benevolent Society, [1812], Washington Benevolent Society Coll., Mass. Hist. Soc.; see also the explanation of admissions policies in [Boston] *Repertory*, Apr. 14, 1814.

[35] Ibid.

[36] Treasurer's Report of the Washington Benevolent Society of Boston, Feb. 13, 1815, Washington Benevolent Society Coll., Mass. Hist. Soc.

[37] Constitution of the Washington Benevolent Society of Boston [1812], *Ibid.*; "List of Stockholders of the Washington Benevolent Society of Pennsylvania," Washington Benevolent Society Papers, Hist. Soc. of Penna.

[38] [Rutland, Vt.] *Herald*, Mar. 21, 1812; there is no evidence of participation by females of any description in meetings of Washington Benevolent Societies on a regular basis.

tions such as butchers were few and far between.[39] Contemporary ob-observers reached this same conclusion. A Republican in Salem, Massachusetts, noted that "the body of these associations is of young lawyers and merchant clerks."[40]

Table XX. Occupations of Members of the Washington Benevolent
Societies of Philadelphia, New York, and Boston

| | Philadelphia | | New York | | Boston | |
	Number	Per cent	Number	Per cent	Number	Per cent
Independent	38	1.8	9	1.3	0	0
Professional	281	13.6	103	14.9	153	12.1
Merchants	320	14.9	122	17.7	399	31.8
Manufacturers	20	.9	1	.2	2	.2
Shopkeepers	509	22.5	131	19.3	296	22.9
Artists	13	.6	1	.2	5	.4
Mechanics	691	31.6	190	27.9	309	24.3
Clerks	165	7.7	35	5.1	68	4.8
Laborers	139	6.6	90	12.8	44	3.4
Farmers	2	.1	4	.6	1	.1
Total	2,188	100.0	686	100.0	1,277	100.0

Many of the members were quite young. A Republican in New Hampshire observed that "the novelty of these societies has excited numbers to join them, particularly the young and credulous."[41] There were always a few Revolutionary veterans on hand at patriotic festivals, propped up along the walls between papier-mâché busts of Washington and transparencies of the battle of Bunker Hill, but the societies did not attract many old-school gentlemen; as young Peter Augustus Jay reported to his father, "many gentlemen kept aloof."[42] A few Federalists actually opposed it. Among them was Col. John Eager Howard, who re-fused to have any part of the Washington Society of Maryland after it was formed in Baltimore in 1810. The wife of the president of the society, Mrs. Robert Goodloe Harper, was thoroughly disgusted. "I think he does more harm to the cause," she wrote angrily to her husband, "by

[39] A Dictionary, containing names, places of business, and residence of the mem-bers of the Washington Benevolent Society of Massachusetts (Boston, 1813); membership list with street addresses and occupations, dated June 1810, Wash-ington Benevolent Society Coll., New York Hist. Soc.; "Index to Autographs in the original subscription book of Members of the Washington Benevolent Society of Philadelphia," [circa] 1814–1828, Washington Benevolent Society Papers, Hist. Soc. of Penna.

[40] Bentley, Diary, IV, 87 (Mar. 3, 1812). A young Federalist in New York de-scribed the men at a meeting of the Washington Benevolent Society there as consisting of "substantial shopkeepers and mechanics, of men of the middling class;" Peter Augustus Jay to John Jay, Feb. 23, 1810, in Jay Papers, Columbia Univ. Library; Johnston, Correspondence of Jay, IV, 326–327.

[41] [Concord, N. H.] New Hampshire Patriot, Mar. 2, 1813.

[42] Peter Augustus Jay to John Jay, Feb. 23, 1810, in Jay Papers, Columbia Univ. Library.

opposing everything that is proposed by the party, than any other man in the country."[43] Opposition of another kind came from merchants who regarded the organization as merely another trick of the politicians to wheedle money out of them. Kitty Harper, who took a most unladylike interest in the affairs of the Federal Party, was even more disgusted with the merchants than with old Colonel Howard. "A selfish, mercenary, money making set of men," she called them, "who deserve in case of bustle to have their property taken and houses burnt!"[44]

The Washington Societies, of course, claimed to be charitable associations, and some were in fact quite active in humanitarian work. The wealthy Washington Society of Pennsylvania was particularly active in benevolent work. Some of its members received weekly support from the society. Others were given occasional cash assistance, help in obtaining employment, free legal advice and medical care, firewood and warm clothing in cold weather, aid in recovery of debts or the satisfaction of creditors. In 1813 this society raised one thousand dollars for the relief of families of soldiers in the field. Other societies maintained free schools, as did the Washington Society of Maryland in Baltimore.[45] But other groups could point to little in the way of good works. The benevolent expenditures of the Washington Benevolent Society of Massachusetts were laughably small—in 1813, for example, only ten dollars went to charity out of total expenses of $1,721.70.[46]

As the Republican editors never wearied of pointing out, charity was not a major concern of most Washington Benevolent Societies.[47] Their purposes were always predominantly political. The founders of the societies were invariably the handful of young Federalists who had founded and dominated the state committee organizations.[48] In confidential correspondence these men spoke openly of "the political purposes for which the society was instituted."[49]

[43] Catherine (Carroll) Harper to Robert Goodloe Harper, Mar. 5, 1810, in Harper-Pennington Papers, Md. Hist. Soc.

[44] Ibid., see Table XVI.

[45] *Summary Statement of the Washington Benevolent Society of Pennsylvania;* in 1812, the recipient of this charity, the Washington Free School, had a student body of 109; Alexander Contee Hanson to Robert Goodloe Harper, Feb. 23, 1812, in Harper-Pennington Papers, Md. Hist. Soc.; see also [Baltimore, Md.] *Federal Republican,* July 8, 1811; [Boston, Mass.] *New England Palladium,* Feb. 23, Mar. 4, 1814.

[46] In 1814, $35.00 out of $856.23; in 1815, $13.00 out of $748.54; Annual Treasurer's Reports, 1813–1815, Washington Benevolent Society Coll., Mass. Hist. Soc.

[47] Robinson, "Washington Benevolent Societies," pp. 278–279.

[48] Alexander Contee Hanson to Robert Goodloe Harper, Mar. 3, 1810, in Harper Papers, Library of Congress; *Summary Statement of the Washington Benevolent Society of Pennsylvania;* [Boston] *New England Palladium,* Feb. 25, 1812; Dixon Ryan Fox, "Washington Benevolent Society," pp. 30–36.

[49] Records of the Standing Committee of the Washington Benevolent Society of Massachusetts, Feb. 8, 1821; Robinson, "Washington Benevolent Societies," p. 280.

In public the societies sometimes wore the mask of impartiality, but scarcely anyone was deceived. There can be little doubt that most members were Federalists—if not all of them. The Boston society was in fact directly descended from the "Young Federalists."[50] Sometimes the thin veneer of impartiality was altogether discarded. An orator before the society of Windsor, Vermont, announced candidly that one of its purposes was to "correct the political sentiments of the people."[51]

When a recruit was admitted to membership, he was required to take a solemn oath which bound him to support the Constitution of the United States and the regulations of the Washington Benevolent Society. The latter usually required him to be true to "Washington principles," or in the words of the Boston society's constitution, "to oppose all encroachments of Democracy, Aristorcracy, or Despotism."[52]

Some societies gave their members a little chapbook to guide them. The "textbook" of the Washington Benevolent Society of Concord, New Hampshire, for example, was a substantial little work of 106 pages. The frontispiece was an engraving of the immortal Washington, with the motto "His path be Ours." Pages two to twelve comprised a short biographical sketch of Washington, written in simple, effective prose and crowded with Federalist propaganda. Pages thirteen to twenty-six were an analysis of the "character of Washington." The remainder was filled up with the ubiquitous Farewell Address and the Constitution of the United States.[53]

Most societies furnished their members with a badge for display at official functions. The emblem of the Washington Benevolent Society of Onondaga County, New York, was a "creamy silk ribbon" which bore a portrait of Washington with a small angel hovering above his head and crowning him with laurel.[54]

There were two quite different kinds of functions, private and public. The former were secret sessions which roused the deepest suspicions of

[50] Dixon Ryan Fox, "Washington Benevolent Society," p. 31; [Boston] *New England Palladium*, July 16, 1811, Feb. 25, 1812.

[51] Robinson, *Jeff. Dem. in N. Eng.*, p. 90; see also [Boston] *New England Palladium*, Nov. 29, 1814; and *The Constitution of the Washington Benevolent Society of Mount Holly, N. J.* (n.p., 1812).

[52] Constitution of the Washington Benevolent Society of Massachusetts, 1812, Washington Benevolent Society Coll., Mass. Hist. Soc. Samuel Elliot specified a three-fold purpose to "moralize and instruct," to "ameliorate distress," and to "unite the American People in bands of political love and harmony under the banners, and in the principles and policy of our beloved and departed Washington." *Address to Members of the Washington Benevolent Society* (Brattleboro, 1812).

[53] *Textbook of the Washington Benevolent Society* (Concord, 1812).

[54] "Notes and Queries," *Pennsylvania Magazine of History and Biography*, XXXII (1908), 374; the badge of the Newburyport society was a white rose tied in a blue ribbon; John Pierpont, *The Portrait* (Boston, 1812), p. 9; after 1800 Federalists imitated French royalists in substituting the white rose for the black cockade as the emblem. Republicans in 1800 had made good use of "Jefferson buckles" of pinchbeck, worn in hats on the front of the crown. [Balto.] *American*, 20 Dec. 1800.

the Jeffersonians.[55] They were held quarterly or monthly, with extra meetings on the eve of important elections, which sometimes lasted far into the night.

Public exercises were more elaborate. Most societies held them three times a year—the Fourth of July, Washington's Birthday, and the anniversary of his first inauguration on April 30, which in some states came at the peak of the political campaign. Often all-day affairs, these intricate public spectacles were carefully planned with astonishing attention to detail. Sometimes they began at dawn, when the party faithful were awakened by a battery of guns, often styled "The Washington Artillerists." Householders along the line of march were instructed to sprinkle the streets with water in order to keep down the dust.[56]

At midday the members of the society and their children, sisters, brothers, cousins, nephews, and nieces collected for a grand parade, reminiscent of a saint's procession in some sunny Catholic land. An illustration is the Boston society's procession on April 30, 1814. In the van marched brightly uniformed militia companies with fifes shrilling, drums beating, and colors flying. Behind them came the officers of the society, "public characters and strangers of distinction," and honored members of the clergy. Next in line were four hundred small children dressed in white, bearing wreaths, garlands, the badge of the Washington Society, and—suspended by chains around their necks—a book ostentatiously labeled "Washington's Legacy." Next were twenty-one youths carrying the society's twenty-one silken banners, commemorating Revolutionary victories, the events of Washington's life, and the names of other American heroes, or representing in allegorical terms such sentiments as "independence," the "union of states," "commerce," "peace," and "national glory." Then came the culmination—borne reverently on a satin cushion was a relic of the great Washington, the gleaming gorget which he had worn in the French and Indian War and which his widow had donated to the Washington Society in Boston. Strung out behind, marching in divisions, was the main body of the society four abreast, a mile and a half long. All this took place in a sudden April downpour that failed to discourage the participants or to extinguish their patriotic ardor.[57]

Nothing but the weather was left to chance. The marshals responsible

[55] Robinson, "Washington Benevolent Societies," pp. 280–282.

[56] [Boston] *New England Palladium*, Mar. 1, July 12, 1814; and *Repertory*, Apr. 30, 1814.

[57] [Boston] *New England Palladium*, Apr. 29, May 3, 1814; the society's painted silk banners were objects of special pride and admiration. The "standard of agriculture" was described as follows: "In the midst of rustic scenery in the front ground are seen a variety of husbandry implements, fruits of the harvest, &c. In the middle ground appears a farm house, and in the rear a village church. On a rock is exhibited the following inscription: 'Sons of New-England venerate the plough . . .' "; [Boston] *Repertory;* Apr. 30, 1814; see also Quincy, *Josiah Quincy,* pp. 308–309.

for seeing that all came off in proper style rehearsed many times be-forehand. One of them left the following record in his Diary:

apr. 21 [1814]   Rode in circus with marshals, preparatory to celebration of the Washington Benevolent Society.
apr. 25   Circus 3 o'clock. Exercise of Marshalls, Washington Benevolent Society.
apr. 28   At circus drilling marshalls.
apr. 30   ˙ Celebration of the Washington Benevolent Society. Officiated as Aid to Chief Marshal.[58]

The Boston procession usually ended in front of Old South Church, where the entire ground floor was reserved for members of the Washington Society and the balcony for their ladies. In 1812 this part of the celebration began with music from the "Lock Hospital Society," a prayer, an ode, a reading of Washington's Farewell Address, another ode, a "sublime" oration by the sentimental young Federalist William Sullivan. Then came still another ode, the benediction, and the recessional. Each of the three odes was delivered by a different person. One of them began:

> And first to that immortal name
> Which we in *social union* bear . . .

Another, addressed to the "Spirit of Washington," besought a second coming:

> Descend, thou hallow'd spirit,
> And guard our native land;
> Where every fiend of faction roams
> And discord waves her brand.[59]

An illustration of the oratory, which was equally grandiloquent, was Robert Goodloe Harper's speech to the Washington Society of Alexandria on February 22, 1810. With the ornate rhetorical flourishes in which he excelled, Harper compared the career of Washington favorably to that of Gustavus Vasa, Alfred, Wallace, Epaminondas, Scipio, Alexander, Caesar, Pompey, Germanicus, Trajan, Julian, Marcus Aurelius, Charlemagne, Tamerlane, Genghis Khan, Attila, Tiberius, Caligula, and Napoleon.[60]

[58] Lewis Tappan, "Pocket Remembrancer," Apr. 21–30, 1814, Tappan Papers, Library of Congress; see also [Annapolis] *Maryland Gazette*, May 19, 1814; although such spectacular displays were, of course, beyond the means of many small rural societies, they did their best. One of the smallest spent $140.00 on silk banners and badges; Robinson, "Washington Benevolent Societies," p. 278.

[59] "Order of Performance for the First Celebration of the Washington Benevolent Society of Massachusetts," Apr. 30, 1812, in Broadsides, Mass. Hist. Soc.; see also "Order of Performances . . . ," "Apr. 30, 1814, ibid.; Song Collection of the Library of Congress, "When Death's Gloomy Angel was bending his Bow," written for the First Anniversary of the Washington Benevolent Society of Pennsylvania, 1813; [New York] *Evening Post*, Feb. 23, 1810.

[60] Robert Goodloe Harper, *Oration on the birth of Washington delivered before the Washington Society of Alexandria* (Alexandria, 1810); [Baltimore] *Federal Republican*, Feb. 26, 1810.

In the evening, as Harper or Sullivan might have said, "Bathos folded her purple cloak and sprightly Myrth skipped upon the scene." The society split into groups and had dinner in the local taverns, which the leaders of the Society would visit in turn.[61] Endless toasts were proposed —to "the day," to "the American fair," to Washington, to all the sentiments emblazoned on the society's silken banners, to whatever worthies happened to be present, and to the confusion of the Jeffersonians. One Federalist gathering drank to "the Tree of our Liberties—May the apes of French policy no longer suspend themselves from its branches, nor the jackals of the French emperor repose in its shade."[62] After these "rude toasts and political insults," as Republicans chose to consider them, the members of the society "sallied at midnight into the streets, yelling and destroying property as a proof that they held fast to the rules of good order and public peace."[63]

When the sun came up again, the celebration was over. The disciples of Washington, with heads athrob and hearts aglow, trudged wearily back to their posts as pillars of society. The dignified portions of these festivals at first were held in churches and meeting houses; the frivolous dinners, in taverns. But as the societies caught on, many of them built their own meeting places. The first of them, possibly the first building ever erected in America for partisan purposes, was Washington Hall in New York City, for which the cornerstone was laid in 1809.[64]

A more elaborate structure was Washington Hall in Philadelphia, which serves as a measure of the affluence of the Washington Society in that city. Federalists began by purchasing William Bingham's imposing mansion for $25,000 in 1813. Shortly afterwards they added two adjoining city lots for $20,000 and erected alongside the Bingham house a very large building on a design by Robert Mills at the cost of $120,000. The main room of this remarkable structure was large enough to accommodate six thousand people. The five thousand spectators who thronged it to witness the dedication of the building in 1816 were in all probability the largest crowd ever gathered under one roof in the country up to that time.[65] This building was by no means unique. Many other societies raised their own "Washington Hall," including those in Baltimore, Albany, Troy, Stockbridge, and Charlestown, Mass.[66]

In organization the Washington Societies were ostensibly democratic.

61 [New York] *Evening Post*, Feb. 22, 1809.

62 Robinson, "Washington Benevolent Societies," p. 283.

63 Bentley, *Diary*, IV, 87; see also [New Brunswick, N. J.] *Fredonian*, Mar. 10, 1814.

64 Tammany Hall in New York City was not erected until the following year; Fox, "Washington Benevolent Society," p. 35.

65 "Summary statement . . . of the Washington Benevolent Society of Pennsylvania."

66 [Boston] *New England Palladium*, July 8, 1814; Fox, "Washington Benevolent Society," p. 35; [Baltimore] *Federal Republican*, Sep. 27, 1811.

The officers of the Philadelphia society, which seems to have been typical in everything but wealth and size, were elected by majority vote upon nomination by an electing committee, also chosen by majority vote. Any officer could be removed by two-thirds vote of the society. Superficially the structure of the Washington Societies was in harmony with the principles of Jefferson.[67] But in practice they were little oligarchies tightly controlled by the young Federalists who had founded them. They kept control of the crucial nominating bodies—the election committee in the Philadelphia society, the standing committee in others—and never let go. Nominations were settled in caucus by these men before the open elections.[68]

It is interesting that gentlemen of the old school such as Cabot, Pickering, King, and Jay did not participate in the establishment of the Washington Societies. Like the state organizations of electioneering committees, the Washington Benevolent Societies were primarily an affair of younger men.

The resources of the Washington Benevolent Societies were at the disposal of the Federalist Party. In some cases, assistance was given in the most direct and useful form—bundles of cash—which were placed in the hands of Federalist county leaders. Thus, a Federalist leader in Baltimore County, Maryland, wrote to the treasurer of the Washington Benevolent Society of Maryland in Baltimore City, "We have received the fifty dollars and it is absolutely necessary that we should have one hundred and fifty more which can be disposed of to great advantage. Everything is going well in the county and with proper exertions we must succeed."[69]

More money was probably contributed less directly. Many constitutions of the societies authorized expenditures at the discretion of the officers, for "the diffusion of useful information among our fellow citizens."[70] Federal printers published the societies' orations, odes, and handbills. This activity had the double effect of increasing the amount of

[67] The officers of the Washington Benevolent Society of Pennsylvania in 1816 included one president; 16 vice-presidents, each a resident in one of 16 wards and districts; 16 secretaries, one for each vice president; one treasurer and deputy; one recording secretary and deputy; one corresponding secretary and deputy; 10 counsellors to render legal assistance; 6 physicians to render medical assistance (these two sets of officers were uncommon); 5 stewards; one doorkeeper; electing committee, 48 members; committee of superintendence, 5 members; school committee, 16 members; committee of publication, 3 members; committee of correspondence, ? members; "Summary statement . . . of the Washington Benevolent Society of Pennsylvania"; see also John F. Mercer to Vergil Maxcy, Mar. 25, 1812, in Galloway-Maxcy-Markoe Papers, Library of Congress.

[68] Mr. Bond [?] to W. Cochran, n.d. Feb. 3 [c. 1814] in Washington Benevolent Society Coll.; Mass. Hist. Soc.; [Elizabethtown, Md.] Maryland Herald, Aug. 14, 1811.

[69] Nicholas M. Bosley to Alexander Contee Hanson, July 23, 1811, "McHenry Letters," p. 319; see also [Windsor] Vt. Republican, 10, 24 Feb. 1812.

[70] Constitution of the Washington Benevolent Society of Mount Holly, N. J.; "Summary Statement . . . of the Washington Benevolent Society of Pennsylvania."

Federal propaganda in circulation and of strengthening the financial position of the printers, who were often teetering on the edge of bankruptcy.[71]

Where Federal committee organization was weak, the Washington Benevolent Societies nominated candidates and directly supervised electioneering campaigns.[72] But in other states they were ancillary to the main organization in the same way that the Tammany Societies supplemented Republican committees.

The political effectiveness of the Washington Benevolent Societies is an open question. Republicans attributed great power to these "hot beds of political poison."[73] A Republican correspondent to the *Green Mountain Farmer* was so alarmed by the "Washington Benevolents" that he suggested the organization of committees of safety in each town to keep an eye on them. In Vermont, men were dismissed from office by Republicans because they belonged to the Washington Benevolent Society. Indeed, some Jeffersonians denounced "self-created secret societies" in language that was reminiscent of Washington.[74]

In Maryland, a Republican charged that the Washington Society officers successfully sought "to persuade every wealthy blockhead of their party to join the society, for although there is no *mettle* in their skulls, yet there is *metal* in their purses." He charged that the society had sent four hundred dollars for electioneering purposes to the little county of Calvert alone, "besides Whiskey, etc. with the sinful hope of debasing the minds of the voters, and pamphlets headed up in barrels."[75] Ridicule, parody, and satire—all the weapons in the editorial arsenals of Jef-

---

[71] [Concord, N. H.] *New Hampshire Patriot*, Feb. 4, 1812.

[72] Robinson, "Washington Benevolent Societies," pp. 276–277; see also the comment of the [Rutland] *Herald*, June 2, 1812; that the societies should call themselves "Benevolent Caucusing Societies." In 1812, under the general supervision of a "grand state caucus" which came together at the sitting of the U. S. Circuit Court of Appeals at Windsor, the societies served as Federalist electioneering committees; for an isolated example of caucusing by a Washington Benevolent Society in Pennsylvania, see [West Chester, Pa.] *Chester and Delaware, Federalist,* Mar. 20, 1816.

[73] See, e.g., [Concord, N.H.] *New Hampshire Patriot*, June 30, 1812.

[74] Robinson, "Washington Benevolent Societies," p. 281; Londonderry, Vt. Baptists were excommunicated for joining the local Washington Benevolent Society; Addison E. Cudworth, *The History of Londonderry*, p. 51. There were several attempts at counterorganization by Republicans, such as the "Patriotic Union Association" in Vermont; [Windsor] Vt. *Republican*, 25 May 1812.

[75] [Baltimore, Md.] *Whig*, Aug. 7, 1811; see also [Easton, Md.] *Star*, Oct. 22, 1811; [Baltimore, Md.] *American*, Aug. 29, 1811. "It was explicitly stated, a few days since, by a gentleman of *high standing* not many miles from Windsor, who is one of the leaders of a secret and treasonable combination to overthrow our present government, that the Washington Benevolent Societies were completely organized, in such manner that their plans could be communicated to almost every part of the Union within 8 or 9 days, that they should, with force of arms, oppose a war with Great Britain; that the General Officers were appointed for that purpose, and were under pay; and that Mr. Madison would lose his head in less than five days after war should thus be declared"—thus the fears of Jeffersonians; [Windsor] Vt. *Republican*, 22, 25, 29 June 1812.

fersonianism—were employed to discredit the Washington "Malevolent" Societies.[76]

The expansion of the Washington Societies ended abruptly in 1815, following the convention at Hartford, the treaty of Ghent, and the battle of New Orleans. But many of them were long a-dying. The Philadelphia Society, for example, continued to meet until the mid 1830s. Most, however, were gone by 1824.

A scholar who has had a brief look at the Washington Societies concluded that "the spirit of the Washington Benevolent Society is not that of nineteenth century Americanism." He thought that "its badges, chaplets, and other mummery" were "absurdly out of place in American politics."[77] But another, more penetrating observer of nineteenth-century America, Alexis de Tocqueville, stressed the significance of free associations in the United States. "Americans of all ages, all conditions, and all dispositions constantly form associations," he noted. "They have not only commercial and manufacturing companies, in which all take part, but associations of a thousand kinds, religious, moral, serious, futile, general or restricted, enormous or diminutive."[78] Tocqueville found that voluntary associations operated as a balance weight to the centrifugal force of individualism in a free society. The startling, if short-lived, success of the Washington Benevolent Societies helps to illuminate a significant and central part of American culture. Voluntary associations of this sort fulfilled a deep and basic purpose in an open, free, and democratic culture. The Washington Benevolent Societies are, thus, another example of the ways in which the Federalists acclimatized themselves to the society in which they lived.

[76] Robinson, "Washington Benevolent Societies," p. 279.
[77] Ibid., p. 285.
[78] Alexis de Tocqueville, *Democracy in America*, 2 vols. (New York, 1951), II, 106.

VII

Federalists and the Press

> *I am persuaded by recent experience that we can do infinitely more by private letters than by newspaper publications.*
>
> —Samuel Henshaw, 1789[1]

> *It is impossible to estimate too highly the importance of News Papers and their effects on the public mind. I do believe it was the great attention paid by democrats to the support and diffusion of the Aurora and a few other papers which procured them the small majority they had at the elections.*
>
> —John Rutledge, Jr., 1801[2]

I

Historians generally agree that the press played a major role in the Jeffersonian triumph of 1800.[3] Indeed, it is difficult to imagine how Jefferson could have won without it. In large towns and little country villages his admirers founded "electioneering papers" which were published "not for profit but 'only patriotic motives.' "[4] They were subsidized and edited by men who believed deeply in democracy, the French Revolution, and the rights of man.[5]

Politics appeared everywhere in these journals. The editor of the Baltimore *American* even managed to make propaganda out of his billing notices. "Never did R. G. HARPER want an appointment—Never did judge [sic] CHASE want a fat salary—Never did Mr. ADAMS want to hold his seat—Nor ever did the Republicans want to turn him out of it, more, that at this crisis the editor of the AMERICAN wants the payment of monies due to him."[6]

[1] Samuel Henshaw to Theodore Sedgwick, Apr. 15, 1789, in Sedgwick Papers, Mass. Hist. Soc.

[2] John Rutledge, Jr., to Harrison Gray Otis, Sept. 15, 1801, in Rutledge Papers, Southern Hist. Coll., Univ. of N. C.

[3] Donald Henderson Stewart, "Jeffersonian Journalism: Newspaper Propaganda and the Development of the Democratic-Republican Party, 1789–1801," (unpub. diss. (Columbia Univ., 1950); Cunningham, *Jeffersonian Republicans*, pp. 166–174.

[4] Prospectus of [Richmond, Va.] *Friend of the People*; [Richmond, Va.] *Virginia Argus*, Jan. 21, 1800.

[5] See, e.g., John Bach McMaster, *The Life and Times of Stephen Girard*, 2 vols. (Philadelphia, 1918), I, 420–422; *Providence Gazette*, Apr. 26, 1800.

[6] [Baltimore, Md.] *American*, Oct. 20, 1800.

The Jeffersonians made great use of pamphlets, handbills, posters, printed tickets, and broadsides of every kind. A Republican leader in Charleston boasted to Jefferson that he and his cohorts had "literally sprinkled Georgia and No. Carolina *from the mountains to the sea*" with electioneering pamphlets.[7] There is no better gauge of Republican use of the press than the bill which their New York City committee managed to run up in the spring elections of 1806 with a single printer, James Cheetham. It runs on for pages—too many to be quoted in full—but we might make a brief excerpt from one day's orders:

[apr] 26

. . . 2 quires circulars for the 1st ward @ $1.		$ 2.
300 posting bills for meeting of 3rd ward		6.
8 quires circulars for 3rd ward on fine post paper, as per order @ $1.		8.
500 hand bills signed pains of memory	12/	7.50
500 concerning the Leander do.		7.50
1000 do of the Atrocious Murder	12/	15.
400 for calling a meeting of 5th ward	16/	8.
200 do. for calling a meeting in 6th ward	16/	4.

The total: $586.08![8]

The Jeffersonians frequently used cartoons to put across their message. One which seems not to have survived featured a cow, with Adams at the head, Charles Cotesworth Pinckney and Rufus King at the tail, Alexander Hamilton milking, and John Jay with his treaty upsetting the bucket. It impressed the Reverend Mr. Bentley so much that he decided to hang it on his wall. "This milking work," he noted in his diary, "has kept mankind slaves ever since man has been known."[9]

Historians of journalism have generally suggested that the Federalist press was numerically stronger than that of the Republicans. The standard estimate assigns two-thirds of the nation's papers to the Federalists in 1800.[10] This estimate is correct but misleading. The Federalists in 1800 had fewer "high-toned" journals, subsidized by parties and controlled by political leaders (see Table XXI).

Earlier in the nineties, of course, they had founded political papers in Philadelphia, most notably the *Gazette of the United States* and *Porcupine's Gazette*. But in 1798 John Fenno, the editor of the former, had perished in a yellow fever epidemic, and two years later William Cobbett, or "Peter Porcupine," sailed home to England and a greater political

[7] Beard, Economic *Origins of Jeffersonian Democracy,* pp. 375–378.

[8] Accounts endorsed "*Printing,* Republican Committee, June 19, 1806," McKesson Papers, New York Hist. Soc.

[9] Bentley, *Diary,* III, 161 (May 28, 1805).

[10] Frank Luther Mott, *American Journalism,* rev. ed. (New York, 1950), p. 122; Luetscher, *Political Machinery,* p. 1; Stewart, "Jeffersonian Journalism," p. 56, has questioned this interpretation.

Table XXI. Summary of American Newspapers by Political
Affiliation, October 1, 1800[a]

State	Strongly Republican	Moderately Republican	Nearly Impartial	Moderately Federalist	Strongly Federalist	Unknown	Total
New Hampshire	1	0	0	8	1	1	11
Vermont	1	0	1	3	0	0	5
Massachusetts	4	1	1	12	5	0	23
Rhode Island	2	0	0	5	0	0	7
Connecticut	3	0	0	11	2	0	16
New York	5	0	5	15	1	4	30
New Jersey	2	1	0	1	2	0	6
Pennsylvania	12	1	1	8	5	7	34
Delaware	2	0	0	0	1	1	4
Maryland	6	1	0	3	2	2	14
Virginia	8	3	0	6	0	4	21
North Carolina	1	0	3	5	0	1	10
South Carolina	0	3	0	3	0	0	6
Georgia	1	1	1	2	0	0	5
Kentucky	0	4	0	0	0	0	4
Tennessee	0	1	1	0	0	0	2
Northwest Territory	0	0	1	1	0	0	2
Southwest Territory	0	0	0	1	0	0	1
Total	48	16	14	84	19	20	201

Federalist papers	103
Republican papers	64
Nearly Impartial	14
Unknown	20
Total	201

[a] For a breakdown of newspapers by state, see Table 1 in Appendix III.

career.[11] Here and there, an isolated Federalist electioneering paper appeared but seldom flourished. One of the few in all of the middle states was the Trenton *Federalist,* founded in 1798, but its principal editor was distinguished mainly for his "small quantity of intellect."[12] One of the few Federalist electioneering papers in New England, the *Western Star* in Stockbridge, Massachusetts, received little encouragement and assist-

[11] "Porcupine's paper does a great deal of good; it is very widely circulated, and much among the middle and town classes; his blunt vulgar language suits them and has a great effect: he keeps Bache and the others a good deal in check; the advantage of having a printer constantly on the watch to detect and expose their lies is considerable and the effects are already obvious"; William Smith to Ralph Izard, May 23, 1797, in Phillips, "S. C. Federalist Correspondence," *American Historical Review,* XIV (1909), 788; for a discussion of Cobbett's career as a Federalist editor, see Mary Elizabeth Clark, *Peter Porcupine in America: The Career of William Cobbett, 1792–1800* (Philadelphia, 1939); for John Fenno, see Christopher Gore to Rufus King, Jan. 18, 1798, in King, *Life and Correspondence of King,* I, 357; and Fisher Ames to Thomas Dwight, Sep. 25, 1798, in Ames, *Works,* I, 240.

[12] J. Wilson to W. Darlington, July 22, 1801, in Darlington Papers, Library of Congress.

ance, either in money or in communications. In the crucial period from October 1800 to February 1801 its editor complained that he had received "no aid whatsoever."[13]

Many printers were Federalists—perhaps as many as two-thirds of them. But they were printers first and political writers second. The distinction was significant. It meant that in the hopes of gratifying Republican customers they often wore the mask of impartiality and gave space to Jeffersonian contributions. Federalists as staunch as John Scull of the *Pittsburgh Gazette* and the Barbers of the Newport *Mercury* felt constrained to admit Republican pieces.[14]

Others, including Barzillai Hudson and George Goodwin of the *Connecticut Courant* and Benjamin Russell of the *Centinel* followed the opinions of their readers rather than the interests of a party. A Connecticut Republican spoke truly when he declared in 1798 that the "*Courant* must be considered the political thermometer of Connecticut."[15] When these editors were forced to choose between public opinion and the opinions of leading Federalists, they chose the former. In 1799 and 1800, when almost every Federalist "of the first rank" was heartily sick of Adams, the *Centinel* remained loyal to him and to the opinions of its readers. Editor Benjamin Russell rejected a piece critical of him even though it had been written by George Cabot himself.[16]

As the tide of political opinion began to ebb in the late nineties, many printers floated with it, drifting slowly out upon the "tempestuous sea of liberty." Editors who had been strong for Adams and the government in 1798 became impartial, or "unpartheyische" as the Pennsylvania Dutchmen called it, in the space of only a year or two. When Charles Holt, a Jeffersonian editor who had been jailed during the Terror, emerged from prison, he was surprised by the "trimming of a great portion of the federal papers."[17] Thus, the printer of the *Lancaster Journal,* a firm Federalist, pretended to be impartial in 1800.[18] The editor of the

[13] Henry Van Schaack to Theodore Sedgwick, Feb. 9, 1801, in Sedgwick Papers, Mass. Hist. Soc.; later in February, though, the Federalists bestirred themselves; see ibid.; cf. Birdsall, *Berkshire County,* pp. 183–184.

[14] Reuben Gold Thwaites, "The Ohio Valley Press before the War of 1812–15," *American Antiquarian Society Proceedings,* XIX (1909), 315; [Newport, R.I.] *Mercury,* Sep. 7, 9, 23, 1800.

[15] James C. Welling, *Connecticut Federalism; or Aristocratic Politics in a Social Democracy* (New York, 1890), p. 10.

[16] George Cabot to Timothy Pickering, Mar. 7, 1799, in Lodge, *Cabot,* p. 225.

[17] [New London, Conn.] *Bee,* Aug. 27, 1800; cited by Stewart, "Jeffersonian Journalism," p. 1135; see also William Cranch to Noah Webster, Mar. 3, 1805, in Noah Webster Papers, New York Public Library; printers were dependent not merely upon their public but also upon postmasters. For an illustration of the way in which Jeffersonian postal employees inhibited Federalist editors, see Ebenezer Andrews to Isaiah Thomas, July 30, Aug. 2, Aug. 4, 1802, in Isaiah Thomas Papers, American Antiquarian Society.

[18] *Lancaster Journal,* Jan. 22, 1800.

New York *Commercial Advertiser* declared flatly—albeit falsely—that "no hostile attempts have been made to revive party spirit by any observations that have appeared in our paper."[19] And even the *Farmer's Museum* in Walpole, N. H. made a practice of printing anti-Federalist pieces.[20]

Federalist leaders generally agreed that Republican journals were much more effective than their own. "One of [the Republicans'] many plans," a Federalist wrote, "has ever been to support with all their best *energies*, both mentally and pecuniarily, their best printers, and with the utmost industry, care and activity, to disseminate their papers and pamphlets. While the Federalists on their part leave their printers to scuffle on the support of their subscribers [which is] I believe a very *flimsy and uncertain daily sustenance*, and to scribble their own way to conquest!"[21]

Many Federalists loftily looked down upon journalism as a grimy, disreputable occupation and a journalist as an inferior being. "There is no *profession*, not even physicians, so badly treated," one newspaperman complained.[22] At a Washington's Birthnight Ball, "friends of order" were scandalized when Dolley Madison made her entrance upon the arm of a "dirty editor."[23] Few wished to soil their own hands with printer's ink.

Old-school gentlemen who cared only for the opinions of the "better sort" of people sometimes failed to see why newspapers should concern themselves with politics at all. When one of them felt that he had been wronged by the Jeffersonian administration, he prepared a vindication and had it printed in a few copies "for particular gentlemen." He did not think it necessary to "exhibit it through any newspaper editor."[24] The gentlemen of the old school, who believed in the power of a speaking elite to rule a silent multitude, persuaded themselves that there was no need to resort to the printing press. "We can do infinitely more by

[19] [New York, N. Y.] *Commercial Advertiser*, Jan. 20, 1800.

[20] Fisher Ames to Theodore Sedgwick, Dec. 4, 1800, in Sedgwick Papers, Mass. Hist. Soc. Isaiah Thomas of the [Worcester] *Massachusetts Spy* was an outspoken Federalist, yet he published the works of Thomas Paine for profit; see Shipton, *Isaiah Thomas*, p. 64.

[21] John Nicholas to Alexander Hamilton, Aug. 4, 1803, in Hamilton Papers, Library of Congress; see also Fisher Ames to John Rutledge, July 30, 1801, in Rutledge Papers, Southern Hist. Coll., Univ. of N. C.; for an illustration, see the financial struggles of John Prentiss, of the *New Hampshire Sentinel*, as detailed in William L. Bauhan, "John Prentiss and the New Hampshire Sentinel 1799–1829" unpub. thesis (Princeton, 1952), pp. 32–34; copy in the American Antiquarian Society.

[22] J. Wilson to W. Darlington, Feb. 27, 1808, in Darlington Papers, Library of Congress.

[23] Harrison Gray Otis to Mrs. Otis, Feb. 24, 1815, in Otis Papers, Mass. Hist. Soc.

[24] Thomas Truxtun to John Adams, Dec. 5, 1804, in Adams Family Papers, reel 403.

private letters than by newspaper publications," one of them wrote revealingly.[25]

Some Federalists went so far as to consider a public discussion of political affairs as "improper."[26] Timothy Dwight equated the reading of newspapers with tavern haunting, drinking, swearing, gambling, and pertness.[27] Such disapproval increased in proportion to the growth of Jeffersonian journals. The establishment of a "little jacobin paper" in Delaware brought at least one Federalist to the edge of hysteria. "Sir," he wrote to the Secretary of State, "I am almost delirious at seeing our once happy country disordered by such infamous instruments."[28]

As the century came to an end, many Federalists became quite shy about meeting the Jeffersonians on their chosen ground. "I wish if possible to avoid appearing in print myself," John Marshall declared.[29] "Political controversy is at all times an invidious task," wrote another.[30] The ultimate expression of this kind came from the pen of a Federalist poet:

> And lo! in meretricious dress,
> Forth comes a strumpet called 'THE PRESS.'
> Whose haggard, unrequested charms
> Rush into every blaggard's arms.
> Ye weak, deluded minds, beware!
> Nought but the outside here is fair!
> Then spurn the offers of her sway
> And kick the loathsome hag away.[31]

2

To many Federalists, the triumph of Thomas Jefferson was an object lesson in the power of the printed word. Shortly before the election of 1800 Fisher Ames had minimized the influence of editors, who, he

[25] Samuel Henshaw to Theodore Sedgwick, Apr. 15, 1789, in Sedgwick Papers, Mass. Hist. Soc.; see also James McHenry to Oliver Wolcott, July 22, 1800, in Hildreth, *History of the U. S.*, V, 375: The conduct of the Federalists, McHenry wrote, "in most, if not all of the states, is tremulous, timid, feeble, deceptive, and cowardly. They write private letters. To whom? To each other. But they do nothing to give a proper direction to the public mind."

[26] Oliver Wolcott to Fisher Ames, 1800, in Williamson, *American Suffrage*, p. 166.

[27] Timothy Dwight, *Travels in New England and New York*, 4 vols. (New Haven, 1821–1822), IV, 12.

[28] Allen McLane to Timothy Pickering, Feb. 8, 1800, in Pickering Papers, Mass. Hist. Soc.; see also John Adams to Timothy Pickering, Aug. 13, 1799, in ibid.; "And now, Sir, what shall I say to you on the subject of Libells and Satyrs, lawless things indeed?" But cf. Fisher Ames's more lofty response to a "jacobin" paper in Boston: "I do not read the *Chronicle*," he wrote majestically. "Abuse is unread and I hope unregarded"; Fisher Ames to Thomas Dwight, July 3, 1794, in Ames, *Works*, I, 145.

[29] John Marshall to Timothy Pickering, Oct. 15, 1798, in Pickering Papers, Mass. Hist. Soc.; see also John Jay to Peter Van Schaack, July 28, 1812, in Johnston, *Correspondence of Jay*; and James McHenry to Timothy Pickering, Oct. 16, 1809, in Pickering Papers, Mass. Hist. Soc.

[30] *Providence Gazette*, Aug. 9, 1800.

[31] [Hartford, Conn.] *Connecticut Courant*, Jan. 5, 1801.

believed, were bound to follow public opinion rather than lead it. "Printers are dependent for bread, writers for popularity," he said. "Neither will dare to tell any truth that readers will not want to hear."[32] But two weeks after Jefferson's inauguration he had reached a conclusion which represented a remarkable reorientation of thought. "The newspapers are an overmatch for any government," he wrote. "They will first overawe and then usurp it. This has been done, and the jacobins owe their triumph to the unceasing use of this engine."[33]

Ames enunciated a slogan which summed up his new attitude (and that of many younger Federalists) toward the press and politics in general. "*Fas est et ab hoste doceri,*" he wrote.[34] With a few other Federalists in Massachusetts, Ames decided to establish an electioneering paper for New England. While Ames himself had no scruples about seeking "to use the passions of the citizens,"[35] he and other old-school gentlemen who joined with him—among them Timothy Dwight and Jedidiah Morse—set their sights higher. It was not to be a "popular" sheet in the unpleasant sense of the word, nor would it use such weapons as scurrility. "Wit and satire should flash like the electrical fire," Ames declared, "but the Palladium should be fastitiously polite and well-bred. It should whip Jacobins as a gentleman would a chimney-sweeper, at arm's length, and keeping aloof from his soot."[36]

There was no intention of reducing political conversation to the lowest common denominator. The object was rather to educate, to uplift, and to purify. "Instead of uneducated printers, shop boys, and raw schoolmasters being, as at present, the chief instructors in politics," Ames wrote, "let the interest of the country be explained and asserted by able men, who have had a concern in the transaction of affairs, who understand those interests, and who will, and ever will, when they try to produce a deep national impression."[37]

[32] Fisher Ames to John Rutledge, Jr., Oct. 16, 1800, in Rutledge Papers, Southern Hist. Coll., Univ. of N. C.

[33] Fisher Ames to Theodore Dwight, Mar. 19, 1801, in Ames, *Works,* I, 294; see also Fisher Ames to Jeremiah Smith, Dec. 14, 1802, in ibid., I, 314. A Connecticut Federalist attributed Republican gains in his own state of more than 1000 votes in 1800 to wide distribution of the New London *Bee,* Hartford *American Mercury,* and the Philadelphia *Aurora* (Windham *Herald,* 23 October 1800).

[34] "It is perfectly proper to be taught by one's enemy;" Fisher Ames to Theodore Dwight, Mar. 19, 1801, ibid., I, 294.

[35] Fisher Ames to John Rutledge, July 30, 1801, in Rutledge Papers, Southern Hist. Coll., Univ. of N. C.

[36] Fisher Ames to Jeremiah Smith, Dec. 14, 1802, in ibid., I, 314; Henry W. de Saussure to Jedidiah Morse, Dec. 31, 1800, in Morse Papers, New York Public Library; Timothy Dwight to Jedidiah Morse, Dec. 19, 1800, in Norcross Papers, Mass. Hist. Soc.

[37] Fisher Ames to Jeremiah Smith, Dec. 14, 1802, in Ames, *Works,* I, 314; see also a similar complaint that papers were generally conducted by "young men just entering life, with little erudition, and much vanity, and what is worse, mechanics who have no education for the business of editors"; [New York, N. Y.] *Spectator,* Jan. 8, 1801.

The new journal was, therefore, to be the *London Gazette* of Federalism, *the* paper of the party, *the* standard of truth and political orthodoxy. Ames confidently believed that when the brilliant light of this political beacon began to illuminate the countryside, "jacobinism would sneak back into dirty lanes and yellow fever courts."[38]

The sponsors of this "engine of order" soon learned how expensive political journalism could be. Only large loans or contributions could sustain an electioneering paper. Even the Philadelphia *Aurora*, perhaps the most successful political sheet in America, only realized a profit of six cents on each annual subscription in a good year. In bad ones it teetered on the brink of bankruptcy.[39]

The New England Federalists who sought to establish a new electioneering paper were not able to secure sufficient financial support. They abandoned their original plans to found a new paper, and decided instead to modify a paper already in existence. Ames announced the change of plan in a letter to one of his close friends. "The *Mercury* or *Palladium* [one journal] is to be the federal paper," he wrote, "and pains are taken to spread it, and gain readers and patrons in all parts of New England."[40] The editor, a young Federal lawyer named Warren Dutton, was described as a man of "talents, learning and taste." "And, what is no less essential," wrote Ames, "he has discretion."[41]

Shortly before the state elections of 1801, the *New England Palladium* thus became a Federalist electioneering paper. Its sponsors sought to give it currency by arranging a year's subscription for every clergyman in Massachusetts, Vermont, and New Hampshire.[42] The paper won immediate popularity among Federalists. Its circulation became considerable, not only in New England but even as far away as South Carolina.[43] The industrious and discreet Mr. Dutton flogged the jacobins in a gentlemanly way and issued frequent appeals for an end to "petty distinctions, little rivalships, or unessential shades of opinion" among the "friends of order."[44]

In Connecticut the young Federalists who established a state organization, gave assistance and comfort to editors who sympathized with "the Cause," which made them less dependent upon the public and more dependent upon the party. The Hartford *Connecticut Courant*, the Litchfield *Monitor*, and other Federal papers were generously subsidized with

[38] Fisher Ames to Christopher Gore, Dec. 13, 1802, in Ames, *Works*, I, 310.
[39] Kurtz, *Presidency of John Adams*, p. 299.
[40] Fisher Ames to Thomas Dwight, Mar. 19, 1801, in Ames, *Works*, I, 295.
[41] Ibid.
[42] Ibid.; see also Levi Lincoln to Thomas Jefferson, July 5, 1801, in Jefferson Papers, Library of Congress; and [Boston, Mass.] *Independent Chronicle*, Sep. 3, 1801; and [Warren, R. I.] *Bristol County Register*, Mar. 31, 1801.
[43] Henry W. De Saussure to John Rutledge, Jr., Aug. 23, 1801, in Rutledge Papers, Southern Hist. Coll., Univ. of N. C.
[44] [Boston, Mass.] *New England Palladium*, Nov. 19, 1801.

money raised among "Gentlemen of Property and liberal Minds."[45] Every town committee was instructed to act as subscription agents for Hudson and Goodwin, editors of the *Courant*. Other funds were used to pay for papers which the committees were requested "to distribute gratis in each town, in addition to what shall be subscribed for."[46]

In New Hampshire, shortly after Federalists had organized themselves into committees, opposition papers commented on the way "their newspapers have been enlarged, without an addition of subscribers, suddenly and at once in various parts of the state."[47]

Meanwhile, Federalists in New York City, who were dissatisfied by the "drowzy" tone of Noah Webster's *Commercial Advertiser*, also established a political paper. A group of them, including Robert Troup and Alexander Hamilton, managed to secure an "extraordinary patronage" of approximately ten thousand dollars for a daily to be called the *Evening Post*.[48] Its editor, William Coleman, a man of considerable learning and intellectual refinement, was offered the princely income of two thousand dollars annually.[49]

When the New York *Evening Post* made its first appearance on November 16, 1801, friends and enemies alike praised it as a masterpiece of literary and journalistic craftsmanship. Even James Callendar considered it "the most elegant piece of workmanship we have seen, either in Europe or America."[50] Its strong white rag paper and fine, clean type contrasted with the blue paper and battered fonts of many early American journals.

The tone of the paper was equally elevated. Although it was undeniably an electioneering journal, sponsored by a group of Federalists for partisan purposes, its editor claimed to be impartial. "This paper shall be equally free to all parties," Coleman declared in his prospectus.[51] At least one of the *Post's* sponsors wished that he were not quite so correct.

[45] Unaddressed Circular dated July 9, 1804, in Simeon Baldwin Papers, Yale Univ. Library.

[46] Ibid.; Theodore Dwight et al. to Elias Shipman et al., Jan. 30, 1805, in Simeon Baldwin Papers, Yale University.

[47] [Walpole, N.H.] *Political Observer*, Aug. 18, 1804; the *N.H. Sentinel*, for example, had been struggling on its own resources since its founding in 1799. In the same year that Plumer's committees began to function, it suddenly increased in size and improved its appearance; Bauhan, "N.H. Sentinel," p. 66.

[48] Nevins, *New York Evening Post*, pp. 17ff.

[49] Theodore Ellemont to Noah Webster, Sep. 21, 1801, in Noah Webster Papers, New York Public Library; Samuel Bayard to Noah Webster, Oct. 13 1801, in ibid.; for Coleman's account of Hamilton's involvement, see Hilliard, *Jeremiah Mason*, p. 33.

[50] Nevins, *New York Evening Post*, p. 20.

[51] [New York, N. Y.] *Evening Post*, Nov. 17, 1801; the tone of the paper was very similar to that of the *Palladium*. Compare, for example, its quiet plea for party unity: "The cause of Federalism has received as much injury from the indiscreet contentions . . . among those who profess to be its friends, as from the open assault of its enemies"; ibid., Nov. 17, 1801.

"Coleman is very jealous and devoted to the federal cause," wrote Robert Troup in his cynical way, "but his paper is that of the scholar and the gentleman."[52]

The story was the same in every major city. Philadelphia Federalists put new life into the old *Gazette of the United States* by giving aid and encouragement to its able young editor, Enos Bronson, who took it over on November 2, 1801.[53] In Baltimore, Federalists led by Robert Goodloe Harper collected a capital of eight thousand dollars and used it to found the *Republican; or, Anti-Democrat* with a "very excellent printing office" and a large circulation in Maryland. Like the *Evening Post*, this paper made claims of independence, but its patronage was an open secret.[54] In the District of Columbia, Federalist Congressmen and Georgetown merchants supported the *Washington Federalist*.[55] Virginia Federalists, led by John Nicholas and John Marshall, joined together to lend aid and encouragement to editors of Federalist sympathies in the Old Dominion.[56]

Before 1800 the most decidedly federal paper in North Carolina was the *Minerva*. A few years afterward it became an electioneering paper with a new name, the *Minerva; or, Anti-Jacobin*. It had substantial assistance from local Federalists—a fund was opened among wealthy gentlemen to defray the cost of six hundred annual subscriptions for free distribution to "men of democratic principles of a moderate kind." Leading Federalists were appointed in each Congressional election district, and in turn in many of the counties to be responsible for the dissemination of the paper.[57]

[52] Robert Troup to Rufus King, June 6, 1802, King, *Life and Correspondence of King*, IV, 136.

[53] Burton Alva Konkle, "Enos Bronson, 1774–1823," *Pennsylvania Magazine of History and Biography*, LVII (1953), 355–358. Another Federalist paper published in Philadelphia was Major William Jackson's *Political and Commercial Register*, which first appeared on July 2, 1804. Jackson was an able if somewhat unstable character who had served as secretary of the Constitutional Convention in 1787. This paper was often quoted by Federalists but not apparently subsidized by them; see William Duane to Thomas Jefferson, Nov. 12, 1801, in Thomas Jefferson Papers, Library of Congress.

[54] [Baltimore, Md.] *Republican; or, Anti-Democrat*, July 29, 1803; [Easton, Md.] *Star*, Jan. 31, 1804; Uriah Tracy to Robert Goodloe Harper, Jan. 15, 1804, in Miscellaneous Manuscripts, New York Public Library; Nevins, *New York Evening Post*, p. 17; [Wilmington, Del.] *True Republican*, June 6, 1809.

[55] For the checkered career of the *Washington Federalist*, see Uriah Tracy to Robert Goodloe Harper, Jan. 15, 1804; Robert Goodloe Harper to Uriah Tracy, Jan. 20, 1804, in Miscellaneous Manuscripts, New York Public Library; Archibald Lee to Robert Beverley, Sep. 15, 1808, in Rutledge Papers, Southern Hist. Coll., Univ. of N. C.; [Boston, Mass.] *New England Palladium*, Dec. 11, 1804; Archibald Lee to Dwight Foster, Sep. 16, 1808, in Broadsides, American Antiquarian Society.

[56] John Nicholas to Alexander Hamilton, Aug. 4, 1803, in Hamilton Papers, Library of Congress.

[57] [Raleigh, N. C.] *Minerva; or, Anti-Jacobin*, May 16, 1803; Duncan Cameron to John Moore, Sep. 2, 1802, in Moore Papers, Duke Univ. Library, pub. in Dodd, "Macon Papers," III, 36–38; Blackwell P. Robinson, *William R. Davie* (Chapel Hill, 1957), pp. 361–363.

South Carolina Federalists complained in 1801 that they were "very illy off for a good press."[58] Henry W. De Saussure thought that "it would be of infinite service if we could procure an able, sensible, virtuous, well-informed man who could conduct a paper in the manner [of] the *Palladium*.[59] Late in 1802 Federalists in Charleston imported an editor, Loring Andrews, from the northern states and encouraged him in the establishment of a new daily Federalist paper, the *Charleston Courier*. Its patronage must have been quite extensive, for by 1805 it was strong enough to survive the death of its editor.[60]

After the election of 1800, Federalist electioneering papers also appeared in villages and country towns. An important and highly successful electioneering sheet in western Maryland was the *Frederick-town Herald*, established by a group of local Federalists including Roger Brooke Taney in 1802.[61] In Hudson, New York, a sprightly Federalist paper, the *Balance*, edited by Harry Croswell, appeared in 1801.[62] Another Federalist electioneering paper, the *New England Repertory*, was founded in Newburyport in 1803. A year later it moved to Boston.[63] These were but three of many similar events (see Table 2 in Appendix III).

By comparison with many Jeffersonian sheets, these Federalist electioneering papers were remarkable for their restraint. Their editors with few exceptions were indeed "scholars and gentlemen." The papers themselves were perhaps the most distinguished journalistic specimens which the nation had seen.[64]

But they were not without critics, even among Federalists. Despite the participation of some old school gentlemen, others did not approve. Governeur Morris, for example, was under constraint and unremitting pressure to write for the *Evening Post*. Occasionally he yielded, but with an oath and a protest and a promise to himself that each communication would be his last. He gave three reasons for his disapproval: "It may be objected," he wrote bitterly, "firstly that our newspapers abound with political dissertations which few take the trouble to read; secondly that 'tis not easy to enlighten those who are not already possest of more in-

[58] Henry W. De Saussure to John Rutledge, Jr., Sep. 13, 1801, in Rutledge Papers, Southern Hist. Coll., Univ. of N. C.

[59] Ibid., Sass, *News and Courier*, 3–27.

[60] *Charleston Courier*, Jan. 10, 1803; Abraham Nott to John Rutledge, June 26, 1803, in John Rutledge Papers, Southern Hist. Coll., Univ. of N. C.; John Stanly to John Rutledge, Apr. 25, 1807, in ibid.; Henry W. De Saussure to John Rutledge, Jan. 1803, in ibid.; Andrews had been employed by Theodore Sedgwick to edit the *Western Star* in Stockbridge, Mass., from 1789–1797, one of the few Federalist electioneering papers outside the large cities before 1800.

[61] *Frederick-town Herald*, July 3, Aug. 8, 1802; Swisher, *Taney*, p. 44.

[62] [Hudson, N. Y.] *Balance*, May 21, 1808.

[63] [Newburyport, Mass.] *New England Repertory*, July 6, 1803; Benjamin Whitwell to Theophilus Parsons, Aug. 3, 1804, in Columbia Univ. Coll., Columbia Univ.

[64] Schouler, *History of the United States*, II, 31.

formation than man in general can spare time to acquire, and thirdly that it would be presumption in one to protrude the Reflections and Experience of only thirty years on a Community, every member of which is a Statesman born."[65]

An altogether different kind of criticism came from such younger Federalists as John Rutledge. He had no basic objection to the establishment of Federalist electioneering papers—quite the contrary. "Much good might be done by having our newspapers well supported," he believed. "Men of talents should assist them with their pens, and the rich and timid with their purses."[66] Rutledge criticized the early Federalist electioneering papers for not going far enough, for devoting too much space to measured and moderate apologies for the old order. "They should no longer be champions of a fallen administration, but of the people," he argued. Rutledge was no democrat, no defender of popular government in a Jeffersonian sense. His hope was to get close to the people in order to gain control of them. "If Jefferson cannot be ousted but by this sort of *cant*," he wrote candidly, "we must have recourse to it."[67]

Rutledge's disagreement with the editors and sponsors of the early Federalist electioneering papers became a quarrel in 1802, when he suggested to Elias Boudinot Caldwell of the *Washington Federalist* that the "spirit" of this languishing paper might be improved by adding James Callendar to its staff. Callendar was an unprincipled and unattractive scribbler who had been "the most abusive opponent of John Adams' administration" while in the pay of Jefferson.[68] By 1802 he had turned against his old employer and was available to the Federalists.

Editor Caldwell was shocked and angered by Rutledge's suggestion. "However the spirit of the paper might be increased by such an arrangement," he replied indignantly, "its reputation would certainly be lost. It would be found very difficult to support, much more, to associate with a man whose character has been so completely damned to infamy."[69] As Caldwell warmed to his subject, he revealed the gap between moderate Federalists like himself and men like Rutledge who favored more extreme measures. "I do not conceive a newspaper intended as much to gratify resentment or party spirit as to convince those who have been deceived," Caldwell wrote. "It is certainly incorrect to imitate the conduct we condemn."[70]

[65] Gouverneur Morris to Jonathan Dayton, Dec. 18, 1805, in Morris Papers, Library of Congress; see also Rufus King to Gouverneur Morris, July 17, 1805, in Morris Papers, Columbia Univ. Library.

[66] John Rutledge, Jr. to Harrison Gray Otis, Apr. 3, 1803, in Otis Papers, Mass. Hist. Soc.

[67] Ibid.

[68] Cunningham, *Jeffersonian Republicans*, p. 170.

[69] Elias Boudinot Caldwell to John Rutledge, Jr., Aug. 17, 1802, in Rutledge Papers, Southern Hist. Coll., Univ. of N. C.

[70] Ibid.

Such plans as Rutledge's soon triumphed over objections such as Caldwell's. Gradually more extreme Federalist electioneering papers began to appear, inexpensive sheets of no journalistic merit that came and went with astonishing rapidity. The birth and death of one was celebrated by a Republican rival with the following memorable lines:

> But two years old the creature was,
> A dark complexioned slut,
> Filthy and lying all about;
> But now her mouth is shut.[71]

The expenses of these sheets were pared to the bone. Type was ancient and sometimes almost illegible; paper was cheap blue stuff. Standards of editing were generally undistinguished. In the newspaper wars of the new Republic, Gresham's Law prevailed. Bad journals drove out good. An example is a sequence of electioneering sheets in Hudson, New York. The men of the Federal party set up Harry Croswell's *Balance* in 1801. Local Republicans quickly countered with a printer of their own persuasion—Charles Holt, who put out a paper called the *Bee*. The Federalist editor, Croswell, responded by filling the *Balance* so full of invective that he had to publish another journal for his advertisements, the Hudson *Advertiser*. When the *Bee* replied in kind, Croswell launched a third paper, the *Wasp*, which became a symbol of unrestrained scurrility. A witness to this activity commemorated it in an epic poem that could be sung to the tune of Yankee Doodle:

> There's Charlie Holt is come to town
> A proper lad with types, sir.
> The Democrats have fetched him here
> To give the federals stripes, sir.
>
> The Balance-folks seem cruel 'fraid
> That he'll pull down their scales, sir.
> And so they got a pokerish wasp,
> To sting him with his tail, sir.[72]

The most important of more extreme Federalist papers was the *Federal Republican,* published in Baltimore until its young editor, a Hotspur named Alexander Contee Hanson, was chased out of town by a mob. This journal first appeared in 1808 under the sponsorship of an "association of gentlemen," to fill the place of the now defunct Baltimore *Anti-Democrat* as the principal organ of Maryland Federalism.[73] The amount of its capital is unknown, but it must have been considerable, for

---

[71] Robinson, *Jeff. Dem. in N. Eng.*, p. 70.

[72] [New York, N. Y.] *Evening Post,* Aug. 17, 1802; Clarence S. Brigham, *History and Bibliography of American Newspapers, 1690–1820,* 2 vols. (Worcester, Mass., 1947), I, 583.

[73] [Baltimore, Md.] *Federal Republican,* July 4, 1808; [Philadelphia, Pa.] *United States Gazette,* June 24, 1808.

in 1818 Hanson sold out for twelve thousand dollars.[74] The "association of gentlemen" was limited to young men. "There is scarcely a respectably old Federalist involved," a Republican commented.[75]

These radical Federalist electioneering papers outstripped their comparatively restrained predecessors in the zeal with which they defended the "Cause" and attacked its enemies. In place of the traditional protestations of impartiality, their partisanship was open and unashamed. The prospectus of the Cooperstown *Switch*, for example, was a candid declaration of intent:

> To seek, to find, the kennel'd pack,
> To lacerate the Rascals back.
> Detect their crimes, expose their pranks,
> And put to flight their ragged ranks.[76]

The titles of some of these sheets—*Scourge, Switch*, and *Wasp*—suggest the wild abandon with which their editors lashed out at Republicans. In the course of its brief career, the Boston *Scourge* was the defendent in ninety-nine libel suits, an average of three per issue.[77]

The activity of the young Federalists, particularly after 1808, in establishing new journals and encouraging old ones was astounding. The Boston Central Committee made a survey of newspapers in New England which carefully listed each press which might be of use to the "Cause," the assistance which it was receiving and the assistance which it still needed.[78] To one Republican it seemed that "the Federalists are purchasing all the *Presses* in New England whose proprietors are mercenary enough to comply with their wishes."[79] Overtures were even made to a Democratic electioneering editor, Isaac Hill of the *New Hampshire Patriot*, without success.[80] There was a steady augmentation of political material in old and well established papers edited by men of Federalist sympathies after 1800. The Stockbridge *Western Star* is an illustration. Its commentary increased from 10.5 per cent of total news space in 1790 to 16.9 per cent in 1801 to 26.6 per cent in 1810.[81]

---

[74] Alexander Contee Hanson to George Carbin Washington, Dec. 29, 1818, in Hanson-Washington Papers, Md. Hist. Soc.

[75] [Wilmington, N. C.] *True Republican*, June 6, 1809.

[76] [Cooperstown, N. Y.] *Impartial Observer*, Mar. 4, 1809; cited in Milton W. Hamilton, *The Country Printer, New York State, 1785–1830* (New York, 1936), p. 188.

[77] See *Rutland Herald*, May 13, 1812.

[78] Survey of Newspapers in New England, n. d. [c. 1808], in Otis Papers, Mass. Hist. Soc.

[79] [Murfreesborough, N. C.] *Hornet*, Oct. 8, 1812.

[80] Ibid.; the Windsor, Vt. *Washingtonian* was reportedly subsidized by the local Washington Benevolent Society; see [Windsor, Vt.] *Vermont Republican*, Feb. 24, 1812.

[81] This is the estimate of Richard D. Birdsall, *Berkshire County*, p. 189; after 1807 this paper became the [Pittsfield, Mass.] *Berkshire Reporter*.

These extreme Federalist electioneering papers were more accessible to the people than more dignified dailies such as the *Post* and the *Courier*, which had cost eight to ten dollars annually, plus postage. The weeklies which followed were as cheap as $1.50 a year, three cents an issue, which sometimes amounted to less than the cost of postage alone for the dailies. At least one electioneering paper published an edition on cheap paper at a reduced rate.[82]

Sometimes, at election times, whole editions of these papers were distributed free. An example was a special weekly extra edition of the Boston *Weekly Messenger*, a paper which had been "set up with great pains, trouble, and expense by the Federal party."[83] Its editor announced that "any persons, friendly to the federal cause, may be supplied gratis with these papers for the purpose of carrying them into the country."[84] Other Federal printers departed from the traditional practice of American editors and offered short-term subscriptions for a few months before elections.[85]

More important, latter-day Federalist electioneering papers addressed themselves directly to the people. Their editors made themselves masters of "propaganda"—a word just coming into common usage.[86] They provided an example which was quickly emulated by many of the older Federalist papers.

Federal printers attempted to reach the people by improving the visual impact of their papers. Even in large cities, editors of electioneering

[82] Abraham Nott to John Rutledge, June 26, 1803, in Rutledge Papers, Southern Hist. Coll., Univ. of N. C. [Windsor, Vt.] *Washingtonian*, June 27, 1814; July 23, 1810. It is difficult to determine the reach of American newspapers. Quantification is impossible (but cf. Stewart, *Jeff. Journalism*, p. 27.) Contemporary estimates varied considerably. The Poughkeepsie, N. Y. *Political Barometer* estimated that two thirds of the families along the post routes did not receive a paper. "There are yet many families of property who do not receive or read any periodical," its editor declared (June 8, 1802). But in Connecticut, the Hartford *Courant* observed that "almost every family in Connecticut is supplied with a weekly gazette" (Jan. 26, 1801).

[83] Harrison Gray Otis to William Sullivan, Oct. 23, 1812, in Miscellaneous Manuscripts, New York Public Library; see also [Windsor, Vt.] *Vermont Republican*, July 20, 1812.

[84] [Boston, Mass.] *New England Palladium*, Mar. 27, 1812.

[85] [Baltimore, Md.] *Federal Republican*, Aug. 12, 1809. The editors accepted almost anything in lieu of cash. One announced that "the following articles of country produce will be received in payment for the newspaper; viz; Beef, pork, flour, indian corn and meal, oats, butter, cheese, lard, fowls, eggs, sauce of almost any kind, wool, flax, honey, beeswax, tallows, candles"; [Columbus, Ohio] *Western Intelligencer*; see also [Hanover] *Dartmouth Gazette*, 3 Jan. 1801. Dec. 10, 1814; Clarence S. Brigham, *Journals and Journeymen* (Philadelphia, 1950), p. 26; see also [Wilkesbarre, Pa.] *Luzerne County Federalist*, May 6, 1808; this practice, of course, was commonplace long before parties developed.

[86] [Boston, Mass.] *New England Palladium*, Mar.–Apr. 1812; [Albany, N. Y.] *Balance*, Jan. 6–Feb. 2, 1810; [Exeter, N. H.] *Constitutionalist*, Feb. 19, 1811; Porter G. Perrin, "The Life and Works of Thomas Greene Fessenden," in *University of Maine Studies*, 2nd. Ser., IV (1925), 113.

journals placed important political information on the front page instead of advertisements.[87] On important occasions they used double-width columns and display types—roman, italic, and black-letter.[88] For major stories they developed eye-catching headlines in sixty-point type, such as "Borrowing in time of Peace!"[89] Cartoons and caricatures were also used with effect. A striking and familiar example is the famous "Gerrymander," which first appeared in Federalist papers during the Massachusetts campaigns of 1812 and 1813.[90] During the Embargo, Federalist editors frequently used a terrapin withdrawing into its shell to symbolize the administration's policy.[91]

Cartoons, caricatures, and typographical flourishes were eminently useful to the Federalist editors, but were never more than the means of drawing attention to a written message. Always and inevitably the main reliance remained the printed word. But there were many devices which served to sharpen the edge of an appeal. The Federalist editors showed that they understood these techniques very well. After 1800 they made themselves masters of the art of popular rhetoric.[92] The awkwardness of early efforts suggest that these usages did not come easily. An anti-Jeffersonian address to Philadelphia mechanics concluded thus: "Was it for this, ye useful and respectable men, was it for this that you gave your suffrage to his elevation?" The reaction of a "useful and respectable mechanic" to the plea can well be imagined.[93] Such titles as "Anti-

[87] [Boston, Mass.] *New England Palladium*, Feb. 28–Mar. 13, 1812.

[88] Hamilton, *Country Printer in N. Y.*, p. 13; [Raleigh, N. C.] *Minerva*, Aug. 29, 1803; [New Bern, N. C.] *Carolina Federal Republican*, extra, Aug. 4, 1812.

[89] [Boston, Mass.] *New England Palladium*, Mar. 6, 1812; see also [Windsor, Vt.] *Washingtonian*, Aug. 28, 1816.

[90] It was not the work of Gilbert Stuart, as was generally believed, but of an obscure Federalist named Elkaneh Tisdale. After the defeat of Gerry in 1813, another cartoon appeared in the Federal papers—the scrawny skeleton of a Gerrymander with the caption, "Hatched 1812, Died 1813"; John Ward Dean, "The Gerrymander," *New England Historical and Genealogical Register*, XXVII (1873), 421, XLVI (1892), 374–383.

[91] [New York, N. Y.] *Evening Post*, Feb. 6, 1809; for Federalist cartoons on other subjects, see [Albany, N. Y.] *Balance*, Apr. 21, 1809; Fee, *New Jersey*, p. 202; [Boston, Mass.] *New England Palladium*, Feb. 21, 1815; [Boston, Mass.] *Repertory*, May 19, 1807, Sep. 6, 1808, Mar. 17, 1814; *Portland Gazette*, Jan. 2, 1809; [Bristol, R. I.] *Mt. Hope Eagle*, May 30, 1807; [Boston, Mass.] *Scourge*, Oct. 7, 1811; [Worcester, Mass.] *Spy*, Mar. 25, 1807; [Boston, Mass.] *Columbian Centinel*, Mar. 14, 1807.

[92] There had been some similar activity on the part of Federalist editors before 1800, particularly in New York State; see Young, *Democratic Republican Movement in New York*, pp. 396–426.

[93] [Philadelphia, Pa.] *Political and Commercial Register*, July 3, 1804; see also the taunts of Jeffersonians in the [Portland, Maine] *Eastern Argus*, Sep. 6, 1804: "A *Federalist* a few days since, accosted a *Republican*—'Well, sir, we intend to try pamphleteering in the business of choosing Federal Electors as your party did in the choice of Governor.' 'Did you,' says the *Republican*, 'ever hear the story of the monkey, who having seen a man shave himself, stole the razor to try his skill at shaving, and thereby gave himself a mortal wound?'"

Jacobin" or *"Anti-Democrat"* fell into desuetude; instead, Federal papers began to call themselves *The People's Friend, The People's Advocate,* or *Volksfreund.*

Even the *New England Palladium,* one of the most staid of the party's electioneering papers, provides many examples of the folksiness which Federal editors affected: headlines such as "Look, Neighbors, Look!" or "Friends and Fellow Citizens, Read these Names!"[94] Reports of Federalist mass meetings in the *Palladium* were headed "Voice of the People," or "People's Meeting," or even "Vox Populi, Vox Dei"![95] Federalists were described generically as "Friends of the Poor," "Friends of the People," "The Yeomanry of New-England" or even "Friends of Equal Rights."[96]

Federal candidates were treated in the same fashion. A man as thoroughly elitistic as Harrison Gray Otis was billed as "the man of the people."[97] Even John Quincy Adams, dour and aloof, received the following endorsement when he ran for office in 1802: ". . . vote for Jack Adams: He is the seamen's and mechanic's friend: can do his duty aloft or below, and was brought up by his father, our old Federal Commodore."[98] Federalist contributors, writing, perhaps, at polished mahoghany desks, signed their political epistles to the people with such pseudonyms as "A Poor Man of the Country," or "One of the People," or "Thousands."[99]

Republicans were disgusted. They enlarged their papers, and filled them with reminders of the Federalist strictures against the people before 1800. "These same federals," one of them wrote bitterly, "are the very men who now call themselves the *exclusive friends of the poor man's rights!* Where is your memory? Where is their shame?" "Trust them not," warned another. "They are wolves in sheep's clothing," cried a third.[100]

Every propaganda technique listed in twentieth-century manuals can

---

[94] [Boston, Mass.] *New England Palladium,* Mar. 6, 1812.

[95] Ibid., Sep. 9, 1808; Feb. 3, 1809; Mar. 24, July 10, 17, 1812; Feb. 1, 1814; see also [New York, N. Y.] *Evening Post,* Sep. 30, 1812; *Portland Gazette,* Mar. 27, 1809.

[96] [Boston, Mass.] *New England Palladium,* Mar. 31, 1807; Mar. 17, 1812; Nov. 23, 1813.

[97] Ibid., Aug. 6, 1813.

[98] [New York, N. Y.] *Evening Post,* Nov. 3, 1802; a similar campaign was undertaken on behalf of Platt in the New York election of 1810. See [Hudson, N. Y.] *Northern Whig,* Jan. 26, 1810.

[99] [New York, N. Y.] *Evening Post,* Dec. 25, 1807; Mar. 25, 1808; [Annapolis, Md.] *Maryland Gazette,* Sep. 17, 1818; [New York, N. Y.] *Evening Post,* Oct. 7, 1802; [Albany, N. Y.] *Balance,* Jan. 26, 1810; there was much of this before 1800, of course, but more afterward, and also a noticeable diminution of such antidemocratic pen names as "Aristides" or "Phocion."

[100] [Baltimore, Md.] *Whig,* Aug. 10, 1811; Aug. 17, 1813; [Baltimore, Md.] *American,* Aug. 8, 1811; a piece signed "Demosthenes" in the handwriting of William Plumer, Oct. 20, 1812, in Plumer Papers, Library of Congress; [Portland, Me.] *Eastern Argus,* Nov. 1, 1804; [Bristol, R. I.] *Mt. Hope Eagle,* Mar. 28, 1807. See, e.g., the enlargement of Republican papers of New Hampshire & Vermont in response to Federalist efforts, as described in [Windsor, Vt.] *Washingtonian,* 27 Aug. 1810.

be found, finely developed in Federal electioneering sheets.[101] Much was made of slogans and catchwords. For Caleb Strong's gubernatorial campaigns in Massachusetts, rallying cries included "The Long Pull, The STRONG Pull, The Pull Altogether." Another was "STRONG in the field! STRONG in the Cabinet! STRONG in the hearts of the People!"[102] Intricate issues were summarized in a few phrases or reduced to a line of wretched verse. "How fertile is the genius of Federalism in furnishing *low doggerel* epithets to be applied on any occasion," a Republican paper complained.[103] Political problems which might have stymied Solomon were resolved in a pun or an epigram. The Embargo was dismissed in an anagram:

"O, grab em;" says King Tom.
"O, grab me;" says the merchant, "for what in God's name?"

"Go bar em;" says King Tom.
"Go bar me;" says the farmer.
"Aye, that I will says the Embargo."[104]

Federalists, who were seeking to win elections by influencing voters, learned, in the words of Fisher Ames, "to rely upon the effect of repetition."[105] Editors ran the same cant words and phrases in their columns over and over again. Such slogans as "Peace, Union, and Commerce" in 1812 were drummed into the ears of their readers.

Federalist political writers also appreciated the value of humor in attracting and holding a reader's attention. Sometimes their jokes were as primitive as one which was current in the New York electioneering papers during the Embargo: "Why had Democratic barbers doubled the price of a shave? Because Democratic faces were twice as long."[106] Or they could be as feculent as an electioneering song to the tune of the Rogue's march:

Great Jefferson first shall have command
Next Aaron like Moses shall head the state band;
Brockholst as good a Repub: as ever p—s-t,
Next stands fairest on the list.
If the New York Phaeton should the reins hold,
He'll scorch all your bottoms black as pit coal.[107]

Or they might be as scandalous as a song titled "Moll Carey," from the pen of the young Federalist Theodore Dwight, who, in the judgment of

[101] See, e.g., Curtis D. MacDougall, *Understanding Public Opinion* (New York, 1952).

[102] Edwin C. Rozwenc, "Caleb Strong: The Last of the River Gods," *The Northampton Book* (Northampton, 1954), pp. 56–76.

[103] [Bristol, R. I.] *Mt. Hope Eagle*, Feb. 28, 1807.

[104] [New York, N. Y.] *Evening Post*, Feb. 6, 1809.

[105] Fisher Ames to Timothy Pickering, Jan. 1, 1807, in Pickering Papers, Mass. Hist. Soc.

[106] [New York, N. Y.] *Evening Post*, Apr. 28, 1808.

[107] "A *New* Arsecotcia Song" [1804], in Broadsides, New York Public Library.

Fisher Ames, "knows well the avenues to New England minds." It was a satire upon a Republican meeting in New Haven led by a clergyman of "unblemished reputation" named Levi Ives. Moll Carey, it might be noted, was the madam of a notorious New York brothel:

> Behold a motley crew
> Comes crowding o'er the Green
> Of every Shape and Hue,
> Complexion, form and mein.
>
> [chorus] With deafening noise
> Drunkards and Whores
> And rogues in scores
> They all rejoice.
>
> . . . Ye tribes of faction join
> Your daughters and your wives
> Moll Carey's come to dine
> And dance with Deacon Ives.[108]

Interspersed with humor was bathos. For every important Federalist occasion there was a throbbing ode to:

> Dear Liberty, that lovely flower
> That vanisheth e'en in an hour.

The Embargo and the War of 1812 occasioned many choice specimens. Among them:

> The hopeless race of sailors move
> Half famished o'er the plain.
> For bread hard industry has strove
> Alas! the strife is vain.[109]

"Omnibus words," as twentieth-century publicists call them, were used by Federal editors with frequency and effect. "Identification" techniques, subtle and crude, were also in evidence. In the Massachusetts elections of 1808, Federal candidates were identified with "Washington, Adams, New England, virtue, and liberty." The usefulness of the so-called "band wagon" technique was also fully apparent to Federal editors.[110]

Not all Federalists condoned this unrestrained exploitation of popular journalism. One of them declared, "The federalists behave scandalously. I read pieces in their newspapers which degrade them below the charac-

---

[108] [Hartford, Conn.] *Connecticut Courant*, Mar. 2, 1803; Fisher Ames to Josiah Quincy, Jan. 27, 1807, in Ames, *Works*, I, 390; It was, of course, without even a shadow of substance; see also [New York, N. Y.] *Evening Post*, Oct. 29, 1808; William Cullen Bryant, *The Embargo*, ed. Thomas O. Mabbott (Gainesville, 1955), p. 40.

[109] Undated broadside, New York Public Library.

[110] [Boston, Mass.] *New England Palladium*, Aug. 23, 1808; [Exeter, N. H.] *Constitutionalist*, May 21, 1810; *Portland Gazette*, Oct. 17, 1800.

ter of rational freemen."[111] But such behavior continued until the party disintegrated. Federal political writers spoke in their own defense: "In times like this, it is right to appeal to the people, not in the attitude and language of sedition and rebellion, but in the attitude of argument and expostulation."[112]

The most eminent student of early American newspapers speaks of the early national period as the "dark age of American journalism."[113] His judgment is understandable. Never, not even in the heyday of Pulitzer and Hearst, were American papers as scurrilous and irresponsible as in the young republic. In Boston, for example, a Republican electioneering paper portrayed a Federalist rival thus: "That polluted vehicle of misrepresentation and falsehood, the Daily Advertiser, is a most plentiful outpouring of malignancy and gall, well adopted to be the Boston branch of the Georgetown Common Sewer."[114] By 1816, many Americans would have agreed with Thomas Jefferson's evaluation of his nation's newspapers. "I rarely think them worth reading," he wrote, "and almost never worth notice."[115]

But behind the smoke and flame of party strife, developments of deep significance were taking place. The American press was becoming increasingly popular; partisan politics served as the catalyst. In American history, popular journalism preceded mass journalism. Before the development of high-speed presses and pulp paper made possible a penny daily, American editors had already begun to refine the techniques of popular journalism, and nowhere more than in electioneering papers. At the same time, the chief purpose of a newspaper, the dissemination of news, was not neglected. Indeed, party competition was productive here, too. Two examples illustrate the point.

First, federal editors of electioneering papers sought to regularize the collection of information, which had previously been a hit-or-miss affair, as material happened to fall into the hands of printers.[116] In 1806, Charles Prentiss, editor of the Washington Federalist, worked out a primitive news service. For ten dollars a week he undertook to supply accounts

---

111 John Gorham to Leverett Saltonstall, n. d., in Saltonstall Papers, Mass. Hist. Soc.; see also Ebenezer Huntington to Rufus King, Dec. 25, 1812, with the draft of King's reply, in King Papers, New York Hist. Soc.; Charles Carroll of Carrollton to Robert Goodloe Harper, July 4, 1811, in Harper-Pennington Papers, Md. Hist. Soc.

112 [Philadelphia, Pa.] Freeman's Journal, Jan. 3, 1810.

113 Frank Luther Mott, History of American Journalism, 3rd edn. (New York, 1962), pp. 167–180.

114 [Boston, Mass.] Patriot, Feb. 19, 1814. By Daily Advertiser was meant the Repertory; the Georgetown Common Sewer was, of course, the Federal Republican.

115 Thomas Jefferson to James Monroe, Feb. 4, 1816, in Ford, Writings of Thomas Jefferson, X, 18.

116 Newark Gazette, Feb. 25, 1800; see also a Democratic editor's allusion to "the privilege taken in their editorial capacities by many of my typographical brethren of inventing news." James Wilson to William Darlington, Jan. 6, 1802, in Darlington Papers, Library of Congress.

of Washington affairs, at least twice weekly. He guaranteed that accounts of Congressional debates would be dispatched within twenty-four hours of the event. Prentiss's news service functioned sporadically for five years. It was less than a resounding success, but nevertheless it constituted an interesting and significant attempt to deal with the central problem of news gathering.[117]

Another interesting if embryonic development was that of the editorial as a regular feature, separate from news columns. The *Courier* was, according to a local historian, the first paper in South Carolina to present "regular and pronounced editorial expressions of opinion."[118] At the same time, according to the historian of the Pittsburgh *Gazette*, "the evolution of the editorial" became apparent in that paper as well.[119]

When the development of the editorial and systematic news gathering are added to the methodological devices discussed earlier—the expanded use of front-page news, cartoons, headlines, display types, double columns, the application of rhetorical techniques such as folksiness, simplification, identification, omnibus phrases, and repetition—we gain a new perspective on the "dark age of American journalism."

[117] Benjamin Russell to Charles Prentiss, Dec. 1, Dec. 20, 1806, Dec. 5, 1811, in Prentiss Papers, American Antiquarian Soc.; it is possible that similar arrangements were made between Prentiss and editors of southern Federalist papers. The Democratic editors of Charleston complained to Madison that they were regularly scooped on events in Washington by the editors of the *Courier*. See Wolfe, *Jeff. Dem. in S. C.*, p. 248.

[118] Ibid., p. 182.

[119] Andrews, *Pittsburgh Post Gazette*, p. 6.

VIII

A Party in Search of an Issue

Popular gales sometimes blow hard, but they don't blow long. The man who has the courage to face them will at last out-face them.

—GEORGE CABOT, 1797

We must court popular favor. We must study popular opinion and accomodate measures to what it is.

—FISHER AMES, 1801[1]

I

The Federalists who created party organizations in the states, emulated the electioneering techniques of their opponents, founded Washington Benevolent Societies, and sponsored a political press clearly perceived that they labored in vain, unless they found a message which appealed to the public. After 1800 they set out in search of an issue which could carry them to victory and power. They never found one, just as they never succeeded in erasing the stigma which the Jeffersonians had affixed to Federalism during the 1790s. But if the Federalists' search for an issue is not a success story, it is a highly significant one. It provides another manifestation of the way in which the ideals of the old school slowly faded away; another demonstration of the way in which younger Federalists came to terms with the world in which they lived; another measure of the expansion of democracy in America.

There is nothing to be gained by a chronological recitation of the Federalists' search for an issue, year by year, campaign by campaign. This approach to the problem would obscure its solution. To uncover the deep changes which were occuring in the structure of American politics during the period 1800–1816, it is necessary to look beneath the day-to-day events which have absorbed the attention of political historians. We must seek out the logic of change itself, and make *it* the framework of our analysis.

The men who led the Federalists before 1800—George Washington, George Cabot, John Jay, and other gentlemen of the old school—believed

---

[1] George Cabot to Oliver Wolcott, Apr, 7, 1797, in Lodge *Cabot* p. 120; I read "last" for "least." Fisher Ames to John Rutledge, Jr., Jan. 26, 1801, in Rutledge Papers, Southern Hist. Coll., Univ. of N. C.

that the sacred duty of a public man was to pursue the "common good" without permitting himself to be distracted by the opinions of his friends and constituents, by opinions merely popular. In their minds, a politician who sought merely to follow public opinion was derelict in his duty, devoid of honor and integrity, guilty of wanton and reckless political behavior.[2]

A North Carolina Federalist who lived beyond his time, William Richardson Davie, ran for office in 1803 and addressed the public in the following way: "I desire that it may be clearly understood, that I never have, and that I never will, surrender my principles to the opinions of any man, or description of men, either in or out of power; and that I wish no man to vote for me, who is not willing to leave me free to pursue the good of my Country according to the best of my judgment, without respect either to party men or party views."[3] There was much to be said for this ideal, but after 1800 it did not appeal to the true sovereigns of America—the people. The "great and independent character" of General Davie attracted fewer votes than the "puny mind" of his Republican rival.[4] Two years later the General withdrew "in silent dignity" from the state.[5]

But after the inauguration of Thomas Jefferson, other Federalists realized that the idealism of the old school was no longer relevant to the realities of American public life. "There is one particular in which, I think, the leading gentlemen of the Washington school have uniformly erred," Noah Webster declared. "They have attempted to resist the force

[2] See above, ch. I.

[3] William R. Davie to the voters, dtd. May 2, 1803, in W. R. Davie Papers, Southern Hist. Coll., Univ. of N. C.

[4] Gilpatrick, *Jeffersonian Democracy in N. C.*, p. 168n.

[5] Ibid., p. 168; see also William R. Davie to John Steele, Sep. 25, 1803, in Henry M. Wagstaff, ed., *The Papers of John Steele*, 2 vols. (Raleigh, 1924), I, 414–415; for similar utterances by older Federalists, see Jonathan Jackson, *Thoughts upon the Political Situation of the United States of America in which that of Massachusetts is more Particularly Considered* (Worcester, 1788), p. 185; Ames, *Works*, II, 3; Parsons, *Memoir of Theophilus Parsons*, p. 99; [Boston, Mass.] *Gazette*, Mar. 19, 1787. Samuel Chase's views are noticed in Philip A. Crowl, *Maryland During and After the Revolution* (Baltimore, 1943), p. 464; see also James Wilson in Elliot, *Debates*, II, 420. An interesting debate took place in the First Congress over Thomas Tudor Tucker's proposed amendment guaranteeing the right of instruction to the people. With but two exceptions it was supported by men who later became Jeffersonians, and opposed by Representatives who called themselves Federalists in 1800; see *Annals of Congress*, 1st Cong., 1st Sess. 733–747 (Aug. 15, 1789). Younger Federalists sometimes took the same position; see Abijah Bigelow to his wife, July 4, 1813, in *American Antiquarian Society Proceedings*, XL (1930), 367; Robert Goodloe Harper, "Address to his Constituents," *Works* (Baltimore, 1814), p. 42; and Gaylord Griswold in *Annals of Congress*, 8th Cong., 1st Sess., 664 (Dec. 7, 1803). For the contrasting opinions of Jeffersonians, see Maclay, *Journal*, pp. 387–389; Eugene T. Mudge, *The Social Philosophy of John Taylor of Caroline* (New York, 1939), p. 96; Clement Eaton, "Southern Senators and the Right of Instruction," *Journal of Southern History*, XVIII (1952), 305; [Nashville, Tenn.] *Whig*, Dec. 2, 1812.

of public opinion instead of falling into the current with a view to direct it. In this they have manifested more integrity than address. They are men of independent minds and unsuspected honor and honesty, and appear to consider it wrong to yield their own opinions, in the minutest particular, in favor of such as are more popular. But in this, I think, they err, either from scrupulous regard to *principle,* or from mistaking the means by which all popular governments are to be managed."[6] The only question in the minds of Federalists who were still active after 1800—except for a few curmudgeons like Pickering—was whether the ideals of the old-school gentlemen should be abandoned in part or dropped altogether.

Noah Webster, a transitional figure, was moderate on this question. He believed that a politician could find a middle position without destroying himself. "Between the unbending firmness of an H[amilto]n, the obsequiousness of a J[efferso]n," he wrote, "there is a way to preserve the confidence of the populace, without a sacrifice of integrity."[7] He hoped that at least something could be salvaged from the wreck of old-school Federalism: "Honest, independent men of talents should yield so far to popular opinion, as to retain the confidence of the people; for without that confidence, they are lost in the scale of political measures. But with it they may gradually wean the people from their foolish schemes and correct their opinions. . . . If they do not lead the people, fools and knaves will."[8]

Another moderate was James A. Bayard. Like Webster, he realized that the ancient ideal of rugged independence was no longer tenable. "We shall probably pay more attention to public opinion than we have heretofore done, and take more pains not merely to do right things, but to do them in an acceptable manner," he wrote to Hamilton, but hastened to add, "you may rely that no eagerness to recover lost power will betray [the Federalists] into any doctrines or compromises repugnant or dangerous to their former principles."[9]

Much more extreme was Fisher Ames. In 1807, he declared, "Invincible popular notions may be let alone, or touched without wounding them. For, I repeat, the skill of the business is to attempt only what is

[6] Noah Webster to Rufus King, July 6, 1807, in King, *Life and Correspondence of King,* V, 37–38; see also Noah Webster to Rufus King, May 5, 1806, in ibid., IV, 515: "The great question seems to be whether the time has arrived when the current of public opinion in favor of the present administration can be arrested and turned."

[7] Ibid.

[8] Ibid.

[9] James A. Bayard to Alexander Hamilton, Apr. 12, 1802, in Bayard Letterbook, New York Public Library; see also James A. Bayard to Richard Bassett, Jan. 25, 1802, in Bayard Papers, Library of Congress; Theodore Sedgwick to John Rutledge, June 3, 1801, in Rutledge Papers, Southern Hist. Coll., Univ. of N. C.; James A. Bayard to Robert Goodloe Harper, Jan. 30, 1804, in Donnan, ed., *Bayard,* pp. 159–161.

practicable, and some of the popular tenets are false yet sacred, and therefore respectable."[10]

It would appear that Ames was more typical than Bayard and Webster, for after 1800 the Federalists made many compromises which were indeed repugnant to their former principles. Gradually they came to terms with every major argument of the Jeffersonians—majoritarianism, individuality, the ever-broadening concept of equality, states' rights, even agrarianism and Anglophobia. In their search for a popular issue and an attractive position, in their zeal to show that they were indeed "identified with the public," the Federalists sharply shifted their arguments. An independent and astute Vermont editor, Peter Houghton, observed in 1809, "As different as light is from darkness, as different as our benevolent religion is from the worship of Belial, so different is the political doctrines, character, and conduct of the leaders of modern Federalists from those of Washington."[11]

This is not to suggest that the Federalists became Jeffersonian Democrats. Certainly they did not. But more and more, they began to sound like Jeffersonians. After 1800, they gradually identified themselves with a concept of public responsibility which contrasted sharply with the ideals of the old Washington school. Thus, a Federalist mass meeting in 1809 resolved that "those who administer a free government are literally the servants of the people, bound to pursue such a course, and adopt such measures, as the people shall approve."[12] In the same vein, the prospectus of a Federalist electioneering paper in 1810 declared, "In a monarchy, the object of *duty* is to serve the KING—in a Republic, to serve the PEOPLE."[13]

There were many Federalists, of course, who steadfastly refused to style themselves subservient to popular opinion, even in appearance. In every large city on the Atlantic seaboard, these relics of an older and simpler world collected in lonely little cliques. Near the city of Boston they comprised the so-called "Essex Junto," which after 1800 had scarcely anything to do with either Essex County or junto politics, but was merely "a society of friends," as a fringe member, Timothy Pickering, described it. Almost every day these gentlemen could be found in the office of the Suffolk Insurance Company, which was "more noted for its daily political harangues than for its semi-annual dividends." Presiding

[10] Fisher Ames to Josiah Quincy, Nov. 19, 1807, in Ames, *Works*, I, 403; see also Fisher Ames to Theodore Dwight, Mar. 19, 1801, in ibid., I, 293, quoted in part at the opening of this chapter; and Fisher Ames to John Rutledge, July 30, 1801, in Rutledge Papers, Southern Hist. Coll., Univ. of N. C.; for Alexander Hamilton, who was again close to Ames, see Alexander Hamilton to James McHenry, Aug. 27, 1800, in Hamilton, ed., *Works*, X, 388.

[11] [Brattleboro, Vt.] *Independent Freeholder*, Dec. 3, 1809.

[12] [Boston, Mass.] *New England Palladium*, May 19, 1809.

[13] Humphrey Marshall to Harrison Gray Otis, Apr. 16, 1810, in Otis Papers, Mass. Hist. Soc.

at the gatherings was the slovenly, sharp-tempered chief justice of Massachusetts, Theophilus Parsons (his law students called him Theawfullest Parsons). Elderly gentlemen rose before him and delivered "set speeches such as would not have been out of place in the Senate."[14]

In Charleston, they organized among themselves the "Mutton Chop Club," which met every other Wednesday at Sally Seymour's in Tradd Street. At New York, they established the "Friendly Club" and the "Sub-Rosa Society." Behind barred doors and shuttered windows they drank to each other's integrity and to the good old way. In their cups, they muttered darkly about Procrustes' bed and Pandora's box.[15]

A few of these men remained active in public life. Their refusal to be daunted by defeat might be easier to admire if they had ever learned from it. Gouverneur Morris is an example of this mentality. He continued to speak in public of the "Ignorance and Presumption" of the "general mass" and the "false notions of their Power and Importance."[16] Other Federalists were appalled. In 1814, shortly before Morris was to deliver an oration, Rufus King wrote to John Jay, "notwithstanding our admiration for his rare talents and extensive information, I should, I confess, like that you and I should see the discourse before it is pronounced. Cannot this be brought about?"[17]

2

The Federalists moved toward Jeffersonian principles by stages. At first, they tried merely to make their old antidemocratic ways seem acceptable to the people. The Baltimore *Republican; or Anti-Democrat* sought to defend balanced government in rather heavy-handed popular language which concluded: "O people! Is not this enough for the preservation of liberty, and the security of property?"[18] A folksy Federalist who called himself "Bill Bobstay" prepared an address for seamen in behalf of "Tim Pick" and his principles. "He has been true to your liberty," Bill Bobstay wrote, "but don't misunderstand me, Jack; I don't

---

[14] Timothy Pickering to George H. Rose, Mar. 22, 1808, in Pickering Papers, Mass. Hist. Soc.; Lodge, *Cabot*, pp. 17–22; Henry Adams, *New England Federalism*, pp. 368–370; Sigma [Lucius Manlius Sargent], *Reminiscences of Samuel Dexter* (Boston, 1857), pp. 54, 83, 84–5, 88. Another meeting place in Boston was the Social Law Library; [Boston, Mass.] *New England Palladium*, June 13, 1806.

[15] Alfred Huger to the Charleston [?] *Evening Post*, Nov. 22, 1871, "Notes and Queries," *South Carolina Historical and Genealogical Magazine*, I, (1900), 101; Sub Rosa Society Papers, New York Historical Society; Allan Nevins, *The New York Evening Post*, p. 15.

[16] Gouverneur Morris, "An Address to the People of New York on the present State of Affairs," n. d. [c. 1812], in Morris Papers, Columbia Univ. Library.

[17] Rufus King to John Jay, June 20, 1814, in Johnston, ed., *Correspondence of Jay*, IV, 374f.

[18] [New York, N. Y.] *Evening Post*, Aug. 2, 1803.

mean the liberty of every man's being captain."[19] By the odd combination of Jeffersonian rhetoric and anti-Jeffersonian principles, the Federalists, in a phrase of an opponent, "attempted to excite a passion of jealousy in the people against themselves."[20]

A good specimen of Federalist rhetoric after 1800 is the following, which incidentally added a cliché to the American language. It is from Charles Miner's *Essays from the Desk of Poor Robert the Scribe* (Doylestown, Pa., 1815), pp. 1–5.

When I was a little boy, Messrs. Printers, I remember one cold winter's morning, I was accosted by a smiling man, with an axe on his shoulder— "My pretty boy," said he, "has your father a Grindstone?" "Yes Sir," said I. "You are a fine little fellow," said he, "will you let me grind my axe on it?" Pleased with his compliment of "fine little fellow,"—"O yes Sir," I answered, "it is down in the shop." "And will you, my man," said he, patting me on the head, "get a little hot water?" How could I refuse? I ran and soon brought a kettle full. "How old are you, and what's your name," continued he, without waiting for a reply—"I am sure you are one of the finest lads that I have ever seen, will you just turn a few minutes for me?" Tickled with the flattery, like a little fool, I went to work, and bitterly did I rue the day. It was a new axe—and I toiled, and tugged, till I was almost tired to death. The school bell rung, and I could not get away;—my hands were blistered, and it was not half-ground. At length, however, the axe was sharpened, and the man turned to me with "Now you little rascal, you've played the truant—scud to school, or you'll buy it." Alas, thought I, it was hard enough to turn grindstone this cold day; but now to be called "little rascal" was too much. It sunk deep in my mind, and often have I thought of it since—

When I see a merchant, over polite to his customers—begging them to taste a little brandy, and throwing half his goods on the counter—thinks I— *That man has an axe to grind.*

When I see a man of doubtful character, patting a girl on the cheek— praising her sparkling eye and ruby lip, and giving her a sly squeeze—Beware my girl, thinks I, or you will find to your sorrow, *that you have been turning grindstone for a villain.*

When I see a man flattering the people—making great professions of attachment to liberty, who is in private life a tyrant—Methinks, look out, good people, *That fellow would set you to turning grindstone.*

When I see a man hoisted into office by party spirit—without a single qualification to render him either respectable or useful—Alas! methinks, deluded people, *you are doomed for a season to turn a grindstone for a booby.*

But more and more, Federalists began to borrow Jeffersonian principles as well as Jeffersonian rhetoric. With increasing skill and facility they sought to demonstrate that the "Democrats" were hostile to true

[19] Ibid., Nov. 5, 1802.

[20] [Boston, Mass.] *Independent Chronicle*, July 18, 1803; for other examples, see [Boston, Mass.] *Repertory*, Jan. 6, 30, Mar. 17, 1807; [New York, N. Y.] *Evening Post*, Dec. 31, 1801, [Portsmouth, N. H.] *New Hampshire Gazette*, Aug. 11, 1801; *Frederick-town Herald*, Nov. 13, 1802; [Hartford, Conn.] *Connecticut Courant*, Dec. 7, 1801; [Raleigh, N. C.] *Star*, Aug. 21, 1812; [Boston, Mass.] *New England Palladium*, Jan. 15, Feb. 19, 1805, May 6, 1805; [Keene, N. H.] *New Hampshire Sentinel*, July 28, 1804.

majoritarianism. At the same time they identified themselves with this concept.

The Federalists defined republicanism, for which they stood, as majority rule and democracy as its opposite. The *New England Palladium* put it this way: " 'The majority ought to govern,' says REPUBLICANISM. But what says DEMOCRACY? Why, 'Employ every trick and strategem to get the minority in power when my followers compose the minority.' "[21]

The Federalists represented their opponents as hostile to majority rule in four specific ways: first, as "mobocrats"; second, as a little clique of self-serving office seekers who sought to impose themselves upon the decent majority of the community; third, as aristocratic Virginia slaveholders who were over ruling the rest of the nation by means of the three-fifths compromise; fourth, as tools of the tyrant Napoleon rather than the servants of the American people. In most cases these arguments implicitly accepted the majority principle; in some cases they explicitly endorsed it.

Perhaps the most common of these four interpretations was the Democrats as mobocrats. It rested upon a basic and essential distinction, "of the highest importance," as one Federalist put it, "between the *people* and the *mob* or *populace*. By the latter I designate certain of the lowest class in the community, who are alike destitute of property and principle, and may be emphatically stiled the *rabble*. . . . By people I mean the great body of American farmers, merchants, mechanics, etc."[22] In confidential correspondence this distinction tended to be rather fuzzy. One Federalist wrote of "the mob, i.e., the people." And Gouverneur Morris wrote to J. C. Mountflorence:

By this word Mob I mean not so much the indigent as the vicious, hotheaded and inconsiderate Part of the Community together with that numerous Host of Tools, which Knaves do work with, called fools. These folks form the majority of all empires, kingdoms and commonwealths, and, of course, where not restrained by political Institutions or coerced by an armed force, possess the efficient power: And as power so possessed must needs be abused, it follows in direct consequence that the affairs of a democracy will ever be in the hands of weak and wicked men unless [except] when distress or danger shall compel a reluctant people to chuse [sic] a wise and virtuous administration. From this you will perhaps infer that Democracy is a bad Species of Government but there we shall disagree for I hold that it is no government at all, but in fact the death or dissolution of others systems, or the passage from one kind of a government to another. What the new system may be, time alone can discover.[23]

---

[21] [Boston, Mass.] *New England Palladium*, Apr. 7, 1807.
[22] [New York, N. Y.] *Evening Post*, Apr. 22, 1805.
[23] Jacob Bigelow, Jr., to Rev. Jacob Bigelow, Apr. 16, 1807, in Misc. Bound MSS, Mass. Hist. Soc.; Morris to Mountflorence, June 22, 1805, in Morris Papers, Library of Congress.

But in public they were more careful with their terms. A Federalist editor pointed out that to denounce the Jeffersonians as a "multitude of swine" was not to denounce the "swinish multitude."[24]

The editors of the large Federalist papers gave as much publicity as possible to whatever civil disorder could be laid at the door of the Democratic administration. Their efforts were particularly effective after the bloody Baltimore riots of 1812, in which a pro-administration mob twice wrecked the offices of the Baltimore *Federal Republican,* murdered one venerable relic of the Revolution, and maimed another. This unpleasant incident, compounded by the incompetence of Democratic city officials, was described in vivid detail by almost every Federalist paper in the country, protested by scores of Federalist meetings, and solemnly investigated by the Federalist majority in the Maryland General Assembly.[25] "The horrors of Baltimore," one editor wrote, "seem to leave the Septembrizers of Paris, in point of ferocity, quite in the background."[26] A casual reader of Federalist accounts might have obtained the impression that President Madison himself had marched at the head of the rioters.[27] The fact that Federalist mobs ran loose in many a staid New England town during that same smouldering summer passed unnoticed in the Federalist papers.[28] But their readers were never permitted to forget about the Baltimore riots. In Maryland the story of how a mob of Madisonians had trampled decency, order, and honest sensibilities of the largest part of the community into the dust of Baltimore's dung-strewn streets was retold at every election time until the party disappeared.[29]

[24] [Boston, Mass.] *New England Palladium,* Nov. 12, 1805; see also, in the same journal, July 16, 1805, an account of a Jeffersonian Independence Day celebration in New Hampshire, in which sixty democrats looked so disrespectable in appearance that they were not permitted to march in procession, but detailed to keep watch and walk around the liberty pole.

[25] [New Bern, N. C.] *Carolina Federal Republican,* Aug. 7, 1812; *Martinsburgh Gazette,* Aug. 7, 21, Sep. 4, 1812; [Boston, Mass.] *New England Palladium,* Aug. 7, 1812.

[26] Ibid., Aug. 7, 1812; the riot, however horrible it may have been, lost nothing in the telling:

> Hark!—'tis the Daemon!—at the door he treads!
> Alecto's mantle shrouds his hundred heads;—
> Back fly the bolts;—his bloody eye balls glare;—
> Long dangling snakes hiss in his horrent hair;—
> Blue Flames of sulpher issue from his jaws;—
> Each giant hand a naked daggar draws;—
> The steely clashing echoes from the walls,
> And at his feet the hoary LINGAN falls!
> 　　　　　　　　　　Pierpont, *The Portrait,* p. 32.

[27] "Madison's MOB!" Aug. 2, 1812, in Broadsides, Mass. Hist. Soc.

[28] Republicans claimed that Federalist mobs terrorized New Haven, Milford, Litchfield, Boston, Plymouth, Newburyport, and the towns of Rhode Island; [Concord, N. H.] *New-Hampshire Patriot,* Aug. 11, 1812; [Philadelphia, Pa.] *Aurora,* July 2, Aug. 2, 1798.

[29] [Annapolis, Md.] *Maryland Gazette,* Aug. 17, 1820.

The theme of these reiterations was always the same: the mob against the majority, Jeffersonians versus the people.[30]

A second way, closely related to the first, in which the Federalists sought to discredit the Jeffersonians as antimajoritarian was by describing them as a pack of self-serving office seekers, unscrupulous demagogues who were exploiting the majority to advance themselves. "What is democracy?" one Federalist asked himself. His answer: "A system of falsehood. How has it prevailed? By the disciplined spirit, the enterprizing, the hardy and incessant exertions of its followers." And another writer: "The *Aurora* editor still continues to talk about *Democracy.*— But there can be no *Democracy:*—For, if we may be allowed a sort of Hibernianism, *Democracy* would be Aristocracy—and of the worst kind. No set of Rulers in a government founded on an aristocratic system, would ever have so much power over their subjects, as the leaders of a Democracy would have over their followers.—the former would rule the body, the latter the body & mind."[31]

Republicans and Federalists vied with one another not only in creating their own elaborate organizations but also in exposing each other's. The young Federalist poet William Cullen Bryant first made his name by a poem in which he attacked the demagoguery of the Democrats:

> . . . Hark! the murmuring meed
> Of hoarse applause, from yonder shed proceed;
> Enter and view the gaping concourse there,
> Intent with gaping mouth, and stupid stare;
> While in the midst their supple leader stands,
> Harangues aloud, and flourishes his hands;
> To adulation tunes his servile throat,
> And sues successful for each blockhead's vote.[32]

Sometimes the Federalists argued that their opponents had no principles at all. One of them rhymed:

---

[30] [New Bern, N. C.] *Carolina Federal Republican,* Aug. 7, 1812; *Martinsburgh Gazette,* Aug. 7, 21, Sep. 14, 1812; [Georgetown, Md.] *Federal Republican,* July 29, 1812; [Boston, Mass.] *New England Palladium,* Aug. 7, 1812; [New York, N. Y.] *Evening Post,* July 31–Aug. 6, 1812; [Philadelphia, Pa.] *Gazette of the United States,* Oct. 20, 1812; [Exeter, N. H.] *Constitutionalist,* Aug. 4, 1812; [Windsor, Vt.] *Washingtonian,* Aug. 10, 1812. The mob response of administration journals lent itself to Federalist purposes; see [Washington, D. C.] *National Intelligencer,* Oct. 15, 1812; for other disturbances used by Federalist papers to identify Jeffersonian Democracy with mobocracy, see [Boston, Mass.] *New England Palladium,* Oct. 25, 1808 (another incident in Baltimore); ibid., Feb. 10, 1809, for a riot in Philadelphia against a Federalist mass meeting; ibid., May 4, 1810, for a riot in New York City; [Boston, Mass.] *New England Palladium,* Aug. 7, 1812, *Portland Gazette,* May 9, 1808, for two other riots in the same town; see also ibid., July 3, Oct. 16, Nov. 6, 1812, Oct. 19, 1813; [New York, N. Y.] *Evening Post,* Apr. 28, 1810.

[31] [New York, N. Y.] *Evening Post,* June 1, 1803; the [Boston, Mass.] *New England Palladium,* Dec. 4, 1807.

[32] Bryant, *The Embargo,* pp. 23–24.

> . . . I'll unmask the Democrat
> Your sometimes this thing, sometimes that.
> Whose life is one dishonest shuffle,
> Lest he perchance the *mob* should ruffle.[33]

And the Exeter, N. H., *Constitutionalist* on March 1, 1814, denounced the Democrats thus: "*Office-holders, Office seekers, Pimps* . . . this *Host* of worse than Egyptian locusts, now preying upon the very Vitals of the public must *starve* or *steal* or *cheat.*" Another asked scornfully: "Whoever heard of any dissention among the Jacobins about their principles? As well might the naked ladies of *Otaheite* be expected to quarrel about the fashions."[34] And another:

> The noise they make, a few mistake
> for patriotic squeaking
> You may depend that's not their end;
> They're all for office seeking.[35]

And still another, entitled "Oppressed Humanity" and written to the tune "A cobler there was, and he liv'd in a stall":

> I'm a full-blooded democrat lately come over,
> And now my dear honies I'm living in clover,
> A Halter and gibet I've left, do you see,
> For a *snug little place* in a country that's free.
>   *Derry down, down, down, derry down. . . .*
>
> *Five thousand* a year—'tis excellent wages,
> For cursing a country and damning its sages;
> Indeed my dear jonies, whilst democrats reign,
> We'll all fill our pockets, says Paddy Duane.
>   *Derry down, &c.*

Here again the theme was Jeffersonian office seekers versus the majority. The Federalists in Canterbury, Connecticut, passed on April 3, 1804, this resolution denouncing Jeffersonian organization as dangerous to majority rule: "Voted, that it is the duty of every good citizen of this state to resist all attempts to encroach upon the freedom of elections. Voted, that secret caucuses and electioneering cabals are of ruinous tendency, and ought to be holden in abhorrence by all honest men."[36]

A third common theme of Federalist controversial literature was that their opponents, though professedly democratic, were in fact a dynasty of Virginia planter-aristocrats who merely masqueraded as friends of the people. Federal polemicists throughout the period repeatedly referred to

[33] Fessenden, *Democracy Unveiled*, p. 2.

[34] [Boston, Mass.] *Centinel*, Feb. 11, 1801.

[35] [New York, N. Y.] Evening Post, Oct. 28, 1802; see also the issues for Dec. 11, 1802, and June 1, 1803; [Boston, Mass.] *New England Palladium*, May 6, Nov. 21, 1806.

[36] Poem publ. [New York, N. Y.] *Evening Post*, June 7, 1803; Federalist resolution publ. [Boston, Mass.] *New England Palladium*, May 1, 1804.

"slave driving nabobs of Virginia, who would fain conceal their designs of domination beneath the mask of liberty, and a pretended zeal for the rights of the people."[37] New Englanders were particularly bitter about the three-fifths compromise. By means of elaborate computation, they sometimes tried to show that were it not for this provision in the Constitution, Jefferson would never have been elected President. They ruminated on the possibility that the Jeffersonians might find an even more favorable ratio of representation:

> A southern negro is, you see, man
> Already three-fifths of a freeman
> And when Virginia gets the staff,
> He'll be a freeman and a half.[38]

In these arguments there was an implicit, and sometimes an explicit, endorsement of direct majority rule. One Federal body thus resolved, in true Jeffersonian style, that "a pure majority shall govern."[39]

Federalists also undertook to represent American Democrats as tools of the tyrant Bonaparte, the bloodstained Corsican bandit, the "enemy of the human race." Jefferson and Madison were alternately depicted as his dupes and his henchmen. Federalists circulated the rumor that a Democratic paper had declared that Napoleon was "destined by Heaven to rule the world."[40] A Republican stump orator was quoted as having said that "if the French should land here as enemies he would treat them as friends."[41]

In the new republic, majoritarianism was an expansive ideal, less easily defined in terms of being than becoming. It implied that power and legitimacy should derive from the will of the majority, not merely in some remote way but as directly as possible. It was, most of all, an ever larger commitment to equality—*all* men should vote, *any* man could hold office.[42]

[37] Fessenden, *Democracy Unveiled*, p. 3; see also Fisher Ames, "Dangers of American Liberty," 1805, in Ames, *Works*, II, 358; [Boston, Mass.] *New England Palladium*, Dec. 4, 1807; [New York, N. Y.] *Evening Post*, Sep. 21–Oct. 13, 1808; *A defense of the Legislature of Massachusetts, or the Rights of New England Vindicated* (Boston, 1804), p. 10, cited in Williamson, *American Suffrage*, p. 175; according to a Jeffersonian, this was the leading Federalist issue in the Delaware campaign of 1802. See Caesar Rodney to Thomas Jefferson, May 16, 1802, in Jefferson Papers, Library of Congress.

[38] Fessenden, *Democracy Unveiled*, p. 106.

[39] [New Bern, N. C.] *Carolina Federal Republican*, Mar. 14, 1812.

[40] "Let every Federalist do his duty, and Massachusetts will yet be saved," Apr. 1811, in Broadsides, Mass. Hist. Soc.; [Boston, Mass.] *New England Palladium*, Mar. 13, Aug. 19, 1808.

[41] Ibid., Oct. 28, 1808, Sep. 13, 1811.

[42] This enlargement of the majority principle can be followed in the writings of the great majoritarian, Thomas Jefferson, from the "Rights of British America" to *Notes on Virginia* to the First Inaugural Address to a cycle of letters in 1816, especially to John Taylor (May 28, 1816) and Samuel Kercheval (July 12, 1816). See Adrienne Koch and William Peden, *The Life and Selected Writings of Thomas Jefferson* (New York, 1944), pp. 293–311, 187–293, 321–325, 668–676.

"Rotation in office" is a rallying cry that has been set down in our history books as a Jacksonian phenomenon. But it was a part of Jeffersonian rhetoric before the War of 1812 and was even taken over by the Federalists.[43] It was, of course, utterly corrosive of "old School" principles. Through the 'nineties, Friends of Order had contended that only the wise and good could bear the burdens of responsibility, that natural leaders should be trusted with power for periods as long as possible. But after the election of 1800, younger Federalists learned to speak another language. "Rotation in office *is one of the first republican principles,*" one of them declared.[44] In North Carolina another ran for office with the following platform: "In all republican governments (of which ours is most happily one) it has been deemed essential to the preservation of correct principles that due regard should be had to *rotation in office.*"[45]

A favorite means by which gentlemen of the old school had hoped to render representatives independent of their constituents, within an elective process, was secret legislative sessions. At least one of them continued to defend it after 1800. "I love the practice of closed doors," Richard Peters wrote to Timothy Pickering, "and wish very much that all your business was, in its progressive stages, so transacted. This would be treason in the eyes of the inquisitive & jealous Citizens of this free and enlightened Hemisphere."[46] Treason, indeed! Here, too, younger Federalists did a swift about-face. "In republics there should be no secrets," one announced. "If a knowledge of the situation of the public, and of the conduct of men in office is withheld from public view, it is impossible for the people to think or act correctly as members of the body politic."[47]

A broadly based electorate was, as we have seen, perfectly compatible

[43] See, e.g., "Thoughts on the subject of the ensuing Election," Apr. 1, 1800, in Broadsides, New York Public Library.

[44] [Windsor, Vt.] *Washingtonian,* Aug. 24, 1812.

[45] Duncan Cameron, "To the Freemen of the District Composed of the Counties of Wake, Orange and Chatham," June 1808, in Cameron Papers, Southern Hist. Coll., Univ. of N. C.; see also [Boston, Mass.] *New England Palladium,* Jan. 8, 1808, June 28, 1811; [New York, N. Y.] *Evening Post,* Oct. 29, 1806. There is at least one instance of Federalists using this issue before 1800—in New York, during the early 'nineties; see A. F. Young, "Democratic-Republican Movement in New York," p. 395.

[46] Richard Peters to Timothy Pickering, Feb. 26, 1806, in Pickering Papers, Mass. Hist. Soc.

[47] *Portland Gazette,* Sep. 26, 1808; see also William Gaston's maiden speech, *Annals of Congress,* 13th Cong. 1st Sess., 119; Schauinger, *Gaston,* p. 67; in one case, at least, this was an honest conversion, an honest response to the secret sessions of the 8th Congress. See Robert Beverley to John Rutledge, Feb. 15, 1808, in Rutledge Papers, Southern Hist. Coll., Univ. of N. C.: "Secrecy is a dangerous [illegible] of power in the hands of any set of men, but even those who hold the national purse determine in secret to vote away and possibly to squander millions, they cease to be the constitutional guardians of those rights they have been chosen to protect. Our people contribute money with great reluctance. I can hardly suppose it compatible with this national close-fistedness to allow their pockets to be rifled without a why or a wherefore."

with the elitism of the old school. But *universal* suffrage was another matter. The enfranchisement of the unpropertied was opposed by most, if not all, of the Federalists of the "Washington school." Even some of the more cynical of the younger men, such as Harrison Gray Otis, who as we shall see was willing to sacrifice nearly every other principle on the altar of success, refused to go as far as advocating universal suffrage.[48]

But in Maryland a group of young Federalists were nothing loath. Led by young John Hanson Thomas of Frederick County, they were as outspoken as any Jeffersonian for an end to property qualifications for voting and officeholding, for popular election of governor and state senators, and for abolition of religious tests. A few older Federalists, especially Philip Barton Key and Michael Taney, were associated with this movement before 1800, but it was primarily an affair of younger men after 1801. The most prominent and prestigious old-school gentlemen in the state, Charles Carroll of Carrollton and James McHenry, were unalterably opposed. Samuel Chase blamed the agitation on "degenerate sons" of the Revolutionary generation.[49]

Pennsylvania Federalists swallowed their scruples in the gubernatorial election in 1808 and supported James Ross, who ostensibly favored universal suffrage. But it was clearly a marriage of convenience. "What a miserable state of society we are in," a young Federalist wrote, "when in order to insure Mr. Ross's election by persuading People to vote for him, you are compelled to recommend him for opinions, which, if he still entertains them, prove him to be wholly unfit to fill your gubernatorial chair. You declare he is a friend to universal suffrage, which is the very rock upon which we are about being shipwrecked."[50]

In New England, after 1800, at least a few Federalists argued that their party should take up the cause of suffrage reform. John Felch of Connecticut believed that taxpayer suffrage was "a popular theme" and "*timely.*" He argued sensibly that the Democrats would gain more votes by taxpayer suffrage as an issue than as an enactment. But it seems that

---

[48] See Harrison Gray Otis to John Rutledge, Jan. 29, 1802, in Rutledge Papers, Southern Hist. Coll., Univ. of N. C.; see also, similar scruples strengthened by a solid attachment to interest which appear in John Rutledge to Harrison Gray Otis, Nov. 10, 1812, in Otis Papers, Mass. Hist. Soc.: "In a frenzy of democracy, our legislature the last year abolished one of the oldest laws in their statute book, the right of suffrage, which has always been restricted to the freeholders, was made universal. Altho' a very great change has been made in the politics of Charleston, yet at the late election we were overwhelmed by 13 wretches who are without local habitation." See also, [Philadelphia, Pa.] *Political and Commercial Register*, Aug. 25, 1804.

[49] Williamson, *American Suffrage*, pp. 139–146; J. T. Scharf, *History of Maryland*, 3 vols. (Baltimore, 1879), II, 29–32 [Georgetown, Md.] *Federal Republican*, Sep. 15, 1813; "The Challenge Accepted," 1819, in Broadsides, Md. Hist. Soc.

[50] D. B. Ogden to William Meredith, Sep. 27, 1808, in Meredith Papers, Hist. Soc. of Penna.

the larger portion of his comrades remained hostile to universal suffrage.[51]

Jeffersonians made the most of the opportunities which the inconsistencies of their opponents provided. One editor ragged the latter-day Federalists as "semi-demycrats":

> Since things so sadly go against 'em
> And luck and demys e'en convinced 'em
> Our Feds their former ground despise
> And feel an itch for compromise.[52]

And a European visitor, who endeavored to discover the source of the partisan battle in campaign literature, was unable even to find a genuine difference. "They equally lay claim to the title of Republicans," he wrote. "It is somewhat singular that there should be a difference at all."[53]

3

As it was with majority rule, so also with minority rights. Nothing is quite as startling as the unabashed zeal with which Federalists courted the minority groups who had been the chief victims of their repressive legislation during the nineties. Before 1800, they had been extremely hostile to "united Irishmen" as they tended to label every man who came from the Emerald Isle. In 1797 young Harrison Gray Otis made a famous speech against the "hordes of wild Irishmen" who were beginning to appear in the large cities.[54] After 1800, however, they sometimes sang a different tune. While continuing to pander to anti-Hibernian prejudices of "native Americans," they sought to conciliate the Irish too. "There are

[51] John Felch to Jonathan Trumbull, Sep. 3, 1803, cited by Williamson, *American Suffrage*, p. 168n; for other examples of Federalist support for suffrage reform, see Bentley, *Diary*, 418, (Feb. 24, 1809); J. R. Pole, "Jeff. Dem. and Fed. Dilemma in N. J.," p. 271; "Right of Suffrage," 1811 [R. I.], in Broadsides, American Antiquarian Society. On the question of reapportionment the Federalists varied from state to state, depending on whether their strongest counties were under- or over-represented. In Maryland, where they were in command of overrepresented counties, they resisted any step in the direction of reapportionment. But in Virginia, the situations and the arguments of the parties were reversed. There the Federalists, after 1808, were dominant in the counties west of the Blue Ridge, and the champions of reform. In Massachusetts, Federalists demanded large representation for Boston. [Boston, Mass.] *New England Palladium*, May 10, 1805; Ambler, *Sectionalism in Virginia*, pp. 61–99.

[52] [Bristol, R.I.] *Mt. Hope Eagle*, Feb. 21, 1807.

[53] Melish, *Travels*, I, 55–68. See [New York] *Evening Post*, 3 Apr. 1805: "It is said, that a gentleman having told Mr. Randolph that he was considered as having turned Federalist, received this laconic reply, 'It is false, Sir, I have not changed; but the Federalists have become good Republicans.'"

[54] Morison, *Otis*, I, 108; for other examples, see Uriah Tracy to Oliver Wolcott, Aug. 7, 1800, in Gibbs, *Administration of Washington and Adams*, II, 399; [New York, N. Y.] *Evening Post*, Apr. 30, 1808; Williamson, *American Suffrage*, p. 113; [New York, N. Y.] *Commercial Advertiser*, Sep. 25, 1800; [Boston, Mass.] *New England Palladium*, Apr. 15, 1803; William Rawle to Timothy Pickering, Jan. 5, 1804, in Pickering Papers, Mass. Hist. Soc.

few Federalists who will not join in the wish of *Erin go Bragh*," a Federalist paper proclaimed in 1805.[55] A rousing Federalist electioneering march called "Platt and Liberty," written for "the New York election" in 1810, included a stanza in praise of the melting pot:

> Come Dutch and Yankees, Irish, Scot,
> With intermixed relation;
> From whence we come it matters not;
> *We all make, now, one nation.*[56]

Philadelphia Federalists went so far as to include in their organization a "committee to aid in the naturalization of foreigners."[57] Efforts were made to play up Irish support for Federal candidates, and to make the Democrats appear anti-Irish.[58]

The Federalists also altered their expressed opinions about the place of Jews in American society. During the 1790s there had been a wide and fetid stream of antisemitism in Federalist thought. So strong was it, in fact, that it drove even wealthy Jewish merchants into the Jeffersonian party. An influential member of the Philadelphia Jewish community announced in a public letter to the *Aurora*, "I am a jew, and if for no other reason, for that reason am I a republican."[59] In Philadelphia after 1800, however (probably the only place except Charleston where a Jewish "vote" existed in the early national period) the Federalists

---

[55] [Boston, Mass.] *New England Palladium*, Aug. 13, 1805; for an appeal to nativism, see [Newburyport, Mass.] *Repertory*, July 6, 1803; *Portland Gazette*, Nov. 28, 1808: "It *is a fact*, that at this moment, a *great majority of free, native Americans are Federalists*; and it is believed, that never was a time, when this was not the case. . . . Thus then the AMERICAN PEOPLE ARE FEDERAL: and if they were at liberty to choose a Government for *themselves*, it would be a *Federal Government*.

[56] "Platt and Liberty," [1810], in Broadsides, New York Public Library; in the same campaign the New York *Evening Post* (Apr. 25, 1810), called out: "To the Polls!—To the Polls!—Federal Republicans, whether native or adopted, away to the polls, and retrieve your country."

[57] Higginbotham, *Keystone in the Democratic Arch*, p. 282; in Herkimer County, N.Y., Federalists learned to balance their tickets—one-third German, two-thirds English; Benton, *Herkimer County*, p. 266; and in Lancaster County they rotated English, Scotch-Irish, and German candidates; Klein, "Early Lancaster County Politics," *Penna. History*, III (1936), 100–101.

[58] See, e.g., the publicity attending an endorsement of Federal candidates, by "St. Patrick's Congregation" in Butler County, Pennsylvania, [Wilkesbarre, Pa.] *Luzerne County Federalist*, June 24, 1800; see also [Charleston, S. C.] *Courier*, Oct. 12, 1812; [Boston, Mass.] *New England Palladium*, May 23, 1809.

[59] [Philadelphia, Pa.] *Aurora*, Aug. 13, 1800; for anti-Jewish statements by Federalists, see Wilson, *History of Pittsburgh*, p. 744; [Philadelphia, Pa.] *Gazette of the United States*, July 16, 1800; [Newark, N. J.] *Gazette*, July 22, 1800. A Federal mob was exhorted to treat B. F. Bache as they would "a Turk, A Jew, a Jacobin, or a dog"; E. Wolf et al., *The History of the Jews in Philadelphia* (Philadelphia, 1957), p. 206; antisemitism was not entirely unknown among Jeffersonians; see [Wilmington, Del.] *True Republican*, Jan. 24, 1809; Mann, *Yankee Jeffersonian*, p. 46; but Jefferson cemented his Jewish support by appointing Reuben Etting as United States Attorney in Baltimore; see Memorandum dated Mar. 8, 1801, in Jefferson Papers, Library of Congress.

soon showed signs that they had recognized the political dangers, if not the moral obliquities, of antisemitism. From 1806 onward, a Jew was usually on the most important Federalist electioneering committees in the City of Brotherly Love.[60] Of course, in other parts of the country Federalists continued to capitalize upon antisemitism.[61]

Before 1800, even in northern states, Federal polemicists were openly contemptuous of Negroes. They sneered at a respected citizen of Philadelphia as "Citizen Sambo,"[62] and during the election of 1800 tastelessly made an issue of "Mr. Jefferson's Congo Harem," in such a way as to imply that he was guilty not merely of fornication but bestiality.[63] They accused the Democrats of bringing Negroes to the polls and lamented that in New York City the elections "in no small degree depend on that class of people who secrete less by the kidneys and more by the glands of the skin, which gives them a strong and disagreeable odor."[64]

Federalists at first tried to reduce the idea of equality to absurdity by extending it to Negroes. They publicized a song allegedly sung by a leader of a slave revolt, "Quashee."

> Our massa Jefferson he say
> Dat all mans free alike are born;
> Den tell me, why should Quashee stay
> To tend de cow and hoe de corn?
> Huzza for massa Jefferson.
>
> And if all mans alike be free,
> Why should de one, more dan his broder,
> Hab house and corn? For poor Quashee
> No hab de one no hab de oder.
> Huzza for massa Jefferson.

It was double-edged satire, designed to cut against Jefferson and Negroes too, as was this story:

"Liberty and Equality," shouted my companions in the public stage, because I made a remark, which they thought savoured a little of aristocracy—"Liberty and Equality," echoed an African tinker, who had for several miles rode on the baggage seat, behind the carriage—"Halloa, massa driver, stop a bit! stop, stop I say d—n me, if I don't ride with the other passengers; for I pay

[60] Wolf, Jews in Phila., p. 218; [Philadelphia, Pa.] Political and Commercial Register, Oct. 5, 1808; see also the sympathy of the Chillicothe Supporter, Mar. 24, 1810, for "individuals of the Jewish community" persecuted by Bonaparte.

[61] Scharf, History of Maryland, p. 152.

[62] Wolf, Jews in Phila., p. 209.

[63] James Parton, "The Presidential Election of 1800," Atlantic, XVII (July 1873), 28.

[64] [New York, N. Y.] Evening Post, May 27, 1803; this, of course, was an allusion to Jefferson's Notes on Virginia; see also "More Notes on Virginia; ". . . Mr. Jefferson asserts, that the only chosen people of God are the labourers in the earth. Now as the only labourers in the earth of Virginia are the Black People, we hope in future [sic] the friends of Mr. Jefferson will be more explicit"; [Newark] Gazette, July 1, 1800.

as much as any of 'em! I'm pounded to pumice here behind, the seats are so rough! Equal rights, the good fellows say—I'll ride with them."

"Democratic consistency requires," said WILLIAM, "that the poor African have a seat with us; for he has been bruised shamefully; and his money is as good as ours!" At this expression he cast his sack of tools across his shoulders and jumping up before, rode on the seat with the driver. Soon the Democrats, who had clamored so much about equal rights, complained that the negro was offensive, and should take his former seat, or be left. Their solicitations finally prevailed with the driver, and the poor tinker, having paid his stage hire, was compelled to go on foot. Such is democratic equality. I beseech our philosophical president, in some future essay, or in the revision of his *Notes on Virginia,* to prove, for the benefit of his friends, the promotion of genuine democratic equality, that the effluvia excited by perspiration, from the skin of Africans, is not disagreeable. It may possibly prevent his partisans, from treating innocent black men like brutes.[65]

At the same time, however, Federalists were increasingly aware of the importance of the Negro vote in northern states. A Republican in eastern Massachusetts complained of their attempts in Boston to win over Prince Hall, "an African and a person of great influence upon his colour in Boston . . . a person to whom they [the Federalists] refer with confidence their principal affairs. The clergy were introduced to him, and the principal gentlemen took note of him." In Salem, a free Negro was vouched for by several of the leading citizens, including a Marston and a Derby.[66] And the following broadside, distributed in the New York election of 1808, is of interest here:

A BLACK JOKE! ! ![67]

LET every American peruse the following, written by [William] COLEMAN, whose heart is blacker than his highly COLORED Federal Friends.—Let him ponder on the contents, and say, who are the base, slanderous, VIPERS of America! Shame upon you Federalists! If your hearts were not impervious to remorse, your very consciences would mark your faces still more infamous than your acts are flagitious! ! !

The following are a set of Resolutions published in the Evening Post—A Tory-English-Jacobinic Newspaper—look at, read, and pronounce the sentence of your insulted country! ! !

At *a General Meeting of the Electors of* COLOUR, *held at* Heyer's *Long Room, Chatham-street, on Monday Evening,* April 25, 1808, Nicholas Smith *was called to the Chair, and* Robert Sidney *appointed Secretary, the following Resolutions were unanimously agreed to:* —

Resolved, That we consider the EMBARGO as being extremely injurious to the labouring class of citizens, and entirely produced by Executive imbecility and Foreign influence.

[65] The poem in ibid., Sep. 1, 1802; the stagecoach story in [Boston, Mass.] *New England Palladium,* Sep. 10, 1805; see also a "do-you-want-your-daughter-to-marry-a-nigger" argument in *Port Folio,* May 23, 1801, which alleged that miscegenation would be the fruit of the Jeffersonian movement.

[66] Bentley, *Diary,* II, 379 (July 11, 1801) and 429 (May 3, 1802); see also [Boston, Mass.] *Independent Chronicle,* Jan. 29, 1801.

[67] Broadsides, Apr. 25, 1808, New York Hist. Soc.

Resolved, That during the twelve years of the Federal Administration the Country was prosperous and happy, and that the firm and dignified conduct pursued by them calls loudly for the support of all real friends of the country.

Resolved, That this Meeting will support the AMERICAN TICKET at the present Election, by all just and honourable means.

Resolved, That this Meeting be adjourned to meet at the same place, every Evening during the Election, and that notice thereof be given in the public papers.

> *Published by order of the Meeting,*
> Nicholas Smith, Chairman,
> Robert Sidney, Secretary.

Negroes were useful to Federalists in another way. In Massachusetts and New York an overworked electioneering theme was the condition of slaves in Virginia and South Carolina. A letter from Charleston that was published by the *Palladium* claimed that "there are many plantations in this neighborhood upon which the slaves are absolutely *naked.* Yet this unfeeling treatment of *human creatures* is thought a matter scarcely worthy of attention. You will hear a Carolina planter who talks loudly about Democracy, and detests the very name of a Federalist, speak of a *gang of negroes* (the term expressive of a number of slaves) as though they were a pack of hounds. Nay, the very dogs are better fed and provided for than they, and yet their masters, with all the insolence of jacobinic demagogues, refuse to allow the appellation of *Republican* to another Federalist who truly respects the rights of man."[68]

In southern states Federalists were sometimes extremely hostile to Negroes and friendly to the institution of slavery. John Rutledge, Junior, is a famous example. But other southern Federalists were more similar in attitude to their northern colleagues. Robert Goodloe Harper argued that the Negro was unassimilable into white culture, but not inferior to whites.[69] The Virginia Federalist Robert Beverley was as bitter a critic of slavery as any New Englander.[70]

In Jeffersonian America, the Federalists themselves became a persecuted minority group. After 1800, these old "rulers" of the nation were forced to fight for rights and privileges which they had denied to Democrats during the 1790s. The same leaders who had favored rigorous enforcement of the Sedition Law became outstanding defenders of free expression. Federal mass meetings opened with an affirmation of the right of assembly and ended by solemnly resolving the right of petition.[71]

---

[68] [Boston, Mass.] *New England Palladium,* Feb. 21, 1812; See also Sep. 19, 1805.

[69] Robert Goodloe Harper, *A Letter . . . to Elias B. Caldwell, Esq.* (Baltimore, 1818).

[70] Robert Beverley to John Rutledge, Jan. 20, 1801, in Rutledge Papers, Southern Hist. Coll., Univ. of N. C.; see also [Raleigh, N. C.] *Minerva,* Apr. 30, 1804.

[71] [Boston, Mass.] *New England Palladium,* Sep. 13, 16, Oct. 25, 1808, Aug. 3, 1813; [Windsor, Vt.] *Washingtonian,* May 13, 1811.

The multiplication of Federalist electioneering newspapers made freedom of the press the crux of the libertarian controversy. After the Wetmore case, in 1802, the roles of the parties were reversed. "The *Federalists* discover a most dishonorable inconsistency of conduct, when in and out of power," a Republican complained in this connection.[72] And the Elizabethtown *New Jersey Journal* on July 28, 1812, said:

In the address of the meeting of fourth of July at Trenton, we find the Federalists warmly advocating *freedom of speech and freedom of the press!* How mutable are things in this mundane system? What was your language in 1798? Who passed the gag law? Who the Sedition law? Truly, Federalism is an *igneus fatuus* [sic]. It blows hot and blows cold.

But the record of Republicans was no better; with a few conspicuous exceptions, they too showed a most dishonorable inconsistency when in and out of office. Leonard Levy has recently shown how the Jeffersonians lost much of their enthusiasm for freedom of the press after Jefferson came to power. But the important thing is that the Federalists picked up the thread of free discussion and carried it through a period of Jeffersonian "despoliation."[73] Alexander Hamilton's famous defence of Harry Croswell was but one of many similar acts by Federalists, in which the authors of the Sedition Act argued for an enlarged conception of free expression, and Jeffersonians argued for the narrow Blackstonian law of seditious libel.[74] Some Federalists defined freedom of the press even more broadly than Jeffersonians had in 1798. One of them even raised the question of news sources by denouncing secret sessions as an infringement of a free press.[75]

Federal editors' right of free expression was in actuality menaced less by Republican prosecuting attorneys than by mobs. The great Baltimore riots of 1812 were not, unhappily, an isolated phenomenon. In New Jersey, the Federal editor of the *Essex Patriot* published a letter which he had received: "Your damned tory paper will serve a Baltimore trick if it don't quit printing federal lies about the republicans. If your shop

---

[72] Barnabas Bidwell to E. Kirby, Sep. 20, 1803, in Kirby Papers, Duke Univ. Library.

[73] Leonard W. Levy, *Legacy of Suppression* (Cambridge, 1960), p. 297.

[74] For the Croswell case, see D. B. Ogden to William Meredith, May 26, 1804, in Meredith Papers, Hist. Soc. of Penna, which reports that Harison's role was more important than Hamilton's; see also the manuscript volume titled *Croswell ads the People* in Kent's hand, New York Public Library; [New York, N. Y.] *Evening Post,* Jan. 29, 1803; for other Republican infringements, real and threatened, see A. C. Hanson to Robert Goodloe Harper, Feb. 10, 1809, in Harper Papers, Library of Congress; [New York, N. Y.] *Evening Post,* Nov. 17, 1801; [Boston, Mass.] *New England Palladium,* May 31, 1803, Jan. 12, 1808; Thomas Boylston Adams to John Quincy Adams, July 10, July 18, 1803, John Quincy Adams to Thomas Boylston Adams, Aug. 19, 1803, in Adams Family Papers, reel 402; Henry W. De Saussure to John Rutledge, Feb. 14, 1803, in Rutledge Papers, Southern Hist. Coll., Univ. of N. C.

[75] [Boston, Mass.] *New England Palladium,* Oct. 27, 1807.

is burnt low and your ears cut off 'tis not any more than what you deserve and will get." Five months later, the office of the *Patriot* was burned to the ground.[76]

Freedom of worship also became a Federalist watchword, even while some members of the party were still defending an established church.[77] They attempted to portray Jefferson as a militant atheist who not merely rejected God but hated Him. A Federal contributor to the Hudson *Balance* undertook to prove two propositions:

First—That Mr. Jefferson is an infidel. And *Secondly*—That he would be pleased with a subversion of Christianity in this country.[78]

In many little ways, Federalists labored to dissolve the connection between Jefferson and liberty. They tried even to separate him from the Declaration of Independence by means of a few doctored letters, and the astonishing argument that if all the basic ideas came from John Locke, and if a committee had been responsible for the final phraseology, then Jefferson's contribution must necessarily have been meager.[79]

This sordid search for an issue by the Federalists after their fall from power masked a reorientation of fundamental significance. For generations, government had been the servant of the better sort of people. But with the defection of Adams in 1799 and the election of Jefferson in 1800 this connection was dissolved. In the first chapter we considered a tendency of old-school Federalists to think in terms of an organic, functional society, of the people (*all* the people) as one moral whole, of government as a strong and active agency of regulation and control. This set of assumptions contrasts sharply with a recent view of Jeffersonian thought as resting upon a consciousness of individuality, a metaphysical atomism, a sense of individual autonomy and self-sufficiency, free of restraint or regulation.[80]

[76] [Elizabeth-town] *Essex Patriot*, Mar. 9, Oct. 20, 1813; see also E. Pennington to Timothy Pickering, July 6, 1812, in Pickering Papers, Mass. Hist. Soc.; [New York, N. Y.] *Evening Post*, Sep. 15, 1802; challenges were another very real hazard: see, e.g. "E. Bronson, Editor of the United States Gazette" 1809, in Broadsides, American Antiquarian Soc.

[77] See, e.g., the resolutions in favor of "free exercise of religion" in New Hampshire; [Exeter, N. H.] *Constitutionalist*, Mar. 12, 1811.

[78] [Hudson, N. Y.] *Balance*, Nov. 6, 1802; see also Pierpont, *The Portrait*, p. 23n.

[79] Charles Warren, "The Doctored Letters of John Adams," *Mass. Hist. Soc. Proceedings*, LXVIII (1952), 160–170.

[80] Roland Van Zandt, *The Metaphysical Foundations of American History* (The Hague, 1959), pp. 99–202. It is instructive to contrast Jeffersonian attitudes toward Adam Smith with those of older Federalists. Mahlon Dickerson, for example, wrote "Finished reading Smith's Wealth of Nations 3 vols. the best book in the English language. (bible excepted.)"; Diary, Feb. 2, 1795, Dickerson Papers, N. J. Hist. Soc. Rufus King, on the other hand, wrote, "I have just been reading Smith's *Wealth of Nations;* if his theory is just, our plans are all wrong." King to Gerry, 5 June 1785, in *King*, I, 109.

The simple fact of Jeffersonian victory would have been reason enough for an agonizing reappraisal of traditional assumptions by Federalists. But several specific acts of Democratic administrations after 1800 served as catalysts, making the reaction more swift and sweeping. The various and sundry embargoes, nonintercourse and nonimportation acts had many consequences which were never intended by their authors. One which historians have never noticed was a startling Federalist *démarche* on a question of high importance—the economic relationship between government and the individual, between public policy and private enterprise.

Before 1800, Federalists had never challenged the right of government to regulate trade or to embargo it altogether. But by 1808 they were attacking "Jefferson's Embargo" as not merely inexpedient but immoral. It is true, of course, that an old-school Federalist in Massachusetts upheld the constitutionality of the measure, but he was an exceptional figure. More typical was the editor of the Charleston *Courier*, who defined an embargo as "a restraint upon the liberty of a mercantile nation." The only rallying cry which Federalists used in every political campaign in every state, from 1808 to 1814, was "Free Trade," the "Rights of Commerce."[81]

Eight years of Jeffersonian measures generally, and fifteen months of the Long Embargo in particular were more than enough to change mercantilists into free-traders. If their new *laissez-faire* attitudes were never developed into a formal academic system, they comprised a coherent and conscious body of thought nonetheless. In Congress, for example, Josiah Quincy declared: "This is the misfortune of the policy of the embargo, that you undertake by your laws to do what laws never did do—what they never can do. You undertake to protect better the property of an individual than his own sense of personal interest would enable him to protect it. The interests which society has in the property of the merchant, are much better secured by his own prudence and understanding of his business, than by any general law."[82]

The Jeffersonian ideal of minimal government was best epitomized

---

[81] Henry Adams, *Hist. U.S.*, IV, 268; [Charleston] *Courier*, Jan. 12, 1808. See also [New Bern] *Carolina Federal Republican*, Feb. 1, 1812; [Wilkesbarre] *Luzerne County Federalist*, Sep. 26, 1808; "March Meeting," Mar. 10, 1809, in Broadsides, American Antiquarian Society; [Boston] *New England Palladium*, Apr. 1, 1808; "At a General Assembly of the State of Connecticut," October, 1808, in Broadsides, N. Y. Hist. Soc.; [N. Y.] *Evening Post*, Apr. 27, 1808; for Federalist support of embargoes before 1800 see Kurtz, *Presidency of John Adams*, p. 396; Miller, *Hamilton*, p. 135.

[82] *Annals of Congress*, 10 Cong, 1 Sess., col. 2076 (Apr. 11, 1808); a few days later he added, "The best guarantees of the interest society has in the wealth of the members which compose it, are the industry, intelligence and enterprise of the individual proprietors, strengthened as they always are by the knowledge of business, and quickened by that which gives the keenest edge to human ingenuity—self-interest"; ibid., col. 2204-5 (Apr. 19, 1808). See also Quincy to Otis, Nov. 8, 1811, in Otis Papers, Mass. Hist. Soc. Daniel Webster argued in much the same vein; see Carey, *Webster as an Economist*, pp. 21, 197. For similar arguments by

by Jefferson himself in his first inaugural address. "A wise and frugal government," his familiar sentence runs, "which shall restrain men from injuring one another, which shall leave them otherwise free to regulate their own pursuits of industry and improvement, and shall not take from the mouth of labor the bread it has earned. This is the sum of good government, and this is necessary to close the circle of our felicities."[83]

His sentiments were doubly appropriate to the occasion, for economy as a general principle was an issue which helped to secure his election. Federalists and Republicans were of one mind as to its importance. "Every puny prater," Theodore Sedgwick wrote angrily, "who talks much of the interest of the people, the necessity of public economy, the importance of calculating every public measure on the principle of taking the least possible of 'the fruits of labor from the mouth which earns it' is sure of an affectionate reception from the people." Jeffersonian exploitation of the economy issue was in Federalist eyes pure demagoguery, proof of depravity, a measure of political irresponsibility.[84]

Yet, after 1800, young Federalists borrowed the economy issue and used it without restraint, not merely in isolated cases of public extravagance but as a general principle discussed in generic terms, precisely as Jeffersonians had used it before 1800. "Gold is the God of the American people," a young Federalist cynically declared. "The purse strings are their political religion."[85]

Federalists in other contexts, see [N. Y.] *Evening Post*, Sep. 30, 1806, in which the gift of stalls to butchers by the city was opposed by Federalists and made into an electioneering issue. "The prime duty of a free government," one Federalist declared, "is to treat all men alike, leaving their prosperity and success to depend upon their integrity, industry and skill." See also Federalist opposition to public workshops as "destructive of mechanic enterprize and industry"; ibid., Apr. 25, 1803. In an election broadside, a Federalist denounced Jeffersonian restraints as subversive of three "inalienable rights," the "right of acquiring property," the "right of enjoying it as we will," and the "right of alienating it." "The Constitution Gone," 1808, in Broadsides, American Antiquarian Society.

[83] Koch and Peden, *Jefferson*, p. 323.

[84] Sedgwick to King, Dec. 14, 1801, in King, *Life and Corres. of King*, IV, 34. For a Jeffersonian view see Meriwether Jones to Creed Taylor, Apr. 9, 1799, in Bruce-Randolph Coll. Va. State Library: "I hope my friend in your conversations with the people, you frequently recur to governmental expenses:—it is an ample field, and one on which the people ought to be well informed.— 'Tis in vain in the present temper of the United States to talk of *principles;* from that there has been a considerable defection: we ought therefore to bring our arguments home to their feelings— I am sorry to speak so ill of the *sovereign people*, but they have really become very mercenary, and of consequence opposed to War expenses. Let *peace and economy* then be our constant theme." For Federalist condemnations see Israel Thorndike to Nathan Read, in Read Papers, Essex Institute, Jan. 2, 1801; K. K. Van Rensselaer to Peter Van Schaack, Jan. 29, 1802, in Van Rensselaer Papers, New York Hist. Soc.; Henry Van Schaack to Sedgwick, Dec. 23, 1800, in Sedgwick Papers, Mass. Hist. Soc.; Otis to Rutledge, July 15, 1807, in Rutledge Papers, Southern Hist. Coll., Univ. of N. C.

[85] Job Purdy to Daniel Webster, May 5, 1815, in Webster Papers, Library of Congress; cited in Livermore, *Twilight of Federalism*, p. 14.

"Who wants to know how the people's money goes?" a Federalist agitator asked. "I, says one, for I pay something towards it."[86] The famous "Two Million Act" was the occasion of much Federal pamphleteering. "From whom do all these MILLIONS flow?" one piece inquired. "FROM US, THE PEOPLE; the poor pack-horses of false ambitious demagogues, who squander away by millions, live in palaces, and now riot in security and luxury, whilst the whole nation, farmers, merchants, mechanics, are reduced to ruin and confusion, and the very bread is taken from the mouth of the labouring poor." On the larger question of the economic role of government, as on the smaller one of constitutional interpretation, John Adams's comment was to the point. "Our two great parties have crossed over the valley, and taken possession of each other's mountain," that lonely observer noted.[87]

4

Majority rule and minority rights were not the only themes which Federalists borrowed from their enemies. None of the precepts of the old school remained sacred; all of the Jacobinical slogans of the nineties were seized upon by erstwhile Friends of Order.

In their days of power and glory, Federalists had regarded Jeffersonian appeals to the agrarian prejudices of the American people as pure cant. The interdependence of commerce and agriculture was a self-evident truth. "The present administration . . . talks of their attachment to the *Agricultural* interest," a Federalist declared. "What can they do for it, if they neglect commerce? Agriculture wants neither arms nor treaties to protect it; if commerce flourishes it is sure to prosper; if commerce is neglected, the farmer's industry is labour in vain. He cannot store his pork and beef and corn for posterity."[88]

The anticommercial bias of Jeffersonian publicists may have been an economic absurdity, but as a political weapon it was very effective. After 1800, Federalists borrowed it without regard for truth or consistency. In Frederick County, Maryland, one of them declared, "In an agricul-

86 N. Y. *Evening Post*, Mar. 8, 1809.

87 Ibid., Jan. 28, 1808. For other examples of exploitation of the economy issue by Federalists, see Warren *Bristol County Register*, Mar. 11, 1809; Charleston *Courier*, May 26, 1809; Chillicothe *Supporter*, June 23, 1810; "Count the Cost," 1814, Broadsides, American Antiquarian Society; Trenton *Federalist*, June 24, 1811; Hartford *Connecticut Courant*, Feb. 8, 22, July 5, Aug. 30, Sep. 6, 1802; Boston *New England Palladium*, Feb. 12, 1802, Sep. 27, 1803, Apr. 20, 1810; "Election Address," [1808?] Gouverneur Morris Papers, Columbia University Library; John Stanly to William Gaston, Nov. 11, 1814, Gaston Papers, Southern Hist. Coll., Univ. N. C.; C. A. Rodney to Jefferson, May 16, 1802, Jefferson Papers, Library of Congress. Even before Jefferson's election, Federalists in N. Y. were applying this issue against the Clintonians. See "To the Electors of the State of New York," n. d., Am. Broadsides, N. Y. Hist. Soc. John Adams to William Plumer, in Plumer, *Life of Plumer*, p. 403.

88 Boston *Repertory*, Mar. 30, 1807; Hamilton, *Works*, ed. Lodge, V, 4ff.

tural country like ours, wherever the farming and the commercial interests have equal claims, the *commercial* interest ought to yield to the farming, since the farming interest is the great and general interest of the country." Maryland Federalists in particular found an appeal to agrarianism very useful, for their strength was in small rural counties which were jealous of Baltimore, the most Jeffersonian city in the nation. In the context of the reapportionment controversy of 1819, a Federal meeting resolved that "it would be the height of madness to bend the steady yeomanry of the country, the honest and hardy cultivators of the soil and all the industrious mechanics of our village and country places, as victims to the overpowering influence of the ever varying and fickle population of a great commercial city."[89] But the Federalist flirtation with the politics of agrarianism was not restricted to Maryland. Even in Boston, party publicists made much of "blithe yeomen" and "bounteous flocks."[90]

If agrarianism was one emotion which Federalists learned to play upon, Anglophobia was another. There were moments when they were willing to sacrifice even their sympathy for England on the altar of success. They regarded the British constitution as the fountainhead of American freedom and the only "free government" in Europe. They saluted "England's fast-anchored isle" as the world's best hope, the only bulwark in the way of French aggression.[91] But even in that nation's darkest hour, Federalists coolly contemplated an abandonment of traditional policies for the sake of power.

Fisher Ames had pointed the way as early as 1805. To Timothy Pickering he wrote, "The conduct of Great Britain is undoubtedly unpopular,

[89] *Frederick-Town Herald*, Sep. 3, 1803; Annapolis *Maryland Gazette*, Aug. 26, 1819; see also ibid., Aug. 15, 1816, Sep. 2, 30, 1819; Baltimore *Federal Gazette*, Aug. 14, 1800; Baltimore *Federal Republican*, Aug. 22, 1809; Aug. 26, 1811; Georgetown *Federal Republican*, Aug. 18, 1813; Aug. 29, Sep. 21, Oct. 10, 1815; "To the Polls! Freemen of Frederick County," 1819, in Broadsides, Md. Hist. Soc.

[90] "Ode written for the Washington Benevolent Society," May 1, 1815, in Broadsides, Mass. Hist. Soc. See also William Cullen Bryant's "The Contented Ploughman," published in *Embargo*, p. 62. Its subject was an honest and staunchly Federalist yeoman, happy in his work and faithful in his attachment to the cause of order.

> "His pleasure is his daily toil,
> On no fantastic visions built;
> His treasure is the teeming soil,
> His boon a conscience void of guilt.

See also Boston *Columbian Centinel*, Mar. 12, 1800; Portland *Gazette*, Jan. 23, 1809; Boston *New England Palladium*, Oct. 11, 1808; Robinson, *Jeff. Dem. in N. Eng.*, pp. 42–44.

[91] "Not a free government exists [in Europe] but in the land of our forefathers," [Boston, Mass.] *Repertory*, Mar. 19, 1807; for a Republican comment on Anglophobia, see Hugh Williamson to Thomas Jefferson, July 6, 1801, in Thomas Jefferson Papers, Library of Congress: "In my endeavours to discover the most prevailing argument by which the strength of the republican party has been constantly increasing, I have seen none so general, conclusive and well understood, as a fixed dislike to the English nation."

which, in our country, is a test of right and wrong. Inquiry usually stops at that point. I hope the federalists will be very shy, therefore, and cautious how they come out as the avowed apologists for England. It is for our best interest that we ought to provide; and that we may be permitted to do it in any degree. I hope the Feds will not needlessly make themselves unpopular by vindicating British principles."[92]

Other Federalists were thinking along the same lines. In 1811 and 1812, Josiah Quincy and Harrison Gray Otis were on the point of reversing their party's foreign policy. Quincy took the initiative. He wrote home to Otis on November 26, 1811, "My own opinion concerning the fault of the conduct of the federalists has been the zeal with which they have advocated every point between this country and Great Britain, in favour of the latter." He suggested that the Federalists could destroy the administration by calling for war with Great Britain and claimed that he was "very far from being alone in these sentiments."[93]

Older Federalists strongly disagreed. One of them, Christopher Gore, described what was going on for the benefit of Rufus King in New York. He reported that "many of the middle-aged and ardent politicians of our Section of [the] Country have become tired of waiting for Place and Distinction." Gore thought they meant "to join Democracy in the cry against G. B. and declare that war with her was preferable to commercial restrictions; that many Federalists had been wrong; they had been more British than the British themselves, and it was necessary this opprobrium should be got rid of, by encouraging opposition to England and uniting in the Vulgar abuse, which was belched out against her Power and her Enormities. They should then attain the Favour of Democracy and controul and direct the Councils of the Mild and amiable men

92 Fisher Ames to Timothy Pickering, Dec. 2, 1805, in Ames, *Works*, I, 344; see also memo in the hand of Rufus King, n. d. [1812?], in King, V, 262: "The Revolution left a mass of prejudices upon the People against England, and in favour of France. Our Government is popular, the People are the fountain of power; by their favour can ambitious men acquire eminence. Upon these data are our Parties founded. . . ."

93 Josiah Quincy to Harrison Gray Otis, Nov. 8, 26, 1811, in Otis Papers, Mass. Hist. Soc.; H. D. Sedgwick to Harmanus Bleecker, Dec. 16, 1811, in Sedgwick Papers II, Mass. Hist. Soc.: "Many of our friends here are much alarmed by the course which they fear the federal representation is taking in Congress. Mr. Quincy wrote a long letter to Mr. Otis some time since intimating that a war with England was better than the present state of things—& that it was the only mode whereby we could be relieved from the non-intercourse. Mr. Otis for a time seemed to be of the same opinion, but most of the federalists here generally feel so strong a repugnance to any such course, that whether from being overpowered by the general sentiment or from a real change of opinion, I know not, but he certainly now holds different language—Mr. Lloyd's sentiments would seem from his expression of them to his friends to be in co-incidence with Mr. Q's . . . be good enough to inform me whether the federalists really design to sanction by their countenance a war with England—Such a total revolution in plan & conduct, if in truth it is adopted, I am sure is not without good reason, though of that reason I happen to be ignorant."

who fill her Ranks, to the Glory of the Nation and their own Distinction."[94]

Such a dramatic reversal of position was too radical to be executed by the men who invented it. The great wave of popular indignation against the War which swept over the northern states wrote finis to this contemplated revolution in Federalist foreign policy.

Of all the issues which Federalists borrowed from Jeffersonians, none is better known than their appeal to New England sectionalism which grew gradually into a flirtation with disunion. There is no better example of the Federalists' appeal to the prejudices of the people.

Between 1800 and 1814 there were two disunionist movements in New England, separate and distinct. The first began soon after Jefferson's inauguration and reached a climax in the winter of 1803–1804. Its principals were a little group of Federalists in Congress, led by that battered relic of the old school, Timothy Pickering. Pickering did not sit in the inner circles of New England Federalism. He sometimes complained very bitterly about the way in which the Federalists at Boston checked and frustrated him.[95] He was valued by the younger leaders of the party as a living monument to old-school virtues, as "the copatriot and friend of the immortal Washington."[96] They named their children after him, visited his farm, toasted him on the Fourth of July, and published his pamphlets, but paid little attention to his opinions on party strategy.

Only twice did Pickering put his influence to a test; twice it was found wanting. The first occasion came in 1804, when Pickering decided that disunion might check the contagion of democracy. He won support among Federalists in Washington who were driven to desperation by a

[94] [Christopher Gore to Rufus King, Oct. 5, 1812, in King, *Correspondence of King*, V, 282]; these "middle-aged" politicians were the men whom I have called "young Federalists." In 1812 their ages ranged from 52 to 22 (at the very youngest). See also Christopher Gore to Rufus King, Feb. 7, 1812, in King, *Correspondence of King*, V, 257: "The ladder by which these men mean to ascend to power and consequence is inveighing against G. Britain." For other examples of Federalists' appeals to Anglophobia, see Wolfe, *Jeff. Dem. in S. C.*, p. 216; the Pearce incident in New York harbor, [New York, N. Y.] *Evening Post*, Apr. 26, 28, May 2, 1806; D. B. Ogden to William Meredith, Mar. 3, Apr. 5, 1806, in Meredith Papers, Hist. Soc. of Penna.; Benjamin Russell to Charles Prentiss, Dec. 2, 1807, in Prentiss Papers, American Antiquarian Society, which specifies targets of an address, including "a touch at England"; see also Richard Peters to Timothy Pickering, Dec. 3, 1808, in Pickering Papers, Mass. Hist. Soc.; and a Federal electioneering broadside, "Direct Tax," Nov. 1, 1808, went so far as to attack "British influence" in Jefferson's administration! Broadsides, American Antiquarian Society.

[95] See, e.g., Timothy Pickering to John Lowell, Nov. 7, 1814, in Lodge, *Cabot*, pp. 539–542; Timothy Pickering to Samuel Putnam, Feb. 4, 1814, in Pickering Papers, Mass. Hist. Soc.

[96] [Boston, Mass.] *New England Palladium*, Sep. 9, 1808; *Pittsburgh Gazette*, June 28, 1811; this despite the true facts of Pickering's career; see also, W. W. Van Ness to Timothy Pickering, Apr. 10, 1814, J. H. Thomas to Timothy Pickering, Jan. 16, 1814, in Pickering Papers, Mass. Hist. Soc.

crushing sense of their own impotence, but when Pickering wrote home to New England, he failed to convince anyone. The men who supposedly comprised the "Essex Junto" did not like his plan, and politely but firmly told him so. The young Federalists, except for William Plumer, paid no attention to it but went their own way, with the party behind them. Pickering's Northern Confederacy scheme melted away in the spring of 1804.[97]

The second disunion movement was altogether separate and infinitely more serious. Pickering really had little to do with it, though he tried unsuccessfully to take it over.[98] It began as a response to the economic policies of Jeffersonian administrations. Ironically, it flourished among Jefferson's "chosen people," the yeomanry of the Connecticut Valley.[99]

Although this movement began independently of young Federalist leaders in Boston, they saw an opportunity in it, an issue which could be turned to partisan advantage. Harrison Gray Otis described the game in a letter to Josiah Quincy: "This temper, you are sensible, must not be extinguished for want of sympathy, nor permitted to burst forth into imprudent excess," he declared. As early as 1808 Otis contemplated a convention in Hartford "for the purpose of providing some mode of relief that may not be *inconsistent with the union of these states.*"[100]

[97] Timothy Pickering to Richard Peters, Dec. 24, 1803, Timothy Pickering to George Cabot, Jan. 29, 1804, George Cabot to Timothy Pickering, Feb. 14, Mar. 7, 1804, n. d. [marked received Mar. 9, 1804], Stephen Higginson To Timothy Pickering, Mar. 17, 1804, in Pickering Papers, Mass. Hist. Soc.; Henry Adams, *Documents relating to New England Federalism*, pp. 338–342, 346–349, 353, 361–362; George Cabot to Rufus King, Mar. 17, 1804, in King, *Life and Correspondence of King*, IV, 372.

[98] Fisher Ames to Timothy Pickering, Mar. 17, 1804, Fisher Ames to Stephen Higginson, Jan. 27, 1804, in Pickering Papers, Mass. Hist. Soc.; Plumer, *Life of Plumer*, p. 298. A sole exception was Theodore Lyman; Theodore Lyman to Timothy Pickering, Feb. 29, 1804, in Pickering Papers, Mass. Hist. Soc.; see also William Plumer to Thomas W. Thompson, Feb. 1, 1804; to James Sheafe, Feb. 22, 1804; to Jedidiah Morse, Mar. 10, 1804; in Plumer Papers, Library of Congress; for negotiations with Aaron Burr see Uriah Tracy to Aaron Burr, Mar. 29, 1802; James Hillhouse to Aaron Burr, Dec. 20 [1803?]; in Burr Papers, American Antiquarian Society; for efforts of Cabot to keep Pickering from reviving his conspiracy, see Cabot to Pickering, Mar. 12, 20, 1808, Oct. 5, 1808, in Pickering Papers, Mass. Hist. Soc.; Timothy Pickering to Samuel Putnam, Feb. 4, 1814, in King, *Life and Correspondence of King*, V, 391–393; Timothy Pickering to Caleb Strong, Oct. 12, 1814, ibid., V, 394–398; Morison, *Otis*, II, 88.

[99] George Gibbs to Oliver Wolcott, July 30, 1812, in Wolcott Papers, Library of Congress; Noah Webster to Daniel Webster, Sep. 6, 1834, in Webster Papers, Library of Congress; Joseph L. Lyman to Noah Webster, Jan. 15, 1814, in Webster Papers, New York Public Library; Morison, *Otis*, II, 78–109; Rozwenc, "Caleb Strong, p. 71. For disunionist sentiment in coastal areas see Labaree, *Patriots and Partisans*, p. 154; and "Who are the Federal Leaders in Buckspont," 1812, in Broadsides, American Antiquarian Society; Bentley, *Diary*, III, 352 (Apr. 23, 1808).

[100] Harrison Gray Otis to John Rutledge, Dec. 15, 1808, in Rutledge Papers, Southern Hist. Coll., Univ. of N. C.; Otis to Josiah Quincy, Dec. 15, 1808, in Morison, *Otis*, II, 4–6; but cf. the more belligerent tone of Harrison Gray Otis to

With few exceptions, disunion was never the object of young Federalist leaders in New England. Most wished merely to play upon sectional loyalties for political purposes. Party organs in New England—the *Palladium,* the *Courant,* and others—printed many inflammatory pieces, but few which were genuinely secessionist.[101]

This appeal to sectional pride was more successful than its sponsors may have wished. Otis had noted in December 1808 that "the spirit of the yeomanry in this state is raising to a point which will require restraint rather than the excitement of those who are supposed to influence and lead them." The initiative passed to the people. The young Federalists suddenly found themselves in the uncomfortable and even dangerous position of a rider thrown and dragged behind his horse that he had spurred once too often.[102]

The simile is inexact, for the Federalists never entirely lost control. After two years of war, they called the famous meeting at Hartford and managed to keep a firm grip upon its proceedings.[103] It is interesting that extremists such as Pickering and John Lowell, who had their hearts set on disunion, were dead against the Hartford Convention. Opinion in the Connecticut River Valley was not satisfied by its moderate proposals. A citizen of Northampton wrote to his son in Boston, "What think you of the proceedings of the convention? Our Federalists were much disappointed, saying that they dared not adopt any energetic measures, but would go on in the way of supplication till the chains that

---

John Rutledge, Jan. 3, 1809, in Rutledge Papers, Southern Hist. Coll., Univ. of N. C.: "Either of these measures would convulse the Union. I have little doubt that the Legislatures of the 5 Eastern States will recommend a convention after the next election, for the purpose of presenting [illegible] amendments to the Constitution, which if resisted by the Southern States, after a fair and patient exposition of our interests, will but too probably be followed by consequences which I never love to contemplate, much less to put in black & white." — An informed opinion, deserving of serious consideration was that of James Loring, who declared "It is highly probable that the Hartford Convention owes its origin more especially to the [Washington Benevolent Societies] than to the Essex Junto," *Hundred Boston Orators,* p. 369.

[101] [Hartford, Conn.] *Connecticut Courant,* June 23, 1800; [Boston, Mass.] *New England Palladium,* Nov. 9, 1804, Mar. 28, Sep. 16, Nov. 29, 1808: Aug. 1, 1809, Mar. 20, July 21, Aug. 7, 1812, Sep. 6, 23, 1814. The tone of Jeffersonian papers did not help: "The federalists of New-England bluster about a division of the union, and threaten to confederate and establish a government independent of the middle and southern states. They dare not do it; they have neither the courage to attempt nor the means to effect it . . ." [Nashville, Tenn.] *Clarion,* July 30, 1813. — Plumer had an interesting comment upon the tactics of federal party leaders after he shifted to the other side: "The leading Federalists are practising upon Napoleon's maxim of *dividing the people from their government,*" which was not, of course, the same thing as dividing the government itself; Turner, *Plumer,* p. 187.

[102] Morison, *Otis,* II, 4–6, passim; the exceptions included John Lowell, Jr., "the Boston rebel," and William Plumer.

[103] Ibid., II, 78–124.

are preparing to bind them to the earth were riveted." Only an unexpected peace rescued Otis and his colleagues from their predicament.[104]

The Federalists' exploitation of sectional emotions in New England stimulated counteremotions in the rest of the nation. The blue lights that burned along the coast of Connecticut, signaling to a British squadron that the *Stephen Decatur* was trying to break through the blockade, became the symbol of Federalism. It was unfair, but not entirely unwarranted.

It ought to be noted that the same Federal leaders who sought to play upon the sectional loyalties of the New England "yeomanry" also appealed to the developing emotions of American nationalism with complete disregard for consistency. The odes and orations of the Washington Benevolent Societies made much of patriotic sentiments, rampant eagles, and Columbian images. The Federalists as a party celebrated American naval victories with an almost xenophobic ferver.[105]

In March 1813, for example, they sponsored a Washington Naval Ball at Boston's Exchange Coffee House, a festival of patriotism "open to the public." The rooms were decorated with national banners, victory columns, signal flags of the various American commanders, and transparencies of Washington, the frigate *Constitution*, the captures of *Guerrière*, *Frolic*, and *Macedonian*, the destruction of *Java*, and of course the banners of the Washington Benevolent Society. Seven hundred celebrants attended. The *Palladium* boasted that "the splendor of the ball was never equalled in this town, and we believe was never surpassed in the United States."[106] A year later, when Commodore Perry

[104] Arthur Bryant to William Cullen Bryant, Jan. 25, 1815, in Godwin, *Bryant*, I, 133; see also A. C. Hanson to Robert Goodloe Harper, Jan. 13, 1815, in Hanson Papers, Hall of Records, Annapolis, Md.: "There are two descriptions of men who are disappointed by the result of the Hartford Convention—the Jacobins who wished them to commit treason, and that clan of Federalists whose impatience prompts them to a short course of relief. It was Mr. King's influence more than any man's that restrained the convention." See also John Stanly to William Gaston, Nov. 11, 1814, William Davie to William Gaston, Feb. 4, 1815, in Gaston Papers, Southern Hist. Coll., Univ. of N. C.; Robinson, *Davie*, p. 390. — For the mission of Otis, Sullivan, and Perkins to the Capitol, see S. E. Morison, "The Massachusetts Embassy to Washington, 1815," *Massachusetts Historical Society Proceedings*, XLVIII (1915), 343–351; see also the wry comment of Lewis Condict to Mahlon Dickerson, Feb. 15, 1815, in Dickerson Papers, New Jersey Hist. Soc.: "Harry Otis is here in a most pitiful plight. He is pregnant with most weighty concerns—the period of gestation is expired, and he is 'groaning to be delivered,' but finds no accoucheur."

[105] One of the few issues which the Federalists consistently supported from 1800 to their disintegration was a strong navy. They had christened Jefferson's gunboat appropriations the "democratic sinking fund." The American victories at sea in 1812 were interpreted by them as vindication for their navy policy, and they outstripped the Republicans in their celebrations of them; [New York, N. Y.] *Evening Post*, July 12, 1808.

[106] [Boston, Mass.] *New England Palladium*, Mar. 12, 1813.

came to Boston, Federalists lined the streets and greeted him "till hoarse."[107]

5

Slowly, painfully, Federalists learned that they must avoid a head-on clash with democracy. "Names are influential things," one wrote. "Much has been effected by the term Democratic republican—In my opinion it is time to leave this distinction."[108] When they spoke of the Balance after 1800, it was in a sense quite different from that of old John Adams. "The sovereign people hold an awful scale or BALANCE," a young Federalist wrote, "and their hand will never fail to weigh correct."[109]

From 1800 to our own time, no major political party has failed to pay lip service to Jeffersonian ideals. Antidemocracy was banished to the moss-hung plantations of the South and the musty pages of literary magazines. Now and again a few gentlemen of the old school emerged from retirement to order back the tide of universal suffrage, or a southern statesman, safely in retirement, would compose a treatise on political theory. But antidemocracy was politically dead, and so were any politicians who sought to act upon it.[110]

The Federalists' search for an issue is remarkable not merely for their recognition of Jeffersonian ideals but also for the spirit in which they went about it. Political defeat taught them to respect the people, if not to admire them. The consequence was political practices lower than even the lowest of Jeffersonian acts during the nineties. Federal appeals to the people, like those of the Whigs in 1840, bordered upon pure demagoguery. "Their love and hate, their hopes and fears are only to be addressed," Fisher Ames candidly declared. "Logic is not worth chopping."[111]

[107] Lewis Tappan, "Pocket Remembrancer," Aug. 2, 1814, in Tappan Papers, Library of Congress; see also *Norfolk Gazette*, Sep. 28, 1812; [Boston, Mass.] *New England Palladium*, Sep. 1, 1812; [Hartford, Conn.] *Connecticut-Courant*, July 13, Nov. 30, 1813; O. H. Perry to Thomas Francis et al., in Meredith Papers, Historical Society of Penna.

[108] E[lizur?] Goodrich to S[imeon] Baldwin, Feb. 20, 1804, in Baldwin Papers, Yale Univ. Library.

[109] [Albany, N. Y.] *Balance*, Jan. 2, 1810. This investigator would heartily endorse Sanford W. Higginbotham's conclusion that "in the matter of popular government, the Federalists for the most part had discovered that it was impossible to gain political control on the frankly avowed principle of the rule of 'the wealthy, the wise, and the good.' Most of them were now [1809] willing to accede to the necessity of paying deference to the principle of popular sovereignty"; Higginbotham, *The Keystone in the Democratic Arch*, p. 178.

[110] For a survey of antidemocratic thought in America after the Federalists, and of Thoreau, Calhoun, and Brownson as antidemocrats, see Donald Ray Harkness, "Crosscurrents: American Antidemocracy from Jackson to the Civil War," unpub. diss. (Univ. of Minnesota, 1955).

[111] Ames to ?, n. d. [1806?], in Miscellaneous Manuscripts, New York Public Library.

Ames, as should be clear by now, was not representative of all Federalists. While younger men labored with him to construct a Federal party and to rally the people behind it, the gentlemen of the old school could be overheard in the background chanting their disapproval. "Is it [wise] policy," one wrote, "to confirm the worst part of the mass in their folly and prejudice by making use of the paltry arguments of the old opposition in order to bring into contempt the present administration?"[112] Richard Peters was of the same opinion: "Times are too ticklish to play a game, and make hazardous moves merely to alarm and put to flight an adversary," he exclaimed. "I never passionately admired the celebrated feat of good old Sampson, who to destroy his enemies, pulled away the pillars of a building, with the certainty of being crushed under its ruins."[113]

"We must court popular favor," Fisher Ames had said in 1801. "We must study popular opinion and accomodate measures to what it is." Though many younger men labored beside him, the candor, the stubborn independence of a Peters or a Pickering could nullify all their efforts. Federalism, a Democrat observed in 1807, was "approaching to a *metaphysical* as well as a *physical* NIHILITY."[114]

The Federalists search for an issue after 1800 was a double failure— they failed to find an issue which could carry them to victory, and they failed to erase the destructive stereotype of Federalism which Democrats had stamped upon the minds of the people. In 1788, two political parties claimed the name Federalist; by 1815, it was an epithet, a smear word. "The people have been made to tremble at the name of Federalism," Moss Kent declared.[115] Pertinent in this connection is "A recipe to make a modern federalist," in the collection of the New York Historical Society:

Take the Heart of a contemptible Hypocrite, five scruples of liars tongues, four drachms of the hatred of Truth, five Drops of the Spirit of Oliver Cromwell, one gallon of Robertsperian blood, One Do of the treason of Benedict Arnold, One pound of Burr's conspiracy, one do. of bribery and corruption, eight ounces of Purdyism with an equal quantity of quidism, and fifteen drops of AntiChrist with the sanguinary appetite of a cannibal. Put the whole

---

[112] J. E. Hall to J. Q. Adams, Jan. 5, 1804, in Adams Family Papers, reel 403.

[113] Richard Peters to Timothy Pickering, Apr. 17, 1808, in Pickering Papers, Mass. Hist. Soc.

[114] Fisher Ames to John Rutledge, Jan. 26, 1801, in Rutledge Papers, Southern Hist. Coll., Univ. of N. C.; see also [Bristol, R. I.] *Mt. Hope Eagle*, Feb. 28, 1807; [Washington, D. C.] *National Intelligencer*, Oct. 6, 1812, which described the Federalists as "anythingarians."

[115] Moss Kent to James Kent, Apr. 30, 1807, in Kent Papers, Library of Congress; see also ? to Duncan Cameron, July 21, 1808, in Cameron Papers, Univ. of N. C.: "Among [the people] you hear of nothing but tories, Monarchists, Warhawks, Oppressors, British partizans, taxmakers applied to the name of Federalists— Indeed the word Federalist alone without the aid of expletives represents to their affrighted imaginations every thing that is base and infamous. . . ." In Indiana, a man accused of being a Federalist collected $1000. damages. O. H. Smith, *Early Times in Indiana*, pp. 98–99.

compound into the mortar of discord and pound it with the pestle of malice and sift through the skin of a quiddical apostate scoundrel into the vessel of rebellion and steep it over the fire of sedition 24 hours. Then strain it through the instrument of treason; then put it into the bottle of British influences and work it with Toryism, and let it settle till the election.

Sixteen years of national defeat, from 1800 to 1816, had a cumulative effect which was irresistible. Although embargoes and war brought a brief resurgence, both issues proved destructive of Federalism in the end—reinforcing Republican charges of toryism, monarchism, and Anglophilia. When Joseph Story publicly declared that George III could find a more faithful ministry in Boston than in London, he needed nothing more than Pickering's pamphlets to sustain his point. The unlucky coincidence of events at Hartford, Ghent, and New Orleans provided the *coup de grâce*. The War of 1812 was the only war in American history which was not followed by a resurgence of the conservative party. The opportunity was there; but the party was not.

Nevertheless, a revolution had occurred in American conservatism. "The open *dissent* of federalism," a Jeffersonian declared, "is much less to be feared by the republican yeomanry of the country, than their feigned *assent*. Heresy is never so insinuating and pervicious [sic] as when it marches under false colours."[116]

[116] [Bristol, R. I.] *Mt. Hope Eagle*, 21 Feb. 1807.

IX

Federalists and Democracy, 1800–1816

> Federalists of our age must be content with the past. It would
> be most unworthy to affect to have changed our opinions. I
> would not suffer the self-humiliation & reproaches of the
> changelings I could name, for the highest offices and ap-
> plause that could be given them.
>
> —RUFUS KING, 1816

> Having once fully and fairly plunged into the great moral and
> political revolution which is fixing the destiny of the world,
> it is absurd to imagine that . . . we shall be able to withdraw
> from it.
>
> —CHARLES WILLING HARE, 1812[1]

I

It is difficult for a twentieth-century American to comprehend the
depth of party feeling in the period 1800–1816. Political questions
possessed an urgency beyond all comparison with the milk-and-water
contests of today. The new nation was simultaneously pursuing experiments in independence and in republicanism; and the outcome of both
were in doubt. The Western world appeared to be approaching chaos;
political events succeeded one another with unprecedented force and
speed. Of all the monarchs of important states in 1789, not one remained
securely seated on his throne in 1815. The changes had often been
violent—the king of France, guillotined; the king of Sweden, shot; the
czar of Russia, strangled in his bed. The crowned heads of England and
Portugal had lost their reason; the ruler of the Sicilies had lost his throne.
Republics had fared no better—Venice, Switzerland, the Low Countries,
all subverted or subdued.[2]

The era of the early republic has been described, in a global context,
as a *saeculum politicum*. Religiosity had lost its centrality; economics

[1] Rufus King to Christopher Gore, 15 May 1816, in *King*, V, 535; Chares Willing
Hare to Harrison Gray Otis, Dec. 7, 1812, in Otis Papers, Mass. Hist. Soc.

[2] For the international setting, see R. R. Palmer, *The Age of Democratic Revolution; A Political History of Europe and America, 1760–1800* (Princeton, 1959) and
Jacques Godechot, *La Grande Nation: L'Expansion Révolutionnaire de la France
dans le Monde, 1789–1799*, 2 vols. (Paris, 1956). Godechot, unhappily, was misled
in one respect by standard American accounts of the Jeffersonian era. "Une certaine
stabilisation semble se dessiner vers 1800," he writes, "avec l'avènement de Bonaparte en France, l'élection de Jefferson aux Etats-Unis" (I, 17).

had not yet exercised its fascination upon the minds of many men. And in the new nation, where society was comparatively simple and life was hard and often lonely, political activity was the most important outlet for emotions, the only sustained source of entertainment.

All of these factors may help to make more comprehensible the intensity of partisan commitment. But whatever the factors may have been, the fact itself is clear. According to William Plumer, Boston in 1806 was "a vast pile of cumbustibles [sic], and a spark may produce a flame that will end in mobs and spread blood and destruction through the streets." Parson Bentley observed that in Salem in 1809 "parties hate each other as much as the French and English hate each [other] in time of war." And in Philadelphia during the summer of 1812 a moderate, pro-war Federalist wrote, "So embittered are the minds of the parties, that I fear the first blood that flows may very possibly be shed in civil strife."[3]

Human relationships of every kind were shaped and colored by the party rivalry. There are accounts on record of fathers disinheriting sons and of husbands separating from wives because of contrasting party commitments. Plumer noted that "many go so far as to dismiss their truckmen, mechanics and seamen who differ with them in politics." A Federalist lady in Connecticut, Elizabeth Baldwin, discharged her maid because she was a Democrat.[4]

As an English traveler observed, politics reached even into the "graves of the dead." In Essex County, Massachusetts, a Federalist relative of Timothy Pickering deliberately disrupted funeral services for a Republican neighbor. And in Norfolk County, Massachusetts, Jeffersonian Nathaniel Ames refused to witness the interment of his own brother after the Federal party "snatched" the "putrid corpse" and gave it a "political funeral."[5]

It is difficult to conceive of any kind of collective enterprise which

[3] Plumer, *Diary*, June 5, 1806, in Plumer Papers, Library of Congress; Bentley, *Diary*, III, 479 (24 Nov. 1809); F. M. Gilbert to Mrs. Sarah Hillhouse, June 20, July 24, 1812, in Alexander-Hillhouse Papers, Southern Hist. Coll., Univ. of N. C.; see also J. C. Calhoun to James McBride, June 23, 1813, in Meriwether, ed., *Papers of Calhoun*, I, 177; John Thaw to Charles Bird, Oct. 16, 1804, *West. Penna. Hist.*, XV (1933), 329; Theodore Foster to Dwight Foster, July 6, 1806, in Foster Papers, American Antiquarian Society.

[4] "Account of the Lineage of the Brown Family," typescript, 23 Feb. 1865, in Ambler-Brown Papers, Duke University Library; [Norristown, Penna.], *True Republican*, May 24, 1801; Plumer, *Diary* (June 5, 1806), in Plumer Papers, Library of Congress; Elizabeth Baldwin to Simeon Baldwin, Nov. 17, 1804, in Baldwin Papers, Yale Univ. Library.

[5] Edward A. Kendall, *Travels through the Northern Parts of the United States . . .*, 2 vols. (New York, 1809), II, 131; Bentley, *Diary*, III, 356 (May 1, 1808); Charles Warren, *Jacobin and Junto* (Cambridge, 1931), p. 222; see also Jeremiah Schuyler's comment on the death of Nicholas Snyder: "Another God-Damned Democrat has gone to Hell, and I wish they all were there." Williamson, *American Suffrage*, p. 161.

was not affected by party feeling. Justice itself, unhappily, was not blind to the conflict. In Pennsylvania a Jeffersonian jurist wore a liberty cap as he sat upon his bench. The militia was infected—in elections of officers there were party tickets. William Bentley declared that "every club in the choice of its members, even an association against fire, [considered] whether they will oppose the government." Federalists of Charleston, South Carolina, gained control of the Library Society and refused to admit Jeffersonians. Massachusetts Republicans and Federalists had their own candidates for the presidency of the Historical Society, and the former made an electioneering issue of the "aristocratic" Boston Atheneum. The Federalists of Salem gained a predominance in the Dancing Assembly and drove out all Republicans. The latter organized their own cotillion and competed for the "best music."[6]

Even the ladies, in this masculine society, became involved in the party conflict. Feminine fashions revealed the allegiance of the wearer —a foreign traveler was startled to discover that he could "discern a pretty *Democrat* a la mode *Francaise,* and a sweet little *Federalist* a la mode *Anglaise.*" The new ideas which were in the air prompted at least a few oppressed members of the second sex to reflect upon their subordinate position. A New England newspaper describes a mass meeting of women in Vermont which punctuated its proceedings with "the soft, clear musical discharge of a small cannon, a fit emblem of female eloquence." Among the toasts: "Liberty and Equality with our Companions—may we never be driven to the point where degradation and dishonor begin."[7]

Gatherings such as this were, of course, infrequent, but the interest which women were taking in political questions was an object of general concern among men, Federalists and Jeffersonians alike. "A woman in politics is like a monkey in a toy shop," one outraged husband declared. "She can do no good, and may do harm."[8]

[6] Robert Goodloe Harper to Vergil Maxcy, July 13, 1809, in Galloway-Maxcy-Markoe Papers, Library of Congress; Samuel Chase's lawyers defended him in his impeachment trial by arguing that his partisanship was a common characteristic of the American judiciary; Charles Evans, *Report of the Trial of Samuel Chase* (Baltimore, 1805), pp. 208–251. [Boston, Mass.] *New England Palladium,* Mar. 10, 1807, July 12, 1814; Fisher Ames to Jeremiah Smith, Dec. 14, 1802, Ames, *Works,* I, 316; Bentley, *Diary,* III 5 (Jan. 25, 1803), III, 226 (May 4, 1806), III, 413 (Jan. 30, 1809), III, 203 (Dec. 4, 1805), when William Gray supported the Republican administration during the embargo he was "excluded from all his former associations"; ibid., III, 47, (Feb. 19, 1809); Col. John Williams to William Lenoir, Oct. 29, 1804, in Lenoir Papers, Southern Hist. Coll., Univ. of N. C.; Wolfe, *Jeff. Dem. in S. C.,* p. 261; see also Republican attacks upon "the aristocratic" Boston Atheneum, [Boston, Mass.] *Independent Chronicle,* May 21, 1807.

[7] John Lambert, *Travels through Canada and the United States. . . ,* 2 vols. (London, 1813), II, 91; [Boston, Mass.] *New England Palladium,* date lost.

[8] [Norristown, Pa.] *True Republican,* May 24, 1801; see also [Portland, Me.] *Eastern Argus,* May 3, 1805; *Port Folio,* June 20, 1801; Jeremiah Mason to wife, Jan. 23, 1814; in Hilliard, *Mason,* p. 26.

Taverns tended to be Federal or Republican. Senator Samuel Smith of Maryland, who by error "stopped at a Federal Tavern," was subjected to much embarrassment before he was permitted to depart. A Federalist who strayed into a "Republican tavern" paid for his blunder with a beating. Discomfort was the price of party disagreement. In New Jersey, an amusing indicator of the depth of partisan commitment was noted by L. Q. C. Elmer: "About the year 1800 Levi Leake of Deerfield, brother of the eminent lawyer Samuel Leake, and a warm Federalist, commenced building a new house. . . . Before it was finished, Mr. Jefferson was elected President, which so displeased him that he made a vow that he would not complete the building until the Federalists came again into power. As this never happened the building remained near twenty years unoccupied."[9]

Party labels became value-terms. A Philadelphia fishmonger of the Jeffersonian persuasion advertised the quality of his cargo by "carrying a flag on which was displayed in glaring letters, 'Republican shad.' " A Democratic grocer in Ohio habitually referred to the rats who infested his store as "damned Federalists." The wrong party label served as the ultimate insult. James L. Petigru, a gentlemen of South Carolina, ran afoul of a bully who "lavished upon him all the foul epithets he could remember or invent." Petrigru kept his temper until his assailant called him "a damned Federal." "The words were no sooner uttered than a blow, altogether unexpected, laid him in the sand."[10]

The intensity of partisan loyalty, which paralleled the expansion of popular participation in politics, often spilled over into violence. A Republican reported from Dover, Delaware, that "we have here the times of turmoil and difficulty. Some of the most astonishing outrages and violence have taken place. Some of our oldest citizens declare that they have never witnessed anything equal to them since *Black Monday* in 1776." Political mobs, even "well-dressed mobs" of Federalists terrorized American towns. More than one New England town meeting dissolved into a melee between Federalists who sat on one side of the meetinghouse and Jeffersonians who occupied the other. Similar events were not unknown even among Jefferson's chosen people. A North Carolinian named John Halloway "had the misfortune to have his right ear bitten off . . . at the election of Coxe's ferry."[11]

[9] [Baltimore, Md.] *Federal Republican*, Sep. 22, 1809; Wyatt, *G.Q.K. Taylor*, p. 7; see also Gouverneur Morris, Diary, June 7, 1807, in Morris Papers, Library of Congress; [Boston, Mass.] *New England Palladium* Nov. 5, 1805, May 24, 1814; [Salem, Mass.] *Impartial Register*, May 29, 1800; Jonathan Fisher, *Diary*, Jan. 25, 1808; cited in Mary Ellen Chase, *Jonathan Fisher*, p. 236; Elmer, *History of Cumberland County, New Jersey*, p. 43.

[10] [Philadelphia, Pa.] *Political and Commercial Register*, Apr. 29, 1808; [Chillicothe, Ohio] *Supporter*, Feb. 9, 1809.

[11] John Fisher to Caesar Rodney, Sep. 7, 1804, in Fisher Papers, N. Y. Hist. Soc.; [Elizabeth-town] *New Jersey Journal*, Aug. 18, 1812. For other examples, see above, p. 157 and Williamson, *American Suffrage*, p. 176. And see the account of a sham

The duello, which had been common in colonial America, came into fashion during the period of intense party rivalry. "The practice of duelling," an editor lamented, "has of late become so prevalent that scarce a mail arrives but brings accounts of one or more." Men fought in the streets with pistols, muskets, knives, fists, canes, cudgels, bottles, and swords. In Salem, young Joseph Story and a Federalist antagonist exchanged "fisty cuffs" over politics. During the summer of 1806 there was an ugly "political murder" in Boston. A Federalist, Thomas Selfridge, quarreled with a Republican editor, Benjamin Austin, called him out, and posted him. Austin's son deliberately attempted a premeditated assault on Selfridge in the street, but was shot and killed by his intended victim. Federalists defended Selfridge, Republicans made young Austin a martyr, and the incident became a *cause célèbre*. Mobs met and clashed; Selfridge was hanged in effigy as far away as New York.[12]

In New York City, William Coleman, the Federalist editor, duelled with the Republican harbormaster and shot him dead; on another occasion, Coleman narrowly survived a street encounter with a Republican physician who tried to perform a "surgical operation" on him with a stiletto. In Albany, two septuagenarians, one Republican, the other Federalist, fought with canes in the street and severely wounded one another. And of course there was the famous "interview" at Weehawken between Aaron Burr and his great Federalist enemy. Hamilton fell mortally wounded on the same ground where his son Philip had been killed in a political duel in 1801. The fact that so many of the "better sort of people" engaged in bloody battles shows that violence in the early republic was not a consequence of increased popular participation

---

battle at Concord in which politics intruded. Result: 28 casualties, some serious. *New England Palladium*, Oct. 13, 1812. In Mississippi Territory a group of Republicans endeavored to organize a "hanging party" to rid their country of Federalists; *Raleigh Star*, Oct. 16, 1812. See also affidavits of J. S. West, William McClure, George Lane, William Blackledge, and James Whitfield, March 1798, typescript in Gaston Papers, Southern Hist. Coll., Univ. of N. C.; and James Wilson to William Darlington, May 8, 1802, in Darlington Papers, Library of Congress. "A story has frequently been told of the meeting of two citizens opposed in politics; one was in the wagon returning home from a political gathering, and the other on foot. The footman asked the other 'how it had went.' The other, stopping his horse, replied, 'come here and I will tell you.' He came, but as soon as he was within reach the rider up with his fist and knocked him down, saying, 'so it did went,' and drove off." Schoonmaker, *History of Kingston*, p. 400.

12 [Walpole, N. H.] *Farmer's Museum*, June 9, 1800; see similar statements in [Hartford, Conn.] *Connecticut Courant*, Aug. 11, 1800; [Raleigh, N. C.] *North Carolina Star*, June 28, 1810; William Johnson to James Kent, May 18, 1798, in Kent Papers, Library of Congress; Bentley, *Diary*, III, 18 (Apr. 2, 1803); Warren, *Jacobin and Junto*, pp. 183–214; Robinson, *Jeff. Dem. in N. Eng.*, p. 121; Warren, *John Collins Warren*, I, 65; and see an account of a duel between two brothers of different political persuasions—"a sad example of political enthusiasm"; Albany *Centinel*, 23 Sep. 1800.

in politics, but of the intensity of political commitment which appeared on every level of American society.[13]

Even in the Halls of Congress, violence which spilled over from the party rivalry came to be accepted as part of American political life in the period 1800–1816. It had not been so in 1797, when Federalist Roger Griswold and Republican Mathew Lyon went at each other literally hammer and tongs, in the chamber of the House of Representatives. Shocked colleagues seriously contemplated their expulsion. But seven years later, two feuding Republican Congressmen, Joseph Hopper Nicholson and Michael Leib, pummeled each other in the Lobby for an hour and seventeen minutes, until Leib finally yielded. Both men were knocked down and covered with blood. A spectator who described the fight expressed disapproval only of the fact that his favorite, Leib, had failed to use his left.[14]

2

All of this impressionistic evidence may serve to explain the voting statistics collected by McCormick and Pole. An examination of Table XXII will show that in four states, Massachusetts, New Hampshire, New Jersey, and Pennsylvania, there was a significant expansion of voter participation in the period 1798–1816. In Massachusetts, participation rose gradually in the period 1799–1803, and more rapidly from 1804 to 1809, reaching a high of 64 per cent in the latter year. After a slight dip, participation rose even higher in 1812, to 68 per cent of adult white males. In New Hampshire a similar but even more striking pattern appears; in the gubernatorial election participation rose to the extraordinary height of 81 per cent of adult white males.

[13] "Brief Statement of Facts which led to and attended the Affray . . ." Apr. 27, 1807, in Amer. Broadsides, N. Y. Hist. Soc.; Mrs. James Kent to James Kent, Apr. 25, 1804, in Kent Papers, Library of Congress; Charles H. Levermore, "The Rise of Metropolitan Journalism, 1800–1840," Amer. Hist. Rev., VI (1901), 449; D. B. Ogden to William Meredith, Jan. 19, 1807, in Meredith Papers, Hist. Soc. of Penna.; Miller, Hamilton, pp. 548–49, 567–76; for other political duels see Brigham, Journals and Journeymen, p. 68; John Fisher to Caesar A. Rodney, Jan. 19, 1804, in John Fisher Papers, N. Y. Hist. Soc.; A. C. Hanson to Wm. Meredith, Apr. 20, 1811, in Meredith Papers, Hist. Soc. Penna.; Samuel Taylor to Creed Taylor, Oct. 20, 1798, in Bruce-Randolph Papers, Va. State Library; J. Q. Adams, Memoirs, I, 517; [Chillicothe] Supporter, Sep. 22, 1810.

[14] [N. Y.] Evening Post, Dec. 13, 1805. For other outbreaks of violence in Congress, see Capers, Calhoun, pp. 39; Plumer to John Park, Feb. 14, 1804, in Plumer Papers, Library of Congress; Silas Betton to John Cotton Smith, Feb. 2, 1805, in John Cotton Smith Papers, Library of Congress; Simeon Baldwin, memo dated Feb. 12, 1804, in Baldwin Papers, Yale Univ. Library; Horace Binney to John Sergeant, Feb. 11, 1816, in Sergeant Papers, Hist. Soc. Penna.; for disorder in state legislatures, see Williamson, American Suffrage, p. 171; and Higginbotham, Keystone in the Democratic Arch, p. 109.

Table XXII. Voter Participation in State Elections, 1790–1826

NOTE: All elections gubernatorial except New Jersey.

am = adult males
awm = adult white males
fam = free adult males

Year	New Hampshire		Massachusetts		New Jersey		Pennsylvania	
1790	24%	awm[b]	17%	awm[b]	27%	awm[b]	31%	fam[b]
1791	28	awm[b]	17	awm[b]				
1792	27	awm[b]	17	awm[b]				
1793	29	awm[b]	18	awm[b]			27	fam[b]
1794	31	awm[b]	22	awm[b]				
1795	27	awm[b]	16	awm[b]				
1796	30	awm[b]	24	awm[b]	26	awm[b]	26	fam[b]
1797	30	awm[b]	22	awm[b]				
1798	33	awm[b]	18	awm[b]	46	awm		
1799	32	awm[b]	28	awm[b]			56	fam
1800	44	am	31	awm	68	awm		
1801	40	am	37	awm				
1802	48	am	39	awm			47	fam
1803	53	am	33	awm	31	awm[a]		
1804	60	am	41	awm				
1805	68	am	47	awm			55	fam
1806	49	am[a]	55	awm	35	awm[a]		
1807	39	am[a]	58	awm				
1808	36	am[a]	56	awm	70	awm	70	fam
1809	70	am	64	awm				
1810	71	am	61	awm				
1811	70	am	55	awm			33	fam[a]
1812	69	am	68	awm				
1813	75	am	64	awm				
1814	81	am	64	awm	67	awm	43	fam
1815	74	am	59	awm				
1816	77	am	59	awm				
1817	70	am	50	awm			61	fam
1818	61	am	41	awm				
1819	45	am[a]	46	awm				
1820	45	am[a]	47	awm	9	awm[a]	64	fam
1821	45	am[a]	42	awm				
1822	44	am[a]	41	awm				
1823	54	am[a]	53	awm			64	fam
1824	54	am[a]	58	awm	31	awm[a]		
1825	52	am[a]	29	awm[a]				
1826	52	am[a]	30	awm[a]	40	awm[a]	28	fam[a]

SOURCE: Articles by McCormick and Pole cited in n. 6 above; McCormick, *The History of Voting in New Jersey* (New Brunswick, 1953), p. 121.

[a] Not contested by Federalists.   [b] No clear party cleavage.

Table XXIII. Voter Participation in Maryland
Congressional Elections, 1812

	Free Adult white males voting (in per cent)
Alleghany	80%
Anne Arundel	75
Baltimore	61[a]
Calvert	47[b]
Caroline	88
Cecil	41[a]
Dorchester	93
Frederick	88
Harford	55[a]
Kent	47[a]
Montgomery	77
Prince George's	100
Queen Anne's	68[c]
St. Mary's	40[b]
Somerset	79
Talbot	90
Washington	81
Worcester	80

NOTE: Candidates of both parties competed in all counties except those otherwise indicated.

SOURCE: Pole, "Constitutional Reform and Election Statistics in Maryland, 1790–1812," pp. 291–292; Maryland State Papers, Election Returns, 1812, Hall of Records, Annapolis, Md.; and files of the following newspapers for Oct., 1812: [Baltimore, Md.] American, [Elizabethtown, Md.] Maryland Herald, [Georgetown, Md.] Federal Republican, and [Washington, D. C.] National Intelligencer; Pole's calculations are inaccurate for Baltimore County. The figure which he lists as total votes cast (4,966) was in fact the number of votes received by only a single candidate, Isaac McKim. There were two others, Moore and Little; a second error of Pole's, however, more than cancels this one out, and is responsible for his conclusion that more than 100 per cent of free white adult males actually voted. He has computed McKim's votes for the county without the town, when in fact they were for both town and county.

[a] No opposition to Republican candidates.
[b] No opposition to Federalist candidates.
[c] No opposition to Republican candidates for delegates, who were elected on the same day as Congressmen.

In the middle states a slightly different pattern prevailed. Voting participation rose during the 1790s more rapidly than in New England, a clear consequence of the greater efforts and more efficient organizations of both parties during that decade. Thus, we see the figures of 56 per cent (free adult males) for Pennsylvania in 1799 and 68 per cent for New Jersey in 1800. But in these two middle states, as in New England, participation reached new heights after 1800—70 per cent in both states in the election of 1808.

Table XXIV. Voter Participation in North Carolina
Congressional Elections, 1812

District	County	Free adult white males voting (in per cent)	Average participation throughout district (each county rated equally)
Morgan	Burke	65%	65.2%[a]
	Lincoln	48	
	Buncombe	76	
	Rutherford	68	
Hillsboro	Orange	100	90.0[c]
	Chatham	80	
Rockingham	Rockingham	72	73.8[a]
	Guilford	71	
	Caswell	71	
	Person	89	
	Randolph	66	
Fayetteville	Cumberland	68	77.8[b]
	Robeson	76	
	Richmond	82	
	Montgomery	77	
	Anson	88	
	Moore	76	

SOURCE: Pole, "Election Statistics in North Carolina, to 1861," p. 227; Gilpatrick, *Jeffersonian Democrats in North Carolina*, pp. 241–244.

[a] No Federalist candidates.
[b] No Republican candidates.
[c] Competition between Federalist and Republican candidates.

It will be noted that these figures correlate very closely with the political activity of the younger Federalists. In both Massachusetts and New Hampshire, systematic state organization appeared in 1804, the year of a sudden surge of participation. Organizational efforts were constant in Massachusetts, and participation rose steadily (except for a drop in 1810); but in New Hampshire the trend is slightly more complicated by the defection of William Plumer and the consequent dislocation of Federalist organization. But after Federalist reorganization had been achieved in 1809, participation began to climb again.

In Pennsylvania, the highest level appears in 1808, the year in which Federalists made their greatest effort. The last year in which a federal gubernatorial candidate competed was 1823, when 64 per cent of free adult males voted. After that campaign a sudden drop in participation occurred. The same trend appears in New Jersey.

For Maryland and North Carolina, where Federalists were strong after 1808, J. R. Pole has compiled election returns by county (Tables XXIII and XXIV). They show that voter participation was high in districts and counties where party competition was intense: in Hillsboro District, N. C., and in Maryland's counties of Alleghany, Caroline, Dorchester, Frederick, Prince-George's, and Talbot. Voter participation was low where one party or the other had gained a clear hegemony.

In one-party states, participation did not rise as it did where the party rivalry was keen. Virginia Federalists, though strong in portions of their state, were never able to compete on a statewide front. The highest known level of participation in the Old Dominion before 1824 was 26 per cent, in the election of 1800.[15]

Nothing in this chapter, or in any other, is meant to suggest that the expansion of voter participation was caused solely, or even primarily by the Federalists. What has been demonstrated in preceding pages for that party is even more true of their opponents. Jeffersonians were the innovators of most party techniques and the most effective exploiters of nearly all. However active and industrious the Federalists may have been, their competitors were always a step ahead.[16]

The argument, rather, is this: that the most sudden and sweeping expansion of voter participation came after two popularly oriented political parties began to compete with one another. The period 1798–1814, the period of contraction in France, was America's age of Democratic revolution, in which the agency of change was not the action of one party but the interaction of two. It is perhaps true that Federalists may have served after 1800 to drive Jeffersonians further to the left than the latter may have wished to go, and that this fact, rather than the absence of Federalist opposition, explains the fragmentation of Jeffersonian groups in Pennsylvania and other states. It is perhaps accurate to say that Republican courtship of the people was more ardent than it would otherwise have been had the Federalists responded differently to the rise of the Democratic-Republican party. Certainly the new-model political behavior that manifested itself in the new republic was disagreeable to more than a few self-styled friends of the people "Attended the ward elections at Kerr's tavern," wrote a Jersey Jeffersonian, ". . . almost suffocated with a variety of stinks."[17]

15 Pole, "Representation in Va.," pp. 16–50; McCormick, "New Perspectives on Jacksonian Politics," p. 292. Virginia Federalists made their most energetic state-wide effort in 1800; see also Purcell, *Connecticut in Transition*, pp. 188–89.

16 See Noble Cunningham's excellent studies of the Republicans, *The Jeffersonian Republicans, 1789–1801* (Chapel Hill, 1957) and *The Jeffersonians in Power* (Chapel Hill, 1963).

17 Mahlon Dickerson, Diary, Oct. 2, 1802, in Dickerson Coll., N. J. Hist. Soc. It is interesting to note that, in the opinion of Monroe, "it was evidently a maxim of policy in the late president [Jefferson], to keep alive the federal party, as I presume to keep alive, in the *spirit of party*, the republican one. As he was sup-

These two suggestions must remain hypothetical, until a student of the Jeffersonian movement undertakes to test them. But two facts from which they derive seem clear. First, younger Federalists responded to the Jeffersonian movement with more energy and flexibility than has previously been believed. Secondly, Jeffersonians *and* Federalists together after 1800 contributed in a major way to the erosion of the "habit of subordination," to the evaporation of the deferential spirit, which had been in progress since the War of Independence and would continue into and beyond the age of Jackson.

3

The sudden expansion of popular participation in the period 1800–1816 is not the only indication of significant structural changes in American politics. New patterns of political ethics were apparent, and new forms of political corruption, as well. New kinds of men were holding public office, even on the national level.

Two ethical changes were most apparent. First, party loyalty entered the pantheon of political virtue. It is true, of course, that many older Federalists could never accept the idea of a party. As late as 1808 Noah Webster wrote, "The present struggle of parties with us are of no use. At most they produce only alternate temporary triumphs, while the best interests of the country are overlooked and sacrificed." To another gentleman of the old school he proposed the creation of a third force in American politics, an antiparty party, an "association of American patriots," who might thus manage to destroy the spirit of party and to purify the corrupted American experiment.[18] The concern of clergymen expressed itself in Lemuel Crooker's *A Remedy for Party Spirit*, advertised in the Rutland *Herald*, May 13, 1812, and in Daniel Ostrander's *Circular to the Ministers and Members of the Methodist Episcopal Church in the State of N. Y.*, which latter work began: "Brethren and Friends, 'two great parties unhappily divide the people of this country.' My design is not to persuade you to unite your influence in support of any party; but to guard you against the imposition from either, and to

---

ported by the latter, and it necessarily gained strength daily, it was the easiest way to preserve his own ascendancy in publick affairs, and in his opinion, I presume, the cause." Monroe to George Hay, 8 June 1809. *Bulletin of the New York Public Library*, V, 378. Another characterized Congressional contests as scrub races, in which "the slowest and meanest horse is always sure to win." *Annals of Congress*, 14th Cong., 2d sess., 556 (Jan. 1817).

[18] Noah Webster to Oliver Wolcott, May 13, 1808, in Noah Webster Papers, N. Y. Public Library; Ostrander's circular dtd. 1810, in Broadsides, Amer. Antiq. Soc. See also Francis Scott Key to John Randolph of Roanoke, Nov. 27, 1813, Howard Papers, Md. Hist. Soc.; John Marshall to Timothy Pickering, Feb. 28, 1811, Pickering Papers, Mass. Hist. Soc.; Chauncey Langdon to John Cotton Smith, Oct. 15, 1808, Helen Evartson Smith Coll., N. Y. Hist. Soc.

set before you the danger and evil that may result from your entering too deeply into the spirit of electioneering, which now rages like a pestilence in our land . . . the souls of Federal Republicans and Republican Federalists are equally precious . . . Shall we carry our bible in one hand and a bundle of electioneering handbills in the other?"

But other men were unable to make a simple value judgment about party organization. William Trigg wrote, "I have sometimes thought the name of party degrading to Government. At others I think its operation serviceable, as their convolutions appear to have something of the effect of the physical atmosphere. It purifies the system and seems conducive to energetick spirit and prevents the calm which is apt to lull human nature and prevent that active sprightliness by which alone we can expect to retain our present state of republicanism and independence." And still others identified completely with their party. The indispensable tool of statesman and timeserver alike, the essential political artifact, party was metamorphosed from an abomination to a necessary evil to a positive good.[19]

A second ethical change concerned the relationship of politicians to the people, the recognition of popular will as a standard of right. What ended as morality began as necessity. An effective vote-getter in New York, when asked for the secret of his popularity, replied candidly, "To tell the truth, *when my troops won't follow me, I follow them.*" Something of the same mood is apparent in a statement by a North Carolina Federalist who reported to a friend, "I have been in stinking quarter, sifting the minds of the people."[20]

We have seen some evidence of this reorientation among Federalists in the preceding chapter. Let us note here one extraordinary rhetorical flourish by an elegant young New York Federalist, Barent Gardenier. In Congress in 1809 a Republican denounced protests against the Embargo as "rebellion." Gardenier saw his chance and made the most of it. "Sir," he exclaimed, "I cannot find a word to express my ideas at hearing the majesty of the people assailed in this way; and as a representative of the people, I will not endure it; it is abominable." When Federalist Charles Goldsborough of Maryland could publicly acknowledge that a representative was the mouth of his constituents; when young Alexander Contee Hanson, in Congress, could describe himself as a tribune of the people, not merely responsible for their

19 William Trigg to John Preston, Feb. 23, 1800, in Preston Papers, Va. Hist. Soc.; D. B. Ogden to Wm. Meredith, June 29, 1812, in Meredith Papers, Hist. Soc. of Pa.; see also Gavin Hogg to James Iredell, Dec. 24, 1814, in Iredell Papers, Duke Univ. Library; John Stanly to John Rutledge, Apr. 25, 1803, in Rutledge Papers, Southern Hist. Coll., Univ. of N. C.; Barent Gardenier to Rufus King, Dec. 29, 1809, in King Papers, N. Y. Hist. Soc.; Alexander Contee Hanson to George Corbin Washington, Dec. 16, 1817, in Hanson-Washington Papers, Md. Hist. Soc.

20 Hammond, *Political Parties in New York*, I, 75; B. Rainey to Duncan Cameron, June 27, 1808, in Cameron Papers, Southern Hist. Coll., Univ. of N. C.

interests but responsive to their will, a new ethical pattern was emergent, if not entirely internalized.[21]

The appearance of new standards of political responsibility ran parallel to the growth of new forms of irresponsibility. Old-school gentlemen saw this change merely as the increase of corruption. "The dems have turned old honesty out-of-doors," one of them wrote. But more precisely, new and uniquely democratic forms of corruption replaced older forms associated with elitist rule. In the heyday of the old-school Federalists, when gentlemen predominated in the government, many public men tended to look upon special political favors as a gentleman's natural right. A few did not scruple to use public resources for the private advantage of the "better sort of people."[22]

The classic example of irresponsibility of this sort was the Robinson scandal in prerevolutionary Virginia. At the time of his death in 1765, John Robinson was "the topmost figure in the political structure of colonial Virginia," Speaker of the Assembly and Treasurer of the Colony. After he died, an auditor discovered that no less than one hundred thousand pounds was unaccountably missing from the treasury. Investigation revealed that it had been "lent" without interest to land-poor members of ruling families who needed ready cash. Robinson used scarcely a penny of it in his own interest. He had merely placed the resources of the government at the disposal of the "wise and good."[23]

There is no other case as spectacular as the Robinson affair, but smaller instances suggest that the Speaker's values were by no means unique. Old-school Federalists frequently sought special favors for the speaking elite at the expense of the silent multitude. Charles Nisbet, arch antidemocrat and Scottish clergyman, sought in 1800 to have his private letters carried free, and was angry when refused. To another clergyman he wrote self-righteously, "I have desired . . . to get this letter franked by some of [the Pennsylvania Congressmen], by which means I might have the pleasure of corresponding with you, at least as long as Congress remains at Philadelphia, and perhaps afterwards

[21] *Annals of Congress,* 10th Cong., 2d Sess., col. 1260–61 (Jan. 31, 1809); 13th Cong., 1st Sess., col. 114 (May 31, 1813); 13th Cong., 3d Sess., col. 1217 (Jan. 24, 1813).

[22] T. Dawes to N. Webster, June 18, 1806, in Noah Webster Papers, New York Public Library; see also Noah Webster to Rufus King, Apr. 27, 1807, in King, *Life and Correspondence of King,* V, 34: "The influence used in your N. York elections, if it should not produce riots & bloodshed, exhibits a melancholy state of moral and political corruption." See also M. Stokes to Duncan Cameron, Nov. 22, 1814, in Cameron Papers, Southern Hist. Coll., Univ. of N. C.: "It is possible you may not be Elected, but if you are not it will be for the very reason that the Athenian gave in the case of banishment. *I am tired of hearing of Aristides the just.* . . . See also Moss Kent to James Kent, Jan. 1, 1816, in Kent Papers, Library of Congress; Henry St. George Tucker to James Garnett, Aug. 3, 1811, in Tucker Papers, Duke Univ. Library.

[23] David John Mays, *Edmund Pendleton, 1721–1803,* 2 vols. (Cambridge, Mass., 1952), I, 174–208, 358–385; Freeman, *Washington,* III, 152–178.

too, as the new seat of government is much nearer this place than Philadelphia. On coming to this country I flattered myself that I might correspond with Men of Letters in different states without putting them to any expence, but on mentioning this to some of our representatives my proposal was received with sullen silence, as Learning is in no estimation among them, and they only correspond with such demagogues as may be useful to securing their re-election."[24]

As the "better sort of people" withdrew, this peculiar form of public irresponsibility, this tendency to regard the government as the last refuge of a gentleman, slowly died away. A new and peculiarly democratic system of political corruption replaced it. The "spoils system" was more than merely a matter of appointing one's friends to office and removing one's enemies, which is undoubtedly as old as government itself. It was the use of the power and patronage of the government to strengthen party machinery for the purpose of winning votes and influencing elections. This system became widespread in America with the Jeffersonian victory in 1800. The moderation of Jefferson himself is well known, but more significant is the immoderation of his followers.[25]

[24] Charles Nisbet to Jedidiah Morse, Jan. 4, 1800, in Dreer Coll., Hist. Soc. of Pa.; I am indebted to Wilson Smith for this letter. Another example is an episode in 1816 involving the old school gentleman, Charles Biddle of Philadelphia, and his good friend, Thomas Truxtun. Biddle told it well: "A few weeks before the general election this year, I thought it would be of great service to my friend Truxtun if he could do so, to reside upon his farm in Jersey in the summer and in the winter [move to] the city, and to be Deputy Sheriff. Having very little to do, and his estate not being productive, I thought he wanted some employment, and this office would employ him and he could make more by it than would maintain his family. At this time the Deputy Sheriff, Elliot, who was a very good officer, had been agreed upon by the Federal conferees to be run as Sheriff. When I mentioned Truxtun they all agreed he deserved the office, but [they objected] that he was a Jerseyman, and could not be commissioned if he had a majority of votes, that it was too late to think of him, and that by running him we should get in a democrat for a Sheriff. My opinion being otherwise I went with him all over the county and some other of his friends and myself using our exertions we got him elected." Then Biddle went to Harrisburg and by sheer stubbornness obtained Truxtun's commission. *Autobiography*, 354. John C. Miller's statement that "during their tenure of power no Federalist officer was found guilty of malfeasance," *Federalist Era*, 115, is literally true, but only because none were convicted. Jonathan Dayton, for example, stole $18,000 from the U.S. Treasury, but other Federalists made him disgorge it; see Oliver Wolcott to George Cabot, June 18, 1800, Lodge, *Cabot*, 280.

[25] There had been something of this in the "court" parties of the colonial period and in the mother country, too. But see the revisionist conclusion of Sir Lewis Namier, that in eighteenth-century England "corruption was not a shower-bath from above, constructed by Walpole, the Pelhams, or George III, but a waterspout springing from the rock of freedom to meet the demands of the people. Political bullying starts usually from above, the demand for benefits from below; the two between them made eighteenth-century elections"; Namier, *The Structure of Politics at the Accession of George III*, 2d edn. (London, 1957), p. 104. The spoils system did exist before 1800, but only in proportion to popular participation. Between political structure in 1730 and in 1830 there are differences of degree which are so great that they can be considered differences of kind.

When Jeffersonians gained control of the New York Common Council in 1804, they immediately removed every officer except the keepers of the prison and the almshouse. All other officeholders were replaced by party workers for the purpose of strengthening party organization. Another example was the use of patronage by the Madisonian administration in Philadelphia during the campaign of 1812. Joseph Hopkinson described it: "The whole force of the administration has been exerted here, by the means of customs house officers and other dependents, but more by a skillful distribution of army contracts. Camp kettles, canteens, cloathing, sadlery, etc. have been making in every part of town, and to the people thus employed, the war is a very agreeable event [sic]."[26]

We have seen that Federalists as well as Republicans learned to speak of "rotation of office"; and whenever an opportunity presented itself, they practiced what they preached. In every state government which they won after 1800, in all of New England, New York, New Jersey, Delaware, and Maryland, they began their administration by "cleaning the Augean stables." When they regained control of the New Hampshire state government they made a mockery of judicial independence by abolishing the entire judiciary at a blow and appointing a new one. Adoption by Jeffersonians *and* Federalists made the spoils system an accepted feature of American political life, before the Jacksonians expanded it on the national level.[27]

[26] I. N. P. Stokes, *Iconography of Manhattan Island*, 6 vols. (New York, 1895–1928, V, 1429. Joseph Hopkinson to Harrison Gray Otis, Oct. 16, 1812, in Otis Papers, Mass. Hist. Soc.; see also Thomas McKean to Thomas Jefferson, Dec. 15, 1800; Thomas Jefferson to Thomas McKean, Jan. 27, 1801, in Jefferson Papers, Library of Congress; Thomas McKean to Thomas Jefferson, July 20, 1801, in McKean Papers, Historical Soc. of Penna.; James Wilson to William Darlington, May 27, 1802, in Darlington Papers, Library of Congress; Thomas F. Newton to James Madison, Mar. 12, 1813, *William and Mary Quarterly*, 2nd. Ser. XVI (1936), 201.

[27] [Georgetown, Md.] *Federal Republican*, Oct. 19, 1812; see also Hatch Hill and Isaac Hill to William Gaston, July 1, 1813, in Gaston Papers, Southern Hist. Coll., Univ. of N. C.; John Rodman to Harmanus Bleecker, Feb. 15, 1813, in Rice, *Bleecker*, p. 57; Stokes, *Iconography of Manhattan*, V, 1451; Richard Stockton to Jonathan Rhea, Dec. 17, 1814, in Stockton Papers, New Jersey Hist. Soc.; [Newark, N. J.] *Centinel*, Oct. 20, 1812; [Frederick-town, Md.] *Star of Federalism*, Oct. 2, 1818; James P. Heath to Vergil Maxcy, Nov. 22, 1816, in Galloway-Maxcy-Markoe Papers, Library of Congress; Robert Troup to Rufus King, Feb. 17, 1807, in King, *Life and Correspondence of King*, V, 10; Morison, *Jeremiah Smith*, p. 265; Mathews, *Recollections of Men and Events*, pp. 118–119; an old-school response to the spoils system appears in Benjamin Lincoln to subordinates in Customs, 19 Nov. 1802: "I know gentlemen that I may appeal to you with the highest confidence that you will assent to the truth of the declaration that I have never attempted to controul your political creeds, or influence any of your votes in the choice of officers at any of our public meetings. . . . If any of you . . . have in public walks vilified the Chief Magistrate of the Union [Jefferson] in terms rude and indecent and should justify yourselves herein you only exercise your rights, I have to ask that you will in future recollect that there is an infinite difference between Right and propriety of exercising that right"; Shipton, *Sibley's Harvard Graduates*, XII, 437.

4

The new realities of American public life—enlarged popular participation, and the emergence of parties—altered the structure of government as well as the structure of politics. Oratory lost much of its
significance in legislative proceedings. "The business of speaking in
the Senate has become on most subjects of little importance and seldom
changes a single vote," William Plumer declared. "On a few intricate
and important subjects, debates are useful and interesting. But in general by the time a senator has been speaking ten minutes it is rare that
there is a quorum within the bar."[28]

James Hillhouse manifested much the same reaction. "I have not the
smallest expectation or hope," he wrote, "that the vote of a single member will be changed by the most impressive eloquence, or arguments
the most conclusive. All questions are settled in private meetings and
every member composing the majority of both houses comes pledged
to support the measures so agreed on. I feel very little inclined to remain
long in this situation."[29]

The restraints which accompanied the development of party discipline
and the democratization of political power were intolerable to men such
as Hillhouse, who had been raised to conceive of government as the
province of gentlemen. An English visitor to America observed in 1809
that "men of property and talents have been so annoyed by the servile
means necessary to gain power, and by the violence and licentiousness
connected with it, they are generally shrinking from the scene."[30]

We have chronicled the changing of the guard within the Federal
Party, the retirement of the old school, the emergence of new men,
masters of the main chance, experts in the art of the possible, spokes-
men for a new and covert elitism. It is interesting that these new men
described even more striking transitions. Harrison Gray Otis complained
that "the lowest and most ordinary classes of the people are converted
into a cast out of which all the favorites and officers of government are
selected. The metamorphosis from blacksmiths and shoemakers into
civil and military officers is as regular as that of caterpillers into butter-
flies." A few years earlier, William Plumer had written into his diary

---

[28] William Plumer to William Plumer, Jr., Mar. 15, 1806, in Plumer Papers,
Library of Congress. "Instead of debating measures in the House, motions were
often made for a postponement to give members an opportunity *to talk the matter
over in their lodgings.* And the reason assigned in those bald terms. There seemed
to be a pretty general prejudice against all who had or pretended to have more
information or knowledge than the general herd." Jeremiah Smith to William
Plumer, Jan. 5, 1806, ibid. See also David Campbell to Edward Campbell, Jan. 30,
1814, in David Campbell Papers, Duke Univ. Library.

[29] James Hillhouse to Simeon Baldwin, Feb. 18, 1802, in Baldwin Papers, Yale
Univ. Library.

[30] John Howe to [?], n.d., [circa May, 1809], "Reports of John Howe," 345.

an account of a meeting with a Jeffersonian Representative. "At a public tavern," he began, "I found Peter Carlton, member of Congress elect. His clothing and hat were mean, and what was worse, he lived in the kitchen and associated with men of the lowest classes, though I urged him to go into the parlour. He ventured in to dine, but at the table sat with the meanest persons who were admitted and after dinner retired." The same value judgment was more explicit in Archibald Murphey's "Address to the Freeholders of Orange County," dated June 3, 1814:

> Politics have become a trade, in which bankrupts of fortune and reputation are master-workmen, and the idle, the profligate, the dissipated and the factious are apprentices. When a man gets out of business he turns politician, undertakes to instruct his neighbors about their rights and the administration of their government; and just at the moment when he loses his prudence in managing his own affairs he gets wisdom for managing the affairs of the nation.[31]

To Friends of Order there sometimes seemed to be no end of Peter Carltons. The young Federalist Harmanus Bleecker wrote, "National councils in which wheelwrights, innkeepers and butchers make a figure cannot be respectable." Another Federalist, William Barry Grove, complained that many Congressmen were "good for nothing unless you had a *logrolling* or *corn shucking* on Capitol Hill."[32]

Was this merely the grousing of a disgruntled minority? A recent study of the social origins of important national officeholders in the administrations of Adams, Jefferson, and Jackson suggests that Plumer, Otis, Bleecker, and Grove knew what they were talking about. After a careful investigation, Sidney Aronson tells us that "the most significant conclusion that emerges from this data is that the Jeffersonians were more akin to the Jacksonians than to the Federalists. Jacksonian Democracy was not a noticeable departure from the Jeffersonian but rather a continuation or moderate extension of the earlier egalitarian movement." In Aronson's study, the differences among the three are muted, as might be expected from the offices to which he confined his

---

[31] Otis to John Rutledge, Jr., Mar. 15, 1803, in Rutledge Papers, Southern Hist. Coll., Univ. of N. C.; see also Gouverneur Morris to David Parish, Jan. 5, 1812, Morris Papers, Library of Congress; Plumer, Diary, June 11, 1807, Plumer Papers, Library of Congress; see also W. B. Grove to William Gaston, 8 July 1813, Gaston Papers, U. N. C., described congressmen as "upstart backwoods semi-savages."

[32] Harmanus Bleecker to Theodore Sedgwick., June 12, 1812, in Sedgwick Papers, Mass. Hist. Soc.; William Barry Grove to William Gaston, July 8, 1813, in Gaston Papers, Southern Hist. Coll., Univ. of N. C.; see also Charles Biddle, *Autobiography*, p. 313; A. Russell to David Campbell, Dec. 6, 1808, in Campbell Papers, Duke University Library; Jeremiah Mason to Mrs. Mason, Mar. 20, 1814, in Hilliard *Mason*, p. 87; Gouverneur Morris to Rufus King, Mar. 23, 1814, in King, *Life and Correspondence of King*, V. 389; Moses H. Hopkins to Dr. Jones, July 5, 1805, in Calvin Jones Papers, Southern Hist. Coll., Univ. of N. C.; Quincy, *Josiah Quincy, pp.* 243, 303, 329.

attention. It is to be hoped that he will follow up his investigation with a study of lower officeholders, or state officeholders, or legislative figures, all of which might show more extreme divergences. But be this as it may, the fact remains that greater differences appear between officeholders in the 1790s and in the 1800s than between the 1800s and the 1830s.[33]

5

This investigation began with an epistolary conversation between two gentlemen of the old school, David Sewall and Robert Treat Paine, who agreed in 1810 that America's experiment in Republicanism had gone awry, that the spirit of its War for Independence had degenerated into "selfishness and democracy." Their values, of course, are debatable; but the fact of change is clear. A new society, with new ethics and new corruptions, a new progressive spirit and a new conservatism, was in process of becoming. The pervasive holism and honest undisguised elitism of the old school had become anachronisms.

The great social revolution which Sewall and Paine were unable to accept or to approve had begun long before the election of 1800 and would continue after the War of 1812. But there is no period in American history in which fundamental change proceeded with greater power, speed, and effect than in this most obscure of periods. And there is no better reflection of that change than the careers of those most obscure of American party leaders, the men who called themselves Federalists in the era of Jeffersonian democracy.

[33] Sidney H. Aronson, *Status and Kinship in the Higher Civil Service* (Cambridge, 1964), pp. 60–61, 99, 198–99.

APPENDIX I

Patterns of Partisan Allegiance, 1800

> *Never was there a more singular and mysterious state of parties. The plot of an old Spanish play is not more complicated with underplot. I scarcely trust myself with the attempt to unfold it.*
>
> —FISHER AMES, 1800[1]

The difficult problem of defining Federalism in social terms was not central to this project. Nevertheless, relevant material of two kinds came to light—impressionistic opinions of Federalists and Jeffersonians, and fragmentary election returns. The evidence is grossly incomplete, and conclusions from it are necessarily tentative. But on the theory that it is better to light one candle than to curse the darkness, they are offered here, for whatever they may be worth.

I have found no single pattern of partisan allegiance in 1800, no magic monism which unlocks the inner secrets of political behavior. There was surely no simple symmetry of political conviction and economic interest, no clean-cut cleavage between wealth and poverty, between agriculture and commerce, between realty and personalty holdings, between city-dwellers and countryfolk, between northern merchants and southern planters, between subsistence and commercial farmers, between hardy frontiersmen and effete easterners, between orthodox Calvinists and other religious groups.

There were many patterns of political allegiance—all of them intricate in the extreme. Taken together, they present a picture of bewildering, disheartening complexity. Each serves to qualify all others; they lie superimposed one upon another, blending, shading, mixing, merging in an infinity of shapes and colors. But notwithstanding their complexity, clear patterns do appear, and some patterns are clearly more important than others. Contemporaries described them, and we can detect them in election returns. The object here is to discuss them in order of importance—to peel them back, one by one, with all due care for their fragility, caution for their intricacy and respect for many researchers who have gone before.

Before we begin, the weary reader must bear with one more qualification. Although partisan feeling was very high in 1800, higher than

[1] Fisher Ames to Rufus King, 15 July 1800, in *King*, III, 275.

ever before, the two parties did not divide the nation between them. Only in the Congress, where the parties had first appeared, were men either Federalists or Jeffersonians. During the 1790s, party rivalry spread slowly outward from Philadelphia, like ripples on the surface of a pond, sweeping first through the middle states, then into New England and the southern states. The rate of diffusion seems to have been roughly proportional to the rate of travel and the density of population.[2]

The cities appear to have been well ahead of the countryside; states east of the Hudson seem to have been affected before states south of the Potomac. John Rutledge, Jr., summering in Rhode Island in 1798, noted that the "political line of distinction which separates parties here [Newport], does not extend to South Carolina." Two years later, however, the Palmetto State had caught up. "Hitherto the distinction of political parties has been marked by a very faint line," Thomas Pinckney wrote from Charleston. "This line is however becoming every day more distinct, and by the next election of President we shall probably arrive at the same acme of political rancour and malevolence which the Pennsylvanians seem to have first reached, and which has diffused itself pretty generally on all sides."[3]

In the most remote states, party distinctions appear to have had little meaning even as late as 1800. It was said of Vermont that "all goes there by barter and that offices are trucked off to Feds and Jacobins without much discrimination." At the opposite end of the Republic there was scarcely any discrimination at all. A man could read the *Georgia Gazette* in 1800 without learning that a presidential election was taking place; in voting for Congressmen in that state in the same year there was no visible sign of party consciousness among the electorate. Eight years later, when party lines were clearer in most states, a Federalist in Savannah wrote that "the ancient distinctions between federalist and republican are almost lost in the interior of the state."[4]

Political growth in the Mississippi Valley was also retarded by distance and dispersion. A westerner declared in 1800 that the "most numerous

---

[2] Cunningham, *Jeffersonian Republicans*, pp. 255–257; see C. O. Paullin, *Atlas of the Historical Geography of the U. S.* (Washington, 1932), "Phyladelphia is the Heart, the Censorium, the Pineal Gland of the U. S. in Politics." John Adams to Jefferson, 3 Mar. 1814, Cappon, ed., *Adams-Jefferson Letters*, II, 426.

[3] John Rutledge, Jr., to Bishop Robert Smith, Aug. 14, 1798; Thomas Pinckney to Rutledge, 23 Sep. 1800, in Rutledge Papers, Southern Hist. Coll., Univ. of N. C. Pinckney's observations would appear to describe North Carolina as well. "Parties in this district become more and more defined. It is not the personal good qualities of a candidate that are inquired for; whether he is a Federalist or not, is all the question"; Charles W. Harris to Robert Harris, 12 May 1800, in "Harris Letters," *Sprunt Studies*, No. 14, p. 71.

[4] [Savannah] *Georgia Gazette*, 18 June–25 Dec. 1800; John MacPherson Berrien to John Rutledge, Jr. 3 Oct. 1808, in Rutledge Papers, Southern Hist. Coll., Univ. of N. C.

class" was not firmly committed to either side. Despite persistent efforts by Frederick Jackson Turner's disciples to demonstrate that the frontier was an accelerator of political change, it would appear that political techniques even in the most advanced western state, Kentucky, were in 1800 roughly on a par with colonial practices in coastal settlements. Our discussion of partisan patterns might be more fruitful if we would leave by the side those distant states and territories in which party consciousness was not sufficiently clear to be meaningful.[5]

I

The most pervasive pattern of partisan allegiance derived from the existence of established and entrenched elites in the new republic. Americans who analyzed the structure of their society sometimes divided it into two groups—the better sort and the meaner sort, the respectable and the ambitious. "Society consists of two classes," a Friend of Order declared, "of those who have something and want to keep it, and of the rabble who have got nothing and are ever ready to be stirred up to get it."[6]

The distinction, of course, was not between those who had something and those who had nothing, not simply between wealth and poverty, but between attainment and aspiration, between those who had and those who hungered. The most hungry, the most ambitious, the most "mean" from an elitist perspective were men who had much and wanted more—men who wished to add respectability to riches, or riches to popular influence. Thus conceived, the political pattern was clear. The established elites in most states were Federalist; their challengers were Jeffersonian. Recent students of the period, even those most critical of Beard's generalizations, would appear to accept this one. "The complex array of entrenched officials, together with the older county families and their professional and mercantile allies, led the Federalist party," an anti-Beard historian of the Massachusetts Jeffersonians has recently written; the Republicans on the other hand "attracted persons either outside the elite or enjoying a recently acquired and insecure position in local society. They were often new men who came from rising families that had been excluded from the highest levels of influence and standing."[7]

[5] William Dunbar to Winthrop Sargent, 29 Oct. 1800, in Sargent Papers, Mass. Hist. Soc.; see the description of electioneering practices in Kentucky in [Lexington] Kentucky Gazette, 13 Mar. 1800; and an article calling for greater political sophistication on eastern models in ibid., 27 Feb. 1800.

[6] Thomas Dwight to Hannah Dwight, 21 Jan. 1802, in Dwight-Howard Papers, Mass. Hist. Soc.; Robinson, Jeff. Dem. in N. Eng., passim.

[7] Goodman, Democratic-Republicans of Mass., p. 75; Robinson, Jefferson Dem. in N. Eng., p. 110; Purcell, Conn. in Transition, p. 229; Fee, Aristocracy to Democracy in N. J., Higginbotham, Keystone in the Democratic Arch, p. 382; Munroe, Federalist Delaware, p. 213, Ambler, Sectionalism in Va., passim. Gilpatrick, Jeff. Dem. in N. C., Wolfe, Jeff. Dem. in S. C., pp. 6, 13, 49, 81-2.

It goes without saying that Federalists claimed the elites as their own. "Here as everywhere," a Connecticut gentleman wrote, "the men of talents, information and property, yea and I may add honesty and integrity are found among the Federalists." Their claims were recognized by Jeffersonians, who used different value-terms but to describe the same facts. A New England Republican labeled the Federalists of his town the "prigarchy." John Binns of Pennsylvania conceded that Federalism commanded the support of "everything that considers itself a part of the natural aristocracy." A Jeffersonian editor in Delaware wrote, "The Federalists boasted that the weight of talents is on their side; it cannot be denied that this has been the case." In South Carolina, Charles Pinckney, "Blackguard Charlie," the family Democrat, acknowledged "the weight of talent, wealth, and personal and family influence brought against us."[8]

This brute fact of early American politics explains much of the emotive power of the Jeffersonian cause. A Rhode Island Republican summarized his resentment in a stanza:

> These men I hate 'cause they despised me
> With deep contempt—and 'cause they advis'd me,
> To hold my tongue when th'was debate
> And not betray my want of wit.

It also explains the immediacy of one of the most important of Jeffersonian rallying cries—"It is principles, not men, that democrats ought to support," a Marylander insisted. "It may seem like a paradox, but yet no less true, that good men may support bad political principles."[9]

The claims of Federalists and the complaints of Jeffersonians were reinforced by the observations of foreign travelers in the new republic. British or French, republican or monarchist, bourgeois or noble, nearly all agreed that in America the "gentle," the people of the "better sort" were generally Federalist; the meaner sort were Jeffersonian.[10]

Gentility in America as in England meant, most of all, old riches. By European standards, of course, personal fortunes in the new republic were neither old nor large, but they were sufficient to sustain an exclu-

8 Cyrus Allen to Kilbourne Whitman, 30 Oct. 1808, in Misc. Bd. Mss., Mass. Hist. Soc.; Nathaniel Ames, "Diary," 4 Nov. 1796, *Dedham Hist. Register*, VII (1896), 116; Higginbotham, *Keystone in Demo. Arch*, p. 23; [Wilmington] *Mirror of the Times*, 16 Mar. 1804; Pinckney to Jefferson, Dec. 1800, *Amer. Hist. Rev.*, IV (1898), 122.
9 "To All Good People of the State of Rhode Island," n.d., in Broadsides, Amer. Antiq. Soc.; Easton *Star and Eastern Shore General Advertiser*, 5 Sep. 1809.
10 John Howe to George Prevost, 5 May 1808, "Reports of John Howe," p. 81; Louis A. F. Beaujour, *Sketch of the United States of North America at the Commencement of the Nineteenth Century* (London, 1814), pp. 128–130; Charles William Jansen, *The Stranger in America 1793–1806*, Carl S. Driver, ed., (N. Y., 1935), p. 133; anon., *A View of the State of Parties in America* (Edinburgh, 1812), pp. 50–56.

sive elitism in society and politics. There is an abundance of impressionistic testimony to a connection between established wealth and Federalist
politics, but the most persuasive evidence, perhaps, appears in voting
returns for the three largest American cities in 1800 New York City
Federalists were strong in wards 1, 2, and 3, where assessments were
high, houses were large, lots were scarce and addresses were
fashionable. The Philadelphia returns reflect a traditional prejudice
among the "best people" against living in the ends of the town, near
the Northern Liberties and Southwark. The exclusive neighborhoods
in Baltimore lay within the central and western wards; the least respectable addresses were towards Fell's Point.[11]

These patterns may have been clearer in the large cities than in rural
counties, but they do not appear to have differed in kind. John Adams's
observation in 1787 that three or four families comprised a little elite
in almost every New England village would appear to be true in 1800;
and the little elites would seem to have been generally Federalist. Similar
statements appear for almost every part of the Republic—even Mississippi Territory, where Federalist Winthrop Sargent wrote of "dispassionate men of cultivated minds" who were "firmly attached to good order
by Families and Wealth."[12]

Federalists could not, of course, claim that all of the wealth of the
nation was behind them. "Rich, overgrown rich men are to be found
among every description of politics," a New York Federalist declared.
But Friends of Order could claim most of the old wealth of the republic,
and once again their claims were ratified by opponents. William Bentley,
a Republican, noted that his party had "rich men not high in reputation."
Many a Federal family sought to stave off the challenge of new-rich
Republican rivals. The Derbys and Crowninshields of Salem are surely

[11] Beard, *Econ. Origins of Jeff. Dem.*, pp. 383–87; New York *Commercial Advertiser*, 5, 7 May 1800; I. N. P. Stokes, *Iconography of Manhattan Island*, 6
vols. (New York, 1895–1928), V, 502; [Philadelphia] *Aurora*, 2, 17 Oct. 1800;
[Philadelphia] *Gaz. U. S.*, 16 Oct. 1800; anon., *Phila. Scrapple*, (Philadelphia, 1956),
p. 3; J. T. Scharf and T. Westcott, *Hist. of Philadelphia*, 3 vols., (Philadelphia,
1844), I, 511; J. T. Scharf, *Chronicles of Baltimore*, (Baltimore, 1874), p. 281;
Baltimore *Telegraphe*, 11 Nov. 1800; [Baltimore] *Fed. Gazette*, 11 Nov. 1800; maps
of election returns in these cities, plotted by wards, appear in my "Federalists and
Democracy" on file at The Johns Hopkins University Library.

[12] Adams, *Works*, IV, 393; Winthrop Sargent in Dunbar Rowland, ed., *Mississippi Territorial Archives, 1798–1803* (Nashville, 1905) 185; George Salmon to
James McHenry, 7 Oct. 1798, McHenry Papers, Md. Hist. Soc.; Oswald Tilghman,
History of Talbot County, Md., I, 144; George Gibbs to Oliver Wolcott, 30 July
1812, Wolcott Papers, Library of Congress; Troup to King, 6 May 1799, *King*, III,
14; Higginbotham, *Keystone in the Democratic Arch*, 11–12, 382. "How many
instances have you and I known of these monopolies of county administration!
I know a county in which a particular family (a numerous one) got possession
of the bench, and for a whole generation, never admitted a man on it who was
not of its clan or connection. I know a country now of 1500. militia, of whom
60. are federalists. Its court is of 30. members of whom 20. are federalists."
Jefferson to John Taylor, 21 July 1816, Ford, *Jefferson*, X, 53.

the most conspicuous examples. The gentry of Baltimore county, the Howards and Ridgelys and Carrolls, unwillingly surrendered their local power to parvenu Republican merchants such as the Smiths and Mc-Kims. In New Castle County, Delaware, new manufacturing families such as the Du Ponts were Republican; their influence rapidly outran that of the older Federalist gentry. The Browns of Providence faced, and outfaced, a host of rising Republican merchants and manufacturers. Jeffersonian *arrivistes* in Pittsburgh were not welcomed to the drawing rooms and dancing assemblies of the Federalist "connexion" nor into the commercial affairs of the town; and at the opposite end of Pennsylvania, Stephen Girard suffered similar snubs from Philadelphia Federalists. The same pattern appears, albeit less clearly, in Virginia and the Carolinas. Randolphs and Jeffersons notwithstanding, voting returns and impressionistic evidence suggest that the scions of splendid colonial families in the tidewater—Beverleys and Pages, Fitzhughs and Carters —either entered Federal ranks or withdrew from active politics.[13]

A sense of elitism derived not merely from old wealth but from occupation as well. Men who held positions of power and prominence in 1800 tended toward Federalism. The same qualifications entered above also apply here, of course. Inherited power operated like ancient riches, to distinguish old families from new. Republicans, Federalists, and neutral observers agreed. John Binns of Pennsylvania, who declared that "everything that considers itself a part of the natural aristocracy" tended toward Federalism, defined aristocracy in occupational terms—"nearly all the lawyers, nearly all the merchants, most of the parsons, many of the physicians." There have been occasional efforts at quantification. Sanford Higginbotham investigated the occupations of Federalist and Republican electioneering committeemen in Philadelphia, 1811, and found that 51 per cent of the Federalists were merchants and lawyers, against 17 per cent of the Republicans; 27 per cent of Federalists were mechanics, artisans and small shopkeepers against 37 per cent of their opponents. In 1809 a Republican in Windsor, Vermont, calculated that of twenty-two lawyers in Windsor County, seventeen were Federalist; of thirty-three merchants, twenty-four were federal.[14]

[13] Pickering to Hazen Kimball, 5 Jan. 1814, in Pickering Papers, Mass. Hist. Soc.; Bentley, *Diary*, III, 350; [New York] *Evening Post*, 14 Dec. 1801; Goodman, *Democratic-Republicans of Mass.*, pp. 114–115, 120–124; Munroe, *Federalist Delaware*, p. 224; Danforth, "Pictures of Providence," *R. I. Hist.*, X (1951), 7; Tarleton Bates to Frederick Bates, 28 Jan. 1804, W. *Pa. Hist.*, XII (1930), 49; K. L. Brown, "Stephen Girard's Bank," *Pa. Mag. Hist. Biog.*, LXVI (1942), 29–55; Federalists did occasionally claim nearly all the wealth of the nation, but their claims were refuted by Jeffersonians; Ames, *Works*, II, 116; cf. [Boston] *Independent Chronicle*, 31 Dec. 1801.

[14] Higginbotham, *Keystone in the Democratic Arch.*, pp. 326–382; Robinson, *Jeffersonian Democracy in New England*, p. 110; Fox, *Decline of Aristocracy*, ch. I; Fee, *New Jersey*, p. 269.

Lawyers appear to have been more generally Federalist than merchants, and more active and zealous as well. Sweeping attacks upon attorneys were a common theme of Republican editors, and apparently with reason. Federal nominating meetings often coincided with court sessions and bar meetings.[15] On the other hand, a common complaint of active Federalists was the lack of enthusiasm which merchants showed for the "cause of order." Jeremiah Mason's lament in 1813 was representative. The merchants, he wrote "are of all classes of society the least apt to make a manly opposition. They have never acted with the least concert, and have always in the end quietly submitted. Gain is their great object. They will never enter into a contest with the Government in which no money can be made."[16]

"Merchant" was a term which was at once much less precise and much more inclusive than "lawyer," embracing many different kinds of entrepreneurial activity, and many different degrees of wealth and respectability. An English traveler distinguished between "principal merchants" and "small merchants," the former tending toward Federalism, the latter toward Jeffersonian principles. William Bentley noted that the richest and the poorest citizens of Salem were generally Federalist, and the middling families Republican. In Delaware a Democrat declared that Federalists were the "wealthy and powerful," who having tasted privilege "wished to confirm themselves in it, and hand it down as a patrimony to their children by endeavoring to fix a government more energetic and more restraining to the liberties of the people." Republicans he identified as "the middling ranks" and the "industrious poor" who desired "to keep the door open, thro' which merit and industry may reach the highest summit of power, equally with the wealthiest."[17]

There were, of course, men in trade whose politics were shaped by profit-seeking in the most direct sense. Dry-goods merchants, who dealt mostly in English goods, appear to have leaned toward the "British" rather than the "French" party; merchants such as Girard who traded with France were in the other camp. But it should be noted that commercial connections with England were old and well established; merchants who operated within them were less apt to be new men than those who entered the newer sector of French trade. Similarly, contemporaries often distinguished between Federalist merchants and Democratic manufacturers. An English visitor to Philadelphia believed that "the party names they assumed were merely other terms for im-

---

[15] [Portland] *Eastern Argus,* 11 Oct. 1804, 29 Mar. 1805; [New York] *American Citizen,* 3 May 1800; [Chillicothe] *Supporter,* 11 Aug. 1800; Fox, *Decline of Aristocracy,* pp. 11–17, Higginbotham, *Keystone in the Democratic Arch.,* p. 79; Benton, *Herkimer Co., N. Y.,* p. 257.

[16] Jeremiah Mason to Rev. Jesse Appleton, 21 Dec. 1813, in Hilliard, *Mason,* pp. 69–72; see above, ch. II.

[17] Lambert, *Travels,* II, 90; "To the Citizens of Newcastle County," 1804, in Broadsides, Amer. Antiq. Soc.; Bentley, *Diary,* IV, 17.

porters and manufacturers." The profit motive clearly operated in the case of Henry Smith, a wealthy Jeffersonian distiller in Providence, Rhode Island, who blazoned the side of his factory with the slogan "liberty, equality and no excise!" But immediate economic interest may have been less important than the transcendent fact that manufacturing money was often new money, and commercial families were more apt to be entrenched.[18]

Patterns among artisans, craftsmen, and petty shopkeepers reflect the same general theme. Occupations which appeared least "respectable," and most mobile though not necessarily the most impoverished, were markedly enthusiastic for Jefferson. The butchers of Philadelphia, often affluent but rarely respectable, were "distinguished among their fellow-citizens, for their support and attachment to Republican principles." The cartmen of New York City showed similar political attitudes. "Indigo pedlars" in Connecticut, who were regarded as a species of gypsy by the sober citizenry of that stable and conservative state, were decidedly Democratic in 1800.[19]

Two other occupational patterns of partisan allegiance, which reflected a sense of elitism and of "respectability," are sufficiently clear to be meaningful. Naval officers in the new nation appear to have been generally Federalists. Jefferson's "gunboat policy" may have been a factor, but the habit of command, as we have seen with Commodore Truxtun, provided a deeper basis for rapport with the "cause of order."[20] On the other hand, physicians more than any other profession leaned toward Jeffersonian ideas. Gideon Granger, for example, described physicians as "generally friends of equal liberty." Other observers agreed in the fact and in its explanation—no other profession was "so badly treated."[21]

Old wealth and respectable callings were but two of many distinguishing characteristics of the American elite, which tended toward Federalism in its politics in 1800. Another was education. The higher the attained level of formal schooling, the more likely was a firm Federalist

---

[18] [Boston] *New England Palladium*, 21 Oct. 1806; Melish, *Travels*, I, 167; see also P. A. Jay to John Jay, 7 May 1813, in Jay Papers, Columbia Univ.; Danforth "Pictures of Providence," *R. I. Hist.*, X (1951), 7. The republicanism of manufacturers was no more than a tendency, of course. It was probably true that Federalists owned most of the manufacturing establishments of the nation, as the *Palladium* claimed. But a relative distinction between the politics of merchants and manufacturers would remain valid.

[19] Michael Fry and Nathan Coleman to Jefferson, 17 Oct. 1801, in Jefferson Papers, Library of Congress; [New York] *Am. Citizen*, 7 May 1800; [Hartford] *Connecticut Courant*, 1 Sep. 1800; see also Timothy Dwight's strictures against boatmen in *Travels*, VII, 485.

[20] Abijah Bigelow to wife, 9 Dec. 1812, *Amer. Antiq. Soc. Proceedings*, XL (1930), 345 [Exeter] *Constitutionalist*, 29 Dec. 1812; Wolfe, *Jeff. Dem. S. C.*, p. 278.

[21] Granger to Jefferson, 20 Jun. 1805, in Jefferson Papers, Library of Congress; James Wilson to Wm. Darlington, 27 Feb. 1808, in Darlington Papers, Library of Congress; [Chillicothe] *Supporter*, 4 July 1809.

commitment. Federalists often entered this claim; Jeffersonians acknowledged its validity. Gideon Granger complained to Jefferson that in
Connecticut there were "at least four hundred men of public education
and prospects for four or five of us to contend with." A Massachusetts
Republican lamented that though his political friends were often "men
of firm minds," they "were not qualified by education to plead or write."[22]

Table I. Formal Education of Federalists and Republicans
in the Sixth Congress

Attained level	Federalists Number	Per cent	Republicans Number	Per cent
Private tutors	5	7.5	0	0
College graduate	34	50.8	12	25.5
Attended college	6	9.0	8	17.0
Lower schools	21	31.2	22	46.9
Unknown	1	1.5	5	10.6
Total	67	100.0	47	100.0

SOURCE: Party affiliations are taken from Dauer, *Adams Federalists;* educational
level, from *Biographical Directory of the American Congress* and *Dictionary of
American Biography.* Efforts were also made to trace Congressmen listed here
as unknown in registers, alumni catalogues and directories of American colleges
founded before 1795. Those so listed in all probability did not advance beyond
the lower schools.

A comparison of the educational level of Federalist and Jeffersonian
Representatives in Congress in 1800 (see Table I) reveals a clear
disparity.

The colleges of the new nation were, if not Federalist, at least decidedly
hostile to Jefferson. The trend was most apparent in New England
institutions but by no means confined to them alone. A Princeton undergraduate wrote in 1800 that "the students are in general on the federal
side; this cannot, I fear, be said of the people at large." Similar evidence
exists for Columbia, Brown, and even the new colleges in North Carolina, Georgia, and later in Kentucky. An exception was William and
Mary, where the students refused to wear crepe for the death of Washington and received the news of Jefferson's election with "joy almost
bordered on madness."[23]

[22] For Federalist claims see Warren, *Autobiography and Journals of John C.
Warren,* I, 65; D. B. Ogden to Wm. Meredith, 1 May 1805, in Meredith Papers,
Hist. Soc. Penna.; Jeremiah Smith to Wm. Plumer, 5 Jan. 1806, in Plumer Papers,
Library of Congress; John Tabb to William Shaw, 25 May 1807, in Misc. Bd Mss.,
Mass. Hist. Soc.; Quincy, *Figures of the Past,* p. 192; for Jeffersonians, see Gideon
Granger to Thomas Jefferson, 18 Oct. 1800, in Jefferson Papers, Library of Con-
gress; Bentley, *Diary,* II, 176; Robinson, *Jeff. Dem. in New Eng.,* pp. 106, 113.

[23] There were periodic eruptions of Republican zeal among the undergraduates,
perhaps primarily because their professors were so staunchly Federalist. But for
the predominantly Federal cast of trustees, teachers and students alike see Fred-

The anti-Jeffersonian bias of the colleges was equally evident in the other "literary institutions" of the Republic, from the Boston Athenaeum to the Charleston Library Society. Republicans excluded from these particular associations sometimes displayed a general enmity toward literary institutions of any kind. There were of course many exceptional men in the party of Jefferson, whom New England Federalists, incidentally regarded as "a scholar among gentlemen, but not a scholar among scholars." But there was also more than a trace of an anti-intellectual prejudice. Unlike federal fear of "visionary" philosophizing, it was directed against settled institutions of learning, against metaphysics, erudition, and formal scholarship. The most elevated expression of this prejudice is perhaps Jefferson's fulminations against "abstraction." A more crude manifestation was a New York Jeffersonian who denounced Gouverneur Morris because "he knows too much."[24]

In addition to formal education, any accomplishment, habit, custom, quality, prejudice, or predilection which tended to distinguish those who had from those who hungered, tended also to distinguish a Federalist from a Jeffersonian in a descriptive if not a causal way. Physical appearance?

> Apollo views with honest pride,
> His fav'rites all on Fed'ral side.

So at least boasted a Federalist, and he may well have been right. Modes of dress? A Democrat distinguished the parties as "ruffle-men" and "apron men." The phrase "silk-stocking district" first characterized Federalist constituencies.[25]

---

erick Beasley to William Gaston, 3 May 1800, Gaston Papers, Univ. N. C.; Ezekiel Baer to John Bacon, 28 Dec. 1801, Gallatin Papers, N. Y. Hist. Soc.; Birdsall, *Berkshire Co.*, 137–8; Robinson, *Jeff. Dem. in New England*, 110; Fox, *Decline of Aristocracy*, 29; A. D. Murphey to John Scott, 23 Feb. 1801, Hoyt, *Murphey Papers*, I, 1–2. Gilpatrick, *Jeff. Dem. in N. C.*, 129–130; Phillips, *Sectionalism in Ga.*, 92–93; for William and Mary see J. S. Watson to David Watson, 24 Dec. 1799, 2 Mar. 1801, *William and Mary Quarterly*, 29 (1921) 152, 161–162; and [New London] *Bee*, 26 Mar. 1800. Dickinson College appears to have been divided; see James Somervell to Samuel Marsteller, 1 Feb. 1813, Duke Univ. Library; Dartmouth in Hilliard, *Mason*, 169; and for Transylvania, Lexington *Western Monitor*, 10 Nov. 1815.

24 Wolfe, *Jeff. Dem. S. C.*, p. 261; [Boston] *Independent Chronicle*, May 21, 1807; Bentley, *Diary*, II, 226; Boorstin, *Lost World of Thomas Jefferson*, pp. 128–139; Gouverneur Morris to John Parish, 9 May 1806, in Morris Papers, Library of Congress.

25 [Boston] *New England Palladium*, 6 Nov. 1804; Cooperstown *Otsego Herald*, 3 May 1798. Charles Biddle, in his *Autobiography*, pp. 330–331n, tells an anecdote which makes clear the importance of dress as an emblem of elitism. Edward Badger, a Pennsylvania lawyer, gentleman and Federalist was riding to Lancaster, wearing a short coat which was rarely adopted by the best people. Late in the day he stopped to ask about an inn kept by a certain Mr. Slough. "Oh yes, be sure," came a stranger's reply, "Slough he keeps a good house, but that won't do for you and me, for none but gentlemen go there." Badger vowed and declared that he would never wear a short jacket again.

There were many exceptions, to be sure—exceptional men at the top and bottom of American society. Some there were who regarded themselves as full-fledged members of the elite, without any apparent reason. Some years after the fall of the Federalists, Francis Parkman came across an individual who serves as an illustration. In one of his excursions through the north woods, Parkman met a squatter who seemed at first almost a caricature of the American Democrat—and yet he was an anti-Democrat. Sitting at supper in his cabin, "squatting on his home-made chair, shirt-sleeves rolled up to the elbows, bushy hair straggling over his eyes, attacking his meal, as if his life depended on his efforts," he astonished his Brahmin guest by declaiming against "levelling democracy" and "the bed of Procrustes." This man was a Whig; thirty years earlier he would have been a Federalist.[26]

At the upper end of American society, of course, there were others who for reasons of principle or political aggrandizement led the peaceable revolution against the entrenched elites. They qualify the general pattern but do not contradict it. "Although there are no nobles in America," a Frenchman had written in 1786, "there is a class of men denominated 'gentlemen,' and although many of these men have betrayed the interests of their order to gain popularity, there reigns among them a connection so much more intimate as they almost all of them dread the efforts of the people to despoil them of their possessions." His conclusion still held true in 1800.[27]

2

The class of men denominated "gentlemen" could not, of course account for all of the votes which Federalist candidates received in 1800. A geographical analysis of voting patterns in the elections of that year suggest that particularly heavy concentrations of Federalist voters were to be found in the following areas:[27a]

1. The North Shore of New England, including Essex County, Mass., Rockingham and Hillsborough Counties, N.H., and York and Cumberland Counties, Maine.

2. The Connecticut River Valley, including Hartford County, Conn., Worcester and Hampshire Counties in Massachusetts, Grafton and Cheshire Counties in New Hampshire and Windham, Windsor, and Caledonia Counties in Vermont.

3. The middle counties of Rhode Island—Kent and Bristol.

[26] Quoted in Howard Doughty, *Francis Parkman* (New York, 1962), p. 56.

[27] Otto to Vergennes, 10 Oct. 1786, in George Bancroft, *History of the Formation of the Constitution* (New York, 1882), II, 399–400.

[27a] These generalizations rest upon voting returns for the election of 1800, gathered from state archives and newspapers. Maps indicating strength in each state, plotted by town and county, appear in my "Federalists and Democracy," The Johns Hopkins University Library.

4. The old Dutch counties of the Hudson Valley, including Columbia, Rensselaer, and Albany Counties in New York and Bergen County in New Jersey.

5. The counties of West Jersey, and the central portions of that state—Burlington, Somerset, Middlesex, Monmouth, Hunterdon, Gloucester, Salem, Cumberland, and Cape May.

6. Philadelphia and the southeastern counties of Pennsylvania, including Adams, Chester, Delaware, and Lancaster.

7. Luzerne County in northeastern Pennsylvania.

8. The "Delmarva" Peninsula, as it is now called, including Kent and Sussex Counties in Delaware; Dorchester, Worcester, and Somerset Counties in Maryland, and Virginia's Accomack and Northampton Counties.

9. Tidewater Maryland and Virginia—Charles, St. Mary's, and Prince George's Counties in the former state, Loudoun, Westmoreland, Fairfax, Stafford, James City, New Kent, Henrico, and Charles City Counties in the Old Dominion.

10. The upper Cape Fear counties of North Carolina, in Fayetteville and Salisbury Districts.

11. The southern coastal counties of North Carolina, in New Bern and Wilmington Districts.

12. The South Carolina low country, including Cheraw and Georgetown, Charleston, and Orangeburg and Beaufort Districts.

13. The Valley of Virginia, western Virginia, and western Maryland, including Alleghany County Md., and Hampshire, Hardy, Pendleton, Augusta, Rockbridge, and Greenbrier Counties in Virginia.

Manning Dauer, the only scholar since Charles Beard to publish a nationwide analysis of the socioeconomic basis of the party dispute in the 1790s, has suggested a qualified Beardian hypothesis. Extreme Federalists, he writes, were to be found in "commercial and shipping" areas of the nation, "Half-Federalists" generally in "exporting-agricultural sections," which raised cash crops and sold them abroad. The centers of Jeffersonian strength, according to Dauer, were the "more self-sufficient farming sections."[28]

Dauer's evidence does not sustain his conclusions. He suggests five specific ways of distinguishing Federalist from Republican farming areas—soil type, export statistics, ratio of slaves to whites in southern states, wealth per capita, and accessibility to markets. But voting patterns in the 1790s generally and in 1800 particularly do not correlate with any of these variables.[29]

[28] Dauer, *Adams Federalists*, pp. 7, 18–25, 275–287.

[29] Dauer's generalizations from soil types derive from Paullin, *Atlas of the Historical Geography of the U. S.*, Plate 2C, which does not sustain him. The brown, gravelly, and stony loams of New England and New York were farmed by Federalists and Republicans alike. In New Jersey and North Carolina, Federalists subsisted on soils which were essentially sand. The richest soil in the latter state was reputed to be in the northeastern corner—Jeffersonian country (Gilpatrick, *Jeff. Dem. in N. C.*, p. 13). By 1800, the clay loams of the Piedmont in Virginia and Baltimore, Harford, and Frederick Counties in Maryland—all Jeffersonian—were surely richer than the coastal regions where good soil had been mined nearly to exhaustion (Craven, *Soil Exhaustion*, passim) Dauer's generalizations

There are other patterns which appear more clearly in the voting returns for 1800. Most of the Federalist regions enumerated above had one set of characteristics in common, they were mature, static, homogeneous, and ingrown. Jeffersonian areas on the other hand tended to be immature, fluid, and dynamic.

The most staunchly Federalist region in the nation was the Connecticut River Valley. Timothy Dwight wrote of it, "The inhabitants of the valley might be said in several respects to possess a common character;

---

from soil types would appear to hold for South Carolina and western Virginia, but scarcely anywhere else. Export statistics by state, from which Dauer also generalizes, are not helpful. County of origin is unknown and domestic consumption is ignored; the figures are more representative of port facilities than anything else. But even assuming the relevance of state export statistics to the problem, there is certainly no "direct correlation" with Federalist voting strength, as Dauer claims. The states in which exports (excluding re-exports) were lowest —less than $5.00 per capita per year, included N. H., Vt., Conn., N. J., Del., and N. C. In all but Vt. and N. C., Federalists were strong; and in N. C., Federalism would remain stronger through the Jeffersonian era than in any other southern state. The states where exports were highest, more than $12.00 per capita, were Mass. and Md., Penna. and N. Y., R. I. and S. C., of which two were Federalist, two Republican, and two divided in 1800 and afterwards. Slave ratios are equally inconclusive. Only in S. C. do they correlate with Federalist strength. In N. C., slaves were numerous in the northeastern corner of the state, which voted Jeffersonian; they were comparatively few in the upper Cape Fear region, where Federalism was strongest. In Va., the slave ratio was high in the Federalist tidewater counties, but also in the southside counties which were Jeffersonian. The ratio was low in Federalist counties in the west. Federalist counties in Md. were in the same fashion both high (Charles) and low (Alleghany); so also, Jeffersonian counties such as Queen Anne's had a high ratio of slaves; Harford County had a very low one. Per capita wealth is generally unknown, though a conclusion could be drawn from the census of 1800 and assessments for the Federal Land Tax of 1799, a laborious task which neither Mr. Dauer nor I have undertaken to perform. Dauer does list the state land tax per capita for Massachusetts in 1796, but there is not even the "fair correspondence" which Dauer claims. Two of the three wealthiest counties, Norfolk and Middlesex, were described by a Federalist as "dens of unclean beasts" (Thomas Dwight to Theodore Sedgwick, 11 Apr. 1800, in Sedgwick Papers, Mass. Hist. Soc.); Hampshire County, the most Federal in the state, was less affluent according to this indicator than Worcester and Essex, which were more nearly divided, and Plymouth, which was Jeffersonian. Accessibility to markets does not correlate with party allegiance. Many Jeffersonian areas were more accessible than Federalist areas—Norfolk and Middlesex Counties in Massachusetts, Suffolk, Queens, Westchester, Rockland, Dutchess, and Orange in New York; Essex in New Jersey; Bucks, Montgomery and Berks in Pennsylvania; Harford, Anne Arundel, and Baltimore Counties in Maryland. The Jeffersonian counties of Virginia were exporting large crops as early as 1791 (Edward Carrington to Hamilton, 4 Oct. 1791, in *William and Mary Quarterly*, 2d series, II (1922), 139). as were the northeastern counties of North Carolina. On the other hand, the Connecticut River Valley was in Timothy Dwight's description (Dwight, *Travels*, III, 333) "remote from a market;" most agricultural goods appear to have been carried out by wagon across the interior of the state, rather than floated down the rock strewn river. Turnpikes and river improvements were only beginning to expand commercial opportunities.

Finally, another of Dauer's suggestions that "in general, the Half-Federalists, as those who deviated from the Hamiltonian orthodoxy are called, are to be found in farming sections," is not sustained by his evidence. Such a conclusion certainly and, in all the different states resemble each other more than their fellow citizens, who live on the coast. This similarity is derived from their descent, their education, their local crcumstances, and their mutual intercourse. In the older settlements most of the inhabitants are natives of this valley, and those who are not, yield to the influence of a character which they continually see all around them."[30]

Dwight described the "sobriety" and "good order" of the inhabitants of the Valley—and many other men of all persuasions agreed with him. "The yeomanry of the towns on and near this river in Massachusetts," another Federalist wrote, "are in their principles, habits and manners and in their police [policy] as far as a difference of government will admit, very like the stable yeomanry of Connecticut—not extremely liable to change." Still a third Federalist summarized in a sentence, "We keep more to our Old Habits, being composed chiefly of the descendants of Old Settlers."[31]

The same qualities appear among the people of the second most staunchly Federalist region, the Delmarva peninsula, including lower Delaware, Maryland's southeastern shore and the two Virginia counties. Writing of lower Delaware, John Munroe has observed, "the people were largely of English stock, inbreeding was common among them, and, with the passage of time, isolation and homogeneity bulwarked the customs and attitudes of their forbears." As Munroe succinctly states, it was a region which cherished "ancient virtues and accustomed procedures."[32]

A historian of New Jersey, Richard P. McCormick, has written of the "stability" of society in West Jersey, with its "relatively homogeneous population and its pronounced ruralness." A Pennsylvania historian has observed that the southeastern counties of that state were marked by "the habits of a mature society" early in the nineteenth century. There are similar descriptions of tidewater Maryland and Virginia, the Cape Fear region of North Carolina and the South Carolina low country.[33]

---

does not appear on the face of the maps which Dauer included. As far as leading Federalists and Independents are concerned, those few who stood with Adams in 1800 (Knox, Otis, Dexter, Gerry, Reed, the Fenners, the Trumbulls, Rush, Chase, Craik, Stoddert, and Marshall) were nearly all merchants or commercial lawyers. The acidulous comments of Federalists who were displeased with Adams in 1800 (nearly all the leaders in 'the first rank') suggest that commercial men were generally better pleased by Adams' temperate foreign and domestic policies than by more reckless alternatives of the "High Federalists."

[30] Dwight, *Travels*, III, 333; see also [Boston] *Repertory*, 15 May 1807, in which Federalists are described as "quiet men."

[31] Jabez Colton to Simeon Baldwin 31 Dec. 1804, Baldwin Papers, Yale University Library; Thomas Dwight to John Williams, 2 Dec. 1802, Dwight-Howard Papers, Mass. Hist. Soc.

[32] Munroe, *Federalist Delaware*, p. 239.

[33] Richard McCormick, *Experiment in Independence: New Jersey in the Critical Period* (New Brunswick, 1950), p. 45; Philip Shriver Klein, *Pennsylvania Politics,*

Jeffersonian areas, on the other hand, appear to have shown a different set of characteristics. Timothy Dwight's notorious comments upon that "Nazareth of anti-Federalism," western Vermont, as populated by "the discontented, the enterprising, the ambitious and the covetous," may perhaps be taken as something more than a measure of one Federalist's irascibility. Dynamism, expansion, and mobility appear, generally, to have distinguished Republican regions from those in which Federalism flourished.[34]

Impressionistic evidence is reinforced by demographic statistics. The single variable which correlates more closely than any other with voting behavior in 1800 is the rate of population growth as revealed in the censuses of 1790, 1800, and 1810. The most Federalist state in the nation, Connecticut, had the smallest growth rate—6 per cent in the 1790s, 4 per cent in the first decade of the nineteenth century. Population increase in the Connecticut Valley (except its northernmost reaches) was equally small in the period 1800–1810: 6 per cent in Worcester County, Massachusetts; 5 per cent in Hampshire County, Massachusetts; 2 percent in Cheshire County, New Hampshire; 4 per cent in Windham County, Vermont; and 7 per cent in Windsor County, Vermont.

These Valley counties were growing more slowly than the Republican counties in eastern Massachusetts, nearly all of which had growth rates of 11 per cent to 25 per cent in the same period. Essex County, Massachusetts, showed a low growth rate (6 per cent) in the 1790s when it voted Federalist; but in the 1800s, when it drifted into the Republican camp, its rate of growth was 18 per cent.[35]

In the middle states, the same generalizations can be made. The most Federal counties of New York were Albany and Columbia; the first was nearly static (2 per cent population rise, 1800–1810) and in the second, population was actually declining. Rensselaer and Washington Counties, also Federalist, showed higher rates of population increase (20 and 23 per cent respectively in 1800–1810) but were still far behind the extraordinary New York average, 78 per cent. In New Jersey the three decidedly Republican counties of Morris, Essex and Sussex had growth rates of 23, 17 and 13 per cent; the Federalist counties of Bergen, Burlington, and Hunterdon had rates of 10, 13 and 14 per cent. Federalist counties in southeastern Pennsylvania—Adams, Delaware, Chester, and

---

1817–1832 (Philadelphia, 1940), pp. 4–5; Avery O. Craven, *Soil Exhaustion as a Factor in the Agricultural History of Virginia and Maryland, 1606–1860* (Urbana, Ill.), pp. 72–121; William A. Schaper, "Sectionalism and Representation in South Carolina," *Amer. Hist. Assn. Annual Report for 1906,* I, 253–258, 433–452.

[34] Dwight, *Travels,* III, 458. See also *Providence Gazette,* 15 Nov. 1800.

[35] Growth rates of counties in eastern Massachusetts were as follows—Bristol, 11 per cent; Barnstable, 15 per cent; Plymouth, 17 per cent; Middlesex 13 per cent; Norfolk, probably more than 25 per cent, Nantucket, 21 per cent. Only Dukes, 5 per cent, was more static than Federalist counties.

Lancaster—showed increases of 10–23 per cent between 1800 and 1810, in a state which was growing at the rate of 35 per cent.

States south of the Mason-Dixon line were much the same. In Delaware's one Republican county, Newcastle, growth rate during the 1790s was 30 per cent; in Federalist Kent County population increase in the same period was 3 per cent, and in Sussex the population was declining. Maryland's Republican counties were growing rapidly; Federalist counties in southern Maryland were losing population. Alleghany County in western Maryland, decidedly Federalist, was not a frontier area, as has sometimes been suggested, but a stagnant backwater in which population was also falling. Federalist Virginia—the Eastern shore, Potomac Valley, and the tidewater counties—was in process of depopulation. In western Virginia, the counties which showed heavy concentrations of Federalists —Berkeley, Hampshire, Hardy, Pendleton, Bath, Augusta, Rockbridge, Botetourt, and Greenbrier—were altogether losing population during the decade 1800–1810. In North Carolina, Republican Districts such as Hillsborough and Morgan were increasing during the 1790s at the rates of 34 and 47 per cent; Federalist areas—New Bern, Wilmington, and Fayetteville—were increasing at rates of 9, 15, and 21 per cent.[36]

There were exceptions, of course. Grafton, Rockingham, and Hillsborough Counties in New Hampshire, Cumberland County in Maine, Caledonia and Orleans in Vermont, Oneida, Ontario, Steuben, Chenango, and Tioga Counties in New York, Luzerne County in Pennsylvania, and the Salisbury District in North Carolina were areas with high rates of population increase which voted Federalist in 1800. Nearly all of them, however would shift to the Republican side within two or three years. There were also a few Republican counties with low rates of increase— Dukes in Massachusetts, Dutchess in New York, Newport and Washington Counties in Rhode Island, Queen Anne's in Maryland; Caroline, Louisa, Isle of Wight, Surry, Nansemond, Mathews, Brunswick, Greenville, Chesterfield, Goochland, Prince Edward, Charlotte, and Montgomery Counties in Virginia, and Edenton District in North Carolina. But altogether, there are fewer exceptions to this generalization than to any other. During the period 1800–1815, the trend would become even more clear.[37]

Population increase would appear to be a more significant indicator than length of settlement or density of population. The southeastern counties of Massachusetts, for example, appear to have been surprisingly

36 In the absence of total population figures for Virginia and Md. counties, calculations are made from white adult males between the ages of 26 and 45. All others are taken from figures listed in the U.S. censuses of 1790, 1800, and 1810, for total county population.

37 See, e.g., on the shift of Tioga County, N. Y., populated by "a rude fierce people," and showing a high growth rate, into the Republican camp in 1802, James Kent, "Journal," 1802, in Kent Papers, Library of Congress.

dynamic. And it might seem at first sight that that the lower Hudson counties of New York, with Long Island, should have been as mature, stable, and static as the middle Hudson counties which voted Federalist. But these southern counties, particularly Suffolk, Queens, Kings, and Westchester, had been the scene of extensive confiscations of loyalist property which by the 1790s were beginning to be broken up into smaller holdings. Census returns for all these counties show growth rates of 10 to 50 per cent.[38] Similarly, the most dynamic urban areas tended to be Jeffersonian—Baltimore, a rough, disorderly boom-town in the new republic, was decidedly Republican. Philadelphia, increasing more slowly, was Federalist.[39]

The descriptive pattern is clear; but causal implications are more problematical. The "meaner sort" in stable, static areas, those who voted Federalist, could be divided into two groups—those who had no objection to elitist government and those who had no opportunity or liberty to make an objection. The motivation of the first group may have been of the sort which Erich Fromm has described in *Escape from Freedom.* A stable, structured society in a world of change and conflict may have been for them a source of security, a means of identity. Economic interests may have been involved, as they surely were in the case of a Federalist barber in the District of Columbia. "What Presidents we might have, sir!" he declared. "Just look at Daggett of Connecticut and Stockton of New Jersey! [Both prominent Federalists.] What queues they have got, sir—as big as your wrist, and powdered every day, sir, like real gentlemen as they are. Such men, sir, would confer dignity upon the chief magistracy, but this little Jim Madison, with a queue no bigger than a pipe stem! Sir, it is enough to make a man forswear his country!" A hunger for the orders and distinctions of a deferential society was not limited to the "best of people."[40]

On the other hand, there were surely other men who were so entangled in the web of social and economic connections that they were unable to escape—bound to their station not by psychic need but by fear and interest. A Pennsylvania Federalist, Charles Biddle, detailed an example:

Enos Clark, an honest Irish tenant of mine, called upon me the morning of the election in much distress. He said just as he was putting in his ticket, one of his friends called him to come down; that he put in the ticket and came to him, when he said, "Clark, do you know what you have been doing?" "Yes, to be sure, I have been putting in the ticket that D. S_____ gave me,

[38] Harry B. Yoshpe, *Disposition of Loyalist Estates in the Southern District of the State of New York* (New York, 1939), pp. 113–120.

[39] A related pattern which reinforces growth rates and also conforms to patterns of partisan allegiance is the fertility ratio of whites, in America. The gross reproduction rate in 1800 was generally low in Federalist areas, high in Republican ones. See A. J. Jaffe, "Differential Fertility in the White Population in Early America," *Journal of Heredity,* XXXI (1940), 407–411.

[40] S. G. Goodrich, *Recollections,* I, 131–32.

and he, you know, is one of us." "Damn you; do you not know you have been voting against your landlord, who has been so kind, and so good to your family?" "I hope it is not so, Mr. Biddle, for I would not do that for all the world." I comforted the poor fellow, by assuring him that on this occasion I did not want his vote."[41]

Internal emigration in the new republic may have served as a social filter, to separate the "discontented, the enterprising, the ambitious and the covetous" from such men as the Washington barber, who had an economic and psychological involvement in a deferential society, and from men such as Biddle's tenant, who was perhaps in too deep to escape or even to protest. Men who remained in the most stable and slowly changing parts of the nation, whether because they were unable or willing to leave, were for the same reasons apt to be "Friends of Order" on election day.[42]

3

There were, of course, many other patterns of partisan allegiance which added complexity and color to the general problem. All are important, and as many will be discussed as the limitations of time and space allow. But in the judgment of this investigator they were subordinate to major patterns described above—they were the "underplot" of this old American tragedy, the images and shadows of a larger theme.

Partisan identity in 1800 reflected, among many other things, previous and prior political loyalties. Of these, perhaps the most important allegiance was to one's state. Larger states tended toward Republicanism; smaller ones to Federalism. The three behemoths, Virginia, Pennsylvania, and New York, were the pillars of the Jeffersonian movement. Federalism flourished better in their smaller neighbors, Connecticut, New Jersey, Delaware, Maryland, and North Carolina. Clear exceptions, of course, would be Massachusetts and Rhode Island.

[41] Biddle, *Autobiography*, p. 330.

[42] To argue thus is, of course, to touch upon the wooly problem of the frontier as "safety valve" (see Murray Kane, "Some Considerations on the Safety-Valve Doctrine," *Miss. Valley Hist. Rev.*, XXIII (1936), 169–188; Carter Goodrich and Sol Davison, "The Wage Earner in the Westward Movement," *Pol. Science Quarterly*, L (1935), pp. 161–185; LI (1936), 61–116; Fred A. Shannon, "A Post Mortem on the Labor-Safety-Valve Theory," *Agricultural History*, XVII (1945), 31–37). It may be true that men who had greatest cause for discontent were least able to ameliorate their condition by emigration, either westward to the frontier or eastward to the city. But what of the men who could lead a social movement—men who had much but wanted more? From a conservative perspective, these were the "dangerous" men—and the beneficiaries of the frontier and the expanding cities. The voting patterns of Luzerne County in Penna. and western New York would suggest that many New England emigrants were Federalists. But cf. J. Cook to Jefferson, 21 Oct. 1801, Jefferson Papers, Library of Congress. "These days there is not an Emigrant from Connecticut within this county," he wrote from Marietta, "but what is really a friend to your honor and a true Republican." Boston emigrants, however, he characterized as "hauty," "overbearing," and Federalist.

American statesmen demonstrated in 1800 that they were thinking of their states first when they addressed themselves to national interests. Such considerations acted upon Bayard, the young Delaware Federalist, when he shifted his vote from Burr to Jefferson. "Representing the smallest state in the Union without resources which could furnish the means of self-protection," he wrote, "I was compelled by the obligations of a sacred duty so to act as not to hazard the constitution upon which the political existence of the state depends."[43]

Ancient rivalries between state and state, often of colonial origin, also operated in 1800. Yorkers and Yankees who had traditionally viewed each other with suspicion and even with enmity, divided on the party question—New York strongly for Jefferson, Connecticut more strongly for Adams. New Jersey, the barrel bunged at both ends by its neighbors, was also affected. "Who wish to bring New-Jersey back to their *tributary* state?" a Federalist asked, "The friends of Jefferson in New York and Pennsylvania."[44]

Virginia's neighbors, Maryland and North Carolina, showed a similar jealousy of the Old Dominion. Charles Harris was one of many Federalists in his state who complained bitterly of "our republican neighbors, the Virginians." An old-school gentleman of the Old North State declared, "the real source of our divisions . . . originates in whether Virginia shall be everything, and other states NOTHING."[45] Another state whose citizens were also jealous of Virginia was Massachusetts. Ames believed that "two causes make our affairs turbulent, the ambition of Virginia and the spirit of jacobinism." A Republican agreed. "There is much state pride in Massachusetts," he wrote, "and federalism has been kept from sinking there by raising jealousies against Virginia."[46]

[43] James A. Bayard to John Adams, 19 Feb. 1801, in Adams Papers, reel 400. Personal considerations may have been important in this case. "I fear that the Virginia pride, will never truly appreciate a Delaware character," Bayard wrote to Caesar Rodney, 10 Dec. 1803, in Bayard Papers, New York Pub. Library; see also Lewis R. Morris to Rutledge, 27 Nov. 1803, in Rutledge Papers, Univ. of N. C.

[44] "Citizens of New-Jersey," 1800, in Broadsides, N. J. Hist. Soc.

[45] Charles W. Harris to Robert Harris, 15 Sep. 1800, in Harris Papers, Univ. of N. C.; W. R. Davie to John Steele, 25 Sep. 1803, cited in Robinson, *Davie*, p. 374.

[46] Ames to Jeremiah Smith, 14 Dec. 1802, in Ames, *Works*, I, 314; Robinson, *Jeff. Dem. in N. Eng.*, p. 152; Otis to Rutledge, 18 Oct. 1801, in Rutledge Papers, Univ. of N. C.; [Boston] *Ind. Chronicle*, 15 Oct. 1801. Fear of Virginia was reinforced, of course, by the expansion of new western states which seemed her colonies to Federalists, and with reason. In 1802, four of seven U. S. Senators and Representatives from Kentucky and Tennessee were Virginia born and bred; see *Biographical Directory of the American Congress*, and compare the exaggerated fears and statistics of the [New York] *Evening Post*, 3 Mar. 1802, which reported that 57 members of Congress were natives of the Ancient Dominion. In fact only 30 were, of whom 21 represented Virginia herself. It might be noted here that although patterns of partisan allegiance did follow state boundaries they did not follow sectional lines, at least in terms of north versus south. Sectional consciousness did exist—at least one New Englander who strayed into Virginia wrote home that he felt "more secure on the other side of the Potomac." (Tristram Dalton to Gouver-

In each of these state rivalries, the large state was Jeffersonian and the little one Federalist. One other rivalry operated in the opposite direction. Federalists of Massachusetts and Connecticut were neither surprised nor particularly sorry that Rhode Island should "lend the dirty mantle of its infamy to the nakedness of Sans-culottism." To Fisher Ames it seemed that "Rhode Island *should* be wrong."[47]

In addition to state loyalties, local attachments were reflected in voting patterns in 1800. Most apparent were rivalries between towns— Salem versus Marblehead, Providence versus Newport were two of many. Perhaps the most important conflict of this kind appeared in Maryland, between the "two great contending parties in this state, to wit: the Baltimore and Patowmack interests," of which the former was Republican, the latter Federalist.[48]

More pervasive, more generally operative, were family connections and conflicts in a society which was still strongly familial. The "Family Compact of Connecticut" is much the most famous example, which Beard enumerated in detail. The Essex clique in eastern Massachusetts was joined by marriage bonds. In Delaware the Bayards, Bassetts, and Claytons, the Dagworthys, Mitchells, and Wellses, the Johnses and Van Dykes intermarried. The Federal Party in that state was one extended cousinage, with ties to New Jersey Federalists through the Stocktons and to Maryland Federalists through the Ridgelys. In the latter state, the Harpers and the Carrolls, Taneys and Keys, Goldsboroughs, Hansons, Ridgelys, Steretts, and Platers intertwined in the same fashion.[49]

---

neur Morris, 12 Jan. 1804, in Morris Papers, Columbia University). But there were no northern and southern parties in 1800. It was the great fear of public men that such parties would soon develop. "The time is not far distant," William Plumer wrote, "when the present parties shall be no more—and parties will then derive their names from geographical lines—a southern and western party, and an eastern party will and must exist. For our separate interests will create them." (Plumer to Daniel Plumer, 7 Feb. 1804, in Plumer Papers, Library of Congress). Geographical divisions appeared in the election of the speaker of the House of Representatives in December, 1799, and cut cleanly across party lines. (John Rutledge to Bishop Smith, 3 Dec. 1799, in Rutledge Papers, Univ. of N. C.)

47 Ames to Jeremiah Smith, 14 Dec. 1802, in Ames, *Works*, I, 314; to this rivalry could be added another that was beginning to appear in 1800 between Massachusetts and the counties of Maine which sought autonomy. It would become more important in the period 1800–1816. See Goodman, *Democratic-Republicans of Massachusetts*, pp. 118–127, 131–132, 155–162, for a discussion of the religious and economic intricacies of this rivalry.

48 [Boston] *Independent Chronicle*, 9 July 1801; Robinson, *Jeff. Dem. in N. Eng.*, p. 83; [Annapolis] *Maryland Gazette*, 14 Aug. 1800; Benjamin Stoddert to John Templeman, n. d., in Stoddert Papers, Library of Congress.

49 Beard, *Econ. Origins of Jeff. Dem.*, p. 364; Fischer, "Myth of the Essex Junto," p. 197; J. D. Phillips in *Essex Institute Hist. Colls.*, XXXIII (1897), 299; [Boston] *New England Palladium*, 25 Mar. 1803; Munroe, *Federalist Delaware*, passim; Conrad, *Delaware*, III, 830; *Sussex Co. Records*, 295–317; G. P. Fisher, "Recollections of Dover in 1824," *Hist. Soc. Del. Papers*, LV, 24–27; Fischer, "Metamorphosis of Maryland Federalism," pp. 9–11.

Family connections also appeared among Republicans. Gallatin married into the Nicholsons, who were connected to Randolphs, who were connected to Jeffersons and the Nicholas clan, who were tied by two marriages to the Smiths of Baltimore. The classic case is New York politics, of course. On the Republican side were two great connections— the Clinton-Osgood-Bailey clan and the Livingston-Lewis-Armstrong-Tillotson-Cutting group. On a lower level, families of Jeffersonians as well as Federalists functioned and thought as political units. In Maine, the following Republican clique, on the Federal payroll:

Joshua Wingate, esq.	Postmaster in Hallowell.
Joshua Wingate, jun.	Collector at Bath.
James Wingate	Postmaster at Portland.
John Wingate	Commissary for troops at Hallowell.
Joseph Wingate	[Indian Agent]

And another in Frederick County, Maryland, in the same year, 1803:

David Shriver, Esq. a delegate to the General Assembly.
Abraham Shriver, his son, an associate justice of Frederick County court.
Andrew Shriver, ditto, a Justice of the Peace.
Andrew Shriver, a Justice of the Levy Court.
John Schley, a son-in-law of David Shriver, a Justice of the Peace.
John Schley, a Justice of the Orphan's Court.
Henry Leatherman, father-in-law of one of the Shrivers, a Supervisor of the Roads [and] supplier to the Jail and Courthouse, &c &c.[50]

At least one prior political conflict which had affected many parts of the new nation was reflected in the voting patterns of 1800. Men who had been Tories in the Revolution, and regions which were heavily populated with them, tended to be Federalist. Leaders of the Federal Party were, of course, more than a little uncomfortable about that fact, but in private correspondence they cheerfully acknowledged it. "Soon after we regained possession of New York," Robert Troup wrote, "we permitted the Tories to enlist under our banners; and they have since manfully fought by our side in every important battle we have had with the democracy; some of them in the character of officers, others in those

[50] *Letters on the Richmond Party*, #1; "To the Independent Electors of the State [of N. Y.], *N. Y. Election Broadsides*, p. 29; see John Adams in Jefferson, 15 Nov. 1813, in Cappon, ed. *Adams-Jefferson Letters*, II, 401. "In New York it is a struggle of Family Feuds"; see also Sedgwick to King, 24 Aug. 1802, in *King*, IV, 162. "The great line of division by which parties are separated in other states is more obscurely marked there [N. Y.] than anywhere else—the people are more under the dominion of personal influence." The local cliques were described by Federalists and republished in the [Boston] *N. Eng. Palladium*, 1 Mar. and 23 Sep. 1803, from local journals. Another state in which family connections were important was Rhode Island; see Hamilton to Bayard, 6 Aug. 1800, in Lodge, *Hamilton*, X, 386; the full reach of family influence in early American politics remains to be established by a careful student of genealogy and local history; this investigator can only endorse J. F. Jameson's suggestion that an important dissertation could be written upon the subject of early American mothers-in-law.

of common soldiers." Areas in which Tories had been numerous and in which Federalism flourished included, in addition to New York City, downstate Delaware, Virginia's eastern shore, Norfolk, and the Cape Fear region around Fayetteville, North Carolina.[51]

Revolutionary Whigs, on the other hand, were divided; each party traced its lineage back to 1776 and cherished its own particular Revolutionary heroes. One pattern within this group appears—men who served as officers for extended periods in the Continental Army tended toward Federalism. Despite many exceptions, Monroe, Armstrong, Smith and others, Beveridge's suggestion that John Marshall's national principles, and perhaps his elitism, were strengthened if not originally implanted by his military experience.[52]

Another early conflict is less easily related to the events of 1800. It is difficult to establish a clear connection between the Federalist-Republican division in 1800 and the Federalist-anti-Federalist cleavage in 1788. The cautious conclusions of Noble Cunningham are generally sustained by my research. In New York and Pennsylvania there were continuities between the parties to the argument 1787–1788, and the more structured parties of 1800. But in other states similar patterns do not appear. Of the four most prominent anti-Federalists in Maryland, three became Federalists in 1800. A Jeffersonian wrote of Delaware in 1800 that "most opponents of the Constitution in 1787 are now friends of order." In North Carolina, the Federalist regions of 1800 had been "anti-Federalist ten years earlier. An able secondary account of Virginia politics minimizes continuities in that state as well. New England requires more thorough research—but there was surely little continuity in New Hampshire. Massachusetts and Connecticut remain doubtful.[53]

[51] Troup to King, 4 Apr. 1809, in *King*, V, 148; [New York] *American Citizen*, 22 Mar. 1800; Hammond, *Pol. Parties N. Y.*, I, 223.

[52] Beveridge, *John Marshall*, I, 144–147.

[53] Cunningham, *Jeffersonian Republicans*, pp. 3, 23, 142, 218; Tinkcom, *Republicans and Federalists in Penna.*, p. 31; Young, "The Democratic-Republican Movement in New York State, 1788–97"; Harry Ammon, "The Formation of the Republican Party in Virginia," pp. 309–310; Fischer, "Metamorphosis of Maryland Federalism," p. 10; [Wilmington] *Mirror*, 5 Apr. 1800; Samuel Miller to John Jay, 17 Mar. 1800, in *Jay*, IV, 263; Goodman, *The Democratic-Republicans of Mass*, takes no clear position on this question, but stresses the "fluidity of politics" in Massachusetts during the '90s. Charles Beard's efforts to establish a relationship between the contests of 1789 and 1800 are not merely inconclusive, as Cunningham has pointed out (p. 23n) but grossly inaccurate. Forty-two members of the Convention can be clearly connected to one or the other party in 1800. Of these, seventeen (not Beard's twelve) contradict the Beardian hypothesis; twenty-five (not thirty-one) support it. Federalists of 1787 who became Jeffersonians included Baldwin, Blount, Butler, Dickinson, Few, Gilman, William Houstoun, Langdon, Madison, Alexander Martin, Charles Pinckney, Randolph, Rutledge, Spaight, and Wythe. Two anti-Federalists became Federalists in 1800, Martin and Yates. Unclassifiable are Brearly, Carroll, Franklin, Gorham, Houston, Jenifer, Livingston, McClurg, Mason, Robert Morris, Pierce, Sherman, and Williamson; cf. Beard, *Economic Origins of Jeffersonian*

4

Ethnic voting patterns in 1800 were clear to contemporary observers of political behavior. The Irish, who were beginning to pour into the great "flour cities" of the middle states and into New England as well, were overwhelmingly Republican. Many were political refugees; all felt the bite of prejudice in the Anglo-American republic. There were the inevitable exceptions—Irishmen such as Thomas FitzSimons who had emigrated before the War of Independence and became an important Federalist in Pennsylvania. But Republicans and Federalists agreed upon the rule.[54]

French immigrants appear to have been as generally Republican as the Irish, notwithstanding an occasional *émigré* who became a "friend of order and good government." Of 311 Frenchmen who voted in Charleston in 1812, all but seven favored the Republican ticket. The six or seven hundred Frenchmen who had settled in Philadelphia by 1808 were reported to be nearly unanimous for the Democratic cause.[55]

The Germans of Pennsylvania and Maryland had generally voted for Federalist candidates in the mid 1790s, but in 1800 were generally, if not enthusiastically, Republican. Contemporaries explained the shift as a reaction to the threat of direct taxation and to the repression of Fries' Rebellion. In 1805 they would show a clear preference for moderate rather than radical Republicans. In 1814, the threat of Republican taxes would drive many of them back to the Federalists.[56]

Free Negroes, in the states which permitted them to vote, appear to have been divided; torn, perhaps, between the ideals of the Republican movement and its slave-owning leadership. Courted by both parties on

Democracy, pp. 34–84. There is, as Beard claims, impressionistic testimony supporting his hypothesis, but there is also much against it. In North Carolina, for example, an attempt to demonstrate in 1806 that a politician was a Federalist of the latter-day variety supplied as evidence the fact that he had opposed the Constitution in 1788! Untitled circular, July 1806, in Lenoir Papers, Southern Hist. Coll., Univ. of N. C.

[54] King, *Life and Corresp. of King*, II, 635–648; V, 15–20; "Federal Persecution," 1802, in Broadsides, Library of Congress; John Adams to James Lloyd, 14 Feb. 1815, in Adams-Lloyd Letters, Harvard Univ., P. A. Jay to John Jay, 18 Feb. 1808, in Jay Papers, Columbia Univ.; Morison, *Otis*, I, 108; Howe to Prevost, c. May, 1809, *Amer. Hist. Rev.*, XVII (1913), 344; Ames to Gore, 18 Dec. 1798, in Ames, *Works*, I, 247; [Boston] *New England Palladium*, 7 Feb. 1804, 29 Aug. 1809; Robert Troup to Peter Van Schaack, 27 Oct. 1799, in Van Schaack Papers, Library of Congress.

[55] [Boston] *New England Palladium*, 21 Oct. 1808; Rutledge to Otis, to Nov. 1812, in Otis Papers, Mass. Hist. Soc.; C. J. Ingersoll to King, 11 May 1807, in *King*, V, 36; Echeverria, *Mirage in the West*, p. 187.

[56] Adams to Jefferson, 15 Nov. 1813, in Cappon, ed., *Adams-Jefferson Letters*, II, 401; Adams to James Lloyd, 14 Feb. 1815, in Adams-Lloyd Letters, Harvard Univ.; C. W. Hare to Otis, 21 Oct. 1814, in Otis Papers, Mass. Hist. Soc.; Andreas Dorpalen, "The German Element in Early Penna. Politics," *Penna. Hist.*, IX (1942), 176–190.

election day, spurned by both parties through the rest of the year, they appear to have split their votes.[57]

Only two non-English ethnic groups leaned to Federalism in 1800 and afterwards: the old Dutch families of the Hudson valley, and Scottish merchants and factors who were sufficiently numerous to be politically significant in Richmond, Norfolk, New Bern, Wilmington, Charleston, and Savannah. Altogether, the party which in 1800 sometimes called itself "Federal-American" or "True-American" or "American-Republican" was deeply suspicious of all men who were not old-stock Anglo-American and received their hostility in turn.[58]

5

Religious patterns were of great importance in 1800. In New England, the established Congregational churches were, despite recent attempts at reinterpretation, bastions of Federalism. But New England's establishments had acquired many enemies by 1800, both within and without their folds, and most were Jeffersonian. The ripples of revivalism which continued to overspread New England contributed to the fragmentation of the Congregational churches which had begun early in the century. And wherever a religious controversy appeared in the quiet New England countryside, it blurred into the partisan conflict. Specific alignments were difficult to predict, but from theological commitments one generalization is indisputable—a religious faction in Massachusetts, Connecticut, or New Hampshire which felt that it had more to gain than lose from a union of church and state was certain to be Federalist. Edwardsian Calvinists who suspected the establishments of a tendency toward Arminianism, Unitarianism, or worse were, in the judgment of Parson Bentley, more often Jeffersonian than not. On the other side, some Unitarians and many Universalists who found the prevailing temper of the established churches to be too orthodox, were, in John Adams's considered opinion, rarely in the Federal camp. And of course nearly all the sects and denominations which were expanding in New England were apt to be Jeffersonian—be they Irish Catholic or Anabaptist, Methodist or Episcopalian.[59]

[57] [Hartford] Conn. Courant, 7 Sep. 1803; Bentley, Diary, IV, 90; II, 366; [Boston] Ind. Chronicle, 3 Nov. 1800; 29 Jan. 1801; [New York] Evening Post, 10 Apr. 1805.
[58] Fox, Decline of Aristocracy in New York, pp. 31–34; Biddle, Autobiography, pp. 325–326; Baltimore Federal Republican, 17 July 1811; Boston Centinel, 22 Mar. 1800; Leonard Chester to Ephraim Kirby, 26 Sep. 1800, in Kirby Papers, Duke Univ. Library.
[59] It is very difficult to estimate the reach of Jeffersonian politics among the Congregational clergy of New England. One of them wrote from New Haven, "Being the only Democratical Preacher in the state who dares to speak I am, of course, the object of persecution." J. Gemmel to Ashbel Green, 7 Nov. 1800, in Gratz Coll. (Clergy), Hist. Soc. Penna. How many did not dare to speak out remains an open question. Bentley, Diary, III, 364–365; Adams to Lloyd, 14 Feb. 1815, in Adams-

In other parts of the Union, three religious groups were generally Jeffersonian—Baptists, Jews, and Irish Catholics. The Baptist Church in Londonderry, Vermont, which excommunicated four of its members for joining the Washington Benevolent Society, appears to have been representative in its politics if not in its zeal. Even in Virginia it was said that Baptists were "almost universally Republican."[60]

Notice was taken in chapter VIII of Jews in politics, and specifically of Benjamin Nones, who publicly declared, "I am a Jew, and if for no other reason, for that reason am I a republican." There were exceptions— Jacob Henry, the North Carolina Jew who figured in a notable test of religious liberty, had been the victim of discrimination less for his religion, perhaps, than his politics—he was a Federalist. But notwithstanding this and other exceptions, the antisemitism which appeared in Federalist tracts during the 1790s had effectively alienated another minority group.[61]

The Irish and French voters who supported Jefferson in 1800 were, of course, generally Catholic. Their religion did not cause their political commitment, but a descriptive pattern is clear. On the other hand, English Catholics in Maryland were described as Federalist "almost without exception."[62]

Two other religious groups were generally Federalist—Methodists on the Delmarva peninsula, and Scotch-Irish Presbyterians in western Virginia and the Cape Fear region of North Carolina. Jefferson himself wrote that "the string of counties at the Western foot of the Blue ridge settled originally by Irish presbyterians [composes] precisely the tory [Federalist] district of the state." Local historians have discussed the relevance of Methodism to Federalist strength in Delmarva, and of Presbyterianism in the Cape Fear region.[63]

Lloyd Letters, Harvard Univ.; William Hart to Ephraim Kirby, 12 Apr. 1803, in Kirby Papers, Duke Univ.; Hall, *Benjamin Tallmadge*, p. 187; [Boston] *N. Eng. Palladium*, 11 June 1811; Robinson, *Jeff. Dem. N. Eng.*, p. 132; Goodman, *Democratic-Republicans of Mass.*, pp. 86–96; Sedgwick to King, 24 Aug. 1802, in *King*, IV, 161; [Warren] *Bristol Co. Register*, 1 Apr. 1809; Chase, *Jonathan Fisher*, pp. 236–237; Dwight, *Travels*, II, 65; M. Cutler to Pickering, 5 Jan. 1809, in Pickering Papers, Mass. Hist. Soc.; Mead, *Taylor*, p. 44, Joslin, *Poultney*, pp. 74–75.

[60] Cudworth, *Londonderry*, p. 51; [Philadelphia] *Aurora*, 2 Oct. 1800; one can wonder whether Republicans or Baptists gained more from their association; surely it was mutually advantageous. Bentley, *Diary*, II, 409; Dwight, *Travels*, II, 34; Jeremiah Smith to William Plumer, 11 Mar. 1804, in Plumer Papers, Library of Congress; [New London] *Bee*, 8 Oct. 1800.

[61] [Phila.] *Aurora*, 13 Aug. 1800; memo dated 8 Mar. 1801, in Jefferson Papers, Library of Congress; [Philadelphia] *Gazette of the U. S.*, 16 July 1800; Schauinger, *William Gaston*, p. 54; antisemitism was not restricted to Federalists; see Mann, *Yankee Jeffersonian*, p. 46; [Chillicothe] *Supporter*, 24 Mar. 1810.

[62] Thomas Dwight to wife, 28 Dec. 1804, in Dwight-Howard Papers, Mass. Hist. Soc.

[63] Jefferson to Horatio Gates Spofford, 10 Jan. 1816, in Ford, *Jefferson*, X, 13; Munroe, *Federalist Delaware*, pp. 239–40; Gilpatrick, *Jeffersonian Democracy in N. C.*, pp. 18 passim.

6

Each of these patterns, as has already been noted, served to qualify all the others. Men were caught up by them in different and often conflicting and sometimes unique ways. It remains only to remind the reader that these patterns are descriptive and not necessarily causal. Did men take possession of the land, or did the land take possession of them? Were they masters or servants of their interests? Dilemmas such as this cannot be resolved by appeals to historical evidence. The historian must yield to the theologian.

APPENDIX II

Federalist Leaders, 1800–1816

> *All history becomes subjective; in other words there is properly*
> *no history, only biography. Every mind must know the whole*
> *lesson for itself.*
> —Ralph Waldo Emerson

> *Here is an ant-heap, with the human ants hurrying in long*
> *files along their various paths.*
> —Sir Lewis Namier

Whether Emerson or Namier learned the secret, a historian will never be able to tell. But any historical generalization must come down, in the end, to human cases. This swollen appendix is designed to specify the thesis which has been argued in preceding chapters. There are many exceptions to the general rules, many subtle shadings. The contrast between old Federalists and younger men was not between all and nothing, but between much and little. There were variations by section, by state, by county and of course by individual. We are dealing in tendencies and trends, in probabilities and proportions.

The following sketches are not meant to be balanced biographies, but brief and often impressionistic intersections of individual lives and the general patterns which are relevant to this study. The sketches are arranged geographically by state. Within each state, Federalist leaders are divided into three groups—gentlemen of the old school, transitional figures, and young Federalists. Men in the first group were nearly always born before 1760; those in the third group, after that date. Birth dates of transitional figures were for the most part between 1755 and 1765.

At the risk of redundancy, the following interpretation is central to this work. Older Federalists conceptualized in terms of a collectivized commonwealth, tightly regulated and elaborately structured. They favored "energy in government," within a republican frame. Though they often "stood" for office, they rarely "ran." After the French Revolution, they rarely disguised their contempt for democracy, political parties, popular opinion, and all the paraphernalia of Jeffersonian politics. Younger Federalists sought to use Jeffersonian ideas and innovations for their own elitist purposes—partisanship, popular rhetoric, libertarian ideology, the ideal of minimal government. These are the polarities,

227

which of course some men approached more nearly than others. The transitional figures are those who cannot be clearly associated with either group.

All biographical information not otherwise credited is obtained from the *Dictionary of American Biography*, the *Biographical Directory of the American Congress*, or standard studies listed alphabetically by subject in the *Harvard Guide to American History*. The Annals of Congress are cited throughout as *AC*. A full, formal bibliography of works consulted in the preparation of the first draft of this work appears in "Federalists and Democracy," vol. II, pp. 505–572, in the Library of The Johns Hopkins University.

NEW HAMPSHIRE

Federalists of the Old School

CILLEY, BRADBURY (1760–1831), b. Nottingham, N. H.; educated in lower schools; wealthy farmer residing in Nottingham. U. S. Marshal, 1798–1802; unobtrusive backbencher in Congress, 1813–1817. "A rich, conservative, patriotic country squire," Cilley appears to have been a specimen of William Sullivan's "gentry of the interior," much like Theodore Sedgwick (q.v.) in his inherited prejudices. [Elliott Cogswell, *History of Nottingham* (Manchester, N. H., 1878), p. 184; J. P. Cilley, *Cilley Genealogy* (Augusta, 1877), p. 19; Lynn Turner, *William Plumer*, pp. 136–37.]

FOSTER, ABIEL (1735–1806) b. Andover, Mass.; A.B., Harvard, 1756; Congregational minister in Canterbury, N. H., 1761–1779; Continental Congress, 1783–1785; U. S. Congress, 1789–1791, 1795–1803; N. H. Senate, 1791–1794. The stiff and stubborn elitism of this reticent gentleman is described by William Plumer in *N. H. State Papers*, 21 (1892), 798–799. [See also J. O. Lyford, *Canterbury, N. H.* (2 vols., Concord, 1912) I, 15 passim.; Reginald Foster, *Foster Genealogy* (Chicago, 1889), pp. 197–199; and his letters in Burnett, ed., *Letters of Members of the Continental Congress*, VII, VIII passim.]

FARRAR, TIMOTHY (1747–1849), b. Lincoln, Mass.; A.B., Harvard, 1767; prosperous farmer in Ipswich, N. H.; though lacking in legal training, he held many judicial positions in his state, 1775–1816. His son, Timothy Farrar (1788–1874) was a prominent young Federalist in New Hampshire, partner, friend, and confidant of Daniel Webster (q.v.). Friendly characterizations of Farrar, Senior, comprised a conventional catalogue of old school virtues: piety, frankness, independence. Antagonists saw the same traits as bigotry, rudeness, and aloofness. [Timothy Farrar Clary, *Discourse Occasioned by the Centennial Anniversary of Hon. Timothy Farrar* (Andover, 1847); Lyford, *Canterbury*, I, 327.]

FREEMAN, JONATHAN (1745–1808), b. Mansfield, Conn.; educated in local schools; militia service in the Revolution; wealthy farmer in Hanover, N. H.; member, N. H. House of Representatives, 1787–1789; N. H. Senate, 1789–1794; Council, 1789–1797; U.S. Congress, 1797–1801. Though his voting record was decidedly Federalist, Freeman's most important recorded speech was a protest against the partisan spirit which he observed in fellow friends of order, such as Robert Goodloe Harper and William Loughton Smith (qq.v.). He declaimed against the "use, or rather abuse, of the terms federalist and anti-federalist" by administration supporters in the 1790's, and denounced efforts by Alexander Hamilton (q.v.) and others to bring discipline and coherence to a Federal party in Congress. [AC 5/1/88–93, 23 May 1797; see also Plumer's characterization in *N. H. State Papers*, 21 (1892), 799.]

GILMAN, JOHN TAYLOR (1753–1828), b. Exeter, N. H.; educated in local schools; minuteman in 1775; shipbuilder and sometime merchant, banker, speculator in securities and Maine lands, gentleman farmer. N. H. House of Representatives, 1779, 1781, 1810–1811; Continental Congress, 1782–1783; State Treasurer, 1791; Governor, 1794–1805, 1813–1816; president, Board of Trustees, Phillips Exeter Academy, 1795–1827; trustee of Dartmouth, 1794–1805, 1813–1819. With Oliver Peabody and Samuel Tenney (qq.v.), Gilman was a pivotal figure in the so-called "Exeter Junto," a little clique of conservative gentlemen, united by temperament, principle, and state patronage. Gilman's hankering for "high-toned government" and his haughty contempt for the people appear in his attempt as state treasurer to maintain taxes beyond the needs of the state, "to habituate the people to paying them." [Turner, *William Plumer*, p. 41.] His many ponderous public statements as governor (published in the *Journals* of the New Hampshire House of Representatives) overflow with old-school didacticism, preaching patience, restraint, and order to the people, honesty, firmness, benevolence, and public service to their natural rulers. In his private character Gilman was the personification of old school precepts, winning even the grudging admiration of his quondam friend and political rival William Plumer. "He openly and freely expressed his opinion of men and measures. He neither attempted to conceal or equivocate . . . a contempt for sordid intrigue. . . . A firm, unbending Federalist, [he] could not, like his brothers Nicholas and Nathaniel, barter his creed for his office." [*N. H. State Papers*, 22 (1893), 830–835.]

LIVERMORE, SAMUEL (1732–1803), b. Waltham, Mass.; A.B., Princeton, 1752; lawyer and large landowner residing in Holderness, N. H.; Continental Congress, 1785; chief justice N. H. Supreme Court, 1782–1789; member N. H. ratifying convention, 1788; U. S. Congress, 1789–1793; U. S. Senate, 1793–1801. During the 1780's, Livermore used the traditional techniques of magnate politics to establish a predominant influence in northern New Hampshire; His role in the ratification of the Constitution may have been decisive [MacDonald, *We the People*, pp. 238–242]. But in the age of Jefferson he appears as an anachronism [Plumer's sketch in *N. H. State Papers*, 21 (1892), 816–18]. Livermore's principles appear in an *Address on the Death of George Washington* [Walter Eliot Thwing, *The Livermore Family of America* (Boston, 1902), pp. 82–88]; and see also his opposition to T. T. Tucker's proposed amendment on the right of the people to instruct their representative [*AC*, 1/1/742 15 Aug. 1789].

OLCOTT, SIMEON (1735–1815), b. Bolten, Conn.; A.B., Yale, 1761; lawyer practising in Charlestown, N. H.; N. H. House of Representatives, 1772–1773; holder of many judicial offices in N. H., 1773–1800; U. S. Senate., 1801–1805. Olcott has been described as "honest but inept" [Turner, *Plumer*, p. 81]. An undisguised elitist, he was "frank even to bluntness, and avoided studiously every species of dissimulation" [Dexter, *Yale Graduates*, II, 712; see also *N. H. State Papers*, 22 (1893), 836–837].

PEABODY, OLIVER (1753–1831), b. Exeter, N. H.?; A.B., Harvard, 1773; studied law with Theophilus Parsons (q.v.); lawyer residing in Exeter; probate judge, Rockingham Co., and sometime state treasurer. A central figure in the "Exeter Junto," he manifested the same "curious indifference to public opinion" which characterized that group as a whole. If John Taylor Gilman personifies the virtues of the old school, Oliver Peabody represents its vices. The odor of corruption clung persistently to his public reputation. As Treasurer, he did not carefully discriminate between private and public money in his possession and placed state funds at the disposal of the "wise and good" for purposes of private speculation [articles signed "Veritas" and dated Oct. 1812, in Plumer Papers, Library of Congress; Turner, *Plumer*, pp. 68–69, passim.; Bell, *Exeter* (1888), p. 357].

SHEAFE, JAMES (1755–1829), b. Portsmouth, N. H., son of a merchant; A.B., Harvard, 1774; wealthy import merchant in Portsmouth; a Loyalist, he was arrested and jailed during the Revolution; N. H. Assembly, 1788–1790; N. H. Senate, 1791, 1793, 1799; Council, 1799; U. S. Congress,

1799–1801; U. S. Senate, 1801–1802. A gentleman of great dignity and honest integrity, he had become active in a partisan way in 1795, attempting to organize the sober citizenry of his town against the expanding Republican interest, and was assaulted by a mob for his efforts [Brewster, *Rambles in Old Portsmouth*, II, 126–137]. Sheafe was one of a handful of merchants who remained politically active after 1800. "As Cooke said of Tiba Hall's *principles* that they were *no principles* and if he was *any-thing*—he was a *nothingarian*—so of our merchants—so of our merchants always excepting James Sheafe and a few others" [Jeremiah Smith to William Plumer, in Plumer Papers, Library of Congress]. In 1816 Sheafe was persuaded to accept the empty honor of a Federalist nomination for the governorship. In the brutal campaign which followed, his great wealth (more that $1,000,000 plus large tracts of N. H. lands), haughty bearing, and Tory past made him an easy mark for Jeffersonian writers, who caricatured his old-school ideals with abandon and deadly effect [Turner, *Plumer*, p. 237]. His honest republicanism appears in his response to the proposed northern confederacy scheme of 1804. "As a commercial man," he wrote, "I should dread such an event. Our consequence abroad will be lowered to nothing" [Sheafe to Plumer, 7 Mar. 1804, in Plumer Papers, Library of Congress; T. E. Satterthwaite, *Sheafe Family* (1923), pp. 54–59].

TENNEY, SAMUEL (1748–1816), b. Byfield, Mass.; A.B., Harvard, 1772; served in the Continental army; physician not practising in 1800. Apparently independent, he occupied himself with "literary, historical and scientific studies," and politics. Judge of Probate, Rockingham County, 1793–1800; U. S. Congress, 1800–1807. In Washington he spoke rarely, but voted invariably against the Jeffersonian administration. Plumer's acid assessment was "a man of strong prejudices—of feeble intellect; indolent and unacquainted with men" [Turner, *Plumer*, p. 78n]. Tenney owed his power and influence to his secure status as a member of the "Exeter Junto." In 1812 he was prevailed upon to serve as chairman of a county convention, but collaborated more fully with younger Federalists. [Bell, *Exeter*, p. 382; and see also Plumer, ms. diary, 17 Nov. 1805, Library of Congress.]

WINGATE, PAINE (1739–1838), b. Amesbury, Mass., a clergyman's son; A.B., Harvard, 1759; Congregational clergyman in Hampton Falls, N. H., 1763–1776, and Stratham, N. H., thereafter. State House of Representatives, 1783, 1795; Continental Congress, 1787–1788; U. S. Senate, 1789–1793; U. S. Congress, 1793–1795; Judge, Superior Court, N. H., 1798–1809. He conceived of his republicanism as a *via media*, a compromise, an honorable adjustment in the spirit of 1689. Of "political enthusiasts," he had a general horror (to Pickering, 4 Dec. 1804, in Pickering Papers,

Mass. Hist. Soc.) and counseled caution to both parties. "In the present time of political ferment, many are in danger of running into one or another of extremes" [fragment of a public address, n.d., Charles E. L. Wingate. *Life and Letters of Paine Wingate*, 2 vols. (Medford, 1930), II, 465–466]. But there was no doubt as to which extreme he feared more. "The lawless fury of the ignorant multitude let loose and unrestrained in the torrent of their passions is a more dangerous and fatal tyranny than that of a single despot" [ibid]. Young Federalists succeeded in bringing him out to a county convention in 1812, where he served in an honorific capacity but party organizers were advised by this relic of an earlier society to avoid "base means" in their pursuit of victory and power. [Exeter *Constitutionalist*, 25 Aug., 1812; see also Wingate, *Life and Letters of Paine Wingate*, II, 507–514.]

Transitional Figures

GORDON, WILLIAM (1763–1802), b. near Boston, Mass.; A.B., Harvard, 1779; lawyer residing in Amherst, N. H.; State Senate, 1794–1795; U. S. Congress, 1797–1800; State Attorney General, 1800–1802. In Gordon's Congressional speeches there was a spirit of malice, a vindictive harshness of tone and content which did not characterize John Taylor Gilman's more mellow utterances. In the bitter debates of June 1798 he suggested that the Constitution might permit friends of order to intervene in the states with military force, to preserve peculiarly Federalist forms of republicanism. "The United States have guaranteed to the individual states a Republican form of Government; but, if one state admit so many aliens into it as to produce a change in its system of Government, the United States would be obliged to use force to recover it" [*AC*, 5/2/1785, 19 June 1798]. In discussion of a motion by Robert Goodloe Harper to distribute extra copies of the Sedition Act to counteract alleged Republican misrepresentation (Republicans amended the motion to include those parts of the Constitution which they claimed were violated by the Sedition Act), Gordon commented, "What was the object of the selection? To enable the people to decide whether these laws are constitutional or not. What would be the consequence? A mob, or large collection of people, will be brought together" [ibid., 5/3/2448 14 Dec. 1798].

SMITH, JEREMIAH (1759–1842), b. Peterboro, N. H.; attended Harvard and graduated from Rutgers, 1780; served briefly in the Revolution; lawyer residing in Peterboro, Exeter, and Dover, N. H.; State House of Representatives, 1788–1791; U. S. Congress, 1791–1797; U. S. District Attorney, 1797–1800; chief justice N. H. Superior Court, 1802–1809; governor, 1809–1810; chief justice N. H. Supreme Court, 1813–1816.

His first response to the Jeffersonian movement was that of the old school —contempt and revulsion. Commenting on Republican machinery, he asked "Did you believe 15 years ago that a thing of this kind could happen in New England?" [to Plumer, 22 Feb. 1804, in Plumer Papers, Library of Congress]. But he perceived that the precepts of the old school bore small relevance to the realities of Jeffersonian America. "Federalism can suit only a virtuous state of society. These times demand other principles and other systems." [Turner, *Plumer*, p. 143]. Conscious that "Federalism has a good many unpopular men in its ranks" [to Plumer, 28 Jan. 1804, in Plumer Papers, Library of Congress], he undertook to improve its public image, joining younger men in the effort to sustain a popularly oriented conservative counterforce (see, e.g., "The Constitution," [1808] Broadsides, Amer. Antiq. Soc.). Plumer was constrained to comment that Smith was motivated by a "love of . . . vulgar popularity" [Turner, *Plumer*, p. 188; Morison, *Jeremith Smith*, passim.]

Young Federalists

ATHERTON, CHARLES HUMPHREY (1773–1853), b. Amherst, N. H.; A.B., Harvard, 1794; read law in the office of William Gordon (q.v.), lawyer in Amherst, gentleman farmer and president of the Hillsborough Agricultural Society, large landowner, banker; leader of Hillsborough Federalists; U. S. Congress, 1815–1817. As Congressman, he publicly courted "the great mass of the American population," defended a binding relationship between a representative and his constituents, and advocated minimal government. "I shall act, sir, upon a different principle. I say retrench; and if I cannot have retrenchment when I would, I will take it when I can. . . . It is written there is a time for peace; we have had it. That there is a time for war; we have had that also. I hope the leaf is not torn from our political bible which says there is a time for retrenchment. . . . Dash, yes, sir, dash the Circean cup from the mouth of sycophants, contractors, and office-seekers. Do not enervate the American Hercules by steeping him in the hot-bed of executive patronage. . . . Here, then, let gentlemen direct their caution, and not to the great mass of the American population, where there is no danger of the enemy. Moderate the car of State." [AC 14/1/900–904, 5 Feb. 1816; Daniel F. Secomb, *History of Amherst* (Concord, 1883), p. 123 passim.; see also Atherton's earlier *Oration pronounced in . . . Amherst* (1798) and *Oration delivered at Concord* (1799).]

BEALS, EPHRAIM (1785–1831), b. Boston, Mass.; editor, printer of the Exeter *Constitutionalist*. His paper was dedicated to the proposition that "the people should be ever vigilant and scrutinize the conduct of their rulers." Edited in this spirit, it became the principal organ of New Hampshire young Federalists—popular in tone, intensely partisan in content (see, e.g., 21 May 1810; and see also Boston *Columbian Centinel*, 13 July 1831).

BLAISDELL, DANIEL (1762–1833), b. Amesbury, Mass.; educated in local schools; served briefly in the Revolution; farmer, lawyer in Canaan, N. H., from 1780; Baptist, one of the few outside of Rhode Island who were Federal in politics. N. H. House of Representatives, 1793, 1795, 1799, 1812–1813, 1824–1825; Council, 1803–1808; N. H. Senate, 1814–1815; U. S. Congress, 1809–1811. Actively engaged with William Plumer (q.v.) and other young Federalists in the effort to organize an effective, popular Federal party in N. H., Blaisdell was specially responsible in 1804 for maintaining communications throughout the state. His sons made weekly trips with letters and newspapers, and he himself was prosecuted in Federal courts for "carrying letters without postal authority" [Turner, *Plumer*, p. 146n]. A speech in Congress is a good specimen of young Federalist rhetoric. Attempting to taint the administration with the odor of Napoleonic despotism, he denounced its foreign policy for tending "to throw this people into the embraces of that monster, at whose perfidy and corruption Lucifer blushes and Hell itself stands astonished." His climax: "What American can read this correspondence without laying his hand upon his heart and exclaiming, O my Government, my Government . . ." [AC 11/3/1039–1056, 26 Feb. 1811; see also William A. Wallace, *The History of Canaan* (Concord, 1910), p. 64 passim; and Windsor *Washingtonian*, 23 July 1810].

COOKE, PHINEAS (1781–1853), b. Hadley, Mass.; A.B., Williams, 1803; studied law; later entered the ministry; pastor at Acworth, N. H., 1814–1829; Lebanon, 1829–1848. Active in the organization of the Washington Benevolent Societies, Cooke's *Oration delivered at Keene, N. H., before the Washington Benevolent Society* (1813) was a direct appeal to "the common sense of the common people" [see also Calvin Durfee, *Williams Biographical Annals* (Boston, 1871), p. 247].

CROSBY, OLIVER (1769–1851), this obscure young lawyer, a resident of Dover, N. H., and member of the First Church (Congregational) there, was one of six young Federalists who met secretly in Concord, 4 July 1804, to organize a Federal party in N. H. "None of them had any close relations with either the Exeter Junto or the Portsmouth aristocracy. They were eminently practical men, not too deeply concerned with the protocols of eighteenth-century politics and willing to learn from their adversaries" [Turner, *Plumer*, p. 144]. Scattered information on Crosby appears in Dover Historical Society *Collections*, I (1894), pp. 63, 213; and Portsmouth *N. H. Gazette*, 16 Sep. 1800; he published *Proposals for reprinting by subscription, The History of New Hampshire* (Dover, 1812).

CUTTS, CHARLES (1769–1846), b. Portsmouth, N. H.; A.B., Harvard, 1789; lawyer in Portsmouth; N. H. House of Representatives, 1803–1810 (speaker, 1807–1808, 1810); U. S. Senate, 1810–1813; secretary, U. S. Senate, 1814–1825; removed to Fairfax County, Va. A central figure in the second N. H. Federalist organization, created after the defection of William Plumer (q.v.), Cutts was an experienced hand at the quiet labor that Jeremiah Smith called "woodchuck work." His particular concern was the thankless task of persuading Portsmouth merchants to contribute to "liberal appropriations for c[anvassin]g purposes" [Cutts to Daniel Webster, 23 June 1813, in Webster Papers, Library of Congress]. Unlike his elders among the Portsmouth gentry, he understood that "to retain our present political ascendancy requires more systematic arrangements" [ibid.]. [See also Charles Brewster, *Rambles About Portsmouth*, 2 vols. (Portsmouth, 1869), II, 142.]

GATES, ISAAC (1777–1852), b. Harvard, Mass.; A.B., Harvard, 1802; lawyer in Concord, N. H.; later returned to Massachusetts [Henry S. Nourse, *History of the Town of Harvard* (1894), p. 430]. Active in the Washington Societies, his *Oration, pronounced publicly, at Bedford N. H., before the Washington Benevolent Society* (Concord, 1814) asks rhetorically, "What must the friends of the Constitution and the interests of our country do, when an organized portion of the citizens, and a set of adopted outcasts, labor incessantly . . . ?" His answer: labor incessantly against them, organize and "disseminate correct information among the *People.*"

KENT, WILLIAM (1765–1840), b. Charlestown, Mass.; educated in apprenticeship; merchant, banker in Concord, N. H. [Nathaniel Bouten, *History of Concord* (Concord, 1856), pp. 594–596]. One of the six young Federalists who met secretly in Concord, in 1804 [Turner, *Plumer*, p. 144], he was again active in the bolder second effort to organize New Hampshire Federalism for a vote-seeking competition with the Democrats, not in the subterranean way of 1804, but openly and with solicitous attention to the people. "We had a meeting at Stickney's Hall last Thursday evening without disguise, organized as we ought, & adjourned to the day previous to the election at 2 *o'clock* in the afternoon," Kent wrote. "We don't care how bright the sun then may shine upon us, & I am confident we lose nothing here by taking *tall ground*" [to Daniel Webster, 28 Feb. [1810?], in Webster Papers, Library of Congress].

LIVERMORE, SOLOMON KIDDER (1779–1859), b. Wilton, N. H.; A.B., Harvard, 1802; teacher, 1802–1803, in Cambridge, Mass.; thereafter a lawyer in Dover, N. H. Livermore was prominent in the Washington Societies. His *Oration pronounced at Temple* (Amherst, 1809) was an interesting effort to justify partisan competition to doubting Federalists. "If we oppose rulers who acknowledge no law but their own whim and caprice, and who transgress legitimate authority; if we oppose laws repugnant to the Constitution, impolitic and unjust; we thereby support government, and merit approbation, as friends of order, and advocates of republicanism" [p. 10].

MASON, JEREMIAH (1768–1848), b. Lebanon, Conn.; A.B., Yale, 1788; lawyer in Westminster, Vt. (1791–1794), Walpole (1794–1797), and Portsmouth, N. H. (1798–1832); thereafter in Boston. Attorney General N. H., 1802–1805; U S. Senate, 1813–1817; N. H. House of Representatives, 1820–1821, 1824; president Portsmouth branch, Bank of the United States, 1825–1829. Mason was active in the second Federalist organization [to Moses Payson, 15 Oct. 1816, in Misc. Bound Coll., Mass. Hist. Soc.; Cutts to Webster, 23 June 1813, in Webster Papers, Library of Congress]. He operated on the premise that the Federalists "ought to follow and not lead public opinion" [to Jesse Appleton, 29 Jan. 1814, in Hilliard, *Jeremiah Mason,* pp. 82–83].

MOORE, HUMPHREY (1778–1871), b. Princeton, Mass.; A.B., Harvard, 1799; Congregational minister in Milford, N. H. [Henry A. Hazen, *The Congregational and Presbyterian Ministry and Church of N. H.* (1875), pp. 17, 21, 51]. Active in the Washington Societies, his *Oration delivered at Bedford* (1815) is a young Federalist endorsement of "equal rights."

PERKINS, MATTHEW (1788–1826), b. Sanbornton, N. H.; A.B., Middlebury, 1812; lawyer in Sanbornton, later removed to New York City [W. E. Howard, *Catalogue of the Officers and Students of Middlebury College,* p. 43]. His *Oration delivered . . . in Sanbornton* (Concord, 1813) is an apologia for the right of dissent from rulers and measures, and an awkward attempt to justify partisan opposition.

PLUMER, WILLIAM (1759–1850): see above, chapter II.

PRENTISS, JOHN (1778–1873), b. Reading, Mass., son of a clergyman; apprenticed to Thomas Adams, printer of the Republican *Independent Chronicle,* 1792–1795. Editor of the Leominster *Rural Register,* 1797; *Political Focus,* 1799; and the *New Hampshire Sentinel,* 1799–1847. His paper developed the positive-good doctrine of party rivalry. "No republic can long exist without parties. We have no affinity with the 'calm of despotism,' preferring rather the 'boisterous sea of liberty,'—a free press and free communion of thoughts" [Wm. L. Bauhan, *John*

Prentiss and the New Hampshire Sentinel, 1799–1829 (unpubl. thesis, Princeton, 1952), pp. 45f.]. It is interesting to note that the size of the *Sentinel* suddenly increased in 1804, and the masthead was new-modeled in a more popular form in the same year, when the first firm federal organization appeared in New Hampshire [ibid., pp. 66, 67] —clear circumstantial evidence of an understanding between Prentiss and political leaders.

SULLIVAN, GEORGE (1771–1838), b. Durham, N. H., son of John Sullivan; A.B., Harvard, 1790; lawyer in Exeter, N. H.; State House of Representatives, 1805, 1813–1814; N. H. Attorney General, 1805–1806, 1816–1835; U. S. Congress, 1811–1813; N. H. Senate, 1814–1816 [Bell, *Exeter, N. H.*, passim]. His *Oration pronounced on the 4th of July, 1816* (Boston, 1816) was another popularly oriented [p. 9] positive-good justification of partisanship. "Parties are the soul of free government" [p. 17]. See also his *Speech . . . at the late Rockingham Convention* (Concord, 1812).

THOMPSON, THOMAS WESTON (1766–1821), b. Boston; A.B., Harvard, 1786; lawyer practicing in Salisbury, N. H., from 1791 to 1810, and in Concord, N. H., thereafter. Postmaster, Salisbury, 1798–1803; N. H. House of Representatives, 1807–1808, 1813–1814 (speaker 1813–1814); U. S. Congress, 1805–1807; N. H. Treasurer, 1809–1811; U. S. Senate, 1814–1817. Thompson was a party wheel-horse who provided strength and continuity from the secret meeting in Concord which he attended in 1804, to his death sixteen years later. "I do what I can to give a right direction to public opinion," he wrote to Plumer. ". . . I believe I can be as useful or more so out of office as in" [27 Feb. 1804, in Plumer Papers, Library of Congress]. Though he had first resolved to devote himself to "objects of public benefit without regard to popular opinion" [ibid.], he grew gradually more respectful of the latter [to Webster, 17 Feb. 1810, in Webster Papers, Library of Congress]. After the apostasy of Plumer, Thompson became the central figure in N. H. Federalist organization [see his pirated circulars in Concord *N. H. Patriot*, 13 Oct. 1812]. In 1812 he also attended the presidential nominating meeting in New York. [to Meredith, 12 Oct. 1812, in Meredith Papers, Hist. Soc. Penna.].

VOSE, ROGER (1763–1841), b. Milton, Mass.; son of a small farmer; A.B., Harvard, 1790; lawyer in Walpole, N. H. State Senate, 1798, 1809–1810, 1812; U. S. Congress, 1813–1817; N. H. House of Representatives, 1818; jurist, 1818–1825 [Ellen Vose, *Robert Vose and his Descendants* (Boston, 1932), pp. 183–184]. Another participant in the secret meeting of 1804, his exertions continued after the departure of Plumer from Federalist ranks. Vose became the most important Federal leader in the Walpole area; through him communications and decisions affecting that neighborhood were channeled. [Kent to Webster, 28 Feb. [1810?], in Webster Papers, Library of Congress].

WEBSTER, DANIEL (1782–1852), b. Salisbury, N. H.; A.B., Dartmouth, 1802; studied law with Thomas W. Thompson and Christopher Gore (qq.v.); lawyer in Boscawen (to 1807), Portsmouth (to 1816), and Boston; U. S. Congress, 1813–1817 (N. H.), 1823–1827 (Mass.;) U. S. Senate, 1827–1841, 1845–1850; Secretary of State, 1841–1843, 1850–1852. Throughout his tortuous career, it is difficult to find any other consistency than his hunger for power and his zeal for the protection of property and privilege within the American democracy. Striking shifts of posture and lesser principle can certainly be traced through Webster's Federalist period. In his early *Oration pronounced at Hanover* (1800), he articulated the collectivized ideals of the old school. But in his *Appeal to the Old Whigs* (1805) and his *Anniversary Address delivered before the Federal Gentlemen of Concord* (1806) the social consciousness was eroded, and a Burkean justification of militant party, as a league of like-minded gentlemen, appears. Six years later, Webster's *Address delivered before the Washington Benevolent Society at Portsmouth* (1812), his "harangue" at the Rockingham Convention, and his famous Congressional speeches were more popular in orientation. The Federal Party was conceived as a mass movement of the people against a tyrannizing government. Elitist purposes remained constant; but phrases and particular commitments had changed. Webster had learned a lesson from the Revolutionist. "Was it Mirabeau who has told us that words are things? They are indeed things, and things of mighty influence" [Current, *Daniel Webster*, p. 47]. If his efforts to "put a period to the popularity of the administration" [to Thomas W. Thompson, 15 Mar. 1808, in Misc. Bound Coll., Mass. Hist. Soc.] were unavailing, he had broken clearly and decisively with the conservatism of the old school—and identified himself with another—demagogic, deceitful, but dishearteningly effective, in the course of the nineteenth century. [see Current, *Webster*, pp. 91–114, on later manifestations]. The free trade economics of the young Webster are familiar [Carey, *Webster as an Economist*, pp. 21, 197]; if he later changed his mind about the tariff and the Bank, his economic conservatism remained individualized, atomistic in a way which contrasted with the ideals of gentlemen of the old school [cf. Webster on property rights and old school conceptions of property as discussed in my "Myth of the Essex Junto," pp. 199–213]. There could conceivably be another version of "The Devil and Daniel Webster," in which the same Revolutionary shades would sit in judgment upon Webster himself, pleading the cause of his new conservatism. Whatever their verdict might have been upon the man himself, ours cannot be as harsh as John Quincy Adams's,

who cursed his "ravenous ambition and rotten heart." The tragic dilemma
of Daniel Webster was not a private affair; it was part of the tragedy of
a generation of American conservatives who learned most of the vices
of their democratic opponents but few of their virtues—a generation
which inherited an ethical pattern no longer relevant to social realities.

WOODWARD, WILLIAM H. (1774–1818), b.?; A.B., Dartmouth, 1792;
lawyer and jurist in Hanover. A participant in the secret meeting of
1804, he remained a Federalist after Plumer switched sides, but himself
joined the Jeffersonians in 1816 [Turner, *Plumer*, pp. 144, 251; Cyrus
Perkins, *Eulogy on Hon. William Woodward* (Hanover, 1818), pp.
10–14; John K. Lord, *A History of the Town of Hanover* (Hanover,
1928), pp. 53, 163; Lord, *Dartmouth College*, p. 99].

VERMONT

Federalists of the Old School

BARRETT, JOHN (1731–1806), b. Boston, Mass.; moved to Vermont,
1771; military service in Revolution; farmer and miller in Springfield,
Vt.; his real estate was appraised at $22,500 in 1806; active Congrega-
tionalist. With Samuel Cobb, Samuel Lewis, and Lewis R. Morris (q.v.),
Col. Barrett was the core of an old-fashioned "connexion" which derived
its power from the deferential spirit of society in the upper Connecticut
Valley and its cement from a web of economic and familial ties. Unwilling to adapt to changing social circumstances, Col. Barrett's clique was
unable to preserve its political influence against the Jeffersonian challenge, 1800–1804. [C. H. Hubbard & Justus Dartt, *History of the Town of
Springfield* (Boston, 1895), pp. 215 passim.]

BUCK, DANIEL (1753–1816), b. Hebron, Conn.; educated in local schools;
lost an arm at Bennington; lawyer residing in Norwich, Vt., 1784–1805,
Chelsea, Vt. 1805–1806; Vt. Council, 1792; Assembly, 1793–1794,
(speaker), 1806–1807; U. S. Congress, 1795–1797. In two powerful
speeches on Jay's Treaty he took a holistic view of his society as "a complete moral person," governed by "the conjoint and united will of the
great mass and body of the people." But the "dispassionate will of the
nation" was to be determined by its constituted authorities; and was
not to be confused with "popular clamor, which originates in discontent,
is fostered in violence and passion, and stimulated by the intrigues of
interested and ambitious individuals" [AC 4/1/430–435, 703–717, 7
Mar., 24 Mar., 1796]. His old-school ideals did not permit him to participate in party opposition. After the elections of 1800 he declared, "the

duty of every federalist [is] to retire from office and leave the government entirely in the hands of the republicans, in order to promote the peace and happiness of the country" [Scioto *Gazette*, 3 Dec. 1800].

CHIPMAN, NATHANIEL (1752–1843), b. Salisbury, Conn.; A.B., Yale, 1777; lt. in Continental Army; lawyer in Tinmouth, Vt.; Vt. Assembly, 1784–1785, 1806–1811; Vt. Supreme Court, 1786–1789; chief justice, 1789–1791, 1796–1797, 1813–1815; U. S. District Judge, 1791–1794; U. S. Senate, 1797–1803. His formal *Sketches of the Principles of Government* (1793) is an able exposition of old-school ideals, not anti-democratic but openly elitist and deeply socialized [see also Roy J. Honeywell, "Nathaniel Chipman," *New England Quarterly*, V (1932), 355–384, and George L. Montagno, "Nathaniel Chipman's Political Primer," *Vermont History*, XXIX (1961), 103–110]. An effective and un-scrupulous practitioner of magnate politics [*DAB*, IV, 63], he responded to Jeffersonian techniques with righteous fury [Daniel Chipman, *Life of Nathaniel Chipman* (Boston, 1846), pp. 394–402]. In 1812, however, he was persuaded to become a backer of the Windsor *Washingtonian* and to attend Federal electioneering meetings [Windsor *Washingtonian*, 18 May 1812; Chilton Williamson, *Vermont in Quandary*, p. 264].

HALL, LOT (1757–1809), b. Barnstable Co., Mass.; educated in local schools; served in Continental Navy; studied law with Shearjashub Bourne (q.v.); removed to Vermont, 1782, where he became a promi-nent lawyer and jurist. His charge to a Windham County grand jury, 1798, is a good statement of old-school principles—"order," "restraint," and "propriety" are his conceptual units, a stable, structured republican society his political ideal. [Benjamin Hall, *History of Eastern Vermont* (New York, 1858), pp. 662–665.]

MORRIS, LEWIS RICHARD (1760–1825), b. Scarsdale, N. Y.; son of the colony's chief justice and nephew of Gouverneur Morris (q.v.); edu-cated privately; served briefly in Revolution, 1776; gentleman farmer, speculator in Vermont and New York lands; Vt. Assembly, 1795–1797, 1803–1808; U. S. Congress, 1797–1803. A political mediocrity, Morris's greatest distinction was his wealth; and his greatest accomplishment appears to have been his horsemanship. "It is related of him that in the street of Springfield he picked up a lady's glove from the ground while riding at full speed, and returned it to her with a courtly bow" [Hubbard & Dartt, *Springfield*, p. 15, passim]. His response to the Jeffer-sonian movement was couched in a characteristic equestrian metaphor. "Poor United States! For all our governments are going to the Devil full gallop—and even the Man of the People will not be able to manage them long" [to Wm. Meredith, 11 Jan. 1804, in Meredith Papers, Hist. Soc.

Penna.; see also his speech in *AC* 5/2/1008, 12 Feb. 1798]. But in 1812 Morris, like Chipman, was brought out to electioneering meetings [Windsor *Washingtonian*, 18 May 1812] and contributed to that newspaper [Williamson, *Vermont in Quandary*, p. 264].

PAINE, ELIJAH (1757–1842), b. Brooklyn, Conn.; A.B., Harvard, 1781; served briefly in the Revolution; removed to Vermont 1784, resident of Williamstown. His interests were a microcosm of the American economy —he was at once a practicing lawyer, large-scale farmer (1200 sheep in 1812), owner of saw and grist mills, pioneer textile manufacturer (his factory absorbed an investment of $40,000), banker, speculator in lands and securities. As a jurist (Vt. Supreme Court, 1791–1795; U. S. District judge, 1801–1842) Paine was "known rather for strict discipline than for deep learning." As a politician (Vt. Assembly, 1787–1791; U. S. Senate, 1795–1801) he was described as "destitute of duplicity, and scorned covert design." As a man he was "inflexibly upright in conduct, a stable member of society" [H. D. Paine, *Paine Family Records*, II (1883), 142; there are many anecdotes, all suggestive of his open elitism, in D. P. Thompson, *History of Montpelier*, pp. 53–54; and John Gregor, *Northfield, Vt.*, pp. 59–62]. His only published work, *A Collection of Facts in Regard to Liberia* (Woodstock, 1839), shows a deep religiosity (p. 8) and a pervasive social sense (p. 13).

TICHENOR, ISAAC (1754–1838), b. Newark, N. J.?; A.B., Princeton, 1775; commissary in the Continental Army; lawyer in Bennington; Vt. Assembly, 1781–1784; Council, 1787–1792; State Board of Censors, 1792–1813, U. S. Senate, 1796–1797, 1815–1821; governor of Vt., 1797–1806, 1808; Vt. Supreme Court, 1790–1794, Chief Justice, 1795–1796. Tichenor was a hearty, back-slapping, practical-joking extrovert [Keene *N. H. Sentinel*, 28 Mar. 1801], but by the Jeffersonian movement he was not amused. A speech published in the *Amherst Village Messenger*, 15 Nov. 1800, reveals his inflexible attachment to the "cause of order," and to a graduated society [see also Tichenor to Noah Webster, 14 Dec. 1795, in Webster Papers, N. Y. Public Library].

Transitional Figures

CHIPMAN, DANIEL (1765–1850), b. Salisbury, Conn.; A.B., Dartmouth, 1788; studied law with brother Nathaniel (q.v.); practiced in Middlebury, Vt., 1794–1828; professor of law, Middlebury College, 1806–1818; Vt. Assembly, 1798–1808, 1812–1814, 1818, 1821 (speaker 1813–1814); Council, 1808; U. S. Congress, 1815–1816. Chipman participated actively in such partisan ventures as the Washington Benevolent Societies; but his public statements conformed to old-school ideals. [Windsor *Washing-*

tonian, 6 Dec. 1813; Kilbourne, *Litchfield Co., Conn.*, p. 81; Swift, *Middlebury, Vt.*, pp. 264–270.]

CHITTENDEN, MARTIN (1763–1840), b. Salisbury, Conn.; A.B., Dartmouth, 1789; country merchant, farmer, jurist in Jericho, Vt.; Vt. Assembly, 1790–1796; justice, Chittenden Co. Court, 1793–1795, Chief Justice, 1796–1813; U. S. Congress, 1803–1813; Governor of Vt., 1814–1815. Enemies conceded that he was "an honest man and a good farmer"; his friends claimed nothing more than simple competence in the performance of his public tasks [Windsor Vt. *Republican*, 26 Aug. 1811; *Washingtonian*, 19 Aug. 1811]. A Thanksgiving Proclamation from his pen began and ended with the conventional old-school formulation of rulers and people, but in Congress he spoke in an almost egalitarian vein [ibid., 22 Nov. 1813; *AC* 10/1/1181–1182, 1209; 15, 17 Dec. 1809]. He also advocated strict economy in government expenditures [ibid., 8/1/574, 18 Nov. 1803. Kilbourne, *Litchfield Co., Conn.*, p. 89; C. H. Haydon et al., *History of Jericho* (1916), I, 432–434].

LANGDON, CHAUNCEY (1763–1830), b. Farmington, Conn.; A.B., Yale, 1787; lawyer in Castleton and Windsor, Vt.; Register of Probate, 1792–1797; Judge of Probate, 1798–1799; Vt. Council, 1808, 1823–1830; Vt. Assembly, 1813–1814, 1817, 1819–1820, 1822; U. S. Congress, 1815–1817; active Congregationalist; trustee Middlebury College, 1811–1830. His *Oration delivered at Castleton* (Middlebury, 1812) and *Address upon the reading of the Declaration of Independence* (1814) condemn the poisonous partisanship of "Virginia tarantulae" in old-school terms, but exhort Federalists to partisan activity. A reconciliation of sorts appears in private statements that a resurgent federal party could destroy partisanship by the defeat of its rival [Langdon to John Cotton Smith, 15 Oct. 1808, 21 Sep. 1813, in Helen Smith Coll., N. Y. Hist. Soc.].

LYON, ASA (1763–1841), b. Pomfret, Conn.; A.B., Dartmouth, 1790; Congregational minister in Grand Isle, Vt.; Vt. Assembly, 1799–1802, 1804–1806, 1808, 1810–1814; Council, 1808; judge, County Court, 1805–1809, 1813–1814; U. S. Congress, 1815–1817. His *Depravity and Misery of Man* (Middlebury, 1815) invokes old-school ideals but also includes an extraordinary plea for partisan exertion in the form of a gloss upon the text "Many should run to and fro, and knowledge should be increased" [p. 17]. See also his major speech on treaties and domestic law [*AC*, 14/1/884–897, 4 Feb. 1816].

MARSH, CHARLES (1765–1849), b. Lebanon, Conn.; A.B., Dartmouth, 1786; attended Tapping Reeve's (q.v.) law school in Litchfield, Conn.; lawyer in Woodstock, Vt; U. S. District Attorney, 1797–1801; U. S.

Congress, 1815–1817; member American Colonization Society; trustee of Dartmouth, 1809–1849. His *Essay on the Amendments proposed to the Constitution of the State of Vermont* (Hanover, N. H., 1814) begins with the old-school ideal of paternalist government—" Its legitimate objects are the restraint of the wicked and the protection of the weak" [p. 6]— and attacks caucuses—"more vile and hateful than nests of unclean birds"—and mass meetings—"polluting feasts of selfishness and party spirit"—regardless of which party sponsored them. In practice, however, his record is less consistent. He publicly condemned the Washington Societies and refused to join them, but consented to serve on electioneering committees [Windsor *Washingtonian*, 18 May 1812; see also, James Barrett, "Charles Marsh," *Vt. Hist. Soc. Proceedings*, (1870), passim].

NOYES, JOHN (1764–1841), b. Atkinson, N. H.; A.B., Dartmouth, 1795; merchant in Brattleboro, Vt., dealing in potash (downriver) and general merchandise (upriver); reputedly one of the wealthiest men in his county [M. R. Cabot, *Annals of Brattleboro* (1921), I, 247–248]. His *Oration, delivered in Brattleboro* (1811) was an appeal from the innovating spirit of the times to the ancient ideals of the old school. Of the Democrats he declared, "Disdaining to travel the old, and well-beaten paths of wisdom and experience, they are perched upon the aerial car of the balloon, without a compass or a star for a guide, or a chart with which to direct their course" [p. 11]. But he served regularly on party committees [Windsor *Washingtonian*, 18 May 1812].

Young Federalists

DUNHAM, JOSIAH (1769–1844), b. Columbia, Conn.; A.B., Dartmouth, 1789; teacher and journalist in Windham Co., Vt. [Edward S. Moseley, *Mosley Family* (Newburyport, 1878), pp. 26, 47–48; Lord, *Hanover, N.H.*, passim; Isaac Dunham, *Dunham Genealogy* (Norwich, 1907), p. 81]. Dunham was the central figure in Vermont Federalism, editor of the most important Federalist newspaper, advisor to governors, representative of his state in national and sectional meetings, founder of Washington Societies, and member of electioneering committees [Windsor *Washingtonian*, 18 May 1812; Windsor *Vt. Republican*, 11 Mar., 15 July, 4 Nov. 1811]. His two most important public addresses [both titled *An Oration . . . pronounced at Windsor* (1812 and 1814)] were partisan, without apology, disguise, or restraint. His text was the Declaration of Independence rather than the Constitution; he declared himself in favor of equality [1814, p. 9] and minimal government ("commerce and freedom always flourish and decay together," *ibid.*, p. 12) and pandered to popular prejudices which Jeffersonians had so skillfully exploited— agrarianism, anglophobia, etc. He was a favorite target for Republican editors, who declaimed against his hypocrisy and hunger for power [see Windsor Vt. *Republican* as cited, and Hector Benevolus (pseudonym), *The Hartford Convention in an Uproar* Windsor, 1815, frontis., passim].

ELLIOT, JAMES (1775–1839), b. Gloucester, Mass.; educated in apprenticeship; clerk in a country store, 1789–1793; sergeant and junior officer, U. S. Army, 1793–1796; lawyer in Brattleboro, sometime journalist; U. S. Congress, 1803–1809; Vt. Assembly, 1801–1803, 1818–1819, 1837–1838 [Cabot, *Annals of Brattleboro*, I, 213–215]. His bewildered biographer writes, "Officially he was a Federalist, which is the one mystery of his life. He was a democrat in his principles" [*DAB*, VI, 92]. In 1798 he composed an electioneering "Ode to Equality" [*Poetical and Misc. Works* (Greenfield, 1798), p. 46]:

All hail, divine Equality! Benignant daughter of History.
Sister and Friend of Godlike Liberty! Descend from the Ethereal Plains!

This was no passing phase. In 1808 he declaimed upon liberty, equality and minimal government in Jeffersonian terms [*AC*, 10/1/1772, 11 Mar. 1808].

ELLIOT, SAMUEL (1777–1845), b. Gloucester, Mass., brother of James Elliot (q.v.); education unknown; clerk in a Brattleboro store, 1800; lawyer, 1804. An activist in the Washington Societies of Vermont, his *Address* (Brattleboro, 1812), asks his political colleagues to acknowledge that "the Federalists were haughty in power" and to identify themselves with minimal government, direct popular sovereignty, and even "rotation in office" [p. 12]. See also his similar *Oration pronounced at West Springfield* (Bennington, 1803).

HALL, WILLIAM, JR. (1774–1831), b. Salem, N. H.; attended local schools; miller and country merchant engaged in downriver trade (lumber) from Bellows Falls, Vt. Hall was the only Vermonter to be seated in the Hartford Convention, having been elected by a mass meeting in Windham Co., Vt. [Morison, *Otis*, II, 108n; Adams, *New England Federalism*, p. 252; L. S. Hayes, *History of the Town of Rockingham, Vt.* (Bellows Falls, 1907), p. 672]. I have found no specimen of his politics.

JEWETT, LUTHER (1772–1860), b. Canterbury, Conn.; A.B., Dartmouth, 1795; physician practising in Putney, Vt., until c. 1820; Congregational minister in Newbury, Vt., 1821–1828; editor and publisher of *Farmer's Herald*, St. Johnsbury, 1828–1832; U. S. Congress, 1815–1817. His Independence Day Oration [Windsor *Washingtonian*, 24 Aug. 1812] is at once an appeal to the people to take a more active role in politics and to Federalists to seek popular support. [See also Edward T. Fairbanks, *St. Johnsbury, Vt.* (1914), pp. 183–185.]

POMROY (var., PUMROY), THOMAS MERRICK (1782–1843), b. Northampton, Mass.; printer, publisher, bookseller in Northampton and later Windsor, Vt.; He replaced Josiah Dunham (q.v.) as editor of the *Washingtonian*, and regularly published editorials and electioneering addresses which were openly partisan and popularly oriented [see, e.g., 3 Jan. 1814]. He also served as secretary (the most important office) of the Washington Society of Windsor, the most active in the state [ibid., 21 Feb. 1814; see also Albert A. Pomeroy, *Pomeroy Family* (Toledo, 1912), p. 2389].

PRENTISS, SAMUEL (1782–1857), b. Stonington, Conn.; attended lower schools in Northfield, Mass.; privately tutored; lawyer practising in Montpelier, Vt., 1803–1822; Vt. Assembly, 1824–1825; U. S. Senate (Whig), 1831–1842; U. S. District Judge, 1842–1857. His *Oration pronounced at Plainfield* (Montpelier, 1812) was an appeal for the organization of a new "Republican-Federal" Party and for an effort to "diffuse correct information, to awaken a spirit of candid inquiry, to induce men to regard measures more than men, to destroy the odious influence of party names, to abolish the invidious and unreal distinction between the words Federal and Republican" [p. 33]. "Perilous as the times are," he declared, "what [is] more proper than to associate ourselves?" [p. 36]. [See also Philips, "Samuel Prentiss," passim; and Kelton, *Montpelier*, pp. 447–451.]

WALLACE, JOHN (1790–1826), b. Newbury, Vt.; attended Dartmouth; teacher in New Salem, Mass., 1808–1811; lawyer in Newbury, Vt., 1811–1826. His *Oration, delivered at New Salem* (Greenfield, Mass., 1809), attacked the "mishapen mask of French Democracy [p. 5] but flattered the virtue and power of the "good citizens of Massachusetts" [p. 13]. See also his *Oration delivered before the Washington Benevolent Society in Newbury, Vt.* (Windsor, 1812) and F. H. Wells, *Newbury, Vt.*, p. 722.

MASSACHUSETTS

Federalists of the Old School

ADAMS, JOHN (1735–1826): see above, chapter I.

BARTLETT, BAILEY (1750–1830), b. Haverhill, Mass.; attended local schools; retail merchant in Haverhill; State House of Representatives, 1781–1784, 1788; State Senate, 1789; U. S. Congress, 1797–1801. The politics of this taciturn gentleman can perhaps be inferred from his thoughts on church government. Insisting upon the irrelevance of such "polemical topics" as free will and predestination, he simply suggested a spirit of "due subordination" to Godly leaders [(Bartlett), *Remarks on the*

Proceedings of the Episcopal Convention (Boston, 1786), pp. 4, 7; Hurd, *Essex County, Mass.*, II, 2009].

BAYLIES, WILLIAM (1743–1826), b. Dighton, Mass.; attended Harvard; physician and import merchant in Dighton; not to be confused with his son, William Baylies, Jr., a Jeffersonian. In an *Oration pronounced at Middleborough, at a Meeting of the Federal Republicans* (Boston, 1808) he counseled caution and patience to his young colleagues. "Society is essential to our happiness—Society cannot exist without the protection of Government. Government, therefore, is . . . a blessing which every man will consider it his duty to preserve. . . . Subjection to the powers that be, is the dictate of reason, and the injunction of revelation" [pp. 6–8].

BROOKS, JOHN (1752–1816), b. Medford, Mass.; educated in local schools; studied medicine with Dr. Simon Tufts, Medford; served in the Continental Army; physician residing in Medford. His *Eulogy on General Washington* (Boston, 1800) was heavy with the conventional wisdom of the old school. Washington, "the Aristides, as well as the Fabius of the age," was presented as the personification of elitist ethics—his dignity, independence, and integrity were singled out for special commendation. The career of the model statesman suggested to Brooks that pursuit of popular participation was doubly disagreeable—unseemly and unnecessary. Had not the true "friend of the people found the people to be his friends?" General Brooks also described his model state—a "government of energy," sustained by "sentiment and habit" rather than by forcible restraint, an arrangement which he regarded as the fruit of America's eighteenth-century political experience. Another pamphlet from his pen, *A Discourse delivered before the Humane Society* (Boston, 1795), is colored by a sense of *noblesse oblige*. But in the long years of defeat, Brooks would be more suggestible than his inflexible contemporaries. He encouraged the organization of Washington Societies and took an active part in caucuses and county conventions. As governor of Massachusetts, 1816–1823, his artful dodging belied a carefully contrived electioneering image of a simple-soldier-in-politics [Boston *N. Eng. Palladium*, extra, 7 Apr. 1817].

CABOT, GEORGE (1751–1823): see above, chapter I.

CUTLER, MANASSEH (1742–1823), b. Killingly, Conn.; A.B., Yale, 1765; chaplain in the Continental Army; Congregational clergyman in Hamilton, Mass.; physician, nonpractising lawyer; speculator in western lands. State House of Representatives, 1800; U. S. Congress, 1801–1805. His *Sermon, delivered at Hamilton* (Salem, 1799) was a warning to "an ungrateful and disobedient people" that a jealousy of rulers had been "carried to a dangerous extreme" and that the majority should rest content with its one political responsibility, the election of wise and good rulers, "leaving the administration of government to the wisdom of those in whose hands the people have placed it" [pp. 21, 16, 28]. Fourteen years in the political desert left no noticeable marks upon the mind of Manasseh Cutler. His *Century Discourse, delivered at Hamilton* (1814) and his *Discourse, delivered in Salem* (1813) are in the same spirit. He labored in the electioneering campaign of 1800—"I sat up till after 2 o'clock to prepare votes" [W. P. & J. P. Cutler, *Life, Journals and Correspondence of Rev. Manasseh Cutler*, 2 vols. (Cincinnati, 1888), II, 41]—but soon succumbed to despair. [See Cutler to Francis Low, 30 Nov. 1803, *Essex Institute Historical Collections*, 39 (1903), pp. 321–323].

DANA, FRANCIS (1743–1811), b. Charlestown, Mass.; A.B., Harvard, 1762; Mass. Council, 1776–1780; Continental Congress, 1776–1778; Diplomatic Service, 1779–1783; Continental Congress, 1784; justice, Mass. Supreme Court, 1785–1791; Chief Justice, 1791–1806. His personal dignity and public decorum befitted an old-school gentleman who had married two fortunes and inherited a third. A "high-strung man, sensitive as to manners and conduct, and intolerant of anything underhand or mean or rude," he carefully "kept up, in his manner of life, the style of olden times" [R. H. Dana, "Francis Dana," *Penna. Mag. Hist. & Biog.*, I (1877), pp. 86–95; Cresson, *Francis Dana*, passim; Thomas Dawes to Noah Webster, 9 Feb. 1795, in Webster Papers, N. Y. Pub. Library]. His old-fashioned, functional conservatism appears most clearly in his judicial decisions [see, e.g., Amory *v.* Gilman, *Reports of Cases . . . In the Supreme Judicial Court of . . . Massachusetts* (Boston, 1883), II (1806), 1–13; Hamilton *v.* Boiden, ibid., I (1804), 50–53, and Wales *v.* Stetson, ibid., II (1806), 143–146; as discussed in my, "Myth of the Essex Junto," pp. 202–203]. His hatred of partisan politics and stubborn refusal to participate in them after 1800 appear in Dana to Pickering, n.d. [1804], in Pickering Papers, Mass. Hist. Soc., quoted in chapter I, above.

DANE, NATHAN (1752–1835), b. Ipswich, Mass.; A.B., Harvard, 1778; lawyer residing in Beverly, Mass. State House of Representatives, 1782–1785; Continental Congress, 1785–1788; State Senate, 1790–1791, 1794–1797; he emerged from a long retirement to serve in the Hartford Convention, 1814. Dane's politics were deeply republican, and his model republic mirrored the traditional arrangements of Puritan New England. It was government by consent "of every freeman" [to King, 8 Oct. 1785, in *King*, I, 67–68], but consent to men rather than measures, to natural rulers chosen from the wise and good [see my "Myth of the Essex Junto," pp. 202–213]. Dane's preference for a government "restored to its former firmness and order" appears in his "Address before the Mass. House of Representatives" [Burnett, *Letters of Members of the Continental Congress*, VIII, 504] and Dane to Gorham [ibid., p. 613]. For his holistic conservatism see his *General Abridgement and Digest of American Law* (Boston, 1823–1829), I, 87.

DWIGHT, THOMAS (1758–1819), b. Springfield, Mass.; A.B., Harvard, 1778; lawyer in Springfield; State House of Representatives, 1794–1795; State Senate, 1796–1803; U. S. Congress, 1803–1805; Governor's Council, 1808–1809. His political ideal was a collectivized commonwealth in which "the good people" placed their trust in "rulers" [to Theodore Sedgwick, 13 July 1790, in Sedgwick Papers, Mass. Hist. Soc.]. But he was pessimistic about its chances for survival. "A man will soon, without the imputation of indelicacy, be able to hawk himself in the highways as an excellent candidate for the highest promotion, with as much freedom and vociferation as your market men now cry codfish and lobsters" [to Sedgwick, 7 Feb. 1789, ibid.]. He regarded the Jeffersonian movement with fear and loathing, dismissing its ideology as "Gallic Bastard Jeffersonian lingo" [to John Williams, 8 Apr. 1802, in Dwight-Howard Papers, Mass. Hist. Soc.] and its techniques as "means which are contemptible in the eyes of honest men, such as frequent private associations, riding and running from place to place, writing and preaching constantly against the government itself and more against the administration of it" [to Sedgwick, 11 Apr. 1800, in Sedgwick Papers]. Though he stood for office, he refused to run after it or to engage in an active pursuit of public opinion. "If the government, with the present weakness of its executive branch, cannot be supported without a resort to those contemptible measures which distinguish the exertions of its enemies, I can easily foresee its rapid dissolution" [ibid.]. He refused outright to participate in party affairs [to John Williams, 21 May 1802, 5 July 1805, in Dwight-Howard Papers] but continued to conduct himself with old-school propriety, fearing that the "full tide of successful experiment" would "inundate and sweep away liberty, property and law [to John Williams, 19 May 1803], hoping for Divine intervention [to John Williams, 2 Apr. 1802].

FOSTER, DWIGHT (1757–1823), b. Brookfield, Mass., brother of Theodore Foster (q.v.); A.B., Brown, 1774; lawyer in Brookfield, Mass.; member, State House of Representatives, 1791–1792, 1808–1809; U. S. Congress, 1793–1800; U. S. Senate, 1800–1803; chief justice, Court of Common Pleas, 1801–1811. In Congress, Foster conformed to old-school ethics, publicly declaring that he was "alike indifferent to censure and applause" [*AC*, 5/2/1614, 7 May 1798]. He labored consistently to extend the independence and efficiency of "constituted authority" [ibid., 4/1/1173, 26 Apr. 1796]; and when administrative decisions became questions of general interest, as in the consideration of Jay's Treaty, he preferred the "opinion of many of the best informed mercantile characters" to that of the people [ibid.]. During the French crisis he was more mindful of "the liberty of his country" than of individual freedom [ibid., 5/2/1614, 7 May 1798]. Throughout his career he favored energy in government, particularly its active intervention in the economy [ibid., 3/1/413, 31 Jan, 1794]. He did, however, participate in the committee organization of Connecticut Valley Federalism in 1811 [Otis et al. to Foster, 6 Apr. 1811, in Broadsides, Amer. Antiq. Soc.; see also Joseph Allen et al. to Foster, 13 Mar. 1815, ibid.].

GOODHUE, BENJAMIN (1748–1814), b. Salem, Mass.; A.B., Harvard, 1766; import merchant in Salem; State House of Representatives, 1780–1782; State Senate, 1786–1788; U. S. Congress, 1789–1796; U. S. Senate, 1796–1800. Ideologically conservative, his commitment to "order and good government" permitted no compromise with the principles and practices of the Jeffersonian movement [Goodhue to Nathan Read, 29 Nov. 1800, in Read Papers, Essex Institute; see also his condemnation of the "many toad eaters in Boston," his fellow merchants, in Goodhue to Pickering, 5 Oct. 1799, in Pickering Papers]. During the 1790s he manifested a touching faith in the virtue of the American people. "You may depend upon it, that it will not be in the power of the inconsiderately or the determinedly vicious, to shake the great body, either of the merchants, or the yeomanry of our country, from their attachment to order, or a reverence for their own government" [to Wolcott, 1 Aug. 1795, in Gibbs, *Administrations of Washington and Adams*, I, 221; to Stephen Goodhue, 2 Apr. 1796, 9 Apr. 1796, in Goodhue Papers, Essex Institute]. The events of 1800 not merely defeated but disarmed him; in retirement and deep despair, he drifted slowly into alcoholism. "His habits since his return have given him no influence in society, and as he rose gradually to public notice, so he insensibly passed away from his former friendships and notice, being habitually and publickly intemperate" [Bentley, *Diary*, IV, 271]. On rare occasions he was permitted to serve on Federalist committees [*Repertory*, 27 Mar. 1807] but he took neither an active nor a leading part.

HIGGINSON, STEPHEN (1743–1828), b. Salem, Mass.; attended common schools; import merchant in Boston; Continental Congress, 1782–1783; naval officer of Boston port, 1797–1808. His holism, deep conservatism, and open elitism appear in *The Writings of Laco* (Boston, 1789), quoted in chapter I above and more fully in my "Myth of the Essex Junto." His idealized conception of energy in government appears in Higginson to Arthur Lee, 1783, in Jameson, ed., "Letters of Stephen Higginson," pp. 711–713. He also favored energy and unity among friends of order: "In times like the present it is provoking to hear men talk of their independence, their candour, their love of conciliation, and their aversion to party" [to Wolcott, 11 July 1798, in Gibbs, *Administrations of Washington and Adams*, II, 70]. But he never countenanced, and firmly condemned the popularly oriented political behavior of such younger men as Harrison Gray Otis and John Quincy Adams (see above chapter II).

JACKSON, JONATHAN (1743–1810), b. Boston, Mass.; A.B., Harvard, 1761; import merchant in Boston (sometime partner of Stephen Higginson); banker; member, State House of Representatives, 1777; Continental Congress, 1782; State Senate, 1789; U. S. Marshal, 1789–1791; State Treasurer, 1802–1806. His *Thoughts upon the Political Situation of the United States* (Worcester, 1788), a conservative critique of the U. S. Constitution, is a classic statement of the functional conservatism of the old school [see my "Myth of the Essex Junto," pp. 201–216, for many extracts]. [For his economic policy, see K. W. Porter, *Jacksons and Lees*, I, 100–112; and for his open elitism, James Jackson, *Reminiscences*, p. 30.]

KNOX, HENRY (1750–1806), b. Boston; attended Boston Latin School; bookseller in Boston before the Revolution; afterwards a gentleman farmer and land speculator residing in Thomaston, Maine. Major general in the Continental Army; Secretary of War, 1785–1794. Knox had no fear of a broadened base of popular participation in the choice of rulers; indeed, he declared, "I cannot hesitate to prefer democracy to every form of government, though I am convinced of its faults and that it does not confer the greatest security to property" [this in 1785; quoted in North Callahan, *Henry Knox* (New York, 1958), p. 235]. But his "democracy" was an elitist conception, reminiscent of Cotton Mather's "status popularis" [*Magnalia Christi Americana* . . . (Hartford, 1820), I, 395]. If the people were to choose their rulers, they were to be ruled by a government of the "best people," possessed of energy and power. A plan from Knox's pen for federal union went far beyond the forms that were adopted in elitist spirit and concentrated power. "The state systems are the accursed thing which will prevent our being a nation," Knox wrote. "The democracy might be managed, nay, it would remedy itself after being sufficiently fermented; but the vile State governments are sources of pollution, which will contaminate the American name for ages —machines that must produce ill, but cannot produce good; smite them in the name of God and the people" [to Rufus King, 15 July 1787, in *King*, I, 228]. Knox was prepared to make such exertions in the cause of order as might "unite and brace the public mind" [to John Adams, 19 Mar. 1797, in Adams, *Works,* VIII, 532] but not to appear to bend before the will of the people. A Jeffersonian would defeat him in 1804, by denouncing him as a "natural aristocrat" [Robinson, *Jeffersonian Democracy in New England,* p. 46].

LINCOLN, BENJAMIN (1733–1810), b. Hingham, Mass.; received "a good common education"; farmer in Hingham, speculator in securities and Maine lands. Major general in Continental Army; Secretary of War, 1781–1783; commander of militia army which suppressed Shays' Rebellion; collector of port of Boston, 1789–1807. In the last-named capacity this somnolent student of old-school precepts issued the following order to his subordinates in 1802: "If any of you . . . have in the public walks vilified the chief Magistrate of the Union in terms rude and indecent and should justify yourselves herein you only exercise your rights, I have to ask that you will in future recollect that there is an infinite difference between Right and the propriety of exercising that right" [quoted in Shipton, *Sibley's Harvard Graduates,* XII, 437]. If Gen. Lincoln's job was at stake, so also were his principles.

LOWELL, JOHN (1743–1802), b. Newburyport, Mass.; A.B., Harvard, 1760; served briefly in the Revolutionary militia; lawyer in Newburyport to 1777, Boston thereafter. Member, Mass. House of Representatives, 1778, 1780–1782; Continental Congress, 1782–1783; Mass. Senate, 1784–1785; judge, Mass. court of appeals, 1784–1789; U. S. District Court, 1789–1801; U. S. Circuit Court, 1801–1802. His *Eulogy, on the honourable James Bowdoin* (Boston, 1791) is a conventional statement of old-school ideals [pp. 12, 18]. Honest in his elitist politics even to a fault, his enemies satirized him as "lawyer Candour" [Harrison Gray Otis, *Biographical Sketch of the Late Judge Lowell* (Boston, 1849), p. 5]. He did, however, participate in at least one caucus in 1800 [Cutler, *Manasseh Cutler,* II, 41].

LYMAN, SAMUEL (1749–1802), b. Goshen, Conn.; A.B., Yale, 1770; lawyer residing in Springfield from 1784; member Mass. House of Representatives, 1786–88; State Senate, 1790–93; U. S. Congress, 1795–1800; justice court of common pleas, 1791–1800; his estate at his death was appraised at $7000. A full expression of his old-school conservatism was his farewell address to his constituents [published in New London *Conn. Gazette,* 23 July 1800]. He repudiated a "spirit of surmise and jealousy" which he sensed among the people, instructing them that "a higher degree of liberty cannot exist without endangering the whole," and that "nothing is so unequal as equality." Lyman counseled all Americans "to divest themselves of party animosity and to live together like brothers" under a Federalist administration. He analyzed the arguments among friends of order in 1800 not as a dispute over particular military or economic measures, but rather as a general "division as to the degree of hatred and animosity necessary to be used in order to destroy all opposition to Government. A small party, I suppose, sincerely believe, that a few bold strokes would silence all opposition; others say no, let it be done by civility and sound argument; so here they are at issue; but their ultimate views are the same." [For an unfriendly Federal comment, see Wolcott to Fisher Ames, 10 Aug. 1800, in Gibbs, *Administrations of Washington and Adams*, II, 400.]

LYMAN, THEODORE (1755–1839), b. York, Me.?; educated in lower schools; Boston merchant in East Indies and China trade; resided at a country seat in Waltham, Mass.; his wife, Lydia Williams, was a niece of Timothy Pickering (q.v.). His own ethics are reflected in his condemnation of young Federalist Harrison Gray Otis for "timidity" in the face of popular opinion, and for a consequent inconsistency in the defence of functional republicanism [to Pickering, 16 Sep. 1796, in Pickering Papers, Mass. Hist. Soc.]. One of the few Massachusetts Federalists who were prepared to act upon Timothy Pickering's desperate disunionist conspiracy in 1804 (and even Lyman counseled "patient waiting with prudent management"), he was unable to find others who were even willing to "freely converse" upon that dark subject [to Pickering, 29 Feb. 1804, in Lodge, *Cabot*, p. 446].

MASON, JONATHAN (1756–1831), b. Boston, Mass.; A.B., Princeton, 1774; lawyer practising in Boston; member, Mass. House of Representatives, 1786–1796; Council, 1797–1798; Mass. Senate, 1799–1800; U. S. Senate, 1800–1803. His *Oration delivered Mar. 6, 1780* (Boston, 1780), in commemoration of the Boston massacre, was a plea for the preservation of the New England way—"Let not party-rage, private animosities, or self-interested motives succeed that religious attachment to the public weal which has brought us successful thus far" [p. 22]. In the 1790s he disapproved of Otis's desire to "please everybody." To that young Federalist, Mason wrote peremptorily, "You individually are to stand at your Post, *firm*—I mean by that word—industrious, constant, decisive, complaisant, always to be found by your party, & never to retreat" [to Otis, 4 Dec. 1797, in Morison, *Otis*, I, 77]. Thus willing to see party discipline established among friends of order, Mason was however unable to approve of the pursuit of popular favor, after the fashion of Jefferson's friends. "Fabian prudence was never more necessary. We have a singular enemy, extremely powerful, but extremely diseased" [to Otis, 26 Mar. 1798, in Morison, *Otis*, I, 91]. A year later he declared, "The old way

which is most commonly the best way—is to jogg on steadily, inde-
pendantly, & firmly" [to Otis, 27 Feb. 1799, in ibid., I, 173].

MATTOON, EBENEZER (1755–1843), b. North Amherst, Mass.; A.B.,
Dartmouth, 1776; major in Continental Army; farmer in Amherst, Mass.
Mattoon was "a good singer, extravagantly fond of music" [Cutler,
Manasseh Cutler, II, 52], but his voice was not well suited for concert.
Of party discipline he knew little; for party exertions he cared less.
"Resistance is vain at present," he wrote to Thomas Dwight, 11 Feb.
1802, "the Federalists may as well go home. They do no good here, and
I am led to think hasten our ruin by any attempts to prevent it." Mattoon
believed that as long as there was "a fatal blindness or rather obstinacy
prevailing with the majority" there was nothing to be done. He
anticipated anarchy—"The federal government is dead and damned.
We may creep over its remains, but ere long attend it to the grave
and bury it under arms" [Dwight-Howard Papers, Mass. Hist. Soc.].

MORSE, JEDIDIAH (1761–1826), b. Woodstock, Conn.; A.B., Yale, 1783;
Congregationalist clergyman in Charlestown, Mass. Deeply conservative,
even by Federalist standards, his sermon on *The Duty of Resignation
under Afflictions* (Boston, 1796) came close to the doctrine of passive
obedience. Although he was one of many New England clergymen who
were asked to assist in the encouragement of a Federal electioneering
paper, the *Palladium*, he was not active in partisan undertakings. A letter
to Judge Breese, 15 Mar. 1800, expressed his antipathy to the "Jacobin
spirit," and to secret party organization [Morse Papers, N. Y. Public
Library].

OTIS, SAMUEL ALLYNE (1740–1814), b. Barnstable, Mass.; A.B., Harvard, 1759; merchant in Boston to 1789; member, Mass. House of
Representatives, 1776, 1784–1787; Continental Congress, 1787–1788;
secretary, U. S. Senate, 1789–1814. The public spirit and physicial
stamina of this "uniform whig" was such that in thirty years of service
he never missed a day of public business [H. G. Otis to John Rutledge, 14
Sep. 1801, in Rutledge Papers, Univ. of N. C.; Loring, *100 Boston Orators*,
p. 190]. The austere elitism of his politics appears in his complaint
against the blinding "glare of popularity" [to Sedgwick, 13 Oct. 1788, in
Sedgwick Papers, Mass. Hist. Soc.] and also in his opposition to "frolics"
sponsored by Federal friends in 1788 to celebrate their great success
and bind the people to them. "I don't know but we are in danger of
running to excess in regard to processions. Perhaps my gravity and
aversion to parade may have induced this opinion" [to Thacher, 17 July
1788, in Burnett, *Letters of Members of the Continental Congress*, VIII,

763]. After 1800, his commercial prospects having gone aglimmering, Otis was dependent upon his office and understandably reluctant to participate actively in the Federalist opposition [Otis to Wadsworth, 12 Jan. 1789, in ibid.; H. G. Otis to Rutledge, 14 Sep. 1801].

PARSONS, THEOPHILUS (1750–1813), b. Byfield, Mass.; son of a clergyman; A.B., Harvard, 1769; studied law under Edmund Trowbridge; practised in Newburyport to 1800, Boston thereafter; married Elizabeth Greenleaf, 1780. As a "moderate whig" [to John Waite, 12 Mar. 1776, in Parsons, *Memoir of Theophilus Parsons*, p. 38] he was a powerful figure in the Essex Convention of 1778, where he composed the *Essex Result* (published as an appendix in ibid., pp. 359–402). Though partly cribbed from John Adams, it is an expression of an elitism much deeper than that more moderate conservatives. (Many extracts appear in my "Myth of the Essex Junto," passim). In the Mass. convention of 1779–1780, he worked at cross-purposes with John Adams, who wished to confine the "natural aristocracy" in a single chamber, where it could only do good. Parsons preferred to extend its power throughout the government, without check or balance. He acquiesced reluctantly in the "governour's negative," which he privately described as a concession made "to please the people" [to Dana, 3 Aug. 1780, in Dana Papers, Mass. Hist. Soc.]. As chief justice of the Mass. Supreme Court, 1806–1813, Parsons' decisions on the law of property made clear his distance from nineteenth-century American conservatives who elevated possession to a sacred right as a barrier against the people. Parsons, still conceptualizing in terms of a government safely in the hands of the elite, defined property as an "alienable right," subject to the will of rulers and the needs of the state [*Essex Result*, pp. 15, 21–22; "First Mass. Turnpike Corp. *v.* Field," *Mass. Reports*, III (1807) 201–208; "Amory *v.* Gilman," ibid., II (1806) 1–13.] Parsons' horror of the substance and the forms of the Jeffersonian movement appear in a letter to John Jay, 5 May 1800, *Jay*, IV, 267–70. Although he occasionally attended party meetings, and helped to establish an electioneering journal, the *Repertory* [Benjamin Whitwell to Parsons, 3 Aug. 1804, in Columbia University Coll., Columbia University], the influence and activity of this reputed manager of Massachusetts Federalism appears greatly exaggerated. "To the close of his life he took an interest in the politics of the State, and exerted an influence upon them; but not, I am persuaded, so great an influence as was imputed to him," his son wrote. "I doubt whether he ever attended a public meeting of any kind during the last twenty years of his life [1793–1813]. . . . I cannot recall any one gathering, great or small, in the office or anywhere in the house, for political purposes. No doubt there were such meetings, but they were never frequent; and very few took place, I think, during the last ten years of his life" [Parsons, *Memoir of Parsons*, pp. 123, 131, 132].

PICKERING, TIMOTHY (1745–1829), b. Salem, Mass.; A.B., Harvard, 1765; colonel and quartermaster-general in Continental Army; U. S. Postmaster General, 1791–1795; Secretary of War, 1795; Secretary of State, 1795–1800; U. S. Senate, 1803–1811; Mass. Council, 1812; U. S. Congress, 1813–1817; nonpractising lawyer, small farmer in Salem and Wenham, Mass. In the age of Jefferson, he was probably the worst-hated man in the nation. This fact, coupled with the accessibility of his massive papers, the number of his virulent pamphlet-assaults upon Republican administrations, and the violence of his prejudices, has led historians hostile to the latter-day Federalists from Henry Adams to Irving Brant to make him the central figure in the federal party after 1800. Without questioning Pickering's prominence in the period 1800–1820, one might challenge the extent of his power and influence among his brother-Federalists. In 1804 and 1812, his influence was tested and found wanting (see above, chapter 8). He was not a member of the most important Massachusetts committees, and there is evidence that in 1808 he was deliberately kept uninformed of a secret Federalist meeting in New York to settle questions of national strategy (see above, chapter 4). Pickering personifies a dilemma which young Federalists never resolved. What could be done with older men, Revolutionary heroes, friends of Washington, founders of the nation, who persisted in their open and honest elitism? "In voting for the compensation law, as in every other act of my public life," Pickering wrote piously, "I did not take time to consider whether it would be popular or unpopular; but simply whether the measure was just and right" [to Jacob Ashton, 29 Oct. 1816, in Pickering, IV, 277]. The depth of Pickering's unpopularity suggests that his commitment was as constant as he claimed. One of his outrageous pamphlets, which Republican editors invariably gave wide circulation, was more influential in its operation upon the public mind than a dozen carefully contrived young Federalist efforts to establish a popular base for their covert elitism. [There is much in Pickering's pamphlets and personal papers on his old-school ideals; see, e.g., "The Road to Power in a Free State," 16 Apr. 1813, in Pickering Papers, Mass. Hist. Soc.; for his disapproval of young Federalists, see Pickering to King, 9 Feb. 1808, in King, V, 71; Pickering to Lowell, 7 Nov. 1814, in Lodge, Cabot, pp. 539–541; Pickering to Samuel Putnam, 4 Feb. 1814, in Pickering Papers, Mass. Hist. Soc.; Pickering to Higginson, 23 Dec. 1799, in Morison, Otis, I, 166; for their disapproval of him, see Otis to Josiah Quincy, n.d., in Edmund Quincy, Josiah Quincy, Jr., p. 242; for his biography see Edward Hake Phillips, "The Public Career of Timothy Pickering," (unpub. diss., Harvard, 1950); Octavius Pickering and Charles W. Upham, The Life of Timothy Pickering, 4 vols. (Boston, 1867–1873); H. P. Prentiss, Timothy Pickering as the Leader of New England Federalism, 1800–1815 (Salem, 1934); and Henry

Cabot Lodge, "Timothy Pickering," *Studies in History* (Boston, 1884), pp. 182–223.]

READ, NATHAN (1759–1849), b. Warren, Mass.; A.B., Harvard, 1781; apothecary, iron manufacturer in Essex County, Mass.; removed to Belfast, Me., in 1807; U. S. Congress, 1800–1803; judge, Essex County Court of Common Pleas, 1803; same office in Hancock County, 1807. His unyielding opposition to the "spirit of innovation" which he sensed in the Jeffersonian movement, and to the "political quackery" of its principles and practices,. appears in Read to William Prescott, 5 Jan. 1802, and Read to Israel Thorndike, 17 Jan. 1802, in Read Papers, Essex Institute.

REED, JOHN (1751–1831), b. Framingham, Mass.; his father a clergyman; A.B., Yale, 1772; served in the Continental Navy; Congregationalist clergyman in West Bridgewater, Mass.; father of John Reed (1781–1860), q.v. U. S. Congress, 1795–1801. His speech of 5 Mar. 1798 [AC 5/2/1202–1207] was an elitist argument for "responsibility in government." See also, *Sermon by Rev. Dr. Reed* (Boston, 1815).

SEDGWICK, THEODORE (1746–1813): see above, chapter I.

SEWALL, SAMUEL (1757–1814), b. Boston, Mass.; A.B., Harvard, 1776; lawyer practising in Marblehead; removed to Wiscasset, Me. Member, Mass. House of Representatives, 1784, 1788–1796; U. S. Congress, 1796–1800; associate justice, Mass. Supreme Court, 1801–1813; chief justice, 1813–1814. A powerful and prominent Congressman who stands much in need of a biography, he took the conventional old-school view of his job—"It is the duty of every member to consider himself as the representative of the whole union" [AC 5/2/941–945, 26 Jan. 1798]. If he was more *suaviter in modo* than such fiery young Federalist colleagues as Robert Goodloe Harper (q.v.), he was almost equally *fortiter in re.* "Liberty is security," he declared, "destroy security, therefore, and you destroy liberty." From this premise he reasoned to the conclusion that party opposition to "Executive authority" was "a sort of treason against the peaceful enjoyment by the people of their liberty" [ibid.]. In his *Communication from the Hon. Samuel Sewall and the Hon. Nathan Dane* (Boston, 1805), society is idealized as an organism, a moral entity. Government is portrayed in paternalistic terms as an active force in the hands of an aristocracy of talents and virtue for the primary purpose of protecting the weak against the strong.

SHEPARD, WILLIAM (1737–1817), b. Westfield, Mass., son of a tanner; attended common schools; served as a colonel in Continental Army throughout the war; assisted in suppression of Shays' Rebellion; member, Mass. House of Representatives, 1785–1786; Governor's Council, 1792–1796; U. S. Representative, 1797–1803; gentleman farmer in Westfield [Isaac Knapp, *Sermon delivered at Westfield* (Springfield, 1818) passim]. In Congress, Gen. Shepard declared his determination to "hold fast that which is good," in the face of many doubtful experiments [*AC*, 6/2/291, Jan. 1800]. He did not hesitate to express his contempt for young Federalists such as Robert Goodloe Harper (q.v.) who were attempting to build a popularly based Federal party [ibid., 5/2/1943 15 June 1798]. His old-school conception of representation and public ethics appears in ibid., 5/2/982, 9 Feb. 1798.

STRONG, CALEB (1745–1819), b. Northampton, Mass.; A.B., Harvard, 1764; lawyer in Northampton, Mass.; member, Mass. House of Representatives, 1776–1778; Mass. Senate, 1780–1788; U. S. Senate, 1789–1796; Mass. Governor, 1800–1807, 1812–1816. His political and social ideas appear in *Patriotism and Piety, The Speeches of His Excellency, Caleb Strong, Esq.* (Boston, 1812). In 1801, he declared that even if Jeffersonians should revolutionize the state government, friends of order should not resort to "faction" [p. 39]. In addition to the conventional old-school formulas for society, government, morality and the laws, Strong's speeches included interesting comments upon the subject of education. "It is not enough to teach children to read and write, and understand the first rules of arithmetic," he wrote, "it is also of importance to habituate them to restraint" [p. 40]. Despite the austerity of his manners and the simplicity of his habits (a "man who lives a hundred miles from salt water, whose wife wears blue stockings, and who, with his household, calls hasty pudding luxury," Ames to Gore, 5 Mar. 1800, I Ames, 277), he was regarded by Fisher Ames as a man "set apart to be a governor" [ibid.]. [See also *Amer. Hist. Rev.*, IV (1899), 328–331; XLIII (1937–1938), 553–566; Edwin C. Rozwenc, "Caleb Strong: The last of the River Gods," *The Northampton Book* (Northampton, Mass., 1954), pp. 56–76; Henry Cabot Lodge, "Caleb Strong," *Studies in History*, pp. 224–262; and Alden Bradford, *Caleb Strong* (Boston, 1820).]

SUMNER, INCREASE (1746–1799), b. Roxbury, Mass., his father a middling prosperous farmer; attended Harvard; studied law with Samuel Quincy and practised in Boston. Associate Justice, Mass. Supreme Court, 1782–1797; Governor of Mass., 1797–1799. His moderation, restraint, and general hostility to partisanship either federal or Republican appears in Boston *Ind. Chronicle*, 20 Feb. 1800. To the General Court he declared in 1798, "I hold it an article in my political creed, that the People and their Government are inseparably united; and that whoever attempts to divide them, cannot be viewed in any other light, than as aiming a blow at the main pillar" [*Speech . . . 2 June 1798* (Boston, 1798), p. 19n].

TAGGART, SAMUEL (1754–1825), b. Londonderry, N. H.; A.B., Dartmouth, 1774; Presbyterian clergyman in Colrain, Franklin Co., Mass. U. S. Congress, 1803–1817. He was not a leading member of the Federal minority—"I have, for the most part, contented myself to giving my vote in silence" [*AC*, 12/1/1639]—but in occasional speeches he consistently defended a deeply conservative and openly elitist view of society and politics. "Innovations in a national system, I humbly conceive, ought never to be admitted without the most imperious necessity. They are, at all times, a matter of hazardous experiment. . . . Facilis descensus Averni, sed revocare gradum, hic labor, hoc opus" [sic; *AC* 8/1/728–729, 34, 8 Dec. 1803]. It is interesting to note that he opposed the embargo, not with the arguments of younger Federalists, but rather as an unwise and unconstitutional measure which would destroy the confidence of the people in their magistrates [*AC*, 10/2/864–886, 17 Dec. 1808]. For his attitudes on party and democracy, which he publicly attacked, see "Letters of Samuel Taggart, Representative in Congress," *Amer. Antiq. Soc. Proceedings*, 33 (1923), 113–116, 134–141, and see also his *Address to the Independent Electors of Hampshire District* (1811).

THACHER (var., THATCHER), GEORGE (1754–1824), b. Yarmouth, Mass.; A.B., Harvard, 1776; made one cruise in a Revolutionary privateer; lawyer residing in Biddeford, Me.; Continental Congress, 1787; U. S. Congress, 1789–1801; associate judge, Mass. Supreme Court, 1800–1820, Maine Supreme Court, 1820–1824. Thacher was a freethinker in religion but deeply conservative in his politics. "The overthrow of Rome," he declared in Congress, "was accomplished by mobs (something of which have been seen in this country), [by] a kind of democratic societies, by demagogues, getting the rabble about them, and getting on the backs of fools, rode the government down. . . . If a stop is not put to them we shall soon experience a similar fate. Nothing is more easy than to assert that liberty has always been destroyed by an excess of power in the Executives of Governments. But I believe it has more frequently been destroyed by democratic mobs, by the erection of whiskey poles and liberty poles, and by discontented Representatives going home to their constituents, and setting them against the Government" [*AC*, 5/2/1114, 28 Feb. 1798].

WADSWORTH, PELEG (1748–1829), b. Duxbury, Mass.; A.B., Harvard, 1769; officer in the Continental Army; merchant, land agent, speculator residing in Portland (1784–1807) and Wadsworth Hall, Oxford County, Me.; Mass. Senate, 1792; U. S. Congress, 1793–1807. His advisory opinion on the Hartford Convention suggests that having lived through the Jeffersonian era, he had learned nothing. "It would be best to deliberate with closed doors, from prudential motives, and because a concourse would put a restraint on freedom of debate, and the business would be done in half the time without spectators" [Morison, *Otis*, II, 140].

Transitional Figures

AMES, FISHER (1758–1808): see above, chapter I.

DEXTER, SAMUEL (1761–1816), b. Boston, Mass.; A.B., Harvard, 1781; lawyer residing in Roxbury; member, Mass. House of Representatives, 1788–1790; U. S. Congress, 1793–1795; U. S. Senate, 1799–1800; Secretary of War, 1800; Secretary of the Treasury, 1801. Moderate in his republican principles, conciliatory by temperament, "Ambi" Dexter, as Federal friends called him, was constitutionally unable to become a partisan of any stripe. But with many complaints and hesitations he collaborated fitfully in the construction of Federalist machinery in Boston [J. Q. Adams, *Memoirs*, 5 Apr. 1807, II, pp. 466–467; Dexter, *Reminiscences*, pp. 68, 84]. In 1812 he tried a deeper game. Refusing to attend the Federalists' nominating meeting in New York City, he reminded Harrison Gray Otis of the heavy handicap under which the young Federalists labored—"When Piso [sic] conspired against Nero it was proposed to make Seneca emperor; to this two objections of some weight appeared, 1st that it was not possible to make a sufficient party to put him in; & 2dly that if he were in he could not stay a moment in office, such was the state of public manners. Gov. Jay could no more play President than Seneca could Emperor" [to Otis, 12 Sep. 1812, in Morison, *Otis*, I, 319]. Dexter formed a different plan. "The great object is to prevent our annihilation as a commercial nation. . . . If these objects can best be obtained by a [permanent] coalition with a portion of the opposite party, why should pride or passion prevent it?" [ibid.]. Dexter found encouragement only from the other side; he received Republican votes in the Mass. gubernatorial elections of 1814–1816, and Madison offered him the post of minister to Spain. Dexter rejected the latter, insisting publicly that he was a Federalist [Dexter, *Address to the Electors of Massachusetts* (Boston, 1814)]. His hope was fusion on Federalist terms rather than on those of the administration, but all in vain.

GORE, CHRISTOPHER (1758–1827), b. Boston, son of a prosperous Tory artisan; A.B., Harvard, 1776; brief military service in the Revolution; studied law with John Lowell, Sr. (q.v.); lawyer and gentleman farmer residing in Waltham [Helen R. Pinkney, "Christopher Gore, A Federalist of Massachusetts," (unpubl. diss., Radcliffe, 1942), p. 12, passim]. Too old to count himself among the younger generation, whom he anathematized as "vulgar" in their hunger for "place and distinction" and in their willingness to pursue popular favor in order to get it [Gore to King, 5 Oct. 1812, in *King*, V, 282], Gore was nevertheless too young to join the old school in its retreat. He shared in the effort to organize Massachusetts Federalism, serving regularly as a member of the state Central Committee [Gore to Bristol County Committee, 25 Mar. 1807, in Misc. Bound Coll., Mass. Hist. Soc.]. As governor, 1809–1810, he made electioneering trips through the state and "mixed with the different classes of his constituents," breaking with New England tradition [Ripley, *Christopher Gore*, p. 9]. As U. S. Senator, 1813–1816, he joined younger Federalists in their flirtation with free trade [*AC*, 13/2/602–611, 27 Jan. 1814]. After the disintegration of the federal party, he became a National Republican [Gore to Daniel Webster, 11 May 1824, in *Writings and Speeches of Daniel Webster*, XVII, 351].

HOLMES, ABIEL (1763–1837), b. Woodstock, Conn., son of a physician; A.B., Yale, 1783; m. Mary Stiles (daughter of Ezra Stiles) and Sarah Wendell (daughter of Oliver Wendell); Congregationalist clergyman in Georgia, and from 1792, in Cambridge, Mass. His *Sermon preached at Cambridge* . . . (Boston, 1799) praised the old school virtues of Increase Sumner (q.v.) and delineated an ideal political system in which all the people elected "good rulers" who governed by "example and authority." But his *Address delivered before the Washington Benevolent Society* (Cambridge, 1813) was in another spirit—a free use of Jeffersonian ideology for partisan Federalist purposes. He bent before "the majesty of the people" and urged party workers to "never despair of the Commonwealth. Do your duty and God will save it." Altogether, his polemic was an unusual effort to lend divine sanction to a popularly oriented conservative political party. "Let the eyes of the people be on 'the faithful of the land,' " he piously declared.

HULBERT, JOHN WHITEFIELD (1770–1831), b. Alford, Mass.; A.B., Harvard, 1795; lawyer practising in Alford; director Berkshire Bank, Pittsfield, Mass.; U. S. Congress, 1814–1817; removed to Cayuga County, N. Y., 1817. Hulbert was out of step with, and openly critical of, his young Federalist colleagues. "The deliberate opinion of the people, I will always respect," he declared, but in Congress he attacked both "Federal and Democratic Demagogues" [*AC* 14/2/321, 553, Jan. 1817]. Hulbert remained loyal to the old-school ideal of energy in government. "Mr. H. said he was one of those who never believed that the Executive patronage was too great in this country. He would rather see it increased than lessened" [ibid., 14/1/445, 2 Jan. 1816]. He supported measures to this end, including the second Bank of the United States [ibid., 14/1/ 1339, 5 Apr. 1816]; he did, however, oppose a large military establishment in time of peace [ibid., 14/1/424, 2 Jan. 1816]. He was disagreeably surprised at the voting conduct of his brother Federalists, and refused to join them in their flirtation with minimal government. "Mr. H. said he would not part with his friends unless they thrust him off, but he would prefer parting with his friends to parting with his conscience" [ibid., 14/1/1343, 5 Apr. 1816]. Hulbert was a strong nationalist when many young Federalists were moving in the opposite direction. In a brief but very interesting speech he sought to refurbish old-school holism within a nationalistic frame, defining the nation, rather than society, as a "moral person" [ibid., 14/1/999, Feb. 1816].

LEE, SILAS (1760–1814), b. Concord, Mass.; A.B., Harvard, 1784; lawyer, jurist in Wiscasset, Me.; member, Mass. House of Representatives, 1793, 1797–1798; U. S. Congress, 1799–1801, where his voting record was strongly Federalist [Dauer, *Adams Federalists*, pp. 318, 323]. After the elections of 1800, Lee worked out his own private compromise with the Jeffersonian movement. He covertly served it, but did not publickly repudiate his Federalism. "This masked course of procedure," a Republican drily observed, "is sometimes useful" [Goodman, *Democratic-Republicans of Mass.*, pp. 146–147]. It was useful to Silas Lee as well. Appointed U. S. Attorney for Maine by Jefferson, he served from 1802 to 1814; simultaneously, he held a Federalist state appointment as probate judge.

RUSSELL, BENJAMIN (1761–1845), b. Boston, Mass., son of an artisan; attended lower schools; apprenticed to Isaiah Thomas in the printing trade; private soldier in the Revolution. From 1784 to 1828, he edited the Boston *Centinel* (title varied); member, Mass. House of Representatives, 1805–1821, 1828–1835; State Senate, 1822, 1825; Council, 1836–1837; president, Boston Board of Health. In his first issue of the *Centinel* he declared, "Uninfluenced by party, we aim only to be just" [24 Mar. 1784]. That this was more than merely a masthead motto, even as late as 1800, is evidenced in the general dissatisfaction of party Federalists, tacitly expressed in their support of an electioneering paper in the *Palladium*. But by 1805 he was deeply involved in partisan activity [Benjamin Russell to Charles Prentiss, 16 Apr. 1805, in Prentiss Papers, Amer. Antiq. Soc.]. His paper received support from the Federal party after the founding of the *Palladium;* its content suggests that it served the cause in the southeastern counties of Massachusetts. Russell himself also was among the founders of the Washington Society in Boston; he was active in the powerful Initial Caucuses, and labored to improve and extend party discipline among Boston Federalists [Morison, *Otis*, I, 295].

THORNDIKE, ISRAEL (1755–1832), b. Beverly, Mass., to a family of impoverished farmer-seamen; attended common schools; served in privateers during the Revolution; merchant residing in Beverly to 1810, Boston thereafter; at his death his fortune exceeded one million dollars. In 1801, his old-fashioned elitism and mercantilist economic ideas [Thorndike to Nathan Read, 2 Jan. 1801; see also J. D. Forbes, *Israel Thorndike, Federalist Financier* (New York, 1953), pp. 99–133] were similar to other members of the Essex clique, George Cabot, Theophilus Parsons, Stephen Higginson, and Jonathan Jackson (qq.v.), with whom he was intimate. But unlike any other member of that fabled junto, he was regularly a member of Federalist electioneering committees, including the Central Committee [Otis to Sullivan, 17 Aug. 1812, in Misc. Mss., N. Y. Public Library; Morison, *Otis*, I, 318. See also my "Myth of the Essex Junto," pp. 198, 234, passim].

WELLES, ARNOLD (1761–1827), insurance company president in Boston. In the 1790s he publicly identified himself with the open elitism of the old school, quoting Ogilvie thus:

'Tis just:—The noble mind by fortune raised,
And warmed by strong benevolence to spread
Its happiness to all; displays to man
His maker's image. To a god-like few
Heaven gives at once the virtue and the power.

[*An Address to . . . the Mass. Charitable Soc.* (Boston, 1797)]. But as founder and first president of the Washington Society in Boston, he associated himself with the covert elitism of the young Federalists.

Young Federalists

ADAMS, BENJAMIN (1764–1837), b. Mendon, Mass.; A.B., Brown, 1788; lawyer residing in Uxbridge, Mass.; member, Mass. House of Representatives, 1809–1814; U. S. Congress, 1816–1821 [Andrew N. Adams, *A Genealogical History of Henry Adams* (Rutland, Vt., 1898), p. 410]. Adams spoke rarely in Congress; but he was prominent among young Federalists who sought to exploit the slavery question shortly *before* the Missouri question became a crisis [*AC*, 15/1/837, 29 Jan. 1818]. He was also active in debate upon the Missouri question itself, and clearly with a view to its impact on public opinion [ibid., 16/2/1236–

1237, 26 Feb. 1821; see also Glover Moore, *The Missouri Controversy 1819–1821* (Lexington, Ky., 1953), p. 178; as modified by Livermore, *The Twilight of Federalism*, pp. 88–97].

ADAMS, JOHN QUINCY (1767–1848): see above, chapter II.

BIGELOW, ABIJAH (1775–1860), b. Westminster, Mass.; A.B., Dartmouth, 1795; lawyer residing in Leominster, and after 1817, in Worcester; member, Mass. House of Representatives, 1807–1809; U. S. Congress, 1810–1815. His ethics and attitudes echoed old-school ideals —"I should always wish to have my political conduct be such as to meet the approbation of my constituents," he wrote to his wife, "but this wish should never induce me to act directly contrary to the dictates of my conscience" ["Letters of Abijah Bigelow," *Amer. Antiq. Soc. Proceedings*, n.s., XL (1930), 367]. But he participated in party operations in Worcester County, belonging regularly to county and town committees [Benjamin Ferris et al. to Abijah Bigelow, 18 Aug. 1812, and many similar circulars in Broadsides Coll., Amer. Antiq. Soc.]. Although he remained faithful to old-school economic ideals, he brought popular rhetoric to their defense [see his "bread from the mouth of labor" speech, AC 12/2/878, 23 Jan. 1813]. Bigelow was the compiler of *The Voter's Guide: Or, The Powers, Duty and Privileges of the Constitutional Voters in the Commonwealth of Massachusetts* (Leominster, 1807), a compendium of extracts from Montesquieu and Paley, Blair, Burgh, Rollin, Washington, and Caleb Strong, critical of party spirit and crowded with the conventional wisdom of the old school. But the fact that Bigelow undertook such a work was in itself significant. Acknowledging the fact of expanding popular power and participation, he declared that in America the "difference is not essential" between "representative republicanism and democracy." With many other young Federalists, Bigelow took an agnostic view of political philosophy. Quoting with approval Pope's statement, "For forms of government, let fools contest," which had so infuriated John Adams and others of the Revolutionary generation, Bigelow commented, "We firmly believe there is more truth and justice in the remark, than many speculative and theoretical writers are willing to admit" [p. 11].

BIGELOW, TIMOTHY (1767–1821), b. Worcester, Mass.; A.B., Harvard, 1782; studied law with Levi Lincoln; practised law in Boston and resided in Medford, Mass. As speaker of the Massachusetts House of Representatives (1805–1806, 1808–1810, 1812–1820) and as a member of the Central Committee, he was a powerful figure in the Federalist organization in Massachusetts. His *Address delivered on the 3d Anni-*

versary of the Washington Benevolent Society (Boston, 1814) was an apologia for popularly oriented partisan activity [pp. 10–11, 14] which paid lip service to equality [p. 8], popular sovereignty [p. 14], minimal government [p. 7], and the freedom of speech, press, and assembly [p. 18] which the Federal party required.

BRADBURY, GEORGE (1770–1823), b. Falmouth, Mass.; A.B., Harvard, 1789; lawyer in Portland; member, Mass. House of Representatives, 1806–1810, 1811–1812; U. S. Congress, 1813–1817. Although Bradbury, in his own words, "was not in the habit of obtruding his opinions and views of subjects upon the House" [AC 14/1/918, 7 Feb. 1816], he openly articulated a conception of representation as an agency, a particular responsibility for the special interests and needs of the electing constituency [ibid.; see also 14/2/806–807, 31 Jan. 1817], abandoning the old-school ideal of representation as a trust, an enlarged responsibility for the transcendent interests of the nation, and society. He also spoke against a tariff, on the ground that commerce could best look after itself. Though he acknowledged the right of government to regulate the trade of its citizens, he questioned its expediency. "To restore this trade is, indeed, all important; but I am disposed to think it cannot be effected by measures merely compulsory," he declared. "The restrictive energies of this country have, in my judgment, had a fair experiment; and, as was observed on another occasion the other day, 'been found wanting'" [ibid., 14/1/919, 7 Feb. 1816].

CHANNING, FRANCIS DANA (1775–1811), b. Newport, R. I.; A.B., Harvard, 1794; lawyer in Boston; as a member of the powerful Central Committee in Boston, he promoted party organization among Massachusetts Federalists and exhorted local committees to active competition with Jeffersonians for popular support [Channing et al. to Thomas W. Ward et al., 10 Apr. 1810; Channing et al. to Abijah Bigelow et al., 13 Apr. 1810, in Broadsides, Amer. Antiq. Soc.].

DANE, JOSEPH (1778–1858), b. Beverly, Mass.; A.B., Harvard, 1799; lawyer in Kennebunk, Me.; U. S. Congress, 1820–1823. His *Oration pronounced at Kennebunk* (1809) was an effort to turn libertarian and egalitarian ideas against the Jeffersonians and to establish a popular base for the Federal cause of covert elitism.

DERBY, ELIAS HASKET (1766–1826), b. Salem, Mass.; attended Harvard; import merchant in Salem; later, manufacturer of broadcloth. Derby was active in the Federalist "political club," which introduced the "zeal of caucussing" to Salem [*Life, Journals and Correspondence of Rev. Manasseh Cutler*, II, 42].

DEXTER, FRANKLIN (1793–1857), b. Charlestown, Mass.; A.B., Harvard, 1812; m. Catherine, daughter of William Prescott (q.v.); lawyer practising in Boston. His *Oration delivered July 4th, 1819* (Boston, 1819) was a restrained young Federalist appeal to the "enlightened spirit of liberty." Echoes of an older conservatism ring throughout, however.

DUTTON, WARREN (1774–1857), b. East Haddam, Conn.; A.B., Yale, 1797; studied theology with Timothy Dwight (q.v.); after 1800, lawyer and journalist in Boston, and editor of the *New England Palladium* (see above, chapter VII). His *Oration pronounced July 4, 1805* (Boston, 1805) conceded a point to the old school—"popular governments are destroyed by popular means"—but contended that they could only be preserved and controlled in the same way. Exhorting Federalists of Massachusetts to active competition for popular support, he warned, "The timid and the wary, who fear to act, lest they should be acted upon, who hope to obtain favor from their neutrality, will find that the evils of anarchy will fall indiscriminately" [p. 15].

DWIGHT, JOSIAH (1767–1821), b. Springfield?, Mass.; A.B., Harvard, 1786; country merchant in business with his brother-in-law, William T. Edwards; resident of Stockbridge, Mass. As chairman of Federalist county committees, he promoted the policies of the Central Committee, and labored to unify a party beneath it. Seeking to "excite the attention of the people" to his cause, he circulated pamphlets through western Massachusetts, arranged nominating meetings, sponsored Washington Societies, and took a leading role in the dangerous game of playing upon the sectional prejudices of the New England yeomanry [Dwight to Otis, 18 Nov. 1805, 16 Mar. 1808, in Morison, *Otis*, I, 312–313, 333].

ELWELL, ROBERT (c. 1765–1824), b. Gloucester, Mass., son of a merchant; himself a merchant residing in Gloucester; member, Mass. House of Representatives, 1810–1812; a central figure in the Federalist organization in his town, he organized and controlled public meetings, and looked after communications with the Central Committee in Boston ["A meeting of Federalists of Gloucester," n.d. [1815], in Misc. Mss., Mass. Hist. Soc.; John J. Babson, *History of the Town of Gloucester* (1860), p. 510].

EDWARDS, WILLIAM (1770–1851), b. Northampton, Mass.; trained as a tanner; his many innovations revolutionized his calling; he became the operator of the largest tannery in the U.S.; m. Rebecca, sister of Lewis Tappan (q.v.); committee chairman in his county, and a leader of the Federal party in Northampton, where he resided. Edwards also served as an emissary between Massachusetts and New York Federalists; he later removed to the latter state [William H. Edwards, *Timothy and Rhoda Edwards* (Cincinnati, 1903), passim; A. E. Winship, *Jukes-Edwards, A Study in Education and Heredity* (Harrisburg, 1903), pp. 67–73; Morison, *Otis,* I, 313, II, 29].

HALE, NATHAN (1784–1863), b. Westhampton, Mass.; A.B., Williams, 1804; lawyer, journalist in Boston, later president of the Boston and Worcester Railroad. He organized and led meetings of "the young Federalists of Boston" and was a member of the standing committee of the Washington Society, urging his young friends to "every fair and honorable exertion" [Boston *New Eng. Palladium,* 16 July 1811; Loring, *Hundred Boston Orators,* pp. 368–369]. Hale was best known as editor of the *Weekly Messenger* and the *Daily Advertiser,* Mass. Hist. Soc. *Pro.* XVIII (1881) 270–279.

JACKSON, CHARLES (1775–1855), b. Newburyport, Mass.; A.B., Harvard, 1793; studied law with Theophilus Parsons (q.v.) and practised in Boston. His *Oration delivered before . . . St. Peter's Lodge* (1798) articulated a covert elitism. The people, he declared, were not to be controlled by "inventing new systems of morality—It is not by 'wire-drawn' dissertations on soul duties—by amplifying and straining to hyperbole the sentiments of philanthropy and universal beneficence. It is by the silent but powerful influence of habit and example." As a regular member of the Central Committee, Jackson sought to reinforce habit and example by the silent but powerful influence of a party organization [Morison, *Otis,* I, 318–319].

JARVIS, WILLIAM (1780–1836), b. near Boston, Mass.; son of Charles Jarvis; lawyer residing in Stockbridge and Pittsfield, Mass.; member, Mass. House of Representatives, 1821–1824. A Federalist despite his name and parentage, his *Oration delivered at Pittsfield* (Stockbridge, 1812) found a new meaning in the old text of Bolingbroke. "Let us not neglect, in our party, such means as are in our power to keep the cause of truth, of reason, of virtue, and of liberty alive." He specified two prior objectives—the dissemination of the Federal message among "the great mass of the citizens" and the organization of a Federal party "to unite in good men" [George A. Jarvis, *The Jarvis Family* (Hartford, 1879), p. 208].

KING, CYRUS (1772–1817), b. Scarboro, Me.; A.B., Columbia, 1794; secretary to his half-brother, Rufus King (q.v.) in England, 1796; lawyer in Saco, Me.; U. S. Congress, 1813–1817. After Daniel Webster (q.v.), King stood foremost among the "Federal demagogues" whom John W.

Hulbert (q.v.) condemned in Congress. In speeches addressed less to Congressional colleagues than to his constituents [AC 13/2/1076, 20 Jan. 1814] he pandered to Jeffersonian prejudices, delivering impassioned harangues in defence of direct popular sovereignty and minimal government [see, e.g., his demagogic speeches against the Bank of the United States, AC, 13/3/450, 22 Oct. 1814, and against the compensation bill, 14/2/503–507, 14 Jan. 1817]. King's use of democratic ideology extended even to extracts from Thomas Paine's most radical pamphlets, quoted against the administration [13/3/721, 3 Dec. 1814].

KNAPP, SAMUEL LORENZO (1783–1838), b. Newburyport, Mass.; A.B., Dartmouth, 1804; lawyer practising in Newburyport and prominent young Federalist polemist; founder and secretary of the Washington Society in his town [Currier, Newburyport, II, 135–136]. His Oration delivered before the Associated Disciples of Washington (1812) was an argument for "unceasing assiduity" in partisan activity [p. 14]. He undertook the task of persuading older Federalists to support young party leaders [p. 15] at the same time that he sought to attract the very young, who were just entering upon adulthood [p. 21].

LLOYD, JAMES (1769–1831), b. Boston, Mass.; A.B., Harvard, 1787; import merchant and banker in Boston; member, Mass. House of Representatives, 1800–1801; Mass. Senate, 1804; U. S. Senate, 1808–1813, 1822–1826. In the Senate, he served as the guardian of the interests of Boston's mercantile community [AC, 12/1/228–235, 6 May 1812]. But he made full use of democratic rhetoric, even declaring, "In this country it may emphatically be said the vox populi is the vox Dei" [ibid., 10/2/422, 21 Feb. 1809]. Though he favored a strong navy and a national bank, he generally endorsed strict interpretation of the Constitution, minimal government, and the sanctity of property [ibid., 10/2/254, 19 Dec. 1809]. In 1814, he labored with other young Federalists to control the rampant sectionalism of New England, which his widely read speeches on the embargo and the war had helped to stimulate. But even when he tried to cool the fiery spirit of secessionism, he sought to do so "without refrigerating the popular zeal" against the administration [Morison, Otis, II, 88–92].

LONGFELLOW, STEPHEN (1775?–1849), b. Gorham, Cumberland Co., Me.; A.B., Harvard, 1798; lawyer practising in Portland; member, Mass. House of Representatives, 1814–1815; delegate to the Hartford Convention; U. S. Congress, 1823–1825. His Oration Pronounced July 4, 1804 (Portland, 1804) attacked Republican electioneering but exhorted friends of order to similar partisan activity. In 1814, he was engaged in Otis's game—seeking to rouse the people of New England by appeals to their sectional pride. "I hope and trust there is sufficient energy and spirit in the people of New England to vindicate their rights at every hazard," he declared. But he joined in the effort to prevent that spirit from issuing in secession [Boston *Weekly Messenger*, 2 Dec. 1814; Morison, *Otis*, II, 115, 189, 191]. In Congress, he urged retirement.

LOWELL, JOHN (1769–1840), b. Newburyport, Mass., son of John Lowell (1743–1802) q.v.; A.B., Harvard, 1786; lawyer, gentleman farmer residing in Roxbury, Mass. This prolific pamphleteer and popular caucus orator was as extreme as Timothy Pickering in his hostility to the national administration and to the Union as well. Though honored by his alma mater with an LL.D., he was not trusted by other young Federalists [Quincy, *Josiah Quincy*, pp. 241–242]. Lowell reciprocated their suspicion, describing Otis, who was so much more sensitive to the set and drift of popular opinion, as "naturally timid and frequently wavering— today bold, and tomorrow like a hare quivering in every breeze" [Morison, *Otis*, II, 116]. The party leaders of Boston made good use of his particular talents in the great mass meetings at Fanueil Hall, where he exploited the pseudo-democratic rhetoric of young Federalists with the same abandon that characterized his criticism of the administration [Boston *New Eng. Palladium*, 2 Apr. 1811]. But the fact that his name was absent from the roster of the Central Committee before 1819 suggests that he was not admitted to the inner councils, by party leaders who feared his sectionalist fervor during the Madisonian era. In the Missouri controversy, however, he took a much more moderate part, helping Otis to quiet the New England temper [William Tudor to Rufus King, 12 Feb. 1820, in *King*, VI, 273]. Thereafter, he became more acceptable at the headquarters of good principles; indeed, they were removed to his home, where Federal caucuses convened in 1823 [Lowell to Otis, 26 Feb. 1823, in Morison, *Otis*, II, 253].

LYMAN, JOSEPH (1767–1847), b. Northampton, Mass.; A.B., Yale, 1783; studied law with Caleb Strong (q.v.) and practised in Northampton, Mass., where he held many town and county offices. In December, 1800, Lyman appears to have been in something very near to a state of shock. "The restlessness of the people under such unrivalled prosperity derived from an excellent administration is one of the strange things in the history of man," he wrote in wonder and bewilderment [to Sedgwick, 28 Dec. 1800; in Sedgwick Papers, Mass. Hist. Soc.]. But he was an early and active participant in the organization of a Federal party in the Connecticut Valley. He convened private meetings of "the most discreet and intelligent inhabitants of the old county of Hampshire" to concert policy [to Noah Webster, 5 Jan. 1814, in Webster Papers, N. Y. Public Library] and public meetings to attract popular support [Morison, *Otis*, II, 87]. A member of the Hartford Convention, he played a major part in the sectional movement.

LYMAN, THEODORE (1792–1849), b. Boston, son of Theodore Lyman (1755–1839) q.v.; A.B., Harvard, 1810; independently wealthy, he made a full-time hobby of political journalism. Lyman was a choice specimen of that spectacular political hybrid, *Federalis Jacksonians*. In his *Oration presented July 4, 1820* (Boston, 1820), an invocation of "the freedom and equality of man" [p. 7], he brought Jeffersonian rhetoric to the defense of the federal party. After the crippling defeat of 1824, he wrote to Daniel Webster, "It appears to me that the Federal party in Massachusetts and the great mass of the Federalists themselves is as democratic as the democrats—the only difference is that the last are known by that name—certainly a great advantage if it has secured the voices of those who are carried along by the current of society. . . .The increase of democratic talent, respectability and wealth in Boston the last two years, entirely owing to gradual secessions, is very great and having once begun, will constantly be greater. What can we do, therefore, having lost our own fortress, but take the enemy's camp" [quoted in Livermore, *Twilight of Federalism*, p. 119]. Lyman acted upon his own suggestion, becoming editor of the *Jackson Republican*, in which he attacked John Quincy Adams (q.v.) for allegedly retaining old-fashioned federal principles. "The leading trait in the opinions of Mr. Adams is a distrust of the qualifications of the people, in matters of government. His opinions were formed in the school of Burke, who adopted it as a leading principle, that government is, in sound theory, if not in its actual origin, a *compact*, in which the people and the government are respectively the contracting parties. Our government, on the other hand, derives entirely from the people" [quoted in ibid., p. 220].

MESSINGER, DANIEL (1768–1846), b. Wrentham, Norfolk Co., Mass.; educated in common schools; hatter (manufacturer and retailer) in Boston [Boston *Repertory*, 19 Mar. 1808; John Ward Dean, "Memoir of Daniel Messinger of Boston," *New Eng. Hist. and Gen. Quarterly*, XVI (1862), 305–307]. He was prominent among "a number of young men of this town" who established the Washington Benevolent Society, being elected vice-president [Boston *New England Palladium*, 25 Feb. 1812]. A regular member of both the State Central Committee and the Boston Town Committee in the Federalist organization, Messinger put his name to many committee communications and exhortations to bring out the vote for Federal candidates [see, e.g., "Sir, At a very numerous and respectable convention . . ." 20 Mar. 1806, in Broadsides, Essex Institute; "To the Federal Republicans," 21 Mar. 1820, in Broadsides, Mass. Hist. Soc.].

MILLS, ELIJAH HUNT (1776–1829), b. Chesterfield, Mass.; A.B., Williams, 1797; lawyer in Northampton, Mass.; member, Mass. Senate, 1811; U. S. Congress, 1815–1819, Mass. House of Representatives, 1820 (speaker); U. S. Senate, 1821–1827. Mills was an exceptional figure among the young Federalists. He participated in the creation of an organized opposition party—"Painful indeed is the task to proclaim the follies and expose the wickedness of our rulers. But these are no ordinary times" [An Oration Pronounced at Northampton (1813)]. On occasion, he was not above the use of popular rhetoric [AC 15/2/1144, 9 Feb. 1819]. But Mills was one of the few young Federalists who continued to articulate in public the social and political ideals of the old school. In debate on the Compensation Law, which was the occasion of much "Federal demagoguery" from men such as Cyrus King and Daniel Webster (qq.v.), Mills openly proclaimed his contempt for democracy. "No, sir, I did not obtain the honor of a seat in this House by flattering the prejudices of my constituents," he declared. ". . . Much less do I come in forma pauperis, to propitiate the offended majesty of the people, by a sacrifice of opinions, deliberately formed and honestly entertained, upon the altar of popular favor" [ibid., 14/2/658, 20 Jan. 1817]. Mills warmed to his subject, and with the fervor of deep conviction he said, " 'The voice of the people is the voice of God,' is a maxim which, by a perversion of its true meaning, has become more fallacious in principle, and more dangerous in its consequences, than any other which the frenzy of political madness can conceive. It has prostrated the wisdom of the ages, and drenched the earth with the blood of its inhabitants. In one respect, indeed, does 'the voice of the people' sometimes resemble the 'voice of the Almighty,' in the terror of its power, rather than the perfection of its wisdom" [ibid., p. 663]. Mills preferred to hark unto "the still small voice of reason." But having gone this far, Mills was unable to stop. The climax of his speech was an orgasm of oratorical imagery, in which the voice of the people was the "lightning" and "thunder," "tornado" and "earthquake," "fire" and "flood," "whirlpool" and "tidal wave" [pp. 663–664]. Outbursts such as this were rare, even in the speeches of Mills himself. His accustomed mood was a quiet determination—not merely conservative but reactionary—to restore the American republic to its original purity [see, e.g., ibid., 17/2/128, 16 Jan. 1823; 18/1/59, 29 Dec. 1823]. In 1824 he supported Jackson, whom he took to be a gentleman worthy of Federalist backing—"his manners, though formed in the wilds of the west, exceedingly polished and polite" [Mills to wife, 22 Jan. 1824, in Henry Cabot Lodge, "Letters of Hon. Elijah H. Mills," *Mass. Hist. Soc. Proceedings*, XIX (1881–1882), 12–53, 41].

OTIS, HARRISON GRAY (1765–1848): see above, chapter II.

PERKINS, THOMAS HANDASYD (1764–1854), b. Boston, Mass.; educated in common schools; import merchant (heavy investments in China trade) and banker in Boston. His heavy profits, partly gained in the opium trade [Briggs, *Cabot Family*, II, 573], sustained many philanthropies, including the Boston Athenaeum, the Mass. General Hospital, and the Perkins School for the Blind. Perkins was unusual among New England merchants for the depth of his political commitment and the breadth of his involvement. He served not merely in state offices (Mass. House of Representatives, 1806–1807, 1821; Mass. Senate, 1805, 1813, 1817, 1822–1823) but also as a member of the Federalists' State Central Committee ["Treason Detected! Or, the Federal Circular Exposed" (1811), in Broadsides, Amer. Antiq. Soc.; Perkins to Sullivan, 10 May 1811, in Morison, *Otis*, I 316], as president of mass meetings [*Palladium*, 2 Apr. 1811], and in 1815 as a member of the Mass. "embassy" to Washington. As late as 1822 he was working indefatigably to unify the federal party in Boston and to enlarge its popular base [Perkins to Otis, 5 Apr. 1822, in Morison, *Otis*, II, 251–253; Boston *Centinel* 10 Apr. 1822]. Timothy Pickering (q.v.) condemned him, in language similar to that employed to describe Harrison Gray Otis and John Quincy Adams (qq.v.), as an unscrupulous office-seeker [to William Coleman, 30 Apr. 1827, in Pickering Papers, Mass. Hist. Soc.].

PHILLIPS, JOHN (1770–1823), b. Boston, Mass.; attended Harvard; read law with Thomas Dawes and practised in Boston. His *Oration pronounced July 4, 1794* (Boston, 1794) was a paean, in old-school fashion, to government by "sages and heroes." But after 1800, as president of the Mass. Senate and as a regular member of the state Central Committee he exhorted his federal brethren to assist in the establishment of a popularly oriented party. "Above all," he wrote, "let every man be urged and engaged to attend the elections, and let arrangements be made to bring out by all honorable means the greatest possible strength" [to Theodore Sedgwick, 8 Mar. 1809, in Sedgwick Papers, Mass. Hist. Soc.]. In 1822, with the joint support of the Federal organization and the insurgent "middling interest," he was elected first mayor of Boston [Quincy, *Josiah Quincy*, p. 393; Morison, *Otis*, II, 239].

PICKMAN, BENJAMIN (1763–1843), b. Salem, Mass.; A.B., Harvard, 1784; married daughter of Elias H. Derby; studied law but abandoned it for commerce; president of the Salem Bank, and colonel of the Salem Regiment; member, Mass. House of Representatives, 1797–1802, 1812–1813; Mass. Senate, 1803; Mass. Council, 1805, 1808, 1813–1814, 1819–1821; U. S. Congress, 1809–1811. This man, whose supper parties were thought "worthy of a palace and a prince," chose to identify himself to the public as "one who before the Embargo got his Bread by the Sweat of his Brow," suggesting that a wealthy merchant-banker was a labouring man. Active in the Federalist organization in Essex County, he supplied a slogan for the cause of covert elitism. "We must follow, instead of leading, the public opinion," he declared [AC, 11/2/1290, 20 Jan. 1810; cf. his private thoughts in Pickman to Nathan Read, 28 Dec. 1801, in Read Papers, Essex Institute].

POLLARD, BENJAMIN (1780–1836), b. Boston; lawyer in Boston; clerk, Mass. House of Representatives, 1811–1815; City Marshal, 1822–1836 [Maurice J. Pollard, *History of the Pollard Family* (Dover, 1961), p. 78; Boston *Centinel*, 23 Nov. 1836]. A favorite caucus orator [*Palladium*, 2 Apr. 1811], his oratorical efforts to woo the people to the federal party are satirized in *The Boston Assemblage, or a Peep at Caucus Hall . . . by Tristram Trap'em Esq.* (Boston, 1812).

PRESCOTT, WILLIAM (1762–1844), b. Pepperell, Me.; A.B., Harvard, 1789; studied law with Nathan Dane (q.v.); lawyer, jurist in Beverly, 1787–1789, Salem to 1808, and Boston thereafter. For twenty-five years he sat either in the General Court or on the Governor's Council. His response to the debacle of 1800 was that of the old school. "There is perhaps something to hope from this experiment which we are obliged to try; if the people should find that the government is not administered with purer hands, nor their burthens lightened, nor the general prosperity increased, they may perhaps become less jealous and more contented in the future" [Prescott to Nathan Read, 22 Dec. 1800, in Read Papers, Essex Institute]. But after this fragile reed was broken in 1804, he took an active and leading part in the organization of a federal party in Massachusetts, sitting in the seats of partisan power, serving on the Central Committee [Otis to Sullivan, 17 Aug. 1812, in Misc. Mss., N. Y. Public Library]. He would also be a member of the Hartford Convention [P. G. Young, *The Stay and the Staff Taken Away: A Discourse Occasioned by the Death of the Hon. William Prescott* (Boston, 1844)].

QUINCY, JOSIAH (1772–1864), b. Boston, Mass.; A.B., Harvard, 1790; lawyer practising in Boston; member, Mass. Senate, 1804–1805, 1813–1820; U. S. Congress, 1805–1813; Mass. House of Representatives, 1821–1822 (speaker, 1822); mayor of Boston, 1823–1829; president, Harvard, 1829–1845. Unlike gentlemen of the old school who regarded political service as a duty, or a hobby, Quincy "intended *ab initio* to pursue politics as a profession" [Otis to Phillips, 1818, in Quincy, *Josiah Quincy*, p. 375]. When he entered upon public life, he was appalled but impressed by the professionalism of his opponents, and disheartened by the disorder of the federal cause. "Men who hesitate at everything contend at unequal odds with men who stick at nothing. A degree of organization has been effected in the opposite party unexampled, I suspect, in this country since the revolutionary committees of 1775" [to John Quincy Adams, 23 Nov. 1804, in Adams Family Papers, Mass. Hist. Soc.].

Rejecting the weak response of the old-school Federalists, whom he contemptuously described as "cautious politicians, who are always prophets by retrospect; men who neither devise nor execute" [ibid., 15 Dec. 1804], Quincy participated in the organization of Massachusetts Federalism, participating in open caucuses [*Palladium*, 2 Apr. 1811], serving as vice-president of the Washington Benevolent Society, and exhorting Federalists throughout New England to improve their party machinery and offer more effective competition for popular favor [to Noah Webster, 30 June 1806, in Webster Papers, N. Y. Pub. Library]. Quincy himself accepted the fact of party conflict and even welcomed it. "The state of things may be wholesome," he wrote. ". . . We shall have enough 'tossing about,' but that keeps the faculties in play" [Quincy, *Josiah Quincy*, p. 254]. Except for his support of the insurgent "middling interest" in 1822, which may have been an effort on his part to enlarge the popular base of Boston Federalism [cf. Quincy, *Josiah Quincy*, p. 393, and Morison, *Otis*, II, 239], he generally subordinated himself to party discipline [Quincy, *Josiah Quincy*, p. 94] and continued to identify himself as a Federalist as late as 1861, though voting for Whig and Republican candidates [ibid., p. 538]. The intensity of his partisanship appears in an attempt to impeach President Jefferson in January 1809, five weeks before the inauguration of Madison. Quincy's resolution was lost by a vote of 117 to 1, his own [AC, 10/2/1182, 25 Jan. 1809]. But he gained a notoriety which led Republicans whose political purity was in doubt to vindicate themselves by assaulting him in Congress. Quincy, in a letter to his wife, reported a conversation with Felix Grundy of Tennessee, "a perfect political jockey, and as good-humored as he is cunning. He said to me yesterday, 'Quincy, I thought I had abused you enough, but I find it will not do.'—'Why, what is the matter now? I do not mean to speak again.'—'No matter; by heavens, I must give you another thrashing'—'Why so?'—'Why, the truth is, a damned fellow has set up against me in my district,—a perfect Jacobin, as much worse than I am as worse can be. Now, except Tim Pickering, there is no man in the United States so perfectly hated by the people of my district as yourself. You must therefore excuse me. By God, I must abuse you, or I shall never get re-elected" [Quincy, *Josiah Quincy*, p. 303]. That such hatred developed is one of the many ironies of Quincy's public career. Without indulging in the demagoguery of other young Federalists, he sought an "honorable popularity" for himself and his party [to John Quincy Adams, 15 Dec. 1804, in Adams Family Papers], seeking in 1811–1812 to abandon the traditional foreign policy of his party and to exploit the anglophobia of the American people [Quincy to Otis, 8, 26 Nov. 1811, in Otis Papers, Mass. Hist. Soc.]. The result of an experiment in this direction was disappointing to him. "My fate is odd," he wrote. "By some I am thought such a raving Federalist as to be shrewdly suspected of being one of Henry's confidants; by others that I am so strongly hostile to the British that I am in danger of turning Democrat. The truth is, that there is an intermediate ground for an American politician to stand upon. That I seek, and when I think I have found it I shall not hesitate to defend it, let who will shake or wonder" [Quincy, *Josiah Quincy*, p. 253; see also his flirtation with the ideology of free trade, in chapter VIII, above; which must, however, be qualified by his interventionist acts as mayor of Boston]. The tone and spirit of his public speeches were a similar compromise. He professed to love the people, but declared that "The love of the people exactly resembles an honorable passion for a woman. In both cases, those whom in the days of courtship, extolled them as angels, never failed, in the time of attained power, to treat them as brutes; while those who truly loved them would not hesitate to remonstrate gently, even at the hazard of their displeasures, and to point out where their true happiness sat, where it always sits—enthroned between truth and virtue" [as reported in the Providence *American*, 24 Feb. 1809].

REED, JOHN (1781–1860), b. West Bridgewater, Mass.; A.B., Brown, 1803; academy principal, lawyer in Yarmouth, Mass.; U. S. Congress, 1813–1817; 1821–1841; Whig Lieutenant Governor of Mass., 1845–1851. In Congress he spoke only on the immediate interests of his district, argued for a close relationship between constituents and their agent-representative, and also advocated the consent of an interested minority to legislation of vital and particular importance, thus prefiguring the political theory of John C. Calhoun [AC, 14/1/739, 23 Jan. 1816; 18/1/1880–1888, 23 Mar. 1824].

REED, WILLIAM (1776–1837), b. Marblehead, Mass.; "limited education"; import merchant in Marblehead, Mass.; U. S. Congress, 1811–1815. His Congressional speeches, like those of John Reed (q.v.), were confined largely to the special interests of his mercantile constituency. In their defense, he paraphrased the political economy of Adam Smith. "Sir, I tremble," he said on the subject of the war embargo, "lest the only benefit I had ever anticipated for the immense sacrifices on this experiment, viz.: a practical demonstration of the axiom 'that interested individuals are the best judges of their own affairs,' and that much legislation ever distracts and destroys commerce . . ." [AC 13/1/1980, 5 Apr. 1814]. Yet so bitter was his partisanship that he voted against repeal of the embargo, on the avowed ground that "I am disinclined to its removal at the moment when the correction of the public mind is in rapid progression, and when a short time, without any new sacrifice, will so far cleanse the body politic, as to leave no further hopes to the expedients of quackery" [ibid., 1980, 2001–2002]. He was joined by a small handful of young Federalists, including Elisha Potter of Rhode Island (q.v.).

SEDGWICK, HENRY DWIGHT (1785–1831), b. Stockbridge, Mass.; A.B., Williams, 1804; lawyer in Stockbridge, and sometime journalist in Boston, where he edited the *Weekly Messenger*. A member of county committees and a tireless, self-effacing worker in the cause of party unity. In the 1811 campaign he was a sort of roving ambassador for the Central Committee, moving through western Massachusetts to intercept trouble before it could disrupt the electioneering effort. "My concern is *business* & not elegance—I shall go to every nook in the county where I can do the most good," he reported to William Sullivan (q.v.) [20 Apr. 1811, in Columbia Univ. Coll., Columbia Univ. Library]. Though he was cool to Quincy's suggestion for a reversal of foreign policy, he declared his willingness to go along, if it should be the will of the party [to Harmanus Bleecker, 16 Dec. 1811, in Sedgwick Papers, Mass. Hist. Soc.]. He embraced the laissez-faire principles of young Federalists wholeheartedly, however; in 1831 he would found a Free Trade Convention in Philadelphia [B. W. Dwight, *Descendents of John Dwight* (New York, 1874), II, 746].

STEDMAN, WILLIAM (1765–1831), b. Cambridge, Mass.; A.B. Harvard, 1784; lawyer practising in Lancaster, Mass.; U. S. Congress, 1803–1810. He played a leading part in the Worcester County organization ["To the Friends of Peace and Union," 8 Mar. 1814, in Broadsides, Amer. Antiq. Soc.]. In eight years of Congressional debate, his only major speech took a Jeffersonian view of appropriations, in which the legislature specified allocations in full detail [AC, 10/2/1975, 5 Apr. 1808].

SULLIVAN, WILLIAM (1774–1839), b. Biddeford, Me.; A.B., Harvard, 1792; lawyer, independently wealthy after 1829 through his wife's inheritance. As vice-president of the Washington Society in Boston and as a regular member of the Central Committee, he helped to concert party policy and to exhort local committees to get out the Federal vote [Sullivan et al. to Timothy Bigelow, 9 Feb. 1810, in Broadsides, Mass. Hist. Soc.; Sullivan et al. to Thomas W. Ward et al., 26 Feb. 1813, and to Dwight Foster, same date, in Broadsides, Mass. Hist. Soc.]. His memoirs, *Familiar Letters on Public Characters and Public Events* (Boston, 1834), leave an impression of firm independence and old-school integrity which is not merely inaccurate but positively deceitful. He was active in interstate politics, attending the New York meeting in 1812 [*Public Men of the Revolution*, p. 291] and was one of the Massachusetts ambassadors to Washington in 1815 [Morison, *Otis*, II, 160–173].

TAPPAN, LEWIS (1788–1873), b. Northampton, Mass.; educated in town schools; dry goods merchant residing in Boston. In his twenties this future abolitionist made Federalism his cause. His model was Alexander Hamilton, his guide "the great Locke" [Pocket Remembrancer, n.d. (post 1814), Lewis Tappan Papers, Library of Congress; Tappan to Benjamin Tappan, 9 Mar. 1818, in Benjamin Tappan Papers, Library of Congress]. Tappan was of two minds about political partisanship. "I will not justify men with parties; it is not generous; but it is sometimes expedient that one should adhere to a party although some measures do not appear just to him," he wrote [to Benjamin Tappan, 27 Dec. 1813, in Benjamin Tappan Papers, Library of Congress]. But he overcame his doubts and took an active part in the affairs of the Washington Society in Boston, attended caucuses, chaired ward committees, and distributed electioneering material [Pocket Remembrancer, 21–30 Apr. 1814, in Lewis Tappan Papers; Boston *New Eng. Palladium*, 25 Mar. 1814].

VAN SCHAACK, HENRY (c.1765–1845), b. Kinderhook, N. Y., son of Peter Van Schaack, q.v.; lawyer residing in Pittsfield, Mass., c.1781–1807 [J. E. A. Smith, *The History of Pittsfield* (Springfield, 1876), II, 7, passim]. He willingly subordinated himself to party discipline [to Theodore Sedgwick, 7 Feb. 1800, in Sedgwick Papers, Mass. Hist. Soc.]. After the retirement of Theodore Sedgwick (q.v.) he became "the leading political manager of Berkshire" [Birdsall, *Berkshire County*, p. 81; Van Schaack to Sedgwick, 9 Feb. 1801, in Sedgwick Papers].

WALDO, DANIEL (1763–1845), b. Boston, Mass.; educated in lower schools; hardware merchant in Worcester, Mass.; held many county and town offices; delegate to the Hartford Convention; State Senator, 1816–1819. Waldo was the central figure in the Federalist organization in Worcester, chairman of the County Committee, and founder of the Washington Benevolent Society in his town [Waldo et al. to Abijah Bigelow, 23 Mar. 1813, in Broadsides, Amer. Antiq. Soc.; untitled broadside in the same collection dated 1 Dec. 1813; Waldo et al. to Abraham Low et al., 7 Mar. 1812, in Broadsides, Mass. Hist. Soc.].

WARD, ARTEMAS (1762–1847), b. Shrewsbury, Mass.; A.B., Harvard, 1783; lawyer, jurist in Boston and after 1800 in Charlestown, Mass.

Member, Mass. House of Representatives, 1796–1800, 1811; U. S. Congress, 1813–1817; State Senate, 1818–1819. He served the Federal party in the usu·ª variety of ways—member, State Central Committee, officer of the Washington Society in Boston, and caucus orator. In Congress, his speeches were cast in libertarian language and addressed to the voters of his state. [AC 13/2/1812, 5 Mar. 1814; 13/3/904, 14 Dec. 1814].

WHITWELL, BENJAMIN (1772–1825), b. Boston, Mass.; A.B., Harvard, 1790; studied law with John Sprague, married his daughter and moved to Maine, where he practised in Hallowell and Augusta [North, *History of Augusta,* passim]. Whitwell helped to establish a net of Federalist committees in Maine; he was also the projector of political fraternities, sponsor of electioneering newspapers, and coordinator of campaigns, all in order to awaken "the sleeping Sampson of Federalism" [Whitwell to Otis, 31 July 1804, in Otis Papers, Mass. Hist. Soc.; to William Sullivan, 24 Aug. 1804, and to Theophilus Parsons, 3 Aug. 1804, in Columbia Univ. Coll., Columbia Univ. Library].

WILDE, SAMUEL SUMNER (1771–1855), b. Taunton, Mass.; A.B., Dartmouth, 1789; lawyer and jurist in Hallowell, Me.; member, Mass. House of Representatives, 1798–1799; delegate to the Hartford Convention; associate justice, Supreme Courts of Mass. and Me., 1815–1850. In the 1790s Wilde made an early effort to use popular, libertarian language in the Federal cause. "Let us once more rally, round the *pole of liberty,*" he declared, in a year when other Federalists were engaged in cutting them down [*Oration delivered at Thomaston, July 4, 1797* (Hallowell, 1797)]. He collaborated with his friend Benjamin Whitwell in seeking to systematize Maine Federalism; a friend and correspondent of Harrison Gray Otis (q.v.), he was an important link between the Federalists of Maine and the Central Committee in Boston [Whitwell to Sullivan, 24 Aug. 1804, Columbia Univ. Coll.; Morison, *Otis,* I, 234].

RHODE ISLAND

Federalists of the Old School

BOURN, BENJAMIN (1755–1808), b. Bristol, R. I.; A.B., Harvard, 1775; served briefly in the Continental Army as quartermaster of the second R. I. Regt.; lawyer practising in Providence. Bourn was a member of a "political club" in Providence which included Jabez Bowen and John Brown (qq.v.) among its members, and which appears to have been the headquarters of national principles in Rhode Island during the 1780s and 1790s. After the state's belated entry into the Union, this convivial clique of like-minded men gained its reward in the form of federal patronage:

Bourn's share alone amounted to a lucrative customs office and two U. S. judgeships. As Rhode Island's first U. S. Congressman (1790–1796), Bourn was a quiet backbencher; but his occasional speeches suggest the peculiar quality of Rhode Island Federalism. Like friends of order in every state, he sought to strengthen respect and deference to "constituted authorities" [AC 4/1/1106, 20 Apr. 1796]. But at the same time he showed an aversion to measures "disagreeable to the people," which rarely appeared in older Federalists of other states [ibid., 4/1/844–845, 1 Apr. 1796]. Without actively engaging in partisan rivalry, without pursuing popular opinion with the directness of younger Federalists, he sought the middle way, "republican firmness and political wisdom, which dignify the nation and endear its government to the people" [Address to John Adams, 1798, quoted in Wm. R. Sprague, *Annals of the Town of Providence* (Providence, 1843), p. 369].

BOWEN, JABEZ (1739–1815), b. Providence, R. I.; physician, owner of the largest apothecary shop in Providence; m. Polly Brown, cousin of John Brown (q.v.), and shared in the manufacturing and commercial enterprises of that family; wealthy speculator in land, goods, and paper; his many state offices included the lieutenant governorship, 1784–1786; active also in church affairs (Congregational) and chancellor of R. I. College [G. S. Kimball, *Providence in Colonial Times* (Boston, 1912), pp. 302, passim; Mack Thompson, *Moses Brown*, p. 262; MacDonald, *We the People*, p. 342]. The contours of his public career paralleled those of Bourn's. A member of the Hopkins faction before the Revolution, and of the "political club" in Providence, his active support of the U. S. Constitution was rewarded with a ripe plum, the office of Commissioner of Loans, with a salary of six hundred dollars [Lovejoy, *Rhode Island Politics and the American Revolution*, p. 114; Jabez Bowen et al. to Thomas Allen et al., 31 Mar. 1790, in Broadsides, Mass. Hist. Soc.; "Additional Estimate of Monies," 6 Aug. 1790, in Syrett, ed., *Papers of Alexander Hamilton*, VI, 536]. A contemporary described him as "emphatically a gentleman of the old school, dignified in his deportment and rather aristocratic in his bearing" [Danforth, "Pictures of Providence," *R. I. History* 10 (1950), 195–199]. But though he favored "energy in government" in conventional old-school fashion, his public statements discovered a healthy respect for popular opinions [*To the Freemen of the State of Rhode Island* (Providence, 1786)]. After the Embargo, he assisted in the organization of the Federal party in his state [Bowen et al. to Henry Comstock, 22 Aug. 1810, in Broadsides, Amer. Antiq. Soc.].

BROWN, JOHN (1736–1803), b. Providence, R. I.; educated in local schools; merchant in the West Indian, African, and China trades; manufacturer of candles, rum, and iron products; banker and speculator;

trustee and treasurer of Brown University. Crude, vain, expansive, aggressive, his career was more crowded with acts than words. A member of the Sons of Liberty in Providence, he was the central figure in the *Gaspee* affair [William R. Leslie, "The Gaspee Affair," *Miss. Valley Hist. Rev.*, 39 (1952), 233–256; James B. Hedges, *The Browns of Providence Plantations* (Cambridge, 1952), pp. 208–213]. After Rhode Island's ratification of the U. S. Constitution, an act which Brown strongly supported, his bank was used for the deposit of federal funds in Rhode Island [Thompson, *Moses Brown*, p. 252]. As U. S. Congressman (1799–1801) he took small part in debate but spoke out against the growth of party consciousness, which he regarded as nothing better than a bad joke, and in defense of slavery. "He did not hold a slave in the world, he said, but he was as much for supporting the rights and property of those who did, as though he was a slave owner. He considered this as much personal property as a farm or a ship" [AC 6/1/232–233, 2 Jan. 1800]. But an admonitory letter to his son James suggests that he cherished the elitist ideals of the old school, and after the fashion of Rhode Island Federalism, combined them with a tough-minded appraisal of popular power. "You have an Education and may probably have a considerable Fortin [sic] if Heaven doeth not lift her Rod against us," he wrote. "Why should you not give a part of your time to the Publick, its a Duty the man of welth and abillitys owes his Fellow men. I wish you to take a seat in our General Assembly in my Place Next Spring, provided you do not cross the Atlantic. You must not suffer yourself to be Hortey [haughty], high-minded nor so proud as to look Down on those of a Smaller kind of Mortalls but learn so much of the Courtyer as to please the poore as well as the Rich. Mr. Howall is a good examplar [David Howell, q.v.]" [F. H. Brown, "A Colonial Merchant to his Son," *R. I. Hist. Colls.*, 34 (1941), 47–57].

FOSTER, THEODORE (1752–1828), b. Brookfield, Mass.; brother of Dwight Foster, q.v.; A.B., Brown, 1770; lawyer in Providence; town clerk, 1775–1787; secretary, R. I. Board of War, 1776–1781; member, R. I. General Assembly, 1776–1782, 1812–1816; U. S. Senate, 1790–1803; a relation of the Fenners, and a trimmer in his politics, untrammeled by party dependency. In the 1790s his voting record was decidedly Federalist, but at the end of the century he became a correspondent of Thomas Jefferson, and after the Embargo returned to the Federal side [W. E. Foster, "Sketch of the Life and Services of Theodore Foster," *R. I. Hist. Colls.*, VII (1885), 111–134].

HOWELL, DAVID (1747–1824), b. Morristown, N. J.; A.B., Princeton, 1766; lawyer practising in Providence; tutor in Brown, 1766–1769, professor, 1769–1779, 1790–1824, and acting president, 1791–1792;

member, Continental Congress, 1782–1785; U. S. District Judge, 1812–1824. Notwithstanding his famous indiscretion [Burnett, *Continental Congress*, pp. 530–534], he was a model of old-school decorum, the personification of its precepts. At the end of the war, he reaffirmed his commitment to "serve the people and the cause of real liberty," and remained faithful to it, in his fashion [to Moses Brown, 24 Aug. 1783, in Burnett, *Letters of Members of the Continental Congress*, VII, 280]. Though an elitist in his own politics [to William Greene, 23 Aug. 1785, in ibid., VIII, 198–200], he was openly hostile to the vices of the American elite, critical of speculators generally and of "men vulgarly called Land robbers, or Land-Sharks" [to William Greene, 29 Apr. 1785, in ibid., VIII, 106–107]. The critical period was in his view primarily a moral crisis in which the republican virtue of America was threatened by prosperity. "Wealth begets luxury, luxury corrupts," he wrote, "corruption and a general depravity of manners [are] fatal to the freedom of any country" [to Thomas Hazard, 26 Aug. 1783, in ibid., VIII, 839]. He was equally critical of party spirit, which he condemned as a "poisonous influence" in the affairs of a republic [to Wm. Greene, 24 Dec. 1783, in ibid., VIII, 839]. Altogether, the most impressive testimonial to his character is that of John Brown, cited above.

JONES, WILLIAM (1753–1822), b. Newport; served in Continental Army; speaker, R. I. General Assembly, 1809–1811; governor, 1811–1817. His electioneering pamphlet *To the Freemen of Rhode Island* (n.p., 1817) contains the conventional wisdom of the old school, but tempered by a concern for popular rights and prejudices. On the subject of the great Embargo he had earlier declared, "The dissolution of the Union may be more surely and speedily effected by the systematic oppression of the government than by the inconsiderate disobedience of the people" [Address to the General Assembly, 1808, quoted in Samuel H. Allen, "The Federal Ascendancy of 1812," *Narragansett Historical Register* 7 (1889), 381–394]. Altogether, Jones appears as another representative of old-school Federalism in Rhode Island—openly articulating the twin ideals of elitism in society and energy in government, but attentive to the drift of public opinion.

LYMAN, DANIEL (1756–1830), b. Durham, Conn.; A.B., Yale, 1776; served in the Continental Army; lawyer and textile manufacturer in Newport; Surveyor of Newport District, 1790–1802; chief justice of Rhode Island, 1812–1816 [Peter J. Coleman, *The Transformation of Rhode Island, 1790–1860* (Providence, 1963), p. 82n; Morison, *Otis*, I, 136; Dexter, *Yale Graduates*, III, 615]. Lyman headed the Rhode Island delegation to the Hartford Convention; his eminence in that body is evidence of the respect in which his Federal brethren held him [Morison,

Otis, I, 137, 144, 156]. With his Rhode Island contemporaries, however, he was notably respectful of popular power, running for public office in 1815 as a "Real Friend of the People" [Allen, "The Federal Ascendancy in 1812," p. 393].

MARTIN, SIMEON (1755–1819), merchant and gentleman farmer in Newport, holder of many civil and military offices in his state. If he shared with other Federalists a preference for government by an elite of birth and wealth and breeding, Martin was more responsive to popular pressures than some of his confreres thought proper. A presidential elector in 1800, he discarded his vote for Charles Cotesworth Pinckney because Republicans were particularly successful in arousing the suspicions of the people in the northern part of the state that the Federalist intrigue against the incumbent president might prove successful [W. V. King to John Rutledge, 23 Dec. 1800, in Rutledge Papers, Univ. of N. C.].

OLNEY, JEREMIAH (1744–1812), as Collector of Customs for Providence, demonstrated an extraordinary diligence in the enforcement of the revenue laws, even against such powerful Federalist merchants as Welcome Arnold and John Brown. In the face of economic and social pressure which must have made his position nearly untenable, he wrote to Hamilton for an increase in his remuneration. "Officers of the customs, who faithfully discharge their duties to the public, have ever, in this Country, met the censure and ill-will of the generality of the merchants. . . . The Law will, at times, bear hard upon them all; and if the Collectors do not then favor them more than consists with a due execution thereof, they are almost sure to lose the esteem of those who were their friends, and to gain the enmity of those who before wished them well. This consideration forcibly points out the expediency of placing those officers in an independent situation, in respect to their emoluments; lest from the smallness of their income, they should be privately tempted to wink at breaches of the law. . . . But while I hold [my office], I mean unproductive as it is, to continue a strict and impartial discharge of the trust reposed in me, regardless of my own Popularity and the consequent loss of Friends" [to Hamilton, 6 Jan. 1791, in White, *The Federalists*, pp. 307–308]. To men such as Olney, the old-school ideal of independence implied more than a disdain for popular pressures; but as the opposition of Arnold and Brown suggest, his was a minority opinion.

WARD, SAMUEL (1756–1832), b. Westerly, R. I., son of Gov. Samuel Ward; A.B., Brown, 1772; served in the Continental Army; East India merchant and wealthy landowner in Warwick, R. I. Moderate in his national principles, restrained in his elitism, he served the cause of order with dignity and effect [John Ward, *Memoir of Samuel Ward*, pp. 15, passim].

Young Federalists

BURRILL, JAMES (1772–1820), b. Providence, R. I.; A.B., Brown, 1788; studied law with Theodore Foster and David Howell (qq.v.) and practised in Providence. Burrill was an architect of the fusionist policy of 1806–1808, by which the two parties agreed to unite in a division of the spoils —Jeffersonians taking the governor, secretary, and treasurer; Federalists the lieutenant governor and attorney general. Burrill was elected in the latter capacity. In the succeeding nine-year period, Burrill was the central figure in the creation of an active, vote-seeking Federal organization in Providence which was far advanced beyond anything that town had seen in the factional strife of the eighteenth century [Walter R. Danforth, himself a party functionary, describes the organization and Burrill's part in it in "Pictures of Providence in the Past," *R. I. History*, 10 (1951), 1–13, 45–60, 85–96; see also Allen, "The Federal Ascendancy of 1812," pp. 381–394]. For Burrill's use of popular rhetoric, see *At a Convention of Delegates from the Eight Towns in the Counties of Providence and Bristol* (1796), in which he declared his faith in a democratic republican-ism—"The great body of the people will never intentionally do wrong."

CHAMPLIN, CHRISTOPHER GRANT (1768–1840), b. Newport; A.B., Harvard, 1786; merchant, banker, gentleman farmer, and proud owner of the "largest barn in Rhode Island" [Timothy Bigelow, *Diary of a Visit to Newport*, p. 8] As U. S. Congressman (1797–1801) and U. S. Senator (1809–1811) he demonstrated a talent for Federalist demagoguery, speaking to and for his constituents [*AC*, 5/2/974–975, 8 Feb. 1798]. In the politics of his state he helped to order the efforts of his party ["To the Freemen of the State of Rhode Island," 19 Aug. 1800, in Broadside bound under that date in the Library of Congress file of the Newport *Mercury*; see also extracts from his letters published in George C. Mason, *Remini-scences of Newport* (Newport, 1884, pp. 97–103].

HAZARD, BENJAMIN (1770–1841), b. Middletown, Conn.; A.B., Brown, 1792; son-in-law of Daniel Lyman (q.v.); merchant, manufacturer in Newport. From 1809 to 1840 Hazard represented his town in the R. I. General Assembly, winning sixty-two consecutive popular elections; he was also among Rhode Island's delegation to the Hartford Convention [Morison, *Otis*, II, 136]. This skillful politician organized one of the most efficient Federalist machines in the nation—a cluster of committees which mustered the most aged citizens and the very young, the blind and the halt. One of the youngest members of this federal organization, himself too young to vote, later described his particular role in the semi-annual renewal of Hazard's plurality. "I constituted one of a company of electioneering juveniles," he wrote. "It was made their duty to wait upon the aged and infirm voters of the right stamp, and accompany them to the polls. One of them, Mr. Jabez Dennison, I was directed to attend; a most excellent man, and universally respected, except on voting days. He was partially paralyzed in one side and suffered from a contraction of his fingers. Previous to reaching the State House, I placed in the hand least affected the State 'prox' " [George C. Channing, *Early Recollections of Newport, 1793–1811* (Newport, 1868), pp. 186–187].

JACKSON, RICHARD (1764–1838), b. Providence, R. I.; attended lower schools; merchant, textile manufacturer, insurance company president in Providence; U. S. Congress, 1808–1815. In Congress, he spoke for the interest of his "suffering constituents" and made use of the rhetoric of his opponents. "The American people are a cool calculating people, and know what is best," he declared [AC 10/2/812, 10 Dec. 1808]. He argued laissez-faire economics in the debates on the Embargo, remarking that "commerce was like water, which, if left to seek its own course, would find its level, and if left to regulate itself, articles would always find their way to places where they are wanted for consumption" [ibid., 10/2/881–882, 17 Dec. 1808; and see also Jackson and Elisha R. Potter, *Address . . . to their Constituents* (1812), pp. 3, 20].

MASON, JAMES BROWN (1775–1819), b. Thompson, Windham Co., Conn.; A.B., Brown, 1791; physician in Charleston, S. C., 1795–1798; merchant in Providence, R. I., 1798–1819; member R. I. General Assembly, 1804–1814 (speaker, 1812–1814); U. S. Congress, 1815–1819. Mason helped to arrange the open caucuses of Rhode Island Federalists in Newport from 1808 to 1820, by which body the most vital decisions were made—including the decision to abandon the "coalition" or "fusion" policy with the Fenner party. Mason led the young Federalists of his state away from the ethical patterns of the old school and into the nineteenth century. "I hope too rigid an adherence to old principles will not preclude us (at this alarming crisis) from the choice of the least of two evils," he wrote to Otis (11 July 1808, in Otis Papers, Mass. Hist. Soc.; see also Neil Andrews, "Development of the Nominating Convention in Rhode Island," *R. I. Hist. Soc. Pubs.,* I (1893–1894), 258–269].

NOYES, THOMAS (1769–1837?), a gentleman farmer residing in Westerly. Noyes ran for Congress in 1800 as "A Real Farmer, and a Uniform Friend to the Rights and Liberties of the People" [Broadside, n.p., n.d., Evans #38374].

POTTER, ELISHA REYNOLDS (1764–1835), b. Little Rest, R. I.; educated in apprenticeship to a blacksmith, and attended Plainfield Academy; served as a private soldier in the Revolution; lawyer, gentleman farmer in South Kingston, R. I.; member, R. I. General Assembly, 1793–1796 (speaker, 1795–1796), 1798–1808 (speaker, 1802, 1806–1808, 1816–1835); U. S. Congress, 1796–1797, 1809–1815. His defeat, as Federalist gubernatorial nominee in 1818, marked the end of his party's control of the Rhode Island government. A man of great presence and enormous size—he paid for two seats when he traveled by coach—he "seemed to carry about with him a certain homespun certificate of authority, which made it natural for lesser men to accept his conclusions" [Josiah Quincy, *Figures of the Past*, p. 232]. His devotion to the Federal party was nearly complete; in a Congressional caucus, after the Federalists had found themselves to be a minority of eleven and had convened to consider surrender, Potter said, "Friends, just remember that we are as many as the Apostles after Judas had deserted them. Think what *they* did, and fight it out" [ibid., p. 232]. But Josiah Quincy's recollection of Potter's "uncompromising" response to the Jeffersonian movement is not sustained by the texts of his Congressional speeches. Potter made much use of Jeffersonian rhetoric. "It is not only the right but the duty of the majority to govern," he declared [AC 14/2/1101, 21 Jan. 1814; 14/2/1814, 8 Feb. 1814]. He contended that the party dispute, by 1809, was only a question of ins and outs. "The division is not so much among the people as it is among those who want the people's money," he said. Potter argued that in a republic a party system was a positive good. "That there are parties in the United States cannot be denied, and that it is for the interest of the people that it should be so is equally true; and I could wish, let whatever party have the ascendency in the United States, that they may have but a small majority, which will make them more attentive to business, and more circumspect in their conduct" [AC 11/2/761–762, 19 Dec. 1809].

CONNECTICUT

Federalists of the Old School

BRACE, JONATHAN (1754–1837), b. Harwinton, Conn., son of a "substantial farmer;" attended Yale; studied law with Oliver Ellsworth (q.v.); and practised in Hartford, Conn.; member, Conn. General Assembly, 1788, 1790–1794; Assistant, 1798, 1808–1818; U. S. Congress, 1798–1800; probate judge, 1809–1824; mayor of Hartford, 1815–1824; Conn. Senate, 1819–1820 [Dexter, *Yale Graduates*, IV, 101–103]. Brace, it will be noted, simultaneously held high executive, legislative, and judicial offices in his state, where pluralism was prevalent during the Federalist era and the ideal of a separation of powers was honored in the breach. Self-interest was sustained by principle. The transcendent holism of the old school, the consciousness of social and political interdependency which was articulated with increasing clarity by older Federalists as the Jeffersonian movement gathered strength and power, reinforced a determination that power should not be divided but rather united in the hands of "natural rulers," who would remain ultimately responsible to the people but more directly responsive to a certain self-evident sense of the "public good." The same mood appears in Jonathan Brace's quaint comments upon partisanship: "I do not think that those gentlemen who are in the habit of supporting all the measures of government ought to be denominated a *party*; those only who oppose such measures deserve that appellation—especially in all free governments" [AC 6/1/2633, 11 Jan. 1799]. For his refusal to court popularity, see Kilbourne, *Litchfield County*, pp. 121–125.

COIT, JOSHUA (1758–1798), b. New London, Conn.; A.B., Harvard, 1776; lawyer practising in New London, Conn.; member, Conn. General Assembly, 1784–1785, 1789–1790, 1792; U. S. Congress, 1793–1798. In Congress, Coit generally voted with the Federalist administration on routine questions, but his independence on military and foreign policy in the first session of the fifth Congress infuriated his brother Federalists. Coit's Congressional conduct was not an effort to trim to political winds; rather it derived from a union of principle and temperament. He described himself as "constitutionally inclined to moderation—not capable of feeling the warmth which appears to me to have existed in the parties which have agitated our public councils since I have been among them, & not perfectly approving at all times of measures pursued by either." This natural inclination interacted with old-school ethics. "I could find no path to satisfy myself in," he wrote, "but to form my judgment on the best information I could get, and to act on each individual measure as appeared to me right" [quoted in Chester McArthur Destler, *Joshua Coit* (Middletown, Conn., 1962), pp. 100–101]. To other old-school gentlemen, he seemed to carry moderation to excess. "In times like the present, when dangers, novel in their kind and terrible in their aspect, press us on every side," wrote Stephen Higginson (q.v.), "it is provoking to hear men talk of their independence, their candour, their love of conciliation, and their aversion to party, like Mr. Coit" [to Oliver Wolcott, Jr., 11 July 1798, in Gibbs, *Administrations of Washington and Adams*, II, 70–71].

DANA, SAMUEL WHITTLESEY (1760–1830), b. Wallingford, Conn.; A.B., Yale, 1775; lawyer residing in Middletown, Conn.; member, Conn. General Assembly, 1789–1796; U. S. Congress, 1797–1810; U. S. Senator,

1810–1821; mayor of Middletown, 1822–1830. This self-styled "states-man of the school of Washington" [to Pickering, 30 Jan. 1812, in Pickering Papers, Mass. Hist. Soc.] was much respected by his colleagues for "deep erudition" [Plumer to Wm. Plumer, Jr., 30 Dec. 1805,—Plumer Papers, Library of Congress]. He articulated his ideals in a full, formal treatise, *Essay on Political Society* (Philadelphia, 1800), which deserves to be more widely known, as an extended statement of old-school ideas. Society is divided into two classes—"the rich, the few, the rulers" and "the poor, the many, the ruled." Liberty receives a very narrow definition, as "exemption from useless restraint" [p. 18], and government is divided, in order that society may be unified [pp. 50–51]. See also his *Specimen of Republican Institutions* (Philadelphia, 1802).

DAVENPORT, JOHN (1752–1830), b. Stamford, Conn.; A.B., Yale, 1770; served in the Continental Army; lawyer residing in Stamford; member, Conn. General Assembly, 1776–1796; U. S. Congress, 1799–1817 [Hunt-ington, *History of Stamford*, pp. 369–370; Dexter, *Yale Graduates*, III, 377–379]. In nine Congresses he appears never to have made a major speech. Plumer described him as a "blunt unpolished countryman," most remarkable for "zeal and bigotry of superstition" [to Wm. Plumer, Jr., 30 Dec. 1805, in Plumer Papers, Library of Congress]. His letters discover the conventional wisdom of the old school [to John Cotton Smith, 15 Dec. 1808, in J. C. Smith Papers, Library of Congress].

DWIGHT, TIMOTHY (1752–1817), b. Northampton, Mass.; A.B., Yale, 1769; served in the Continental Army as a chaplain; Congregational clergyman; gentleman farmer, president of Yale, 1795–1817. Dwight was never a party leader; with a few exceptions, such as his support of the *New England Palladium* [to Jedidiah Morse, 19 Dec. 1800, in Norcross Papers, Mass. Hist. Soc.], he rarely engaged in direct partisan activity. Though Republicans called him the pope of Connecticut, his influence and involvement was largely confined to the spiritual realm. Though he contributed his considerable talents to the cause of order, writing and speaking for the instruction of his neighbors, he never descended to the depths of aggressive and abusive partisanship which characterized the polemics of his younger brother Theodore (q.v.). President Dwight's famous warning that "we may see our wives and daughters the victims of legal prostitution; soberly dishonoured; speci-ously polluted," was not a direct electioneering assault upon Thomas Jefferson in 1800 but a Fourth of July Oration in 1798 in which Dwight was discussing the consequences of "illuminatism" and French Infidelity and in which the only names named were those of Frenchmen—Voltaire and Marat particularly [*The Duty of Americans in the Present Crisis* (1798), p. 20; Charles E. Cunningham, *Timothy Dwight* (New York,

1942), p. 396; cf. Beard, *Economic Origins of Jeffersonian Democracy*, pp. 365–366; Adams, *New England in the Republic*, p. 222; Morison and Commager, *The Growth of the American Republic* (5th edn., New York, 1962), I, 359n]. After the election of 1800, Dwight was not merely anti-Jeffersonian, but antipolitical. He advised one of his sons to keep clear of "political contentions and disputes. Leave these things to those who love them and make it your care to do what is good and right in the sight of God and to make the most of your time and present advantages" [to B. W. Dwight, 8 Dec. 1801, quoted in Cunningham, *Timothy Dwight*, p. 343]. In his own time and place, Dwight was perhaps respected most widely not as a politician or a theologian but as a teacher. His pedagogy, as much as his public pronouncements, epitomizes his old-school idealism. Scorning the coercive discipline of his contemporaries, he dominated his students by the firmness of his manner and the force of his personality rather than by "fines and floggings." He rarely resorted even to public reproof, fearing that such humiliation would drive a child to deceit and deep resentment; Dwight preferred private persuasion and gentle correction to public chastisement of any kind. At the same time he sought to foster a sense of community among his students by discouraging competition among them and by awarding "little prizes" not for outreaching the performance of others but for improving upon their own accomplishments. If he feared the force of passion in almost every form, he felt the value of "tenderness and love."

> Convince, ere you correct, and prove
> You punish, not from rage, but love;
> And teach them, with persuasion mild,
> You hate the fault, but love the child.

Dwight's pedagogic means were notably liberal; but the end remained indoctrination, not of precepts and phrases but of habits.

> Habits alone thro' life endure,
> Habits alone your child secure:
> To habit, bid the blessings grow,
> Habits alone yield good below.

Here was Dwight's ultimate weapon—his answer to the social disorder which he saw in the Jeffersonian movement. His prescription for political sickness came down to the three great educational institutions of his society, family, church and school, serving together to sustain the steady habits of New England [Dwight, *Greenfield Hill: a Poem in seven parts* (New York, 1794); *Decisions of Questions discussed by the Senior Class in Yale College* (New York, 1833); Denison Olmsted, "President Dwight as a Teacher," *American Journal of Education*, V (1858), 566–585; Cunningham, *Dwight*, pp. 146–170; for his political views explicitly stated see *Virtuous Rulers a National Blessing* (Hartford, 1791); *A Discourse, delivered at New-Haven, Feb. 22, 1800* (New Haven, 1800); and "Farmer Johnson's Political Catechism," *New England Palladium,* 31 Mar.–8 May 1801].

EDMOND, WILLIAM (1755–1858), b. Woodbury, Conn.; his father was a native of Ireland who emigrated c. 1755; A.B., Yale, 1777; served in the Continental Army; lawyer, jurist, and gentleman farmer in Newtown, Conn. [Ezra L. Johnson, *Newtown's History* (Newtown, Conn., 1917), p. 198]. Member, Conn. General Assembly, 1791–1797, 1801–1802; U. S. Congress, 1797–1801; associate justice, Conn. Supreme Court, 1805–1819. In Congressional debate he took the conventional old-school view of representation as transcending the particular interests of one's constituents [*AC,* 5/3/2647, 12 Jan. 1798], condemned the spirit of faction in a fashion similar to Jonathan Brace (q.v.), circumscribed the right of petition to preclude Congressional reception of documents which appeared "seditious" [ibid., 5/2/1716, 15 May 1798], and criticized not merely "self-created societies" but "self-created orators" as well [ibid., 5/3/2455, 15 Dec. 1798].

ELLSWORTH, OLIVER (1745–1807), b. Windsor, Conn.; A.B., Princeton, 1776; studied theology, but abandoned it for law, building a very large practice in central Connecticut, and a substantial fortune as well [Wm. G. Brown, *The Life of Oliver Ellsworth* (New York, 1905), pp. 30–41; McDonald, *We the People,* pp. 46–47]. Member, Conn. General Assembly, 1775–1776; Continental Congress, 1777–1784; Governor's Council, 1780–1785, 1801–1807; member, U. S. Constitutional Convention; U. S. Senator, 1789–1796; chief justice, U. S. Supreme Court, 1796–1799; Envoy Extraordinary to France, 1799–1801. Ellsworth's personality was perfectly suited to the deferential society in which he was bred. "His presence was tall, dignified and commanding," Timothy Dwight wrote, "and his manners, though wholly destitute of haughtiness and arrogance, were such as irresistibly to excite in others, wherever he was present, the sense of inferiority" [Dwight, *Travels in New England,* I, 41]. Ellsworth strongly supported Hamilton's fiscal policies, acquiesced in Adams's diplomatic *démarche,* and bitterly condemned the politics of Jefferson. A fellow Congressman recorded the following conversation in 1796: "I was one evening sitting alone with Mr. Ellsworth, when I asked him the question, why the apprehensions of Mr. Jefferson's being President should occasion so much alarm? at the same time observing that it could not be supposed he was an enemy to his country, or would designedly do anything to injure the Government. Mr. Ellsworth, after a short pause, replied, 'No, it is not apprehended that Jefferson is an enemy to his country, or that he would designedly do anything wrong. But it is known he is a visionary man, an enthusiastic disciple of the French Revolution, and an enemy to whatever would encourage commercial enterprise, or give energy to government. It is apprehended that, if he were President, he would take little or no responsibility to himself. The nation would be, as it were, without a head. Everything would be referred to Congress. A lax, intriguing kind of policy would be adopted: and while arts were practised to give direction to public sentiment, Mr. Jefferson would affect to be directed by the will of the nation. There would be no national energy" [Flanders, *Lives and Times of Chief Justices*, pp. 177–178]. After the election of 1800, Ellsworth wrote cynically, "So the anti-Feds are now to support their own administration, and take a turn rolling stones up hill. Good men will get a breathing spell, and the credulous will learn the game of *out and in*" [quoted in Brown, *Ellsworth*, p. 323]. But the game was not for him. He withdrew from public life and busied himself in the bucolic pleasures of his farm, writing essays and letters for the improvement of American agriculture. "Happy would it be," he wrote, "if other good qualities could be as easily renewed as those of land. Would to God there were some kind of tillage also by which a republic that once loses its virtue might be restored to virtue again" [ibid., p. 337].

Hopkins, Lemuel (1750–1801), b. Waterbury, Conn.; A.B., Yale, 1771; physician practising in Litchfield to 1784, Hartford thereafter [*Memorial History of Hartford*, I, 158; Timothy Hopkins, *John Hopkins and Some of his Descendents* (n.p., 1932), p. 160]. His importance in this story derives from the popularity of his sardonic political satire—*The Anarchiad* (New Haven, 1787), *The Democratiad* (Philadelphia, 1795), *The Echo, or a Satirical Poem on the Virtuous Ten* (Hartford, 1795), *The Guillotina, or a Democratic Dirge* (Philadelphia, 1796). It has been remarked that Hopkins was a better physician than a poet, to which one might add that he was a better poet than a politician. But his verses probably reached a wider audience than the speeches of Ames or the pamphlets of Cobbett. All of his productions were admonitions to the people and to their leaders, each to serve in his proper station:

> Yes, there are men who fiercely burn
> Your Constitution to o'er turn,
> To blast the Sages of your Choice,
> They wield the pen and ply the voice
> Nor long will Talents tempt th'affray,
> Where Virtue gains Contempt for pay. [*Guillotina*]

All condemned the form, as well as the substance of the Jeffersonian movement.

Huntington, Ebenezer (1754–1834), b. Norwich, Conn.; A.B., Yale, 1775; colonel in the Continental Army; merchant, banker, speculator in land and securities residing in Norwich, Conn.; U. S. Congress, 1810–1811, 1817–1819. His letters during the Revolution contain the holistic ideals of the old school [Huntington to Andrew Huntington, 8 Jan. 1780, in Huntington Papers, Conn. Hist. Soc. *Colls.*, XX, 436–438). A Congressional speech advocating the use of the militia for purposes of political indoctrination suggests that his principles and prejudices were very little changed by the Jeffersonian movement [*AC* 11/2/2411–2418, appendix].

JOHNSON, WILLIAM SAMUEL (1727–1819), b. Stratford, Conn.; A.B., Yale, 1744, Harvard, 1747; lawyer residing in Stratford, Conn.; member, Conn. General Assembly, 1761, 1765; delegate to the Stamp Act Congress; Governor's Council, 1766, 1771–1775; Continental Congress, 1784–1787; U. S. Senate, 1789–1791; president, Columbia College, 1787–1800. Always loyal to his old-fashioned political principles, he never became a partisan in their defense. "The theme of Johnson's long career," writes his biographer, "is one of conciliation; or, to phrase it differently, his whole life was a quest for harmony and peace" [G. C. Groce, Jr., *William Samuel Johnson* (New York, 1937), p. 193]. He supported Hamilton's financial program, but did not assist in the organization of a Federal party [ibid., pp. 170–171, 67, 192]. In retirement after 1800, he lingered on for twenty years, a living monument to the old way. Timothy Dwight (q.v.) described him in 1815 as "the representative of his contemporaries of a former age, whom time has spared for the purpose of pointing out to their children the true policy of this state [E. E. Beardsley, *Life and Times of William Samuel Johnson* (New York, 1876), p. 167].

REEVE, TAPPING (1744–1823), b. Brookhaven, L. I.; A.B., Princeton, 1765; lawyer, jurist in Litchfield, Conn.; founder of the first law school in the United States (1784). Reeve was a member of the so-called "Jockey Club" in Litchfield, a junto of like-minded men who guarded the path to power in their town. They were not organized in the formal fashion of the young Federalist Committeemen, but were joined together by a web of family relationships, by interlocking economic interests, and by a unity of principle, prejudice, and purpose. The Litchfield group does not appear to have been a brotherhood, like the so-called "Essex Junto." The camaraderie of that more famous group was conspicuously absent on Litchfield Hill. After 1800, especially, private feuds, personal jealousies, and petty rivalships threatened to disrupt the group and destroy its influence. But a sense of common purpose remained more powerful in public affairs. Similar cliques existed in most well-established New England communities; the Litchfield Junto was unusual only in the talents of its leaders—besides Reeve, Benjamin Tallmadge, John Allen, and Uriah Tracy (qq.v.), James Gould, Julius Deming, Frederick Wolcott,

Charles Butler and Oliver Boardman—and in the extent of their involvement in state and national affairs. Reeve's political attitudes appear in *The Sixth of August, or the Litchfield Festival. An Address to the People of Connecticut* (Hartford, 1806), an interesting disquisition in old-school fashion on passion and politics, an angry repudiation of the means and ends of the Jeffersonian Republicans, and an idealization of the symbiotic relationship between rulers and people which older Federalists remembered as the strength and glory of pre-Revolutionary American society.

SWIFT, ZEPHANIAH (1759–1823), b. Wareham, Mass.; A.B., Yale, 1778; lawyer residing in Windham, Conn.; member, Conn. Assembly, 1787–1793, 1820–1822; U. S. Congress, 1793–1797; secretary, U. S. mission to France, 1800; justice, Conn. Supreme Court, 1801; chief justice, 1806–1819; delegate to the Hartford Convention [Ellen Larned, *Windham County*, II, 212 passim]. His *System of the Laws* is a full and explicit description of Connecticut's Republican polity, as older Federalists understood it—with its orders and distinctions, its deferential spirit, its deep-rooted communitarian consciousness, a structured republicanism in which the people were urged to place their confidence in government by sages and to disregard the clamorous appeals of party [I, 55–56]. Swift, a gentleman of candor and liberality—in the eighteenth-century meanings of those words—acted upon his ideals. He disdained "arts of intrigue" in public affairs, and stood for office without the support of "party, family influence or wealth" [Swift, *A Second Address to the Rev. Moses C. Welch* (Windham, 1796), p. 24].

TALLMADGE, BENJAMIN (1754–1835), b. Brookhaven, L. I.; A.B., Yale, 1773; colonel in the Continental Army; merchant, (worth about $150,000) banker in Litchfield, Conn.; member of the "Litchfield Junto" with Tapping Reeve (q.v.); U. S. Congress, 1801–1817. William Plumer described him as marked by "plain sound sense which is so necessary to render any man what he is, a *man of business*"; and a year later as "a zealous bigot. He often sends to eternal perdition those who do not go every sunday to Chh., believe as he professes, and pay the priest" [Plumer to Wm. Plumer, Jr., 30 Dec. 1805; Plumer, *Diary*, 21 Mar. 1806, in Plumer Papers, Library of Congress]. Tallmadge was one of a remarkably large number of Federalists who in the late 1780s and early 1790s professed to a faith in "democracy." In 1793 he described the Constitution as "a free Democratic Government" [quoted in Hall, *Benjamin Tallmadge*, p. 167] But his democracy was one in which constituted authorities led rather than followed the people. "The National Legislature," he said, "not only gives law but also a kind of political tone to our country. It ought therefore to be a school not only of sound policy and good Government, but also of urbanity and politeness. . . . It may be hoped that [our constituents] will imitate our example" [AC 7/2/936–948, 2 Mar. 1802]. Democratic-Republicanism, as Tallmadge chose to call this polity before a party claimed that name, meant order and stability in society, energy in government, virtuous restraint in the people, and responsibility in their natural rulers. It meant equality defined in narrow, legal terms, and liberty defined in terms of the common good. Its natural enemies were partisanship and demagoguery [ibid., 10/1/1584–1592, 8 Feb. 1808].

TREADWELL, JOHN (1745–1823), b. Farmington, Conn., son of a mechanic; A.B., Yale, 1767; lawyer in Farmington, Conn.; member, Conn. Assembly, 1776–1785; Clerk, Court of Probate, 1777–1784; Continental Congress, 1785–1786; Council, 1786–1797; Lieutenant Governor, 1798–1809; Governor, 1809–1811. The personality of this "stiff man" conformed to the Jeffersonian caricature of Connecticut Federalism. In religion a "hyper-Calvinist" and in politics a stubborn, unreconstructed elitist of the old school, his enforcement of sabbatarian laws made his state a byword for bigotry in the new nation [Purcell, *Connecticut in Transition*, p. 286]. Younger Federalists such as Chauncey Goodrich and Roger Griswold (qq.v.) were appalled, but older gentlemen idealized his independence and steadiness,

> Like Cato firm, like Aristides just,
> Like rigid Cincinnatus nobly poor

[Olmstead, *Memoir of John Treadwell*, p. 25].

TRUMBULL, JONATHAN (1740–1809), b. Lebanon, Conn.; A.B., Harvard, 1759; served in the Continental Army (aide-de-campe to Washington in 1780); U. S. Congress, 1789–1795 (speaker, 1791–1793); U. S. Senate, 1795–1796; Lieutenant Governor of Conn., 1796–1797; Governor, 1797–1809. His gubernatorial messages were sober warnings aganist the progress of French principles in the American republic. "Situated as the United States are," he said, "the arms of France are not to be dreaded—but their arts of seduction and their intrigues at division and disunion, fill me with apprehension and caution. . . . Among numberless other artifices which at this time are bro't into operation, two great engines which are made use of by our enemies against us, are French infidelity, and French philosophy:—The one, operating to the destruction of all religious sentiments—the other, unhinging every social and human tie, by which societies are cemented" [Oct., 1798, *Public Records of Connecticut*, IX, 461]. Trumbull urged friends of order to prepare for the worst—he recommended "the purchase, at publick expence, of a number of stands of good fire arms, to be lodged in public stores and to be used on any sudden emergency" [*ibid.*, May, 1798, 460]

Transitional Figures

ALLEN, JOHN (1763–1812), b. Great Barrington, Mass.; attended common schools; lawyer residing in Litchfield, Conn., after 1785; member, Conn. Assembly, 1793–1796; U. S. Congress, 1797–1799; Conn. Council, 1800–1806; a member of the federal connection in his town with Tapping Reeve (q.v.) and others [P. K. Kilbourne, *Biog. History of Litchfield County* (New York, 1851), p. 353]. Allen's extraordinary virulence perhaps requires a somatic interpretation; but it should be noted that his instability was shared by his transitional contemporaries, too young to share the sweet dream of a "silent multitude," too old to acquiesce in new realities. Whatever the cause, Allen himself testified to his trouble—"I confess, sir, that I have not that perfect command of myself, I have not that iron system of nerves which I could wish" [AC 5/2/1476, 20 Apr. 1798]. He had no patience for "Constitutional questions, theories, doubts, nice distinctions, learned metaphysicial disquisitions and long speeches" [ibid., 1482] but reacted to the Jeffersonian movement with fear and loathing. Privately he found a refuge of sorts in a crypto-royalism which has been already discussed (chapter I, above). Publicly he declared, "The people I venerate; they are truly sovereign; but a section, a part of the citizens, a town, city, or a mob, I know them not; if they oppose the laws they are insurgents and rebels; they are not the people" [ibid., 5/2/2096, 5 July 1798]. He repudiated party organization, and on the subject of the press declared, "Liberty of the press and of opinion is calculated to destroy all confidence between man and man; it leads to the dissolution of every bond of union; it cuts asunder every ligament that unites man to his family, man to his neighbor, man to his society, and to government" [ibid., 2098]. Pursuing the organic imagery of the old school to a scatological extreme, he described his Jeffersonian antagonists as "morbid excrescences upon the body politic," putrid pustules to be removed, if necessary, by a surgical operation" [ibid., 5/3/2800, 30 Jan. 1799].

GOODRICH, CHAUNCEY (1759–1815), b. Durham, Conn.; son of a clergyman; A.B., Yale, 1776; m. Mary Anne Wolcott, daughter of Oliver Wolcott; teacher and tutor in New Haven, 1776–1781; lawyer in Harvard, Conn.; member, Conn. Assembly, 1793–1794; U. S. Congress, 1795–1801; Council, 1802–1807; U. S. Senator, 1807–1813; lieutenant governor, 1813–1815; mayor of Hartford, 1812–1815, delegate to the Hartford Convention [Hollister, *History of Conn.*, II, 634–640; Dexter, *Yale Graduates*, III, 609–611]. The Jeffersonian movement, which he regarded as mere "bullyism," he repudiated in the usual way. In 1793, he believed that there was no cause for concern. "A noisy set of demagogues make a rant, and it seems as if they were about breaking up the foundations, but the great body of men move slowly, but move with sure success" [to Oliver Wolcott, 17 Feb. 1793, in Gibbs, *Administrations of Washington and Adams*, I, 88]. But seven years later he labored to improve the newspaper resources of Federalism and to align his party with public opinion. "The public temper," he wrote, "is more than usually fastidious about public expense; they care more about that than British influence, or monarchy. The strong passion of the country is money. Take all taxes together, they pay pretty large sums" [to Oliver Wolcott, 26 Apr. 1800, in ibid., II, 411]. Goodrich was scornful of and separate from the younger generation—"No little imp or greenhorn, come from mother's womb since 1776, is to say anything about it," he wrote [to Oliver Wolcott, 19 June 1800, in ibid., II, 373]. But he was also critical of the older generation. "Those who claim to be master spirits are unmanageable spirits everywhere," he declared. "Wanting discretion, which alone leads to wise and elevated political conduct, they generally lose the battle. This, for a long time, has been one of the infirmities of our friends. It is certainly a grievous misfortune, perhaps a fatal one" [to ?, 4 Feb. 1814, Gratz Coll., Hist. Soc. Penna.].

HILLHOUSE, JAMES (1754–1832), b. Montville, Conn.; A.B., Yale, 1773; served in the Governor's Foot Guards during the Revolution; lawyer in New Haven, Conn.; General Assembly, 1780–1785; Council, 1789–1791; U. S. Congress, 1791–1796; U. S. Senator, 1796–1810, when he resigned to become commissioner of the Conn. School Fund, 1810–1825; also treasurer, Yale College, 1782–1832, and member of the Hartford Convention. His personality, according to Plumer, was "a sample of Connecticut cunning, mixed with the manners of low life" [to William Plumer, Jr., 30 Dec. 1805, in Plumer Papers, Library of Congress]. His principles, when he gave them full and fair expression, were those of the old school. Partisan appeal for popular support was "teaching the people to trample on the Constitutional Authorities" [AC 10/2/27, 21 Nov. 1808; see also Hillhouse to Noah Webster, 22 Apr. 1808, in Webster Papers, N. Y. Pub. Library, and to Simeon Baldwin, 18 Feb. 1802, in Baldwin Papers, Yale Univ. Library]. But in response to the revolutionary events of Jefferson's administration, he proposed Constitutional amendments which would have weakened the power of government and enlarged the influence of the electorate by more frequent elections, rotation in office, the consent of both houses for appointments, the choice of the president by lot, and the abolition of the vice-presidency (see above, chapter I). The response of Federalists was summarized in that of Richard Peters (q.v.). "In all 'the circle of vacillating opinion,' I have never seen anything which has so completely astounded me as our friend Hillhouse's Resolutions. Those of the old school wonder and lament.

Those of the new seminary are too cunning to be operated upon" [to Pickering, 17 Apr. 1808, in Pickering Papers, Mass. Hist. Soc.].

TRACY, URIAH: see above, Chapter I.

WEBSTER, NOAH (1758–1843), b. West Hartford, Conn.; A.B., Yale, 1778; served briefly in the Revolution; teacher, 1779–1783, in Goshen, N. Y.; journalist in New York City (to 1788, 1793–1798); lawyer in Hartford, 1788–1793; writer in New Haven, 1798–1812, and in Amherst, Mass., 1812–1822; resident of New Haven thereafter. His desperate Constitutional expedients (see above, ch. I) were typical of the transitional group. His attempt to organize an anti-party party (ch. IX) and his belief that an honest politician could take a middle ground between old-school aloofness and Jeffersonian plasticity (ch. VIII) have also been described. But he was persuaded to serve upon Federal electioneering committees and to participate in appeals for popular support [John Caldwell et al. to Webster, 30 Jan. 1805, in Baldwin Papers, Yale Univ. Library].

Young Federalists

BALDWIN, SIMEON (1761–1851), b. Norwich, Conn.; his father a farmer and blacksmith; A.B., Yale, 1781; lawyer, jurist in New Haven; town clerk, 1789–1800; U. S. Congress, 1803–1805; associate justice, Supreme Court, 1806–1817; mayor of New Haven, 1851 [Dexter, *Yale Graduates*, IV, 179–180]. In Congress, Baldwin was a proud member of the "little band of Federalists." "Tho constantly foiled and frequently much discouraged they still continue to make repeated and vigorous exertions," he wrote [to Elizabeth Baldwin, 10 Jan. 1803, in Baldwin Papers, Yale]. The same perseverance, which appeared so rarely among men of the old school, is reflected in Baldwin's active participation in the creation of a federal party organization in his state, 1804–1806—complete with open caucus (itself no innovation in Conn.), committees of correspondence and of "vigilance," door-to-door campaigns and broad support for Federal journalists and pamphleteers (see above, chapter III). Without attempting to rationalize his partisan pursuit of popular support, he paused only to ask his friends, "What are we coming to?" [to M. B. Whittlesey, 25 Nov. 1804, in Baldwin Papers, Yale].

CALDWELL, JOHN, a member of the Central Committee in Hartford, he was asked to look after the party treasury, to "superintend the raising and distribution of the funds which are well known to be indispensable to the accomplishment of the great object in view" [Caldwell et al. to Elias Shipman et al., 30 Jan. 1805, in Baldwin Papers, Yale].

DAGGETT, DAVID (1764–1851), b. Attleboro, Mass.; A.B., Yale, 1783; studied law with Charles Chauncey and practised in New Haven; member, Conn. Assembly, 1791–1796 (speaker, 1794–1796); Council, 1797, 1809–1813; U. S. Senate, 1813–1816; justice, Conn. Supreme Court, 1826–1832, chief justice, 1832–1834; mayor of New Haven, 1828. Daggett, known for his skill at "political wire-working" [Beecher, *Autobiography*, I, 257–261], was an active participant in the federal party organization which he helped to create. He also served as the party's most prolific polemicist. His pamphlet, *Facts are Stubborn Things* (Hartford, 1803), written at the request of the Central Committee at Hartford and disseminated widely by them through county and town committees [Caldwell et al. to Shipman et al., 30 Jan. 1805, in Baldwin Papers, Yale], was an electioneering address which began and ended with an attack upon the practise of electioneering, a heavy-handed appeal to "common laborers and mechanics," but most of all to Connecticut's conservative yeoman farmers. In this and other pamphlets Daggett broadly condemned "theorists" and "reforms" and was particularly critical of universal suffrage [*Count the Cost* (Hartford, 1804); and the earlier *Sunbeams May Be Extracted from Cucumbers, but the Process is Tedious* (New Haven, 1799), the latter including, incidentally, interesting admonitions on child-rearing practices]. But his conservatism possessed a different quality from that of the old school. He manifested little nostalgia for the colonial past. "This state, and many others, were under a most perfect aristocracy—The name we truly disowned, yet quietly submitted to a government essentially autocratic" [*Oration delivered in . . . 1787*]. Daggett paid lip service to popular sovereignty in more fulsome terms than his elders used, describing Connecticut as "more than almost any government upon earth, it is the legitimate child of the people" [ibid.]. He openly and positively defended party spirit [*Sunbeams*], and articulated the ideal of minimal government on both the state and national levels [*Steady Habits Vindicated; AC* 13/3/71, 15 Nov. 1814].

DWIGHT, THEODORE (1764–1846), b. Northampton, Mass.; his father a prosperous merchant with deep roots in the New England soil; Theodore Dwight's maternal grandfather was Jonathan Edwards, his cousin was Aaron Burr, and his older brother was Timothy Dwight (q.v.). After "preparatory studies," he practised law in Haddam and Hartford; and was editor of the Hartford *Connecticut Courant* and the *Connecticut Mirror* to 1815, and the Albany *Daily Advertiser*, 1815–1817, all powerful Federalist electioneering papers; and the New York *Daily Advertiser*,

1817–1835. His public offices—U. S. Congressman, 1806–1807; Conn. Council, 1809–1815; secretary of the Hartford Convention, 1814—were less important than his party posts. As the de facto head of the Hartford Committee, he was the central figure in the Federal party organization in Connecticut. Though Dwight ran his party machine in strict secrecy—instructing county committeemen to take "particular care" that "written instructions do not go out of your own hands on any occasion" [to Simeon Baldwin, 9 July 1804, in Baldwin Papers]—the circulars which survive among the manuscripts of Simeon Baldwin serve to document his extraordinary exertions. No aspect of partisan activity escaped his attention, but two objects concerned him above others. First, he endeavored to reach every freeman in the state who might vote for a federal candidate; to this end, he urged subdivision of local committees and personal visits by party workers. "One personal intercourse will accomplish more than a hundred messages," he believed. He also encouraged voter registration campaigns, federal committees being urged to see that all qualified "young men" in every town were admitted as Freemen. His second object was to adjust the principles of the party to popular prejudices; local committees were asked to report to the county and state committees on the state of public opinion—on questions in the minds of the people which demanded attention, and on issues which could be exploited. At the same time, Dwight sought to dress the public pronouncements of Connecticut Federalism in homespun. "The stile and manner of political disquisitions should be plain and perspicuous [sic] and they should not be of tedious length. *Multum in parvo* [sic] should always be remembered" [Dwight to Baldwin, 9 July 1804, Dec. 1804, Jan. 1805, 27 Mar. 1805, 21 Aug. 1806, in Baldwin Papers, Yale]. Dwight himself remembered, in his pamphleteering, which was marked by some of the most outrageous—but incisive—scurrility in the annals of the republic [*The Political Greenhouse for the Year of 1798* (Hartford, 1799), *Oration delivered at Hartford* (Hartford, 1801); Dwight deserves a full biography, which he has yet to receive].

GODDARD, CALVIN (1768–1842), b. Shrewsbury, Mass.; A.B., Dartmouth, 1786; lawyer, banker, manufacturer residing in Plainfield, and after 1807, in Norwich, Conn.; member, Conn. Assembly, 1795–1801, 1807 (speaker); U. S. Congress, 1801–1805; Council, 1808–1815; delegate to the Hartford Convention; Mayor of Norwich, 1814–1834. In Congress he supported a powerful judiciary as a device for controlling the power of the people and preserving property [AC 8/1/721, 24 Feb. 1802], but strongly favored economy and retrenchment for the executive [ibid., 7/1/1088, 26 Mar. 1802; 8/1/611, 21 Nov. 1803] and regarded the legislature as an arena in which Representatives fought for the particular interests of their constituents [8/2/714, 28 Nov. 1804; 8/1/430,

24 Oct. 1803]. He also borrowed Jeffersonian rhetoric to defend the right of free speech, assembly and petition [ibid., 8/2/946, 9 Jan. 1805].

GOODRICH, ELIZUR (1761–1849), b. Durham, Conn.; brother of Chauncey Goodrich (q.v.); A.B., Yale, 1779; lawyer practising in New Haven; member, Conn. Assembly, 1795–1802, and simultaneously U. S. Congressman, 1799–1801; appointed Collector of Customs in New Haven, 1801, his removal was made a *cause célèbre* by Federalist pamphleteers; Conn. Council, 1803–1818; judge, probate court, 1802–1818; mayor of New Haven, 1803–1822, holding offices in the three branches of government for the greater part of his career. Elizur Goodrich's words and acts suggest a greater flexibility than those of his older brother. He worked to organize a federal party [to Simeon Baldwin, 27 Jan. 1805, in Baldwin Papers, Yale] and also to popularize its image. "Names are influential things—and much has been effected by the term Democratic Republican. In my opinion it is time to leave this distinction" [ibid., 20 Feb. 1804]. In the judgment of this young Federalist, friends of order could preserve their influence, even on the national level, which was not openly anti-democratic, but anti-southern and anti-slavery.

GRISWOLD, ROGER (1762–1812), b. Lyme, Conn.; son of a Conn. governor; A.B., Yale, 1780; lawyer residing in Norwich and after 1794 in Lyme, Conn. U. S. Congress, 1795–1805; justice, Conn. Supreme Court, 1807; lieutenant governor, 1809–1811; governor, 1811–1812. His public career, which included a famous fracas with Mathew Lyon on the floor of the House of Representatives, and complicity in Timothy Pickering's (q.v.) conspiracy of 1804, was unstable and occasionally violent. But he consistently identified himself with a federal party and sought to promote its interests even at the cost of the holistic ideals of the old school. When the unpopularity of the clergy and their stiff sabbatarian friend John Treadwell threatened political disaster, Griswold organized a revolt: "We have served the clergy long enough. We must take another man and let them take care of themselves" [Beecher, *Autobiography*, I, 260–261]. For his attempt to make popular appeals and to align his party with such popular issues as economy, see Griswold to John Rutledge, Jr., 14 Dec. 1801, 15 Apr. 1802, in Rutledge Papers, Southern Hist. Coll., Univ. of N.C.

HALL, JOHN (1783–1847), b. Ellington, Conn.; son of a prosperous merchant; A.B., Yale, 1802; tutor, 1805–1807; after a brief career in commerce, he settled as a gentleman farmer in Tolland, Conn., and was active on local committees and in the Washington Society. His *Oration delivered at Tolland* (Hartford, 1814) was an extended apologia for partisan opposition to constituted authorities. "Overweening confidence in those who are entrusted with the Government, is another fruitful source of our calamities. To repose a suitable confidence in those whom we ourselves have elected to office, is commendable. It is fit that we consider them to be right, until their conduct proves them to be wrong. . . . [But] never to doubt the political honesty and capacity of their leaders, and never to suffer their conduct to be impeached, seems among certain people, to be standing orders of the day. What could be more dangerous to the liberties of the people?"

LAW, LYMAN (1770–1815), b. New London, Conn.; son of a prominent lawyer and jurist; A.B., Yale, 1791; lawyer practising in New London; member, Conn. General Assembly, 1801–1802, 1806, 1809–1810, 1819, 1826; U. S. Congress, 1811–1817 [Dexter, *Yale Graduates*, IV, 718–719]. In Congressional debate he articulated the young Federalist ideal of the representative as an agent of his constituents and the servant of their interests, pandered to the people of his district and of the nation, sought to improve the popular image of Federalism, defended the right of the people to judge their elected officers, advocated the ideal of economy in public expenditures, and argued that commerce could flourish best where the people have "the fruits of their labor secured by just and equal laws; where the property cannot be taken from the owner without his consent" [AC, 12/1/896, 21 Jan. 1812; 12/2/537–538, 5 Jan. 1813; 13/1/1123, 24 Jan. 1814; 13/3/939–950, 17 Dec. 1814].

MOSELEY, JONATHAN OGDEN (1762–1838), b. East Haddam, Conn.; A.B., Yale, 1780; lawyer practising in East Haddam, Conn.; General Assembly, 1794–1804; U. S. Congress, 1805–1821 [Dexter, *Yale Graduates*, IV, 153–154]. His attitudes and articulated principles were similar to those of Lyman Law (q.v.)—openly partisan without qualification or apology [AC 10/1/1977–1979, 6 Apr. 1808; 13/3/830, 9 Dec. 1814] and without suggesting that popular opinion was a rule of right, urged it as a rule of thumb. "Would any gentleman professing an attachment to a republican form of government, a government of laws founded on the affections of the people, wish to have recourse to such an . . . odious and unpopular measure?" [AC 10/2/1333, 3 Feb. 1809]. He made frequent use of libertarian language and popular arguments (13/1/1125, 24 Jan. 1814; 12/3/482, 2 Jan. 1813; 9/2/234–235, 31 Dec. 1806; 10/2/629, 1 Dec. 1808; 10/2/1019, 5 Jan. 1809; 10/2/1332, 3 Feb. 1809].

PERKINS, ELIAS (1767–1845), b. Lisbon, Conn.; A.B., Yale, 1786; lawyer practising in New London; member, Conn. Assembly, 1795–1800, 1814–1815; U. S. Congress, 1801–1803; chief justice, New Haven County Court, 1807–1825; mayor of New London, 1829–1832. Active in the

Federal committee organization in Connecticut, he sought to turn Federal eyes toward the people, and vice versa. "It must be wisdom in the friends of order to improve the present sensibility of the nation to our political advantage," he wrote frankly [to Roger Griswold, 18 Jan. 1800, quoted in E. & E. Salisbury, *Family Histories and Genealogies*, II, 95–97; M. E. Perkins, *Chronicles of a Conn. Family*, pp. 129, 158–159].

PITKIN, TIMOTHY (1766–1847), b. Farmington, Conn., son of a clergyman; A.B., Yale, 1785; studied law with Oliver Ellsworth (q.v.) and practised in Farmington; member, Conn. Assembly, 1790, 1792, 1794–1805 (speaker, 1803–1805); U. S. Congress, 1805–1819; Conn. House of Representatives, 1819–1830. Pitkin sought a "middle passage through which we can steer our political ship," in domestic as well as foreign affairs [AC 10/2/1225, 27 Jan. 1809]. He preserved the dignity and decorum of older Federalists, but the substance of his Congressional speeches marked a departure from their precepts. He spoke for retrenchment of governmental expenditures and reduction of governmental power. "The president of the United States has now more power than is consistent with the simplicity of Republican Government. If this Government will ever be wrecked, it will be on the rock of Presidential Power" [ibid., 12/2/467, 29 Dec. 1812]. Pitkin could never be called a "Federal demagogue," like Cyrus King (q.v.). But he reminded the Democratic Republicans, "This is a Government of the People. . . . Our Government, said Mr. P., is not a Government (in this branch especially) of energy. It is a Government of confidence" [ibid., 11/3/407, 14 Dec. 1810]. In other speeches he claimed to speak in the name of the American people [11/1/389, 22 June 1809; 11/2/1729–1730, 3 Apr. 1810], embraced partisanship without apology [12/1/1181, 9 Mar. 1812], and consistently defended the right of the people to assemble, petition, and peaceably oppose their government [11/2/733, 14 Dec. 1809] at the same time that he insisted upon the most strict respect for rights of private property [10/2/983, 5 Jan. 1809; 12/2/180, 4 Nov. 1812].

NEW YORK

Federalists of the Old School

BENSON, EGBERT (1746–1833), b. New York City; A.B., Columbia, 1765; studied law with John Morin Scott; attorney, jurist; first attorney general of New York, 1777–1789; N. Y. Assembly, 1777–1781, 1788; associate judge, N. Y. Supreme Court, 1784–1801; Continental Congress, 1784–1788; U. S. Congress, 1789–1793, 1813; a "prophane bachelor" with homes in New York City and Jamaica, L. I. [Syrett, *Hamilton*, III, 683;

Thompson, *Long Island*, I, 487–490]. Even in his early career, Benson was remarkable for his political independence ["H. G. Letter III," 22 Feb. 1789, in ibid., V, 268]. But after 1800 he reluctantly yielded to the entreaty of younger friends and loaned the weight of his reputation to their partisan cause. "The Federalists have been generally brought out," wrote James Kent (q.v.). "The passions of party have carried the generality of them along the turbulent current of the times. Even Judge Benson has yielded to the current" [to Mrs. Kent, 26 Apr. 1804, in Kent Papers, Library of Congress].

COOPER, WILLIAM (1754–1809): see above, Chapter I.

FISH, NICHOLAS (1758–1833), b. New York City, son of a wealthy merchant; attended Princeton; studied law with John Morin Scott; served in the Continental Army; lawyer and speculator in New York lands; Episcopal vestryman, 1805–1821, and warden, 1821–1835; N. Y. alderman, 1806–1817; unsuccessful Federal candidate for Lieutenant Governor, 1810, 1811. Known as a "great disciplinarian" in military, domestic, and political affairs, this dignified and decorative gentleman of the old school instinctively repudiated the Jeffersonian movement. Its principles, he wrote, comprised a "general plan of disorganization" compounded of "modern philosophy, of French jacobinism, and local prejudice" [to Arthur Noble, 25 July 1802, in Stuyvesant Fish, ed., *1600–1914* (New York, 1942), pp. 80–82; Lester Warren Fish, *The Fish Family in England and America* (Rutland, Vt., 1948), pp. 323–324]. He participated in partisan activity after 1800, presiding over Federal meetings in New York City [New York *Evening Post*, 18 Aug. 1812]. Gouverneur Morris (q.v.) described him as "popular without Vulgarity" [to Abraham Van Vechten, 6 Jan. 1810, in Morris Papers, Library of Congress].

GLEN, HENRY (1739–1814), b. Schenectady, N. Y.; served in Continental Army; member, N. Y. Provincial Congresses, 1774–1776; N. Y. Assembly, 1786–1787, 1810; U. S. Congress, 1793–1801 [Austin Yates, *Schenectady County* (New York, 1902), pp. 102, 127, 135]. A quiet backbencher in the Congress, his voting record discovered a zeal for energy in government. In Dauer's voting charts, he opposed the administration on only two minor questions in six years [Dauer, *Adams Federalists*, pp. 288–320]. Like other New York Federalists of the old school, he appeared much less reluctant to engage in partisan activity after 1800 than contemporaries in other states. In 1808 he served as chairman of a federal committee of correspondence in Schenectady, appointed "to attend to and promote the Federal Cause by all lawful and honourable means" [Glen et al to Pickering, 25, 27 May 1808, in Pickering Papers, Mass. Hist. Soc.].

HARISON, RICHARD (1748–1829), b. New York City, son of a prominent lawyer; privately educated; a lawyer of Tory leanings, his fortune was much diminished by the Revolution, but by 1799 he was again regarded as a man of wealth—his town house alone appraised at £ 2500 [E. B. O'Callaghan, "Biographical Sketch of Francis Harison," *N. Y. Gen. & Biog. Record*, IX (1878), 49–51; Boston *Columbian Centinel*, 12 Dec. 1829; McDonald, *We the People*, p. 147]. Harison was a member of the N. Y. Assembly, 1788–1789, and U. S. District Attorney for New York, 1789–1801. His speeches in the New York Ratifying Convention, 1788, were delivered in defence of "vigorous government"; his conception of representation was that of the old school—the legislator was not an agent or ambassador of his constituents, but a disinterested contemplator of the good of the whole. For this and his generally holistic view of society see Francis Childs, *Debates and Proceedings of the Convention of the State of New York* (New York, 1788), pp. 48, 68; and Syrett, ed., *Hamilton*, V, 104, 413. Like other older New York Federalists, he shared in a sustained partisan effort after 1800, not in the streets, but in private meetings [Troup to King, 12 Jan. 1810, in *King*, V, 185].

HOBART, JOHN SLOSS (1738–1805), b. Fairfield Conn., son of a clergyman; A.B., Yale, 1757; lawyer in New York City; member N. Y. Provincial Congress, 1775–1777; Justice, N. Y. Supreme Court, 1777–1798; U. S. Senator, 1798; U. S. District Judge, 1798–1805. Hobart's politics appear to have been essentially those of John Jay (q.v.). He dismissed Jeffersonian principles as mere "envy" and "malevolence" [to Jay, 18 Nov. 1795, *Jay*, IV, 195–196] and, like Jay, refused to stoop to partisan opposition [ibid., pp. 128, 237; Hammond, *Political Parties in New York*, I, 110–111; Dexter, *Yale Graduates*, II, 465–467].

JAY, JOHN (1745–1829): see above, chapter I.

KENT, JAMES (1763–1847), b. Fredericksburgh, N. Y.; grad. Yale, 1781; lawyer, jurist, professor of law (Columbia), resident of New York City after 1793. For Kent the Federal cause was "the cause of Virtue and of Truth and of laws and of liberty"—and by the last term he meant "true old English & old common law liberty" [Kent to Moss Kent, 21 May 1799, in Kent Papers, Library of Congress]. Though active during the 1790s [Kent to Moss Kent, 8 Jan. 1797, in Kent Papers, Library of Congress], he never abandoned his hatred of partisan politics or disguised his elitist prejudices [Fox, *Decline of Aristocracy in the Politics of New York*, pp. 34, 143]. "Everybody seems to be occupied with the two polluted factions," he wrote. "I keep quite aloof and mind my court" [Kent to Mrs. Kent, 20 Apr. 1804, in Kent Papers, Library of Congress]. Of such young Federalists as Elisha Williams and T. P. Grosvenor (qq.v.)

he once declared, "Oh! These politicians! What trouble and vexation do they not cause! For myself I have been content to eat my cake in peace" [Van Buren, *Autobiography*, p. 63]. In 1816 he declared, "I have nothing to do with meetings or nominations, but my wishes for the honor and success of the federal party (as containing more virtue and juster views than any other party) are ardent and unceasing" [Kent to King, 16 Feb. 1816, in *King*, V, 508].

KING, RUFUS (1755–1827), b. Scarboro, Me.; A.B., Harvard, 1777; served briefly in the Continental Army; read law with Theophilus Parsons (q.v.); member, Mass. House of Representatives, 1782; Continental Congress, 1784–1787; U. S. Constitutional Convention, 1787; Mass. Ratifying Convention, 1788; removed to New York City in 1788; member, N. Y. Assembly, 1789–1790; U. S. Senate, 1789–1796; U. S. Minister to Great Britain, 1796–1803; U. S. Senate, 1813–1825. After his return to the United States in 1804, King was deeply disturbed by the state of American politics—not merely by the weakness of the Federal cause but by fundamental changes in patterns of political behavior. In an unpublished essay titled "Words," he displayed his doubts about the ideology of American politics in the Jeffersonian era and about the expansion of party consciousness. "Words without meaning, or with wrong meaning have especially of late years done great harm," he wrote. "Liberty, Love of Country, Federalism, Republicanism, Democracy, Jacobin, Glory, Philosophy, and Honor are words in the mouth of everyone and without any precision used by any one; the abuse of words is as pernicious as the abuse of things. Apostacy is another word of Party. The majority are careless or ignorant. Such a man is an apostate, says some impudent Quack, because he separates from the Party with which he commenced his career; the Calumny is believed and Character is lost. What is Glory, what is Patriotism, what is apostacy? are they names or things?" [*King*, V, 96]. King was also troubled by the conduct of the coming generation of American politicians, both Federal and Democratic. "Neither a democratical nor a federal President could in the actual State of parties do anything to remove our present evils, or to prevent their recurrence," he wrote. "All palliatives, such as the mere change of President among Democrats, or between them and federalists, will have the effect, not only to postpone the chance of reform, but to weaken the faculty of making it, should the opportunity occur. They would have this effect by the more complete conversion of political parties into political factions; by the inevitable progress of corruption and by the difficulty which daily increases of confining the young men of the Country to a political Creed which is sure to prevent them from sharing in public distinctions" [to Gore, 19 Sep. 1812, in *King*, V, 279]. King sought to live quietly in retirement. "I pass my time in the bosom of my family, thinking and saying as little as I can upon the subject of politicks," he wrote [to George Hammond, 12 Dec. 1808, in *King*, V, 122]. Colleagues criticized him for his apathy. "That you have become disgusted with the politics of our country can excite no surprise," Gore told him. "Some of your friends, however, complain that you do not take a more active part in the affairs of New York, and think that your exertions might materially affect the cause of order and freedom" [to King, 5 May 1811, in *King*, V, 245; and see the more angry remarks of David B. Ogden to Wm. Meredith, 11 Apr. 1806, in Meredith Papers, Hist. Soc. Penna.]. On uncommon occasions, he was dragged by the heels into party gatherings. "Went to Town, and attended the Peace meeting," King noted in his Diary, "though without the zeal and animation ascribed to me by the Evening Post" [*King*, V, 271]. In 1813, a union of Federalists and dissident Democrats elected him to the Senate. "This appointment," King wrote to a close friend, "has been made without solicitation, nay, without the expression, or existence of a wish for it on my part" [to Gore, 14 Feb. 1813, in *King*, V, 294]. There he remained for a dozen years, a ghostly figure from the Washingtonian past, a living relic to be visited by tourists, like Mt. Vernon; a personification of a political philosophy so remote that such a politician as Thomas Hart Benton could regard it as a curiosity [Benton, *Thirty Years View*, I, 57–58]. King professed to many doubts about the future of American republicanism. But he was clear in his own mind upon two points. First, he understood that the Constitutional devices which he had helped to develop could not in themselves serve old-school purposes. "We have been the visionary men," he wrote, "who have believed, as many have, that mere Paper Constitutions, without those moral and political habits and opinions, which alone give solidity and support to any Government, would be sufficient to protect and preserve the equal Rights of the weak against the strong, of the honest agt. the dishonest, of the wise and faithful friends of free Govt. against the wicked and ambitious" [to Gore, 8 May 1816, in *King*, V, 534]. Secondly, he knew that he was too old to adjust his ideals to new realities. "It has probably become the real interest & policy of the Country, that the Democracy should pursue its own natural Course. Federalists of our age must be content with the past. It would be most unworthy to affect to have changed our opinions" [to Gore, 15 May 1816, in *King*, V, 535].

LAURANCE, JOHN (1750–1810), b. Cornwall, England; settled in New York, 1767, educated in lower schools; lawyer in New York City; served in the Continental Army; Continental Congress, 1785–1787; N. Y. Senate, 1789; U. S. Congress, 1789–1793; U. S. District Judge, 1794–1796; U. S. Senate, 1796–1810. In Congress, he spoke and voted for energy in government, and made no secret of his impatience with the debates on the bill of rights, which he described as "speculative amendments upon an untried constitution" [AC 1/1/706, 13 Aug. 1789]. He took the conventional old-school view of representation. "Every member on this floor ought to consider himself the representative of the whole Union, and not of the particular district which had chosen him" [ibid., 1/1/746, 15 Aug. 1789]. Though his letters in the 1790s manifest the conventional hatred of "passion and party" [to King, 16 Apr. 1794, in *King*, I, 561], Laurance participated in the partisan effort in New York City, serving as chairman of federal nominating meetings [N.Y. *Evening Post*, 22 Apr. 1802; Alexander, "John Laurance," *N.Y. Hist.*, XXV (1944), 35–45].

LENOX, ROBERT (1759–1839), b. Kirkcudbright, Scotland; emigrated to New York City, 1776; educated in lower schools; served as a commissary in British service during the Revolution; after the war, made an immense fortune, reputedly the largest in New York City, in the East India trade. He also engaged in banking, insurance, and land speculation; was president of the N. Y. Chamber of Commerce, elder of the First Presbyterian Church, and an active contributor to many philanthropic and educational enterprises. Lenox and his friend Archibald Gracie were characterized as "two violent Scotch Federalists, who would gladly banish the Republican party to Botany bay, if they had the power" [quoted in Livermore, *Twilight of Federalism*, p. 22]. The feeling was probably not mutual—this dour Scot, with his great riches and stiff "unswerving integrity," was more useful to his political enemies than to his friends. An unfounded myth that his father had been keeper of the infamous Jersey Prison Ship and that Lenox himself had been involved in that unhappy chapter of events, permitted New York Republicans to campaign against British atrocities in more than one pivotal election [New York *Argus*, 25 Dec. 1795; New York *American Citizen*, 24 Feb., 1 Mar. 1802; New York *Evening Post*, 25 Feb. 1802; James Lenox Banks, *Genealogical Notes Concerning the Banks and Allied Families* (New York, 1938), pp. 85–90].

MOFFITT, HOSEA (1757–1825), b. Stephentown, N. Y.; educated in lower schools; served in the Continental Army; farmer residing in Stephentown, N. Y.; member, N. Y. Assembly, 1794–1795, 1801; town supervisor, 1806–1809; sheriff, Rensselaer Co., 1810–1811; U. S. Congress, 1813–1817. Moffitt was another of the older New York Federalists who participated in a partisan organization during the 1790s [Hosea Moffitt et al. to Peter Van Schaack, 14 Mar. 1798, in Van Schaack Papers, Library of Congress].

MORRIS, GOUVERNEUR (1752–1816), b. Morrisania, N. Y.; A.B., Columbia, 1768; lawyer practising in Philadelphia and New York, gentleman farmer with an estate at Morrisania, N. Y.; member, N. Y. Provincial Congresses, 1775–1777; N. Y. Assembly, 1777–1778; Continental Congress, 1777–1778; Asst. Minister of Finance, 1781–1785. U. S. Constitutional Convention, 1787; Commissioner to England, 1790–1791; Minister to France, 1792–1794; U. S. Senate, 1800–1803. Morris personifies another another variety of old-school Federalism, not included in chapter I, which flourished in the fashionable salons of New York and Philadelphia. We might meet him on the road, as another Federalist did. "Thursday night at 10 o'clock," John Rutledge wrote, "I arrived in the dark and rain at Pomfret, where I heard a chattering of French, and upon entering the Inn found Gouverneur Morris with two french Valêts—a french travelling companion, and his hair buckled up in about one hundred Papilliottes [curlers]. His wooden leg, papilliottes, french attendants, and french conversation made his Host, Hostess, their daughters, and grand Daughters, with the whole family, including the Hostler and Betty the Cook maid, stare most prodigiously; and gave me some idea how the natives looked when poor Cooke made his Entrée at the friendly Isles" [Rutledge to Otis, 17 July 1803, in Morison, Otis, I, 278]. There was nothing austere about Morris, none of the gravitas that characterized George Cabot, John Jay, and George Washington (qq.v.). But in an effete, even Frenchified way, his principles were much the same. He shared their deep conservatism. "Let it be remembered that nothing human is perfect, and that every change is hazardous," he warned [to Aaron Ogden, 28 Dec. 1804, in Morris Papers, Library of Congress]. He took the same holistic view of society and believed that "high-toned government" was necessary to social preservation, for without the intervention of a controlling power, the strong would devour the weak. "That which theorists call Natural Equality," he wrote, "would be reduced in practice to this relation of Tyrant to Beast." Man was made for society; "a social creature can have no rights inconsistent with the social state" [Morris, "Equality" (n.d.), in Morris Papers, Columbia Univ. Library]. He called himself a Republican, but that identity was less than complete. "In adopting a republican form of government, I not only took it as a Man does his Wife, for better or for worse, but what few Men do with their Wives, I took it knowing all its bad qualities," he wrote. Its worst quality, of course, was its dependence upon the soundness of the majority. "The dangerous doctrine that the Public Will, expressed by a numerical majority, is in all cases to be obeyed, arises from a perverse confusion of ideas and leads to horrible results" [to John Dickinson, 23 May 1803; to Uriah Tracy, 5 Jan. 1804, in Morris Papers, Library of Congress]. He always insisted upon a distinction between republicanism and democracy; the difference, it appears, was less a matter of institutional arrangements than of habits and attitudes and modes of behavior.

"Government becomes the result of character, manners and condition," he declared. Cast in this form, the distinction was brittle but clear, and as long as a deferential spirit lingered in American society, it was meaningful. But to sustain the difference after the spirit of subordination had evaporated in the party heat of the 1790s was a problem which neither Morris nor any other old-school Federalist managed to resolve. He believed that even the most high-toned government could do little in America "when unsupported by popular sentiment." After 1800 he also believed that there was "a moral tendency, and in some cases even a physical disposition, among the people of this country to overturn the government" [Morris to Aaron Ogden, 28 Dec. 1804, in Morris Papers, Library of Congress]. Other "friends of order" found an answer of sorts —a species of covert elitism, a popular, vote-seeking federal party. But it was not the answer for Morris—to him it meant "two holes in the stocking" instead of merely one (see above, chapter III). His colleagues begged him to labor in the partisan cause, and he did serve in a small way, writing occasional newspaper articles, and attending "for the first Time in my Life" a "popular meeting" in 1809 [to Jonathan Mason, 3 Mar. 1809, in Morris Papers, Library of Congress]. But other men led—he followed with the greatest reluctance. "Hamilton tells me I *must* take an active part in our public affairs," he wrote. "This is a painful idea, every way" [Morris, "Diary," 5 Jan. 1799, 6 Apr. 1800, in Morris Papers, Library of Congress]. When he was invited to join the committee organization in New York, he recoiled in shocked disapproval. "The times are indeed difficult and menacing," he declared, "but the freeholders of this County are not, I believe, convinced that Circumstances as yet require a revolutionary Organization" [to Wm. Henderson et al., 9 Mar. 1809, in Morris Papers, Library of Congress]. But if Morris found no solution to America's political problems, he remained optimistic about his nation's future, in a most astonishing way. "Something may happen to arrest this progress to Anarchy," he wrote. "I indulge flattering hopes but should be puzzled to assign any rational ground" [Morris to John Penn, n.d., [1805?], in Anne Cary Morris, ed., *Diary and Letters of Gouverneur Morris*, II, 466; Morris to John Eager Howard, 20 Nov. 1804, in Morris Papers, Library of Congress].

SANDS, COMFORT (1748–1834), b. Cowneck, N. Y.; "a good school education"; wealthy banker and import merchant in New York City; N. Y. Assembly, 1778; Director of the Bank of N. Y., 1784–1798; president, New York Chamber of Commerce, 1794–1798 [Temple Prime, *Descent of Comfort Sands* (New York, 1897), passim]. Sands was another member of the New York mercantile community which carried elitism to the edge of arrogance. It was he who allegedly declared publicly that "no poor man can be honest" [East, *Business Enterprise*, p. 259].

SCHUYLER, PHILIP JOHN (1733–1804), b. Albany, N. Y.; educated by a tutor; large landowner, miller, speculator in land and timber residing in Albany, N. Y.; major general in the Continental Army; member, Continental Congress, 1775–1777, 1778–1781; N. Y. Senate, 1780–1784, 1786–1790, 1792–1797; U. S. Senate, 1789–1791, 1797–1798. Schuyler was a central figure in an eighteenth-century "connexion" of landed families in the upper Hudson Valley and a master of eighteenth-century magnate politics.

VAN SCHAACK, PETER (1747?–1832), b. Kinderhook, N. Y.; A.B., Columbia, 1766; m. daughter of Henry Cruger, studied law with Peter Silvester and William Smith and practiced in New York City. His politics were conservatively Whiggish in the period 1765–1775, but he backed away from the Revolutionary movement after the fighting began. He wandered from state to state and finally to Britain, from whence he returned in 1785, after seven years exile, to his home in Kinderhook, N. Y. His office, like Tapping Reeve's (q.v.) formal school in Litchfield, Conn., became a nursery for young Federalist lawyers [H. C. Van Schaack, *Peter Van Schaack* (New York, 1842), pp. 7–9, 54–76, passim]. Van Schaack worked actively but quietly in the Federal cause during the 1790s. His letters are crowded with the conventional condemnations of "the Hydra of Faction" [to Theodore Sedgwick, 25 Dec. 1799, in Sedgwick Papers, Mass. Hist. Soc.]. But in the elections of 1792, 1795, 1798, 1800, and 1801 he was a faithful party worker. "I am busy writing letters as a Secretary of State or rather as a member of a *revolutionary committee*," the Kinderhook Tory wrote in 1800. "I trust that we may in one instance imitate the Jacobins" [to Sedgwick, 7 Apr. 1800, in Sedgwick Papers; many of his letters survive in the Van Schaack Papers, Library of Congress].

VARICK, RICHARD (1753–1831), b. Hackensack, N. J.; educated in lower schools; lawyer in New York City; served in the Continental Army; recorder of New York City, 1783–1789; mayor, 1789–1801; active in many philanthropic enterprises, including the American Bible Society and the New York City Humane Society [E. R. Purple, "Contributions to the History of the Ancient Families of New York," *N. Y. Gen. & Biog. Record* (Jan. 1877), pp. 16–20, 92; Griffin, *Their Brothers' Keepers*, pp. 28 passim]. Varick was described by a friendly observer as "a severe magistrate, an upright and honorable man, somewhat austere and lofty in his manner" [Duer, *Reminiscences*, p. 29]. As mayor of New York, his strict enforcement of the laws, particularly against men suspected of jacobinical tendencies, and his haughty manner made him one of the least popular men in the city. "Is it lawful to make use of the Devil to serve in [the] good cause?" he asked a brother Federalist. Varick thought not [to Abraham Van Vechten, 18 Mar. 1810, in Varick Papers,

N. Y. Hist. Soc.]. As haughty in defeat as he had been in power, he refused to subordinate himself to the discipline of a party, and in a violent quarrel with other New York Federalists in 1810 nearly wrecked the party in that city [Troup to King, 13, 27 Feb. 1810, in King Papers, N. Y. Hist. Soc.; Fox, *Decline of Aristocracy in New York*, p. 111].

Transitional Figures

COLEMAN, WILLIAM (1766–1829), b. Boston, Mass., perhaps in the poorhouse; patronized by Theodore Sedgwick (q.v.) and other older Federalists, he attended Andover Academy, studied law with Robert Treat Paine, and settled in New York City as a lawyer and journalist, becoming editor of the New York *Evening Post* in 1801. Though he made a profession of partisanship, he did so with dignity and restraint [see the cynical comment of Robert Troup, in chapter VII above]. The same elevated tone which characterized his newspaper appeared also in his polemical electioneering pamphlets, addressed to the people's reason, not to their passions. For a specimen of his style, see *An Appeal to the People . . .* (New York, 1810): "The time approaches, and it assuredly will, when an indignant and abused and insulted people will insist on an answer to it:—when they will demand their answer, in a tone that will carry dismay into the walls of the palace. . . ."

GRISWOLD, GAYLORD (1767–1809), b. Windsor, Hartford Co., Conn.; his father was a man of "great wealth and influence"; A.B., Yale, 1787; emigrated with Thomas R. Gold (q.v.) to Herkimer County, N. Y., where he practised law; member, N. Y. Assembly, 1796–1798; U. S. Congress, 1803–1805. A central figure in the federal committee organization in Herkimer County, his whole-hearted acceptance of partisanship separated him from Federalists of the old school. But he clung to other old-fashioned ideals, among them the conception of representation not as an agency but as a trust [AC 8/1/664, 7 Dec. 1803; for his activity in his county, see Benton, *Herkimer Co.*, pp. 314–316].

HAMILTON, ALEXANDER (1755?–1804): see above, chapter I.

PLATT, JONAS (1769–1834), b. Poughkeepsie, N. Y.; son of a prosperous lawyer and farmer; attended a French academy in Montreal, Canada; studied law under Richard Varick (q.v.); lawyer, jurist residing in Whitesboro, Oneida Co., N. Y.; clerk of Herkimer Co., 1791–1798; and of Oneida Co., 1798–1802; N. Y. Assembly, 1796; U. S. Congress, 1799–1801; unsuccessful federal candidate for governor, 1810; N. Y. Senate, 1810–1813; justice, N. Y. Supreme Court, 1814–1821 [Thompson, *Long Island*, II, 475; Wager, *Oneida Co.*, p. 253; Cookingham, *Oneida Co.*, p. 253]. Platt's prejudices were those of the old school. "We want your aid to give stability to the cause of virtue and merit," he wrote to James Kent (q.v.). "This part of the state is under the curse of browbeating influence—Men's characters are not known, and the state of society is not properly graduated" [13 Dec. 1796, in Kent Papers, Library of Congress]. In the early stages of his career he openly expressed these views [Morris S. Miller, *Address* (Whitestown, 1810), includes excerpts from Platt's speeches]; but in 1810 Platt was represented in his gubernatorial campaign as a "man of the people" and a "conscientious friend of the equal rights of man" [*An Address to the Independent Electors*, (n.p., 1810), p. 5]. Platt tried to live the part, even to the point of enflaming class animosities. "My colleagues from the western district who oppose this bill may, if they please, lick the crumbs which fall from the rich man's table," he declared. "As the representative of freemen, I disdain such mean condescension. I shall never turn swiss [mercenary] and enter into foreign service. May my tongue lose its utterance if my voice be ever raised in opposition to what I know to be the best interest of those whom I represent" [ibid.].

RADCLIFF, JACOB (1764–1844), b. Rhinebeck, N. Y., son of a wealthy landowner and Revolutionary general; A.B., Princeton, 1783; lawyer practising in Poughkeepsie, N. Y., and later in New York City; mayor of New York City, 1810, 1815–1817; Radcliff made no secret of his elitist attitudes [Hurd, *Long Island*, I, 349]. He did, however, participate in organized partisan activity on both state and national levels [Radcliff et al. to Committee at Martlings, 2 July 1807, in McKesson Papers, N. Y. Hist. Soc.; Radcliff to Mass. Central Committee, 25 Oct. 1808, in Otis Papers, Mass. Hist Soc.]. He was restless under the restraint of party discipline, however, and a perpetual nuisance to federal party leaders. In 1812 one of them noted with pleasure that "Judge Radcliff has made up his mind that his voice is better suited for concert than for solo" [Wm. Meredith to Wm. Sullivan, 17 Oct. 1812, in Columbia Univ. Coll., Columbia Univ. Library]. But the rejoicing was premature—in 1814 he participated in a party revolt by the New York "coodies," Gulian Verplanck, Hugh Maxwell (qq.v.), and others, against Federal leaders who were promoting an amalgamation with De Witt Clinton's renegade Republican following [Fox, *Decline of Aristocracy in New York*, p. 203].

TROUP, ROBERT (1757–1832), b. N. Y.; A.B., Columbia; studied law with John Jay and Wm. Peters; lt. col. in the Continental Army; secretary, Boards of War and Treasury; lawyer, land agent, speculator residing in Geneva, N. Y. Troup, in his heart of hearts, appears to have been a monarchist—he wrote privately of "such as do not admire (and I confess myself of this number) the republican system [to King, 6 June 1802, in

King, IV, 135], The events of 1800 did not surprise him. "Our system is just where it is by nature intended to be—in the hands of demagogues, and I think it will not be an easy work to rescue it from them" [to King, 9 Apr. 1802, in *King* IV, 104]. Nevertheless, he was prepared to try, and labored tirelessly for thirty years against "democracy" in New York [Troup to Nicholas Low, 18 Aug. 1789, 19 Feb. 1801, in Troup Papers, N.Y. Public Library; to Peter Van Schaack, 2 May 1800, in Van Schaack Papers, Library of Congress; to Gouverneur Morris, 4 Mar. 1809, in Morris Papers, Columbia Univ. Library; to King, 8 Jan. 1810, in King Papers, N. Y. Hist. Soc.].

VAN RENSSELAER, STEPHEN (1764–1839), b. New York City; A.B., Harvard, 1782; wealthy landowner with homes in Rensselaer Co., and Albany, N. Y.; member, N. Y. Assembly, 1789–1791, 1798, 1818; N. Y. Senate, 1791–1796; lieutenant governor of N. Y., 1795–1801; major general in the War of 1812; N. Y. Canal Commission, 1816–1839; U. S. Congress, 1822–1829. Van Rensselaer was a gentleman of the old school in his manners and speech—a splendid specimen of that ponderous political fossil, the high-minded Federalist, a powerful animal in its proper element but pathetically clumsy, weak, and defenceless in competition with the less majestic but more nimble beasts of nineteenth-century American politics. Without hope, he persevered in the cause of order [to King, 22 Oct. 1812, in *King*, V, 286–287], seeking a middle way between partisanship and independence, between the elitism of his youth and the expansive egalitarianism of the new world in which he had the misfortune to mature. Without going as far in his party sense as younger Federalists [to King, 12 Feb. 1813, in *King*, V, 291], he labored faithfully to promote the interest of his Federal friends; after the disintegration of their organization in New York, he helped to organize the so-called "People's Party," an amalgam of Federalists and Clintonian Democrats [Fox, *Decline of Aristocracy in the Politics of New York*, p. 299; see also Livermore, *Twilight of Federalism*, pp. 176–182].

Young Federalists

BLEECKER, HARMANUS (1779–1849), b. Albany, N. Y.; lawyer practicing in Albany; member of the Twelfth Congress; member of State Assembly, 1814, 1815; regent of the University of the State of New York, 1822–1834; chargé d'affaires in the Netherlands, 1837–1842. A "stiff-necked Albany Federalist" [Livermore, *The Twilight of Federalism*, p. 183], his elitism appears in private correspondence [Bleecker to Sedgwick, 12 June 1812, in Sedgwick Papers, Mass. Hist. Soc.]; but in public he sought to strike a more democratic pose. "Is it not better to have the hearts of the people with you," he declared in Congress [AC 12/2/1381, 6 May 1812; see also 1406, 1522–1523, 22 June 1812, 12/3/619, 7 Jan. 1813]. To that end he worked quietly within the formal machinery of New York Federalism [King, *King*, V, 506] and later joined Van Buren's Democratic organization [Van Buren, *Autobiography*, p. 429].

BRACKETT, JOSEPH WARREN (1775–1826), b. Greenland, N. H.; A.B., Dartmouth, 1800; lawyer practicing in New York City. Active in the Washington Benevolent Society, his *Oration delivered July 4, 1810* (Brooklyn, 1810) seeks to rouse the temper of "an enlightened and high spirited people" against their corrupt magistrates and, ineffectually, to erase the party's reputation for haughtiness. "Poverty is no disgrace," he said plaintively.

CADY, DANIEL (1773–1859), born and raised in that nursery of Federalists, Columbia Co., N. Y., son of a farmer; attended public schools and apprenticed to a shoemaker; became a property lawyer with a "large and lucrative practice" and a gentleman farmer residing in Florida and Johnstown, N. Y.; member, State Assembly, 1808–1813; village trustee, 1808, and supervisor 1809, 1810; district attorney, fifth district, 1813; member, fourteenth Congress, 1815–1817; justice, State Supreme Court, 1847–1855. Cady showed scant sympathy for old-school ideals—neither its stubborn independence, nor its belief in "energy in government," nor its devotion to the Union. "My friend Cady is sinking into *ennui*," wrote Moss Kent. "He considers our political body corrupt to the very core, wishes there was a separation of the Union, & thinks Congress will ruin the nation" [Moss Kent to Jas. Kent, 1 Jan. 1816, in Kent Papers, Library of Congress]. He moved toward an ideal of minimal governmental interference in the economy and in society [AC 14/1/1214–1217 (Mar. 14, 1816), 14/2/364 (24 Dec. 1816)], and in his "secretive and taciturn" manner took a leading part in federal party operations in New York [Alden Chester, *Courts and Lawyers of New York* (1925), pp. 1043, 1126; Raymond, *Columbia County*, pp. 44–45; Fox, *Decline of Aristocracy*, p. 178]; he supported Adams in 1824 [Hammond, *Political Parties NY*, II, 191].

COLDEN, CADWALLADER DAVID (1769–1834), b. Flushing, N. Y., to a prominent Tory family; educated in grammar schools in Jamaica, L. I. and London; lawyer in New York City with J. O. Hoffman; district attorney, 1798, 1810; member of Volunteers, War of 1812; member, State Assembly, 1818; mayor, New York, 1818–1820; member, Seventeenth Congress, 1821–1823; member, State Senate, 1824–1827; a founder of the American Academy of Fine Arts and a backer of the Erie Canal. Prominent in New York City Federalist organizations before

1812, he followed Clinton thereafter, calling himself an Independent Republican, and later led the so-called "People's Party" (populated largely with Federalists). As mayor of New York and U. S. Congressman, he practiced and preached retrenchment and economy [AC 17/1/666, 7 Jan. 1822; 17/1/577, 17/1/1004, 11 Feb. 1822; 17/1/1706, 27 Apr. 1822; 17/2/1073, 21 Feb. 1823; 17/2/492, 6 Jan. 1823].

CROSWELL, HARRY (1777–1858), b. West Hartford, Conn.; secondary education; clerk in a country store and printer's helper; Federalist editor and printer. Croswell addressed the people with less restraint and fewer scruples than Coleman. His new-modeled federal principles appear in the prospectus of his newspaper—"The sovereign people hold an awful scale or BALANCE; and their hand will never fail to weigh correct" [Albany Centinel, 2 Jan. 1810]—a far cry from Adams's use of the word. Croswell's political career ended abruptly in 1814, when, after many scrapes, he wearied of his partisan labors and took orders in the Episcopal church.

EMOTT, JAMES (1771–1850), b. Poughkeepsie N. Y. to an old Anglican family; preparatory studies; admitted to the bar, 1790; practiced in Albany until c. 1813, thereafter in Dutchess Co., N. Y.; land commissioner to settle disputes of titles to military reservations in Onondaga Co., 1797; member, State Assembly, 1804; member, Eleventh and Twelfth Congresses, 1809–1813; member, State Assembly, 1814–1817; judge, court of common pleas, Dutchess Co. 1817–1823; judge, second judicial circuit court, 1827–1831. His speech on the conduct of British Minister Francis J. Jackson, in which Emott distinguished between government and administration, is an important document in the difficult process by which young Federalists learned to play the role of an opposition party. "If the president has his duty to perform," Emott declared, "I also have mine. It is not, I trust, necessary in order to evince my respect for the Government, to approbate every Executive measure, or to join with the Administration" [AC, 11/2/805 (20 Dec. 1809)]. He was an active member of the Albany Committee of Correspondence ["In General Committee" (1801), Broadsides, New York Public Library] and attentive to problems of popularity and public opinion [Emott to King, 28 Dec. 1816, in King, VI, 39–41].

FOOTE, EBENEZER (1773–1814), b. Watertown, Conn., the son of a prosperous farmer; attended common schools and Tapping Reeve's law school; admitted to the bar in Connecticut, 1796; settled Lansingburgh, Rensselaer Co., 1797 [Kilbourne, Litchfield Co., Conn., pp. 181–186]. For his attempts to organize a Federalist partisan effort before 1800, see Williamson, American Suffrage, p. 159; but Foote was scandalized by those "unprincipled jacobin Federalists" who sought to return to power behind Clinton and anglophobia [Foote to S. Van Rensselaer, 12 Jan. 1881, in Misc. Mss., N. Y. Pub. Library]. Having begun his career as "Spencer's Foote," a follower of the apostate Ambrose Spencer, he later joined the Democratic-Republican party and supported Jackson until the Bank war [Van Buren, *Autobiography*, p.32].

GARDENIER, BARENT (c.1770?–1822), b. Kingston, N. Y.; preparatory studies; lawyer, journalist; resident of Kingston, N. Y. [Schoonmaker, *History of Kingston*, pp. 418, 451]; member, Tenth and Eleventh Congresses; district attorney, first district, 1813–1815. Gardenier accepted the necessity of a partisan role. "Being attached to [the Federal party]," he said, "is a circumstance in which I feel more pride than any other" [*AC*, 10/2/632, 1 Dec. 1808]. He also accepted the necessity for popular appeals. "I think it no small matter in this Government of ours to be able to catch the public ear," he wrote to Rufus King [Gardenier to King, 26 Jan. 1808, in *King*, V, 68]. He also addressed himself to popular prejudices. "You must either make the government supreme or the people supreme," he declared. "I am for the latter" [*AC*, 11/1/133, 27 May 1809].

GOLD, THOMAS RUGGLES (1764–1827), b. Cornwall, Conn.; A.B., Yale, 1786; lawyer, jurist residing in Oneida Co., N. Y. [Daniel Wager, *Oneida County* (Boston, 1896), pp. 143, 182, 234]; assistant attorney general, New York, 1797–1801; State Senate, 1796–1802; State Assembly, 1808; U. S. Congress, 1809–1813, 1815–1817. Gold was not impressed by the stubborn self-righteousness of such older Federalists as John Jay. "While I shall ever do justice to his integrity of character," he wrote, "I cannot but think there has been wanting a *knowledge of men*, & a disregard of the causes of popular impressions (which are often trifling & capricious) with too unbending & inflexible dispositions on various occasions. Instead of a mixture of the virtues of Cato and Caesar the former character has entirely predominated. Had Cato, instead of fastidiously standing aloof, pent up in Utica (repelling a Union with men whose views were not as pure as his own) joined his name to the arms of Pompey's sons, that day, in Spain on which Caesar fought not for Glory but for Life, would in all probability have put down the Usurper & restored the Republic" [to Sedgwick, 3 Nov. 1800, in Sedgwick Papers, Mass. Hist. Soc.]. Gold himself was not notably fastidious in his appeals to the people of Oneida County [Troup to King, 11 Apr. 1811, in *King*, V, 30]. He took an extended view of the powers of the national government, but tempered to the popular mood [*AC*, 11/3/712, 22 Jan. 1811; 14/1/878, 6 Feb. 1817; for his advocacy of freedom of speech and the right of opposition, see *AC*, 12/1/570, 23 Dec. 1811].

GRISWOLD, JOAB (1769–1814), b. Goshen, Conn.; lawyer and farmer in Herkimer Co., "one of the active & influential men who exerted themselves so successfully and efficiently in upholding the Federal party in the county" [Benton, *History of Herkimer County*, p. 316].

GROSVENOR, THOMAS PEABODY (1780–1817), b. Pomfret, Windham Co., Conn.; A.B., Yale, 1800; studied law with Elisha Williams; lawyer; resident of Hudson, N. Y. to 1815, when he removed to Baltimore [Raymond, *Columbia County*, pp. 39–41]; the brother-in-law of Elisha Williams, (q.v.); member, State Assembly, 1810–1812; U. S. Congress, 1813–1817. A master of popular invective and partisan politics, his *Oration delivered at Christ Church, Hudson* (1806) was a sustained effort to associate Federalists, described as "*men* of the people," with "liberty, equality & rights of man" and to link the opposition to blustering demagogues and "boozy democrats," mere insects of the hour, "buzzing round the rump of the republic." See also *AC* 13/1/116–118, 126, 31 May, 18 June 1813, for a conception of representation which conflicted with that of the old school.

HOFFMAN, JOSIAH OGDEN (1766–1837), b. Newark, N. J.; attended preparatory schools; commercial and maritime lawyer in New York City; his residence was valued at £2000 in 1799 [Wilson *Memorial Hist. New York City*]. Prominent in the New York City Federalist organization, he was a principal backer of DeWitt Clinton [Fox, *Decline of Aristocracy*, p. 167; Hoffman to Meredith, 30 Sep. 1812, Meredith Papers, Hist. Soc. Penn.] until his falling out over patronage in 1819, when he with other Federalists sponsored an anti-Clinton paper. His faction claimed to be "federal in their attachment to the union, and those principles on which it is grounded; republican in their veneration for all the institutions of their native land; and democratic in their deference to the will of the people, among whom they are proud to be included. . . . We mean the people *shall* be rulers. . . . We know no distinctions of class that entitles any man to the title of *public men;* and if there be any such, we are too democratic to acquiesce in so aristocratic an assumption of rank. Our aim is to level all obnoxious distinctions" [quoted in Livermore, *Twilight of Federalism*, p. 58]. Hoffman allied himself with the Tammany faction of New York democrats; in 1828 he voted for Andrew Jackson.

HOPKINS, SAMUEL MILES (1772–1837), b. Salem, Conn.; A.B., Yale, 1791; lawyer residing in New York City; State assembly, 1820–1821; U. S. Congress, 1813–1815; State Senate, 1822; reporter, New York Court of Chancery, 1823–1826; member, N. Y. Prison Commission, 1825–1830; Judge, State Circuit Court, 1832–1836. More restrained in his popular addresses than other younger Federalists [*An Oration delivered before the Washington Benevolent Society* (New York 1809)], he criticized the spirit of French fraternity at the same time that he became one of the leading lights of the Washington Benevolent Society (chairman of the standing committee, Washington Benevolent Society of New York, statement dated Mar. 14, 1810, in Washington Benevolent Society Papers, N. Y. Hist. Soc.].

JAY, PETER AUGUSTUS (1776–1843), b. Elizabeth-town, N. J.; son of John Jay; attended Columbia; lawyer residing in New York City; he was active in the Washington Benevolent Society and New York electioneering committees [Peter A. Jay to John Jay, 28 Feb. 1810, 11 Sep. 1812, in Jay Papers, Columbia Univ. *King*, V, 506]. His public statements became progressively more popular in tone; in 1810 his *Oration delivered before the Washington Benevolent Society* (New York, 1810) began with a distinction between the people and the populace, and proceeded to appeal to the former at the same time that the latter was castigated. Later, however, he sought to extend suffrage more broadly than most Democrats [Fox, *Decline of Aristocracy*, p. 269n].

MAXWELL, HUGH (1787–1873), b. Paisley, Scot.; A.B., Columbia, 1808; lawyer residing in New York City; an orator and leader of the Washington Society. He slipped easily and without apparent embarrassment into Tammany ranks in 1819 [Fox, *Decline of Aristocracy*, pp. 210, 214; see also John Rodman to Harmanus Bleecker, 15 Feb. 1813, in Rice, *Bleecker*, p. 57; and for his private life, Bigelow, *Diary of a Visit to Newport*, p. 11].

OAKLEY, THOMAS JACKSON (1783–1857), b. near Poughkeepsie, N. Y.; A.B., Yale, 1801; lawyer and resident of Poughkeepsie, N. Y.; surrogate, Dutchess County, 1810, 1811; U. S. Congress, 1813–1815; State Assembly, 1816, 1818–1820; attorney general of New York, 1819; U. S. Congress, 1827–1828; Judge, Superior Court of New York City, 1828–1847; appointed Chief Justice, October 1847, a position he held until his death. He was an extraordinarily adroit legislative leader. "He is prompt luminous & pointed," another said, "in the most shrewd and cunning manner he assails the President, yet in such cautious phraseology, that no old Foxes can check" [Fox, *Decline of Aristocracy*, p. 182]. For his acceptance of a partisan role and his labors in behalf of the Federal party, see Oakley to King, 16 Feb. 1816, in *King*, V, 513. He attempted to "unite the views and opinions of the party" in convention etc., and he also believed that the "essential interests of the country" were inseparably connected with the "prosperity and success of the Federal party." The son-in-law of Elisha Williams (q.v.), he voted for Jackson in 1824 [Hammond, II, 255] and was satirized as "Dick Shift" in *The Bucktail Bards*.

OGDEN, DAVID A. (1770–1829), b. Morristown, N. J.; attended Columbia; in 1812 removed to St. Lawrence Co., lawyer in partnership with Alexander Hamilton; associate judge, court of common pleas, St. Lawrence County, N. Y., 1811–1815; State Assembly, 1814–1815; U. S. Congress, 1817–1819; Judge of the Court of Common Pleas, 1820–1824, 1825–1829.

OGDEN, DAVID BAYARD (1775–1849), b. Morrisania, N. Y.; cousin of David A. Ogden, nephew of Gouverneur Morris; A.B., Univ. of Penn., 1792; lawyer residing in New York City. His fear and hatred of democracy which appears in Ogden to Meredith 5 June 1805 [Meredith Papers, Hist. Soc. of Penna.], drove him to partisan activity. "If this country is to be saved," he wrote, "if we are to be spared from that general wreck of freedom, the country, under providence, must owe its salvation to the Federal party" [ibid., 29 June 1812]. See also his statement that Federalists should sacrifice their personal views and pleasured to "the good of the party" [Ogden to S. Van Renssaelaer 24 Jan. 1813, in Ogden Papers, N. Y. Hist. Soc.]. An active leader of the Washington Society [Ogden to Meredith 10 Dec. 1812, in Meredith Papers, Hist. Soc. of Penna.], he attempted to bring older Federalists into active participation [Ogden to Rufus King, 17 Feb. 1816, *King*, V 513–516; New York *Evening Post*, 9 Mar. 1813].

SHIPHERD, ZEBULON RUDD (1768–1841), b. Granville, Washington Co., N. Y.; educated in local schools; lawyer practising in Granville; U. S. Congress, 1813–1815. Shipherd was active in committee work and also in the founding of Washington Societies in New York and Vermont [Windsor *Vt. Republican*, 27 May 1811]. His Congressional speeches are ripe specimens of young Federalist oratory, with much of liberty and equal rights, of widows and orphans, of home and country. He defended the positive-good doctrine of partisanship, and articulated an essentially Jeffersonian ideal of the relationship between government and the people [AC 13/1/1502–23, 18 Feb. 1814; 13/1/1018, 17 Jan. 1814].

TIBBITS, GEORGE (1763–1849), b. Warwick, R. I.; educated in lower schools, merchant, manufacturer, gentleman farmer, and president of the county agricultural society; investor in lands and internal improvements; active Episcopal layman; member, N. Y. Assembly, 1800; U. S. Congress, 1803–1805; unsuccessful candidate for lieutenant governor, 1816; member, N. Y. Prison Commission; Mayor of Troy, 1830–1836 [A. J. Weise, *History of Troy*, pp. 49, passim]. Tibbits was not prominent in Congress, but he took a leading part in federal party affairs in his state and also attended the national meetings in New York (see above, ch. IV).

VAN NESS, WILLIAM W. (1776–1823), b. Claverack, N. Y.; attended lower schools; served in the N. Y. Assembly; Judge of N. Y. Supreme Judicial Court, 1807–1822. In politics and law, Van Ness constructed a career on the arts of popularity. It was said of his courtroom style as an attorney that he won cases "by asking the foreman of the jury for a chew of tobacco" [Fox, *Decline of Aristocracy*, p. 43]. He was deeply engaged in partisan affairs, despite occasional moments of despair [Van Ness to Solomon Van Rensselaer, 18 Mar. 1807, in Catherine Bonney, *Legacy of Historical Gleanings*, 2 vols. (Albany, 1875), II, 158; Van Ness to Samuel M. Hopkins, 8 Nov. 1811, in Misc. Mss., N. Y. Pub. Library]. His skill at lobbying was the subject of a formal legislative investigation [N. Y. General Assembly, Committee on the Official Conduct of William W. Van Ness, *Proceedings* (Albany, 1820), passim]. For a sketch of his character, his early enthusiasm for the French Revolution, and his conversion to the Federal cause, see "Memo on Van Ness," n.d. (circa 1840), in James Kent Papers, Library of Congress.

VAN RENSSELAER, JACOB RUTSEN. According to Dixon Fox, he was "somewhat older than Williams and Van Ness [q.v.], but not less active in the arduous work of party politics, riding far and wide to check up votes, and spending many days and nights in Albany in an unofficial way" [p. 44]. He served nine terms in the N. Y. Assembly, and was a central figure in the Federalists' N. Y. State Convention in 1816 [Van Rensselaer to King, 16 Feb. 1816, in *King*, V, 507–508].

VAN RENSSELAER, KILLIAN KILLIAN (1763–1845), b. Rensselaer Co., N. Y.; attended Yale; lawyer practising in Claverack and Albany; U. S. Congress, 1801–1811. His Congressional speeches prompted the compilers of the *Biographical Directory of the American Congress* to call him a Democrat. But for his active participation in federal party affairs, see Van Rensselaer to Peter Van Schaack, 29 Jan. 1802, in Van Rensselaer Papers, N. Y. Hist. Soc.; and Van Rensselaer to Pickering, 12 July 1808, in Pickering Papers, Mass. Hist. Soc.

VAN VECHTEN, ABRAHAM (1762–1837), b. Catskill, N. Y.; attended Columbia; studied law with John Lansing, and practised in Albany. To Jeffersonians, Van Vechten was a formidable partisan opponent, "much addicted to intrigue" [Hammond, *History of Political Parties in New York*, I, 457]. A Federalist, Robert Troup, said of Van Vechten and

Van Ness (q.v.), "No two men in our whole party seem to be actuated by purer motives than these two men. They certainly work harder for us than any other men, are extremely anxious to promote harmony and prevent desertions [or divisions?]" [to Rufus King, 9 Feb. 1810, in King Papers, N. Y. Hist. Soc]. Van Vechten's manuscripts testify to the accuracy of Troup's observations [Van Vechten to Theodore Dwight, 12 Aug. 1812, in Misc. Mss., N. Y. Pub. Library; to Gouverneur Morris, 4 Apr. 1809, in Morris Papers, Columbia Univ. Library; to Harrison Gray Otis, 21 July 1808, in Otis Papers, Mass. Hist. Soc.]. For Van Vechten's new-modeled conservatism see his *Speech . . . on the important subject of Encreasing the Number of Banks* (n.p., 1811). He would become a leader of the so-called "People's Party" [Fox, *Decline of Aristocracy*, p. 299; and see generally J. B. Van Vechten, *The Van Vechten Genealogy* (Detroit, 1954), pp. 396–399).

VERPLANCK, GULIAN CROMMELIN (1786–1870), b. New York City, son of Daniel Crommelin Verplanck (1762–1834), a transitional Federalist Congressman; A.B., Columbia, 1801; lawyer practising in New York City; member, N. Y. Assembly, 1820–1823; U. S. Congress, 1825–1833; N. Y. Senate, 1838–1841; interested in many educational and philanthropic causes. In the course of his extraordinary career, Verplanck served all four major parties in American political history—first a Federalist, he was a Democrat in his Congressional period, a Whig in the 1840s, and at the very end of his life a Republican. An able sketch by Dixon Ryan Fox [*Decline of Aristocracy*, pp. 160–161) demonstrates his relevance to this investigation. Older Federalists were appalled by Verplanck's aggressive pursuit of popular opinion. In his first important public statement, *An Oration delivered July 4th, 1809* (New York, 1809), this young Federalist declared, "Fellow citizens—to whom do we owe this? To whom do we owe it that we this day met in freedom and in peace? Not to our Pickerings or Bayards, and our Lloyds. No, not to them—though they have done much, though they have deserved well. No—but to the people themselves—the people who had discernment to distinguish their friends from their flatterers." An older Federalist, probably William Coleman, declared in 1811, "Mr. Coody [Verplanck] calls himself a Federalist, because he votes on the Federalist side, and sometimes, I believe, contributes alms to the Federalist purse, but if honest Abimelech would go over to the other party at once, his open apostasy would be of more service to us than either his vote or his money, and for this plain reason, because he now has some little influence among certain Federalists and he exerts it only to do mischief" [quoted in Fox, p. 161]. The mischief for which Verplanck is principally remembered was his opposition, over the pen name of Abimelech Coody, to an alliance between Federalists and Clintonians. He was also centrally involved in the clash between old and young Federalists in 1811, which ended in an unseemly riot at a Columbia commencement [see July, *The Essential New Yorker*, passim; for an interesting perspective, see De Witt Clinton, *An Account of Abimelech Coody* (New York, 1815) and see also Fox, pp. 162–166].

WARNER, HENRY WHITING (1787–1875), a lawyer, practising in New York City [Olivia Stokes, ed., *Letters and Memories of Susan & Anne Bartlett Warner* (New York, 1925), p. 217]. Warner was active on electioneering committees and a leader in the Washington Society. His *Oration* (New York, 1814) delivered before that organization was an exhortation to popular partisan activity. "Popular sentiment is not only the common engine of evil," he declared, "but also the only possible medium of great national reform. You cannot easily mistake the proper course of conduct, or too ardently pursue it. You are required to study and to teach the principles of your political system, to ascertain and assert the rights of the citizen, to guard the limits of Constitutional authority in the government, freely and fully to discuss public measures and characters, to detect intrigue, to expose folly, to chastise iniquity."

WELLS, JOHN (1770–1823), b. Cherry Valley, N. Y.; A.B. Princeton, 1788; studied law with Edward Griswold and practised in New York City. Wells began his partisan career as a leader of an informal voluntary association of "Federalist Young Men," in New York City in the late 1790s, which served as a party auxiliary in a role comparable to that later played by the Washington Society, in which Wells was also active [Wells to Richard Varick, 3 July 1799, in Varick Papers, N. Y. Hist. Soc.]. He also served on party committees, including state corresponding committees [Wells et al. to William Gaston, 25 Aug. 1812, in Gaston Papers, Southern Hist. Coll., Univ. of N. C.]. For his new-fashioned conservatism, see his *Oration, delivered on the Fourth of July, 1798* . . . (New York, 1798), a direct popular appeal in a quasi-Jeffersonian style.

WILLIAMS, ELISHA (1773–1833), b. Pomfret, Conn.; educated in lower schools; attended Tapping Reeve's (q.v.) law school in Litchfield, Conn.; lawyer practising in Hudson, N. Y., and worth perhaps $250,000 at his death. Williams was a prototypical political "boss," in Columbia Co., N. Y. The word is an anachronism, but in its Dutch origin, it bears a relevance to Williams's relationship with his Dutch neighbors. A local historian described him as "the leader of the federal party in this county, and dictated who should go to Congress, but would never consent to be a candidate for that office himself" [Raymond, *Distinguished Men of Columbia County*, pp. 1–21, 105–117]. A frequent visitor to Albany, he was described by Gulian Verplanck (q.v.) as the "known chief of all the lobby tribe" [Dr. *Busby's Edition of the Bucktail Bards containing The Triumvirate and the Epistles of Pindar Puff* (New York, 1819), pp. 25–27]. For his political methods, which appear to have been remarkably similar to those of late nineteenth-century bossism, in use of favors to bind the people to party leaders, see Williams to Abraham Van Vechten, 25 Apr. 1807, in Columbia Univ. Coll., Columbia Univ. Library.

NEW JERSEY

Federalists of the Old School

BEATTY, JOHN (1749–1826), b. Bucks Co., Penn.; A.B., Princeton, 1769; physician practising in Bucks Co., and after 1781 in Princeton and Trenton, N. J.; banker; gentleman farmer; colonel in the Continental Army; member, N. J. Council, 1781–1783; Continental Congress, 1784–1785; N. J. Ratifying Convention, 1787; N. J. Assembly, 1789–1790 (speaker); U. S. Congress, 1793–1795; N. J. Secretary of State, 1795–1805. An exceptional figure among his old-school contemporaries, he actively engaged in electioneering [Trenton *Federalist*, 18 May 1812]. In Congress he was mindful of "the duty he owed to his constituents" [AC, 3/2/1212, 11 Feb. 1795].

BLACK, JOHN (1752–1813), b. Burlington Co., N. J.; educated in lower schools; wealthy farmer and landowner in Springfield, N. J., his estate was estimated at $42,000 at his death [E. M. Woodward, *History of Burlington and Morris Counties* (Philadelphia, 1883), p. 447]. An *Address to the Federal Republicans of Burlington County* (Trenton, 1800), which Black signed and may have written, was a sharp attack upon the means and ends of the Jeffersonian movement. "There is in our country a daring and numerous band of men resolved in the overthrow of public order," he declared. These jacobinical disorganizers could be detected by their desperate tactics. "When we hear *chairmen* spouting sedition to the ignorant, and inflaming the passionate . . . ought we not to suspect that *such* advocates have a bad cause, and that *such* zeal is directed to a bad purpose?" he asked. General Black was unable to fathom the dissatisfaction of the people with a government of unrivalled wisdom and virtue. "Why are we troubled with speeches and handbills, and importunate declaimers against government?" he wondered. He urged the people to ignore the innovators and continue to support "old friends and old principles" [pp. 17, 18, 24].

BOUDINOT, ELIAS (1740–1821), b. Philadelphia, son of a silversmith; attended Franklin's Academy; lawyer and landowner residing in Burlington, N. J. after 1805; active speculator in New Jersey, Pennsylvania, and Ohio lands; Commissary General of Prisoners in the Continental Army, 1776–1779; Continental Congress, 1777–1778, 1781–1784 (president, 1782–1783); U. S. Congress, 1789–1795; Director of U. S. Mint, 1795–1805. His many philanthropic interests included the American Bible Society, of which he was president (1816–1821), and Princeton (trustee, 1772–1821) [George A. Boyd, *Elias Boudinot* (Princeton, 1952), passim]. Boudinot's disapproval of democracy, partisanship, and the tactics of younger Federalists appears in his reaction to the resolutions of James Hillhouse (q.v.). "Perhaps we old fashioned folks may fear more keenly every innovation on the Constitution from former experience of unrestrained power in men of any description," he wrote. "I fear many of our mistakes arise from the fashionable principle, that our government is a republican one—Although this may be true in a strict sense, it is certainly not so in a popular or democratic idea of the term." Boudinot manifested an Adamsonian infatuation for "mixed Government, properly balanced, partaking in wise proportion of all the forms of government." He feared that the tactics of young Federalists and young Republicans together would end in "anarchy and confusion" [to Pickering, 3 June 1808, in Pickering Papers, Mass. Hist. Soc.]. Boudinot preferred a sort of home remedy for social and political problems. The sheet anchor of his conservatism was evangelical religion, disseminated broadly among "every poor family" by the common effort of Protestant Christians of all denominations. Nothing else, he believed, could serve so well "to ameliorate the manners, the tempers and regulate the conduct of the people at large, leading them to greater tenderness and good will" [Boudinot, *An Address delivered before the New-Jersey Bible Society* (Burlington, 1811), p. 12; see also his *Age of Revelation* (Philadelphia, 1801), an answer to Paine's *Age of Reason*]. The institutional manifestation of Boudinot's belief was the American Bible Society and similar groups in which many Federalists joined [see Griffin, *Their Brother's Keepers*, passim].

BOUDINOT, ELISHA (1749–1819), b. Philadelphia, brother of Elias Boudinot (q.v.); educated in lower schools; worked with his brother as commissary of prisoners during the Revolution; lawyer residing in Newark; speculator in lands and securities; justice, N. J. Supreme Court, 1798–1804. Boudinot was more active in partisan politics than his elder brother. He was among a group of Federalists who invaded a Republican Society in 1794 and passed resolutions condemning such organizations as "improper and unnecessary" [Fee, *Transition from Aristocracy to Democracy in N. J.*, p. 40] and participated in an open caucus in 1800 [Trenton *Federalist*, 25 Nov. 1800]. But his principles appear to have been close to his brother's—he described himself as one of the "fellow-travellers of the *old school*" [Elisha Boudinot to Pickering, 24 Feb. 1807, in Pickering Papers, Mass. Hist. Soc.].

CADWALADER, LAMBERT (1742–1823), b. near Trenton, N. J., son of a physician; attended Univ. of Penn.; served in Penn. Provincial Conventions, 1775–1776; lt. col. Continental Army, 1776–1777; member, Continental Congress, 1784–1787; U. S. Congress, 1789–1791, 1793–1795; wealthy landowner residing near Trenton. This eighteenth-century gentleman, whose manners were marked by "good breeding, courtesy and elegance" [Wm. Henry Rawle, "Col. Lambert Cadwalader," *Penna. Mag. Hist. Biog.*, X (1886), 1–14], approved of the creation of an extraconstitutional conservative counterforce against disorganizers—and rationalized it not as a partisan effort in its own right but as "an indirect measure of Government" [to King, 25 Aug. 1793, in *King*, I, 494–495]. He later contributed to the Federal effort in New Jersey, serving as a sponsor of the Trenton *Federalist* [to Pickering, 30 Dec. 1803, in Pickering Papers, Mass. Hist. Soc.].

DAVENPORT, FRANKLIN (1755–1832), b. Philadelphia, a nephew of Benjamin Franklin; educated in lower schools; rose from private to colonel in the Continental Army; member, N. J. Assembly, 1786–1789; U. S. Senate, 1798–1799; U. S. Congress, 1799–1801. He publicly condemned the tactics of the Jeffersonians, specifically the formation of secret societies; Republicans replied that Davenport himself belonged to one [Fee, *Transition from Aristocracy to Democracy in New Jersey*, p. 134]. In 1812 he participated in a Federal "convention," however [Trenton *Federalist*, 21 Sep. 1812; Edes, "Davenport," *Col. Soc. Mass. Pubs.*, X (1906), 356–365].

ELMER, JONATHAN (1745–1817), b. Cumberland Co., N. J.; M.D., Univ. of Penn., 1768; captain, Continental Army, 1775; Continental Congress, 1776–1778, 1781–1784; U. S. Senate, 1789–1791; judge, Cumberland Co. Court, 1802–1804; physician practising in Cumberland Co., active in medical societies, philanthropic and educational affairs. "Formal and stately in his address," Elmer was described by Lucius Horatio Stockton (q.v.) as "an ardent friend of *regulated* liberty" [Brooke More, *Genealogy of the Elmer & More Families* (Boston, 1930), p. 45]. His holistic social ideas, his elitist politics, and his hunger for "high-toned government" appear in his jury charges [ibid., pp. 49–50] and in an address in the Trenton *Federalist*, 20 July 1812.

FRELINGHUYSEN, FREDERICK (1753–1804), b. near Somerville, N. J.; A.B., Princeton, 1773; rose from captain to colonel in the Continental Army; Continental Congress, 1778–1779, 1782–1783; N. J. Assembly, 1784, 1800–1804; N. J. Ratifying Convention, 1787; N. J. Council, 1790–

1792; U. S. Senate, 1793–1796. Frelinghuysen was active in partisan politics, as were many older Federalists in New Jersey [Newark *Gazette,* 25 Nov. 1800]. But he participated in an old-fashioned, elitist spirit. In 1800 he declared publicly, "We cannot all be Washingtons, he was a peculiar favorite of heaven; but we can all be *patriots,* and all Christians. Like him, let us love our country, and in our different stations, exert ourselves to promote its welfare. While we lament a Washington dead, let us honor and support an Adams living" [*Oration on the Death of General George Washington* (New Brunswick, 1800)].

HENDERSON, THOMAS (1743–1824), b. Freehold, N. J.; A.B., Princeton, 1761; physician residing in Freehold, N. J.; member, N. J. Committee of Safety, 1774; rose from lieutenant to colonel in the War for Independence; member, N. J. Assembly, 1780–1784; Council, 1793–1794; acting governor, 1794; U. S. Congress, 1795–1797; judge, county court of common pleas, 1783–1799; Council, 1812–1813. In a major speech on Jay's treaty, Henderson articulated the old-school ideal of representation—the legislator's duty was to serve his country, not his district. He attacked "party views and high raised prejudices" in politics, and declared that "the gentlemen of the opposition appear to me to savor too much of the character of the wolf in sheep's clothing," who in claiming to preserve liberty by appeals to the people were in fact perverting it. The prevailing tone of his speech was a deep conservatism— "I hope we shall, in our career, stop short of changing the times and seasons," he declared [*AC,* 4/1/1158–70, 22 Apr. 1796]. But despite his own prejudices, he showed a considerable respect for popular power. Urging his Federal brethren to moderate their proposed military and tax programs in 1797. "Should we then encourage the agitation of the public mind, already too much agitated, by adopting measures which would prove unpopular and disagreeable?" [ibid., 4/2/1874, 16 Jan. 1797].

KIRKPATRICK, ANDREW (1756–1831), b. Somerset Co., N. J.; son of a Presbyterian clergyman; A.B., Princeton, 1775; after briefly studying theology and serving as a tutor in the Taliaferro family of Virginia, he studied law with William Paterson (q.v.); m. the daughter of Col. John Bayard; settled in New Brunswick, N. J. [James Grant Wilson, *Memorials of Andrew Kirkpatrick* (New York, 1870), pp. 19, passim]. Kirkpatrick was a hanging judge, "a firm believer in capital punishment" [ibid., p. 26]. His dignity, aloofness, and "caustic severity" were said to inspire "the beholder with a respect approaching awe" [ibid., pp. 19, 23]. But the same qualities could arouse other emotions. Kirkpatrick expected deference as his due; when it was not naturally forthcoming, he commanded it. Once, he was driving to his court on a narrow New Jersey road. "Overtaking another vehicle containing two persons going slowly in the same direction, he courteously requested them to permit him to pass, as he was in haste, but when he attempted to go by they obstructed the way, and, with a dog-in-manger spirit, would neither hasten on themselves nor permit the judge to do so; the result was that he arrived half an hour late." From his bench he ordered the arrest of the two tardy travelers and fined them himself for obstructing the Justice [ibid., p. 26]. Jeffersonian journals describe many similar occurrences, all symptomatic of the changing spirit of American society and of the fatal flaw in Federalism—there was surely no more swift and certain way to make an instant Democrat. But if Kirkpatrick contributed to the growth of the Jeffersonian party, he was unprepared to meet it on its own ground. For active partisans of all persuasions he had a deep contempt [ibid., p. 32].

NEILSON, JOHN (1745–1833), b. near New Brunswick, N. J.; attended Univ. of Penn.; merchant in New Brunswick with at least four ships of his own in overseas trade; investor in miscellaneous manufacturing enterprises; rose from captain to brigadier in the War of Independence; Continental Congress, 1778–1779; member, N. J. Ratifying Convention, 1787; N. J. Assembly, 1800–1801. Described by a contemporary as a gentleman of the old school [Trenton *Federalist*, 3 Oct. 1808], he nevertheless served as chairman, perhaps a figurehead, of a Federalist state "convention" in 1812 [ibid., 21 Sep. 1812]. For his strict business ethics, see a biography of his son, Robert Thompson's *Col. James Neilson* (New Brunswick, 1940), pp. 5–8, 13–30, 47.

PATERSON, WILLIAM (1745–1806), b. County Antrim, Ireland; emigrated 1747; his father was an itinerant peddler who prospered in the new world; A.B., Princeton, 1763; lawyer residing in New Brunswick after 1783; speculator in loyalist estates; attorney general of N. J., 1776–1783; U. S. Constitutional Convention, 1787; U. S. Senate, 1789–1790; governor, N. J., 1790–1793; associate justice, U. S. Supreme Court, 1793–1806 [Gertrude S. Wood, *William Paterson of New Jersey* (Fair Lawn, N. J., 1933), passim]. If he manifested a conventional horror of the Jeffersonian movement [*The Charge of Judge Paterson to the Jury* (Philadelphia, 1796), p. 24, passim], he spoke in an extraordinarily popular vein in the Great Convention. "The democratic spirit beats high," he declared. "We must follow the People; the People will not follow us—The plan must be accommodated to the public mind—consult the genius, the Temper, the Habits, the Prejudices of the People" ["Papers of William Paterson," *Amer. Hist. Rev.*, IX (1904), 310–340]. Paterson remains a puzzle; a fresh biographical study would be very useful.

RUTHERFURD, JOHN (1760–1840), b. New York City; A.B., Princeton, 1779; lawyer, gentleman farmer residing near Allamuchy, N. J., and later near Passaic, N. J.; member, N. J. Assembly, 1788–1789; U. S. Senate, 1791–1798. Rutherfurd's elitism and his preference for a structured society appear in his "Notes on the State of New Jersey" [*N. J. Hist. Soc. Proceedings*, 2d ser., I (1867), 79–89] and particularly in his comments on higher education. "It must be owned that the Farmers, and middle Class of People run too much to sending their sons to Colleges, which unfits them for their Employments, greatly overstocks the learned Professions, gives other ideas beyond their circumstances, makes too many Candidates for public offices, and contributes to prolonging the annual Elections, which sometimes throws the Country idle for ten days or even more, and occasions Animosities even among near Relations that the rest of the year hardly make up" [pp. 81–82].

SINNICKSON, THOMAS (1744–1817), b. near Salem, N. J.; educated in lower schools; captain, Continental Army; member, N. J. Assembly, 1777, 1782, 1784–1785, 1787–1788; U. S. Congress, 1789–1791, 1797–1799; merchant in Salem, N. J. Sinnickson was the reputed author of *Plain Truth; or, an Address to the Citizens of New-Jersey and to the Inhabitants of the County of Salem in Particular* (n.p., 1812), a didactic, popular address heavy with nostalgia for "those happy times in which there were a reciprocity of confidence between the *rulers* and the *ruled*" [p. 5]. This idealized symbiotic social relationship, more clearly articulated in New England than in the middle states, pervades the entire work. Sinnickson was appointed to attend a Federal state convention in 1814 [Trenton *Federalist*, 27 June 1814].

SMITH, SAMUEL STANHOPE (1750–1819), a Presbyterian clergyman; son-in-law of John Witherspoon; taught classics and moral philosophy at Princeton, 1770–1773, 1779–1812; president of that college, 1795–1812. His sermons, pamphlets, and textbooks articulated old-school ideals. The fullest rendering is his *Moral and Political Philosophy*, 2 vols. (Trenton, 1812), in which he argued that "the mass of the populace is necessarily ignorant . . . and their passions inflamed by the insidious arts, and violent harangues" [II, 295]. His prescription was open balloting and "a selected electoral class" [ibid., II, 298]. In another work he warned, "The passions of a people are dangerous engines of faction and ambition. Often you may rouse them to a destructive fury by a grimace of false patriotism, or a fanaticism of mistaken liberty. But you cannot mark the point beyond which they shall not rise" [*The Divine Goodness of the United States of America* (Philadelphia, 1795), p. 28; and see also his *Evil of Slander* (Boston, 1791), *Oration upon the Death of Gen. George Washington* (Trenton, 1800), *On the Love of Praise* (New Brunswick, 1810), and his correspondence with Timothy Pickering, quoted in chapter I, above].

WALLACE, JOSHUA MADDOX (1752–1819), b. New Jersey ?; A.B., Penn., 1767; lawyer and judge, Burlington Co. Court of Common Pleas. Wallace is an exception, an older Federalist who engaged actively in partisan affairs after 1800, and shared the ambition of younger men to "bring out every vote" and unify the party in an efficient organization [Wallace et al. to George Hancock et al., 26 Oct. 1808, in Ely Papers, N. J. Hist. Soc.].

Transitional Figures

DAYTON, JONATHAN (1760–1824), b. Elizabeth-town, N. J., son of a wealthy merchant; A.B., Princeton, 1776; captain, Continental Army; member, N. J. Assembly, 1786–1787, 1790; U. S. Constitutional Convention, 1787; Continental Congress, 1787–1788; N. J. Council, 1790; U. S. Congress, 1791–1799 (speaker, 1795–1799); U. S. Senate, 1799–1805; lawyer, merchant, speculator in land and securities residing in Elizabeth-town, N. J. Dayton, as a historian has commented, "could usually be found strongly advocating the winning side in public questions" during the 1790s [Kurtz, Presidency of John Adams, p. 39]. But he demonstrated a steady distaste for "intemperate democratical zeal" from 1788, and participated in efforts to organize New Jersey Federalists into an efficient party before 1800 [to Oliver Wolcott, 4 Sep. 1796, in Gibbs, Administrations of Washington and Adams, I, 381; Dayton to Hunter, 29 Dec. 1788, in Dayton Papers, N. J. Hist. Soc.]. The odor of corruption lingers over Dayton's career—he manifested the same weakened moral sense which marked other Federalists of his age—too young to have internalized old-school ethics, too old to have found newer ethical patterns meaningful. In 1800, Secretary of the Treasury Oliver Wolcott (q.v.) discovered that Dayton had pocketed $18,000 in Federal funds entrusted to his care, a serious "breach of trust" as Wolcott himself considered it. Only with difficulty could Dayton be persuaded to make restitution [Wolcott to George Cabot, 18 June 1800, in Lodge, Cabot, p. 280; White, The Federalists, p. 346; J. C. Miller's statement that "during their tenure of power, no Federalist officeholder was found guilty of malfeasance" (Federalist Era, p. 115) is only technically true— none were brought to trial. Self-policing was the principal safeguard]. Dayton was later indicted for his participation in Aaron Burr's conspiracy but not brought to trial. Whatever Burr himself may have had in mind, Dayton appears to have been contemplating disunion [Adams, History of the U. S., III, 234–235].

OGDEN, AARON (1756–1839), b. Elizabeth-town, N. J.; A.B., Princeton, 1773; major, Continental Army; clerk, Essex County, N. J., 1785–1803; U. S. Senate, 1801–1803; Governor of N. J., 1812; U. S. Collector of

Customs, 1830–1839. In the election of 1800 he took an active part, but in the spirit of colonial American politics, he was more interested in the elite than the people and not deeply committed to his party [Ogden to Dayton, 6 Dec. 1800, in Dayton Papers, N. J. Hist. Soc.; Ogden, *Autobiography*, p. 23]. After the Jeffersonian victory was apparent, Ogden stubbornly predicted a happy ending. "The good sense of the American people," he wrote privately, "shall again lead them to place their confidence in such men as have been the constant advocates of sound principles and practices, though perhaps a little unpalatable, in preference to those popular parasites who flatter only for their self-promotion" [to John Rutledge, Jr., 22 Apr. 1803, in Rutledge Papers, Univ. of N. C.; see also AC 7/1/171, 3 Feb. 1802].

STOCKTON, RICHARD (1764–1828), b. Princeton, N. J.; A.B., Princeton, 1779; studied law with his uncle Elisha Boudinot (q.v.); lawyer, gentleman farmer residing at "Morven," near Princeton, N. J.; U. S. Senate, 1796–1799; U. S. Congress, 1813–1815. Stockton's impeccable manners and aristocratic demeanor occasioned his nickname—"Duke." His descendants remember that he despised "the arts of the politician"; nevertheless, he accepted a partisan role and favored "all the exertion which comports with federal integrity" [to Sedgwick, 29 Nov. 1800, in Sedgwick Papers, Mass. Hist. Soc.]. In Congress he defended his right to participate in a party opposition—"Opposition, Sir, can never be put down whilst the Constitution or one shred of it remains," he declared [AC, 13/2/1013, 17 Jan. 1814]. He took the younger Federalists' view of representation, drawing tight "the ties that bind me to my constituents" [ibid., 1014]; and he spoke for minimal government, advocating a "system of rigid economy" in 1815 [13/3/1229, 24 Jan. 1815]. Stockton, despite his dignity, was not above demagoguery. He waved "the good old flag of America" [13/2/1013, 17 Jan. 1814], and once declared piously, "I am the defender of the rights and liberties of the people of these United States, and by the help of God I will defend them" [ibid., 13/2/881, 10 Jan. 1814; see also 13/2/3034–3042, 11 Dec. 1813].

Young Federalists

BAYARD, SAMUEL (1767–1840), b. Philadelphia; A.B., Princeton, 1784; m. the neice of Elias Boudinot (q.v.); U. S. Commissioner of Claims in London, 1794–1798—an "informal appointment," as a "personal representative of the President" [see David L. Sterling, ed., "A Federalist Opposes the Jay Treaty: The Letters of Samuel Bayard," *William and Mary Quarterly*, ser. 3, XVIII (1961), 408–424]. Bayard served as editor of the New York *Daily Advertiser* after his return to America; in 1806 he settled in Princeton, where he became presiding judge of the Somerset

Co. Court of Common Pleas, trustee and treasurer of Princeton, founder of the Princeton Theological Seminary, and a prominent Presbyterian layman. He was an active organizer of Federal meetings in his county [Trenton *Federalist,* 5 Sep. 1808] and served as secretary (the most important office) of a Federal State "Convention" [ibid., 21 Sep. 1812]. His *Address to the Well Disposed* . . . (New York, 1801) is an argument to "the good sense of the people" that "Federal Republicans" are their "true friends."

COXE, WILLIAM (1762–1831), b. Philadelphia; educated in lower schools; merchant, gentleman farmer, horticulturist [U. P. Hedrick, *A History of Horticulture in America to 1860* (New York, 1950), p. 211]; resided near Burlington, N. J.; N. J. Assembly, 1796–1804 (speaker, 1798–1800, 1802), 1806–1809, 1816–1817; U. S. Congress, 1813–1815. His *Address of the Convention to the Free-Electors of New-Jersey* (1814) was a partisan appeal for popular support. The "fundamental rights of the American people," he argued, had been violated by their self-proclaimed protectors—specifically by secret legislative sessions and restraints upon freedom of petition. "The remedy," he said, "is in our *own* hands. Let us all firmly *resolve* (however firmly we must endure *existing* evils with fortitude and patience) that the *freedom of suffrage* shall finally re-establish the Friends of Peace and the Policy of Washington" [pp. 5–7, cf. Pole, "Federalist Dilemma in New Jersey," pp. 278–279].

GRIFFITH, WILLIAM (1766–1826), b. Boundbrook, N. J., son of a physician educated at home; read law with Elisha Boudinot (q.v.) and practised in Burlington, N. J.; member, N. J. Assembly, 1818–1819, 1823–1824; mayor of Burlington, 1824–1826. His *Eumenes: Being a Collection of Papers* (Trenton, 1799) was an interesting apeal for constitutional reform, arrayed in "practical dress" and addressed to "every man's heart." He favored the elimination of the "perfectly disgusting" practice of women's suffrage [p. 33] and disfranchisement of "restless & intriguing, ignorant and vicious" aliens, Negroes, and transients" [p. 19]. But he also advocated the abolition of property qualifications. "Take away from any citizen the right of suffrage, and he is disfranchised," he wrote. "He is a slave among equals. If it were right to discriminate between one citizen and another in this respect, justice would perhaps decide in favor of that class of the community, whose low estate deprived them of influence; the rich and powerful will take care of themselves; the least privilege which the poor should enjoy, is that of giving a solitary vote for their rulers" [p. 47]. Griffith appeared confident of the support of the sober and steady yeomanry, even the most impoverished among them; but not of the rootless, the mobile, the restless. He also urged tightened qualifications for office-holding, longer terms of office, separation of powers, restraints upon pluralism, reapportionment, and provisions for impeachment. The tone of his work was popular. "The people know their interests, and in whom they may confide their management," he declared [p. 19].

HORNBLOWER, JOSEPH COERTEN (1777–1864), b. Belleville, N. J., his father an English civil engineer who emigrated in 1753; attended Orange Academy and studied law with David B. Ogden (q.v.); member, N. J. Assembly, 1829; Republican Presidential Elector, 1860; active in the American Bible Society, the N. J. Colonization Society, first president of the N. J. Historical Society; professor of law at Princeton, 1847–1855; ruling Presbyterian elder. [Wm. Nelson, *Joseph C. Hornblower* (1894), passim]. Hornblower was an active participant in the federal party organization and an open apologist for it. In 1812 he spoke out for "the right of forming and communicating opinion with a view to the public good, in regard to public men" [Trenton *Federalist*, 17 Aug. 1812].

PATERSON, WILLIAM B. (c. 1780–1833), b. N. J.; A.B., Princeton, 1801; served on the N. J. Central Committee in 1808, urging county committees to "active endeavors in the arduous struggle" [Paterson et al. to Jacob Thompson, 1808, in Broadsides, N. J. Hist. Soc.]. His *Oration delivered . . . in the City of New Brunswick* (New Brunswick, 1815) exhorted his Federal neighbors, in a dreary didactic style, to "the general diffusion of sound moral and political information" [p. 13]. He repudiated partisanship but urged the importance of "consistency" in voting [p. 15].

READ, SAMUEL J., as secretary of a Federal meeting in Burlington County, September, 1814, probably drafted its resolution "that this meeting have entire confidence in the virtue, patriotism and valour of the great body of the people." The meeting also declared collectively, "We ask, you, fellow citizens, each of you, *once* more to rouse yourselves. Let not the *right of suffrage* be abandoned when on your vote, perhaps on a single vote, hangs the fate of your Country!" [Trenton *Federalist*, 20 Sep. 1814].

SHERMAN, GEORGE (1774?–1835), b. New Haven, Conn.; educated in apprenticeship; removed to Trenton, N. J., where he edited the *New Jersey State Gazette*, 1799–1800, and the Trenton *Federalist*, 1800–1835. His journal was the most important federal organ in the state and one of the earliest Federal electioneering papers outside the national capital. It was edited in a popular spirit, exhorting the people to avail themselves of their electoral privileges. "If there is any use in elections,"

Sherman wrote, "it is in this—that they enable the people to *change the men* in power" [Trenton *Federalist*, 4 Oct. 1812]. Sherman was a favorite target of Jeffersonian journalists [see the Trenton *True American*, 5 Oct. 1812, 11 Oct. 1813].

STOCKTON, LUCIUS HORATIO (1767–1835), b. Princeton, N. J.; A.B., Princeton, 1787; lawyer residing in Trenton, N. J.; active participant in federal committees, founder of the Washington Benevolent Society in his city. His many public addresses were appeals for party cohesion— "Let us, fellow citizens, unite as brethren" [Trenton *Federalist*, 13 Sep. 1813]. He argued that the government could be secured by Federalists only by means of "the VOICE OF THE PEOPLE, audibly, repeatedly and firmly pronounced," [ibid.; see also 14 Sep. 1812; and Stockton's *Address delivered before the Convention of the Friends of Peace of the State of New Jersey. (Trenton, 1814), passim*].

VAN CLEAVE, JOHN (c. 1776–1826), A.B., Princeton, 1797; physician practising in Hunterdon Co. He may have been the author of *Serious Considerations addressed to the Electors of New-Jersey concerning the Choice of Members of the Legislature in the ensuing Year* (n.p., n.d. [1803], an appeal to farmers and the "poor" for their support. It condemned Jeffersonian societies and described the object of Federalism as the preservation of "social liberty." "Federal patriots promised nothing but *EQUAL RIGHTS* and *EQUAL LAWS*. Every man is equally free to acquire property, fame and office, by his industry, services, and talents."

VROOM, PETER DUMONT (1791–1873), b. Hillsboro, Somerset Co., N. J., son of Col. Peter Vroom (rhymes with Frome), "an old and much respected citizen of Somerset." He studied law with George MacDonald and practised in Hackettstown, Flemington, and Somerville. An active Federalist in his youth, he supported Jackson in 1824, together with most leading young Federalists in New Jersey, and had a long and distinguished career as a Democrat; member, N. J. Assembly, 1826–1827, 1829; governor of New Jersey, 1829–1831, 1833–1836; U. S. Congress, 1839–1841; minister to Prussia, 1853–1857; delegate to the Washington Peace Convention, 1861; Presidential elector for Seymour and Blair, 1868 [L. Q. C. Elmer, *New Jersey*, p. 184]

WALL, GARRET DORSET (1783–1850), b. Middletown, N. J.; educated in a "classical school" in Woodbury, N. J.; lawyer practising in Burlington, N. J.; U. S. District Attorney for New Jersey, 1829; U. S. Senate, 1835–1841; judge, N. J. Court of Errors, 1848–1850. He was active in the Washington Benevolent Societies in New Jersey and prominent in party gatherings, public and private. For his assiduous appeals for popular support, see Trenton *Federalist*, 18 May 1812, 5 July 1813, 13 Sep. 1813.

WILLIAMSON, ISAAC H. (1767–1844), b. Elizabeth-town, N. J., of "an ancient and respectable family"; educated in common schools; studied law with his brother Mathias and practised in Newark, N. J. a Federalist in his first public years, his *Candid Appeal to the Honest Yeomanry of Essex, Morris and Sussex Counties* (n.p., 1808) invoked "rights of the people" in the defence of Federalism. He exhorted the Federalists to more systematic party efforts, and to more energetic campaigns, in pamphlets and newspapers, for popular support [pp. 5, 9]. Williamson broke with the federal party on the issue of the War in 1812, and as a Democratic Republican was elected to the legislature in 1815 and to the governorship, 1817–1829 [Elmer, *New-Jersey*, pp. 173–183].

PENNSYLVANIA

Federalists of the Old School

ADDISON, ALEXANDER (1759–1807), b. Scotland; attended Aberdeen Univ.; became a licensed minister in the Scottish Kirk; emigrated to America, 1785, and settled in Washington Co., Penn.; became a lawyer and jurist [*Penn. Mag. Hist. & Biog.*, VII, 155–158; XIII, 3–4; XIV, 330]. In the early 1790s Addison was generally identified with the expanding Republican "interest" and associated with such men as Albert Gallatin. But by the end of that turbulent decade, he had joined the federal side. Whether his conversion was caused by a horror of the Whiskey Rebellion, or the persuasive power of Alexander Hamilton, or the general progress of political ideology, or a misguided opportunism, or all of these things together, Addison embraced the cause of order with the proverbial zeal of a convert. He might be described as a Federal fundamentalist. "Truth has but one side," he declared, "and listening to error and falsehood is a strange way to discover truth" [quoted in Miller, *Crisis in Freedom*, p. 79]. As presiding judge of Pennsylvania's Fifth Judicial District, this "transmontane Goliath of federalism" used his bench as a political pulpit, a practice for which he was impeached and successfully convicted by a Republican legislature in 1802. In his jury charges he repeatedly considered what he took to be the central political problem in the new nation—the establishment of efficient restraints upon the populace within a republican frame. "Liberty without limit is licentiousness," he said, "and licentiousness is the worst kind of tyranny, a tyranny of all" [*Liberty of Speech, and of the Press.*

A Charge to the Grand Juries . . . (Washington, Penn., 1798), p. 5]. His sheet anchor was the judiciary, which would protect the reputations of republican "rulers," and thus preserve their power, from the libellous assaults of angry demagogues. Libel he defined as "writings, printings, or the like, of an immoral or illegal tendency, and in a more particular sense, any malicious defamations of any person and especially a magistrate" [ibid., p. 8; see also his *Oration on the Rise and Progress of the United States of America, to the Present Crisis, and on the Duties of the Citizens* (Philadelphia, 1798), a familiar argument that power without restraint is never used without abuse. The duty of the citizens, said Addison, was to spurn the Democrats, who wished to place all power in the hands of the people, and to serve the Federal cause, each in his proper station].

ARNDT, JOHN (1748–1814), b. Bucks Co., Penn.; militia captain in the War for Independence; merchant residing in Easton, Penn.; clerk, Orphans Court, Northampton Co., until his removal by Republican Governor Thomas McKean in 1799 [John S. Arndt, *The Story of the Arndts* (Philadelphia, 1922), pp. 124–145; Heller, *Northampton Co., Penn.*, III, 449; McMaster & Stone, *Penn. & the Federal Constitution*, p. 713; *Penn. Archives*, 2d ser., III, 236]. Arndt's open elitism, his social holism, his hatred of the principles and practices of the Democratic-Republicans, and his bewilderment by the drift of popular opinion, appear in correspondence with Pickering [Arndt's letter of 7 Jan. 1804, in Pickering Papers, Mass. Hist. Soc.; and see also Arndt's statement in the Philadelphia *Gazette of the United States*, 20 Feb. 1800]. After his removal Arndt occupied himself mainly with his two hobbies—botany and mineralogy. He was, however, enlisted in the attempt to organize Pennsylvania Federalism in 1808 [Samuel Sitgreaves to John Arndt, 1 Sep. 1808, in Personal Papers Miscellaneous, Sitgreaves, Library of Congress].

BIDDLE, CHARLES (1745–1821), b. Philadelphia, Penn.; attended common schools; privateersman in the War for Independence; merchant and gentleman farmer residing in Philadelphia. Biddle's contempt for the tactics of the Jeffersonian movement, which he regarded as mere pandering to popular opinions and prejudices, are detailed in his *Autobiography*, pp. 329–339. He participated in a Federalist partisan effort in Philadelphia, but on his own terms. If he electioneered actively, he made no effort to disguise his elitism; if he addressed himself to the people, he sought to command their support rather than to court it (see above, ch. V). Biddle was a faithful financial backer of the Federal party in Philadelphia, contributing $1000 to the Washington Society [List of "Stockholders," Washington Society Papers, Hist. Soc. of Penn.].

BINGHAM, WILLIAM (1752–1804), b. Philadelphia, son of a prosperous merchant; A.B., Univ. of Penn., 1768; agent for the Continental Congress in the West Indies, 1777–1780; member, Continental Congress, 1787–1788; Penn. House of Representatives, 1790–1791 (speaker, 1791); Penn. Senate, 1794–1795 (president); U. S. Senate, 1795–1801; wealthy merchant and speculator in lands and securities residing in Philadelphia. The mansion in which Bingham and his wife (nee Anne Willing) presided over gatherings of the "tinsel aristocracy" of Philadelphia became the architectural embodiment of the elitist spirit which infuriated the leaders of the Republican "interest" in Congress. In 1795 the Bingham house was attacked by a street mob which had been inflamed by the oratory of a Republican mass meeting [Tinkcom, *Republicans and Federalists in Penna.*, p. 89]. Bingham was not well thought of, even in federal circles. "Money, money is his sole object, and he feels the weight of it," Abigail Adams wrote. "He is not without some talents, but they are all turned to gain" [*Journal and Correspondence of Abigail Adams Smith*, II, 153–154]. He was also not without his mercantilist ideals—government by the "best" people, to whom their social inferiors should be trained to defer; energetic government, active in the interest of the nation and its natural leaders; a balanced economy, prospering through the prosperity of its mercantile magnates [see Bingham's *A Letter from an American* (Philadelphia, 1784), and see generally Margaret L. Brown's articles in the *Penn. Mag. Hist. & Biog.*, 61 (1937), 286–324, 387–434]. There was no room in this model mercantile community for a party of the Jeffersonian persuasion. It was surely no mere temporal coincidence that Bingham removed to England in 1801, the year of Jefferson's inauguration. He never returned to the United States.

BORDLEY, JOHN BEALE (1727–1804), b. Annapolis, Md.; attended a moving school and was educated by his brother Stephen; lawyer, wealthy planter, agriculturist residing on Wye Island, Md., to 1783, and in or near Philadelphia thereafter. Holder of many public offices in proprietary Maryland, he sympathized with the American cause in the early 1770s, but drew back when the blood-letting began. All his life Bordley remained loyal to the temperate solution of 1688. "One with another," he wrote in 1761, "all Men are equal and every set of Men not criminal is equally entitled to the privileges, indulgences and protection of the community." But he never believed in government by the people. "Popular opinion is no rule of right," he declared, "too often the contrary. Populace is another word for passion & it was never known that the least acquaintance subsisted between Passion and Reason" [to Roger Boyce, 13 July 1761, A.Df.S. in Bordley's Feebook, 1759–1761, in Bordley Family Papers, Md. Hist. Soc.]. His political principles remained constant to his death. The writer of his obituary noted, "He was true to republicanism; and in its only safe and legitimate form, that in which public authority is founded on the people, but guarded against sudden impressions, and fluctuations of their will" [Baltimore *Federal Gazette*, 7 Feb. 1804; see my "John Beale Bordley, Daniel Boorstin, and the American Enlightenment," *Journal of Southern History*, XXVIII (1962), 327–342].

BOUDE, THOMAS (1752–1822), b. Lancaster, Penn.; educated in lower schools; rose from lieut. to major in the Continental Army, 1776–1783; organizer of the Society of the Cincinnati; brigadier in Penn. militia; member, Penn. House of Representatives, 1794–1796; U. S. Congress, 1801–1802; master bricklayer, lumber dealer, building contractor in Columbia, Penn. [Josiah Granville Leach, *History of the Bringhurst Family* (Philadelphia, 1901), pp. 131–133]. A quiet backbencher in Congress, his voting record was generally Federalist, but on such major questions as the naturalization act he judged independently [*AC*, 7/1/ 993, 10 Mar. 1802].

CHEW, BENJAMIN (1722–1810), b. West River, Md., son of a physician; privately educated; studied law in Middle Temple, London; did not participate in the Revolution, and was suspected of Loyalist sympathies; lawyer and jurist in Philadelphia. Chew did not participate actively in the Federal cause, but he associated intimately with its leaders. His influence among his contemporaries derived less from his words and acts than from the impress of his manners and personality. "Were titles and honors herididtary in the United States," a contemporary noted, "a stranger upon entering Mr. Chew's dwelling and being personally introduced to him in the bosom of his family would have been ready to exclaim, 'This is one of the most ancient and well-bred nobles of the land'" [Konkle, *Benjamin Chew*, pp. 320 passim].

CLYMER, GEORGE (1739–1813), b. Philadelphia, Penn.; probably educated in trade; member, Continental Congress, 1776–1778, 1780–1782; member, Penn. House of Representatives, 1785–1788; member, U. S. Constitutional Convention, 1787; U. S. Congress, 1789–1791; collector of excise, 1791–1794; commissioner to the Creek Indians, 1796; import-export merchant, shipbuilder, banker in Philadelphia. His old-school elitism appeared in his conception of representation as trust rather than agency. The right of constituents to instruct their Congressmen he rejected as "a most dangerous principle, utterly destructive of all ideas of an independent and deliberative body, which are essential requisites in the Legislatures of free Governments; they prevent men of abilities and experience from rendering those services to the community that are in their power, destroying the object contemplated by establishing an efficient General Government, and rendering Congress a mere passive machine" [*AC*, 1/1/733–47, 15 Aug. 1789]. He attributed the "disaffection" of western Pennsylvania to the temper of society in that part of the nation—to an atomistic, egalitarian spirit, and to the absence of a rooted ruling elite. "All their men of distinction," he wrote, "are either sordid shopkeepers, crafty lawyers, or candidates for office, not inclined to make personal sacrifices to truth or honor" [to Hamilton, 10 Oct. 1792, in Gibbs, *Administrations of Washington and Adams*, I, 148–149].

COLEMAN, ROBERT (1741–1825), b. County Donegal, Ireland; emigrated to America c.1764; rose from clerk in an iron forge at Reading, Penn., to a wealthy iron manufacturer residing in Lancaster Co. and associate judge of the Lancaster Co. Court, 1791–1805. Coleman was active in the 1790s playing· the ancient game of magnate politics with skill and determination [Tinkcom, *Republicans and Federalists in Penn.*, p. 254]. But in a contest for popular favor, this setaceous specimen of old-school politics competed at a disadvantage. His family crest, a caltrop, captured the spirit of his personality and his political posture in the age of Jefferson [J. L. Delafield, "Notes on the Life and Work of Robert Coleman," *Penn. Mag. Hist. & Biog.*, 36 (1912), 226–230; Egle, "Sketches of Members of the Penn. Convention," ibid., 11 (1887) 71–72; McMaster and Stone, *Penn. and the Federal Constitution*, pp. 724–725].

CRAIG, ISAAC (1741–1825), b. County Down, Ireland, emigrated to America in 1765; major, Continental Army; merchant and manufacturer in Pittsburgh. The son-in-law of John Neville (q.v.), Craig was a member of the kinship family whose political influence and economic power was predominant within the limits of their own city. But they never appear to have developed a popular base for their authority, and stood firm in the face of clamor against the Federal excise [Craig to Henry Knox, 18 July 1794, *Penn. Archives*, 2d ser., IV, 73–74; Agnew, *Allegheny Co.*, p. 44; Craig, *Pittsburgh*, p. 235]

EGE, GEORGE (1748–1829), b. Womelsdorf, Berks Co., Penn.; educated by his uncle, "Baron" H. W. von Stiegel; owner and operator of many iron forges and founderies in Berks County; large landholder and speculator; in 1824 he was reportedly worth $380,000, but died deep in debt. A member of the Penn. House of Representatives, 1783, associate judge of the Berks County Court, 1791–1818, U. S. Congress, 1796–1797, and an active Lutheran layman, Ege was a powerful country magnate who commanded the support of his German neighbors in the early 1790s; but he resigned from the Congress shortly before the "defence" legislation —which would prove so unpopular among the Pennsylvania Germans— was brought to a vote. Ege was nominated as a Presidential elector in 1800 by Federalists in the state senate, but there is no evidence of partisan activity on his part after 1797 [Thompson P. Ege, *History and Genealogy of the Ege Family* (Harrisburg, 1911), pp. 76–79; Benjamin A. Fryer, *Congressional History of Berks, Pennsylvania, District, 1789–1939* (Reading, 1939), pp. 11–17; Tinkcom, *Republicans and Federalists in Penn.*, p. 160].

FITZSIMONS, THOMAS (1741–1811), b. County Tubber, Ireland; emigrated before the War of Independence, in which he served as a militia captain on the American side; member, Continental Congress, 1782–1783; Penn. House of Representatives, 1786–1787; U. S. Constitutional Convention, 1787; U. S. Congress, 1789–1795; wealthy merchant in the East Indian trade, president of the Insurance Co. of North America, director of the Bank of North America, president of the Philadelphia Chamber of Commerce; active Roman Catholic layman. With George Clymer (q.v.), FitzSimons was another member of the mercantile "junto" in Philadelphia which gave strong support to Hamilton's fiscal policies. He was deeply hostile to the Jeffersonians, condemning both "the principles these people hold and their practises" [to Pickering, 18 Jan. 1804, in Pickering Papers, Mass. Hist. Soc.]. In 1794 he proposed that the Congress follow the President in condemning "self-created societies," which, he said, "misrepresenting the conduct of the Government, and disturbing the operation of the laws, and which, by deceiving and inflaming the ignorant and weak, may naturally be supposed to have stimulated and urged the [Whiskey] insurrection." The Democratic Societies, he declared, were "not strictly unlawful, yet not less fatal to good order and true liberty; and reprehensible in the degree that our system of government approaches to perfect political freedom" [AC 3/2/899, 24 Nov. 1794]. FitzSimons was active in the election of 1800, serving as chairman of a Federal nominating meeting [Philadelphia *Gazette U.S.*, 6 Nov. 1800], but he was critical of the national nominating meeting in 1808 [to Otis, 4 Oct, 1808, in Otis Papers, Mass. Hist. Soc.].

GURNEY, FRANCIS (1738–1815), b. Bucks Co., Penn; lieutenant colonel in the Continental Army; wealthy merchant in Philadelphia; trustee of Dickinson College; member Penn. House of Representatives, 1789–1795. Gurney was a doubly exceptional figure—one of a group of older merchants who actively participated in the organization of a popularly oriented conservative party in Philadelphia [Philadelphia *U. S. Gazette*, 8 Mar. 1808]. Others included Levi Hollingsworth and George Latimer (qq.v.) Though merchants often followed Federal banners, they rarely carried them—a burdensome task that was left to the lawyers in most cities. With the principal exception of New York, older Federalists rarely were willing to play a leading part in party affairs during the Jef-

fersonian era. The exceptions among Philadelphia Federalists could
be explained in four ways. First, the location of the federal government
in that city during the 1790s meant a greater intensity of political feeling
than existed in any other part of the Union. Secondly, Philadelphia as
the largest of the American cities may have had the nearest American
counterpart to a European proletariat—it certainly had the doubtful
distinction of the largest mobs which gathered in America during the
1790s. The spectre of American sans-culottism badly frightened the best
people of Philadelphia—it may have startled them into action. Thirdly,
political turbulence was traditional in Philadelphia—provincial elections
in the 1760s had been contested by factions which came closer to modern
parties than any similar groups in colonial America, Popularly oriented
partisan activity may, as a consequence, have been legitimatized.
Fourthly, during the War of Independence political radicals won a victory
in Pennsylvania in the Constitution of 1776, which, although temporary,
was more substantial than any similar radical success in other states
[see generally Charles H. Lincoln, *The Revolutionary Movement in Pennsylvania* (Philadelphia, 1901); David Hawke, *In the Midst of a Revolution* (Philadelphia, 1961); Joan de Lourdes Leonard, "Elections in
Colonial Pennsylvania," *William and Mary Quarterly*, XI (1954), 385–
401; and Tinkcom, *Republicans and Federalists in Penn.*].

HAND, EDWARD (1744–1802), b. County Kings, Ireland; surgeon's mate
in the Royal Irish Regt. ordered to America, 1767; resigned in 1774
and became a physician in Lancaster, Penn.; served in the Continental
Army, rising to brigadier and brevet major general; member, continental
Congress, 1784–1785; after the war, a manufacturer of rifles, surveyor
of excise, and gentleman farmer, participating actively but quietly in
conservative politics. His letters show a conventional prejudice for a
strong government and a structured society, and a hatred of Jeffersonian
forms [*Penn. Mag. Hist. & Biog.*, 33 (1909), 353–360; ibid., 14 (1890),
333; Harris, *Biog. Hist. Lancaster Co.*, pp. 268–269].

HARTLEY, THOMAS (1748–1800), b. Reading, Penn.; attended lower
schools; lawyer practising in York, Penn.; Colonel in the Continental
Army; member, Penn. House of Representatives, 1778; U. S. Congress,
1789–1800. Hartley was not enthusiastic for the Hamiltonian economic
program—he voted against assumption. But in his view of society and
government he was a specimen of the old school. In debate on the
Tucker amendment in 1789, he spoke against Instruction. "Representation is the principle of our Government; the people ought to have confidence in the honor and integrity of those they send forward to transact
their business; their right to instruct them is a problematical subject,"
he declared. "When the passions of the people are excited, instructions

have been resorted to and obtained to answer party purposes; and although the public opinion is generally respectable, yet at such moments it has been known to be wrong; and happy is that Government composed of men of firmness and wisdom to discover and resist popular error. . . . It appears to my mind that the principle of representation is distinct from any agency which may require written instructions. The great end of meeting is to consult for the common good" [AC, 1/1/733–734, 15 Aug. 1789]. In the Sixth Congress, however, Hartley began to vote more often with the Republicans than with the Federalists on major issues. His early death may have interrupted a political conversion [Dauer, Adams Federalists, p. 319]; on the other hand, Hartley may have been attempting to adjust Federal policy to popular prejudices. His speeches of 8 and 22 Jan. 1800 would sustain this interpretation [AC 6/1/273, 392].

HOLLINGSWORTH, LEVI (1739–1824), b. Elkton, Md.; son of a wealthy merchant; served in the Continental Army; flour merchant in Philadelphia. Hollingsworth was another of the older Federalists who took a leading part in partisan affairs during the Jeffersonian era [see Francis Gurney]. A victim of a mob attack in 1779, he had a private reason for concern in these matters [Mary H. Jamar, Hollingsworth Family (Philadelphia, 1944), pp. 41–42; Joseph A. Stewart, Descendants of Valentine Hollingsworth (Louisville, 1925), pp. 42–43]. In 1799, he was chairman of a Central Committee in Philadelphia, which possessed titular authority over a paper organization of federal committees in the counties [Hollingsworth, et al., Address to the Freemen of Penn. (Germantown, 1799); Tinkcom, Republicans and Federalists in Penn., pp. 228–241]. Thereafter, his name regularly appeared on federal committee rosters in Philadelphia [Hollingsworth et al. to James Lewis, 11 Mar. 1808, in American Broadsides, N. Y. Hist. Soc.; Gaz. U. S. 8, 15, 21 Mar. 1808].

INGERSOLL, JARED (1749–1822), b. New Haven, Conn.; A.B., Yale, 1766; moved to Philadelphia, 1771; studied law in Middle Temple, and after the War of Independence married the daughter of Charles Pettit, an enemy of Robert Morris. An able jury lawyer, practising in Philadelphia, he also invested on a very small scale in the coasting trade [McDonald, We the People, p. 64]. Continental Congress, 1780–1781; U. S. Constitutional Convention, 1787; Attorney General of Penn., 1790–1799, 1811–1817; a candidate for the vice-presidency in 1812, he was generally but not universally supported by Federalists and moderate Republicans who voted for De Witt Clinton. In 1814, Ingersoll was an unsuccessful Federal candidate for the U. S. Senate. Moderate in his principles, restrained in his partisanship, Ingersoll was respected by men of all persuasions. Except in the election of 1792, he took small part in electioneering activities [Binney, *Leaders of the Old Bar of Philadelphia*, p. 86; Tinkcom, *Republicans and Federalists in Penn.*, p. 57; Higginbotham, *Keystone in the Democratic Arch*, p. 306].

INSKEEP, JOHN (1757–1834), b. Marlton, N. J.; educated in local schools; served in the Revolutionary militia; removed to Philadelphia, c.1782, where he became a wealthy china and glass merchant, and Federalist mayor of Philadelphia, 1800, 1805–1806. With Hollingsworth and Gurney (qq.v), he was active in electioneering campaigns [H. E. Wallace, "Sketch of John Inskeep," *Penn. Mag. Hist. & Biog.*, 28 (1904), 129–135].

JACKSON, WILLIAM (1759–1828), b. Cumberland, England; emigrated to South Carolina; an orphan, he was raised and educated as a gentleman by Owen Roberts; served in the Continental Army, rising to the rank of major; Assistant Secretary of War, 1782–1783; Secretary to the U. S. Constitutional Convention, 1787, and to the President, 1789–1791; surveyor of Philadelphia, 1795–1802. Jackson was a lawyer by profession, having studied with William Lewis (q.v.), and in 1804 was persuaded to become the editor of the Philadelphia *Political and Commercial Register*. An Episcopalian, he married Elizabeth Willing [Charles Willing Littell, "Maj. William Jackson," *Penn. Mag. Hist. & Biog.*, II (1878), 353–369; T. W. Francis to Otis, 17 Apr. 1804, in Otis Papers, Mass. Hist. Soc.]. His newspaper became a vehicle of old-school ideas, regularly scolding the people for refusing to recognize the authority of their natural leaders [6 July 1804], and articulating holistic social ideals, in which society was represented as an organism with "head, viscera, members and organs," or a building in which the stones were the people and the cement the "public will" [13 July 1804]. Stubbornly independent in his judgment of men and measures, Jackson was a sore trial to younger Federalists who were more mindful of party unity. Alexander Contee Hanson angrily declared that Jackson deserved "to be raked over the coals" for his unwillingness to accept party discipline [to Pickering, 11 Dec. 1809, in Pickering Papers, Mass. Hist. Soc.]. In the Jeffersonian era, Jackson was best known as the author of a *Eulogium on the Character of General Washington* (Philadelphia, 1800), one of most widely disseminated pamphlets which sought to use the shade of the departed leader for partisan advantage.

KIRKPATRICK, ABRAHAM (1749–1817), b. Cecil Co., Md.; moved to Fort Pitt, 1767; captain in the Continental Army; a landed gentleman whose real estate was worth $100,000 at his death, he married the sister of John Neville (q.v.) and became a prominent member of that family connection [Kirk Q. Brigham, *Major Abraham Kirkpatrick* (Pittsburgh, 1911), p. 9]. Kirkpatrick was described as tall, rugged, and of "severe expression." He habitually wore a large cocked hat pulled down over one eye, which had been blinded by a mutinous soldier in the War for Independence. He was openly elitist in his demeanor and unyielding in his politics. According to a man who knew him, he was "distinguished by an integrity the most undeviating. . . . opposition only served to strengthen the energies of his mind" [Pittsburgh *Gazette*, 25 Nov. 1817].

KITTERA, JOHN WILKES (1752–1801), b. near Blue Ball, Lancaster Co., Penn.; A.B., Princeton, 1776; lawyer residing in Lancaster, Penn.; U. S. Congress, 1791–1801; U. S. District Attorney, 1801 [Harris, *Biog. Hist. Lancaster Co.*, p. 345]. His letter "To the Electors of Lancaster County" was a statement of old school ideals—"Obedience and submission to the powers that be," he wrote, "is the duty of all. . . . Government is made for the protection of the weak and virtuous against the powerful and wicked . . . resistance to lawfully elected officials is 'treason against society' " [Baltimore *Federal Gazette*, 18 Aug. 1800]. A similar argument appears in Kittera's speech in Congress, 21 June 1798 [*AC* 5/2/2016].

LATIMER, GEORGE (1750–1825), b. Philadelphia; attended Univ. of Penn.; served in the Continental Army during the Revolution; merchant, director of the Bank of North America, president of the Union Insurance Co., Collector of Customs in Philadelphia, 1798–1804 [*Penna. Mag. Hist. & Biog.*, 11 (1887), 219–220]. Latimer, with Hollingsworth, Gurney, and Inskeep (qq.v.), was a regular member of electioneering committees in Philadelphia [Latimer et al. to James Lewis, 11 Mar. 1808, in American Broadsides, N. Y. Hist. Soc.]. In 1814, however, he was set up as an independent federal candidate for governor against his party's candidate, Isaac Wayne (q.v.); Higginbotham, *Keystone in the Democratic Arch*, p. 299].

LEWIS, WILLIAM (1752–1819), b. Chester Co., Penn.; his father was a "plain and respectable" farmer; educated in a Quaker school; studied law with Nicholas Waln and practised in Philadelphia; judge, U. S. District Court,, 1791–1793 [William Primrose, "William Lewis," *Penn. Mag. Hist. & Biog.*, 20 (1896), 30–40]. Lewis was distinctly a specimen of the old school. "Amusingly anti-gallican, and entirely anti-Jeffersonian," according to Horace Binney (q.v.) "he abominated the gallican invention, as he called it, of pantaloons, and stuck to knee breeches all his life; and under the same prejudice, he adhered to hair powder and cue [sic] because the French revolutionists had first rejected them" [Binney, "William Lewis" ibid., XIV (1890), 3–27, 22]. A standard of Federal orthodoxy, he was eccentric in nothing more significant than his smoking habits (a lighted cigar was perpetually in his mouth, from early morning until he fell asleep. Binney, who shared a room with him once, described how "a cigar was seen firing up from Mr. Lewis's pillow and disappearing in the darkness, like a revolving light on the coast" [ibid., p. 25]. After the elections of 1799 and 1800, he took small part in political affairs. "I supposed it best, for the wayward political opinions that have long convulsed this commonwealth and menaced its dissolution, to be left to their mad career, and to spend their own folly," he wrote in 1805. But he was persuaded in 1805 to appeal for electioneering exertions by Federalists, in alliance with those Republicans who opposed "Jacobinism" [Philadelphia U. S. Gaz., 27 Sep. 1805].

NEVILLE, JOHN (1731–1803), b. near the headwaters of the Occuquan River, Va., served in the French and Indian War and the War for Independence; a large landowner residing near Pittsburgh, he was described as "a man of good English education, of plain and blunt manners" [Ferguson, Early Western Pennsylvania Politics, pp. 113–114; Craig, Pittsburgh, p. 229]. Neville was the patriarch of a political family in Pittsburgh and the personification of the structured society of colonial America. His prominence won him the special attention of rioters in the Whiskey Rebellion, who attacked his home, "Bower Hill," in 1794 [Baldwin, Whiskey Rebels, pp. 47 passim]. After his death his son Presley Neville (1756–1818) became head of the family and chief of the Neville connection.

O'HARA, JAMES (c.1752–1819), b. County Mayo, Ireland; educated in Paris; emigrated to America, 1772; captain in the Continental Army; settled near Pittsburgh, 1790, where he was a tavernkeeper, downriver merchant, and manufacturer of glass products, and an ally of the Nevilles [Anne Hemphill Herbert, Memories of the Darlington Family (Pittsburgh, 1949), pp. 6–15]. For his part in Burr's conspiracy, see Abernethy, The Burr Conspiracy, p. 61.

PETERS, RICHARD (1744–1828), b. Philadelphia, his father a prominent jurist and Penn. politician; A.B., Univ. of Penn., 1761; lawyer, jurist, gentleman farmer residing at "Belmont" near Philadelphia; captain in the Continental Army, 1776; secretary, Board of War, 1776–1781; member, Continental Congress, 1782–1783; Penn. House of Representatives, 1787–1790; Penn. Senate, 1791; U. S. District Judge, 1792–1828. A political spectator after 1800, Peters was displeased by what he saw in the younger generation of federal leaders. "Times are too ticklish to play a Game and make hazardous moves merely to alarm and put to flight an Adversary," he wrote. "I never passionately admired the celebrated feat of good old Sampson; who to destroy his enemies, pulled away the Pillars of a Building, with the certainty of Being crushed among its Ruins" [to Pickering, 17 Apr. 1808, in Pickering Papers, Mass. Hist.

Soc.]. His correspondence with Pickering, quoted in chapter I above, is a rich source for Federalism of the old school—its ideals, prejudices, and pathetic response to the Jeffersonian triumph.

SMITH, THOMAS (1745–1809), b. Aberdeenshire, Scotland; attended Univ. of Edinburgh; emigrated 1769; surveyor, lawyer, gentleman farmer residing in Bedford, Penn., and Philadelphia; member, Penn. House of Representatives, 1776–1780; Continental Congress, 1780–1782, judge, Penn. Supreme Court, 1794–1809. Smith was a picturesque country squire who might have stepped out of the pages of Fielding, an eccentric who, as he moved through Jeffersonian America, was probably followed by barking dogs and small boys with stones and sticks. A young Federalist, Horace Binney, left an unforgettable picture of the old man—"We overtook Judge Smith on the road. He was on horseback, in enormous boots that came above his knees like a fisherman's, a cocked hat exposing his whole face to the fiery sun, and a full cloth dress which had probably been black when he set out, but when we saw him was a most dirty drab. Some fifteen minutes after our arrival he came into the saloon where the company had assembled. His hat was then in his hand, but on his head was a mass of paste made by the powder and pomatum a part of which had run down in white streams upon his face, as red in all the unplastered parts as a boiled lobster, and his immense boots and spurs, broadskirted coat and the rest . . . made him the most extraordinary figure for a summer dinner I have ever seen" [quoted in Konkle, *Thomas Smith*, foreword]. Binney described him as "rough and bearish in his manners, uncouth in his person and address, and was incapable of raising the skin by a reproof without making a gash. But he was a truly honest man, as far as his prejudices, which were probably unknown to himself, would admit" [ibid].

TILGHMAN, WILLIAM (1756–1827), b. Talbot Co., Md., son of a lawyer; A.B., Univ. of Penn., 1772; studied law with Benjamin Chew, 1772–1776; loyalist in the War of Independence; member, Md. General Assembly, 1788–1790; Md. Senate, 1791–1793; removed to Philadelphia, 1794, where he practised law; Chief Justice, Penn. Supreme Court, 1806–1827. Tilghman was unenthusiastic about the Constitution in 1788; but his Federalism in the Jeffersonian era was unequivocal. He did not, however, approve of organized partisan electioneering efforts [Higginbotham, *Keystone in the Democratic Arch*, p. 239].

YEATES, JASPER (1745–1817), b. Philadelphia, son of a merchant; A.B., Univ. of Penn., 1761; wealthy lawyer and jurist residing in Lancaster; his estate would be appraised at $240,000. Yeates served as captain of the Revolutionary militia; chairman of the Committee of Correspondence in Lancaster, 1775–1776; delegate to the Penn. State Convention, 1789; associate justice, Penn. Supreme Court; center of a federal connection in Lancaster—his niece married Edward Hand (q.v.) [C. I. Landis, "Jaspar Yeates and his Times," *Penn. Mag. Hist. & Biog.*, 46 (1922), 231]. Yeates was not as deeply disturbed by the events of 1799 and 1800 as many of his political friends. While they were prodding each other into panic, Yeates was coolly calculating the profits which could be made in the purchase of U. S. securities sold by frightened British investors. As associate justice, he walked softly and urged his brother Federalists to an alliance with conservative Republicans [Higginbotham, *Keystone in the Democratic Arch*, pp. 30, 95].

Transitional Figures

DUNCAN, THOMAS (1760–1827), b. Carlisle, Penn., son of one of the founders of the town; educated privately, studied law with Jaspar Yeates (q.v.), and practiced in Carlisle [Katherine W. Smith, *The Story of Thomas Duncan and his Six Sons* (New York, 1928), pp. 42–43; Nevins, *Men of Mark of Cumberland Valley, Penn.*, p. 204]. A gentleman of quiet dignity, Duncan collaborated in the Federalist partisan effort after 1800, becoming the most important federal figure in Carlisle, chairman of local electioneering committees, and a corresponding member of the Federalist State Committee in 1812. He may have been present at the national nominating meeting in 1812. [Binney et al. to Daniel Webster, 21 Sep. 1812, in Webster Papers, Library of Congress].

RAWLE, WILLIAM (1759–1836), b. Philadelphia, of a loyalist family; educated in Friends Academy; studied law in Middle Temple and practiced law in Philadelphia after his return in 1782. His public addresses, though written for the people, retained the elitism of the old school ["A Letter to the Freemen of Pennsylvania upon the subject of Equal Liberty," undated mss. in Rawle Papers, Hist. Soc. Penn.]. Rawle served on federal committees in Philadelphia from 1792 to the end of the War of 1812 [Tinkcom, *Republicans and Federalists in Penn.*, p. 248; Higginbotham, *Keystone in the Democratic Arch*, p. 20] and was a founder of the Washington Society of Pennsylvania [*Summary Statement*, p. 3; Rawle et al., unaddressed circular, n.d., Washington Society of Penn. Papers, Hist. Soc. Penn.].

ROSS, JAMES (1762–1847), b. near Delta, Penn.; educated in a "classical school"; taught Latin in Washington and Jefferson College; lawyer residing in Pittsburgh; he married into the Woods family, which was closely allied to the Nevilles. Member, State Constitutional Convention, 1790; U. S. Senate, 1794–1803; unsuccessful gubernatorial candidate, 1799, 1802, 1808. His private opinions were those of the old school—

energy in government, orders and distinctions in society. But in the pandemonium of Pennsylvania politics, he had learned to disguise and dissemble his own views, pandering to popular opinions. In the election of 1808 he shocked other Federalists by his zeal for universal manhood suffrage [D. B. Ogden to Meredith, 27 Sep. 1808, in Meredith Papers, Hist. Soc. Penn.; see also Tinkcom, *Republicans and Federalists in Penn.*, pp. 227–230]. In 1824 and 1828 he would become an active backer of Andrew Jackson [Livermore, *Twilight of Federalism*, pp. 156, 203].

SITGREAVES, SAMUEL (1764–1827), b. Philadelphia; educated in lower schools; lawyer practising in Easton, Penn.; member, State Constitutional Convention, 1790; U. S. Congress, 1795–1798; burgess of Easton, 1804–1807; treasurer, Northampton Co., 1816–1819. In private correspondence he expressed his hatred of Jeffersonian principles and practices and his contempt for those "who know no better guide for their opinions than the elusive Vox Populi" [Sitgreaves to Sedgwick, 8 Dec. 1799, in Sedgwick Papers, Mass. Hist. Soc.; see also *Penn. Mag. Hist. & Biog.*, 23 (1899), 410–411]. After 1800, however, he took an active part in efforts to develop a federal party organization in Pennsylvania. Sitgreaves, in Easton, acted as an intermediary between Philadelphia Federalists and Federal leaders in the counties of the upper Delaware Valley [Sitgreaves to John Arndt, 1 Sep. 1808, in Personal Papers Miscellaneous, Sitgreaves, Library of Congress]. But in 1816 he was appalled by the "Conduct of those who still assume the Name of Federalists. Sickened by the frequent Instances of total Defection of Men of high Standing amongst them—and foreseeing, in the Restlessness and Impatience and Equivocation of others, the repeated Occurence of similar Apostasies—I have lost all Confidence in the Integrity of Men [quoted in Livermore, *Twilight of Federalism*, p. 38].

WHARTON, ROBERT (1757–1834), b. Southwark, Penn.; apprenticed to a hatter; wholesale grocer and flour merchant in Philadelphia; holder of many municipal offices. Wharton's response to the Jeffersonian movement is reflected in his deeds—a regular member of electioneering committees in Philadelphia and a prominent participant in public meetings, he also helped to establish the Washington Society of Pennsylvania [Tinkcom, *Republicans and Federalists in Penn.*, p. 228; Higginbotham, *Keystone in the Democratic Arch*, pp. 280, 371; Philadelphia *Poulson's American Daily Advertiser*, 8 Mar. 1834].

Young Federalists

BAYARD, ANDREW (1762–1832), insurance broker residing in Philadelphia, and cousin of James A. Bayard (q.v.). He was a regular member of local electioneering committees, a founder of the Washington Society of Pennsylvania, and a backer of party journals. In 1812 he also served on the national committee of correspondence which communicated with leading Federalists throughout the Union. Bayard gave his support to an effort to organize a new conservative organization out of a coalition of Clintonian Democrats and Federalists. "A new party must be formed," he wrote. ". . . A majority of the people will not rally round a federal standard" [Bayard et al. to Joseph Pearson, 10 Aug. 1812, in Gaston Papers, Southern Hist. Coll., Univ. of N. C.].

BINNEY, HORACE (1780–1875), b. near Philadelphia; A.B., Harvard, 1797; lawyer practising in Philadelphia; member, Penn. House of Representatives, 1806–1807; U. S. Congress, 1833–1834. His interests ranged broadly from the Philadelphia Horticultural Society to the Pennsylvania Railroad, and included many religious and philanthropic causes. In his heart Binney was a monarchist. "The freest and most durable government in the world is a constitutional monarchy, with adequate representation of the people, and a society so graduated and so established as to prevent concussions between monarch and subjects, or sudden mutations. But we have not had the frame, nor perhaps will at any time have the timber to make it," he wrote [quoted in C. C. Binney, *Horace Binney*, p. 450]. But in the politics of Pennsylvania he was active on committees of correspondence, in an effort to organize a popularly oriented conservative party [Binney et al. to Otis, 27 July 1812, in Otis Papers, Mass. Hist. Soc.]. From the age of eight, when he marched in a procession to honor the new U. S. Constitution, he called himself a Federalist; though he preserved the dignity of the old school, he served a partisan cause with energy and constancy.

BRONSON, ENOS (1774–1823), A.B., Yale, 1798; editor, publisher of the *United States Gazette* in Philadelphia [B. A. Konkle, "Enos Bronson," *Penn. Mag. Hist. & Biog.* 57 (1933), 355–358]. Bronson conducted his journal with more restraint than most young Federalist editors, but on occasion he addressed himself to popular ideals and prejudices with great directness. He exploited emotions, such as agrarianism, which Jeffersonians had used, and flattered "the enlightened affections of the American people" [Bronson, *An Address to the people of the United States on the Policy of Maintaining a Permanent Navy* (Philadelphia, 1802), pp. 11–12, 29, 35]. Bronson also was actively engaged in committee work, and was also a founder of the Washington Society in Philadelphia [Bronson to Rutledge, 30 Apr. 1803, in Rutledge Papers, Univ. of N. C.].

BUCHANAN, JAMES (1791–1868), b. Cove Gap, Penn.; his father a prosperous country merchant; A. B., Dickinson, 1809; lawyer residing in

Lancaster, Penn.; member, Penn. House of Representatives, 1814–1815; U. S. Congress, 1821–1831; minister to Russia, 1832–1834; U. S. Senate, 1834–1845; Secretary of State, 1845–1849; minister to Great Britain, 1853–1856; President of U.S., 1857–1861. From the age of seventeen, Buchanan was an active party worker. He served on Federalist committees in Lancaster County and attended "conventions" of township delegates [Philadelphia *Gazette U. S.*, 27 June 1808], and he was prominent in the affairs of the Washington Benevolent Society in Lancaster. His "Oration delivered before the Washington Association of Lancaster" (partly published in *Works of James Buchanan*, I, 2–9) is a general indictment of the "weak and wicked" administration, but avoids a discussion of its ideals, and makes no elitist appeal in the fashion of the old school.

CALDWELL, CHARLES (1772–1853), b. Caswell Co., N. C.; educated by tutors; attended the medical department of the Univ. of Penn.; physician, editor of the *Port Folio;* removed to Lexington, Ky., in 1819, where he practiced medicine and taught at Transylvania Univ. [Caldwell, *Autobiography*, passim]. Unlike his predecessor on the *Port Folio*, Joseph Dennie (q.v.), Caldwell was a party leader in Philadelphia, particularly active in the affairs of the American Republican Society and the Washington Society. His public addresses were specimens of young Federalist demagoguery, in which the Democratic administration was denounced not for Democratic principles but for corruption and "flagrant incapacity" [Caldwell, *An Oration . . . delivered before the Washington Benevolent Society* (Philadelphia, 1814), p. 62; see also his *Oration . . . delivered before the American Republican Society* (Philadelphia, 1810), passim].

CHAPMAN, NATHANIEL (1780–1853), b. "Summerhill," Fairfax Co., Va., his mother an heiress to a Scottish fortune; A.B., Univ. of Penn., 1801; studied medicine with Benjamin Rush, married the cousin of Nicholas Biddle, and pursued a distinguished career in medicine, becomng the first president of the American Medical Association. Chapman was a backer of and contributor to the *United States Gazette* [Konkle, "Enos Bronson," p. 353]. He also undertook to make a science of eloquence, with a view to partisan advantage over Democratic demogogues. "Whatever tends to improve or widen the dominance of speech cannot be an object of indifference to a *Free People*," he wrote in the preface to his *Select Speeches* (5 vols., Philadelphia, 1808). "Eloquence has always been admired and studied, but never with more ardor than by Republicans. . . . Eloquence is power" [pp. 15–16].

CHAUNCEY, CHARLES (1777–1849), b. New Haven, Conn.; A.B., Yale, 1792; lawyer residing in Philadelphia. Chauncey was a supporter of the *United States Gazette*, an officer in the Washington Society, a regular member of Federalist committees, and a secretary of mass meetings. His extraordinary perseverance in the Federal cause appears in a letter to John B. Wallace, 4 Sep. 1816. "I rather think our apple cart is kicked over, but I am not out of heart yet" [Wallace Papers, Hist. Soc. Penn]. He was prominent in the Pennsylvania convention of 1837, speaking for many libertarian measures, including electoral rights, reapportionment, and restricted terms of office.

DENNIE, JOSEPH (1768–1812), b. Boston, Mass., his father a merchant; A.B., Harvard, 1790; studied law and theology; became editor of the *Port Folio* in Philadelphia, 1801. Dennie is a clear exception to the rule —his magazine was open and unrestrained in its elitism, undisguised in its old-school ideals. Dennie did not bother to camouflage "the profound contempt I entertain for the *herd* of society" [Dennie to his family, 6 Sep. 1799, in Pedder, *Joseph Dennie*, p. 172]. His disdain for electioneering was equally great; after 1800 he did not actively participate in partisan affairs. The *Port Folio*, though "highly esteemed by the most respectable ladies of Philadelphia" [Manasseh Cutler to his daughter, 27 Feb. 1803, in Cutler, *Cutler*, II, 131], was of small electioneering significance, except as a weapon in Jeffersonian hands.

HAMILTON, WILLIAM (1771–1820), b. Philadelphia; educated in apprenticeship to a printer, Benjamin Franklin Bache, in Philadelphia; moved to Lancaster, Penn., where he published the Lancaster *Journal*, 1796–1820. Hamilton was a Republican in the early 1790's, after the image of his master. But in Lancaster a conversion to the cause of order was perhaps speeded by the patronage of Robert Coleman and Charles Smith (qq.v.). His journal became an aggressive electioneering sheet, as popular in tone as a Jeffersonian newspaper (see, e.g., 24 Mar. 1810; extra edition of 10 Sep. 1800). Hamilton also held many local offices. As Treasurer of Lancaster County, he defaulted to the amount of $20,000 and died insane [Alex Harris, *Biographical History of Lancaster County*, pp. 267–268].

HARE, CHARLES WILLING (1778–1827), b. Westover, Penn.; lawyer residing in Philadelphia. Hare appears to have been the central figure in the Philadelphia Federalist organization—secretary of the most important corresponding committees, founder of the Washington Society, sponsor of federal journals, orator in mass meetings. Hare appears to have had few interests beyond his career and his party. Politics was his life, a federal resurgence his obsession. The "great moral and political revolution" of his age he accepted as given, and undertook to accomodate his cause to it [Hare to Otis, 7 Dec. 1812, in Otis Papers, Mass.

Hist. Soc.; see also Hare's *Oration delivered before the Washington Benevolent Society,* (Philadelphia, 1813)].

HEMPHILL, JOSEPH (1770–1842), b. Chester Co., Penn.; A.B., Univ. of Penn., 1791; lawyer, jurist, manufacturer of porcelain products in West Chester, Penn., to 1803, when he removed to Philadelphia; member, Penn. House of Representatives, 1797–1800, 1805, 1831–1832; U. S. Congress, 1801–1803, 1819–1826, 1829–1831. His speech on the judiciary system supported the conventional ideal of judges protected from the people and "the reach of a raging party," but he agreed to the Republican maxim that "it is dangerous to the liberties of the people to legislate upon constructive power," and exploited Jeffersonian rhetoric throughout [*AC* 7/1/536–38, 16 Feb. 1802].

HOPKINSON, JOSEPH (1770–1842), b. Philadelphia; A.B., Univ. of Penn., 1786; lawyer practising in Philadelphia; member, U. S. Congress, 1815–1819; removed to Bordentown, N. J., and sat in the New Jersey Legislature, 1820; returned to Philadelphia, 1823; U. S. District Judge, 1828–1842; chairman, Penn. Constitutional Convention, 1837. Hopkinson was a prominent participant in party affairs of every kind in Philadelphia and a regular member of committees of correspondence. He also attended the national nominating meeting in New York City in September 1812. His political activities were those of his generation, as was his bitter partisanship. "Bless the Embargo—thrice bless the President's distributive Proclamation," he wrote to Pickering. ". . . If these things awaken not, we are indeed in the sleep of death" [25 May 1808, in Pickering Papers, Mass. Hist. Soc.]. But his pamphlets and public speeches, more than those of any other prominent young Federalist, were written in old-school spirit. He preserved his elders' elitism, their contempt for popularly oriented posturing, and their holist sense of social relationships. In 1796 he declared that Jeffersonian innovations would

> Make Government a mere Collusion
> And order change into confusion

[*A Congratulatory Epistle to the Redoubtable "Peter Porcupine,"* Philadelphia, 1796]. The same arguments appear in his speeches in the Fourteenth Congress on the Compensation Bill, the Bank of the United States, direct taxes, and commercial regulations.

INGERSOLL, CHARLES JARED (1782–1862), b. Philadelphia; educated privately; lawyer practicing in Philadelphia; U. S. Congress, 1813–1815; U. S. District Attorney, 1815–1829, 1841–1849. Ingersoll, an apostate, had begun his carer as a federal man. To Rufus King he wrote, "You are building a house, I hear—pray heaven the Jacobins mayn't burn or demolish it. . . . But I believe your property is safe in New York—for your democracy's at least an aristocracy, whereas ours is literally a mobocracy, and I fear nothing will bring us back to a level but theocracy or a convulsion" [11 June 1805, in King Papers, N. Y. Hist. Soc.]. But Ingersoll abandoned the Federal cause altogether; like Plumer and John Quincy Adams (qq.v.), he pursued the logic of the young Federalist position to its natural conclusion. As a Jeffersonian in Congress, Ingersoll declared that if the people changed their opinions on a public measure, he would change his. "According to my persuasion," he said, "majority bespeaks popularity, and popularity involves right. I have great faith in the instincts of the people. I prefer those instincts to the reasoning faculties of honorable gentlemen. With their impulse to sustain me, with the *vis a tergo* of popularity to propel me forward, I proceed with a confidence that justice and sound policy are on my side [AC 13/2/1003, 15 Jan. 1814]. An older Federalist, Richard Stockton (q.v.), was scandalized. "Yes, sir," said Stockton angrily, "he was once a Federalist, or pretended to be one, but the storm came and he changed his garments; he perceived in good season the road the mighty crowd had taken; he saw the course the current would pursue; he seized the happy moment, launched his little bark on the boisterous element of popular opinion; he committed himself to the waves, and the wind and the tide wafted him into—*his seat*" [ibid., 1015, 17 Jan. 1814]. Ingersoll also embraced laissez faire, in contexts where he was aligned with Federalists against the administration. "After the experience public creditors have lately had of Congressional kindness and good will," he said, "they might well exclaim, like the French merchants to the economists: 'Laissez nous faire,' let us alone" [AC 13/3/611, 17 Nov. 1814].

MEREDITH, WILLIAM (1772–1839), lawyer, banker residing in Philadelphia. Meredith's political activities covered the full range of party affairs —electioneering, committees of correspondence, the Washington Society, political journalism, etc. He maintained correspondence with federal leaders in most of the northeastern states and was a figure of major importance in interstate federalist politics. For the depth of his partisan zeal and his willingness to borrow the weapons of his opponents, see Meredith to Sullivan, 17 Oct. 1812, Columbia Univ. Coll., Columbia Univ. Library; and D. B. Ogden to Meredith, 24 Oct. 1804, in Meredith Papers, Hist. Soc. Penna.

MILNOR, WILLIAM (1769–1848), b. Philadelphia; attended lower schools; merchant residing in Philadelphia; member U. S. Congress, 1807–1811, 1815–1817, 1821–1822; mayor of Philadelphia, 1829–1830. Milnor occupied a prominent place in the party structure in Philadelphia; as late as 1816 he was still at hard labor attempting to establish committees "of a permanent character" in all states [to Richard Stockton, 21 Aug. 1816, *Penn. Mag. Hist. & Biog.*, VI, 247–249].

MINER, CHARLES (1780–1865), b. Norwich, Conn.; attended lower schools and served as apprentice to a printer in New London, Conn.; removed to Pennsylvania in 1799, where he became editor of the Wilkesbarre *Luzerne Federalist*, 1804–1811, the Philadelphia *Gleaner*, 1811–1816, the Philadelphia *True American*, 1816, and the Westchester *Chester and Delaware Federalist*, 1817, all electioneering sheets. He served in the Penn. House of Representatives, 1807–1808, and U. S. Congress, 1825–1829. A skilled polemist and a master of popular journalism, his work is quoted in chapter VII, above. He also served on federal committees and participated in public meetings [Wilkesbarre *Luzerne Federalist*, 27 May 1808].

SCULL, JOHN (1765–1820), b. Reading, Penn.; educated in lower schools; removed to Pittsburgh, 1786, where he became editor of the Pittsburgh *Gazette*. In the beginning, he tried to make his journal a nonpartisan mirror of the political sentiments of the community; but at the end of the Adams administration his paper became a virulent Federalist electioneering sheet. For the quality of his popular journalism, briefly discussed in Chapter VII, above, see Alston G. Field, "The Press in Western Penn. to 1812," *Western Penn. Hist. Mag.*, XX (1937), 232–259; and Edward Everett, "Jeffersonian Democracy and the *Tree of Liberty*," ibid., XXXII (1949), 11–44.

SERGEANT, JOHN (1779–1852), b. Philadelphia; A.B., Princeton, 1795; lawyer practicing in Philadelphia; member, Penn. House of Representatives, 1808–1810; U. S. Congress, 1815–1823, 1827–1829, 1837–1841. Sergeant occupied a position in Pennsylvania politics between the Federalists and conservative Republicans. The former, who counted him as one of their own, were nevertheless appalled by his time-serving. After he delivered a fulsome oration on Thomas Jefferson in 1826, an older Federalist commented, "Who would have thought that such men as Daniel Webster (q.v.) and Sergeant would have descended to prostitute, yes, to prostitute their talents and sacrifice their regard for consistency, decency and veracity in pronouncing wholesale eulogies on Thomas Jefferson" [Coleman to Pickering, 24 Sep. 1826, in Pickering Papers, Mass. Hist. Soc.].

SMITH, CHARLES (1765–1836), b. Philadelphia?; A.B. Washington College, Md., 1783; lawyer residing in Lancaster, Penn.; cousin of Henry M. Ridgely and son-in-law of Jasper Yeates (qq.v.). Smith was the most prominent young Federalist in Lancaster, a central figure in the active party machine which his party created in that town and county. He was also important in coalition movements with conservative Republicans ["Descendents of Rev. William Smith," *Penn. Mag. Hist. & Biog.*, IV (1880), 380–381; Leon de Valinger, ed., *Ridgely Family Letters*, II, 166; Higginbotham, *Keystone in the Democratic Arch*, pp. 20, 64].

WALLACE, JOHN BRADFORD (1778–1837), b. Somerset Co., N. J.; A.B., Princeton, 1794; lawyer residing in Philadelphia. Wallace was a leader of the "Federalist young gentlemen of Philadelphia," an organized group of men who served first as an auxiliary to the party committees, and gradually took them over [Wallace to Timothy Pickering, 5 Jan. 1801,— Pickering Papers, Mass. Hist. Soc.]. He served regularly on committees of correspondence, and was present at the New York national meeting in 1812.

WALN, ROBERT (1765–1836), b. Philadelphia; attended Friends Academy; import merchant in Philadelphia, operating in the East Indian trade; president of the Philadelphia Insurance Co.; manufacturer of textiles and iron products. As early as 1787, Waln was engaged in organized, popularly oriented conservative party politics, in which Pennsylvania led the nation [Waln to his cousin, 3 Oct. 1787, publ. *Penn. Mag. of Hist. & Biog.* 38 (1914), 502–503]; he would be continuously active until the disruption of Federalism in Philadelphia; a regular member of committees, and a founder of the Washington Benevolent Society [*Summary Statement of the Washington Benevolent Society*, p. 3].

WALSH, ROBERT (1784–1859), b. Baltimore, his father a wealthy merchant; A.B., St. Mary's Seminary, Baltimore, 1806; studied law with Robert Goodloe Harper (q.v.); settled in Philadelphia, where he was successively editor of the *American Register*, 1809–1810, *American Review*, 1811–1812, and the *National Gazette*, 1820–1835. His position appeared in his prospectus. "We are Federal only in reference to the Constitution of the United States," he declared, "and Democratic or Republican relatively to the character of our American institutions" [Livermore, *Twilight of Federalism*, p. 58 which describes his political alignments after the fall of the Federal party].

WATTS, DAVID (1764–1819), b. Cumberland Co., Penn.; his father a prosperous farmer; attended Dickinson College; read law with William Lewis (q.v.) and resided in Carlisle, Penn. His practice carried him over most of the state, and the circle of his political influence expanded in proportion. He was reportedly among the Pennsylvania delegation to the

New York meeting in 1812 [*Biog. Hist. of Cumberland Co.*, p. 193; Higginbotham, *Keystone in the Democratic Arch*, p. 371].

WAYNE, ISAAC (1772–1852), b. near Paoli, Penn.; son of Gen Anthony Wayne; A.B., Dickinson College, 1795; lawyer and gentleman farmer residing in Chester Co., Penn.; member, Penn. House of Representative, 1799–1801, 1806; Penn. Senate, 1810; unsuccessful federal candidate for governor, 1814; U. S. Congress, 1823–1825; colonel in the War of 1812. In 1814, although he was nominated late, Wayne managed to win 30,000 votes, to the incumbent's 50,000, reducing the Republican margin from 47,000 in 1811 to 20,000.

WILKINS, WILLIAM (1779–1865), b. Carlisle, Penn.; attended Dickinson College; studied law with David Watts (q.v.); removed to Pittsburgh where he became a state banker and manufacturer. Wilkins, a party politician by "mental proclivity," served in the Penn. House of Representatives, 1820; U. S. District Judge, 1824–1831; U. S. Senate, 1831–1834; Minister to Russia, 1834–1835; U. S. Congress, 1843–1844; Secretary of War, 1844–1845; Penn. Senate, 1855–1857; Major General, Penn. Home Guards, 1862 (aet. 83!). A Jacksonian after the collapse of the federal party, Wilkins was among the most prominent state bankers who served in the war on the Bank of the United States; but he drifted into the Whig camp after unsuccessfully challenging Van Buren's bid for the vice-presidency and being exiled to Russia [Van Buren, *Autobiography*, pp. 584–590, 723].

DELAWARE

Federalists of the Old School

BASSETT, RICHARD (1745–1815), b. Cecil Co., Md.; educated privately; served in the Revolutionary militia; member, Delaware Senate, 1782; Delaware House of Representatives, 1786; U. S. Constitutional Convention; U. S. Senate, 1789–1793; chief justice, Delaware Court of Common Pleas, 1793–1799; Governor of Delaware, 1799–1801. A lawyer by profession, Bassett was master of Bohemia Manor's six thousand acres and owner of homes in Dover and Wilmington. William Pierce described him as "gentlemanly," a "man of plain sense." Bassett was possessed by three enthusiasms—agricultural improvement, Methodism, and Federalism. Though he actively supported such Enlightenment reforms as the abolition of slavery and the amelioration of penal practices, his attachment to orders and distinctions, his sense of elitism, and his hunger for "energy in government," were open and unqualified. Bassett was not a party leader in the modern sense but the patriarch of a political family (his sons-in-law included Joshua Clayton and James A. Bayard, q.v.), which with other interlocking families comprised an extended cousinage which dominated the society and the politics of Delaware. [Philadelphia *Gazette of the United States*, 21 Aug. 1802; *American State Papers, Miscellaneous*, I, 340; *Delaware House Journal* (1800), pp. 10–15; Borden, *Bayard*, p. 11; Munroe, *Federalist Delaware*, pp. 41 passim; R. E. Pattison, "Life and Character of Richard Bassett," *Historical Society of Delaware Papers*, 29 (1900), 3–19; J. G. Wilson, "A Maryland Manor," *Maryland Historical Society Fund Publications*, 31 (1889), 13–19.]

LATIMER, HENRY (1752–1819), b. Newport, Del.; A.B., Univ. of Penn., 1773; M.D., Edinburgh Medical College, 1775; surgeon in the Continental Army; physician residing in Wilmington, Del.; member, Del. House of Representatives, 1787–1788, 1790 (speaker); U. S. Congress, 1794–1795; U. S. Senate, 1795–1801. Openly contemptuous of the people, Latimer was reported to have publicly declared that "the laboring classes in this country lived too well to be happy and should be reduced to the diet of the Irish." Jeffersonians made the most of this indiscretion. At a mass meeting in 1802, they fired a salute in the Senator's honor—the cannon loaded with an Irish diet of potatoes and herring [Munroe, *Federalist Delaware*, p. 211].

McLANE, ALLEN (1746–1829), b. Philadelphia, his parents "of the middling grade" in society; educated in lower schools; settled in Kent Co., Del., 1774; served in the Continental Army; farmer, with holdings in Kent Co., sometime merchant, and office holder, whose highest post was Collector of the Port of Wilmington [Conrad, *Delaware*, III, 876–877]. McLane's response to the Democratic-Republican movement was conventional. Of Jeffersonian journals he declared to Pickering, "Sir, I am almost delirious at seeing our once happy Country disordered by such infamous incidents" [8 Feb. 1800, in Pickering Papers, Mass. Hist. Soc.]. He blamed the political troubles of the new republic upon the younger generation, "men who did not exist when I was making every sacrifice in the Service of my country," he wrote angrily [to John Steele, 10 Apr. 1798, *Steele Papers*, I, 266–267]. He was, however, reportedly active in the electioneering campaign of 1800, stumping Kent County and warning that a Jeffersonian victory would be followed by an American jacobinical terror, complete with tumbrils and republican marriages [Munroe, *Federalist Delaware*, p. 208].

VINING, JOHN (1758–1802), b. Dover, Del.; educated privately; lawyer residing in Dover, Del:; member, Continental Congress, 1784–1786; Del. House of Representatives, 1787–1788; U. S. Congress 1789–1793;

Del. Senate, 1793; U. S. Senator, 1793–1798. Vining was a leader of a "federal junto" in Dover, which was predominant in the politics of Kent County [Munroe, *Federalist Delaware*, p. 231n; G. P. Fisher, "Recollections of Dover in 1824," *Historical Society of Delaware Papers*, LV, 24–27]. His political prejudices appear in a *Eulogium delivered to a large Concourse of Respectable Citizens . . . in commemoration of the Death of Gen. George Washington* (Philadelphia, 1800). Of events in the 1790s he declared, "When busy faction, the accursed scourge of almost every land, loudly assumed the name of public zeal, dared to raise her head against the government and laws, and would have spread her desolating rage—he had but to give a stretch to his arm, and with his thunder to speak the terror of disobedience and opposition to constituted authorities."

Young Federalists

BAYARD, JAMES ASHETON (1767–1815): see above, chapter II.

BROOM, JAMES MADISON (1776–1850), b. Wilmington, Del.; A.B., Princeton, 1794; lawyer residing in Wilmington, Del. and briefly in Baltimore, 1807; U. S. Congress, 1805–1807; removed to Philadelphia, 1819, where he practiced law until his death. With James A. Bayard, he took a leading part in the direction of Delaware Federalism; state caucuses convened in his drawing room. His Congressional speeches were delivered in defense of economy of governmental expenditures, and liberty from governmental power. After one such philippic, a Virginia Jeffersonian tendered to Broom "congratulations on his conversion to Democracy" [AC 9/2/503–508, 512, 17 Feb. 1807; see also 9/2/308, 13 Jan. 1807, and 9/2/520, 17 Feb. 1807].

CLAYTON, THOMAS (1777?–1854), b. Massey's Crossroads, Md.; attended Newark Academy; lawyer practising in New Castle, Del.; clerk, Del. House of Representatives, 1800; member, 1802–1806, 1810, 1812–1813; Del. Secretary of State, 1808–1810; Del. Senate, 1808; Del. Attorney General, 1810–1815; U. S. Congress, 1815–1817; U. S. Senate, 1824–1827, 1837–1847. Clayton was active in the Federal party organization within his state, urging political friends to be "careful not to suffer the Democrats to get the advantage of us at the Election" [to H. M. Ridgely, 17 Sep. 1801, in de Valinger, *Ridgely Family Letters*, II, 97]. A speech in Congress, however, contained vestiges of old-school principles [AC 14/2/646–649, 20 Jan. 1817].

HORSEY, OUTERBRIDGE (1777–1842), b. Laurel, Sussex Co., Del.; lawyer practicing in Wilmington; member, Del. House of Representatives,

1800–1802; Del. Attorney General, 1806–1810; U. S. Senate, 1810–1821. Another pillar of the Federal party organization in Delaware, extracts from Horsey's political letters are published in Turner, *Records of Sussex Co., Del.*, pp. 301–305. See also his Congressional speeches against the power hunger of the administration [*AC* 11/3/43–55, 28 Dec. 1810; 13/2/708–722, 2 Apr. 1814].

JOHNS, KENSEY (1759–1848), b. Anne Arundel Co., Md.; attended common schools; studied law with Samuel Chase (q.v.); lawyer residing in New Castle, Del.; Johns served on Federal committees and took a prominent role in public party gatherings. In 1801 a Delaware Republican reported to Jefferson that "Bayard, chief justice Johns, and the whole host of federal lawyers set out to convoke meetings of the people and harrangue [sic] them." He complained of their tactics, which allegedly included "forgery, fabrication, bribery, and every species of seduction" [John Vaughan to Jefferson, 10 Oct. 1801, in Jefferson Papers, Library of Congress].

McLANE, LOUIS (1786–1857), b. Smyrna, Del.; attended Delaware College, Newark, Del.; studied law with James A. Bayard (q.v.) and practiced in Wilmington, Del.; U. S. Congress, 1817–1827, U. S. Senate, 1827–1829; Envoy Extraordinary to England, 1829–1831; Secretary of the Treasury, 1831–1833; Secretary of State, 1833–1834; Minister to England, 1845–1846; president of the Baltimore and Ohio Railroad, 1837–1847. Though a Federalist, like his father Allen McLane (q.v.), Louis McLane was born too late to take a leading part in Delaware politics before the War of 1812. But he became one of the most successful Jacksonian Federalists in the nation, remaining loyal to the party and the person of "Old Hickory," though unable to support Jackson's bank policy [Van Buren, *Autobiography*, passim].

RIDGELY, HENRY MOORE (1779–1847), b. Dover, Del.; attended Dickinson College; studied law with Charles Smith (q.v.), and practiced in Dover and Wilmington, Del.; U. S. Congress, 1811–1815; Del. Secretary of State, 1817–1827; U. S. Senator, 1827–1829. For his role in federal party politics, see de Valinger, *Ridgely Family Letters*, II, 87–94; and for his use of popular rhetoric in Congress see *AC* 12/1/1270–1271, 7 Apr. 1812.

WELLS, WILLIAM HILL (1769–1829), b. Burlington, N. J.; educated in lower schools; lawyer and merchant in Dagsboro, Del.; wealthy investor in Pennsylvania oil and Delaware timber; his income from the latter was reputedly $5400 a year; member Del. House of Representatives, 1794–1798; U. S. Senator, 1799–1804, 1813–1817. For a defense of partisan appeals to the people, against the administration, see *AC* 13/2/590, 14 Jan. 1814. Extracts from political correspondence appear in *Sussex County Records*, pp. 295–317.

MARYLAND

Federalists of the Old School

CARROLL, CHARLES, OF CARROLLTON (1737–1832), b. Annapolis, Md.; educated in France and England; lawyer, gentleman farmer and land-owner; in 1776 his fortune was estimated at one million dollars [John Adams to James Warren, 18 Feb. 1776, in Burnett, *Letters of Members of the Continental Congress*, I, 354]; Continental Congress, 1776, 1777–1778, 1780; Maryland Senator, 1777–1800; U. S. Senator, 1789–1792. Even as a young man, Carroll had taken a disdainful view of the "paltry raffle of colony faction." To an English friend he wrote, "We have our political parties among us but they are too trivial and of too little con-sequence for me to relate or you to hear; I shall only observe that they seem to me to spring from the same source in which your factions have theirs: the want of a sufficient number of lucrative offices to gratify the avarice or the ambition of the 'outs'" [Carroll to Edmund Jennings, 3 Nov. 1765, in Thomas M. Field, ed., *Unpublished Letters of Charles Carroll* (New York, 1902), p. 98]. The injection of ideology into partisan disputes gave him one more reason to despise them [Steiner, *James McHenry*, p. 473; Ellen Hart Smith, *Charles Carroll*, p. 249]. After 1800 he was a mere spectator on the political scene, an unwilling witness to a world which he could not accept, and to a society which he could not serve. Younger Federalists complained of his reluctance to contribute to their party cause [A. C. Hanson to J. E. Hall, 16 Dec. 1813, in Hanson Papers, Md. Hist. Soc.]. On rare occasions, he tried to help as best he could, in the anachronistic ways of his youth—herding his tenants to the polls, mobilizing the resources of his extended kinship family. But more often he alternated between moods of apathy and fear. [*Penna. Mag. Hist. & Biog.*, 28 (1904) 217; Carroll to Harper, 28 May 1812, in Row-land, *Carroll*, II, 289.]

CHASE, JEREMIAH TOWNLEY (1748–1828), b. Baltimore, Md.; educated privately; served on Revolutionary committees; Maryland Council, 1780–1784, 1786–1788; Continental Congress, 1783–1784; chief justice, Maryland Court of Appeals, 1789–1824; lawyer and speculator in loyalist lands, residing in Annapolis. Chase was an anti-Federalist in 1787; but in the more fundamental conflict of the 1790s, he served the cause of "order." As a candidate for Presidential elector (Adams) in 1800, he explained why. "No Republican government can exist without confidence in the constituted authorities," he declared. "It is the basis upon which it rests. Jealousy and unjust suspicion, like the moth fretting a garment, whose ravages are unperceived while they are making, will waste and destroy it by imperceptible degrees." Like other older Federalists, Chase boasted of his independence. "I am linked to no party, correspond with no great men," he declared ["To the Citizens and Free Voters of the Fifth District," Baltimore *Federal Gazette*, 11 Sep. 1800].

CHASE, SAMUEL (1741–1811), b. Princess Anne, Md.; educated by his father (an Anglican clergyman) and by tutors; lawyer residing in Baltimore and Annapolis; member, Maryland General Assembly, 1764–1784; Continental Congress, 1774–1778, 1784–1785; agent for Maryland in Great Britain, 1783; judge, Baltimore Criminal Court, 1788; Maryland General Court, 1791–1796; U. S. Supreme Court, 1796–1811. Chase, a heavy investor in confiscated Loyalist property, was an anti-Federalist in 1787 but, with Jeremiah Townley Chase and Luther Martin, became a "friend of government" in the 1790s. One of the least attractive figures of his generation, this "degenerate character" used secret information available to Continental Congressmen to corner the market in flour when the American army was most in need; he was openly attacked by Alexander Hamilton, no enemy to an honorable speculation [Syrett, *Works of Hamilton*, I, 562–582]. But even Chase recognized a political morality and appears to have been quite genuinely shocked by Jeffersonian ideology and techniques [see a letter from his pen in the Petersburg *Intelligencer*, 3 Aug. 1800]. Though in 1800 he conducted a "canvass" for Federal candidates in traditional eighteenth-century style, he never qualified or disguised his elitist prejudices [*American Antiquarian Society Proceedings*, n.s., 27 (1917), 121]. The jury charge which he delivered in Baltimore in 1803, and which was followed by his impeachment, was a full statement of his position. He condemned the "unfairly acquired power" of the administration, repudiated the doctrine of natural rights, declared that "true liberty, in his opinion, did not consist in the possession of equal rights, but in the protection by the law of the person and property of every member of society, however various the grade in society he filled," and insisted that "a monarchy might be free, and a republic in slavery." Chase's outburst had been provoked by the abolition of property qualifications for the suffrage in Maryland, an act which was passed with strong support from younger Federalists. His most bitter words were reserved for young leaders of both parties—"he could not but flush at the degeneracy of sons, who destroyed the fair fabric raised by the patriotism of their fathers." Brought to bay before the Senate, Chase defiantly attacked his attackers, "those who were 'puling in their nurses arms,' whilst I was contributing my utmost aid to lay the groundwork of American liberty" [AC 8/2/96, 231–236; cf. 296–306].

DENT, GEORGE (1756–1813), b. "Windsor Castle," Charles County, Md.; "preparatory studies"; served in the Continental Army; member, Maryland General Assembly, 1782–1790 (speaker, 1788–1790); Maryland Senate, 1791–1792; U. S. Congress, 1793–1801. Dent generally voted with Federalists on routine legislation, but joined the opposition on such major issues as Jay's Treaty, the call for the XYZ papers, and the Alien and Sedition legislation. Respected by both sides, he was once elected speaker *pro tem.* in the partisan Fifth Congress, by "all except two or three scattering votes" [AC, 5/2/1835, 28 May 1798]. In the Sixth Congress, Dent's positions became progressively more Republican; in the House vote on the Presidential election, he supported Jefferson against Burr, and after the inauguration was appointed to the post of Marshall of the District of Columbia. According to Charles County legend, Dent found this reward unsatisfactory and veered back to the Federal side. In 1802, he removed to Georgia and disappeared from public life [Harry Wright Newman, *Charles County Gentry* (Washington, 1940), pp. 37–39].

HINDMAN, WILLIAM (1743–1822), b. Dorchester County, Md.; A.B., Univ. of Penn., 1761; studied law in the Inns of Court; lawyer and planter residing near Wye Landing, Talbot County, Md. Hindman served on Revolutionary Committees, was a member of the Maryland Senate, 1777–1784; Continental Congress, 1784–1788; Maryland Council, 1789–1792; U. S. Congress, 1793–1799; Maryland General Assembly, 1799–1800; U. S. Senate, 1800–1801. Hindman was willing to canvass in the eighteenth-century manner [to James McHenry, 12 Aug. 1798, in McHenry Papers, Md. Hist. Soc.] but unwilling to engage in more systematized and more ideological partisan activity [Baltimore *Federal Gazette,* 14 Oct. 1809; his conventional old school ideals appear in *An Address to the People of Maryland, on the Origin, Purpose and Present State of the French Aggressions* (Philadelphia, 1798), pp. 4, 65, 72, passim. See generally "A Memoir of William Hindman," *Md. Hist. Soc. Fund Pubs.,* 14 (1890), 5–59].

HOWARD, JOHN EAGER (1752–1827), b. Baltimore County, Md.; educated by private tutors; served in the Continental Army; Continental Congress, 1784–1788; Governor of Maryland, 1789–1791; Maryland Senate, 1791–1795; U. S. Senate, 1796–1803; landowner living at "Belvedere," now within Baltimore City. His old-school attitudes are apparent in his opposition to the popularly oriented partisanship of such younger Federalists as Robert Goodloe Harper (q.v.). Mrs. Harper angrily declared that Colonel Howard "does more harm to the cause, by opposing everything that is proposed by the party, than any other man in the country" [to Robert Goodloe Harper, 5 Mar. 1810, in Harper-Pennington Papers, Md. Hist. Soc.].

JOHNSON, THOMAS (1732–1819), b. Calvert County, Md.; raised in Annapolis and trained in the law by Stephen Bordley, brother of John Beale Bordley (q.v.); served on Revolutionary committees; Continental Congress, 1774–1777; Governor of Maryland, 1777–1779; member, Maryland General Assembly, 1780, 1786–1787; Chief Justice, Maryland General Court, 1790–1791; Associate Justice, U. S. Supreme Court, 1791–1793; landowner residing at "Rose Hill," Frederick County, Md. His old-school ideals appear in an intricate letter to George Washington (q.v.): "Those who are clamorous seem to me to be really more afraid of being restrained from doing what they ought not to do, and being compelled to do what they ought to do, than of being obliged to [do] what there is no moral obligation in them to do. I believe there is no American of observation, reflection and candour but will acknowledge Man unhappily needs more government than he imagined" [quoted in Edward S. Delaplaine's serialized biography, *Md. Hist. Mag.*, 21 (1926), 196–198; the biography runs from vol. 14 to 21 (1919–1926), passim].

LLOYD, JAMES (1745–1820), b. near Chestertown, Md.; "pursued classical studies"; served in the Revolutionary militia; U. S. Senate, 1797–1800; lawyer, gentleman farmer residing at "Ratcliff Manor," Talbot Co., Md. [Tilghman, *Talbot County*, I, 132, 228]. Lloyd's greatest prominence derives from his famous first draft of the Sedition Bill, which younger Federalists in the House successfully modified. Equally revealing is an extraordinary *Address to the Citizens of Kent* (Annapolis, 1794) in which he condemned electioneering attacks upon himself, declaring, "Behold, in the opposition to me, an attempt to subvert the laws of our country. . . . How mischievous a thing it is to oppose the government of the state?" [p. 37]. His posture calls to mind a comparable argument in *Iolanthe*:

> The Law is the embodiment
> Of everything that's excellent.
> It has no kind of fault or flaw,
> And I, my Lords, embody the Law.

McHENRY, JAMES (1753–1816), b. County Antrim, Ireland; emigrated 1771; attended Newark Academy and studied medicine with Benjamin Rush; surgeon in the Continental Army; secretary to George Washington (q.v.), 1778–1780; member, Maryland Senate, 1781–1786; Continental

Congress, 1783–1786; member, U. S. Constitutional Convention; Secretary of War, 1796–1800; after 1800 a nonpracticing physician and gentleman farmer living at "Fayetteville," near Baltimore, Md. In 1800 Dr. McHenry accurately diagnosed the wasting disease which was crippling his cause. "Have our party shown they possess the necessary skill and courage to deserve to be continued to govern?" he asked plaintively. ". . . Their conduct, even now . . . is tremulous, timid, feeble, deceptive and cowardly. They write private letters. To whom? To each other, but they do nothing to give a proper direction to the public mind. They observe, even in their conversation, a discreet circumspection generally, ill calculated to diffuse information, or prepare the mass of the people for the result. They meditate in private. Can good come out of such a system?" [to Wolcott, 22 July 1800, in Gibbs, *Administrations of Washington and Adams*, II, 384–385]. But McHenry was not prepared to try the natural remedy. He despised Jeffersonian techniques as "dirty tricks" and "poisoned weapons" which no "honourable man" could handle [to Pickering, 16 Oct. 1809, in Pickering Papers, Mass. Hist. Soc.]. In 1811, however, he was persuaded by Robert Goodloe Harper to serve on an electioneering committee in Baltimore [J. C. Herbert to McHenry, 5 June 1811, in McHenry Papers, Library of Congress].

MARTIN, LUTHER (1748?–1826), b. New Brunswick, N. J.; A. B., Princeton, 1766; school teacher in Maryland, 1766–1771; lawyer, practicing in Virginia and Maryland; Attorney General of Maryland, 1778–1805, 1818–1820; member, Continental Congress, 1784–1785; U. S. Constitutional Convention; counsel for Samuel Chase and Aaron Burr; speculator in land and loyalist property. Martin was another of the Maryland anti-Federalists who joined the latter-day Federalists; in his case, a personal hatred of Thomas Jefferson was decisive. Not a figure of first importance in Maryland politics after 1800, he was occasionally active—offering himself for public office in the traditional spirit of politics in the Chesapeake colonies, without regard to party discipline or popular opinions [Baltimore *Federal Gazette*, 21 Sep. 1811; Baltimore *Federal Republican*, 28 Sep. 1811]. For his principles see Baltimore *Federal Gazette*, 18 Apr. 1801, which make clear the fact that his hostility to Jeffersonian Republicanism was more than mere enmity to Jefferson or friendship to Burr [cf. Beard, *Economic Origins of Jeffersonian Democracy*, p. 53].

OGLE, BENJAMIN (1746–1809), b. Annapolis, Md.; scion of a proud colonial family; educated in England; planter residing at "Belair," Prince George's County, Md., an English country home complete with deer park. The "last of the old-time federalist executives" of Maryland [Buchholz, *Governors of Maryland*, pp. 46–50], his old-school attitudes appeared in his hostility to Robert Goodloe Harper's "bystander" scheme for securing all of Maryland's electoral votes to Federal candidates. Ogle's position was similar to that which John Jay took in New York at the same time on a comparable proposal [Harper to A. C. Hanson, 19 Jan. 1815, in Galloway-Maxcy-Markoe Papers, Library of Congress, describes the incident and details Ogle's part in it].

STODDERT, BENJAMIN (1751–1813), b. Charles County, Md.; educated privately; served in the Continental Army, and as secretary to the Board of War; Secretary of the Navy, 1798–1801; merchant residing in Georgetown and Bladensburg, Md., heavily endebted in 1801. Stoddert was temperamentally unsuited for a partisan role. In 1798 he articulated a "wish to spend my life in retirement and ease without bustle of any kind," a desire which was reinforced by the precarious state of his finances [quoted in Harriet Stoddert Turner, "Memoirs of Benjamin Stoddert," *Columbia Historical Society Records*, 20 (1917), 141–166; p. 152]. His comments upon the passing political scene were the conventional reactions of the old school [Stoddert to John Rutledge, 18 Sep. 1802, 27 Dec. 1807, in Rutledge Papers, Southern Hist. Coll., Univ. of N. C.]. Though he occasionally attended party gatherings and wrote polemics over the signature of a "Maryland Farmer," his comments upon the Baltimore mobs of 1812 suggest that he was thinking in terms of a reunion of the wise and good which would leave little latitude for popular initiative. "Why, for the honor of Balto, is there not an association of all men of property—or not of the respectable Democrats and the Fedts to support the laws . . . the mob is the most powerful auxiliary of the Executive, & this is known at head quarters. But the Union I speak of would overcome the mob. . . . An association (it ought to be written & signed) by the Fedt. alone, might lead to civil war—every good would result from one begun by Jas. Buchanan & such men—and including the Fedts.—and I would make even all the poorer classes sign it" [to McHenry, 15 July 1812, in Steiner, *McHenry*, p. 583; see also Stoddert to Harper, 31 Aug., 16 Nov. 1812, in Harper-Pennington Papers, Md. Hist. Soc.].

TANEY, MICHAEL (1750?–1838?), b. Calvert Co.?, Md.; educated in Europe; wealthy planter residing in Calvert Co., Maryland, in 1782 his holdings amounted to 728 acres and 10 slaves. A bluff, hearty, fox-hunting, duck-shooting Tidewater squire, Taney taught his sons to ride and swim and shoot before they learned to read [Tyler, *Memoir of Roger Brooke Taney*, pp. 28, 55]. In the House of Delegates, where he represented his county for many years, Taney was a firm advocate of suffrage reform, one of the few older Federalists to support that measure. No doctrinaire, he had opposed abolition of entail and primogeniture

[Charles F. Stein, *Calvert County* Baltimore, 1960, pp. 106, 322–325, 373]. His reasons for wishing to extend the franchise remain obscure —perhaps he was thinking in old-school terms of a speaking elite and a silent multitude; or perhaps the penalties imposed upon his Catholic co-religionists in eighteenth-century Maryland had turned him against restraints on political participation. In any case, he was unable to push his suffrage bill through the legislature until after 1800, when he received the support of some Jeffersonians and of such younger Federalists as John Hanson Thomas (q.v.). For the efforts of his young friends to create a Federal party, however, Michael Taney had neither respect nor sympathy. He continued to vote as he pleased and to "offer" when he wished. A serious conflict between him and the state organization was narrowly prevented in 1811 by the intervention of his son, Roger Brooke Taney (q.v.), who persuaded his father to respect the decision of the party as to candidates and issues [Baltimore *Whig*, 10 Aug. 1811].

Transitional Figures

KEY, PHILIP BARTON (1757–1815), b. near Charlestown, Cecil Co., Md.; pursued an "academic career," probably under tutors; served with the British army during the War for Independence, and continued on half pay to 1806; returned to Maryland, 1785, where he lived as a lawyer, planter, and master of "Woodley," near Georgetown, Md.; U. S. Congress, 1807–1813. During the electioneering campaigns of 1800, Key spoke and acted like an old-school Federalist [Annapolis *Md. Gazette*, 4 Sep. 1800; Baltimore *Federal Gazette*, 10 Sep. 1800]. But in the face of sharp criticism of his counter-revolutionary record, he trimmed close to the political winds. In 1807, he delivered a speech on the idea of representation which was essentially Jeffersonian [AC 10/1/909–917, 16 Nov. 1807], and in 1810 appealed to the agrarian emotions of the nation with no apparent sense of embarrassment. "Are the representatives of the landed interest of this country prepared to give this bonum to merchants and manufacturers?" he asked. "No, sir; under God, I hope the agricultural interest will be the first protected, as they are the shield of the country, and will be its defence when war comes. Then you would look to the hardy sons of the soil as a different class, in point of virtue, feeling and principle, from those whom this law would benefit. You would never look at men and boys in workshops for that virtue and spirit in defence that you would justly expect from the yeomanry of the country" [ibid,, 11/2/1906, 18 Apr. 1810].

MURRAY, WILLIAM VANS (1760–1803), b. Cambridge, Dorchester Co., Md.; studied law in the Inns of Court, 1784–1787; practised in Cambridge, Md.; member, Maryland General Assembly, 1791; U. S. Congress,

1791–1797; Minister to the Netherlands, 1797–1801, and special envoy to France, 1799–1800. The conceptual units of Murray's political thought were the steady yeoman-farmers of Dorchester County. He described their behavior in the election of 1796: "Our election closed this evening. The Jefferson candidate got one *vote*. The Adams candidate 582—no riots— noise or seduction. The farmers came in without leaders to support government, they said, by voting for a Fedl. man" [to McHenry, 9 Nov. 1796, in Steiner, *McHenry*, p. 201; see also Murray to J. Q. Adams, 3 Apr. 1802, in Adams Family Papers, reel 401]. Without actively soliciting support, he did his duty, helping to keep the people steady. "I mean next week to ride through the district I represent, and exercise my apostolic powers to the great end of the [Jay] mission, peace and confidence," he wrote [to Oliver Wolcott, 29 Aug. 1795, in Gibbs, *Administrations of Washington and Adams*, I, 228–229]. Although he condemned Democratic societies and demagogic arts, he urged his political friends to organize and act [ibid., and see above, chapter III]. The tone of letters written shortly before his early death suggests that he might have joined with Harper and others to create a Federal party in Maryland [to King, 5 Apr. 1802, *King*, IV, 95].

Young Federalists

BEVERLEY, ROBERT (1769–1843), b. Blandford, Essex Co., Va.; privately educated; lawyer and planter; removed to Georgetown, Md., c.1805 [John McGill, *The Beverley Family of Virginia* (Columbia, S. C., 1956), p. 549]. In the 1790s, his letters manifest an old-fashioned determination to maintain the "firmness of our progenitors" in the face of Jeffersonian innovations [Beverley to John Rutledge, Jr., 2 Apr. 1798, in Rutledge Papers, Southern Hist. Coll., Univ. of N. C.]. After 1800, however, he showed more flexibility, becoming a backer of the Washington *Federalist* [Beverley and Archibald Lee to Dwight Foster, 16 Sep. 1808, in Broadsides, Amer. Antiq. Soc.] and opening his Georgetown home as a clearing-house for communications between northern and southern Federalists [Beverley to John Rutledge, 3 Oct. 1808, in Rutledge Papers].

CALDWELL, ELIAS BOUDINOT (1776–1825), b. Elizabeth-town, N. J.; attended Princeton; studied law with Elias Boudinot (q.v); clerk, United States Supreme Court, 1800–1825; editor of a party paper, the Washington *Federalist*. As a political journalist he was prepared to pursue public opinion, but disagreed sharply with John Rutledge, Jr., as to the heat of that pursuit (see above, chapter VII). In electioneering business he showed the same willingness to work, and the same tender conscience. "There is something contrary to that dignity, that high and honorable ground upon which federalism stands in this intriguing," he wrote at the foot of a political letter [to William Gaston, 1 June, 26 Nov. 1808, in Gaston Papers, Southern Hist. Coll., Univ. of N. C.).

DORSEY, CLEMENT (1778–1848), b. "Oaklands," Anne Arundel Co., Md.; attended St. Johns College, Annapolis; lawyer, planter residing at "Summerseat," Charles County, Md.; U. S. Congress, 1825–1831; U. S. Circuit Judge, 1831–1848 [Newman, *Anne Arundel Gentry*, p. 90]. Dorsey was the leader of a formal Federal organization which developed in Charles County after 1808 [Harper to Dorsey, 25 Sep. 1812, in Harper Papers, Md. Hist. Soc.). He was prominent in legislative caucuses and committees [Dorsey to Levin Winder, n.d., 1814?, in Dorsey Papers, Duke University Library]. His popular-orientation appears in *"An Address to the People of Charles County in reply to 'Something curious.'"* [n.p., 1817].

DORSEY, WALTER (1771–18??), b. Anne Arundel Co. Md.; lawyer in Baltimore City [Newman, *Anne Arundel Gentry*, pp. 90, 103]. Dorsey's party activities included membership in the committee which sponsored the Baltimore *Federal Republican* and sustained it in times of financial difficulty [Dorsey et al. to H. G. Otis, 20 Aug. 1812, in Otis Papers, Mass. Hist. Soc.]; in the steering committee of the Washington Society of Maryland; and in the Baltimore Committee of Correspondence which served as a general committee for the state ["At a Meeting of Gentlemen," 1 June 1815, in Galloway-Maxcy-Markoe Papers, Library of Congress].

FRISBY, RICHARD (1777–1845), b. "Violet Farm," Kent Co., Md.; planter in Kent County to circa 1812, when he removed to Baltimore City [Emory, *Queen Anne's County* (Baltimore, 1950), p. 391]. In 1811 he was de facto head of the Federal organization in Kent [Frisby to McHenry, 29 May 1811, in McHenry Papers, Md. Hist. Soc.]. Thereafter, he sat on the Baltimore Committee ["At a Meeting of Gentlemen," 1 June 1815, in Galloway-Maxcy-Markoe Papers, Library of Congress].

GOLDSBOROUGH, CHARLES (1765–1834), b. "Hunting Creek," Dorchester Co., Md.; A.B., Univ. of Penn., 1784; lawyer and planter residing in Dorchester Co.; member, Maryland Senate, 1791–1795, 1799–1801; U. S. Congress, 1805–1817; Governor of Maryland, 1818–1819 [Elias Jone, *History of Dorchester* (Baltimore, 1925), p. 325; Buchholz, *Governors of Maryland*, pp. 86–90; Warfield, *Founders of Anne Arundel and Howard Counties*, pp. 260–261]. A gentleman of great integrity, he never joined in the pursuit of popular support with the abandon of men such as Harper; nor did he participate in the bitter war for loaves and fishes which disrupted the Federal party in Maryland and brought brother against brother, cousin against country cousin. His gubernatorial election in 1818 was owing principally to the fact that all factions respected his strength of character and "soundness in politics" [A. C. Hanson to George Corbin Washington, 18 Nov. 1818, in Hanson-Washington Papers, Md. Hist. Soc.]. Goldsborough did, however, whole heartedly embrace the young Federalist ideal of government severely limited in its sphere of operations; he favored restraint and even retrenchment upon both state and national levels [AC 14/1/1219, 14 Mar. 1816; 13/3/1217, 24 Jan. 1815; 14/1/1135, 4 Mar. 1816; Hanson to Washington, 18 Nov. 1818, in Hanson-Washington Papers, Md. Hist. Soc.].

GOLDSBOROUGH, ROBERT HENRY (1779–1836), b. "Myrtle Grove," Talbot Co., Md.; A.B., St. Johns College, Annapolis, 1795; planter residing in Talbot Co., Md.; member, Maryland General Assembly, 1804; U. S. Senate, 1813–1819, 1835–1836. At the start of his political career, Goldsborough showed scant sympathy for the effort to organize a popular Federal party in Maryland—he repudiated his own nomination by a Federal caucus as an "unwarrantable liberty" [Easton Star, 15 Oct. 1805]. But six years later he had changed his views, and had become the central figure in the Federalist committee organization in Talbot Co., deeply engaged in the daily labor of partisan politics [Goldsborough et al. to Harper, 1 June 1811, in McHenry Papers, Library of Congress; Easton Star, 1 Oct. 1811; Baltimore Federal Republican, 25 Sep. 1811].

HANSON, ALEXANDER CONTEE (1786–1819), b. Annapolis, Md.; A.B., St. Johns College, Annapolis, 1802; journalist, lawyer, gentleman farmer residing at "Belmont" near Rockville, Md.; member Maryland General Assembly, 1811–1815; U. S. Congress, 1813–1816; U. S. Senate, 1816–1819. An analysis of Hanson's career should be undertaken by a student of abnormal psychology; it is impossible to explain his political behavior in rational terms. His commitment to the "cause" possessed a fanatic intensity; the cause, for him, was the "good old cause" of Washington and Hamilton. In Congress he refused to join the majority of young Federalists in their conversion to the Jeffersonian ideals of economy and minimal government. "I hold, that the principles of Federalism, old and new, as they have been denominated, are the same," he declared. ". . . Can it be supposed that we will now abandon our principles, and shift sides with the majority, because they have been driven to the necessity of adopting them? I will never disown and renounce the holy scriptures though preached by a depraved minister of the Gospel" [AC 14/1/915, 5 Feb. 1816]. With equal fervor he attacked Jeffersonian techniques as incompatible with the integrity of the Federal cause [ibid]. But though his principles were clear and consistent, they bore small relation to his political practices. Obsessed with a lofty vision of political morality, Hanson was most unscrupulous in the lowly details of active partisanship. End sanctified means—any means, even those which seemed to violate his larger purposes. While condemning Jeffersonian techniques, he exploited them in his holy quest, without conscious cunning or a sense of contradiction. This Federal fanatic was active on electioneering committees, and in the Washington Societies. He took upon himself the thankless task of fund-raising, and as editor of the virulent *Federal Republican* in Baltimore and Georgetown, he led in the business of "making regular appeals to the people" [Baltimore *Federal Republican*, 26 Aug. 1809; Hanson to Gaston, 12 June 1814, in Gaston Papers, Southern Hist. Coll., Univ. of N. C.; Bosley to Hanson, 23 July 1811, *Southern Hist. Assn. Pubs.*, 9 (1905) p. 319]. When a Democratic mob destroyed his printing establishment in Baltimore City in 1812, he returned with arms, and nearly achieved a martyrdom which he consciously sought [Hanson to Harper, 6 July 1812, in Harper-Pennington Papers, Md. Hist. Soc.]. After his party returned to power in Maryland, Hanson became an "element of strain and disruption" (Hoffer, *The True Believer*, pp. 112–113). Hatred had become habitual; Hanson turned it toward Federalists whose purposes seemed less lofty than his own, toward moderates such as his brother-in-law Clement Dorsey and his quondam friend, Roger Brooke Taney (qq.v.). As leader of the faction called "Violents," he battled with brother Federalists until the party fell in ruins [for this intricate story, see my "Metamorphosis of Maryland Federalism," pp. 26–29; and John C. Herbert to Vergil Maxcy, 11 Sep., 7 Nov. 1816, in Galloway-Maxcy-Markoe Papers, Library of Congress; Annapolis *Maryland Republican*, 3 Jan., 28 Feb. 1818]. Hanson, it should be noted, was an exceptional figure; true believers in Eric Hoffer's sense were as rare among young Federalists as among the leaders of any other major party in American history.

HARPER, ROBERT GOODLOE (1765?–1825). See above, chapter II.

HERBERT, JOHN CARLYLE (1775–1820), b. Alexandria, Va.; A.B., St. Johns College, Annapolis, 1794; lawyer, planter residing at "Walnut Grange" near Beltsville, Md., after 1805; member, Maryland General Assembly, 1808–1813 (speaker, 1812–1813); U. S. Congress, 1815–1819. Though Herbert's political behavior superficially resembled Alexander Contee Hanson's, in his involvement with the Washington Societies, electioneering committees, party newspapers, and political campaigns, he was a man of a different breed. Cynical, disenchanted, detached, he never identified himself with the Federal party in Hanson's fashion—the party did not represent a "cause," but was merely a convenient vehicle. His extraordinarily candid correspondence with Vergil Maxcy, in the Galloway-Maxcy-Markoe Papers, Library of Congress, have been quoted in nearly every chapter. They comprise the most complete and revealing direct evidence of the young Federalists' pursuit of popular support which this investigator has discovered.

PLATER, JOHN ROUSBY (1767–1831), b. St. Mary's Co., Md.; attended St. Johns College, Annapolis; wealthy planter residing in St. Mary's Co. [M. R. Hodges, *General Index St. Mary's County Wills,* 93]. Plater was the central figure in the Federal organization within St. Mary's County [Plater to James McHenry, 3 June 1811, in Southern Hist. Assn. *Pubs.,* 9 (1905) pp. 317–319].

RIDGELY, CHARLES CARNAN (1760–1829), b. Baltimore Co., Md.; educated privately; wealthy landowner and master of "Hampton," near Towson, Md.; member, Maryland House of Delegates, 1790–1795, Maryland Senate, 1796–1800; Governor of Maryland, 1817 [Buchholz, *Governors of Maryland,* pp. 81–85]. Ridgely was a friend and close associate of Robert Goodloe Harper (q.v.) from "Bystander" days in 1800, to the great meetings of 1811–1815, some of which convened in Ridgely's home ["At a Meeting of Gentlemen," in Galloway-Maxcy-Markoe Papers, Library of Congress].

STEUART, GEORGE HUME (1790–1867), b. Annapolis, Md.; removed to Baltimore, 1794; attended Princeton; studied law with William H. Winder, and practiced in Baltimore and Annapolis [George A. Hanson, *Old Kent* (Baltimore, 1876), pp. 271–272]. Steuart first became active in the Washington Benevolent Societies of Baltimore and Annapolis [Steuart to Lemuel Shaw, 16 July, 13 Aug. 1812, in Washington Society Papers, Mass. Hist. Soc.] His promise was recognized and rewarded by party leaders; in 1815, aet. 25, Steuart was a member of the Baltimore Committee, and a participant in the Hampton meeting ["At a Meeting of Gentlemen," in Galloway-Maxcy-Markoe Papers, Library of Congress].

TANEY, ROGER BROOKE (1777–1864), b. Calvert Co., Md., son of Michael Taney (q.v.); A.B., Dickinson College, 1795; studied law with Jeremiah Townley Chase (q.v.) and practiced in Frederick-town, Md., after 1801. In 1802, Taney and John Hanson Thomas organized a party effort in Frederick Co., complete with committees, mass meetings, barbecues, and a new electioneering journal, the *Frederick-town Herald* [see issues of 3 July, 28 Aug. 1802]. Taney's clumsy first efforts at popular politics were scoffed at by Jeffersonians [Swisher, *Taney,* p. 46], but the growth of Federalist pluralities in Frederick Co. testifies to his success, as does his *Address to the People of Frederick County* [Frederick-town, 1817]. In 1812, Taney became embroiled in an intramural battle which ended in the disintegration of Maryland Federalism a decade later. The fight was largely over patronage, but also over party policy, and particularly over the question of the war. Taney favored support for the administration, and did not approve of the militancy of Alexander Contee Hanson (q.v.). The Taney faction were misleadingly called Coodies, after Verplanck's group in New York; Hanson's friends became "Violents" [see my "Metamorphosis of Maryland Federalism," and cf. Swisher, *Taney*, p. 60; it should be parenthetically noted that Taney's moderate faction favored a Clintonian alliance in 1812, unlike Verplanck's Coodies. Hanson's "Violents" were opposed to a coalition, and were forced into line, partly by Taney himself, who was called a "demi-Federalist" for his cooperation with dissident Democrats, by Hanson's paper (Georgetown *Federal Republican*, 10 Nov. 1813)]. The "coody" sobriquet had become an "unmeaning epithet," when it was most fashionable in Maryland [*Frederick-town Herald*, 8 Mar. 1817].

THOMAS, JOHN HANSON (1779–1815), b. Frederick-town, Md.; attended St. Johns College; studied law with Robert Goodloe Harper (q.v.), and practiced in Frederick-town. Harper worked closely with Thomas in his effort to bring system to the tangled jungle of Maryland Federalism [Harper to Thomas, July 1808, in Harper-Pennington Papers, Md. Hist. Soc.]. His own new-modeled conservatism appears in his strong support for repeal of property qualifications; and in his *Oration delivered at the Presbyterian Meeting House . . . at the request of the Washington Society of Alexandria* [Alexandria, Va., 1807]. Thomas was caught in the middle by the Coody-Violent controversy. He had cooperated closely with Roger Brooke Taney (q.v.) in Frederick Co. politics, but he was a friend of Alexander Contee Hanson (q.v.), and generally agreed with the latter on patronage questions, the war, and De Witt Clinton. When he died suddenly, aet. 36, he was generally regarded as a "Violent."

WAGNER, JACOB (1772–1825), chief clerk of the Department of State, 1798–1806, and afterwards editor of Federalist electioneering newspapers, the Baltimore *North American*, and the Baltimore *Federal Republican*. The virulent irresponsibility of his editorial work was fully equal to Hanson's (q.v.). A specimen is his sensational exposé of Madison's French Citizenship [Baltimore *North American*, 27 July-17 Sep. 1808]. Even brother Federalists were taken aback by his conduct of a partisan press [Archibald Lee to William Gaston, 5 Nov. 1813, in Gaston Papers, Southern Hist. Coll., Univ. N. C.]. Wagner handled much of the printing work for the Federal party in Maryland. Tickets, handbills, broadsides, posters, and pamphlets distributed literally by the barrel throughout the state came from his office [John Murray to Jacob Wagner, 23 July 1811, in McHenry Papers, Library of Congress; Baltimore *Whig*, 7 Aug. 1811].

VIRGINIA
Federalists of the Old School

BLACKBURN, SAMUEL (1759–1835), b. Augusta Co., Va.?; attended Lexington College; lawyer, planter residing in Bath Co., Va.; Federal candidate for Congress, 1811, on an old school platform [Waddell, *Augusta County*, pp. 374, 383, 392, 466; V. W. Raike, *The Blackburn Genealogy* (Washington, 1939) p. 94].

CAMPBELL, ARTHUR (1734–1811), b. Augusta Co., Va.; probably educated in an old field school; planter and speculator in western lands, residing at Abingdon, Washington Co., Va. [L. P. Summers, *History of Southwest Virginia* . . . (Richmond, 1903) p. 748; Abernethy, *Western Lands and the Revolution, passim.*]. From the late 1790s, Campbell identified himself as a Federalist [to Pickering, Aug. 1799, in Pickering Papers, Mass. Hist. Soc.]. In private correspondence he articulated an idea of mixed or balanced government which, in its deep and pervasive holism and in its idealized sense of social concord rather than institutionalized conflict, contrasts clearly with the balanced government of John Adams (q.v.), and is more typical of old school thought than Adams' familiar version. Campbell's argument [to David Campbell in Campbell Papers, Duke University Library] deserves to be quoted at length, as an extraordinarily full statement of the social thought which also appears in Jay, Cabot, and Washington, but not in either Adams or Hamilton, the two conventional models.

Washington Janr. 29 1799

Sir
    At a time when the attention of not only Individuals but also that of whole States are drawn towards the fundamental principles of government, from an alarm that our liberties are in danger. It may not be unacceptable to offer some observations, and opinions, that may be useful in forming a right judgment of public Men and public measures, on which so much depends at this time.
    Democrat and Aristocrat are appellations not unfrequently given, by one party to the other, and both claiming the name of Republican, without either affixing a determinate idea of the terms or defining the characteristics of republicanism.
    Democracy among the ancient nations hath been defined to be a government where the supreme power is lodged with the people, and exercised by them. This form of government has been deemed most consonant to the order of nature, and the freedom of Man: it has been successfully administered in small communitys, but in large and opulent associations, Men soon degenerate to anarchy for under the pleasing name of liberty, licentiousness is introduced, which is only another name for despotism. Licentiousness is the dominion of passion and caprice and violence: Is a contempt of law, right, and justice, as much as arbitrary rule can possibly be.
    Aristocracy has been called a government by the Nobles or where the supreme power was lodged with a few, and for life, and often hereditary. This form would place on one side, all honor and respect, and nothing but

disregard and contempt on the other, here all oppression and violence, and there all patience, and submission, here all convenience and pleasure, and there all labour and indigence. As to Monarchy and kingly powers, it is altogether inadmissible. In democracies, the people may govern well, while a sense of present danger are hanging over them, or where they reverence virtue as the chief good and abhor vice as the worst of evils: Aristocracies may be long upheld, when a sense of honor pervades the body politic, where talents integrity and the love of order, are deemed more necessary than wealth. But an individual invested with the whole sovereign power, cannot from the narrowness of the human mind, extend his views to every department of civil Society. We will unavoidably be exposed to imposition from some quarter or other, even when it is pre-supposed that he is endowed with strong traits of wisdom and good. This administration of consequence can never be marked with that extensive beneficance which results from a *representative government.* It is this latter form, which is best calculated to collect the whole social body. But in Monarchys when the Prince is a tyrant, the names of Master and Slave annihilate all claims of duty, all voluntary offerings of affection and patriotism, and exhibit man to man in a state of warfare, where power is the only right and terror the only obligation. Men may from a sense of fear submit in silence to a King, yet they abhor him in their hearts:—Every such Rule must share all the terror he inspires and *join trembling with his commands.* Knowing himself the enemy of mankind, he can place no confidence in their affection, and make no appeal to their justice.

The *Representative Plan,* or modern Republics, particularly that in America, unites the essentials of each of the above forms, and calls it a representative or mixed government: Or what it might without arrogence assume, the name of *a real Republic.*

For under the Constitution of the United States, every honest station of life is honorable since they are all parts of the great social body. Between the Chief Magistrate, and the people, the great and the mean, the rich and the poor, the acute and the dull, the learned and the ignorant there is no difference, as to the rights of citizenship, but in possession of different powers, and in the discharge of different offices, peculiar to each capacity and—useful to all; and if one of them have a just demand for submission and obedience, for honor and respect, for convenience and ease; the other have as just a claim for protection and defence, for the administration of justice and the preservation of equal liberty, for the supply of their wants, and the relief of their distresses, for *instruction* and *good example.*

From what is already said, you may have a better understanding of the terms *Aristocrat* and *Democrat,* so much used in France in the first years of the Revolution and lately applied to designate parties in America: you will see on the one hand, that all Men are not equal in rights, but only when they mutually perform their *duties,* and that the declaration—"That all Men are by nature equally free and independent. That when they enter into a state of Society they divest themselves of a portion of their liberty to secure the rest."—is not correct. For how can we conclude that all Men by nature are equal?—when daily experience evince, that one [is] stronger another weaker, one wise some foolish, one beautiful another deformed, one dull another ingenious. And we are equally at a loss to understand the arguments in support of the position: That when Men enter into a state of Society they divest themselves of a portion of what nature has bestowed. Does entering into a state of Society, require that Man part of a part of his wit, strength, beauty or ingenuity? The fact is, that we divest ourselves of nothing, but the power to *commit Wrongs,* and enter into a state to *improve every thing.* That from a natural *inequality* may spring a perfect *equality* in respect of every moral and social obligation. Thus instead of us losing by entering into a state of society, we are great gainers; every mental power can better be drawn forth, and acquire an energy in useful exertions, the very corporal faculties, increase in vigour and dexterity.

It is therefore true, that in forming the social body, there must be superiors, inferiors and equals, but as in the natural body, the hands cannot say to the feet we have no need of thee, so in the social, the *Head* and *Heart* cannot say to the rest of the Members, we can do as well without you.

Thus the grand principle of equality of obligation, and of mutual dependence, if adopted in opinion, as it is established in nature, would show the true ground of distinctions among Men. If stations and offices are neither unjustly *usurped*, nor their duties perfidiously and *weakly* performed, the obligation to obedience and submission, is as strong on inferiors, as that of justice and disinterested zeal, for the public good, is on Rulers and Magistrates, and the honor obtained by distinguished abilities, is equally due to their possessors, as the fruits of their honest labour are due to the lower orders of the Community.

Our Representative Plan places the fabric of Society on a firm and lasting foundation, and all the parts of the building however different in point of use or ornament, are so closely connected and necessary to the whole, that none of them can be removed, or defaced without injuring the beauty or the solidity of the structure. A constant balance and reaction of obligation and duty, are thus maintained through all the departments of Society, similar to what we see in nature. These are the principles on which modern republics ought to be founded, this is that *liberty* and *equality*, to which all may aspire, without any danger of disorganizing the *body politic*, it is the system which Men may not only talk about but live up to: It may well be called a Representative government, it is *real republicanism*.

But unfortunately for the happiness of the human race, these are principles, which turbulent and designing Men, may seek to abuse, as an engine for overturning order, and good government, and for introducing that *anarchy*, in the midst of which they may be gainers.

In a Representative government, there is an *equality*, but it implies subordination, an *equality* of wants with a diversity of means of supplying them, an *equality* of obligation with different modes of discharging it. It is an *equality* which by rendering all equally necessary, makes all who faithfully discharge their duties, equally acceptable in the sight of God: but by requiring higher and lower stations, and various distinctions and spheres, establishes different degrees of respectability and honor among Men. It is an *equality* that degrades none, but the tyrant, the ruffian, the thief, the voluptuary, and the sluggard, and exalts all, but these, to the ennobling dignity, of constituent members of the grand Community of mankind, and fellow labourers with God, in advancing the felicity of his moral and intellectual creation. Liberty, equality, legitimate rule and protection, are all thus harmoniously combined, to effect the end of national association, the *public good*—Where *rights* are claimed *duties* must be performed, where submission and obedience are demanded an obligation is implied, for the *Trustee* to be wise and faithful. In fine all government all—associations, whether religious or civil can only rightfully subsist, when there are a reciprocity of obligation, of duty, but more especially, a representative civil association, where inalienable and important rights are to be preserved on one hand, and necessary duties to be observed on—the other. When all this is done, liberty, equality, safety, and happiness, will be the certain result. *It is an—imitation of the Deity, in his government of the World.* As the above cannot be deemed a theoretical plan; but is altogether practical, and salutary; in common life; equally removed from furious jacobinism, and chilling aristocracy, it holds out motives for exertions to those whose talents and opportunities may designate them for conspicuous stations in Society, and rewards for all who aspire to the title of being useful Citizens, of the American Commonwealth.

Accept Sir, this offering of my affectionate Regard.

Arthur Campbell

CARRINGTON, EDWARD (1748–1810), b. Goochland Co., Va.; educated in lower schools; lieutenant colonel in the Continental Army; lawyer, banker, gentleman farmer residing in Richmond, Va.; member Continental Congress, 1785–1786; U. S. Marshal and Collector of Internal Revenue in Virginia, during the 1790s; foreman of the jury in Burr's treason trial; Carrington and John Marshall (q.v.) married sisters. Carrington's response to political events in the new republic was conventional. Of Shays' Rebellion he declared "it certainly originated in the genuine baseness of the people. . . . Man is impatient of restraint, nor will he conform to what is necessary to the good order of society unless he is possessed of discernment and virtue, or the Government under which he lives is efficient" [to Edmund Randolph, *Calendar of Virginia State Papers*, IV, 195–99].

EVANS, THOMAS (c. 1755–1815), b. Accomack Co., Va.; attended William & Mary College; served as a surgeon's mate in the Continental Army; lawyer, planter, residing in Accomack Co. to 1802, when he removed to Wheeling, now W. Va.; member Virginia Assembly, 1780–1781, 1794–1796; U. S. Congress, 1797–1801. A moderate in Congress [*AC* 5/1/69, 22 May 1797], he generally supported the military, economic, and domestic policies of the administration. In the politics of his state, he attacked the Jeffersonian general ticket plan of 1800. "It is an experiment perfectly in the Jacobinical style," he wrote, "rendering laws, when passed, perfectly ineffectual, if not aided by a central committee, who create and direct the affiliated committees in a manner concealed from public view throughout the country. Govt., if such measures may be so called, thus becomes the property of a few daring characters, whilst ancient forms for a while remain, tho' they cannot possibly be more than forms" [to Leven Powell, 30 Oct. 1800, in Dodd, "Correspondence of Col. Leven Powell," *John P. Branch Historical Papers*, I (1901) 54; see also Evans' farewell *Address* to his constituents (n.p., 1801); and Evans to Rutledge, 8 Dec. 1801, in Rutledge Papers, Southern Hist. Coll. Univ. of N. C.].

GOODE, SAMUEL (1756–1822), b. Chesterfield Co., Va.; "preparatory studies"; militia colonel in the War of Independence; lawyer and planter residing near Invermay, Mecklenburg Co., Va.; member Virginia Assembly, 1778–1785; U. S. Congress, 1799–1801 [G. B. Goode, *Virginia Cousins: A Study of the Ancestry and Posterity of John Goode of Whitby* (Richmond, 1887) pp. 96–97]. Elected as a Federalist to the Sixth Congress, Goode's voting record demonstrated his independence [Dauer, *Adams Federalists*, pp. 320, 325].

GRAY, EDWIN (1743–1814?), b. Southampton Co., Va.; attended William and Mary College; Virginia House of Burgesses, 1769–1775; Assembly, 1776, 1779, 1787–1788, 1791; Virginia Senate, 1777–1779; U. S. Congress, 1799–1813; planter residing in Nansemond Co. Va. Gray was first elected to the Congress as a Federalist; after the Yazoo debates in 1804–1805, he worked closely with John Randolph of Roanoke, and participated in the effort of Virginia Quids and Federalists to create a third party behind James Monroe. Throughout his career, Gray was particularly critical of Jeffersonian techniques and electioneering principles [Gray to S. R. Bradley, 21 Jan. 1808, in Gray Papers, Duke University; Gray to Littleton W. Tazewell, 10 Jan., 20 Mar. 1812, in Tazewell Papers, Va. State Library; Gray to Joseph H. Nicholson, 16 Jan. 1810, in Nicholson Papers, Library of Congress].

HENRY, PATRICK (1736–1799) b. Hanover Co., Va.; educated in lower schools; lawyer; member, House of Burgesses, 1765; Continental Congress, 1774–1776; Governor of Virginia, 1776–1779, 1784–1786; House of Delegates, 1780–1784, 1788–1790; anti-Federalist in the Virginia ratifying convention, 1788. If Patrick Henry made a career of *lèse-majesté*, he died a "friend of order." From the fight over Jay's treaty in 1796 to his death in 1799, he generally supported Federal men and measures. Henry denied that he had changed sides or altered his opinions, insisting in 1796 that "I am too old to exchange my former opinions, which have grown up into fixed habits of thinking" [to Mrs. Betsy Aylett, 20 Aug. 1796, William Wirt, *Patrick Henry*, pp. 400–1401). We might take him at his word—the political records of many other old school gentlemen should make clear the fact that there was no necessary or even probable connection between a radical position on imperial questions in the 1760s and Democratic Republicanism, or between anti-Federalism and Jeffersonianism.

In the late 1790s, many factors, small and large, base and noble, contributed to Henry's Federal commitment. Religion was perhaps of major importance—though Henry was not a church-going animal, he drafted a defense of Christianity after reading Paine's *Age of Reason* (Tyler, *Patrick Henry*, pp. 394–395). In the intensely personal politics of the Ancient Dominion, the jealous hatred of Jefferson, and the warm blandishments of Washington and Henry Lee were also significant. But in Henry's words and acts there is also evidence of a fundamental rapport with old school precepts. Demogoguery may have been his chosen weapon, but democracy was never his creed. In 1776 he had warmly praised *Thoughts on Government;* in 1788, he spoke against the Constitution on the grounds that it was too democratic. "To me," he said, "it appears that there is no check in that government. The President, senators, and representatives, all, immediately or mediately, are the choice of the people" [Elliot, *Debates,* III, p. 164]. In the last year of his life Henry attacked the Jeffersonians as mere disorganizers, and declared that the ideals of the French Revolution were "destroying the great pillars of all government and of socal life,—I mean virtue, morality and religion" [to Archibald Blair 8 Jan. 1799, Tyler, *Henry*, p. 409; and see also Henry's speech to the voters of Charlotte Co., in the spring election of 1799, where he was elected as a Federalist to the Virginia House of Delegates, in Wirt, *Henry*, pp. 408–411]. Virginia Federalists made the most of Henry's popularity. Their extraordinary gains in 1799 were due in no small measure to the influence of his name [Georgetown *Washington Federalist*, 23 Oct. 1800]. One might ponder the course of Virginia politics in 1800, if Patrick Henry and George Washington had remained another year upon the scene.

HOPKINS, JOHN (1757–1827), b. Prince William Co., Va., the natural son of a tenant farmer; educated in apprenticeship; laid the groundwork of a fortune as Continental Commissary of Stores during the War of Independence; after 1800 a wealthy merchant and banker in Richmond, Va.; U. S. Commissioner of Loans [Walter Lee Hopkins, *Hopkins of Virginia and Related Families* (Richmond, 1931) pp. 211–215]. This gentleman "of property and integrity" was deeply respected by such older Federalists as Pickering for his candor and independence [Pickering to King, 4 Mar. 1804, *King*, IV, 364]. His expressed opinions were the conventional prejudices of the old school [Hopkins to Pickering, 30 Jan. 1809, in Pickering Papers, Mass. Hist. Soc.].

LEE, HENRY (1756–1818), b. Prince William Co., Va.; A.B., Princeton, 1773; rose from captain to lieutenant colonel in the Continental Army; Continental Congress, 1785–1788; member, Virginia Ratifying Convention, 1788; Governor of Virginia, 1791–1794; U. S. Congress, 1799–1801. His Congressional speeches, and his famous *Oration on the Death of General Washington* were orthodox old school arguments for order and harmony in society, for virtue in the people, and for responsibility in their natural leaders [AC 6/1/1305–1311, 30 Dec. 1799].

MORGAN, DANIEL (c. 1735–1802), b. Hunterdon Co., N. J.; removed to Virginia, c. 1752, where he became a wagoner, farmer, speculator, country merchant, miller, and distiller residing near Winchester, Va.; Morgan rose from captain to brigadier in the Continental Army, and was U. S. Congressman, 1797–1799. His origins and political attitudes closely resemble those of another self-made frontier federalist, William Cooper (q.v.). He spoke of fellow friends of order as "old swords" and "dear boys," and condemned the Democrats to perdition, as "raskels," "scoundrels," and "a parsell of Egg sucking Dogs." Morgan never lost the common touch, and never abandoned a certain directness in his dealings with others. During the Whiskey Rebellion, a tavernkeeper overcharged

Morgan's soldiers for liquor; the general personally "broke his mouth, which closed the business." But if Morgan remained a ruffian, there was a certain commanding dignity in his presence. "The simplicity of his bearing and the nobility of his manner," wrote the marquis de Chastelleux, "reminded me of those ancient Gallic or Germanic chiefs, who, when at peace with the Romans, came to visit them and offer assistance" [*Travels*, II, 581]. The root of Morgan's Federalism may have been the habit of command; few field-grade Revolutionary officers felt comfortable in the Jeffersonian camp. Other factors included religion— atheism and democracy were all of a piece to this God-fearing man—and also important was the respected example of George Washington. Morgan opposed Jay's Treaty until he learned that "the old Horse" favored it. Then, said he, "I shut my pan." Like Washington, Morgan refused to recognize his own partisanship; he regarded Federalism as not a party but the government, and viewed Jeffersonian principles as a "wicked design" for "anarchy." He appears to have been equally disturbed by Jeffersonian practices, and when he ran for public office he boasted of the fact that "no poppular [sic] motive" was involved. [see Don Higginbotham's excellent *Daniel Morgan, Revolutionary Rifleman* (Chapel Hill, 1961) viii, 180–201; and an older but still useful work, James Graham, *Life of General Daniel Morgan* (N. Y., 1856) pp. 18–38].

PARKER, JOSIAH (1751–1810), b. Isle of Wight Co., Va.; "preparatory studies;" lieutenant colonel in the Continental Army; Virginia Assembly, 1780–1781; U. S. Congress, 1789–1801; planter residing at "Macclesfield," Isle of Wight Co., Va. [Augustus G. Parker, *Parkers in America* (Buffalo 1911) pp. 258–261]. Parker was associated with the Republican "interest" in the early 1790s, but in the Fifth and Sixth congresses was an independent "half-Federalist." In 1801, he voted against Jefferson in the disputed Presidential election.

PORTERFIELD, ROBERT (1752–1843), b. in Pennsylvania; served in the Continental Army; after the war, settled as a planter at "Soldier's Retreat," Augusta Co., Va. [Waddell, *Annals of Augusta County*, p. 265 *passim;* Hugh M. McIlhany, *Virginia Families* (Staunton, 1903), pp. 30–31; J. Lewis Peyton, *History of Augusta County* (Staunton, 1882), pp. 317–318]. Porterfield was prominent in the Federal organization which developed in western Virginia during Madison's administration. Though perhaps only a figurehead, he was chairman of state conventions, and a member of the central committee in Staunton [Martinsburgh *Gazette*, 23 Oct. 1812].

POWELL, LEVEN (1737–1810), b. Prince William Co., Va.; educated in lower schools; lieutenant colonel in the Continental Army; member,

Virginia Assembly, 1779, 1787–1788, 1791–1792; U. S. Congress, 1799–1801; farmer (c. 500 acres), miller, country merchant, turnpike investor residing in Loudoun Co., Va. [Charles S. Powell, *History and Genealogies of the Powells in America* (n.p., 1935) pp. 171–172]. His correspondence [published in the *John P. Branch Historical Papers*, I (1901) 111–138, 217–256] conform to the canon of old school orthodoxy.

SHEPHERD, ABRAHAM (1754–1822), b. Mecklenberg Co., Va.; educated in lower schools; served in the Continental Army; settled at Shepherdstown, Va., country merchant, gentleman farmer [Frank C. Shepherd, *History, Genealogies and Biography of the Shepherd and Related Families* (n.p., n.d.) pp. 333–334]. Shepherd's attitudes were those of the old school; but he assisted in the organization of a Federal effort in western Virginia, and attended party conventions at Staunton [Shepherd to Pickering, 4 Oct. 1812, Pickering Papers, Mass. Hist. Soc].

WASHINGTON, GEORGE (1732–1799), b. "Wakefield," Westmoreland Co., Va.; educated in lower schools; lieutenant colonel in the Old French and Indian War; member, Virginia House of Burgesses, 1758–1774; Continental Congress, 1774–75; commander of the Continental Army, 1775–1783; member, U. S. Constitutional Convention, 1787; U. S. President, 1789–1797; wheat farmer residing at "Mt. Vernon," Va. At first sight, Washington seems doubly irrelevant to this investigation of post-1800 Federalism, for he never called himself a Federalist and died in 1799. But on close inspection, there can be no doubt that he identified himself with the Federal Cause. In the last two years of his life, particularly, his disapproval of the Jeffersonian cause became intense. "You could as soon scrub a blackamore white, as to change the principles of a professt Democrat," he wrote angrily. He spoke of Federalists as "we" and Republicans as "they," broke completely with Thomas Jefferson himself, and threw his considerable weight behind Federal candidates in Virginia. His refusal to recognize the basic fact of his partisanship was typical of the old school [Washington to Edward Carrington, May 1, 1796, Washington to James McHenry, Sep. 30, 1798, Washington to Pickering, Sep. 27, 1795; in J. C. FitzPatrick, ed., *Writings of Washington* (39 vols., Washington, 1931–1944) XXXV, 31–32; XXXVI, 474; XXXIV, 315–316; Beveridge, *John Marshall*, II, 374–379; Joseph Charles, *The Origins of the American Party System; Three Essays* (Williamsburg, Va., 1956), 44].

If Washington's physiognomy is familiar to all Americans, his political attitudes remain indistinct. He was, of course, no philosopher, but behind his acts and phrases was a set of attitudes which consistently embodied an "unspoken philosophy," as Douglas Southall Freeman has called it. At every important point, it was entirely compatible with the principles of his friends, George Cabot and John Jay [Douglas Southall Freeman, et al., *George Washington'* (7 vols. N. Y., 1949–1957) V, 469–501; VI, 52–77. See also Harold W. Bradley's "The Political Thinking of George Washington," *Journal of Southern History*, XI (1945) 469–486; and Saul K. Padover, "George Washington—Portrait of a True Conservative," *Social Research*, XXII (1955), 199–222].

The fact is clear, though it may send a shudder through the serried ranks of the Daughters of the American Revolution, that Washington's social attitudes had a collectivist tinge. In place of Jefferson's notion of an individualized pursuit of happiness, Washington spoke of "the aggregate happiness of society, which . . . is, or ought to be, the end of all government." It was rare for him to use the libertarian language which has dominated American political rhetoric since 1800. Instead, he spoke and thought in terms of "the public good," the "interest of the commonwealth," the "benefit of the whole" [Washington to Comte de Moustier, Nov. 1, 1790, Washington to James McHenry, Aug. 22, 1785; Washington to Lafayette, Aug. 15, 1786; Washington to Jefferson, Feb. 25, 1785; Washington to Knox, Feb. 28, 1785; in Fitzpatrick, *Writings of Washington*, XXXI, 142; XXVIII, 9–12, 227–230, 518, 91–94; Bradley, op. cit., pp. 476, 485, rests a similar conclusion on other evidence].

This corporate conception of society was, in Washington's mind, combined with a consciousness of inequalities among men. Like Cabot and Jay, he tended to divide men into the "discerning part of the community" on the one hand, and "the lower class of citizens" on the other. Though he believed that the people "mean well," he was never confident that they could resist the blandishments of "the discontented, the turbulent, the vicious" [Washington to Lafayette, July 25, 1785, May 10, 1786; Washington to Jay, May 18, 1786; Washington to the Trustees of the Alexandria Academy, Dec. 17, 1785, in Fitzpatrick, ed., *Writings of Washington*, XXVIII, 356–358, 420–425, 430–432; Bradley, "Political Thinking of George Washington," pp. 477–480].

Washington was an elitist, but not a doctrinaire opponent of democracy. He firmly declared his allegiance to "the fundamental principle of our Constitution, which enjoins that the will of the majority shall prevail"—at the same time that he expressed a fear that "mankind, left to themselves, are unfit for their own government." These two sentiments, though contradictory in our world, were compatible in Washington's. Their reconciliation lay in the deferential spirit of American society before the Revolution—a habitual subordination which was nowhere more evident than in Virginia. Even a French marquis noticed it. "The government may become democratic, as it is at the present moment," wrote Chastellux, "but the national character, the very spirit of the government, will always be aristocratic" [Washington to Jay, Aug. 1, 1786; Washington to Madison, Mar. 31, 1787; Washington to Gordon,

July 8, 1783, Washington to Harison, Jan. 18, 1784; Washington to Edward Carrington, May 1, 1796; in Fitzpatrick, *Writings of Washington*, XXVIII, 502; XXIX, 190–191; XXVII, 51, 306; XXXV, 31–32; Bradley, "Political Thinking of George Washington," p. 480; Chastellux, *Travels in North America in the Years 1780, 1781, 1782* (2 vols., Williamsburg, 1963), II, 435].

Washington hoped that the people might possess sufficient wisdom to place their trust in "the virtuous and the wise"—to "choose able and honest representatives and leave them [free] in all national questions to determine from the evidence of reason, and the facts which shall be adduced" [George Washington to Bushrod Washington, Sep. 30, Nov. 15, 1786, Fitzpatrick, *Writings of Washington*, XXIX, 21–22, 67. Bradley's interpretation contrasts with mine. Perhaps they should be read in conjunction with Washington to Knox, Sep. 20, 1795, in Fitzpatrick, *Writings of Washington*, XXXIV, 310].

During the 1780s, he was deeply troubled by the course of public affairs in America. For him, at least, this controversial era was undeniably a critical period, but he diagnosed the crisis as moral rather than economic. "Virtue, I fear, has in great degree taken its departure from our land," he wrote to Jay. Ancient social habits, which from time immemorial had served as social cement were crumbling with astonishing speed. "If three years since," he wrote in 1787, "any person had told me . . . I should see such a formidable rebellion against the laws and Constitutions of our own making, as now appears, I should have thought him a bedlamite" [George Washington to John Jay, May 18, 1786, in Johnston, ed., *Jay*, III, 195–196; George Washington to Henry Knox, Feb. 3, 1787, Fitzpatrick, *Writings of Washington*, XXIX, 151–152.

His familiar reaction to Shays' rebellion was characteristic. "What, gracious God, is man! that there should be such inconsistency and perfidiousness in his conduct?" he wrote. Here was no unruffled observation on human nature, but the lamentation of a man who had temporarily lost both faith and hope [George Washington to David Humphreys, Dec. 26, 1786, in Fitzpatrick, *Writings of Washington*, XXIX, 125–126].

But the crisis of the 1780s did not disarm him altogether. Washington saw two remedies. First, a strong government, "a controulling power." To John Jay he wrote sadly, "We have errors to correct. We have probably had too good an opinion of human nature in forming our confederation. Experience has taught us, that men will not adopt and carry into execution measures best calculated for their own good, without the intervention of a coercive power." One cannot know how far Washington wished to extend this "coercive power." During the fight for Jay's treaty he declared that "meetings in opposition to the constituted authorities" were "*at all times*, improper and dangerous." There was always a measure of the martial spirit in this soldier's social attitudes. [George Washington to John Jay, Aug. 1, 1786, in Johnston, ed., *Jay*, III, 207–209; George Washington to John Adams, Aug. 20, 1795, in Fitzpatrick, *Writings of Washington*, XXXIV, 279–280; George Washington to James Ross, Aug. 22, 1795, ibid., XXXIV, 281–282; Washington to Pinckney, Aug. 24, 1795, Ibid., XXXIV, 285–286; Washington to Edmund Randolph, Oct. 16, 1794, Ibid., XXXIV, 2–5; Washington to Jay, Nov. 1, 1794; Ibid., XXXIV, 15–19].

But repression was never near the center of Washington's political thought. The "discontented, the turbulent, and the vicious" might be restrained by the "intervention of a coercive power," but Washington believed that it was "necessary to *conciliate* the good will of the people." To this purpose he prescribed the traditional American panacea, education. In his first annual Message to Congress, he spelled out his purpose—to teach the people "to distinguish between oppression and the necessary exercise of lawful authority, between burthens proceeding from a disregard to their convenience and those resulting from the inevitable exigencies of society, to discriminate the spirit of liberty from that of licentiousness." Not every American advocate of the common school has been driven by a faith in the common man [Washington to Hamilton, Sep. 1, 1796; Washington, First Annual Message, Jan. 8, 1790; ibid., XXX, 491–494; XXXIV, 59–60n; see also Washington to Trustees of Alexandria Academy, Dec. 17, 1785, Ibid., XXVIII, 356–358].

After 1799, Washington-worship assumed the proportions of a cult among the Federalists. There were political factors involved, of course. For partisan purposes, young Federalist party leaders made certain that Washington's "immortal shade" continued to haunt the Democrats, long after his mortal remains had been enshrined at Mount Vernon. But the reverence of the older Federalists cannot be dismissed as mere political posturing. If they made his life their measure of political morality, it was because he shared their assumptions and embodied their ideals. (For the quality of Washington-worship among the Federalists, see Samuel W. Dana to Timothy Pickering, Jan. 30, 1812, in Pickering Papers, Mass. Hist. Soc. For its quantity, see Charles, *Origins of the American Party System*, 49n. Of 2200 titles which issued from American presses in 1800, more than 400 were about Washington).

Transitional Figures

MARSHALL, JOHN (1755–1835), b. Fauquier Co., Va.; educated by a tutor, and in a classical academy; captain in the Continental Army; lawyer, jurist, and gentleman farmer residing in Richmond, Va.; member, Virginia Assembly, 1782–1788; Virginia Council, 1782–1795; Virginia

Ratifying Convention, 1788; U. S. Commissioner in France, 1797–1798; U. S. Congress, 1799–1800; Secretary of State, 1800–1801; Chief Justice, U. S. Supreme Court, 1801–1835; member, Virginia Constitutional Convention, 1829. According to Marshall himself, his political attitudes underwent a change during the 1790s. In his famous speech in the Virginia ratifying convention, he had declared that "We, sir, idolize democracy." By the latter term he appears to have meant a government "where the people hold all powers in their own hands and delegate them cautiously, for short periods, to their servants" [Elliott, *Debates*, III 223–236]. But forty years later, he wrote apologetically of "the wild and enthusiastic democracy with which my political opinions of that day were tinctured" [John Stokes Adams, ed., *An Autobiographical Sketch by John Marshall* (Ann Arbor, 1937), p. 9].

It is difficult to determine precisely what Marshall's political attitudes became in his more conservative phase. His judicial decisions present major problems of interpretation; his private comments are infrequent and inconclusive. In 1800, for example, he wrote of "a current setting against us, of which the force is incalculable. There is a tide in the affairs of nations, of parties, and of individuals. I fear that of real Americanism is on the ebb" [to Otis, 5 Aug. 1800, in Otis Papers, Mass. Hist. Soc.]. The rational content of this emotional commitment remains obscure.

But certainty seems possible on at least two points. Marshall may have been a partisan judge; but he was not a partisan politician. He did not attend Federal party meetings in Richmond [Marshall to C. C. Pinckney, 19 Oct. 1808, in Pinckney Papers, Library of Congress; printed in J. L. Cross, "John Marshall on the French Revolution and on American Politics," *William and Mary Quarterly*, 3d ser., XII (1955) 648]. And he did not enjoy "appearing in print" [to Pickering, 15 Oct. 1798, in Pickering Papers, Mass. Hist. Soc.; cf. Marshall to Bushrod Washington (28?) June 1811, in Marshall Papers, Library of Congress]. In 1808, he wrote to C. C. Pinckney, "Like you, I had absolutely withdrawn myself from the busy circles in which politics are discussed. I devoted to agricultural pursuits the time which could be drawn from professional duty and scarcely ever read a newspaper. My attempts to produce in my own mind an indifference to what was passing around me would I believe have been nearly successful had they not been totally defeated by events so serious in their nature that they really appear to me to place by our own acts the indepen[den]ce of our country in the most serious danger. We appear to me to be unwilling to wait till it shall be wrested from us by violence. I however can only look on with silent and anxious concern. I can render no service" [21 Sep. 1808, in Pinckney Papers, Library of Congress, Cross, "John Marshall," p. 647]. Whether Marshall abstained from partisan activity from principle, or more likely, he was restrained by a variety of personal considerations, including a fear of impeachment, his self-enforced retirement identified him with the old school.

On the second point, however, he was closer to younger Federalists. His writings, both public and private, show a sense of individual autonomy which contrasts with the holism of the old school. Marshall's rendering of the law of property and the law of contract should be viewed in juxtaposition with that of the old school jurist Theophilus Parsons. Only the eye of a trained lawyer can resolve this knotty point; but in the judgment of this untutored investigator, Parsons used contract and property to cement a structured commonwealth, to unify society and government. Marshall, however, planted both ideas as hedges which protected economic privilege from political power, when the latter was no longer safely in the hands of the "best people." Both Parsons and Marshall were elitist; but Parsons was thinking in terms of a deferential society, while Marshall was operating within a more egalitarian frame. His opinions in Fletcher v. Peck, New Jersey v. Wilson, and Dartmouth College v. Woodward, might be measured against Parsons' in Bliss et al. v. Thompson, and First Mass. Turnpike Corp. v. Field et al. [see my "Myth of the Essex Junto," pp. 202–203].

Marshall's private writings are even more illuminating. In 1788, when Parsons and his friends were talking in Hobbesian language, Marshall declared, "The interest of the community is blended and inseparably connected with that of the individual. When he promotes his own, he promotes that of the community" [Elliott, Debates, III, 230]. In 1809, he withdrew from a Virginia corporation because it was subjected to state control. "I consider the interference of the legislature in the management of our private affairs, whether those affairs are committed to a company or remain under individual direction, as equally dangerous and unwise. I have always thought so and I still think so. I may be compelled to subject my property to these interferences, and when compelled I shall submit; but I will not voluntarily expose myself to the exercise of a power which I think so improperly usurped" [Marshall to Greenhow, 17 Oct. 1809, quoted in Beveridge, Marshall, IV, 479–480].

The difference between Parsons and Marshall is, of course, a difference between ins and outs—but ins and outs writ large. American social and political history, in this context, could be divided into two periods: in the first, an elite of birth and wealth and breeding were comparatively secure in their possession of political power; in the second, the elite was, if not out of power, at least fearful of being turned out. The division line might be drawn between Parsons and Marshall.

NICHOLAS, JOHN (c. 1757–1836), b. Buckingham Co., Va.; educated in lower schools; served as a captain in the Continental Army and lieutenant colonel of Virginia militia; planter and large landowner residing in Albemarle Co., Va.; clerk of Albemarle Co., 1792–1815, an office which was hereditary in the Nicholas family; unsuccessful candidate for Congress, 1799. Nicholas is best known for his part in the affair of the Langhorne letter, a fraudulent document written to George Washington by Jefferson's twenty-seven year old nephew, Peter Carr, in the hope of drawing Washington into an indiscretion. Nicholas exposed the game to its intended victim, an act which occasioned the final breach between the late and future Presidents; and which has resulted in angry criticism of Nicholas himself as "a meddler and a marplot," by a Jeffersonian generation of American historians [Manning Dauer, "The Two John Nicholases," *Amer. Hist. Rev.*, 45 (1939–1940) 343; Malone, *Jefferson and the Ordeal of Liberty*, p. 309; Boyd, *Papers of Thomas Jefferson*, XVI, 140]. Whatever the true facts of this unhappy incident may have been, the general response of John Nicholas to the Jeffersonian movement is clear. Living "in the very 'centre' and stronghold of the other man's politics," Nicholas was quite honestly shocked by Jefferson's partisan industry. "The opposition to the govt, to use one of their favorite words, is here 'systemitized'—regular plans are formed, and correspondences, the most designing . . . commenced agt. the unsuspecting and unmarshalled friends of govt" [to Washington, 22 Feb. 1798, *Amer. Hist. Rev.*, 45 (1939–1940), 350]. Knowing little of Jefferson's party affairs but suspecting the worst, Nicholas urged his brother Federalists to comparable exertions [to Hamilton, 4 Aug. 1803, Hamilton Papers, Library of Congress].

Young Federalists

BRECKINRIDGE, JAMES (1763–1833), b. near Fincastle, Botetourt Co., Va.; served briefly in the War for Independence; A.B., William and Mary College, 1785; lawyer and planter residing at "Grove Hill," a "beautiful and gracious" estate in Botetourt Co.; member, Virginia Assembly, 1789–1802, 1806–1808, 1820–1821, 1823–1824; U. S. Congress, 1809–1817. Breckinridge took a leading part in the Federal effort to develop an efficient "American Republican" organization in 1800. He may have been the author of an address to the people [Richmond *Virginia Gazette*, 27 June 1800] which undertook to identify the Jeffersonian movement with "*real* despotism," and the Federal "American Republican" party with genuine American freedom. In Congress, he was a quiet back-bencher, but voted for economy and even retrenchment [AC 13/1/ 381, 30 June 1813].

CAPERTON, HUGH (1781–1847), b. Greenbrier Co., Va.; probably educated in lower schools; "very wealthy" planter and country merchant living near Union, Monroe Co., Va.; sheriff of Monroe Co., 1805; member, Virginia Assembly, 1810–1818, 1826–1830; U. S. Congress, 1813–

1815. Caperton rarely spoke in Congress, but he usually voted with his young Federalist friends for economy and retrenchment.

GRIFFIN, THOMAS (1773–1837), b. Yorktown, Va.; "pursued classical studies;" lawyer, planter residing at "The Mansion," York Co., Va.; member, Virginia Assembly, 1793–1800, 1819–1823, 1827–1830; U. S. Congress, 1803–1805; justice of the Court of Oyer and Terminer, 1796–1810; 1814–1820. His two major speeches in Congress were delivered in defense of the rights of the popular branch of the legislature, reminiscent of the Jeffersonian arguments on Jay's Treaty [8/1/442, 25 Oct. 1803] and in righteous opposition to alleged "star chamber" proceedings by the administration against Samuel Chase [AC, 8/1/856, 7 Jan. 1804]. It is interesting to note that Griffin's response to the assault on the judiciary took this form, rather than that of older Federalists who continued to defend the third branch as a check upon the people.

LEWIS, JOSEPH, JR. (1772–1834), b. in Virginia; planter residing at Upperville, Va.; member, Virginia Assembly, 1799–1803; 1817–1818; U. S. Congress, 1803–1817. Most of Lewis' congressional speeches were delivered in direct defense of the narrow interests of his constituents [AC 8/2/795, 11 Dec. 1804]. On larger questions he invariably was hostile not merely to the enlargment of the powers of the administration, but to the expansion of the powers of government generally [AC 9/1/837, 22 Mar. 1806]. He gave strong support to minority rights and to civil liberties [AC 13/3/772–775, 8 Dec. 1814, an interesting argument for the right of conscientious objection to military service; and AC 11/1/468, 28 June 1809, on the right of petition].

MERCER, CHARLES FENTON (1778–1858), b. Fredericksburg, Va.; A.B., Princeton, 1797; lawyer and planter in Loudoun Co., Va.; Virginia Assembly, 1810–1817; served in the War of 1812; U. S. Congress, 1817–1839. Mercer was prominent in a broad variety of public causes—an honest opponent of slavery, he was an officer in the Virginia Colonization Society; a gentleman improving farmer, he served as vice president of the National Society of Agriculture; an active promoter of public education, he authored a plan for state supported schools in Virginia which Jefferson helped to defeat, as over-centralized. In politics, Mercer was an open Federalist [AC 15/2/799, 26 Jan. 1819], critical of the conduct of Federal leaders in the 1790s. "Yes, said Mr. M., the Federalists suffered themselves to be outwitted in yielding the popular title to their opponents—a prominent cause, I have no doubt, of their ultimate discomfiture" [AC 15/1/642, 9 Jan. 1818]. Mercer did not mean to repeat their blunder—he made full use of popular rhetoric in the Congress, and participated actively in popular party activities in Virginia [AC

15/2/813, 26 Jan. 1819, 15/1/1754, 16 Apr. 1818; C. F. Mercer Diary, C. F. Mercer to J. F. Mercer, 12 Oct. 1810, in Mercer Papers, Va., 15 June 1816, N. J. Hist. Soc.]. On economic legislation, he opposed a national bank, preferring state institutions [AC 15/1/1752, 16, Apr. 1818]. But he favored support of internal improvements [15/1/1284–1312, 12 Mar. 1818] as was to be expected of a man who would become president of the Chesapeake and Ohio Canal Company.

MINOR, JOHN (1761–1816), b. in Virginia; lawyer practicing in Richmond and Fredericksburg [John B. Minor, *The Minor Family of Virginia* (Proffit, Va., n. d.), pp. 10–11, 112–113; Alvin T. Embry, *History of Fredericksburg* (Richmond, 1937), p. 154]. Minor served on a Federal state committee in 1808, which sought to establish a working relation with conservative Republicans in Virginia [Minor et al. to L. W. Tazewell, 19 Feb. 1808, in Tazewell Papers, Va. State Library].

PAGE, ROBERT (1765–1840), b. Gloucester (now Mathews) Co., Va.; attended William and Mary College; served briefly as a captain in the Continental Army; lawyer and planter residing in Frederick (now Clarke) Co., Va.; member, Virginia Assembly, 1795; U.S. Congress, 1799–1801 [Thomas D. Gold, *History of Clarke County*, p. 67]. A quiet Federalist moderate in Congress, Page supported the Alien and Sedition laws, but balked at commercial legislation, including the bankruptcy act. He supported Adams' French policy, rather than the more bellicose line of the "High" Federalists.

RUTHERFOORD, THOMAS (1766–1852), b. Glasgow, Scotland; emigrated to America, *aet.* 18, as agent for his brother's mercantile firm; established a general store in Richmond, Va., dealing in flour, tobacco, and cotton. He was an early backer of the Tredegar iron works, and a gentleman farmer with an estate near Richmond. Rutherfoord was a specimen of the group which Jeffersonians publicly described as the main support of southern Federalism—the unpopular "Tory" Scottish merchants of the coastal cities and market towns. A political liability, his most valuable contribution to the Federal cause was cash for campaign funds [*Richmond Portraits*, p. 182].

SHEFFEY, DANIEL (1770–1830), b. Frederick-town, Md.; "classical studies"; apprenticed as a shoemaker in his father's shop; removed to Wytheville, Va., where he studied law while working at his craft; lawyer residing in Staunton, Va.; member, Virginia Assembly, 1800–1804; 1822–1823; Virginia Senate, 1804–1808; U. S. Congress, 1809–1817 [Peyton, *History of Augusta County*, 357–358; Scharf, *Western Maryland*, I, 469]. In Congress, Sheffey served as a self-appointed defender of the people's rights against alleged infringements by the Republican administration. He made much use of popular rhetoric [AC 11/2/1743, 3 Apr. 1810; 13/1/1299, 10 Feb. 1814, 13/3/847, 10 Dec. 1814], and was aggressive in his partisanship (he voted for a tight embargo law on the grounds that, if the administration "determined to have an Embargo, it might be so rigid as to nauseate and sicken the people") [AC 13/2/1122, 22 Jan. 1814]. With other young Federalists, Sheffey defended partisanship and party politics as not merely a necessary evil but a positive good. "I have lived long enough to learn that there is no essential difference between political parties, except so far as individual virtue and talents go," he declared. "They all act very much alike under like circumstances. Those who have the reins of government in their hands will abuse their power whenever they think they are firmly seated in the public confidence, and nothing but the vigilance of the people, which the opposition of a minority is calculated to keep alive, can save them from the profligacy and corruption to which it will naturally tend" [AC 13/2/1327, 10 Feb. 1814]. On economic questions Sheffey supported the Bank of the United States, and favored national expenditures for internal improvements [11/3/730–747, 22 Jan. 1811; 14/2/886–891, 6 Feb. 1817]. But he also articulated laissez-faire ideas, arguing that trade should be permitted to "find its own channel" [14/2/789–792, 30 Jan. 1817]. Like many other young Federalists, Sheffey wrote regular letters to his constituents which were widely reprinted by Federal journals [New York *Evening Post*, pp. 9–10 Apr. 1813].

STEPHENSON, JAMES (1764–1833), b. Gettysburg, Penn.; moved to Martinsburg, Va., now W. Va., where he resided to his death; member, Virginia Assembly, 1800–1803, U. S. Congress, 1803–1805, 1809–1811, 1822–1825. A quiet back-bencher in Congress, Stephenson regularly voted with his young Federalist colleagues against the Louisiana Purchase, and the foreign policy of the administration, but for its fiscal policy [AC 11/3/826, 24 Jan. 1811].

STRATTON, JOHN (1769–1804), b. "Old Castle," Northampton Co., Va.; attended lower schools; lawyer practicing in Norfolk; member, Virginia Assembly, 1789–1792; U. S. Congress, 1801–1803. Another quiet back-bencher, his steady partisanship appears in his voting record. He was probably the John Stratton who manumitted a slave in Norfolk in 1795, on the simple grounds that "freedom is the Natural right of all Men" [Harriet R. Stratton, *A Book of Strattons* (2 vols., N. Y., 1918) II, 341–342].

STUART, CHARLES AUGUSTUS (c. 1782–1850), b. Greenbrier Co., Va.; A.B., Yale, 1803; married an heiress and settled as a planter near

Staunton, Augusta Co., Va. [Dexter, *Yale Graduates*, V, 620]. Stuart was a member of the Federalist state central committee in Staunton, Va. [Martinsburgh *Gazette*, 23 Oct. 1812].

SWOOPE, JACOB (c. 1768–1832), b. Philadelphia, Penn.; attended lower schools; removed to Staunton, Va., where he became a prosperous country merchant and first mayor of the town under its 1801 charter; U. S. Congress, 1809–1811 [Waddell, *Annals of Augusta County*, pp. 337, 373, 383]. On the rare occasions when Swoope spoke in Congress, it was as a public watchdog for governmental extravagance [*AC* 11/3/832, 28 Jan. 1811]. In Staunton he also served on the Federal state central committee [Martinsburgh *Gazette*, 23 Oct. 1812].

NORTH CAROLINA

Federalists of the Old School

DAVIE, WILLIAM RICHARDSON (1756–1820), b. Cumberland Co., Eng.; emigrated c. 1763; raised by his uncle, a Presbyterian clergyman; A.B., Princeton, 1776; served in the Continental Army; member, North Carolina House of Commons, 1786–1787, 1789, 1791, 1793–1794, 1796, 1798; member, U. S. Constitutional Convention, 1787, and N. C. ratifying conventions; governor of North Carolina, 1798–1799; envoy to France, 1799–1800; lawyer, jurist, gentleman planter residing at Halifax, N. C., and after 1805 at "Tivoli," a plantation on the Catawba River in S. C. [J. G. de Roulhac Hamilton, "William Richardson Davie," *James Sprunt Studies*, VII (1907), 4–23; Robinson, *Davie*, passim]. Davie had taken an active and eventually effective part in the magnate politics of the 1780s, but in the Jeffersonian era, he appears as a living anachronism. In the pivotal year of 1800, when younger Federalists were complaining that Federal printers and polemicists were not sufficiently enterprising, Davie found them too much so [to John Steele, 20 Sep. 1800, in Kemp Battle, ed., "Letters of Davie," *James Sprunt Studies*, VII (1907) 42]. Though he consented to stand for Congress in 1803, he refused to run—made no concessions in principle or practice, and was roundly defeated (see above, chapter V). For efforts by younger men to revivify the Federal cause, he had little sympathy. "The Federal Party is in fact *dead and buried*, and ought to be so considered even by its warmest friends. No good can arise from any attempts towards its resurrection," he wrote in 1806 [Robinson, *Davie*, p. 386]. His own hopes briefly revived after the embargo. "The Great Mass never reason, but they can feel, and will soon begin to clamour," he wrote (ibid., 383). But he soon returned to his accustomed despondency [Davie to William Gaston, 14 Feb. 1815 (marked 1814) in Gaston Papers,

Southern Hist. Coll., Univ. of N. C.]. Davie's Federal commitment can be understood in terms of his social prejudices; but a disdain for the people was reinforced by a deep jealousy of Virginia. In 1814, he suggested a Constitutional amendment which would have prohibited the election of a President from any state more than once in 12 or 16 years [to Gaston, 27 Nov. 1814, ibid.].

DICKSON, JOSEPH (1745–1825), b. Chester Co., Penn.; raised in Rowan Co., N. C.; served with distinction in the War of Independence; member, North Carolina Senate, 1788–1795; U. S. Congress, 1799–1801; Dickson was another unknown soldier in American politics, whose greatest distinction was his heroism at King's Mountain. In the Sixth Congress, he was one of the few North Carolina Federalists who voted consistently with his party. A circular letter, dated 1 May 1800, has not come to light, but from Jeffersonian comments appears to be a statement of old school precepts [Gilpatrick, *Jeffersonian Democracy in North Carolina*, p. 115]. Like William R. Davie (q.v.), Dickson retired from politics and moved out of the state in 1803.

GAITHER, BASIL, a farmer residing in Rowan Co., N. C., referred to as "Colonel Gaither." In 1802 he described himself as "advanced in years." Gaither served in the North Carolina Legislature, 1788–1789, 1791–1797, 1799–1802. He was an unsuccessful Federalist candidate for U. S. Congress in 1803. His address "To the Citizens of the County of Rowan" (1802) was an old school warning against "faction and party-spirit," no mere platitude, as one young Federalist, Alexander Henderson (q.v.), learned in 1800. Gaither refused to support Henderson's candidacy for Congress, openly attacking a "set of men who jump out of the cradle into college, and out of college into government" [*Steele Papers*, I, 327–328; Gilpatrick, *Jeffersonian Democracy in North Carolina*, p. 114n.].

HODGE, ABRAHAM (1755–1805), b. New York City; educated in apprenticeship; established a newspaper in New Bern, N. C., which he continued in Edenton, Halifax, and Raleigh, N. C. [G. W. Paschal, *A History of Printing in North Carolina* (Raleigh, 1946), pp. 11–14, 16, 19, 26, 29]. The restraint of Hodge's journals in the 1790s, and his private correspondence, suggest old school attitudes—a social holism and open elitism, a deep disgust for Jeffersonian principles [Hodge to John Steele, 10 Oct. 1800, in *Steele Papers*, I, 187–188; see also Hodge to Iredell, 1 Dec. 1791, in McRee, *James Iredell*, II, 336]. The partisanship of a paper partly owned by him, the *Minerva*, after 1803, was owing to the energy of his young partner, William Boylan (q.v.).

IREDELL, JAMES (1751–1799), b. Lewes, Sussex, Eng., of an ancient and well-connected family; privately educated; emigrated to Edenton.

N. C., 1768, as Comptroller of Customs; tutored himself in law and began practicing in 1770; appointed Collector of Port Roanoke, 1774–1776; attorney general of N. C., 1779–1781; N. C. Council of State, 1787; Associate Justice, U. S. Supreme Court, 1790–1799. Iredell acquiesced in independence, but not in an American revolution. From 1776 to his death he served the cause of order with constancy and effect. The principles which appear in his satirical "Creed of a Rioter," 1776 [McRee, *Iredell*, I, 335–336] were never qualified or disguised. Iredell's jury charges, during the 1790s are especially full articulations of the conventional old-school response to the Jeffersonian movement. In 1796, he declared, "All governments depend more or less upon the confidence and support of the people for whose benefit they do, or ought, to subsist. But a free government more especially does so, and the freer the government the greater such dependence must be. Every citizen, therefore, of the United States, whatever may be his station or situation, has an important responsibility attached to himself. He owes to his country, by all possible and honorable means, to promote its prosperity, and to do nothing either negligently or with design to counteract it. Considering himself as a member of a single community, which is itself a member of another in a larger sphere, he should reflect that he is only one individual connected with a great number of others, whose authority separately is equal, and each of whose sentiments are entitled to equal deference with his own: That his individual interest, when it comes into competition, must yield to that of the State" [McRee, *Iredell*, II, 484–485].

JOCELIN, AMARIAH, a sea-captain and merchant residing in Wilmington, N. C., he had held minor offices in the Navy Department, 1798–1801. On Oct. 7, 1801, he wrote an extraordinary letter via John Steele (q.v.) to Albert Gallatin, seeking the collectorship of his port. Jocelin candidly declared that he was "one of those whom the spirit of the times has distinguished by the appellation of Federalist," but insisted that he was not a party man, or a politician. He described his disgust with "popular elections, which, generally, being under the management of designing men express nothing fairly and justly." But at the same time he declared his allegiance to "the system of government established in the United States," and his antipathy to "every kind of despotism." The "designing man" who received this letter was unsympathetic. "The man who thinks that 'popular elections generally express nothing fairly & justly' cannot with candor say that he is 'attached to the system of government established in the States,' nor call himself either a federalist or republican" [*Steele Papers*, I, 228].

JOHNSTON, SAMUEL (1733–1816), b. Dundee, Scot.; emigrated to America, 1736; attended lower schools; lawyer and planter residing near

Edenton, N. C.; moderator of Provincial Convention, 1775; N. C. Senate, 1779; Continental Congress, 1780–1782; president, N. C. ratifying conventions, 1788–1789; U. S. Senate, 1789–1793; judge of the N. C. Superior Court, 1800–1803. Johnston's commitment to the cause of order was as consistent as that of James Iredell. In 1776 he complained of North Carolina politics that "Every one who has the least pretensions to be a gentleman is suspected and borne down *per ignobile vulgus*—a set of men without reading, experience, or principle to govern them" [McRee, *Iredell*, I, 339]. Johnston's correspondence with James Iredell in the 1790s combines the same prejudices with Cassandralike prophecies of worse things ahead [McRee, *Iredell*, I, 481, 515, 516]. "Whenever old men form a resolution founded either on religious or political prejudices, however erroneous or unjust," he wrote, "they have seldom liberality or courage enough to alter it" [ibid., II, 503].

MOORE, ALFRED (1775–1810), b. Halifax Co., N. C.; educated in lower schools; served in the Continental Army; Attorney General of N. C., 1782–1790; N. C. House of Commons, 1792; judge, N. C. Superior Courts, 1798; associate justice, U. S. Supreme Court, 1799–1804. Moore's response to the Jeffersonian movement was compounded of loathing and lethargy. "The troubled scene of politics," as he called it, was put out of sight and mind, and even out of his correspondence after 1800 [Moore to John Steele, 17 Feb. 1802, in *Steele Papers*, I, 251–252]. For Steele's comments on his integrity, see ibid., I, 409.

STEELE, JOHN (1764–1815), b. Salisbury, N. C.; attended "Clio's Nursery," and an English academy; cotton planter and country merchant residing near Salisbury, N. C.; a man of substance, his hobby was the breeding of blooded horses. Steele was a member of the N. C. House of Commons, 1787–1788, 1794–1795, 1806, 1811–1813; N. C. Indian commissioner, 1788–1790; U. S. Congress, 1789–1793; comptroller of the U. S. Treasury, 1796–1802; N. C. boundary commissioner, 1805–1814. Steele was one of a group of moderate North Carolina Federalists who received appointments from Jeffersonian Republicans, or retained important posts after 1800. In Steele's case, this appears to be a consequence rather than a cause of his reluctance to engage in active partisan politics. He had no taste for polemical battles, and refused to contribute to Federal journals. "Mr. Jefferson and Mr. Adams have both suffered so much by the licentiousness of the press," he wrote, "that I should be extremely sorry to contribute materials which might increase it" [to (John Haywood?), 24 Dec. 1802, in Haywood Papers, Southern Hist. Coll., Univ. of N. C.]. For young Federalists he had cautionary counsel. "It is best to guard against innovations of all kinds," he wrote to Joseph Pearson [q.v.; 6 Dec. 1804, *Steele Papers*, I, 442]. To Jeffersonians, he advised tolerance and moderation in principles, electioneering practices and appointments policy. When he wrote of the Federal party after 1800, he employed a past tense. "You must notice here as in former letters that I speak of that party as *having been*, because it was in my opinion dissolved at the conclusion of the late general peace when the French revolution terminated, and our proclamation of neutrality of 1793 and the greater part of the measures which grew out of it had their effect" [to Nathaniel Macon, 17 Jan. 1805, in *Steele Papers*, I, 445]. Macon must have been amused by Steele's protest against the administrations "exclusion policy," and by his complaint that the Federalist minority group was treated "worse than Aliens" [ibid.].

Transitional Figures

GROVE, WILLIAM BARRY (1764–1818), b. Fayetteville, N. C.; educated in lower schools; lawyer practicing in Fayetteville; member, N. C. House of Commons, 1786, 1788–1789; member of N. C. ratifying conventions, 1788–1789; U. S. Congress, 1791–1803. In the 1790s, Grove's Congressional speeches were paeans to old-school precepts. But in the heat of the French crisis, he gave way to a violent panic (see above, chapter I). After 1800, he moved toward the position which younger men were taking. Of a Federal legislator he declared, "Purviance has been extremely inattentive to his Country Constituents, not having written a dozen letters to the District by which I apprehend he has lost ground. Tho' tis no evidence of the qualifications of a good Representative to be writing and Courting Popular men, yet something in that way should not be omitted. It gives satisfaction and produces confidence in the Members and in the Government" [to William Gaston, 12 Mar. 1804, in Gaston Papers, Southern Hist. Coll., Univ. of N. C.; see also Grove to Gaston, 8 July 1813, ibid.; and Grove to Rutledge, 7 June 1803, in Rutledge Papers, Southern Hist. Coll., Univ. of N. C.].

HAYWOOD, JOHN (1755–1827), b. Edgecombe Co., N. C.; probably a planter residing near Raleigh, N. C.; first mayor of that town, and treasurer of North Carolina, 1787–1827 [Ashe, *Biographical History of North Carolina*, III, 170, VI, 289–296]. In private correspondence, Haywood bitterly criticized the Jeffersonian administration, and condemned the developing forms of partisan politics [Haywood to John Steele, 23 Feb. 1802, 27 Aug. 1807, in Steele Papers, I, 253; II, 526]. In public, however, he was very circumspect, being understandably reluctant to sacrifice his lucrative state office. Upon his death, an audit disclosed that the treasurership had been more lucrative for Haywood than most people had supposed—nearly $70,000 was missing, added reason for circumspection. Whatever the reason may have been, other Federalists were disgusted with his conduct, with his own private compromise with the age of democratic revolution. Charles W. Harris (q.v.) wrote, "He is wavering and undetermined, and his conduct of late has not only ruined his own popularity, but injured the cause which we expected he would promote" [to Robert Harris, 29 July 1800, in Harris Papers, Southern Hist. Coll., Univ. of N. C.].

POLK, WILLIAM (1758–1834), b. near Charlotte, N. C.; educated in "Queen's College," Charlotte; lieutenant colonel in the Continental Army; surveyor and planter residing near Raleigh, N. C.; served regularly in the N. C. legislature from 1783 to his death; supervisor of internal revenue for N. C. until removed after 1801; president of the N. C. state bank, 1811–1819 [see his autobiography, *Murphey Papers,* II, 400–410]. Much given to fulmination against "that mire of philosophical democracy [in] which we have been wading . . . that Philo-democratic silt in which we have been mired" [to Duncan Cameron, 6, 15 Oct. 1808, in Cameron Papers, Southern Hist. Coll., Univ. of N. C.]. Nevertheless he was active in attempts to organize a popularly-oriented conservative party in North Carolina [Polk to Duncan Cameron, 15 Oct. 1808, in Cameron Papers, Southern Hist. Coll., Univ. of N. C.; Polk to William Gaston, 23 Feb. 1813, in Gaston Papers, Southern Hist. Coll., Univ. of N. C.].

Young Federalists

BAGGE, CHARLES FREDERIC (c. 1770–post 1829), b. Salem, N. C.?; educated in Moravian schools; banker and country merchant residing in Stokes Co., N. C.; member of the N. C. House of Commons, 1813; active in Moravian affairs, and a manager of the N. C. Bible Society [*Records of the Moravians of North Carolina,* V, 2131, 2170; VI, 2795; VII, 3201, 3234]. In the loose, unstructured power relationships of North Carolina politics (neither party appears to have developed a sophisticated network of committees), Bagge's prominence derived from his influence among his Moravian neighbors in Stokes Co. He was generally assigned the credit, or blame, for the strength of his party in Salem, which had a reputation as a "bed of federalism and disaffection" [Bartlett Yancey to Thomas Ruffin, Mar. 1813, in *Ruffin Papers,* I, 133; Gilpatrick, *Jeffersonian Democracy in North Carolina,* p. 203]. He was "written to" by Federal leaders who were anxious to concert electioneering efforts in west-central North Carolina [Polk to Cameron, 6 Oct. 1808, in Cameron Papers, Southern Hist. Coll., Univ. of N. C.; Polk to Steele, 27 Mar. 1813, in *Steele Papers,* II, 707].

BOYLAN, WILLIAM (1777–1861), b. in New Jersey; probably educated in apprenticeship; moved to Fayetteville, N. C., where he became an assistant to his uncle, Abraham Hodge (q.v.), and editor of the *Minerva,* the most important Federal paper in North Carolina, which was subsidized and systematically circulated by Federal leaders in every superior court district in the state (see above, chapter VII). Boylan engaged in an angry rivalry with his principal Jeffersonian competitor, Joseph Gales of the Raleigh *Register,* which descended from editorials to handbills to physical blows [Gilpatrick, *Jeffersonian Democracy in North Carolina,* pp. 136–141, 171–173]. His unavailing efforts to wrest state printing contracts from the hands of Gales grew into a major issue between the parties in the state. Boylan was himself a member of the N. C. House of Commons, and also was active in the organization of electioneering campaigns.

CAMERON, DUNCAN (1777–1853), b. Mecklenberg Co., Va.; educated in local schools; removed to North Carolina in 1798; wealthy lawyer, planter, banker residing in Hillsboro, N. C., 1800–1805, thereafter at "Fairntosh," 15 miles distant; member, N. C. House of Commons, 1802–1823; major general of militia, 1812–1814; judge of Superior Court, 1814–1816; president, N. C. State Bank, 1829–1849; active Episcopalian layman [Ashe, *Biographical History of North Carolina,* III, 43–47]. Cameron was one of the most indefatigable Federal leaders in his state, energetically promoting organized nominations, systematic campaigns, and extensive support for electioneering journals [see, e.g., Cameron to Moore, 2 Sep. 1802, in Moore Papers, Southern Hist. Coll., Univ. of N. C.; John Huske to Cameron, 22 June 1808, Benjamin Rainey to Cameron, 8, 27 June 1808, in Cameron Papers, ibid.]. Cameron made repeated use of Jeffersonian rhetoric in his public addresses, describing himself as "united to the People by every tie which can bind a man to his Country," and "ardently attached to the cause of liberty, the rights of the people" [Cameron to "Dear Sir," 11 June 1808, Cameron "To the Freemen of the District Composed of the Counties of *Wake, Orange* and *Chatham,*" June 1808, in Cameron Papers].

CULPEPPER, JOHN (1761–1841), b. near Wadesboro, Anson Co., N. C.; attended lower schools; Baptist minister residing at Allenton, N. C.; member, U. S. Congress, 1807–1808, 1808–1809, 1813–1817, 1819–1821, 1823–1825, 1827–1829. In his Congressional speeches Culpepper attempted to turn the ideology of the Democratic-Republican movement against the Democratic-Republican administration. Demanding the repeal of the Non-Intercourse Act, he declared, "some gentlemen represent it as disgraceful to yield to the clamors or murmurings of the people. But I consider it the duty of the Representative to repeal a law whenever it is known to be contrary to the wishes of the people" [*AC* 10/2/1497–1498, 21 Feb. 1809]. On the compensation law, however, he took a more old fashioned view of representation, but cloaked it in popular rhetoric [AC 14/2/584–589, 17 Jan. 1817].

DAVIDSON, WILLIAM (1778–1857), b. Charleston, S. C.; educated in local schools; removed to Mecklenburg Co., N. C., c. 1792; wealthy planter and country merchant residing in Charlotte, N. C., after 1820. Davidson was a quiet back-bencher in Congress, 1818–1821, 1827–1830; he was more prominent in state politics, serving in the N. C. Senate, 1813, 1815–1819, 1825, 1827–1830. Davidson was a leading campaign manager for John Quincy Adams in 1828, drawing perhaps half of North Carolina Federalists with him, including John Culpepper, William Gaston (qq.v.), William B. Meares, Thomas P. Devereaux, and James Brownrigg. A nearly equal number of ex-Federalists were Jacksonians in that election. Leading the latter group were William Polk, Archibald Murphey and John Stanly [William S. Hoffmann, *Andrew Jackson and North Carolina Politics* (Chapel Hill, 1958, *James Sprunt Studies* #40), pp. 16–17, 32, passim. For Davidson's life, see J. B. Alexander, *History of Mecklenburg County* (Charlotte, 1902), p. 97].

GASTON, WILLIAM (1778–1844), b. New Bern, N. C.; A.B., Princeton, 1796; lawyer practicing in New Bern, N. C.; member, N. C. Senate, 1800, 1812, 1818–1819; House of Commons, 1807–1809 (speaker, 1808), 1824, 1827–1829; U. S. Congress, 1813–1817; judge, N. C. Supreme Court, 1833–1844; member, N. C. constitutional convention, 1835. In Congress, Gaston delivered an impassioned oration in defense of a democratic republicanism which read like a Jeffersonian tract in the 1790s. He spoke of Representatives as "agents of the people," directly and immediately responsive to their constituents, duty bound to "make known their grievances, their wants, and their wishes" [AC 14/1/699–703, 19 Jan. 1816]. He recognized no fundamental cleavage between his principles and those of the Jeffersonian movement, insisting in 1814 that "the nominal party distinctions, sir, have become mere cabalistic terms. . . . Federalism and Democracy have lost their meaning." [AC 13/1/1576, 18 Feb. 1814]. Gaston never openly condoned partisanship as a positive good, but he did develop the double theme of popular sovereignty and liberty and full and formal statements [see Gaston's "Intemperance of Party," n. d. (1815), in Gaston Papers, Southern Hist. Coll., Univ. of N. C., in which he was against faction but for democracy]. But if he never defended partisanship, he willingly played a leading partisan role, serving on state corresponding committees in presidential years [Gaston to Rutledge, 5 Nov. 1808, in Rutledge Papers, Southern Hist. Coll., Univ. of N. C.; and Gaston to Phila. Corresponding Committee, n. d. (post 28 Aug. 1812), in Gaston

Papers]. His frequent public addresses were aggressive in spirit and popular in tone [Gaston, "To the Freemen of the Counties of Johnston, Wayne, Lenoir, Jones, Carteret and Craven . . .", in Gaston Papers; and see also N. Y. *Evening Post*, 24 Apr. 1813].

GRAHAM, EDWARD (1765–1838), b. New York City, N. Y.; A.B., Princeton, 1785; studied law with John Jay (q.v.), and practiced in New Bern, N. C. Graham was a member of the corresponding committee in New Bern which communicated with Federal leaders in other states. (D. B. Ogden to John Stanley, et al., 21 Oct. 1812, in Gaston Papers, Southern Hist. Coll., Univ. of N. C.; see also Graham to Edward Ruffin, 29 Feb. 1826, in *Ruffin Papers*, I, 342].

HARRIS, CHARLES W. (1771–1804); A.B., Princeton, 1792; "presiding professor," Univ. of N. C., 1796; lawyer practicing in Halifax, N. C., after 1797. Harris' first reactions to the party conflict as it spread in North Carolina during the campaign of 1800, was that of the old school. "Here party influence or omnipotent Brandy (both blind leaders) dictate every thing," he wrote sadly [Harris to Dr. Charles Harris, 5 Apr. 1800, in Harris Papers, Southern Hist. Coll.; see also in the same collection, Harris to Dr. Charles Harris, 29 Aug. 1800, Harris to Robert W. Harris, 12 May, 11 July 1800]. In the next campaign, however, he was himself busily engaged in partisan activity, writing letters to "the most influential men in the different parts of the state," in an effort to organize an opposition [Harris to Duncan Cameron, 9 Jan. 1801, in Cameron Papers, Southern Hist. Coll., Univ. of N. C.].

HENDERSON, ARCHIBALD (1768–1822), b. near Williamsborough, Granville Co., N. C.; attended Warren Co. Academy and Springer "College"; lawyer residing in Salisbury, N. C.; member, U. S. Congress, 1799–1803; N. C. House of Commons, 1807–1809, 1814, 1819, 1820. Henderson's one major speech reported in the *Annals of Congress* was on the judiciary system, which he defended not as a check upon the people, but as the protector of their rights against the aggrandizement of the vicious, the rapacious members of society [AC 7/1/528, 16 Feb. 1802]. In electioneering harangues he developed the same argument more fully, arguing that "the laws were made for the common people" [Foote, *Sketches of N. C.,* p. 260]. Henderson labored to build a party organization in North Carolina, with a view to the only remedy that he saw—"a lasting and radical change in publick opinion" [Henderson to Rutledge, 9 Sep. 1808, in Rutledge Papers, Southern Hist. Coll., Univ. of N. C.; see also Archibald Henderson, "A Federalist of the Old School [sic]" *North Carolina Booklet*, 17 (1917) pp. 1–38].

HILL, WILLIAM HENRY (1767–1809), b. Wilmington, N. C., or Brunswick, N. C.; attended lower schools and studied law in Boston, Mass.; lawyer and planter residing at "Hilton," near Wilmington, N. C.; U. S. District Attorney for N. C., 1790; N. C. Senate, 1794; U. S. Congress, 1799–1803. In a Congressional speech before the election of 1800, Hill was openly contemptuous of Jeffersonians and the people, of partisan efforts to "tickle the ears of an unreflecting populace" [AC 6/1/319, 9 Jan. 1800]. In the next Congress, however, he was much more circumspect [AC 7/1/855–862, 1 Mar. 1802]. Private correspondence reveals his burning hatred of the Jeffersonian movement—"the spirit rages with demoniac as well as democratic fury," he wrote. It also shows his willingness to use party organization against the "jacobin faction," and his disgust with the conduct of an old school gentleman, William R. Davie [Hill to Duncan Cameron, 3 Jan. 1801, in Cameron Papers, Southern Hist. Coll., Univ. of N. C.].

MURPHEY, ARCHIBALD DEBOW (c. 1777–1832), A.B., Univ. of N. C., 1789; lawyer, jurist, professor of ancient languages at the Univ. of N. C., 1800–1801; member, N. C. Senate, 1812. Murphey's private letters establish that he was a *sub rosa* Federalist [see A. D. Murphey to Duncan Cameron, 24 Nov. 1814, in Cameron Papers, Southern Hist. Coll., Univ. of N. C.]. In public, however, he was taken for an independent Republican. He kept clear of Federal gatherings, and his electioneering statements, published in Republican newspapers, were larded with Republican rhetoric [Murphey, "To the Freeholders of Orange County," 3 June 1814, in Cameron Papers]. Private correspondence reveals his disgust for the dirty business of electioneering, his hatred of the political system which required him to touch the great unwashed. But he drove himself to the mark [Murphey to his wife, 24 July 1814, in *Murphey Papers*, I, 73].

PEARSON, JOSEPH (1776–1834), b. Rowan Co., N. C.; educated in lower schools; lawyer, residing in Salisbury, N. C.; U. S. Congress, 1809–1815. Pearson's open and aggressive partisanship brought him to the duelling grounds on more than one occasion. It also brought him to a decision to exploit the principles of his opponents in the cause of a covert elitism. "The people," he declaimed "have a right to know, not only what is done, but how and by whom." The people, he insisted, should be secure "in the right, not only of expressing their opinions fully and openly in relation to the conduct of their rulers, their motives and the tendency of their measures, but also in the right to change those rulers." Pearson made himself into a defender of "freedom," "civil liberties," the right of petition and "publicity of debate," the right of assembly, and liberty of the press—and at a time when all of these ideas needed defense against Jeffersonian depredation [AC 13/1/275–285, 18 June 1813]. His cause may have been corrupted by his hidden purposes, but in embracing it he helped to legitimate the rights for which others were more honestly contending.

STANLY, JOHN (1774–1834), b. New Bern, N. C.; attended Princeton; lawyer practicing in New Bern; member, N. C. House of Commons, 1798–1799, 1812–1815, 1818–1819, 1823–1826; U. S. Congress, 1801–1803, 1809–1811. Stanly's speeches in Congress were conservative in mood—hostile to "novelty," "innovation," the "throes and convulsions of revolution." But at the same time, he described and defended the status quo in Jeffersonian terms. The American polity he pictured as a "Republican Government, founded on, and guaranteeing, the equal rights of man" [AC 7/1/571, 18 Feb. 1802]. He favored no extension of governmental influence. "Your Administration, styling themselves Republican, have professed to desire no patronage," he said sarcastically. "I will take them at their word, my vote shall never increase their patronage, to multiply their dependents. The Crown, which they profess to put away, I will not force upon their brow" [AC 11/3/800, 24 Jan. 1811]. Stanly promoted party organization as best he could, and contributed to the support of Federal journals.

SOUTH CAROLINA

Federalists of the Old School

BARNWELL, JOHN (1748–1799), served with distinction in the Continental Army; a wealthy planter (83 slaves in 1790) residing in Beaufort, S. C. Federal strength in Beaufort was partly due to the influence of an eighteenth-century family "connexion" of which General Barnwell was patriarch. He served as candidate for Presidential elector in 1796, and great hopes were pinned to his participation in the election of 1800. But death, after a stubborn sickness, intervened. South Carolina Federalism conceived of itself as a party of sages, but by the century's end, it was merely "a party of ailing old men" [Rogers, *Evolution of a Federalist, William Loughton Smith* . . . , p. 349; and see also "Barnwell of South Carolina," *South Carolina Historical and Genealogical Magazine* 2 (1901) pp. 54–55].

BEE, THOMAS (1725–1812), b. Charleston, S. C.; attended Oxford University, and studied law in Lincoln's Inn; lawyer and wealthy planter

(184 slaves in 1790) residing in Charleston, S. C.; member, S. C. Commons, 1762–1765, 1772–1776; S. C. Congresses, 1775–1776; S. C. House of Representatives, 1776–1779, 1782 (speaker, 1777–1779); S. C. Council, 1776–1778; S. C. Lieutenant Governor, 1779–1780; Continental Congress, 1780–1782; S. C. Ratifying Convention, 1788; appointed U. S. District Judge, 1790. This venerable specimen of old school attitudes, member of a veritable dynasty of Charleston lawyers, took a lofty view of the developing Jeffersonian movement which he described as mere "ill-behavior" [Bee to James Iredell, 9 Aug. 1793, in McRee, *James Iredell*, II, 398].

GADSDEN, CHRISTOPHER (1723–1805), b. Charleston, S. C.; attended English public schools; import merchant in Charleston; delegate to Stamp Act Congress, 1765; Continental Congress, 1774–1776; served in the Continental Army; Lieutenant Governor of South Carolina, 1778–1780; declined appointment as Governor of the state, 1781. Gadsden is best remembered for his radicalism on imperial questions—in 1770 he appeared to Tory eyes as a "very violent enthusiast," a "meer tribune of the people" [William Bull to Hillsborough, 5 Dec. 1770, in Rogers, *Evolution of a Federalist*, p. 51]. But events after 1776 demonstrated his deep conservatism on domestic questions. Though a bitter anglophobe, who opposed Jay's treaty, he was consistent in his commitment to the cause of order. Gadsden appears to have regarded the Jeffersonian movement as a species of juvenile delinquency. He attributed the political revolution of 1800 to "new-comers cajoled and imposed upon by emissaries from without, and egged on by a numerous or rather innumerable tribe of young law-followers amongst ourselves" [to John Adams, 11 Mar. 1801, Adams, *Works*, IX, 578–580; see also Richard Walsh, "Christopher Gadsden, Radical or Conservative Revolutionary?" *South Carolina Historical Magazine*, 63 (1962) 195–203].

IZARD, RALPH (1742–1804), b. "The Elms," Goose Creek, S. C.; attended Hackney School, and Christ College, Cambridge University; served as American Commissioner to Tuscany, 1776–1779; Continental Congress, 1782–1783; U. S. Senate, 1789–1795; planter residing on Goose Creek, S. C. Izard was reputedly the "richest planter of his day," the owner of five plantations and 500 slaves. A speculator in lands and internal improvements, he has been called "South Carolina's first entrepreneur" [Rogers, *Evolution of a Federalist*, pp. 127–131]. But if Izard's economic interests prefigured the future, his politics echoed the past. Goose Creek Parish was almost a fief of five great families—Deas, Izard, Manigault, Parker and Smith—which together comprised an extended cousinage, closely cemented by marriage, and by a union of sentiment and interest [ibid., p. 126]. His elitist prejudices were unequivocal. "Our Governments tend too much to Democracy," he wrote, "A Handicraftsman thinks an Apprenticeship necessary to make him acquainted with his business. But our Back Countrymen are of opinion that a Politician may be born such, as well as a Poet. I live as much as possible in the Country, and shall continue a Member of the Legislature as long as my Constituents think that I can render them service. In no other situation will I ever be engaged in public business" [to Thomas Jefferson, 10 June 1785, in Boyd, ed., *Jefferson Papers*, VIII, 196; see also W. C. Ford, "Letters of Ralph Izard," *South Carolina Historical and Genealogical Magazine*, II (1901) 194–204; and U. B. Phillips, ed., "South Carolina Federalist Correspondence," *American Historical Review*, XIV (1909) 776–790].

PINCKNEY, CHARLES COTESWORTH (1746–1825), b. Charleston, S. C.; attended Christ Church, Oxford University; studied law in the Middle Temple, and also pursued natural science and military subjects in France; lawyer and wealthy planter residing in Charleston and on Pinckney's Island, S. C. Pinckney served with distinction in the Continental Army, rising to brevet brigadier in 1783; he was a member of the Constitutional Convention, and U. S. Commissioner to France, 1796; in 1800, 1804, and 1808 he was a Federal candidate for the Presidency. In odd moments this versatile man served as president of six jockey clubs, vestryman of three churches, and curator of a small natural history museum in Charleston [Charles Fraser, *Reminiscences of Charleston*, p. 71; O'Neall, *Bench and Bar of South Carolina*, II, 134–137; Charles G. Singer, *South Carolina in the Confederation* (Philadelphia, 1941), pp. 18–21; Carl Bridenbaugh, *Cities in Revolt, Urban Life in America, 1743–1776* (N. Y., 1955), 384; Newport *Mercury*, 14 Oct., 3 Dec. 1800; Warren *Herald of the United States*, 19 Dec. 1800; Providence *Columbian Phoenix*, 5 Nov. 1808].

Pinckney's political prejudices were those of a Whiggish English country gentleman. He expected deference and respect from lesser mortals whom his mother had called the "cottagers." In return he was prepared to offer honest service and responsibility, which he took to be a gentleman's obligation—in the Constitutional Convention, he opposed pay for U. S. senators. At the same time, Pinckney was contemptuous of men whom he openly called "the little demagogues of a petty parish or county" [Elliot, *Debates*, IV, 302; P. A. Adet to French Minister of Foreign Relations, 3 Oct. 1796, F. J. Turner, ed., "Correspondence of French Ministers to the United States," Amer. Hist. Assoc. *Annual Report for 1903*, II, 951; see also Chap. I, above].

In the 1790s, he was a leader of a moderate Federalist faction in South Carolina, a family connection composed largely of Pinckneys and Rutledges. High-toned Federalists were suspicious of his loyalties. "General P.," wrote William Vans Murray, "had been pretty much of the other side and his friends [also]. He had, while here, to my eyes, often the remaining traits of the state politician, and ways of thinking which might make a man a great favorite with a military regiment filled with local politics" [to John Quincy Adams, W. C. Ford, ed., "Letters of William Vans Murray, Amer. Hist. Assoc. *Annual Report for 1912*, p. 530].

In 1800, Pinckney was Presidential timber. He combined a splendid military record with a republican austerity of manners and a reputation for "pure morals." His reactions to John Adams' diplomatic revolution had been satisfactory to the severest critic of the President. And to the public at large he was that most effective of all conservative candidates, the unknown soldier [Warren *Herald of the United States*, 19 Dec. 1800; Pinckney to Pickering, 19 May, 1800, in Pickering Papers, Mass. Hist. Soc.].

His would have been a formidable candidate, indeed, but for three considerations. First, of course, was the embarrassing fact that his party possessed an incumbent. Secondly, Pinckney was reputed to be a Deist—Jeffersonian pamphleteers made full use of this political weakness. Thirdly, Pinckney was a gentleman of the old school; the voters were gratuitously informed that "having served the people" he "could not flatter them" [Warren *Herald of the United States*, 19 Dec. 1800; . . . *The Voice of Warning to Religious Republicans*, (n.p., 1800); for Pinckney's reluctance to participate in party affairs after 1800, see Pinckney to James Milnor, et al., 24 Aug. 1812, Pinckney Papers, Library of Congress; but unlike other older Federalists he encouraged younger men to remain active. See Pinckney to John Rutledge, Jr., 17 Jan. 1803, 24 Aug., 8 Sep., 28 Sep. 1808, in Rutledge Papers, Southern Hist. Coll., Univ. of N. C.; see above, Chap. 1, and see also Rogers, *Evolution of a Federalist*, p. 191, passim].

PINCKNEY, THOMAS (1750–1828), b. Charleston, S. C., brother of Charles Cotesworth Pinckney (*q.v.*); attended Christ Church, Oxford, and French schools; studied law in the Inner Temple; wealthy lawyer and planter residing in Charleston; major in the Continental Army; Governor of South Carolina, 1787–1789; member, S. C. Ratifying Convention, 1788; S. C. House of Representatives, 1791; Minister to Great Britain, 1792–1796; Envoy Extraordinary to Spain, 1794–1795; U. S. Congress, 1797–1801; major general in the War of 1812, but customarily called "Major Pinckney" to distinguish him from "General Pinckney," his elder brother. A Spanish acquaintance described him as "judicious, affable and solid"; an historian has pictured him as "a man of parts, good judgment, elegant person, of impressive personality if of somewhat impressionable character, he moved easily and nobly through a distinguished life, doing well the tasks he was called on to perform, making no great mistake and encountering no measurable public misfortune" [Samuel Flagg Bemis, *Pinckney's Treaty* (2d edition, New Haven, 1960), pp. 249–250].

Thomas Pinckney's Federalist commitment, like that of his brother, appears to have been intuitive and environmental—not closely reasoned or carefully articulated. In the Fifth Congress he demonstrated all the proper old-school instincts without defending them in an elaborately intellectual way. The principal components were an unembarrassed elitism, and a "shoulder to shoulder" sense of social unity [AC, 5/2/866, 19 Jan. 1798]. He endeavored to "avoid in debate all personalities, and those subjects which tend to heat the passions," and was generally impatient with legislators who introduced "abstraction" to discussions [ibid., 5/2/700, 11 Dec. 1797]. He did not hesitate to reprimand younger Federalists, as well as Jeffersonian Republicans, for their partisan spirit [ibid., 5/2/1255, 13 March 1798].

READ, JACOB (1751–1816), b. Christ Church Parish, S. C.; educated in lower schools; studied law in Grey's Inn, London; colonel in South Carolina militia during the War of Independence; members of S. C. House of Representatives, 1781–1782, 1789–1794 (speaker); S. C. Council, 1783–1784; Continental Congress, 1783–1786; U. S. Senate, 1795–1801; lawyer and gentleman farmer residing in Newport, R. I., during the summer months, Charleston, S. C., and Hobcaw Plantation, Christ Church Parish, S. C., in the winter. Read was an unattractive figure who fitted the Jeffersonian stereotype of an "anglo-Federal" tinsel aristocrat. More mindful of his privileges than of his responsibilities, he was an indefatigable and usually unsuccessful place-hunter, urging his claims upon Federal and Republican Presidents without discrimination. In the 1790s he was best known for the intensity of his hostility to France, a prejudice which was reputedly reinforced by British bribes. After 1800, he and his wife were a pathetic pair, utterly at sea in an increasingly egalitarian society. "She amuses the ladies with her rain of complaints & he the gentlemen with his wonderful pomposity," a South Carolina lady wrote [see the sensitive rendering in Rogers, *Evolution of a Federalist*, p. 386; see also Wolfe, *Jeffersonian Democracy in S. C.*, pp. 85–86, 164n.; Turner, ed., "Correspondence of French Ministers," p. 738].

Transitional Figures

GRIMKÉ, JOHN FAUCHERAUD (1759–1819), b. Charleston, S. C.; A.B., Trinity College, Cambridge, 1774; studied law in Middle Temple and served in the Continental Army; member of S. C. Ratifying Convention,

1788; lawyer and jurist residing in Charleston, S. C. (O'Neall, *Bench and Bar of South Carolina*, II, 597). Grimké's *Oration, delivered in St. Philip's Church* (Charleston, 1807) defends the holistic social ideals of the old school by appealing to the popular prejudices which Jeffersonians had so successfully exploited in the 1790s.

SMITH, WILLIAM LOUGHTON (1758–1812), b. Charleston, S. C.; attended preparatory schools in London and Geneva and studied law in Middle Temple during the War of Independence; commercial lawyer, gentleman planter, speculator in securities, real estate, and internal improvements; resident of Charleston; member of S. C. House of Representatives, 1784–1788; U. S. Congress, 1789–1797; Minister to Portugal, 1797–1801. Contemporaries conventionally used a diminutive to describe "priggish little Will"; he was principally known, perhaps unjustly, for the constancy with which he served himself, and for his zeal in the interest of Great Britain. John Rutledge, Jr., called him "a cold-hearted selfish little anglo-american" [Rogers, *Evolution of a Federalist*, pp. 123, 298]. In the early 1790s, Smith's ideology conformed to old-school precepts. An *Address . . . to his Constituents* (Philadelphia, 1794) began and ended with a conception of representation *in personam*, of legislation by disinterested contemplators of the common good, of energy in government and unity in society, and of popularity as a slut who was spreading the French disease throughout the virtuous republic. "When the capricious dame is only to be won by the prostitution of my principles," he wrote, "I shall always turn from her in disgust, nor suffer her meretricious arts to swerve me from the path of duty. I leave it to others of more pliable dispositions to be seduced by her blandishments and to forget in her arms their country's good" (p. 29). The state of Smith's public reputation suggests that he practiced as he preached. According to Hamilton, whose view of this man was more favorable than most, he was "popular with no description of men" [quoted in Rogers, *Evolution of a Federalist*, p. 305]. But after the *Chesapeake* affair he joined the cry against Great Britain, and suddenly shifted parties. Never fully acepted by Jeffersonians, he was cut off from his quondam colleagues who were unable to account for the conversion in terms of either principle or interest. Smith's apostasy has never been explained satisfactorily; probably it never will [see Rogers' excellent biography, *Evolution of a Federalist*, pp. 382, 393].

Young Federalists

ANDREWS, LORING (1767–1805) b. Hingham, Mass; journalist by occupation, he first appears in the politics of Berkshire County, Mass., where he exhorted older Federalists to greater exertions. "We have the most serious evils to dread, if men who can be active continue that apathy which persuades but too much," he wrote, "the fire side and the private circle will not answer to sit in judgment upon the abettors of French intrigue. Influential characters must be active—they must throw off all reserve—they must speak to the people" [to Peter Van Schaack, 6 Apr. 1798, in Van Schaack Papers, Library of Congress]. Later, Andrews moved to Albany, N. Y., where he printed an electioneering paper and served on party committees ["In General Committee," 1801, in Broadsides, N. Y. Public Library]. Still later, he was set up in Charleston as editor of the *Courier*, through which he endeavored to rally the Federal cause in Carolina.

CRAFTS, WILLIAM, JR. (1763–c. 1820), b. Boston, Mass.; A.B. Harvard, 1805; lawyer practicing in Charleston, S. C., where he also labored to preserve the failing Federal interest (Crafts to Quincy, 30 Jan. 1809, Edmund Quincy, *Josiah Quincy*, p. 192). For the popular tone of his conservative politics, see his *Oration on the Birth of Washington, delivered in St. Philip's Church* . . . (Charleston, 1812); his son, William Crafts (1787–1826), was also a Federalist orator.

DE SAUSSURE, HENRY WILLIAM (1763–1839), b. Pocotaligo, Prince William's Parish, S. C.; attended lower schools in Beaufort and Charleston, S. C.; served briefly with the militia during the War of Independence; studied law with Jared Ingersoll and practiced in Charleston and Columbia, S. C. In the late 1790's, de Saussure's reactions were in one sense those of the old school: The conflict between Jeffersonians and Federalists was in his view, "an organized party against the government" (*Address to the Citizens of South Carolina* . . . [Charleston, 1800], p. 9). But he took an active part in the partisan activity of South Carolina Federalists in 1800, working to bring out "all the elderly men" (to John Rutledge, Jr., 14 Aug. 1800, in Rutledge Papers, Univ. of N. C.). He was more prolific of political polemics than any other South Carolina Federalist, after the departure of Robert Goodloe Harper (*q.v.*) from the state [see especially his *Answer to a Dialogue between a Federalist and a Republican* (Charleston, 1800)], and was active in the founding of electioneering newspapers [to Jedidiah Morse, 21 Dec. 1800, in Morse Papers, N. Y. Public Library]. But there were limits to his partisanship. "We shall converse freely and write fully," he declared, "but you know they use some weapons, which we cannot condescend to" [to John Rutledge, Jr., 14 Aug. 1800, in Rutledge Papers, Univ. of N. C.]. After 1808, he yielded to the fatal despair which characterized South Carolina Federalists and largely abandoned the struggle. But he continued to correspond with northern Federalists, urging caution in rousing in a Jeffersonian fashion the sectional passion of New England people. "The heads of parties seldom govern them," de Saussure wrote, "Mr. Pulteney said truly, that the heads of parties in times of trouble were like the heads of serpents, moved on and governed by the tail. I beg then, that our eastern friends would pause, and avoid stirring up those passions among their own people which may become too strong to be controlled" [to Quincy, 21 Jan. 1809, *Quincy*, p. 190].

HUGER, BENJAMIN (1768–1823), b. Charleston, S. C.; attended lower schools; rice planter residing on the Waccamaw River near Georgetown, S. C.; member of S. C. House of Representatives, 1798–1799, 1808–1812; U. S. Congress, 1799–1805, 1815–1817. Huger's Congressional speeches and votes demonstrated his concern for popular opinion. In the 6th Congress, he joined Jeffersonian critics of the Sedition Act, opposing its renewal on the simple grounds that "the great majority of his constituents would not willingly see it again renewed at this time." He also borrowed the arguments of the most libertarian Jeffersonians in the Fifth Congress, contending for "entire freedom of the press" on the premise that "so nice and delicate were the shades of distinction between the licentiousness of the press and a necessary freedom of discussion, that it was upon the whole better . . . to leave the measures of Government and its Administration entirely open to investigation and animadversion, without attempting to repress the eccentricities and exuberances of public discussion by even an ideal restraint" [AC 6/2/928, 21 Jan. 1801]. In 1802 he took a leading part in the Federal effort to capitalize upon Jeffersonian repeal of the carriage tax, but continuation of the salt tax and whiskey tax, arguing for the equal rights of the people and economy of public expenditures [AC 7/1/451–55, 1027–30, 25 Jan. 1802, 18 Mar. 1802]. Huger returned to the latter theme with a vengeance in debates on the Compensation Act in 1816, opposing an increase in pay for representatives of "the good people." Randolph condemned his demagoguery and his conception of representation. "The gentleman had advised us to go home and consult our constituents. Consult them for what? For four-pence-half-penny? Instead of receiving instructions from his constituents on this subject, Mr. R. said, he should instruct them" [AC 14/1/1159–69, 1182, 1183; 7–8 Mar. 1816]. On the question of the revenue and unsettled balances he spoke in a similar spirit. "*Parcere*, to economise, is the word, and a very significant and important word," he declared [AC 14/1/1054, 22 Feb. 1816].

LOWNDES, THOMAS (1766–1843), b. Charleston, S. C.; educated privately and in lower schools; lawyer, planter residing at Charleston and "Oaklands," in the low country; member of S. C. House of Representatives, 1796–1800; U. S. Congress, 1801–1805. Lowndes, with Huger, in the 7th Congress probed relentlessly for a weakness in the popular armor of the Jeffersonian administration. He thought that he found it in the question of repeal of internal taxes on luxury items but not on "necessities" such as cheap sugar, salt, and coffee. "Good God!" he cried, ". . . The people of this country deserve some consideration. This is a new era" [AC 7/1/1923, 17 Mar. 1802].

NOTT, ABRAHAM (1768–1830), b. Saybrook, Conn.; A.B., Yale, 1787; lawyer, practicing in Columbia, S. C.; and gentleman planter; U. S. Congress, 1799–1801. Nott was a quiet back-bencher in Congress; but his voting record suggests a reaction to the Jeffersonian movement which was similar to that of Huger and Lowndes (qq.v.) He bent before the popular breeze, opposing continuation of the Sedition Act. De Saussure complained in 1798 that he was not a party man (to Pickering, 10 Nov. 1798, in Pickering Papers, Mass. Hist. Soc.). But five years later he was actively engaged in the establishment and support of a Federal electioneering paper, which he wished to make as popular and broadly available as possible [to John Rutledge, Jr., 26 June 1803, in Rutledge Papers, Univ. of N. C.].

RUTLEDGE, HENRY MIDDLETON (1775–1844), b. Charleston, S. C., son of Edward Rutledge (1749–1800); educated privately; large landowner; army officer; private secretary to Charles Cotesworth Pinckney in France; resident of Charleston to c. 1806, when he removed to Tennessee. His *Oration delivered in St. Philip's Church* (Charleston, 1804) contains images and shadows of old-school ideas about "virtue and talents," but advances to paean to the people which is decidedly new. "It was reserved for the new world to produce a new people," Rutledge said, . . . a people, who setting at nought all the calculations of a mysterious policy adapted to the systems of old governments, should dare to question the motives of its rulers, and deny its compliance with measures in which its reason refused to acquiesce."

RUTLEDGE, JOHN, JR. See above, Chap. II.

GEORGIA

Federalists of the Old School

CLAY, JOSEPH (1741–1804), b. Beverly, Yorkshire, England; emigrated to Georgia, 1760; commission merchant and lawyer residing in Savannah; member of Council of Safety and Georgia Provisional Congress; major and paymaster in the Continental Army; member of Continental Congress, 1778–1780; trustee of the University of Georgia. As early as 1777, Clay was disturbed about the Constitution of Georgia, "which is so very democratical & has thrown power into such Hands as must ruin the Country"—"into the Hands of those whose ability or situation in Life does not intitle them to it" [quoted in Kenneth Coleman, *The American Revolution in Georgia* (Athens, 1958), p. 85]. His reputation as a latter-day Federalist, after the French Revolution, and as a leader of the cause of order in Savannah suggests that the mood remained constant.

GORDON, AMBROSE (1751–1804), b. New Jersey; an officer in the Continental Army; a staunch Federalist in 1800, open and unrestrained in his contempt for the principles of the Jeffersonian movement, for which he was removed from his Federal office by the new President in 1801 [Armistead C. Gordon, *Gordons in Virginia* (Hackensack, 1918), p. 119].

HABERSHAM, JOSEPH (1751–1815), b. Savannah, Georgia; attended Princeton University; served as colonel in the Continental Army; member of Continental Congress, 1785–1786; merchant in Savannah, Ga.; rice planter, and speculator in Western lands; U. S. Postmaster General, 1795–1801. A moderate, opposed by High-Federalists, his efforts as Postmaster General to place the wise and good in postal office demonstrates his old-school elitism, and his establishment of a Federal-owned mail stage line between Baltimore and Philadelphia, "an early experiment in public ownership," demonstrates his socialized holism [White, *The Federalists*, pp. 177–184; and see also Charles J. Jones, Jr., *Biographical Sketches of the Delegates from Georgia to the Continental Congress* (Boston, 1891), pp. 80–86].

TALIAFERRO, BENJAMIN (1750–1821), b. Amherst Co., Va.; educated in an old field school; major in the Continental Army; planter residing in Wilkes County, Ga.; served in the Georgia Senate; U. S. Congress, 1799–1802; trustee of Univ. of Georgia. Nominally Federalist in Congress, his voting record demonstrated his independence [Nell Watson Sherman, *Taliaferro-Toliver Family Records* (n.p., 1960), p. 92; George K. Gilmer, "Sketch of Benjamin Taliaferro," *Virginia Historical Register* V (1852) 46–48; Dauer, *Adams Federalists*, pp. 318, 323].

Young Federalists

BERRIEN, JOHN MACPHERSON (1781–1856), b. near Princeton, N. J.; moved with his parents to Georgia, 1782; A.B., Princeton, 1796; studied law with Joseph Clay (*q.v.*) and practiced in Savannah; served briefly in the War of 1812; member of Georgia Senate 1822–1823; U. S. Senate, 1825–1829; U. S. Attorney General, 1829–1831; U. S. Senate, 1841–1852. An active Federal Republican, serving as the principal correspondent for Georgia in the Presidential elections of the Jeffersonian era (see above Chap. IV), Berrien became a Jacksonian Democrat, then a Whig, and finally a Native American.

CLARK, JOHN (1766–1832), b. Wake County, N. C.; educated in lower schools; lieutenant in the Continental Army; Governor of Georgia, 1819, 1821. Clark was a leader of a back-country faction in Georgia, which derived its strength principally from North Carolina settlers. In the late 1790s it was a quasi-Federal faction; after the election of 1800, it was nominally Jeffersonian but actively hostile to Jefferson's most faithful friends in Georgia, the Crawford faction. Clark's crypto-Federal faction was thought to be more democratic in its techniques, if not in its principles [Shipp, *Crawford*, p. 68; Coulter, *Georgia*, pp. 242–243].

DOOLY, JOHN MURRAY (1772–1827), b. Lincoln County, Ga.; lawyer, solicitor general, and jurist residing in Lincoln County. Dooly was a friend and follower of John Clark, an ebullient frontier politician who made no secret of his Federal prejudices but never lost a common touch. He was famed throughout the state for his punning humor, and the informality with which he conducted his court. A constant companion, on the bench, was a jug of apple brandy [Louis Knight, *Reminiscences of Famous Georgians* (Atlanta, 1907), pp. 37–42].

NOEL, JOHN Y., a lawyer of Savannah, alderman (1798–1799), and mayor (1801–1802, 1804–1807) of that Federal stronghold in Georgia. His mayoral career demonstrated his young Federalist commitment to minimal government [Thomas Gamble, *History of the City Government of Savannah* (Savannah, 1900), p. 66; see also *Ga. Hist. Quarterly*, I (1917) 30].

OHIO

Federalists of the Old School

GILMAN, BENJAMIN IVES (1766–1833), b. Exeter, N. H.; attended Phillips Exeter Academy; removed to Marietta, Ohio, 1788; merchant, shipbuilder, banker [Mark A. Andrews, *History of Marietta and Washington Co.* (Chicago, 1902), p. 498; Alex. W. Gilman, *Searches into the History of the Gillman or Gilman Family*, London, 1895, pp. 247–249]. His open elitism, and uncompromising hostility to the Jeffersonian movement appears in many letters printed in Mrs. Charles P. Noyes, *A Family History in Letters and Documents* [(2 vols., St. Paul, 1919), passim; Gilman to Winthrop Sargent, 25 Dec. 1812, Sargent Papers, Mass. Hist. Soc.; Chillicothe *Scioto Gazette*, 19 Nov. 1804].

McINTIRE, JOHN (1759–1815), b. Alexandria, Va., innkeeper and merchant; son-in-law of Ebenezer Zane and a central figure in an old-fashioned Federalist "connexion" in Zanesville, Ohio [J. F. Everhart, *History of Muskingum Co., Ohio* (1882), p. 70].

PUTNAM, RUFUS (1738–1824), b. Sutton, Mass.; self educated; farmer, surveyor, miller, land speculator residing in Marietta, Ohio, after 1780. Approaching political questions with an old school sense of respect and confidence in the virtue and restraint of the American people, he was at a loss to explain the events of 1800. ". . . that ignorant barbarous people; governed chiefly by their passions have been often seduced and sometimes by demagogues of no great abilities is not surprising, but that a people so well informed as the American people in general are, should be brought over to support men in office who from the beginning were opposed to our constitution" [Rufus Putnam to Timothy Pickering, 5 Jan. 1804, in Pickering Papers, Mass. Hist. Soc.]. But he suspected that the Jeffersonians would discredit themselves, "the vile measures pursued by those in power will in the end destroy themselves and rescue from oppression the best and most valuable part of the community" [Putnam to Timothy Pickering, 5 Jan. 1804, in Pickering Papers, Mass. Hist. Soc.]. In the meantime, he wished to take no part in public affairs. ". . . be assured, sir, that I am so far from being mortified or depressed in spirit on account of being removed, that I rather glory in the circumstances—By this act of injustice I am placed on the list of a goodly number of political martyrs, who have gone before me at the head of whom I consider General Washington, for although he escaped a violent death yet how they have traduced him. To be counted one of his disciples and suffer death for adhearing to his principles *what an honor,* was it *possible* for Mr. Jefferson to have *done one a greater; certainly not*" [Putnam to Timothy Pickering, 5 Jan. 1804, in Pickering Papers, Mass. Hist. Soc.].

ST. CLAIR, ARTHUR (1784–1818), b. Caithness, Scot.; attended the University of Edinburgh; settled in Pennsylvania, c. 1762; served in the Continental Army; removed to Ohio after the Revolution; farmer, miller, iron manufacturer, member of the Continental Congress, 1785–1787; governor of the Northwest Territory, 1789–1802; titular head of an executive faction in the Northwest Territory, composed largely of lawyers and officeholders united by patronage, but lacking a base of popular support [John Smith to Nathaniel Massie, 22 Jan. 1803, D. M. Massie, in *Life of Nathaniel Massie* (Cincinnati, 1896), p. 222]. Never the tyrant whom Jeffersonians portrayed, he favored "freedom" and purity in elections generally, and specifically the secret ballot [Address to the Territorial Legislature, 5 Nov. 1800, Smith ed., *St. Clair Papers*, II, 501], but was unrestrained in his sense of elitism, and unequivocal in his detestation of Republic societies, party organization and party rage [Speech at Cincinnati, 1802, ibid., 587–597].

WELLS, BEZALEEL (17??–18??), b. in Va.?; banker, landowner, surveyor, woolen manufacturer, speculator, and promoter of Steubenville, Ohio. A frequent Federalist candidate for state office, he managed his campaign in arrogant old school fashion, without an effort at conciliation or active solicitation [Chillicothe *Scioto Gazette*, 19 Nov. 1804, Chillicothe *Supporter*, 4 Aug. 1810].

Young Federalists

BURNET, JACOB (1770–1853), b. Newark, N. J.; graduate of Princeton in 1791; removed to Ohio, 1796; banker, lawyer, judge, president of Cincinnati College and of the Medical College of Ohio. Presbyterian; resident of Cincinnati; old fashioned in his queue and clothing, but not in his politics. His attempt to organize the Federal cause in Ohio and to take their case to the people appears in Charles Willing Byrd to Nathaniel Massie [7, 20 Jan. 1802, D. M. Massie, *Life of Nathaniel Massie* (Cincinnati, 1896), pp. 205–210 and Bond, *Civilization of the Old North West*, p. 121]. For his acquiescence in party and his willingness to exploit popular rhetoric see his autobiographical *Notes on the Northwestern Territory* (1847), pp. 348–349, 476.

CUTLER, EPHRAIM (1767–1853), b. Martha's Vineyard, Mass.; educated in lower schools?; removed to Ohio *c.* 1794; farmer and land speculator; resident of Washington Co. The most important and energetic party leader among Ohio Federalists, he founded a network of committees in Washington Co., managed protean Federalist nominating conventions, and participated in the establishment of the Washington Benevolent Societies [J. P. Cutler, *Life and Times of Ephraim Cutler*, p. 66]. His new-modeled political attitudes appear in *An Oration delivered before the Washington Benevolent Society at Marietta* (Zanesville, 1814), in which he argued for "the right of the people to criticize and oppose magistrates as well as ministers" (p. 5). It was largely owing to Cutler that a Republican could write of Ohio Federalism: "The party is weak here, but damned saucy" [J. Gregory to R. J. Meigs, 8 Aug. 1802, Cutler, *Ephraim Cutler*, p. 66].

EVERETT, DAVID (17??–1813), b. New Hampshire, removed to Marietta O.; lawyer and editor of the Marietta *American Friend*. For his popularly oriented conservative politics, see 24 Apr. 1813, 26 Dec. 1813.

HAMMOND, CHARLES (1779–1840), b. Baltimore Co., Md.; his father a prosperous farmer; education by tutors; removed to Ohio; lawyer, gentleman farmer, editor of St. Clairsville *Ohio Federalist*. See his electioneering "Address to the Citizens" [St. Clairsville *Ohio Federalist*, 29 Sep. 1810], a popular appeal to farmers and "producers" against "lawyers, doctors, merchants and idle young men." His Political Essays published in the Washington *National Intelligencer,* 1820, were highly praised by Jefferson himself [Howe, *Ohio,* I, 311; F. B. Weisenberger, "A Life of Charles Hammond," Ohio Arch. & Hist. Qtly. XLIII (1934) 364].

KENTUCKY

Federalists of the Old School

MARSHALL, HUMPHREY (1760–1841), b. Fauquier Co., Va.; no formal education, later taught by his wife; captain in the Continental Army; removed to Kentucky, 1780; lawyer, surveyor, landowner residing in Frankfort, Ky.; member of Kentucky House of Representatives, 1793, 1807, 1808, and 1823; U. S. Senate, 1795–1801 [A. C. Quisenberry, *Life and Times of Humphrey Marshall* (Winchester, 1892) passim]. "I am almost the only one who gives the Democrats any trouble here," he wrote in 1810. But his sense of isolation did not serve to soften his old school ideals. In his *History of Kentucky* he declared, "A constitution never has, nor ever will be, preserved by a democracy, which counts its majority from the nether end of society, wherein is necessarily embraced the greatest mass of ignorance, and the least attachment to good order, or constitutional restraint" [II; 319; see also Marshall's *The Aliens, A Patriotic Poem* (Philadelphia, 1798)].

SARGENT, WINTHROP (1753–1820), b. Gloucester, Mass.; A.B., Harvard, 1771; served in the Continental Army; secretary of the North West Territory, 1787–1798; Governor of Mississippi Territory, 1798–1801; planter, speculator residing in Frankfort, Ky. Sargent's letters discover the conventional wisdom of the old school [to Pickering, 15 Nov. 1808, in Pickering Papers, Mass. Hist. Soc.]. As Governor of Mississippi Territory, he acted firmly upon his precepts. "I have lived under three despotic governors of the King of Spain," wrote a Democrat privately, "but Gov. Sargent during his administration . . . has evinced a Disposition to be more arbitrary than any of his Despotic predecessors" [Thomas Green to Matthew Clay, 22 Dec. 1800, in Jefferson Papers, Library of Congress].

Transitional Figures

ADAIR, JOHN (1757–1840), b. Chester, S. C.; educated in lower schools; served in the Revolutionary War and in the Indian Wars of 1791–1793; removed to Kentucky, 1786; planter, residing at White Hall, Mercer Co., Ky. Member of Kentucky Constitutional Convention, 1792; Kentucky House of Representatives, 1793–1795, 1798, 1801–1803; U. S.

Senator, 1805–1806; served in the War of 1812; Governor of Kentucky, 1820–1824; U. S. Congress, 1831–1833. Adair was known as a Federalist at the opening of the nineteenth century [Collins, *History of Kentucky*, II, 32–33]. But without repudiating his Federal past, he effectively identified himself with a variety of political reform movements, including prison reform and debtor relief, and gained a reputation for "generous sympathy with the common people" [E. M. Coulter in the *Dictionary of American Biography*].

Young Federalists

AYRES, SAMUEL (17??–18??). In an "Address to the Voters of Fayette County," he summarized his political principles as "free suffrage, frequent elections, and a frequent change of the officers of government, agreeable with the opinions of those great politicians, WASHINGTON and JEFFERSON" [Lexington *Western Monitor*, 26 July 1816; see also ibid. 12 May 1815; and Kentucky Historical Society *Register*, 58 (1960) 332].

DAVEISS, JOSEPH HAMILTON (1774–1811), b. Bedford Co., Va.; briefly attended a Plantation school; studied law with George Nicholas, m. the sister of John Marshall (q.v.); and removed to Kentucky, where he practiced law in Frankfort and Lexington [Collins, *Historical Sketches of Kentucky*, pp. 251–252]. A measure of his commitment to the Federal cause is his middle name, which he adopted in full manhood [Beveridge, *John Marshall*, III, 317]. But his electioneering addresses, which invoked popular power, electoral rights, and rotation in office, are in the words of a Kentucky state historian, "hard to distinguish from Jeffersonian principles" [Connelly and Coulter, *Kentucky*, I, 474].

FISHBACK, JAMES (c. 1775–1845), b. Culpeper Co., Va.; emigrated to Kentucky in 1783, where he was in turn a physician and professor of medicine in Transylvania University (1805); a newspaper editor in Lexington; and after 1816, a Baptist clergyman [George W. Ranck, *History of Lexington* (Cincinnati, 1872), pp. 45, 120, 309]. In the prospectus of his journal, the Federalist *Western Monitor*, he declared, "An honest appeal to the good sense of the people, happily directed and often made, will arrest the progress of error more successfully than any other means." He added, "We adopt Mr. Jefferson's principle of rotation in office."

POPE, JOHN (1770–1845), b. Prince William Co., Va.; "preparatory studies," removed to Kentucky, where he practiced law in Lexington; member, Kentucky House of Representatives, 1802, 1806–1807; U. S.

Senator, 1807–1813; State Senator, 1825–1829; Territorial Governor of Arkansas, 1829–1835; U. S. Congress, 1837–1843. "Very much a Federalist" in 1798–1799, he was "severely censured" by his constituents in 1800 for his opposition to the Kentucky Resolutions. He became a nominal Jeffersonian, but continued to hold "ultra-private conferences" with Humphrey Marshall and Joseph Hamilton Daveiss (qq.v) [Orval W. Baylor, *John Pope, Kentuckian; His Life and Times, 1770–1845* (Cynthia, Ky., 1943), pp. 22–23, 51; Collins, *Kentucky*, passim]. Pope had lost an arm in early life, but he converted that physical handicap into a political advantage. One of his followers delivered a classic electioneering snub to Pope's inveterate rival, Henry Clay. "Och, Mr. Clay," said this citizen, "I have concluded to vote for a man who has but one arm to thrust into the Treasury" [Rancke, *History of Lexington*, p. 163].

SKILLMAN, THOMAS (1786–18??), b. near Princeton, N. J.; educated in common schools; printer in Lexington, Ky., and editor of the *Western Monitor* with James Fishback (q.v.) [Collins, *Kentucky*, II, 229]. In his journal, Skillman described his ideal state as a Christian Democracy. "This democracy," he wrote, "is that form of government in which the sovereign power is lodged in the people, by the delegation of God, and is so apprehended by them, and is used and applied according to the rules and duties which He has given, in order to [preserve] individual social and natural freedom, safety, prosperity and happiness. This democracy stands distinguished from French or Atheistical Democracy" [8 May 1815].

APPENDIX III

Table 1　Political Affiliation of American Newspapers, October 1, 1800

NOTE: The instability of the fourth estate in the new republic, the frequency with which journals acquired new editors and editors acquired new politics, requires an accounting at a specific moment in time. The following list includes all American newspapers published in the first week of October 1800, the height of the fall campaign.

Though most journals had by this date acquired a partisan identity, some were much more partisan than others. In most states there were a few "political prints" which published polemical pieces regularly, were open to one party only, and made no effort to disguise their partisanship. The fact that they sometimes postponed advertisements during electioneering campaigns suggests that their editors were either subsidized by political sponsors, or else sufficiently motivated to subordinate economic interests to electioneering, for brief periods. Other newspapers conformed to a different pattern: domestic political coverage was slight, polemical material minimal, editorial and advertising space open to all parties. The editor often professed impartiality, and his prejudices appeared only in scattered adjectives and occasional comments. Most papers, of course, fell between these poles, but my reading of the following journals suggests that Federalist editors generally approached moderation, while Jeffersonian journals were more open, aggressive, and effective political agencies.

NEW HAMPSHIRE

Amherst *Village Messenger*, little partisan material, moderately Federalist (see issues of 3 May, 14 June, 26 July, 9 Aug. 1800).

Concord *Courier of New Hampshire*, moderately Federalist (9 Aug. 1800).

Dover *Sun*, moderately Federalist, not much political coverage (6 Feb. 1799).

Gilmanton *Gazette*, unknown.

Gilmanton *Rural Museum*, moderately Federalist, not much partisan material (for the affiliation of the editor, see Portsmouth *N.H. Gazette*, 26 Mar. 1800).

Hanover *Dartmouth Gazette,* moderately Federalist (25 Aug. 1800), polemics rarely published.

Keene N.H. *Sentinel,* moderately Federalist (4 Jan., 1 Mar. 1800), admitted Jeffersonian material (25 Jan., 1 Mar. 1800).

Portsmouth *N.H. Gazette,* moderately Federalist (19 Mar. 1800), always primarily a commercial paper (three-fourths advertisements); its political coverage decreased steadily in 1800 as Federalist fortunes dwindled.

Portsmouth *Republican Ledger,* decidedly Republican; much political material (7 Oct., 4 Nov., 1800); for probable subsidization see Northampton *Hampshire Gazette,* 26 Mar. 1800.

Portsmouth *U.S. Oracle of the Day,* decidedly Federalist (15 Mar. 1800) but a heavy preponderance of advertisements left little room for partisan material.

Walpole *Farmer's Weekly Museum,* moderately Federalist; open to Jeffersonians (Ames to Sedgwick, 21 Dec. 1800, Sedgwick Papers, Mass. Hist. Soc.)

VERMONT

Bennington *Vermont Gazette,* decidedly Republican; much political material, most of it partisan (13, 20, 27 Oct. 1800).

Brattleboro *Federal Galaxy,* moderately Federalist (6 Sep. 1800).

Peacham *Green Mountain Patriot,* very moderately Federalist (24 Apr. 1800), but published Republican pieces regularly, professed impartiality, and practiced something very near it.

Rutland *Herald,* moderately Federalist (18 Mar. 1799; 4 Oct. 1802).

Windsor *Spooner's Vermont Journal,* little politics, nearly impartial (16 Aug., 16 Sep. 1800).

MASSACHUSETTS

Boston *Columbian Centinel,* decidedly Federalist, but independently so (George Cabot to Timothy Pickering, Mar. 7, 1799, Lodge, *Cabot,* 225).

Boston *Constitutional Telegraph,* decidedly Republican; subsidized and systematically distributed by New England Republicans (Providence *Gazette,* 26 Apr. 1800).

Boston *Independent Chronicle,* decidedly Republican in the fall, 1800 (8 Sep. 1800); it had previously been more moderate, even to the point of admitting Federalist contributions regularly (31 Mar. 1800); always open to dissident and independent Federalists.

Boston *Massachusetts Mercury,* decidedly Federalist, but not much political material (11 Apr. 1800).

Boston *J. Russell's Gazette, Commercial and Political,* very moderately

Federalist (7 Apr. 1800); primarily a commercial paper; little political material.

Brookfield *Political Repository*, moderately Federalist (7 Jan. 1800); open to both parties (1 Apr. 1800).

Castine *Journal & Universal Advertiser*, moderately Federalist, (30 Oct. 1801); scattered issues suggest that political coverage was minimal, and tailored to the taste of an increasingly Republican audience.

Dedham *Columbian Minerva*, moderately Republican (29 Aug. 1799); not much partisan material.

Greenfield *Gazette*, moderately Federalist (4 Apr. 1800).

Leominster *Telescope*, very moderately Federalist (3 Apr. 1800).

New Bedford *Columbia Courier*, very moderately Federalist (5 Dec. 1800); not much politics.

— Newburyport *Herald*, decidedly Federalist (4 Apr. 1800).

Northampton *Hampshire Gazette* (moderately Federalist) (2, 23 Apr. 1800).

Pittsfield *Sun*, decidedly Republican, but published pieces occasionally for Federalists (14 Oct. 1800).

Portland *Eastern Herald & Gazette of Maine*, moderately Federalist (27 Oct., 3 Nov. 1800).

Portland *Gazette*, very moderately Federalist (15 Apr. 1799).

Portland *Oriental Trumpet*, moderately Federalist (24 Apr. 1800).

Salem *Gazette*, decidedly Federalist after the appearance of its Republican rival, the *Impartial Register*, in May, 1800; previously moderate in tone and content (cf. 25 Feb., 4 Mar., 6 May, 10 Oct. 1800).

Salem *Impartial Register*, decidedly Republican, despite its name (27 Oct. 1800).

Springfield *Federal Spy*, moderately Federalist (24 Feb. 1801).

— Stockbridge *Western Star*, decidedly Federalist; subsidized by Theodore Sedgwick (Birdsall, *Berkshire Co.*, pp. 51, 183–184; [Bidwell] *Sedgwick's Political Will*, p. 5; Henry Van Schaack to Sedgwick, 9 Feb. 1801, in Sedgwick Papers, Mass. Hist. Soc.).

Worchester *Independent Gazeteer*, nearly impartial in tone (2 Jan., 11, 25 Feb. 1800); but its editor was unequivocally Republican in his own politics (1 Apr. 1800); in the context of Worcester Co. politics, it served the Jeffersonian cause.

Worcester *Massachusetts Spy*, moderately Federalist; but printed moderately Jeffersonian pieces (2 Apr. 1800.)

RHODE ISLAND

Newport *Guardian of Liberty*, decidedly Republican; much political material (3 Oct., 10 Oct., 17 Oct. 1880).

Newport *Mercury*, moderately Federalist; but open to Jeffersonians (7, 9, 23 Sep. 1800).

Providence *Gazette*, moderately Federalist; not much politics (27 Sep. 1800); carried Jeffersonian material (15 Nov. 1800).

Providence *Impartial Observer*, decidedly Republican, 27 Oct. 1800.

Providence *Journal*, very moderately Federalist; not much politics; open to Jeffersonians (29 Oct., 5, 19 Nov. 1800).

Providence *U.S. Chronicle*, moderately Federalist, not much politics; admitted Jeffersonian pieces (23 Oct., 13 Nov. 1800).

Warren *Herald of the U.S.*, moderately Federalist, not much partisan material; open to Jeffersonian contributions (18 July, 26 Sep., 14 Nov. 1800).

CONNECTICUT

Danbury *Farmers Journal*, moderately Federalist (14 July 1801).

Danbury *Sun of Liberty*, decidedly Republican (Litchfield *Monitor*, 29 Oct. 1800; New London *Bee*, 24 Sep. 1800; New London *Conn. Gazette*, 3 Sep. 1800).

Hartford *American Mercury*, decidedly Republican; much political material (25 Dec. 1800).

Hartford *Connecticut Courant*, decidedly Federalist; much political material, but cf. Welling, Conn. *Federalism*, p. 10.

Litchfield *The Farmer's Monitor*, decidedly Federalist, (17 Sep. 1800), but for efforts to woo Republican readers see Hall, *Tallmadge*, p. 160.

Middletown *Middlesex Gazette*, moderately Federalist (18 July 1800); open to Jeffersonians (12 Sep. 1800).

New Haven *Connecticut Journal*, moderately Federalist (2 Sep. 1800); little partisan material.

New Haven *Messenger*, very moderately Federalist (22 Apr. 1800); not much partisan material.

New London *Bee*, decidedly Republican (1 Oct. 1800); see also Providence *Gazette*, 26 Apr. 1800.

New London *Connecticut Gazette*, moderately Federalist (26 Mar., 16 July, 3 Sep. 1800); not much partisan material.

New London *Springer's Weekly Oracle*, probably moderately Federalist (18 Sep. 1800).

Newfield *American Telegraphe*, moderately Federalist in 1798; printed both sides (23 May 1798; 19 Apr. 1797; 18 Oct. 1797).

Norwich *Packet*, moderately Federalist (9 Sep. 1800); little partisan material.

Sharon *Rural Gazette*, moderately Federalist (9 June 1800); very little politics.

Stonington *Impartial Journal*, moderately Republican (4 Aug. 1800).

Windham *Herald*, moderately Federalist, 3 July 1800.

New York

Albany *Centinel,* decidedly Federalist (4 Apr. 1800); but heavy percentage of advertisements (c. 75 per cent) left little space for politics. Republicans could purchase room for their own material (21 Mar. 1800).

Albany *Gazette,* moderately Federalist; not much partisan material (6 Oct. 1800).

Albany *Register,* decidedly Republican (21 Mar. 1800; supplement, 2 Dec. 1800).

Ballston *Saratoga Register; or, Farmer's Journal,* nearly impartial; perhaps very moderately Federalist (5 Sept., 21 Nov. 1800).

Brooklyn *Long Island Courier,* nearly impartial; very little partisan material from either side (11 July 1799).

Canandaigua *Ontario Gazette & Genesee Advertiser;* perhaps very moderately Federalist (15 Feb. 1802).

Catskill *Western Constellation,* unknown.

Cooperstown *Otsego Herald,* moderately Federalist (8 Dec. 1796).

Geneva, *Impartial American,* unknown.

Goshen *Orange Patrol,* strongly Republican (13 May, 10 June 1800).

Hudson *Gazette,* moderately Federalist (17 Feb. 1801).

Johnstown *Gazette,* perhaps very moderately Federalist (see Albany *Centinel,* 11 Apr. 1800).

Kingston *Ulster County Gazette,* moderately Federalist (June 4, 1800).

Lansingburgh *Gazette,* moderately Federalist (27 Aug. 1799).

Mt. Pleasant *Impartial Gazette,* unknown.

New York *American Citizen,* decidedly Republican (11 Mar. 1800); supported and subsidized by Jeffersonians (Boston *N.E. Palladium,* 3 July 1804), but occasionally admitted a moderately Federalist contribution.

New York *Commercial Advertiser,* moderately Federalist by the fall of 1800; earlier more decidedly partisan; admitted Republican material (24 Apr. 1800).

New York *Daily Advertiser,* moderately Federalist; primarily a commercial paper with very little politics (17 Apr. 1800).

New York *Gazette and General Advertiser,* moderately Federalist, little politics (9 Apr. 1800).

New York *Mercantile Advertiser,* very moderately Federalist; like most commercial papers, it tended to admit notices for both parties, but turned away the polemics of both (21 Apr. 1800).

New York *Republican Watch Tower,* decidedly Republican (Hamilton, *Country Printer,* p. 149).

New York *Spectator,* moderately Federalist (8 Jan. 1801) (Apr. 19, 23, 1800).

Newburgh *The Rights of Man,* decidedly Republican, much political material, all of a stripe (Hamilton, p. 149).

Poughkeepsie *Journal*, nearly impartial (28 Oct. 1800).

Rome *Columbian Patriotic Gazette*, moderately Federalist.

Salem *Northern Centinel*, very moderately Federalist, not much politics (5 Nov. 1799).

Schenectady *Gazette*, unknown.

Troy *Northern Budget*, nearly impartial, not much politics (22 Oct., 12 Nov., 1800).

Union *American Constellation*, nearly impartial, 22 Nov. 1800.

Utica *Whitestown Gazette and Cato's Patrol*, moderately Federalist (30 June 1800).

New Jersey

Elizabeth-town *New Jersey Journal*, decidedly Republican (22 July, 2 Dec. 1800).

Morristown *Genius of Liberty*, moderately Republican; admitted Federalist pieces (12 Sep. 1799; 4 Apr. 1800).

Newark *Centinel of Freedom*, decidedly Republican; much political material, none Federalist (4 Mar., 25 Mar., 10 Aug. 1800).

Newark *Gazette*, moderately Federalist; open to both sides (4 Feb., 11 Mar. 1800).

New Brunswick *Guardian*, decidedly Federalist (10 July 1800).

Trenton *Federalist*, decidedly Federalist (3 Mar. 1800; see Newark *Centinel of Freedom*, 15 July 1800).

Pennsylvania

Carlisle *Eagle; or, Carlisle Herald*, moderately Federalist (10 Sep. 1800).

Carlisle *Kline's Carlisle Weekly Gazette*, decidedly Republican, much polemical material (13 Aug., 2 Sep. 1800).

Chambersburg *Franklin Repository*, moderately Federalist (24 Sep. 1800).

Doylestown *Farmer's Weekly Journal*, unknown.

Easton *American Eagle*, moderately Republican in 1799 (12 Dec.); decidedly Republican by 25 June 1803.

Greensburg *Farmers Register*, decidedly Republican by Aug. 13, 1803.

Hanover *Pennsylvanische Wochenschaft*, unknown.

Harrisburg *Farmers Instructor*, decidedly Republican (26 Nov. 1800).

Harrisburg *Harrisburger Morgenröthe*, unknown in 1800, decidedly Republican four years later (22, 29 Sep. 1804).

Harrisburg *Oracle of Dauphin*, moderately Federalist, printed material of both parties (15 Sep. 1800).

Huntingdon *Guardian of Liberty*, unknown.

Lancaster *Americanische Staatsbothe*, moderately Federalist (30 Apr. 1800).

Lancaster *Correspondent,* strongly Republican (23, 30 Aug. 1800); German-language paper.

Lancaster *Intelligencer, & Weekly Advertiser,* decidedly Republican, much more political coverage than its rival, the *Journal* (21 Aug. 1799, 30 July 1800).

— Lancaster *Journal,* decidedly Federalist in tone, but carried Jeffersonian pieces (10 Sep. 1800); it appears to have been one of the few Federalist journals which became more strongly Federalist during 1800 (cf. 18 Jan. 1800, 13 Oct. 1800).

Northumberland *Sunbury and Northumberland Gazette,* decidedly Republican in 1794 (10 Dec.), comments by other journals suggest that it was of the same stripe in 1800 (Carlisle *Gazette,* 20 Aug. 1800; Lancaster *Intelligencer,* 14 Aug. 1799).

Philadelphia *Aurora,* decidedly Republican (11 Oct. 1800).

— Philadelphia *Gazette of the United States,* decidedly Federalist; subsidized by Philadelphia merchants (Baltimore *Federal Gazette,* 19 Sep. 1800).

— Philadelphia *Gazette,* decidedly Federalist, but in contrast with Jeffersonian rivals, "dull and somnolent" (Tinkcom, *Republicans and Federalists in Penna.,* p. 257).

Philadelphia *Pennsylvania Gazette,* moderately Federalist (27 Aug. 1800) but very little partisan material, indeed scarcely any politics.

Philadelphia *Poulson's American Daily Advertiser,* moderately Federalist, a commercial, nearly nonpolitical journal (11 Oct. 1800).

Philadelphia *Supporter, or Daily Repast,* seems nearly impartial, not much politics (23 Apr. 1800).

Philadelphia *True American,* moderately Federalist, not much politics (11 Oct. 1800).

— Pittsburgh *Gazette,* decidedly Federalist by Oct. 1800, but published Jeffersonian pieces (Thwaites, "Ohio Valley Press," *Amer. Anti. Soc. Pro.,* XIX [1909], 315).

Pittsburgh *Tree of Liberty,* decidedly Republican (4 July 1801).

Reading *Readinger Adler,* decidedly Republican (27 May, 3 June 1800).

Reading *Weekly Advertiser,* moderately Federalist, not much politics (28 June 1800).

Sunbury *Freiheitsvogel,* unknown, but from comments in Northumberland *Republican Argus,* 24 Dec. 1802, possibly moderately Republican.

Uniontown *Fayette Gazette,* unknown.

Washington *Herald of Liberty,* decidedly Republican (23 Mar. 1801).

Washington *The Western Telegraphe and Washington Advertiser,* unknown (a single issue, 18 July 1797, appears moderately Federalist, however).

Wilkesbarre *Gazette,* decidedly Republican (27 Oct. 1800).

York *Recorder,* decidedly Federalist (2 July 1800).

York *Unpartheyische York Gazette,* decidedly Republican on 7 Sep. 1798, and in view of voting trends among Germans near York, probably at least equally so in 1800.

DELAWARE

Dover *Friend of the People,* decidedly Republican?

Dover *Herald,* unknown.

Wilmington *Mirror of the Times,* decidedly Republican (23 July 1800); its heavy circulation in the lower counties of Delaware suggests organized support (17 Sep. 1800).

Wilmington *Monitor,* decidedly Federalist (see *Mirror,* 19 Nov. 1800).

MARYLAND

Annapolis *Maryland Gazette,* moderately Federalist (see Dec. 1800); carried Jeffersonian material (Balto. *Federal* Gazette, 22, July 1800).

Baltimore *American,* decidedly Republican (28 Oct. 1800).

Baltimore *Federal Gazette,* moderately Federalist (28 July 1800); a commercial paper which carried pieces of both Federalist and Jeffersonian flavor (14 July 1800).

Baltimore *Telegraphe,* moderately Republican, not much politics (22 Oct., 8 Nov. 1800).

Easton *Maryland Herald,* decidedly Federalist (31 Aug. 14, 21 Sep. 1802).

Easton *Republican Star,* decidedly Republican, but open to dissident Federalists (2 Oct. 1804, 15 Oct. 1805).

Elizabeth-town *Maryland Herald,* unknown.

Frederick *Bartgis's Republican Gazette,* decidedly Republican (11, 18 Feb. 1801).

Frederick *Rights of Man,* decidedly Republican (5 Nov. 1800), cf. Stewart, *Jeffersonian Journalism,* appendix.

Georgetown *Cabinet,* decidedly Republican (30 Dec. 1800).

Georgetown, *Centinel of Liberty,* moderately Federalist (24 Dec. 1799).

Georgetown *Friend of the People,* decidedly Republican (see New London *Bee* 15 Oct. 1800 & Georgetown Cabinet, 26 Aug. to 23 Sep. 1800 for its prospectus).

Georgetown *Washington Federalist,* decidedly Federalist (25 Sep. 1800), probably subsidized Uriah Tracy to R. G. Harper, 15 Jan. 1804).

Hagerstown *Westliche Correspondenz,* unknown.

VIRGINIA

Alexandria *Columbian Mirror,* moderately Federalist (11, 18, 23, 30 Oct. 1800).

Alexandria *Times,* moderately Republican, not much politics (12 May 1802).

Fincastle *Herald of Virginia,* unknown, but from the complexion of the *Weekly Advertiser,* a continuation, probably nearly impartial in tone, with little politics (29 May 1801).

Fredericksburg *Genius of Liberty,* decidedly Republican (3 Feb. 1799).

Frederickburg *Virginia Herald,* moderately Federalist, not much politics (5 Apr. 1800).

Leesburg *True American,* unknown.

Lynchburg *Weekly Gazette,* moderately Federalist, not much politics (13 Oct. 1798).

Martinsburg *Berkeley Intelligencer,* moderately Federalist (21 Aug. 1799).

Martinsburg *Republican Atlas,* decidedly Republican (16 Apr. 1801, 4 Nov. 1801).

Norfolk *Epitome of the Times,* decidedly Republican (13 Feb. 1800, 21 Apr. 1801).

Norfolk *Herald,* moderately Federalist (13 Apr. 1799; 27 Nov. 1800).

Petersburg *Intelligencer,* decidedly Republican (26 Oct. 1802).

Petersburg *Republican,* moderately Republican (20 Apr. 1807).

Richmond *Examiner,* decidedly Republican (2 Sep. 1800).

Richmond *Friend of the People,* decidedly Republican (5 July 1800), see also proposals in the New London *Bee,* 12 Feb. 1800, which explicitly identify it as "a political news-paper."

Richmond *Virginia Argus,* moderately Republican (14 Oct. 1800).

Richmond *Virginia Gazette,* moderately Federalist; no copies of this journal have been examined, but the Albany *Centinel* described its politics as "a little inclined toward aristocracy," though the editor professed impartiality.

Staunton *Phenix* [sic], unknown, not much politics (17 July 1799).

Staunton *Political Mirror, or, Scourge of Aristocracy,* decidedly Republican (3 June 1800).

Winchester *Triumph of Liberty,* decidedly Republican; no copies examined, but see comments in the Staunton *Political Mirror,* 5 May 1801.

Winchester *Virginia Centinel,* unknown; earlier files contain little politics (11 May 1795).

NORTH CAROLINA

Edenton *The Encyclopedian Instructor and Farmer's Gazette,* seems nearly impartial, professes neutrality (21 May 1800; see also Edenton *Post Angel,* 10 Sep. 1800).

Edenton *Gazette,* seems nearly impartial, not much politics (19 Nov. 1800).

Edenton *The Post Angel, or Universal Entertainment,* little politics; more than nonpolitical its editor seemed even antipolitical: "Too many poticians is no blessing to a country," he declared on 12 Nov. 1800, a sentiment which may have masked a moderately Federalist commitment.

Halifax *North Carolina Journal,* moderately Federalist in 1797 (7, 14, 21 Aug.).

Lincolnton ?, unknown.

New Bern *Gazette,* moderately Federalist; little politics, but the regularity with which its editor borrowed his news from Federalist papers suggests that he had a similar leaning (23 May, 15 Aug. 1800).

Raleigh *North Carolina Minerva,* moderately Federalist (10 Sep. 1799, 23 Dec. 1800).

Raleigh *Register,* decidedly Republican (15 Apr., 18 Nov. 1800).

Salisbury *North-Carolina Mercury,* moderately Federalist (29 Jan. 1801).

Wilmington *Gazette,* moderately Federalist, printed Jeffersonian contributions (13 June 1799).

SOUTH CAROLINA

Charleston *Carolina Gazette,* moderately Republican, but ran Federalist pieces. Its editor impartially collected subsidies from both sides (see notes in printers copy, 7, 25 Aug. 1800, Amer. Antiq. Soc., Worcester).

Charleston *City Gazette & Daily Advertiser,* moderately Republican, printed both sides (11 Oct. 1800).

Charleston *Federal Carolina Gazette,* moderately Federalist (13 Nov., 25 Dec. 1800).

Charleston *South-Carolina State-Gazette,* moderately Federalist, printing increasing amounts of Jeffersonian material in 1800 (30 June 1800).

Columbia *State Gazette,* moderately Republican (29 Aug. 1800).

Georgetown *Gazette,* moderately Federalist (9 July 1800).

GEORGIA

Augusta *Chronicle,* moderately Republican (11 Oct. 1800).

Augusta *Herald,* moderately Federalist (1 Jan., 19 Mar., 23 Apr. 1800), printed both sides (9 July 1800).

Louisville *Gazette and Republican Journal,* decidedly Republican, subsidized by a local clique (Augusta *Herald,* 11, 25 June 1800).

Savannah *Columbian Museum and Savannah Advertiser,* very moderately Federalist (11 Mar. 1800), ran Jeffersonian contributions (2 May 1800).

Savannah *Georgia Gazette,* not much politics, nearly impartial (16 Oct. 1800).

Kentucky

Frankfort *Guardian of Freedom*, moderately Republican (30 Oct. 1798, 7 July 1802).

Frankfort *Palladium*, moderately Republican (25 Dec. 1798, 24 Feb. 1803).

Lexington *Kentucky Gazette*, moderately Republican (1 Sep. 1800).

Lexington *Stewart's Kentucky Herald*, moderately Republican (8 July 1800).

Tennessee

Knoxville *Impartial Observer*, nearly impartial (Brigham, *Hist. & Bib. Am. Newspapers*, II, 1060).

Nashville *Tennessee Gazette*, moderately Republican, ran Federalist pieces (3 Sep. 1800).

Northwest Territory

Chillicothe *Freeman's Journal*, nearly impartial?

Cincinnati *Western Spy & Hamilton Gazette*, moderately Federalist, not much partisan material (5 Mar. 1800).

Southwest Territory

Natchez *Green's Impartial Observer*, moderately Federalist (24 Jan. 1801).

Table 2   Federalist Electioneering Newspapers, 1800–1820

NOTE: An "Electioneering Paper" is defined here as one which was either founded or subsidized by the Federalists. This list is restricted to papers for which evidence of such a subsidy exists. In addition to direct statements by federal leaders, committees, and editors, the following are considered as evidence of support: total, or near-total absence of advertizements; distribution gratis at election times; the circulation of subscription lists by federal committees; sudden and substantial increase in size or circulation at the commencement of a campaign. Thus limited, the list is a minimal one. It does not include papers which sometimes had the spirit of an electioneering sheet, such as the Burlington *Vermont Centinel* (1801–1820+); Leominster, Mass., *Political Recorder* (1809–1810); New Bedford, Mass., *Mercury* (1807–1820+); Stockbridge *Farmer's Herald* (1808–1814); Bridgeport, Conn., *Patriot of Seventy-Six* (1804); Geneva, N.Y., *Expositor*, 1806–1809; Peterboro, N.Y., *Freeholder*, 1807–1813; Schoharie, N.Y., *True American* (1809–1813); Elizabeth, N.J., *Federal Republican* (1803); New Brunswick, N.J., *Guardian* (1792–1816); Morristown, N.J., *Genius of Liberty* (1808–1811); Bellefonte, Penna., *Independent Republican* (1816–1817); Norristown, Penna., *Herald* (1800–1809); Dover, Del., *Constitutionalist* (1804–1805); Uniontown, Md., *Engine of Liberty* (1816); Leesburg, Va., *Washingtonian* (1808–1820+); Lexington, Va., *Virginia Telegraphe* (1802–1810); Norfolk, Va., *Gazette and Publick Ledger* (1804–1816); Augusta, Ga., *Herald* (1799–1820+); Knoxville, Tenn., *Western Centinel* (1808–1810). Nor does it include Quid papers to which Federalists sometimes contributed, such as the Philadelphia *Freeman's Journal* (1804–1820+) or the Georgetown *Spirit of 'Seventy-Six* (1809–1811).

MAINE DISTRICT

Augusta *Herald of Liberty*, 1810–1815. See North, *History of Augusta*, pp. 395–397.

Buckstown *Gazette of Maine*, 1805–1812. See "Presses in New England," n. d., *circa* 1808, Otis Papers, Mass. Hist. Soc.

Castine *Eagle*, 1809–1812 (Boston *New England Palladium*, Nov. 28, 1809).

Kennebunk *Gazette*, 1805. See Portland *Eastern Argus*, Nov. 30, 1805.

Portland *Freeman's Friend*, 1807–1810. See issue of Sep. 19, 1807.

Portland *Gazette*, 1798–1820+; subsidized by Federalists after 1808. See the issue of Jan. 4, 1808; also "Presses in New England," Otis Papers, Mass. Hist. Soc.

Saco *Freeman's Friend*, 1805–1807. See issue of Aug. 21, 1805.

New Hampshire

Concord *Gazette*, 1806–1819. See issue of July 26, 1806; Concord *New Hampshire Patriot*, May 18, 1819.

Exeter *Constitutionalist*, 1810–1814. See issues of May 14, 1811, July 21, 1812; Boston *New England Palladium*, Apr. 6, 1810.

Haverhill *Coos Courier*, 1808–1810 ("Presses in New England, 1808?, Otis Papers, Mass. Hist. Soc.).

Keene *New Hampshire Sentinel*, 1799–1820+, subsidized and assisted from 1804. See *supra*, p. 137.

Portsmouth *Oracle*, 1803–1820+; subsidized by Federalists after 1804. See, Turner, *William Plumer*, p. 146.

Portsmouth *People's Advocate*, 1816–1817. See issue of Sept. 24, 1816; Brigham, *Hist. & Bib. Am. Newspapers*, I, 483.

Vermont

Bennington *Ploughman; or, Republican Federalist*, 1801–1802. See issues of Aug. 24, 31, 1801.

Brattleboro *Reporter*, 1803–1820+. See issues of Apr. 25, 1804, Apr. 13, 1805; "Presses in New England," 1808?, Otis Papers, Mass. Hist. Soc.

Middlebury *Vermont Mirror*, 1812–1816. See Windsor *Washingtonian*, Oct. 12, 1812.

Windsor *Post Boy and Vermont & New-Hampshire Federal Courier*, 1805–1807. See Newport *Mercury*, Feb. 2, 1805, New York, Evening Post, Feb. 8, 1805; Boston *N. Eng. Palladium*, Aug. 6, 1805.

Windsor *Washingtonian*, 1810–1816. See Windsor *Vermont Republican*, Feb. 24, July 20, 1812.

Massachusetts

Boston *Columbian Centinel & Massachusetts Federalist*, 1790–1820+. See Boston *Independent Chronicle*, Mar. 26, 1801; it is difficult to fix the beginning of Federalist subsidies. Although they may perhaps have existed from 1790, this investigator has found no evidence before 1801. The *Centinel* appears to have been aimed at Federalists along the south shore.

Boston *New England Palladium*, 1803–1820+. See *supra*, p. 136.

Boston *Repertory*, 1804–1820+. Established in Newburyport, July 6,

1803; removed to Boston, Feb. 1804. Its contents were tailored to the taste of Federalists in Essex County and Maine, where it circulated most widely. Editor John Park's denial of patronage in the issue of Oct. 26, 1803 is disproven by Benjamin Whitwell to Theophilus Parsons, Aug. 3, 1804, Columbia University Coll., Columbia Univ. Library.

Boston *Scourge*, 1811. See issues of Aug. 10, Nov. 30, 1811; Providence *Columbian Phenix*, Dec. 7, 1811.

Boston *Weekly Messenger*, 1811–1820+. See H. G. Otis to William Sullivan, Oct. 23, 1812, Otis Papers, Mass. Hist. Soc. This paper appears to have been distributed mainly in Middlesex County.

Greenfield *Franklin Federalist*, 1817. See issue of June 21, 1817.

Haverhill *Merrimack Intelligencer*, 1808–1817. See issue of July 2, 1808; "Presses in New England," 1808?, Otis Papers, Mass. Hist. Soc.

Northampton *Hampshire Gazette*, 1786–1820+; subsidized after 1808. See ibid.

Springfield *Hampden Federalist*, 1812–1820+. See issue of Sep. 10, 1812.

Springfield *Hampshire Federalist*, 1806–1812. See issue of Jan. 7, 1806.

Worcester *Massachusetts Spy*, 1775–1820+. Moderately Federalist in the 1790s; according to Levi Lincoln it was "elevated to the Federal party" in the summer of 1801. See Lincoln to Jefferson, Sep. 16, 1801, Jefferson Papers, Library of Congress.

RHODE ISLAND

Chepatchet *Scourge*, 1811. See issue of Dec. 4, 1811; Brigham, *American Newspapers*, II, 994.

Providence *American*, 1808–1809. See issue of Oct. 20, 1808; Providence *Columbian Phenix*, July 30, 1808; in 1809 its title changed to *Rhode-Island American*, which was probably subsidized during its much longer career, but this investigator has found no evidence.

Providence *Scourge*, 1810. See issue of Aug. 25, 1810; Brigham, *American Newspapers*, II, 1017.

CONNECTICUT

Danbury *Republican Farmer*, see John Caldwell et al. to Elias Shipman et al., Jan. 30, 1805, Baldwin Papers, Yale University Library.

Hartford *Connecticut Courant*, 1764–1820+; subsidized from *circa* 1804. See ibid.

Hartford *Connecticut Mirror*, 1809–1820+; supported closely by the Federalist organization for at least the duration of Theodore Dwight's connection, to 1815. See issue of July 10, 1809.

Litchfield *Monitor*, 1784–1807; subsidized after *circa* 1804. See John

Caldwell et al. to Elias Shipman et al., Jan. 30, 1805, Baldwin Papers, Yale University Library.
New Haven *Herald of Minerva; or, Columbian Ark and Washington Fortress*, 1802. See issues of Oct. 26; Nov. 2, 16, 1802.

NEW YORK

Albany *Advertiser*, 1815–1817. See Job Purdy to Daniel Webster, May 5, 1815, Webster Papers, Library of Congress.

Albany *Balance*, 1809–1811. See issue of Jan. 4, 1809.

Albany *Centinel*, 1797–1806. See issue of Jan. 2, 1801; see also career of Loring Andrews in Brigham, *American Newspapers*, II, 1370; Birdsall, *Berkshire County*, 112.

Albany *Republican Crisis*, 1806–1808. See Hudson *Bee*, Nov. 17, 1807.

Auburn *Western Federalist*, 1809–1816. See issue of Jan. 10, 1816.

Binghamton *Phoenix*, 1814–1819. See Oxford *Gazette*, Aug. 9, 1814.

Buffalo *Gazette*, 1811–1818. See Canandaigua *Ontario Repository*, Mar. 3, 1818, as cited in Hamilton, *Country Printer*, p. 84.

Cooperstown *Federalist*, 1809–1817. See issue of Feb. 3, 1810.

Cooperstown *Switch*. See Hamilton, *Country Printer*, p. 189; the dates of this paper are not known; no copies are known to exist today.

Goshen *Orange County Patriot* (1809–1820+). See issues of May 9, 1809, May 8, 1810, June 19, 1810.

Hudson *Balance*, 1801–1808. See prospectus, May 21, 1801.

Hudson *Northern Whig*, 1809–1820+. See issue of Jan. 3, 1809.

Hudson *Wasp*, 1802–1803. See *supra*, p. 141.

New York *Courier*, 1815–1817. See issue of May 6, 1815; a smaller semiweekly edition of the same paper was titled *The Country Courier*.

New York *Evening Post*, 1801–1820+. See *supra*, pp. 137–138; a semiweekly edition was called the *New York Herald*.

New York *People's Friend*, 1806–1807. See prospectus, n. d., of Stephen C. Carpenter in the American Antiquarian Society; see also the issue of Sep. 1, 1806.

New York *Pelican*, 1808. See issue of Oct. 6, 1808.

New York *Spirit of '76*, 1809. See issue of Mar. 28, 1809; Brigham, *American Newspapers*, I, 693.

New York *Washington Republican*, 1809–1810. See issue of Nov. 25, 1809.

NEW JERSEY

Bridgetown *Washington Whig*, 1815–1820+. See Elmer, *Cumberland County*, p. 57.

Freehold *Spirit of Washington*, 1814–1815. See issue of Feb. 20, 1815.

Removed to Mt. Holly in 1815, and published there under the same title by the same printer. See issue of Mar. 25, 1815.

Newark *New Jersey Telescope*, 1808–1809. See the Newark *Centinel of Freedom*, Aug. 22, 1808.

Trenton *Federalist*, 1798–1820+. See *supra*, n. 12.

PENNSYLVANIA

Carlisle *Herald* (1802–1820+). See Aug. 11, 1802.

Erie *Mirror*, 1808. See proposals dated May 26, 1808.

Lancaster *Journal*, 1794–1820+. See Higginbotham, *Keystone* in the Democratic Arch, p. 20.

Lancaster *Volksfreund*, 1808–1820+. See issue of Sep. 20, 1808.

Philadelphia *United States Gazette*, 1790–1818. See *supra*, p. 138.

Pittsburgh *Gazette*, 1786–1820+; subsidized from about 1801. See W. W. Brackenridge to Jefferson, Jan. 19, 1801, Jefferson Papers, Library of Congress; John Scull to Noah Webster, July 9, 1801, Webster Papers, New York Public Library; Andrews, *Pittsburgh Post-Gazette*, 6.

Westchester *Chester and Delaware Federalist*, 1809–1817. See Chester County Federalist Records, 1808–1811, Historical Society of Pennsylvania.

Wilkesbarre *Luzerne County Federalist*, 1801–1811. See issues of Apr. 15, May 6, 1808.

DELAWARE

Dover *Federal Ark*, 1802–1803. See issue of Sep. 17, 1802; removed to Wilmington in 1803, where it continued under the same editor to 1804.

1227 MARYLAND

Annapolis *Maryland Gazette and Political Intelligencer*, 1745–1820+; subsidized from 1813. See issues of Jan. 28, 1813, Sep. 8, 1814.

Baltimore *Federal Republican*, 1808–1820+. From 1812 to 1816 published in Georgetown. See *supra*, p. 141–142.

Baltimore *North American*, 1808–1809. See Wilmington *True Republican*, June 6, 1809.

Baltimore *People's Friend*, 1816. See issue of May 25, 1816; Brigham, *American Newspapers*, I, 246.

Baltimore *Porcupine*, 1804. See Raleigh *Minerva*, Sep. 10, 1804.

Baltimore *Republican; or, Anti-Democrat*, 1802–1804. See *supra*, n. 54.

Cumberland *Alleghany Federalist*, 1815–1817. See Joseph Smith to Vergil Maxcy, June 30, 1817, Galloway-Maxcy-Markoe Papers, Library of Congress.

Easton *People's Monitor,* 1809–1815. See issue of Mar. 4, 1809.
Frederick-Town *Herald,* 1802–1820+. See *supra,* p. 139.
Frederick-Town *Plain Dealer,* 1813–1814, Sep. 30, 1813.
Frederick-Town *Star of Federalism,* 1816–1820. See R. B. Taney, *Address to the People of Frederick County* (1817). This paper had originated in Uniontown.

District of Columbia

Georgetown *Washington Federalist,* 1800–1809. See *supra,* p. 138.

Virginia

Martinsburgh *Berkeley Intelligencer,* 1799–1809; probably subsidized after 1803.
Richmond *Virginia Patriot,* 1809–1820+. See issue of Dec. 26, 1809.

North Carolina

New Bern *Carolina Federal Republican,* 1809–1820+. See John Stanly to William Gaston, Nov. 11, 1814, Gaston Papers, Southern Historical Coll., Univ. of North Carolina.
Raleigh *Minerva; or, Anti-Jacobin,* 1803–1820+. See p. 138.

South Carolina

Charleston *Courier,* 1803–1820+. See *supra,* n. 58–60; a country edition was published under the title of the *Carolina Weekly Messenger,* from 1806 to 1810.

Georgia

Savannah *Federal Republican Advocate,* 1807. See issue of Sep. 21, 1807.

Ohio

Chillicothe *Supporter,* 1808–1820+. See W. L. Utter, "Saint Tammany in Ohio," *Miss. Valley Hist. Review,* XV (1928) 321; Chillicothe *Scioto Gazette,* Jan. 30, 1809.
St. Clairsville *Ohio Federalist,* 1813–1818. See issue of Nov. 30, 1814; Brigham, *American Newspapers,* II, 814.

Kentucky

Frankfort *American Republic,* 1810–1812. See Humphrey Marshall to Harrison Gray Otis, Apr. 16, 1810; Otis Papers, Mass Hist. Soc.

Index